GH00889804

Air Fryer Cookbook for Beginners

1001 Easy, Quick & Affordable Air Fryer Recipes – Grill, Roast, Fry, and Bake Your Favorite Meals – Tips & Tricks. Suitable for Beginners and Advanced Users

Judy Gambino

Table of Contents

MAIN & LUNCH

Breakfast

1. Ham and Cheese Mini Quiche

Prep Time: 30 minutes

Ingredients

- 1 shortcrust pastry
- 3 oz. chopped ham
- ½cup grated cheese
- 4 eggs, beaten
- 3 tbsp. greek yogurt
- ¼ tsp. garlic powder
- ¼ tsp. salt
- ¼ tsp. black pepper

Instructions

- Preheat the air fryer to 330 degrees F.Take 8 ramekins and sprinkle them with flour to avoid sticking.
- Cut the shortcrust pastry into 8 equal pieces to make 8 mini quiches.Line your ramekins with the pastry.
- Combine all of the other ingredients in a bowl. Divide the filling between the ramekins.
- Cook for 20 minutes

2. Breakfast Banana Bread

Prep Time: 50 minutes

Ingredients

- 1 cup plus
- 1 tbsp. flour
- ¼ tsp. baking soda
- 1 tsp. baking powder
- 1/3 cup sugar
- 2 mashed bananas
- ¼ cup vegetable oil
- 1 egg, beaten
- 1 tsp. vanilla extract
- ¾ cup chopped walnuts
- ¼ tsp. salt
- 2 tbsp. peanut butter2 tbsp. sour cream

Instructions

- Preheat the air fryer to 330 degrees F.
- Spray a small baking dish with cooking spray or grease with butter.
- Combine the flour, salt, baking powder, and baking soda in a bowl.
- In another bowl combine bananas, oil, egg, peanut butter, vanilla, sugar, and sour cream.
- Combine both mixtures gently.
- Stir in the chopped walnuts.
- Pour the batter into the dish.
- Bake for 40 minutes.Let cool before

serving.

3. Baked Kale Omelet

Prep Time: 15 minutes

Ingredients

- 3 eggs
- 3 tbsp. cottage cheese
- 3 tbsp. chopped kale
- ½ tbsp. chopped basil
- ½ tbsp. chopped parsleySalt and pepper, to taste
- 1 tsp. olive oil

Instructions

1. Add oil to your air fryer and preheat it to 330 degrees
2. Beat the eggs with some salt and pepper, in a bowl.
3. Stir in the rest of the Ingredients.Pour the mixture into the air fryer and bake for 10 minutes

4. Tasty Baked Eggs

Preparation time: 10 mins Cooking time: 20 mins

Ingredients:

- 4 eggs
- 1 pound baby spinach, torn
- 7 ounces ham, chopped
- 4 tablespoons milk
- 1 tablespoon olive oil
- Cooking spray
- Salt and black pepper to the taste

Instructions:

- Heat up a pan with the oil over medium heat, add baby spinach, stir cook for a couple of mins and take off heat.
- grease 4 ramekins with cooking spray and divide baby spinach and ham in each.
- Crack an egg in each ramekin, also divide milk, season with salt and pepper, place ramekins in preheated air fryer at 350 degrees F and bake for 20 minutes.
- Serve baked eggs for breakfast.

5. Breakfast Egg Bowls

Preparation time: 10 mins Cooking time: 20 mins

Ingredients:

- 4 dinner rolls, tops cut off and insides scooped out
- 4 tablespoons heavy cream
- 4 eggs
- 4 tablespoons mixed chives and

parsley

- Salt and black pepper to the taste
- 4 tablespoons parmesan, grated

Instructions:

- Arrange dinner rolls on a baking sheet and crack an egg in each.
- Divide heavy cream, mixed herbs in each roll and season with salt and pepper.
- Sprinkle parmesan on top of your rolls, place them in your air fryer and cook at 350 degrees F for 20 minutes.
- Divide your bread bowls on plates and serve for breakfast.

6. Delicious Breakfast Soufflé

Preparation time:10 mins Cooking time: 8 mins

Ingredients:

- 4 eggs, whisked
- 4 tablespoons heavy cream
- A pinch of red chili pepper, crushed
- 2 tablespoons parsley, chopped
- 2 tablespoons chives, chopped
- Salt and black pepper to the taste

Instructions:

- In a bowl, mix eggs with salt, pepper, heavy cream, red chili pepper, parsley and chives, stir well and divide into 4 soufflé dishes.
- Arrange dishes in your air fryer and cook soufflés at 350 degrees F for 8 minutes.
- Serve them hot.

7. Air Fried Sandwich

Preparation time: 10 mins Cooking time: 6 mins

Ingredients:

- 2 English muffins, halved
- 2 eggs
- 2 bacon strips
- Salt and black pepper to the taste

Instructions:

- Crack eggs in your air fryer, add bacon on top, cover and cook at 392 degrees F for 6 minutes.
- Heat up your English muffin halves in your microwave for a few seconds, divide eggs on 2 halves, add bacon on top, season with salt and pepper, cover with the other 2 English muffins and serve for breakfast.

8. Rustic Breakfast

Preparation time: 10 mins Cooking

time: 13 mins

Ingredients:

- 7 ounces baby spinach
- 8 chestnuts mushrooms, halved
- 8 tomatoes, halved
- 1 garlic clove, minced
- 4 chipolatas
- 4 bacon slices, chopped
- Salt and black pepper to the taste
- 4 eggs
- Cooking spray

Instructions:

- Grease a cooking pan with the oil and add tomatoes, garlic and mushrooms.
- Add bacon and chipolatas, also add spinach and crack eggs at the end.
- Season with salt and pepper, place pan in the cooking basket of your air fryer and cook for 13 mins at 350 degrees
- Divide among plates and serve for breakfast.

9. Egg Muffins

Preparation time: 10 mins Cooking time: 15 mins

Ingredients:

- 1 egg
- 2 tablespoons olive oil
- 3 tablespoons milk
- 3.5 ounces white flour
- 1 tablespoon baking powder
- 2 ounces parmesan, grated
- A splash of Worcestershire sauce

Instructions:

- In a bowl, mix egg with flour, oil, baking powder, milk, Worcestershire and parmesan, whisk well and divide into 4 silicon muffin cups.
- Arrange cups in your air fryer's cooking basket, cover and cook at 392, degrees F for 15 minutes.
- Serve warm for breakfast.

10. Polenta Bites

Preparation time: 10 mins Cooking time: 20 mins

Ingredients:

- For the polenta:
- 1 tablespoon butter
- 1 cup cornmeal
- 3 cups water
- Salt and black pepper to the taste
- For the polenta bites:
- 2 tablespoons powdered sugar

Instructions:

- In a pan, mix water with cornmeal, butter, salt and pepper, stir, bring to a boil over medium heat, cook for 10 minutes, take off heat, whisk one more time and keep in the fridge until it's cold. Scoop 1 tablespoon of polenta, shape a ball and place on a working surface.
- Repeat with the rest of the polenta, arrange all the balls in the cooking basket of your air fryer, spray them with cooking spray, cover and cook at 380 degrees F for 8 minutes.
- Arrange polenta bites on plates, sprinkle sugar all over and serve for breakfast.

11. Delicious Breakfast Potatoes

Preparation time: 10 mins Cooking time: 35 mins

Ingredients:

- 2 tablespoons olive oil
- 3 potatoes, cubed
- 1 yellow onion, chopped
- 1 red bell pepper, chopped
- Salt and black pepper to the taste
- 1 teaspoon garlic powder
- 1 teaspoon sweet paprika
- 1 teaspoon onion powder

Instructions:

- Grease your air fryer's basket with olive oil, add potatoes, toss and season with salt and pepper.
- Add onion, bell pepper, garlic powder, paprika and onion powder, toss well, cover and cook at 370 degrees F for 30 minutes.
- Divide potatoes mix on plates and serve for breakfast.

12. Breakfast Sandwich

Prep Time: 10 minutes

Ingredients

- 1 egg
- 1 English muffin
- 2 slices of bacon
- Salt and pepper, to taste

Instructions

- Preheat the air fryer to 395 degrees.Crack the egg into a ramekin.Place the muffin, egg and bacon in the air fryer.
- Cook for 6 minutes.Let cool slightly so you can assemble the sandwich.

- Cut the muffin in half.Place the egg on one half and season with salt and pepper.
- Arrange the bacon on top.Top with the other muffin half.

13. Prosciutto, Mozzarella and Egg in a Cup

Prep Time: 20 minutes

Ingredients

- 2 slices of bread
- 2 prosciutto slices, chopped
- 2 eggs
- 4 tomato slices¼ tsp. balsamic vinegar
- 2 tbsp. grated mozzarella¼ tsp. maple syrup
- 2 tbsp. mayonnaise
- Salt and pepper, to taste

Instructions

- Preheat the air fryer to 320 degrees.
- Grease two large ramekins.Place one bread slice in the bottom of each ramekin.
- Arrange 2 tomato slices on top of each bread slice.Divide the mozzarella between the ramekins.
- Crack the eggs over the mozzarella
- Drizzle with maple syrup and balsamic vinegar.Season with some salt and pepper.
- Cook for 10 minutes, or until desired.

14. Air Fried Shirred Eggs

Prep Time: 20 minutes

Ingredients

- 2 tsp. butter, for greasing
- 4 eggs, divided
- 2 tbsp. heavy cream4 slices of ham
- 3 tbsp. Parmesan cheese
- ¼ tsp. paprika
- ¾ tsp. salt
- ¼ tsp. pepper
- 2 tsp. chopped chives

Instructions

- Preheat the air fryer to 320 degrees F.grease a pie pan with the butter.
- Arrange the ham slices on the bottom of the pan to cover it completely.Use more slices if needed (or less if your pan is smaller).
- Whisk one egg along with the heavy cream, salt and pepper, in a small bowl.Pour the mixture over the ham slices.Crack the other eggs over the ham.

- Sprinkle the Parmesan cheese.
- Cook for 14 minutes.Sprinkle with paprika and garnish with chives.Serve with bread.

15. Very Berry Breakfast Puff

Prep Time: 20 Minutes

Ingredients
- 3 pastry dough sheets
- 2 tbsp. mashed strawberries
- 2 tbsp. mashed raspberries
- ¼ tsp. vanilla extract2 cups cream cheese1 tbsp. honey

Instructions
- Preheat the air fryer to 375 degrees F.
- Divide the cream cheese between the dough sheets and spread it evenly.
- In a small bowl combine the berries, honey and vanilla.
- Divide the mixture between the pastry sheets.Pinch the ends of the sheets, to form puff.
- You can seal them by brushing some water onto the edges, or even better, use egg wash.
- Place the puffs on a lined baking dish.
- Place in the air fryer and cook for 15 minutes

16. Cheese Air Fried Bake

Preparation time: 10 mins Cooking time: 20 mins

Ingredients:
- 4 bacon slices, cooked and crumbled
- 2 cups milk
- 2 and ½ cups cheddar cheese, shredded
- 1 pound breakfast sausage, casings removed and chopped
- 2 eggs
- ½ teaspoon onion powder
- Salt and black pepper to the taste
- 3 tablespoons parsley, chopped
- Cooking spray

Instructions:
- In a bowl, mix eggs with milk, cheese, onion powder, salt, pepper and parsley and whisk well.
- Grease your air fryer with cooking spray, heat it up at 320 degrees F and add bacon and sausage.
- Add eggs mix, spread and cook for 20 minutes.
- Divide among plates and serve.

17. Biscuits Casserole

Preparation time: 10 mins Cooking time: 15 mins

Ingredients:
- 12 ounces biscuits, quartered
- 3 tablespoons flour
- ½ pound sausage, chopped
- A pinch of salt and black pepper
- 2 and ½ cups milk
- Cooking spray

Instructions:
- Grease your air fryer with cooking spray and heat it over 350 degrees F.
- Add biscuits on the bottom and mix with sausage.
- Add flour, milk, salt and pepper, toss a bit and cook for 15 minutes.

18. Turkey Burrito

Preparation time: 10 mins Cooking time: 10 mins

Ingredients:
- 4 slices turkey breast already cooked
- ½ red bell pepper, sliced
- 2 eggs
- 1 small avocado, peeled, pitted and sliced
- 2 tablespoons salsa
- Salt and black pepper to the taste
- 1/8 cup mozzarella cheese, grated
- Tortillas for serving

Instructions:
- In a bowl, whisk eggs with salt and pepper to the taste, pour them in a pan and place it in the air fryer's basket.
- Cook at 400 degrees F for 5 minutes, take pan out of the fryer and transfer eggs to a plate.
- Arrange tortillas on a working surface, divide eggs on them, also divide turkey meat, bell pepper, cheese, salsa and avocado.
- Roll your burritos and place them in your air fryer after you've lined it with some tin foil.
- Heat up the burritos at 300 degrees F for 3 minutes, divide them on plates and serve.

19. Tofu Scramble

Preparation time: 5 mins Cooking time: 30 mins

Ingredients:
- 2 tablespoons soy sauce
- 1 tofu block, cubed
- 1 teaspoon turmeric, ground
- 2 tablespoons extra virgin olive oil
- 4 cups broccoli florets
- ½ teaspoon onion powder
- ½ teaspoon garlic powder
- 2 and ½ cup red potatoes, cubed
- ½ cup yellow onion, chopped
- Salt and black pepper to the taste

Instructions:
- Mix tofu with 1 tablespoon oil, salt, pepper, soy sauce, garlic powder, onion powder, turmeric and onion in a bowl, stir and leave aside.
- In a separate bowl, combine potatoes with the rest of the oil, a pinch of salt and pepper and toss to coat.
- Put potatoes in your air fryer at 350 degrees F and bake for 15 minutes, shaking once.
- Add tofu and its marinade to your air fryer and bake for 15 minutes.
- Add broccoli to the fryer and cook everything for 5 mins more.

20. Oatmeal Casserole

Preparation time: 10 mins Cooking time: 20 mins

Ingredients:
- 2 cups rolled oats
- 1 teaspoon baking powder
- 1/3 cup brown sugar
- 1 teaspoon cinnamon powder
- ½ cup chocolate chips
- 2/3 cup blueberries
- 1 banana, peeled and mashed
- 2 cups milk
- 1 eggs
- 2 tablespoons butter
- 1 teaspoon vanilla extract

Instructions:
- In a bowl, mix sugar with baking powder, cinnamon, chocolate chips, blueberries and banana and stir.
- In a separate bowl, mix eggs with vanilla extract and butter and stir.
- Heat up your air fryer at 320 degrees F, grease with cooking spray and add oats on the bottom.
- Add cinnamon mix and eggs mix, toss and cook for 20 minutes.Stir one more time, divide into bowls and serve for breakfast.

21. Ham Breakfast

Preparation time: 10 mins Cooking time: 15 mins

Ingredients:
- 6 cups French bread, cubed
- 4 ounces green chilies, chopped
- 10 ounces ham, cubed
- 4 ounces cheddar cheese, shredded
- 2 cups milk
- 5 eggs
- 1 tablespoon mustard

Salt and black pepper to the taste

Instructions:
- Heat up your air fryer at 350 degrees F and grease it with cooking spray. In a bowl, mix eggs with milk, cheese, mustard, salt and pepper and stir.
- Add bread cubes in your air fryer and mix with chilies and ham. Add eggs mix, spread and cook for 15 minutes.

22. Tomato and Bacon Breakfast

Preparation time: 10 mins Cooking time: 30 mins

Ingredients:
- 1 pound white bread, cubed
- 1 pound smoked bacon, cooked and chopped
- ¼ cup olive oil
- 1 yellow onion, chopped
- 28 ounces canned tomatoes, chopped
- ½ teaspoon red pepper, crushed
- ½ pound cheddar, shredded
- 2 tablespoons chives, chopped
- ½ pound Monterey jack, shredded
- 2 tablespoons stock
- Salt and black pepper to the taste
- 8 eggs, whisked

Instructions:
- Add the oil to your air fryer and heat it up at 350 degrees F. Add bread, bacon, onion, tomatoes, red pepper and stock and stir.
- Add eggs, cheddar and Monterey jack and cook everything for 20 minutes.
- Divide among plates, sprinkle chives and serve.

23. Tasty Hash

Preparation time: 10 mins Cooking time: 15 mins

Ingredients:
- 16 ounces hash browns
- ¼ cup olive oil
- ½ teaspoon paprika
- ½ teaspoon garlic powder
- Salt and black pepper to the taste
- 1 egg, whisked
- 2 tablespoon chives, chopped
- 1 cup cheddar, shredded

Instructions:
- Add oil to your air fryer, heat it up at 350 degrees F and add hash browns.
- Also add paprika, garlic powder, salt, pepper and egg, toss and cook for 15 minutes.
- Add cheddar and chives, toss, divide among plates and serve.

24. Creamy Hash Browns

Preparation time: 10 mins Cooking time: 20 mins

Ingredients:
- 2 pounds hash browns
- 1 cup whole milk
- 8 bacon slices, chopped
- 9 ounces cream cheese
- 1 yellow onion, chopped
- 1 cup cheddar cheese, shredded
- 6 green onions, chopped
- Salt and black pepper to the taste
- 6 eggs
- Cooking spray

Instructions:
- Heat up your air fryer at 350 degrees F and grease it with cooking spray.
- In a bowl, mix eggs with milk, cream cheese, cheddar cheese, bacon, onion, salt and pepper and whisk well.
- Add hash browns to your air fryer, add eggs mix over them and cook for 20 minutes.

25. Blackberry French Toast

Preparation time: 10 mins Cooking time: 20 mins

Ingredients:
- 1 cup blackberry jam, warm
- 12 ounces bread loaf, cubed
- 8 ounces cream cheese, cubed
- 4 eggs
- 1 teaspoon cinnamon powder
- 2 cups half and half
- ½ cup brown sugar
- 1 teaspoon vanilla extract

Instructions:
- Grease your air fryer with cooking spray and heat it up at 300 degrees F.
- Add blueberry jam on the bottom, layer half of the bread cubes, then add cream cheese and top with the rest of the bread.
- In a bowl, mix eggs with half and half, cinnamon, sugar and vanilla, whisk well and add over bread mix.
- Cook for 20 minutes, divide among plates and serve for breakfast.

26. Smoked Sausage Breakfast Mix

Preparation time: 10 mins Cooking time: 30 mins

Ingredients:
- 1 and ½ pounds smoked sausage, chopped and browned A pinch of salt and black pepper
- 1 and ½ cups grits
- 4 and ½ cups water
- 16 ounces cheddar cheese, shredded
- 1 cup milk
- ¼ teaspoon garlic powder
- 1 and ½ teaspoons thyme, chopped
- Cooking spray
- 4 eggs, whisked

Instructions:
- Put the water in a pot, bring to a boil over medium heat, add grits, stir, cover, cook for 5 mins and take off heat. Add cheese, stir until it melts and mix with milk, thyme, salt, pepper, garlic powder and eggs and whisk really well.
- Heat up your air fryer at 300 degrees F, grease with cooking spray and add browned sausage.
- Add grits mix, spread and cook for 25 minutes.
- Divide among plates and serve for breakfast.

27. Delicious Potato Frittata

Preparation time: 10 mins Cooking time: 20 mins

Ingredients:
- 6 ounces jarred roasted red bell peppers, chopped
- 12 eggs, whisked
- ½ cup parmesan, grated
- 3 garlic cloves, minced
- 2 tablespoons parsley, chopped
- Salt and black pepper to the taste
- 2 tablespoons chives, chopped
- 16 potato wedges
- 6 tablespoons ricotta cheese

Instructions:
- In a bowl, mix eggs with red peppers, garlic, parsley, salt, pepper and ricotta

and whisk well. Heat up your air fryer at 300 degrees F and grease it with cooking spray.

- Add half of the potato wedges on the bottom and sprinkle half of the parmesan all over.
- Add half of the egg mix, add the rest of the potatoes and the rest of the parmesan. Add the rest of the eggs mix, sprinkle chives and cook for 20 minutes.
- Divide among plates and serve for breakfast.

28. Asparagus Frittata

Preparation time: 10 mins Cooking time: 5 mins

Ingredients:

- 4 eggs, whisked
- 2 tablespoons parmesan, grated
- 4 tablespoons milk
- Salt and black pepper to the taste
- 10 asparagus tips, steamed

Instructions:

- In a bowl, mix eggs with parmesan, milk, salt and pepper and whisk well.
- Heat up your air fryer at 400 degrees F and grease with cooking spray.
- Add asparagus, add eggs mix, toss a bit and cook for 5 minutes.
- Divide frittata on plates and serve for breakfast.

29. Air Fried Buffalo Cauliflower

Prep time: 15 mins Cook time: 20 mins

Ingredients

- Cooking spray
- 1 teaspoon of Arrowroot Powder, divided
- 1 teaspoon of Nutritional Yeast separated
- 1 tablespoon of Ghee
- 3/4 cup of Frank's Red Hot Sauce
- 1 large cauliflower head, wash and cut into florets, pat dry

Directions

- Melt ghee over medium heat in a small sauce pan. Add hot Sauce and beat with the ghee.
- Once sauce starts boiling, reduce to low heat and whisk in the arrowroot powder until blended well.
- In a large bowl, add cauliflower and spread 3/4 of the sauce on the cauliflower.
- Mix with your hands until coated very

well.

- Arrange cauliflower in the Air fryer.
- Do this in batches. Sprinkle top of the cauliflower with half teaspoon of nutritional yeast, then spritz with cooking spray and cook at 400 F for 15-20 minutes, shaking the basket every 5-7 mins. during the Cook Time.
- Drizzle cauliflower with the remaining sauce.

30. Banana Bread

Prep Time: 10 mins. Cook Time: 20 mins.

Servings: 8

Ingredients:

- 1 1/3 cups flour
- 1 teaspoon baking soda
- 1 teaspoon baking powder
- ½ cup milk
- 3 bananas, peeled and sliced
- 2/3 cup sugar
- 1 teaspoon ground cinnamon
- 1 teaspoon salt
- ½ cup olive oil

Directions:

- Preheat the Air fryer to 330 o F and grease a loaf pan.
- Mix together all the dry Ingredients with the wet Ingredients to form a dough.
- Place the dough into the prepared loaf pan and transfer into an air fryer basket.
- Cook for about 20 mins. and remove from air fryer.
- Cut the bread into desired size slices and serve warm.

31. Crispy Potato Rosti

Prep Time: 10 mins. Cook Time: 15 mins.

Ingredients:

- ½ pound russet potatoes, peeled and grated roughly
- 1 tablespoon chives, chopped finely
- 2 Tbsp. shallots, minced
- 1/8 cup cheddar cheese
- 3.5 ounces smoked salmon, cut into slices
- 2 Tbsp. sour cream
- 1 tablespoon olive oil
- Salt and black pepper, to taste

Directions :

- Preheat the Air fryer to 365 o F and

grease a pizza pan with the olive oil.

- Mix together potatoes, shallots, chives, cheese, salt and black pepper in a large
- bowl until well combined.
- Transfer the potato mixture into the prepared pizza pan and place in the Air
- fryer basket.
- Cook for about 15 mins. and dish out in a platter.
- Cut the potato rosti into wedges and top with smoked salmon slices and sour
- cream to serve.

32. Healthy Tofu Omelet

Prep Time: 10 mins. Cook Time: 29 mins.

Ingredients:

- ¼ of onion, chopped
- 12-ounce silken tofu, pressed and sliced
- 3 eggs, beaten
- 1 tablespoon chives, chopped
- 1 garlic clove, minced
- 2 teaspoons olive oil
- Salt and black pepper, to taste

Directions:

- Preheat the Air fryer to 355 o F and grease an Air fryer pan with olive oil.
- Add onion and garlic to the greased pan and cook for about 4 minutes.
- Add tofu, mushrooms and chives and season with salt and black pepper.
- Beat the eggs and pour over the tofu mixture.
- Cook for about 25 minutes, poking the eggs twice in between.
- Dish out and serve warm.

33. Yummy Savory French Toasts

- Prep Time: 10 mins. Cook Time: 4 mins.

Ingredients:

- ¼ cup chickpea flour
- 3 Tbsp. onion, chopped finely
- 2 teaspoons green chili, seeded and chopped finely
- Water, as required
- 4 bread slices
- ½ teaspoon red chili powder
- ¼ teaspoon ground turmeric
- ¼ teaspoon ground cumin
- Salt, to taste

Directions:

- Preheat the Air fryer to 375 o F and

line an Air fryer pan with a foil paper.
- Mix together all the Ingredients in a large bowl except the bread slices.
- Spread the mixture over both sides of the bread slices and transfer into the Air fryer pan.
- Cook for about 4 mins. and remove from the Air fryer to serve.

34. Aromatic Potato Hash

Prep Time: 10 mins. Cook Time: 42 mins. Servings: 4

Ingredients:
- 2 teaspoons butter, melted
- 1 medium onion, chopped
- ½ of green bell pepper, seeded and chopped
- 1½ pound russet potatoes, peeled and cubed
- 5 eggs, beaten
- ½ teaspoon dried thyme, crushed
- ½ teaspoon dried savory, crushed
- Salt and black pepper, to taste

Directions:
- Preheat the Air fryer to 390 o F and grease an Air fryer pan with melted butter.
- Put onion and bell pepper in the Air fryer pan and cook for about 5 minutes.
- Add the potatoes, thyme, savory, salt and black pepper and cook for about 30
- minutes.
- Meanwhile, heat a greased skillet on medium heat and stir in the beaten eggs.
- Cook for about 1 minute on each side and remove from the skillet.
- Cut it into small pieces and transfer the egg pieces into the Air fryer pan.
- Cook for about 5 more mins. and serve warm

35. Zucchini Fritters

Prep Time: 15 mins. Cook Time: 7 mins. Servings: 4

Ingredients:
- 10½ ounces zucchini, grated and squeezed
- 7 ounces Halloumi cheese
- ¼ cup all-purpose flour
- 2 eggs
- 1 teaspoon fresh dill, minced
- Salt and black pepper, to taste

Directions:
- Preheat the Air fryer to 360 o F and grease a baking dish.
- Mix together all the Ingredients in a large bowl.
- Make small fritters from this mixture and place them on the prepared baking
- dish.
- Transfer the dish in the Air Fryer basket and cook for about 7 minutes.
- Dish out and serve warm

36. Air Fryer Jalapeno Poppers

Prep Time: 20 mins
Cook Time: 10 mins

Ingredients
- 10 Jalapenos, sliced in half lengthwise
- 10 slices Bacon, cut in half lengthwise
- 8 oz Cream Cheese
- 1 tsp Cumin
- 1 cup Monterey Jack Cheese
- Olive Oil Spray

Directions:
- Use some of the non-stick spray on the air fryer basket.
- Fetch a bowl, put in the cream cheese, cheese and cumin and mix together thoroughly.
- You must prepare your jalapeno before this time, so you have to spoon the cheese mixture into them.
- Use a slice of bacon to wrap around each of the stuffed jalapenos. When you are done wrapping the jalapenos, make use of a toothpick to secure the end firmly.
- Place the air fryer at 370 degrees F and cook for 9 minutes. It should be done at this point. It may, however, be cooked much earlier, just keep an eye out for when the tips of the jalapenos turn a golden brown.
- Remove from the air fryer and allow it to cool. You can serve with any dip of your choice.

37. Shrimp and Rice Breakfast Frittata

Prep time: 15 mins. Cook time: 15 mins.

Ingredients
- Eggs – 4
- Pinch of salt
- Dried basil – ½ tsp.
- Cooked rice – ½ cup
- Chopped cooked shrimp – ½ cup
- Baby spinach – ½ cup
- Grated Monterey Jack cheese – ½ cup

Directions:
- In a bowl, beat the eggs with salt and basil until frothy. Spray a 6x6x2-inch pan with nonstick cooking spray.
- Combine the spinach, shrimp and rice in the prepared pan. Pour the eggs in and sprinkle with cheese.
- Bake at 320F until frittata is puffed and golden brown, about 14 to 18 minutes.

38. Omelette in Bread Cups

Prep time: 12 mins. Cook time: 11 mins.

Ingredients
- Crusty rolls – 4 (3x4-inch)
- Gouda – 4 thin slices
- Eggs – 5
- Heavy cream – 2 tbsp.
- Dried thyme – ½ tsp.
- Precooked bacon – 3 strips, hopped
- Salt and ground pepper to taste

Directions:
- Cut the tops off the rolls and remove the insides with your fingers to make a shell with about ½-inch of bread remaining. Line the rolls with a slice of cheese, pressing them gently, so the cheese conforms to the inside of the
- roll.
- In a bowl, beat the eggs with the heavy cream until combined.
- Stir in the bacon, thyme, salt and pepper.
- Spoon the egg mixture into the rolls over the cheese.
- Bake at 330F until the eggs are puffy and starting to brown on top, about 8 to 12 minutes.

39. Mixed Berry Muffins

Prep time: 15 mins. Cook time: 15 mins.

Ingredients
- Flour – 1 1/3 cups, plus 1 tbsp.
- Baking powder – 2 tsp.
- White sugar – ¼ cup
- Brown sugar – 2 tbsp.
- Eggs – 2
- Whole milk – 2/3 cup
- Safflower oil – 1/3 cup
- Mixed fresh berries – 1 cup

Directions:
- Combine 1 1/3 cups flour, brown sugar, white sugar and baking powder in a bowl and mix well.
- Combine the milk, eggs and oil in another bowl and beat until combined.

- Stir the egg mixture into the dry ingredients just until combined.
- In another bowl, toss the mixed berries with the remaining 1 tbsp. flour until coated. Stir gently into the batter.
- Double up 16 foil muffin cups to make 8 cups. Put 4 cups into the air fryer and fill ¾ full with the batter.
- Bake at 320F until cooked, about 12 to 17 minutes.
- Repeat with the remaining muffin cups and batter.
- Cool and serve.

40. Dutch Pancake

Prep time: 12 mins. Cook time: 15 mins.
Ingredients
- Unsalted butter – 2 tbsp.
- Eggs – 3
- Flour – ½ cup
- Milk – ½ cup
- Vanilla – ½ tsp.
- Sliced fresh strawberries – 1 ½ cups
- Powdered sugar – 2 tbsp.

Directions:
- Preheat the air fryer with a 6x6x2-inch pan in the basket. Add the butter and heat until the butter melts.
- Meanwhile, beat the eggs, milk, flour and vanilla in a bowl until frothy.
- Carefully remove the basket with the pan from the air fryer and tilt, so the butter covers the bottom of the pan. Pour in the batter and put back in the fryer.
- Bake at 330F until the pancake is puffed and golden brown, about 12 to 16 minutes.
- Remove and top with strawberries and powdered sugar.
- Serve.

41. Chocolate-Filled Doughnut Holes

Prep time: 10 mins. Cook time: 12 mins.
Ingredients
- Refrigerated biscuits – 1 (8-count) can
- Semisweet chocolate chips – 24 to 48
- Melted unsalted butter – 3 tbsp.
- Powdered sugar – ¼ cup

Directions:
- Separate and cut each biscuit into thirds.
- Flatten each biscuit piece slightly and put 1 to 2 chocolate chips in the center.
- Wrap the dough around the chocolate

and seal the edges well.
- Brush each doughnut hole with a bit of butter.
- Air-fry in batches at 340F for 8 to 12 minutes.
- Remove and dust with powdered sugar.

42. Spinach and Cheese Omelette

Prep time: 5 mins. Cook time: 8 mins.
Servings: 2
Ingredients
- Eggs – 3
- Shredded cheese – ½ cup
- hopped fresh spinach – 2 tbsp.
- alt and pepper to taste

Directions:
- Whisk the eggs with salt and pepper and place in a flat oven-safe dish.
- Add the cheese and spinach. Do not stir.
- Cook at 390F for 8 mins. in the air fryer.
- Check the consistency of the omelette. Cook for another 2 mins. if a browner omelette is desired.
- Serve and enjoy.

43. Cinnamon Toast

Prep time: 10 mins. Cook time: 5 mins.
Servings: 6
Ingredients
- Butter – 1 stick, soft
- Bread – 12 slices
- Sugar – ½ cup
- Vanilla extract – 1 ½ tsp.
- Cinnamon powder – 1 ½ tsp.

Directions:
- In a bowl, mix soft butter with cinnamon, vanilla and sugar, and whisk well.
- Spread this on bread slices, place them in the air fryer and cook at 400F for 5 minutes.

44. Fingerling Potatoes with Dip

Prep time: 10 mins Cook Time: 15 mins
Ingredients:
- 12 ounces Fingerling Potatoes
- 1 tablespoon Olive Oil
- 1 tablespoon Garlic Powder
- ¼ teaspoon Paprika
- Salt
- Ground Pepper
Ingredients for the Dipping Sauce:
- 1/3 cup Reduced-fat Sour Cream

- 2 Tbsp.Finely Grated Parmesan Cheese
- 1 1/3 Tbsp.Ranch Dressing Mix
- 1 tablespoon White Vinegar
- 1 tablespoon Chopped Fresh Parsley

Directions:
- Start by preheating the air fryer to about 390 degrees F.
- Fetch a bowl and put in the potatoes. After this, add the olive oil, garlic powder, salt, pepper, paprika. Toss the mixture until the potatoes are well covered by the sauce.
- Place the potatoes into the air fryer basket and allow them to cook. The Cook Time should be no more than 15 minutes. It is important to flip the potatoes halfway through to make sure that they are thoroughly cooked.
- Grab a small bowl, put in the mayonnaise, sour cream, Parmesan cheese, ranch dressing mix, and vinegar and mix all, thoroughly. You should do this while the potatoes are in the air fryer.
- When the potatoes are cooked, bring them out from the basket and serve with the dip.

45. Mozzarella Sticks

Prep time: 5 mins Cook Time: 8 mins.
Ingredients:
- 1 package Mozzarella Cheese Sticks, each stick unwrapped and cut in half to make 12 sticks
- 1/4 cup Mayonnaise
- 1 Large Egg
- 1/4 cup All-purpose Flour
- 1/4 cup Fine, Dry Breadcrumbs
- 1/2 teaspoon Onion Powder
- 1/2 teaspoon Garlic Powder
- 1 cup Marinara Sauce, for serving
Directions:
- Begin by preheating the air fryer to 370 degrees F,
- Get a rimmed baking sheet and line it with parchment paper. Place the
- halved cheese sticks on the sheet. When this is done, place this into the refrigerator.
- Put the mayonnaise and egg into a bowl and proceed to whisk. Fetch a larger bowl and put in the flour, onion, breadcrumbs and garlic powder. Whisk to combine all of the mixture.

- Bring out the frozen cheese sticks and dip each into the mayonnaise mixture, and after they are all coated, you should put the sticks into the flour mixture too. After placing in the flour mixture, put them back onto the baking sheet and put them into the refrigerator for at least 10 more minutes.
- Put the mozzarella sticks into the air fryer and fry for at least 5 minutes

46. Stuffed Mushrooms with Sour Milk

Prep time: 30 mins Cook Time: 15 mins

Ingredients:
- 24 Mushrooms, caps and stems diced
- ½ Orange Bell Pepper, diced
- ½ Onion, diced
- 1 Small Carrot, diced
- 2 slices Bacon
- 1 cup Shredded Cheddar Cheese
- ½ cup Sour Cream
- 1 1/2 Tbsp.Shredded Cheddar Cheese

Directions:
- Preheat the air fryer. The temperature should be set for 350 degrees F at least.
- Fetch a skillet and put in the mushroom stems, onion, carrot, orange bell pepper, and bacon. Turn the heat low and place the skillet over it. Cook for 5 mins. while stirring the mixture to make sure it cooks properly.
- After the 5 minutes, put in 1 cup cheddar cheese together with the sour cream. Keep cooking until the cheese melts and the filling is well prepared.
- Place the mushroom caps on the air fryer's baking tray. Put the prepared stuffing into each mushroom cap. When that is done, add 1 1/2 Tbsp.of the cheddar cheese.
- Put the tray into the air fryer and cook. Cooking should not be more than 8 mins. or at least until the cheese has melted.

47. Potato Chips

Prep time: 15 mins Cook Time: 25 mins

Ingredients
- 1 Russet Potato
- 2 Tbsp.Olive Oil
- ½ tablespoon of Salt, to taste

Directions:
- Slice the potatoes thinly. Each slice is not supposed to be more than 3mm.

After this, you have to dry the moisture in the potato and one way to do this is by wrapping the potatoes in paper towels to absorb the moisture.
- When the slices of potatoes are dry, you can transfer to a bowl and then coat the slices in olive oil.
- Place the potatoes on another plate and season with salt. The slices should be placed evenly on the basket. Make sure not to stack them one on top of the other. Also, you may need to spray the basket before you put in the potatoes so as to ensure that they do not stick.
- Cook for ten minutes. You should remove the basket when the chips start to get brown. When you remove the basket, gently remove the potato slices.
- Serve when the potatoes have cooled.

48. Baked Potatoes

Prep time: 2 mins Cook Time: 40 mins

Ingredients:
- 4 Large Baking Potatoes, cleaned
- 2 Tbsp.Olive Oil
- Coarse Kosher Salt
- Pepper
- Garlic Powder
- Parsley
- 1/2 stick Butter, divided
- Sour Cream, optional

Directions:
- Wash the potatoes thoroughly because this recipe does not involve peeling the potatoes. After washing, rub some olive oil on the potatoes.
- Add some seasonings to the potatoes. The seasonings should include pepper, salt, garlic powder and parsley.
- Put the potatoes into the air fryer and cook. The air fryer should be set to about 400 degrees F. Cook Time should be between 40 mins. to 1 hour depending on the size and weight of the potatoes.
- When the potatoes are cooked, slice them open with a sharp knife, then draw back the sides to reveal the insides. Scoop 1 tablespoon of butter into the open part of the potato. Do this for each of them. You could also add some sour milk if you want, to finish up the entire process.

49. Breakfast Bread Pudding

Prep time: 10 mins. Cook time: 22 mins.

Ingredients
- White bread – ½ pound, cubed
- Milk – ¾ cup
- Water – ¾ cup
- Cornstarch – 2 tsp.
- Apple – ½ cup, peeled, cored and chopped
- Honey – 5 tbsp.
- Vanilla extract – 1 tsp.
- Cinnamon powder – 2 tsp.
- Flour – 1 1/3 cup
- Brown sugar – 3/5 cup
- Soft butter – 3 ounces

Directions:
- In a bowl, mix bread, apple, cornstarch, vanilla, cinnamon, honey, milk and water. Whisk well.
- In another bowl, mix butter, sugar and flour, and mix well.
- Press half of the crumble mixture on the bottom of the air fryer, add bread and apple mixture, then add the rest of the crumble and cook at 350F for 22 minutes.
- Divide bread pudding on plates and serve.

50. Shrimp Frittata

Prep time: 10 mins. Cook time: 15 mins.

Ingredients
- Eggs – 4
- Basil – ½ tsp., dried
- Cooking spray
- Salt and black pepper to taste
- Rice – ½ cup, cooked
- Shrimp – ½ cup, cooked, peeled, deveined and chopped
- Baby spinach – ½ cup, chopped
- Monterey jack cheese – ½ cup, grated

Directions:
- In a bowl, mix eggs with basil, pepper and salt. Whisk well.
- Grease your air fryers pan with cooking spray and add rice, shrimp and spinach.
- Add egg mixture, sprinkle cheese all over and cook in the air fryer at 350F for 10 minutes.
- Serve

51. Fluffy Cheesy Omelet

Prep Time: 10 mins. Cook Time: 15 mins.

Ingredients:
- 4 eggs
- 1 large onion, sliced

- 1/8 cup cheddar cheese, grated
- 1/8 cup mozzarella cheese, grated
- Cooking spray
- ¼ teaspoon soy sauce
- Freshly ground black pepper, to taste

Directions:
- Preheat the Air fryer to 360 o F and grease a pan with cooking spray.
- Whisk together eggs, soy sauce and black pepper in a bowl.
- Place onions in the pan and cook for about 10 minutes.
- Pour the egg mixture over onion slices and top evenly with cheese.
- Cook for about 5 more mins. and serve.

52. Crust-Less Quiche

Prep Time: 5 mins. Cook Time: 30 mins.

Ingredients:
- 4 eggs
- ¼ cup onion, chopped
- ½ cup tomatoes, chopped
- ½ cup milk
- 1 cup Gouda cheese, shredded
- Salt, to taste

Directions:
- Preheat the Air fryer to 340 o F and grease 2 ramekins lightly.
- Mix together all the ingredients in a ramekin until well combined.
- Place in the Air fryer and cook for about 30 minutes.
- Dish out and serve

53. Toasties and Sausage in Egg Pond

Prep Time: 10 mins. Cook Time: 22 mins.

Ingredients:
- 3 eggs
- 2 cooked sausages, sliced
- 1 bread slice, cut into sticks
- 1/8 cup mozzarella cheese, grated
- 1/8 cup Parmesan cheese, grated
- ¼ cup cream

Directions:
- Preheat the Air fryer to 365 o F and grease 2 ramekins lightly.
- Whisk together eggs with cream in a bowl and place in the ramekins.
- Stir in the bread and sausage slices in the egg mixture and top with cheese.
- Transfer the ramekins in the Air fryer basket and cook for about 22 minutes.
- Dish out and serve warm.

54. Ham Omelet

Prep Time: 10 mins. Cook Time: 30 mins.

Ingredients:
- 4 small tomatoes, chopped
- 4 eggs
- 2 ham slices
- 1 onion, chopped
- 2 Tbsp.cheddar cheese
- Salt and black pepper, to taste

Directions:
- Preheat the Air fryer to 390 o F and grease an Air fryer pan.
- Place the tomatoes in the Air fryer pan and cook for about 10 minutes.
- Heat a nonstick skillet on medium heat and add onion and ham.
- Stir fry for about 5 mins. and transfer into the Air fryer pan.
- Whisk together eggs, salt and black pepper in a bowl and pour in the Air fryer pan.
- Set the Air fryer to 335 o F and cook for about 15 minutes.

55. Tofu Omelet

Prep Time: 10 mins. Cook Time: 29 mins.

Ingredients:
- ¼ of onion, chopped
- 12-ounce silken tofu, pressed and sliced
- 3 eggs, beaten
- 1 tablespoon chives, chopped
- 1 garlic clove, minced
- 2 teaspoons olive oil
- Salt and black pepper, to taste

Directions:
- Preheat the Air fryer to 355 o F and grease an Air fryer pan with olive oil.
- Add onion and garlic to the greased pan and cook for about 4 minutes.
- Add tofu, mushrooms and chives and season with salt and black pepper.
- Beat the eggs and pour over the tofu mixture.
- Cook for about 25 minutes, poking the eggs twice in between.
- Dish out and serve warm.

56. Breakfast Muffins

Prep Time: 15 minutes

Ingredients
- 1 cup flour¼ cup mashed banana
- ¼ cup powdered sugar

- 1 tsp. milk
- 1 tsp. chopped walnuts
- ½ tsp. baking powder
- ¼ cup oats¼ cup butter,

Instructions
- Preheat the air fryer to 320 degrees
- Place the sugar, walnuts, banana, and butter in a bowl and mix to combine.In another bowl, combine the flour, baking powder and oats.
- Combine the two mixtures together and stir in the milk.Grease a muffin tin and pour the batter in.Bake in your air fryer for 10 minutes.Enjoy.

57. Air Fryer Bacon And Egg Bite Cups

Prep Time: 10 Mins
Cook Time: 15 Mins
Total Time: 25 Mins

Ingredients
- 6 large eggs
- 2 Tbsps of heavy whipping cream or milk (any is fine)
- Salt and pepper to taste
- ¼ cup chopped green peppers
- ¼ cup chopped red peppers
- ¼ cup chopped onions
- ¼ cup chopped fresh spinach
- ½ cup shredded cheddar cheese
- ¼ cup shredded mozzarella cheese
- 3 slices of cooked and crumbled bacon

Instructions
- Add the eggs to a large mixing bowl.
- Add in the cream, salt, and pepper to taste.
- Whisk to combine. Sprinkle in the green peppers, red peppers, onions, spinach, cheeses, and bacon. I like to add only half of the ingredients here.
- Whisk to combine.
- I recommend you place the silicone molds in the air fryer before pouring in the egg mixture.
- This way you don't have to move the filled cups. Pour the egg mixture into each of the silicone molds. I didn't need to spray mine and they didn't stick. If you have not used your molds yet, you may want to spray with cooking spray first to be sure.
- Sprinkle in the remaining half of all of the veggies.
- Cook the egg bites cups for 12-15 mins at 300 degrees. You can test the

center of one with a toothpick.

- When the toothpick comes out clean, the eggs have set.

58. Quick And Easy Air Fryer Sausage

Cook Time: 20 Mins
Total Time: 20 Mins
Servings: 5

Ingredients

- 5 raw and uncooked sausage links

Instructions

- Line the air fryer basket with parchment paper. Parchment paper will soak up the grease and prevent the air fryer from smoking. Place the sausage on top of the paper. It's ok for the sausages to touch.
- Cook for 15 mins at 360 degrees. Open and flip and cook an additional 5 mins or until the sausage reaches an internal temperature of 160 degrees. Use a meat thermometer. You can also flip halfway through.
- Cool before serving.

59. Easy Air Fryer French Toast Sticks

Prep Time: 10 mins
Cook Time: 12 mins
Total Time: 22 mins

Ingredients

- 4 slices Texas Toast bread
- 1 Tbsp melted butter measured solid
- 1 egg beaten
- 2 Tbsp sweetener
- 1 Tsp. ground cinnamon
- 1/4 cup milk
- 1 Tsp. vanilla

Instructions

- Cut each slice of bread into 3 strip pieces.
- Add the beaten egg, sweetener, cinnamon, milk, and vanilla to the bowl with the melted butter. Stir to combine.
- Spray the air fryer basket with cooking oil spray.
- Dredge each piece of bread in the French toast batter. Be careful not to dredge each stick in too much batter. You may run out of batter if so.
- Place the French toast sticks in the air fryer basket. Do not overcrowd.
- Spray with cooking oil.
- Air Fry for 8 mins at 370 degrees.
- Open the air fryer and flip the French toast. Cook for an additional 2-4 mins or until crisp.

60. Rarebit

Prep Time: 15 mins

Ingredients:

- 3 slices of bread
- 1 tsp. smoked paprika
- 2 eggs1 tsp. Dijon mustard
- 4 ½ oz. cheddar cheese, grated
- Salt and pepper, to taste

Instructions

- Toast the bread in the air fryer to your liking.In a bowl, whisk the eggs.
- Stir in the mustard, cheddar and paprika.+
- Season with some salt and pepper.Spread the mixture on the toasts.
- Cook the bread slices for about 10 mins at 360 degrees

61. Paleo Crispy Air Fryer Sweet Potato Hash Browns

Prep Time: 10 mins Cook Time: 20 mins
Soak in water: 20 mins
Total Time: 50 mins

Ingredients

- 4 sweet potatoes peeled
- 2 garlic cloves minced
- 1 Tsp. cinnamon
- 1 Tsp. paprika
- salt and pepper to taste
- 2 teaspoons olive oil

Instructions

- Grate the sweet potatoes using the largest holes of a cheese grater.
- Place the sweet potatoes in a bowl of cold water. Allow the sweet potatoes to soak for 20-25 minutes.
- Soaking the sweet potatoes in cold water will help remove the starch from the potatoes. This makes them crunchy.
- Drain the water from the potatoes and dry them completely using a paper towel.
- Place the potatoes in a dry bowl. Add the olive oil, garlic, paprika, and salt and pepper to taste. Stir to combine the ingredients.
- Add the potatoes to the air fryer.
- Cook for ten mins at 400 degrees.
- Open the air fryer and shake the potatoes. Cook for an additional ten minutes.
- Cool before serving.

62. Easy Air Fryer Hard Boiled Eggs

Cook Time: 16 mins
Cooling: 5 mins
Total Time: 21 mins

Ingredients

- 6 large eggs

Instructions

- Place the eggs on the air fryer basket.
- Air fryer for 16 mins at 260 degrees.
- Open the air fryer and remove the eggs. Place them in a bowl with ice and cold water.
- Allow the eggs to cool for 5 minutes.
- Peel and serve.

63. Air Fryer Blueberry Muffins

Prep Time: 10 mins Cook Time: 15 mins
Total Time: 25 mins

Ingredients

- 1 1/2 cups all-purpose or white whole wheat flour
- 3/4 cup old-fashioned oats (oatmeal)
- 1/2 cup brown sweetener Light brown sugar can be used if preferred
- 1 Tbsp baking powder
- 1/2 Tsp. cinnamon
- 1/2 Tsp. salt
- 1 cup milk
- 1/4 cup melted unsalted butter (at room temperature)
- 2 eggs (at room temperature)
- 2 teaspoons vanilla
- 1 cup blueberries You can use fresh or frozen blueberries. If using frozen, do not thaw.

Instructions

- Combine the flour, rolled oats, salt, cinnamon, brown sweetener, and baking powder in a large mixing bowl. Mix.
- Combine the milk, eggs, vanilla, and butter in a separate medium-sized bowl. Mix using a silicone spoon.
- Add the wet ingredients to the dry ingredients in the mixing bowl. Stir.
- Fold in the blueberries and stir.
- Divide the batter among 12 silicone muffin cups and add them to the air fryer. Spraying the liners with oil is optional. The muffins generally don't stick.
- Place the air fryer at 350 degrees. Monitor the muffins closely for proper cook time, as every model will cook differently. The muffins will need to cook for 11-15 min.. Insert a toothpick

into the middle of a muffin, if it returns clean the muffins have finished baking. Mine was ready at about 13 min..

64. Air Fryer Loaded Hash Browns

Prep Time: 10 mins Cook Time: 20 mins Soak in water: 20 mins Total Time: 50 mins

Ingredients
- 3 russet potatoes
- 1/4 cup chopped green peppers
- 1/4 cup chopped red peppers
- 1/4 cup chopped onions
- 2 garlic cloves chopped
- 1 Tsp. paprika
- salt and pepper to taste
- 2 teaspoons olive oil

Instructions
- Grate the potatoes using the largest holes of a cheese grater.
- Place the potatoes in a bowl of cold water. Allow the potatoes to soak for 20-25 min.. Soaking the potatoes in cold water will help remove the starch from the potatoes. This makes them crunchy.
- Drain the water from the potatoes and dry them completely using a paper towel.
- Place the potatoes in a dry bowl. Add the garlic, paprika, olive oil, and salt and pepper to taste. Stir to combine the ingredients.
- Add the potatoes to the air fryer.
- Cook for ten mins at 400 degrees.
- Open the air fryer and shake the potatoes.
- Add the chopped peppers and onions. Cook for an additional ten minutes.
- Cool before serving.

65. Air Fryer Homemade Strawberry Pop-Tarts

Prep Time: 15 mins Cook Time: 10 mins Total Time: 25 mins

Ingredients
- 2 refrigerated pie crusts
- 1 Tsp. cornstarch
- 1/3 cup low-sugar strawberry preserves
- Cooking oil I used olive oil.
- 1/2 cup plain, non-fat vanilla Greek yogurt
- 1 oz cream cheese I used reduced-fat.
- 1 Tbsp sweetener
- 1 Tsp. sugar sprinkles

Instructions
- Lay the pie crust on a flat working surface. I used a bamboo cutting board.
- Using a knife or pizza cutter, cut the 2 pie crusts into 6 rectangles (3 from each pie crust). Each should be fairly long as you will fold it over to close the pop tart.
- Add the preserves and cornstarch to a bowl and mix well.
- Add a Tbsp of the preserves to the crust. Place the preserves in the upper area of the crust.
- Fold each over to close the pop tarts.
- Using a fork, make imprints in each of the pop tarts, to create vertical and horizontal lines along the edges.
- Place the pop tarts in the Air Fryer. Do not stack, cook in batches if needed. Spray with cooking oil.
- Cook on 370 degrees for 10 min.. You may want to check in on the Pop-Tarts for around 8 mins to ensure they aren't too crisp for your liking.
- Combine the Greek yogurt, cream cheese, and sweetener in a bowl to create the frosting.
- Allow the Pop-Tarts to cool before removing them from the Air Fryer. This is important. If you do not allow them to cool, they may break.
- Remove the pop tarts from the Air Fryer. Top each with the frosting. Sprinkle sugar sprinkles throughout.

66. Air Fried Breakfast Frittata

Prep time: 15 mins Cook time: 20 mins

Ingredients
- Cooking spray
- (Optional) 1 pinch of cayenne pepper
- 1 chopped green onion
- 2 tbsp of diced red bell pepper
- 1/2 cup of Cheddar-Monterey Jack cheese blend, shredded
- 4 lightly beaten eggs
- 1/4 lbs of cooked breakfast sausage, crumbled

Directions
- 1. Heat up the Air fryer to 360 F.
- 2. Mix the cheese, eggs, sausage, cayenne, onion and bell pepper in a bowl
- until well combined.
- 3. Arrange a 6x2-inch nonstick cake pan and spray with cooking spray.
- 4. Pour the Frittata mixture in the sprayed pan.
5. Cook for 18 to 20 minutes until frittata is set.

67. Quick And Easy Air Fryer Grilled Cheese

Prep Time: 5 mins Cook Time: 7 mins Total Time: 12 mins

Ingredients
- 4 slices of bread
- 1 Tbsp butter melted
- 2 slices mild cheddar cheese
- 5-6 slices cooked bacon Optional
- 2 slices mozzarella cheese

Instructions
- Heat the butter in the microwave for 10-15 seconds to soften.
- Spread the butter onto one side of each of the slices of bread.
- Place a slice of buttered bread (butter side down) onto the air fryer basket.
- Load the remaining ingredients in the following order: a slice of cheddar cheese, sliced cooked bacon, a slice of mozzarella cheese, and top with another slice of bread (butter side up).
- If you have an air fryer that is very loud, you will likely need to use a layer rack or trivet to hold down the sandwich to keep it from flying. My Power Air Fryer does not need this, but my louder Black + Decker air fryer requires this to anchor the sandwich and keep it from flying around inside the air fryer.
- Cook for 4 mins at 370 degrees.
- Open the air fryer. Flip the sandwich. Cook for an additional 3 min..
- Remove and serve.

68. Air Fryer Sweet Potato Hash

Prep Time: 10 mins Cook Time: 25 mins Total Time: 35 mins

Ingredients
- 3 medium sweet potatoes Chopped into chunks about 1 inch thick.
- 1/2 cup diced white onions
- 3 slices bacon cooked and crumbled.
- 1/2 cup chopped green peppers
- 2 garlic cloves minced
- 1/3 cup diced celery
- 1 Tbsp olive oil
- 1 Tsp. Tony Chachere Lite Creole Seasoning

- 1/2 Tsp. paprika
- 1/2 Tsp. dried chives

Instructions

- Combine the sweet potato chunks, onions, celery, green peppers, and garlic in a large bowl.
- Drizzle the olive oil throughout and then sprinkle the Tony Chachere Lite Creole Seasoning and paprika. Stir and mix well to combine.
- Add the sweet potato mix to the air fryer basket. Do not overcrowd the basket. Cook in batches if needed.
- Air fry for 10 mins at 400 degrees.
- Open the air fryer and shake the basket. Air fry for an additional 2-7 mins until the sweet potatoes are crisp on the outside and tender to touch when pierced with a fork.
- Sprinkle the crumbled bacon and dried chives throughout.

69. Easy Air Fryer Roasted Potatoes

Prep Time: 10 mins
Cook Time: 15 mins
Total Time: 25 mins

Ingredients

- 2 russet potatoes peeled and sliced into large chunks.
- 1 Tsp. olive oil
- 2 sprigs of fresh rosemary, use 1 sprig if you prefer a hint of rosemary flavor.
- 2 minced garlic cloves
- 1/2 Tsp. onion powder
- salt and pepper to taste
- cooking oil I use olive oil.

Instructions

- Drizzle the potatoes with olive oil and season with garlic, onion powder, salt, and pepper to taste.
- Spray the air fryer basket with cooking oil.
- Add the potatoes to the air fryer basket along with the thyme. Do not overfill the basket. Cook in batches if needed.
- Air fry for 10 mins at 400 degrees.
- Open the air fryer and shake the basket. Air fry for an additional 2-7 mins until the sweet potatoes are crisp on the outside and tender to touch when pierced with a fork.
- Cool before serving.

70. Air Fryer Cinnamon Sugar Donuts

Prep Time: 5 mins Cook Time: 16 mins
Total Time: 21 mins

Ingredients

- 8 oz can of biscuits
- 1 Tsp. ground cinnamon
- 1-2 teaspoons stevia 1/4 cup of table sugar can be substituted
- cooking oil spray I used avocado oil

Instructions

- Lay the biscuits on a flat surface. Use a small circle cookie cutter or a biscuit cutter to cut holes in the middle of the biscuits. I used a protein powder scoop
- Spray the air fryer basket with oil.
- Place the donuts in the air fryer. Spray the donuts with oil. Do not stack the donuts. Cook in two batches if needed.
- Cook for 4 mins at 360 degrees.
- Open the air fryer and flip the donuts. Cook for an additional 4 min..
- Repeat for the remaining donuts.
- Spritz the donuts with additional oil.
- Add the cinnamon and sugar to separate bowls.
- Dip the donuts in the cinnamon and sugar. Serve!

71. Air Fryer Fried Pork Chops Southern Style

Prep Time: 5 mins Cook Time: 20 mins
Optional marinate: 30 mins
Total Time: 25 mins

Ingredients

- 4 pork chops (bone-in or boneless)
- 3 tbsp buttermilk I used fat-free
- 1/4 cup all-purpose flour
- Seasoning Salt to taste You can also use either a chicken or pork rub.
- pepper to taste
- 1 Ziploc bag
- cooking oil spray

Instructions

- Pat the pork chops dry.
- Season the pork chops with the seasoning salt and pepper.
- Drizzle the buttermilk over the pork chops.
- Place the pork chops in a Ziploc bag with the flour. Shake to fully coat.
- Marinate for 30 min.. This step is optional. This helps the flour adhere to the pork chops.
- Place the pork chops in the air fryer. I do not recommend you stack. Cook in

batches if necessary.

- Spray the pork chops with cooking oil.
- Cook the pork chops for 15 mins at 380 degrees. Flip the pork chops over to the other side after 10 minutes.

72. Ninja Foodi Low-Carb Breakfast Casserole {Air Fryer}

Prep Time: 10 Mins Cook Time: 15 Mins
Total Time: 25 Mins

Ingredients

- 1 LB Ground Sausage
- 1/4 Cup Diced White Onion
- 1 Diced Green Bell Pepper
- 8 Whole Eggs, Beaten
- 1/2 Cup Shredded Colby Jack Cheese
- 1 Tsp Fennel Seed
- 1/2 Tsp Garlic Salt

Instructions

- If you are using the Ninja Foodi, use the saute function to brown the sausage in the pot of the food. If you are using an air fryer, you can use a skillet to do this.
- Add in the onion and pepper and cook along with the ground sausage until the veggies are soft and the sausage is cooked.
- Using the 8.75-inch pan or the Air Fryer pan, spray it with non-stick cooking spray.
- Place the ground sausage mixture on the bottom of the pan.
- Top evenly with cheese.
- Pour the beaten eggs evenly over the cheese and sausage.
- Add fennel seed and garlic salt evenly over the eggs.
- Place the rack in the low position in the Ninja Foodi, and then place the pan on top.
- Set to Air Crisp for 15 mins at 390 degrees.
- If you are using an air fryer, place the dish directly into the basket of the air fryer and cook for 15 mins at 390 degrees.
- Carefully remove and serve.

73. Air Fryer Donuts

Prep Time: 10 Mins Cook Time: 5 Mins
Total Time: 15 Mins **Ingredients**

- 16 oz refrigerated flaky jumbo biscuits
- 1/2 c. Granulated white sugar
- 2 tsp ground cinnamon

- 4 tbsp butter melted
- Olive or coconut oil spray

Instructions

- Combine sugar and cinnamon in a shallow bowl; set aside.
- Remove the biscuits from the can, separate them and place them on a flat surface. Use a 1-inch round biscuit cutter (or similarly-sized bottle cap) to cut holes out of the center of each biscuit.
- Lightly coat the air fryer basket with olive or coconut oil spray. Do not use a non-stick spray like Pam because it can damage the coating on the basket.
- Place 4 donuts in a single layer in the air fryer basket. Make sure they are not touching.
- Air Fry at 360 degrees F for 5 mins or until lightly browned.
- Remove donuts from Air Fryer, dip in melted butter then roll in cinnamon sugar to coat. Serve immediately.
-

74. Air Fryer Breakfast Sausage

Prep Time: 10 Mins Cook Time: 10 Mins
Total Time: 20 Mins

Ingredients

- 1 lb ground pork
- 1 lb ground turkey
- 2 tsp fennel seeds
- 2 tsp dry rubbed sage
- 2 tsp garlic powder
- 1 tsp paprika
- 1 tsp sea salt
- 1 tsp dried thyme
- 1 tbsp real maple syrup

Instructions

- Begin by mixing the pork and turkey in a large bowl. In a small bowl, mix the remaining ingredients: fennel, sage, garlic powder, paprika, salt, and thyme. Pour spices into the meat and continue to mix until the spices are completely incorporated.
- Spoon into balls (about 2-3 tbsp of meat), and flatten into patties. Place inside the air fryer, you will probably have to do this in 2 batches.
- Set the temperature to 370 degrees, and cook for 10 minutes. Remove from the air fryer and repeat with the remaining sausage.

75. Crispy Bacon In The Air Fryer

Cook Time: 10 Mins Total Time: 10 Mins

Ingredients

- 1 Pound of Bacon

Instructions

- Add bacon into the air fryer basket, evenly. This may take 2 batches to cook all of the bacon, depending on size.
- Cook at 350 degrees for 5 minutes.
- Turn bacon and cook an additional 5 mins or until your desired crispiness.
- Remove bacon with tongs and place on a paper towel-lined plate.
- Let cool and serve.

76. Air Fryer Breakfast Stuffed Peppers

Prep Time: 5 mins Cook Time: 13 mins
Total Time: 18 mins
Servings: 2

Ingredients

- 1 bell pepper halved, middle seeds removed
- 4 eggs
- 1 tsp olive oil
- 1 pinch salt and pepper
- 1 pinch sriracha flakes for a bit of spice, optional

Instructions

- Cut bell peppers in half lengthwise and remove seeds and middle leaving the edges intact like bowls.
- Use your finger to rub a bit of olive oil just on the exposed edges (where it was cut).
- Crack two eggs into each bell pepper half. Sprinkle with desired spices.
- Set them on a trivet inside your Ninja Foodi or directly inside your other brand of the air fryer.
- Close the lid on your air fryer (the one attached to the Ninja Foodi machine).
- Turn the machine on, press the air crisper button at 390 degrees for 13 mins (times will vary slightly according to how well done you like your egg but this was perfect for us).
- Alternatively, if you'd rather have your bell pepper and eggless brown on the outside add just one egg to your pepper and set the air fryer to 330 degrees for 15 min.. (for an over hard egg consistency)

77. Air Fryer Bacon And Egg Breakfast Biscuit Bombs

Prep Time: 35 Mins Cook Time: 15 Mins
Total: 50 MIN

Ingredients

- Biscuit Bombs
- 4 slices bacon, cut into 1/2-inch pieces
- 1 Tbsp butter
- 2 eggs, beaten
- 1/4 Tsp. pepper
- 1 can (10.2 oz) Pillsbury Grands! Southern Homestyle refrigerated Buttermilk biscuits (5 biscuits)
- 2 oz sharp cheddar cheese, cut into ten 3/4-inch cubes
- Egg Wash
- 1 egg
- 1 Tbsp water

Instruction

- Prevent your screen from going dark while you cook.
- Cut two 8-inch rounds of cooking parchment paper. Place one round at bottom of the air fryer basket. Spray with cooking spray.
- In 10-inch nonstick skillet, cook bacon over medium-high heat until crisp. Remove from pan; place on paper towel. Carefully wipe skillet with a paper towel. Add butter to skillet; melt over medium heat. Add 2 beaten eggs and pepper to skillet; cook until eggs are thickened but still moist, stirring frequently. Remove from heat; stir in bacon. Cool 5 minutes.
- Meanwhile, separate dough into 5 biscuits; separate each biscuit into 2 layers. Press each into a 4-inch round. Spoon 1 heaping tablespoonful of egg mixture onto the center of each round. Top with one piece of cheese. Gently fold edges up and over filling; pinch to seal. In a small bowl, beat the remaining egg and water. Brush biscuits on all sides with egg wash.
- Place 5 of the biscuit bombs, seam sides down, on parchment in the air fryer basket. Spray both sides of the second parchment round with cooking spray. Top biscuit bombs in a basket with a second parchment round, then top with remaining 5 biscuit bombs.
- Set to 325°F; cook 8 min.. Remove top parchment round; using tongs, carefully

turn biscuits, and place in basket in a single layer. Cook 4 to 6 mins longer or until cooked through (at least 165°F).

78. Air Fryer Sausage Breakfast Casserole

Prep Time: 10 Mins Cook Time: 20 Mins
Total Time: 30 Mins

Ingredients
- 1 Lb Hash Browns
- 1 Lb Ground Breakfast Sausage
- 1 Green Bell Pepper Diced
- 1 Red Bell Pepper Diced
- 1 Yellow Bell Pepper Diced
- 1/4 Cup Sweet Onion Diced
- 4 Eggs

Instructions
- Foil line the basket of your air fryer.
- Place the hash browns on the bottom.
- Top it with the uncooked sausage.
- Evenly place the peppers and onions on top.
- Cook on 355* for 10 minutes.
- Open the air fryer and mix up the casserole a bit if needed.
- Crack each egg in a bowl, then pour right on top of the casserole.
- Cook on 355* for another 10 minutes.
- Serve with salt and pepper to taste.

79. Air Fryer Baked Egg Cups w/ Spinach & Cheese

Prep Time: 5 mins Cook Time: 10 mins
Total Time: 15 mins

Ingredients
- 1 large egg
- 1 Tbsp (15 ml) milk or half & half
- 1 Tbsp (15 ml) frozen spinach, thawed (or sautéed fresh spinach)
- 1-2 teaspoons (5 ml) grated cheese
- Salt, to taste
- Black pepper, to taste
- Cooking spray, for muffin cups or ramekins

Instructions
- Spray inside of silicone muffin cups or ramekin with oil spray.
- Add egg, milk, spinach, and cheese into the muffin cup or ramekin.
- Season with salt and pepper. Gently stir ingredients into egg whites without breaking the yolk.
- Air Fry at 330°F for about 6-12 mins (single egg cups usually take about 6 mins - multiple or doubled up cups take

as much as 12. As you add more egg cups, you will need to add more time.)
- Cooking in a ceramic ramekin may take a little longer. If you want runny yolks, cook for less time. Keep checking the eggs after 5 mins to ensure the egg is to your preferred texture.

80. Airfryer French Toast Sticks Recipe

Prep Time: 5 mins Cook Time: 12 mins
Total Time: 17 mins

Ingredients
- 4 pieces bread (whatever kind and thickness desired)
- 2 Tbsp butter (or margarine, softened)
- 2 eggs (gently beaten)
- 1 pinch salt
- 1 pinch cinnamon
- 1 pinch nutmeg
- 1 pinch ground cloves
- 1 tsp icing sugar (and/or maple syrup for garnish and serving)

Instructions
- Preheat Airfryer to 180* Celsius.
- In a bowl, gently beat together two eggs, a sprinkle of salt, a few heavy shakes of cinnamon, and small pinches of both nutmeg and ground cloves.
- Butter both sides of bread slices and cut into strips.
- Dredge each strip in the egg mixture and arrange it in Airfryer (you will have to cook in two batches).
- After 2 mins of cooking, pause the Airfryer, take out the pan, making sure you place the pan on a heat-safe surface and spray the bread with cooking spray.
- Once you have generously coated the strips, flip and spray the second side as well.
- Return pan to the fryer and cook for 4 more min., checking after a couple of mins to ensure they are cooking evenly and not burning.
- When the egg is cooked and the bread is golden brown, remove it from Airfryer and serve immediately.
- To garnish and serve, sprinkle with icing sugar, top with whip cream, drizzle with maple syrup, or serve with a small bowl of syrup for dipping.

81. Air Fryer Breakfast Frittata

Prep Time: 15 mins Cook Time: 20 mins

Total Time: 35 mins

Ingredients
- ¼ pound breakfast sausage fully cooked and crumbled
- 4 eggs, lightly beaten
- ½ cup shredded Cheddar-Monterey Jack cheese blend
- 2 Tbsps red bell pepper, diced
- 1 green onion, chopped
- 1 pinch cayenne pepper (Optional)
- cooking spray

Direction
- Combine sausage, eggs, Cheddar-Monterey Jack cheese, bell pepper. onion, and cayenne in a bowl and mix to combine.
- Preheat the air fryer to 360 degrees F (180 degrees C). Spray a nonstick 6x2-inch cake pan with cooking spray.
- Place egg mixture in the prepared cake pan.
- Cook in the air fryer until frittata is set, 18 to 20 minutes.

82. Breakfast Potatoes In The Air Fryer

Prep Time: 2 mins Cook Time: 15 mins
Total Time: 17 mins
Servings: 2

Ingredients
- 5 medium potatoes, peeled and cut to 1-inch cubes (Yukon Gold works best)
- 1 tbsp oil
- Breakfast Potato Seasoning
- 1/2 tsp kosher salt
- 1/2 tsp smoked paprika
- 1/2 tsp garlic powder
- 1/4 tsp black ground pepper

Instructions
- Preheat the air fryer for about 2-3 mins at 400F degrees. This will give you the crispiest potatoes.
- Meanwhile, toss the potatoes with breakfast potato seasoning and oil until thoroughly coated.
- Spray the air fryer basket with a nonstick spray. Add the potatoes and cook for about 15 min., stopping and shaking the basket 2-3 times throughout to promote even cooking.
- Transfer to a plate and serve right away.

83. Breakfast Bombs

Active Time: 20 Mins Total Time: 25 Mins Yield: Serves 2

Ingredients

- 3 center-cut bacon slices
- 3 large eggs, lightly beaten
- 1 ounce 1/3-less-fat cream cheese, softened
- 1 Tbsp chopped fresh chives
- 4 ounces fresh prepared whole-wheat pizza dough
- Cooking spray

How To Make It

- Cook bacon in a medium skillet over medium until very crisp, about 10 minutes.
- Remove bacon from pan; crumble.
- Add eggs to bacon drippings in pan; cook, stirring often, until almost set but still loose, about 1 minute.
- Transfer eggs to a bowl; stir in cream cheese, chives, and crumbled bacon.
- Divide dough into 4 equal pieces. Roll each piece on a lightly floured surface into a 5-inch circle.
- Place one-fourth of the egg mixture in the center of each dough circle. Brush outside edge of dough with water; wrap dough around egg mixture to form a purse, pinching together dough at the seams.
- Place dough purses in a single layer in an air fryer basket; coat well with cooking spray. Cook at 350°F until golden brown, 5 to 6 min., checking after 4 minutes.

84. Air Fryer Scrambled Eggs

Prep Time: 3 Mins Cook Time: 9 Mins
Total Time: 12 Mins

Ingredients

- 1/3 Tbsp unsalted butter
- 2 eggs
- 2 Tbsps milk
- Salt and pepper to taste
- 1/8 cup cheddar cheese

Instructions

- Place butter in an oven/air fryer-safe pan and place inside the air fryer.
- Cook at 300 degrees until butter is melted, about 2 minutes.
- Whisk together the eggs and milk, then add salt and pepper to taste.
- Place eggs in a pan and cook it at 300 degrees for 3 min., then push eggs to the inside of the pan to stir them around.
- Cook for 2 more mins then add

cheddar cheese, stirring the eggs again.

- Cook 2 more min..
- Remove pan from the air fryer and enjoy them immediately.

85. Air Fryer Banana Bread

Prep Time: 10 mins Cook Time: 28 mins
Total Time: 38 minutes
Servings: 8

Ingredients

- 3/4 c all-purpose flour
- 1/4 tsp baking soda
- 1/4 tsp salt
- 1 egg
- 2 bananas overripe, mashed
- 1/2 tsp vanilla
- 1/4 c sour cream
- 1/4 c vegetable oil
- 1/2 c sugar
- 7" bundt pan

Instructions

- Mix dry ingredients in one bowl and wet in another. Slowly combine the two until flour is incorporated, do not overmix.
- Spray inside of 7" bundt pan with nonstick spray and pour in batter.
- Place inside air fryer basket and close. Set to 310 degrees for 28 min..
- Remove when done and allow to sit in the pan for 5 min.. Then gently flip over on a plate. Drizzle melted frosting on the top, slice, and serve.

86. Easy Air Fryer Breakfast Frittata

Prep Time: 5 min
Cook Time: 10 min
Total Time: 15 mins
Yield: 4 servings

Ingredients

- 4 eggs
- ½ cup shredded sharp cheddar cheese
- ¼ cup fresh spinach, chopped
- 2 scallions, chopped
- 2 Tbsps half and half
- salt and pepper to taste

Instructions

- In a medium bowl, beat eggs with half and half.
- Stir in cheese, spinach, scallions, salt, and pepper.
- Spray a 6" cake pan with cooking spray (very important). Pour mixture into the pan.
- Air fry at 350 degrees (F) for 10-14

min.. A toothpick inserted will come out clean when done.

- Let cool for 5 mins before removing from pan and serving.

87. Air Fryer Breakfast Pizza

Prep Time: 5 Mins Cook Time: 15 Mins
Total Time: 20 Mins

Ingredients

- Crescent Dough
- 3 scrambled eggs
- crumbled sausage
- 1/2 chopped pepper
- 1/2 cup cheddar cheese
- 1/2 cup mozzarella cheese

Instructions

- Spray Pan with oil, Spread dough in the bottom of a Fat daddio or springform pan. Place in the air fryer on 350 for 5 mins or until the top is slightly brown
- Remove from the air fryer . Top with Eggs, sausage, peppers, and cheese, Or use your favorite toppings.
- Place in the air fryer for an additional 5-10 mins or until the top is golden brown.

88. Breakfast Sweet Potato Skins

Prep Time: 7 Mins
Cook Time: 23 Mins
Total Time: 30 Mins

Ingredients

- 2 medium sweet potatoes
- 2 tsp. olive oil
- 4 eggs
- 1/4 c. whole milk
- salt and pepper
- 4 slices cooked bacon
- 2 green onions, sliced

Instructions

- Wash the sweet potatoes and add 3-4 cuts to the potatoes. Microwave for 6-8 minutes, depending on their size until they are soft.
- Using an oven mitt, slice the potatoes in half lengthwise. Scoop out the potato flesh, leaving 1/4 inch around the edges. Save the scooped sweet potato for another use.
- Brush the potato skins with olive oil and sprinkle with sea salt. Arrange the skins in your Air Fryer basket and cook at 400° (or the highest available temp) for 10 min..

- Meanwhile, add the eggs, milk, salt, and pepper to a non-stick skillet. Cook the mixture over medium heat, stirring constantly, until there are no longer any visible liquid eggs.
- Top each cooked potato skin with 1/4 of the scrambled eggs and 1 slice of crumbled bacon. Cover with shredded cheese and cook for 3 min., or until the cheese is melted.
- Serve topped with green onion.

89. Air Fryer French Toast Sticks

Prep Time: 7 Mins Cook Time: 8 Mins
Total Time: 15 Mins

Ingredients
- 12 slices Texas Toast
- 1 cup milk
- 5 large eggs
- 4 tbsp. butter, melted
- 1 tsp. vanilla extract
- 1/4 cup granulated sugar
- 1 tbsp. cinnamon
- Maple syrup, optional

Instructions
- Slice each bread slice into thirds.
- In a bowl, add the milk, eggs, butter, and vanilla. Whisk until combined.
- In a separate bowl, add the cinnamon and sugar.
- Dip each breadstick quickly into the egg mixture.
- Sprinkle the sugar mixture onto both sides.
- Place into the air fryer basket and cook at 350°F for about 8 mins or until just crispy.
- Remove from basket and allow to cool. Serve with maple syrup, if desired.

90. Breakfast Taquitos Recipe

Prep Time: 25 mins
Cook Time: 6 mins
Total Time: 31 mins

Ingredients
- pound ground turkey sausage
- 2 teaspoons onion powder
- 2 cloves garlic minced
- ½ Tsp. salt
- ½ Tsp. pepper
- 6 large eggs
- 16 small low carb flour or whole wheat tortillas
- 1 cup fat-free shredded Mexican blend or cheddar cheese

- 2 Tbsp I Can't Believe It's Not Butter Melted

Instructions
- Preheat oven to 400 F degrees. Lightly spray a 9x13 baking dish with coconut oil In a large skillet, cook sausage until it's is no longer pink. Drain.
- Add garlic and cook until soft. Season with onion powder, salt, and pepper. In a bowl, whisk eggs and pour into the skillet and cook until eggs are scrambled.
- Remove skillet from the stovetop.
- Add mixture to a bowl and set aside.
- Add tortillas to the microwave for 20 seconds.
- This softens them and makes it easier to roll them.
- On a flat surface, top a tortilla with 2 Tbsps of the skillet mixture. Top with a sprinkle of cheese.
- Roll the tortilla tightly and place in the baking dish.
- Brush with melted butter. Repeat until the remaining tortillas are filled.
- Pre-heat Air Fryer to 350° for 1 minute.
- Bake for 3 mins and turn, and bake for an additional 2-3 mins or until tortillas are golden brown and crispy.
- Serve with your favorite toppings!

91. Air Fryer French Toast

Prep Time: 5 mins Cook Time: 9 mins
Total Time: 14 mins

Ingredients
- 2 eggs
- 2 TBS milk, cream, or half and half
- 1/2 tsp ground cinnamon
- 1/2 tsp vanilla extract
- 1 loaf challah or brioche bread, cut into 8 thick slices

Instructions
- In a medium bowl, add egg, milk, vanilla, and cinnamon; whisk to combine completely; set aside
- Make an assembly line: set up whisked egg mixture and bread next to each other.
- Spray the air fryer basket with nonstick oil spray
- Dip the slices of bread into the egg mixture being sure to flip and coat both sides. Lift out of the mixture and allow to drip for a few seconds, then place

into the air fryer basket. Repeat for remaining slices
- Close the Air Fryer. Set to 400 degrees and 5 min.. After 5 minutes, open the basket and carefully flip the french toast slices. Close the air fryer and cook for 3-4 more mins at 400 degrees. *Time may vary slightly depending on the air fryer model.
- Remove the french toast when finished and then cook the remaining french toast slices.
- Serve with warm maple syrup and powdered sugar or your favorite toppings!

92. Air Fryer Breakfast Pockets

Prep Time: 30 mins Cook Time: 15 mins

Ingredients
- 1 lb of ground pork
- 4 whole eggs
- 1 whole egg for egg wash
- 1/3 + 1/4 c of whole milk
- 1-2 ounces of Velveeta cheese
- Salt and pepper to taste
- 2 packages of Pillsbury pie crust 2 crusts to a package
- 2-gallon ziplock bags
- parchment paper
- Cooking spray

Instructions
- Remove pie crusts from the refrigerator.
- Brown and drain the pork.
- Heat 1/4 c milk and cheese in a small pot until melted.
- Whisk 4 eggs, season with salt and pepper, and add remaining milk.
- Scramble eggs in a skillet until almost fully cooked.
- Mix the meat, cheese, and eggs.
- Roll out your pie crust and cut it into a 3-4 inch circle (about the size of a cereal bowl).
- Whisk one egg to make an egg wash.
- Place about 2 tbsps of mix into the middle of each circle.
- Egg wash all edges of the circle.
- Fold the circle creating a moon shape.
- Crimp the folded edges with a fork.
- Layer the pockets in parchment paper and place them in a plastic ziplock bag overnight.
- Once ready to cook, pre-heat your Air

Fryer to 360 degrees.
- Spray each side of the pocket with cooking spray.
- Place pockets in pre-heated Air Fryer for 15 mins or until golden brown.
- Remove from Air Fryer and allow to cool for a few mins before serving.

93. Air Fryer Cheesy Baked Eggs

Prep Time: 4 mins Cook Time: 16 mins
Total Time: 20 mins Servings: 2

Ingredients
- 4 large Eggs
- 2 ounces Smoked gouda, chopped
- Everything bagel seasoning
- Salt and pepper to taste

Instructions
- Spray the inside of each ramekin with cooking spray. Add 2 eggs to each ramekin, then add 1 ounce of chopped gouda to each. Salt and pepper to taste. Sprinkle your everything bagel seasoning on top of each ramekin (as much as you like). Place each ramekin into the air fryer basket. Cook for 400F for 16 min., or until eggs are cooked through. Serve.

94. Low-Carb Air Fryer Bacon And Egg Cups

Prep Time: 10 Mins Cook Time: 10 Mins
Total Time: 20 Mins

Ingredients
- 3 slices bacon, sliced in half
- 6 large eggs
- 1 bunch green onions, optional
- salt and pepper, optional

Instructions
- Arrange 6 baking cups (silicone or paper) in the air fryer basket. Spray with nonstick cooking spray.
- Line cups with bacon slice. Carefully crack an egg into each cup. Season with salt and pepper, if desired.
- Turn the air fryer on to 330° and cook for 10 minutes, until eggs are set. Carefully remove from air fryer and garnish with desired toppings.

95. Air Fryer English Breakfast

Prep Time: 3 mins Cook Time: 15 mins
Total Time:18 mins

Ingredients
- 6 English Sausages
- 6 Bacon Rashers
- 2 Large Tomatoes

- 4 Black Pudding
- ½ Can Baked Beans
- 2 Large Eggs
- 1 Tbsp Whole Milk
- 1 Tsp Butter
- Salt & Pepper

Instructions
- Crack your eggs into a ramekin and stir in butter, milk, and salt and pepper. Place in the air fryer.
- Add to the air fryer bacon rashers, black pudding, and sausages. Slice tomatoes in half and season the top with salt and pepper.
- Close the air fryer basket, making sure first that there is room for each of the breakfast items to cook.
- Then cook for 10 mins at 180c/360f. Though at the 5-minute interval stir your eggs with a fork.
- When the air fryer beeps, check to make sure the eggs are scrambled and remove the scrambled eggs with a kitchen glove or kitchen tongs. Replace the ramekin space with a ramekin of cold baked beans.
- Cook for a further 5 mins at the same temperature.
- When it beeps load your English breakfast ingredients onto a plate and enjoy.

96. Air Fryer Bacon And Egg Toast

Prep Time: 1 Minute Cook Time: 9 Mins
Total Time: 10 Mins

Ingredients
- Butter (if desired)
- 1 slice of bread
- 1 slice of bacon
- 1 egg
- Salt & pepper to taste

Directions
- Butter a slice of bread and place it in the air fryer. Add a slice of bacon around the top of the bread. Add an egg in the middle.
- Close the air fryer and cook for 9 mins at 340 degrees, or until the desired doneness. Salt & pepper to taste. Enjoy!

97. How To Make Bacon In Your Air Fryer

Prep Time: 5 mins
Cook Time: 10 mins
Ingredients:

- 4 pieces of thick-cut bacon
- 2 eggs
- 1 Tbsp butter
- 2 croissants sliced
- 1/2 cup ketchup
- 2 Tbsp apple cider vinegar
- 1 Tbsp molasses
- 1 Tbsp brown sugar
- 1/4 Tsp. mustard powder
- 1/4 Tsp. onion powder
- 1/2 Tbsp Worcestershire sauce
- 1/4 Tsp. liquid smoke

Instructions:
- Preheat your Air fryer to 200 degrees C (or 390 degrees F)
- Lay the bacon strips of your choice flat on the Air fryer tray.
- Cook for 4-5 minutes, then flip the bacon.
- Cook for another 4-5 mins until the desired doneness is reached.
- Air Fryer Bacon With BBQ Sauce Croissants
- Preheat your Air fryer to 200 degrees C (or 390 degrees F)
- Whisk together in a small saucepan the ketchup, apple cider vinegar, molasses, brown sugar, mustard powder, onion powder, Worcestershire sauce, and liquid smoke. Place on medium heat and bring to a simmer, cooking until the sauce thickens slightly.
- Lay the bacon flat on the Airfryer tray and brush with BBQ sauce. Cook for 4-5 min., then flip the bacon and brush the other side of the bacon with sauce. Cook for an additional 5 mins or until the desired doneness is reached.
- Place the croissants into your toaster and toast lightly.
- Melt the butter in a medium-sized frying pan and fry the eggs until they reach your desired doneness. (over-easy is best).
- Place an egg on the bottom of one croissant, followed by two bacon slices and the croissant top. Repeat with the other croissant.
- Serve and enjoy!

98. Air Fryer Bacon

Prep Time: 2 Mins Cook Time: 10 Mins
Total Time: 12 Mins

Ingredients
- 8 ounces bacon about 8 strips

- Water

Instructions

- Preheat the air fryer at 350F for about 5 minutes.
- Pour ¼ cup of water into the bottom of the air fryer to minimize smoke. Make sure the water is not touching the basket or bacon.
- Place bacon in a single layer into the preheated air fryer basket. Feel free to cut bacon strips in half or even in thirds to make it fit nicely.
- Cook for 8 to 10 mins for thinner bacon and 12 to 15 mins for thicker cut bacon.

99. Tasty Cinnamon Toast

Preparation time: 10 minutes Cooking time: 5 minutes Servings: 6

Ingredients:

- 1 stick butter, soft
- 12 bread slices
- ½ cup sugar
- 1 and ½ teaspoon vanilla extract
- 1 and ½ teaspoon cinnamon powder

Directions:

- In a bowl, mix soft butter with sugar, vanilla and cinnamon and whisk well.
- Spread this on bread slices, place them in your air fryer and cook at 400 degrees F for 5 minutes,
- Divide among plates and serve for breakfast.
- Enjoy!

100. Delicious Potato Hash

Preparation time: 10 minutes Cooking time: 25 minutes Servings: 4

Ingredients:

- 1 and ½ potatoes, cubed
- 1 yellow onion, chopped
- 2 teaspoons olive oil
- 1 green bell pepper, chopped
- Salt and black pepper to the taste
- ½ teaspoon thyme, dried
- 2 eggs

Directions:

- Heat up your air fryer at 350 degrees F, add oil, heat it up, add onion, bell pepper, salt and pepper, stir and cook for 5 minutes.
- Add potatoes, thyme and eggs, stir, cover and cook at 360 degrees F for 20 minutes.
- Divide among plates and serve for

breakfast.
- Enjoy!

101. Sweet Breakfast Casserole

Preparation time: 10 minutes Cooking time: 30 minutes Servings: 4

Ingredients:

- 3 tablespoons brown sugar
- 4 tablespoons butter
- 2 tablespoons white sugar
- ½ teaspoon cinnamon powder
- ½ cup flour
- For the casserole:
- 2 eggs
- 2 tablespoons white sugar
- 2 and ½ cups white flour
- 1 teaspoon baking soda
- 1 teaspoon baking powder
- 2 eggs
- ½ cup milk
- 2 cups buttermilk
- 4 tablespoons butter
- Zest from 1 lemon, grated
- 1 and 2/3 cup blueberries

Directions:

- In a bowl, mix eggs with 2 tablespoons white sugar, 2 and ½ cups white flour, baking powder, baking soda, 2 eggs, milk, buttermilk, 4 tablespoons butter, lemon zest and blueberries, stir and pour into a pan that fits your air fryer.
- In another bowls, mix 3 tablespoons brown sugar with 2 tablespoons white sugar, 4 tablespoons butter, ½ cup flour and cinnamon, stir until you obtain a crumble and spread over blueberries mix.
- Place in preheated air fryer and bake at 300 degrees F for 30 minutes.
- Divide among plates and serve for breakfast.
- Enjoy!

102. Eggs Casserole

Preparation time: 10 minutes Cooking time: 25 minutes Servings: 6

Ingredients:

- 1 pound turkey, ground
- 1 tablespoon olive oil
- ½ teaspoon chili powder
- 12 eggs
- 1 sweet potato, cubed
- 1 cup baby spinach
- Salt and black pepper to the taste
- 2 tomatoes, chopped for serving

Directions:

- In a bowl, mix eggs with salt, pepper, chili powder, potato, spinach, turkey and sweet potato and whisk well.
- Heat up your air fryer at 350 degrees F, add oil and heat it up.
- Add eggs mix, spread into your air fryer, cover and cook for 25 minutes.
- Divide among plates and serve for breakfast.
- Enjoy!

103. Sausage, Eggs and Cheese Mix

Preparation time: 10 minutes Cooking time: 20 minutes Servings: 4

Ingredients:

- 10 ounces sausages, cooked and crumbled
- 1 cup cheddar cheese, shredded
- 1 cup mozzarella cheese, shredded
- 8 eggs, whisked
- 1 cup milk
- Salt and black pepper to the taste

Cooking spray

Directions:

- In a bowl, mix sausages with cheese, mozzarella, eggs, milk, salt and pepper and whisk well.
- Heat up your air fryer at 380 degrees F, spray cooking oil, add eggs and sausage mix and cook for 20 minutes.
- Divide among plates and serve.
- Enjoy!

104. Special Corn Flakes Breakfast Casserole

Preparation time: 10 minutes Cooking time: 8 minutes Servings: 5

Ingredients:

- 1/3 cup milk
- 3 teaspoons sugar
- 2 eggs, whisked
- ¼ teaspoon nutmeg, ground
- ¼ cup blueberries
- 4 tablespoons cream cheese, whipped
- 1 and ½ cups corn flakes, crumbled
- 5 bread slices

Directions:

- In a bowl, mix eggs with sugar, nutmeg and milk and whisk well.
- In another bowl, mix cream cheese with blueberries and whisk well.
- Put corn flakes in a third bowl.
- Spread blueberry mix on each bread

slice, then dip in eggs mix and dredge in corn flakes at the end.

- Place bread in your air fryer's basket, heat up at 400 degrees F and bake for 8 minutes.
- Divide among plates and serve for breakfast.
- Enjoy!

105. Ham Breakfast Pie

Preparation time: 10 minutes Cooking time: 25 minutes Servings: 6

Ingredients:

- 16 ounces crescent rolls dough
- 2 eggs, whisked
- 2 cups cheddar cheese, grated
- 1 tablespoon parmesan, grated
- 2 cups ham, cooked and chopped
- Salt and black pepper to the taste
- Cooking spray

Directions:

- Grease your air fryer's pan with cooking spray and press half of the crescent rolls dough on the bottom.
- In a bowl, mix eggs with cheddar cheese, parmesan, salt and pepper, whisk well and add over dough.
- Spread ham, cut the rest of the crescent rolls dough in strips, arrange them over ham and cook at 300 degrees F for 25 minutes.
- Slice pie and serve for breakfast.
- Enjoy!

106. Breakfast Veggie Mix

Preparation time: 10 minutes Cooking time: 25 minutes Servings: 6

Ingredients:

- 1 yellow onion, sliced
- 1 red bell pepper, chopped
- 1 gold potato, chopped
- 2 tablespoons olive oil
- 8 ounces brie, trimmed and cubed
- 12 ounces sourdough bread, cubed
- 4 ounces parmesan, grated
- 8 eggs
- 2 tablespoons mustard
- 3 cups milk
- Salt and black pepper to the taste

Directions:

- Heat up your air fryer at 350 degrees F, add oil, onion, potato and bell pepper and cook for 5 minutes.
- In a bowl, mix eggs with milk, salt, pepper and mustard and whisk well.

- Add bread and brie to your air fryer, add half of the eggs mix and add half of the parmesan as well.
- Add the rest of the bread and parmesan, toss just a little bit and cook for 20 minutes.
- Divide among plates and serve for breakfast.
- Enjoy!

107. Scrambled Eggs

Preparation time: 10 minutes Cooking time: 10 minutes Servings: 2

Ingredients:

- 2 eggs
- 2 tablespoons butter
- Salt and black pepper to the taste
- 1 red bell pepper, chopped
- A pinch of sweet paprika

Directions:

- In a bowl, mix eggs with salt, pepper, paprika and red bell pepper and whisk well.
- Heat up your air fryer at 140 degrees F, add butter and melt it.
- Add eggs mix, stir and cook for 10 minutes.
- Divide scrambled eggs on plates and serve for breakfast.
- Enjoy!

108. Air Fryer Egg Cups

Prep Time: 5 mins Cook Time: 12 mins Total Time: 17 mins

Yield: 8

Ingredients

- 6 large eggs
- 1/2 cup of heavy cream
- (use low-fat milk for WW)
- 1/2 cup of cheddar
- 1/2 pound of breakfast sausage
- 1 tsp of olive oil
- 1 tsp of garlic
- 2 cups of spinach

Instructions

- Heat a nonstick skillet to medium-low.
- Add ground breakfast sausage and cook for 12-16 mins or until cooked through and browned. Crumble the sausage with a wooden spoon or cooking utensil of choice.
- Remove the breakfast sausage from the skillet. Let the sausage cool.
- Add 1 tsp of olive oil and garlic to the skillet. Cook until the garlic is fragrant

and Add the spinach to the skillet and cover; allow to cook 5 min.. Take the spinach out of the pan let it cool as you did with the sausage.

- In a medium bowl add the eggs and milk and whisk until combined. Fold in the cheddar, breakfast sausage, and spinach.
- Place the silicone muffin cups into the air fryer basket and set the temperature to 300 degrees. Fill the cups with the egg mixture (do not overfill). I used a measuring cup to fill the muffin cups.
- Set the air fryer time to 12 min..
- I had egg mixture left over after only cooking six egg cups at a time. My air fryer basket only fit 6 muffin cups in there without overflowing. Will have to cook in batches if there is any leftover.

109. Air Fryer Quiche

Yield: makes 1 Prep time: 10 mins Cook time: 10 mins Total time: 20 mins

Ingredients

- 1 egg
- 3-4 tbsp (45ml-60ml) of heavy cream
- 4-5 tiny broccoli florets
- 1 tbsp (15ml) finely grated cheddar cheese

Instructions

- Whisk together egg and cream. Lightly grease a 5" (13cm) ceramic quiche dish. Distribute broccoli florets on the bottom. Pour in the egg mixture. Top with grated cheddar cheese.
- Air fry at 325F (162C) for 10 min..

More Air Fryer Quiche Fillings:

- Tomato and Mozzarella. Garnish with fresh basil
- Spinach and Cheese
- Cooked bacon and Cheddar
- Mushroom and Thyme
- Smoked Salmon and Dill
- Goat Cheese and Crispy Leeks (cook leeks first in a skillet with olive oil until crispy)

110. Vegan Air Fryer Breakfast Potatoes

Cook Time: 40 mins Total Time: 40 mins

Ingredients

- 3 lb potatoes, diced
- 2 bell peppers, any color, diced
- 1 onion, diced
- 15 oz mushrooms, diced

- 1 1/2 cups or 1-14 oz can black beans, drained
- Lemon Miso Tahini Sauce, optional
- Spinach and avocado for serving, optional

Instructions

- IF AIR FRYING: Add potatoes to the air fryer basket. Cook 20 mins at 400 degrees F (or 205 degrees C), shaking basket frequently.
- Add beans and vegetables and cook 10 - 15 more mins until potatoes are soft or crispy, according to preference.
- IF BAKING: Spread potatoes out on a lined baking tray and bake for 25-30 mins in a 425 degree F (218 degrees C) oven.
- Remove the tray and flip the potatoes. Add your veggies and beans and stir. Put the tray back in the oven for 15-20 more minutes, until the potatoes have started to get crispy and lightly golden brown and until all the veggies have cooked.
- Make the lemon miso tahini sauce by mixing the ingredients in a bowl and thinning the sauce with water if needed.
- Add to a bowl with spinach and whatever else you like (this would be a great complement to tofu scramble, for instance). Top with sauce mixture and enjoy!
- Refrigerate leftovers in an airtight container for up to 5 days. Recommended reheating in the oven, skillet, or air fryer to retain crispiness.

111. Fried Eggs For The Air Fryer

Prep Time: 1 Minute Cook Time: 8 Mins
Total Time: 9 Mins

Ingredients

- 2 Large Eggs
- 2 Tbsps Butter
- Salt And Pepper

Instructions

- Add a small aluminum pan to the basket of an air fryer.
- Add the butter and heat at 350 degrees to melt (approximately 1 minute)
- Crack both eggs into the aluminum pan.
- Return to the air fryer and cook at 325-degrees until your desired

doneness.

112.Turkey Breakfast Sausage - Air Fryer Or Oven Method

Prep Time: 5 Mins Cook Time: 13 Mins
Total Time: 18 Mins

Ingredients

- 1 pound ground turkey
- 1 Tsp. kosher salt
- ½ Tsp. black pepper
- 1 Tsp. fennel seed
- ½ Tsp. ground sage
- ½ Tsp. smoked paprika
- 3/4 Tsp. garlic powder
- 1/8 Tsp. red pepper flakes (or to taste)

Instructions

- Place all the ingredients in a medium bowl and mix well to combine.
- Wet hands with water and form the ground turkey mixture into 12-13 small patties (approximately 1½ tablespoons, each).
- Place the patties on an air fryer baking sheet and cook for 12-13 mins at 350-degrees (or until an instant-read thermometer reached 165-degrees when inserted into the center of a sausage.

113.Air Fryer Mini Breakfast Burritos

Prep Time: 15 mins
Cook Time: 30 mins
Total Time: 45 mins

Ingredient

- ¼ cup Mexican-style chorizo
- 1 Tbsp bacon grease
- ½ cup diced potatoes
- 2 Tbsp chopped onion
- 1 serrano pepper, chopped
- 2 large eggs
- Salt and ground black pepper to taste
- 4 (8 inches) flour tortillas
- Avocado oil cooking spray

Instructions

- Cook chorizo in a large skillet over medium-high heat, stirring frequently until sausage turns a dark red, 6 to 8 min.. Remove from the skillet and set aside.
- Melt bacon grease in the same skillet over medium-high heat. Add diced potatoes and cook, stirring occasionally, 8 to 10 min..
- Add onion and serrano pepper and

continue cooking and stirring until potatoes are fork-tender, onion is translucent, and serrano pepper is soft, 2 to 6 minutes.

- Add eggs and chorizo; stir until cooked and completely incorporated into potato mixture, about 5 minutes. Season with salt and pepper.
- Meanwhile, heat tortillas in a large skillet or directly on the grates of a gas stove until soft and pliable.
- Place 1/3 cup chorizo mixture down the center of each tortilla. Fold top and bottom of tortillas over the filling, then roll each into a burrito shape.
- Mist with cooking spray and place in the basket of an air fryer.
- Air fry at 400 degrees F (200 degrees C) for 4 to 6 minutes.
- Flip each burrito over, mist with cooking spray, and air fry until lightly browned, 2 to 4 mins more.

114.Air Fryer Churros

Prep Time: 5 mins Cook Time: 15 mins
Additional Time: 5 mins Total Time: 25 mins

Ingredient

- ¼ cup butter
- ½ cup milk
- 1 pinch salt
- ½ cup all-purpose flour
- 2 eggs
- ¼ cup white sugar
- ½ Tsp. ground cinnamon

Instructions

- Melt butter in a saucepan over medium-high heat. Pour in milk and add salt. Lower heat to medium and bring to a boil, continuously stirring with a wooden spoon. Quickly add flour all at once. Keep stirring until the dough comes together.
- Remove from heat and let cool for 5 to 7 min..
- Mix in eggs with the wooden spoon until the pastry comes together. Spoon dough into a pastry bag fitted with a large star tip.
- Pipe dough into strips straight into the air fryer basket.
- Air fry churros at 340 degrees F (175 degrees C) for 5 minutes.
- Meanwhile, combine sugar and cinnamon in a small bowl and pour onto

a shallow plate.

- Remove fried churros from the air fryer and roll in the cinnamon-sugar mixture.

Main & Lunch

115. Lunch Egg Rolls

Preparation time: 10 mins Cooking time: 15 mins

Ingredients:

- ½ cup mushrooms, chopped
- ½ cup carrots, grated
- ½ cup zucchini, grated
- 2 green onions, chopped
- 2 tablespoons soy sauce
- 8 egg roll wrappers
- 1 eggs, whisked
- 1 tablespoon cornstarch

Instructions:

- In a bowl, mix carrots with mushrooms, zucchini, green onions and soy sauce and stir well.
- Arrange egg roll wrappers on a working surface, divide veggie mix on each and roll well.
- In a bowl, mix cornstarch with egg, whisk well and brush eggs rolls with this mix.
- Seal edges, place all rolls in your preheated air fryer and cook them at 370 degrees F for 15 minutes.
- Arrange them on a platter and serve them for lunch.

116. Quick Lunch Pizzas

Preparation time: 10 mins Cooking time: 7 mins

Ingredients:

- 4 pitas
- 1 tablespoon olive oil
- ¾ cup pizza sauce
- 4 ounces jarred mushrooms, sliced
- ½ teaspoon basil, dried
- 2 green onions, chopped
- 2 cup mozzarella, grated
- 1 cup grape tomatoes, sliced

Instructions:

- Spread pizza sauce on each pita bread, sprinkle green onions and basil, divide mushrooms and top with cheese.
- Arrange pita pizzas in your air fryer and cook them at 400 degrees F for 7 minutes.
- Top each pizza with tomato slices, divide among plates and serve.

117. Lunch Gnocchi

Preparation time: 10 mins Cooking time: 17 mins

Ingredients:

- 1 yellow onion, chopped
- 1 tablespoon olive oil
- 3 garlic cloves, minced
- 16 ounces gnocchi
- ¼ cup parmesan, grated
- 8 ounces spinach pesto

Instructions:

- Grease your air fryer's pan with olive oil, add gnocchi, onion and garlic, toss, put pan in your air fryer and cook at 400 degrees F for 10 minutes.
- Add pesto, toss and cook for 7 mins more at 350 degrees F.
- Divide among plates and serve for lunch.

118. Vegetable Egg Rolls

Prep time: 15 minutes
Cook time: 10 minutes
Servings: 8

Ingredients

- Chopped mushrooms – ½ cup
- Grated carrots – ½ cup
- Chopped zucchini – ½ cup
- Green onions – 2, chopped
- Low-sodium soy sauce – 2 tbsp.
- Egg roll wrappers – 8
- Cornstarch – 1 tbsp.
- Egg – 1, beaten

Method

- In a bowl, combine the soy sauce, green onions, zucchini, carrots and mushrooms, and stir together.
- Top each egg roll wrapper with 3 tbsp. of the vegetable mixture.
- In a small bowl, combine egg and cornstarch and mix well. Brush some of this mixture on the edges of the egg roll wrappers.
- Roll up the wrappers, enclosing the vegetable filling. Brush some of the egg mixtures on the outside of the egg rolls to seal.
- Air-fry at 390F for 7 to 10 minutes, or until the egg rolls are brown and crunchy.

119. Veggie Toast

Prep time: 10 minutes
Cook time: 15 minutes
Servings: 4

Ingredients

- Red bell pepper – 1, cut into thin strips
- Cremini mushrooms – 1 cup, sliced
- Yellow squash – 1, chopped
- Green onions – 2, sliced
- Olive oil – 1 tbsp.
- Bread – 4 slices
- Butter – 2 tbsp. soft
- Goat cheese – ½ cup, crumbled

Method

In a bowl, mix red bell pepper with oil, green onions, squash and mushrooms. Toss.

Transfer to the air fryer and cook at 350F for 10 minutes. Shake the air fryer basket once and transfer to a bowl.

Spread butter on bread slices and place them in the air fryer.

Cook them at 350F for 5 minutes.

Distribute vegetable mixture on each bread slice.

Top with crumbled cheese and serve.

120. Shrimp Pancake

Prep time: 10 minutes
Cook time: 10 minutes
Servings: 2

Ingredients

- Butter – 1 tbsp.
- Eggs – 3, whisked
- Flour – ½ cup
- Milk – ½ cup
- Salsa – 1 cup
- Small shrimp – 1 cup, peeled and deveined

Method

- Preheat the air fryer at 400F.
- Add fryer pan, add 1 tbsp. butter and melt it.
- Mix eggs with milk and flour in a bowl. Whisk well, pour into the air fryer pan, and spread.
- Cook at 350F for 12 minutes and transfer to a plate.
- Mix shrimp and salsa in a bowl.
- Stir and serve pancake with this on the side.

121. Hot Bacon Sandwiches

Prep time: 10 minutes
Cook time: 7 minutes
Servings: 4

Ingredients

- BBQ sauce – 1/3 cup
- Honey – 2 tbsp.
- Bacon slices – 8, cooked and cut into thirds

- Red bell pepper – 1, sliced
- Yellow bell pepper – 1, sliced
- Pita pockets – 3, halved
- Butter lettuce leaves – 1 ¼ cup, torn
- Tomatoes – 2, sliced

Method
- Mix BBQ sauce with honey in a bowl and whisk well.
- Brush bacon and all bell peppers with this mixture.
- Place them in the air fryer and cook at 350F for 4 minutes.
- Shake fryer and cook them for 2 minutes more.
- Stuff pita pockets with bacon mixture.
- Also, stuff with lettuce and tomatoes.
- Spread the rest of the BBQ sauce on the stuffed pita pockets and serve for lunch.

122. Macaroni and Cheese

Prep time: 10 minutes
Cook time: 30 minutes
Servings: 3
Ingredients
- Macaroni – 1 ½ cups
- Cooking spray
- Heavy cream – ½ cup
- Chicken stock – 1 cup
- Cheddar cheese – ¾ cup, shredded
- Mozzarella cheese – ½ cup, shredded
- Parmesan – ¼ cup, shredded
- Salt and black pepper to taste

Method
- Spray a pan with cooking spray.
- Add macaroni, salt, pepper, parmesan, mozzarella, cheddar cheese, stock
- and heavy cream. Mix well.
- Cook in the air fryer for 30 minutes.
- Serve.

123. Pasta Salad

Prep time: 10 minutes
Cook time: 12 minutes
Servings: 6
Ingredients
- Zucchini – 1, sliced in half and roughly chopped
- Range bell pepper – 1, roughly chopped
- Green bell pepper – 1, roughly chopped
- Red onion – 1, roughly chopped
- Brown mushrooms – 4 ounces, halved
- Salt and black pepper to taste

- Italian seasoning – 1 tsp.
- Penne rigate – 1 pound, cooked
- Cherry tomatoes – 1 cup, halved
- Kalamata olives – ½ cup, pitted and halved
- Olive oil – ¼ cup
- Balsamic vinegar – 3 tbsp.
- Basil – 2 tbsp., chopped

Method
- In a bowl, combine oil, seasoning, pepper, salt, red onion, green bell pepper, orange bell pepper, mushrooms and zucchini. Mix well.
- Cook in the air fryer at 380F for 12 minutes.
- In a bowl, mix the penne pasta with the cooked veggies, basil, vinegar, olive and cherry tomatoes. Toss and serve.

124. Tuna Cobbler

Prep. Time: 15 min Cook Time: 25 min
Servings: 4
Ingredients :
- Water, cold (1/3 cup)
- Tuna, canned, drained (10 ounces)
- Sweet pickle relish (2 tablespoons)
- Mixed vegetables, frozen (1 ½ cups)
- Soup, cream of chicken, condensed (10 ¾ ounces)
- Pimientos, sliced, drained (2 ounces)
- Lemon juice (1 teaspoon)
- Paprika

Directions :
- Preheat the air fryer at 375 degrees Fahrenheit.
- Mist cooking spray into a round casserole (1 ½ quarts).
- Mix the frozen vegetables with milk, soup, lemon juice, relish, pimientos, and tuna in a saucepan. Cook for six to eight minutes over medium heat.
- Fill the casserole with the tuna mixture.
- Mix the biscuit mix with cold water to form a soft dough. Beat for half a minute before dropping by four spoonfuls into the casserole.
- Dust the dish with paprika before air-frying for twenty to twenty-five minutes.

125. Pork Buns

Prep. Time: 20 min
Cook Time: 25 min
Servings: 8
Ingredients :

- Green onions, sliced thinly (3 pieces)
- Egg, beaten (1 piece)
- Pulled pork, diced, w/ barbecue sauce (1 cup)
- Buttermilk biscuits, refrigerated (16 1/3 ounces)
- Soy sauce (1 teaspoon)

Directions :
- Preheat the air fryer at 325 degrees Fahrenheit.
- Use parchment paper to line your baking sheet.
- Combine pork with green onions.
- Separate and press the dough to form 8 four-inch rounds.
- Fill each biscuit round's center with two tablespoons of pork mixture. Cover
- with the dough edges and seal by pinching. Arrange the buns on the sheet and brush with a mixture of soy sauce and egg.
- Cook in the air fryer for twenty to twenty-five minutes.

126. Tuna Spinach Casserole

Prep. Time: 30 min
Cook Time: 25 min
Servings: 8
Ingredients :
- Mushroom soup, creamy (18 ounces)
- Milk (1/2 cup)
- White tuna, solid, in-water, drained (12 ounces)
- Crescent dinner rolls, refrigerated (8 ounces)
- Egg noodles, wide, uncooked (8 ounces)
- Cheddar cheese, shredded (8 ounces)
- Spinach, chopped, frozen, thawed, drained (9 ounces)
- Lemon peel grated (2 teaspoons)

Directions :
- Preheat the oven at 350 degrees Fahrenheit.
- Mist cooking spray onto a glass baking dish (11x7-inch).
- Follow package Directions in cooking and draining the noodles.
- Stir the cheese (1 ½ cups) and soup together in a skillet heated on medium.
- Once cheese melts, stir in your noodles, milk, spinach, tuna, and lemon peel. Once bubbling, pour into the prepped dish.

- Unroll the dough and sprinkle with remaining cheese (1/2 cup). Roll up dough and pinch at the seams to seal. Slice into 8 portions and place over the tuna mixture.
- Air-fry for twenty to twenty-five minutes.

127.Crispy Hot Sauce Chicken

Prep. Time: 5 minutes
Cook Time: 30 minutes
Total Time: 35 minutes
Servings: 4
Ingredients :
- 2 cups buttermilk
- 1 tbsp hot sauce
- 1 whole chicken, cut up
- 1 cup Kentucky Kernel flour
- Oil for spraying
Directions :
- Whisk hot sauce with buttermilk in a large bowl.
- Add chicken pieces to the buttermilk mixture and marinate for 1 hour in the refrigerator.
- Dredge the chicken through seasoned flour and shake off the excess.
- Place the coated chicken in the air fryer basket and spray them with cooking oil.
- Return the fryer basket to the air fryer and cook on air fry mode for 30 minutes at 380 degrees F.
- Flip the chicken pieces once cooked half way through.
- Enjoy right away.

128.Tofu Sushi Burrito

Prep. Time: 5 minutes
Cook Time: 15 minutes
Total Time: 20 minutes
Servings: 2
Ingredients :
- ¼ block extra firm tofu, pressed and sliced
- 1 tbsp low-sodium soy sauce
- ¼ tsp ground ginger
- ¼ tsp garlic powder
- Sriracha sauce, to taste
- 2 cups cooked sushi rice
- 2 sheets nori
Filling:
- ¼ avocado, sliced
- 3 tbsp mango, sliced
- 1 green onion, finely chopped

- 2 tbsp pickled ginger
- 2 tbsp panko breadcrumbs
Directions :
- Whisk ginger, garlic, soy sauce, sriracha sauce, and tofu in a large bowl.
- Let them marinate for 10 minutes then transfer them to the air fryer basket.
- Return the fryer basket to the air fryer and cook on air fry mode for 15 minutes at 370 degrees F.
- Toss the tofu cubes after 8 minutes then resume cooking.
- Spread a nori sheet on a work surface and top it with a layer of sushi rice.
- Place tofu and half of the other filling Ingredients over the rice.
- Roll the sheet tightly to secure the filling inside.
- Repeat the same steps to make another sushi roll.

129.Air Fryer Fried Chicken:

Prep time: 8 minutes
Cook Time: 50 minutes
Servings: 6
Ingredients:
- Half Whole Chicken
- ½ cup Hot Sauce
- ½ cup Buttermilk
Ingredients for the Seasoning
- ¾ cup All-purpose Flour
- 2 tsp Seasoning Salt
- 1 tsp Garlic Powder
- 1 tsp Onion Powder
- 1 tsp Italian Seasoning
- ½ tsp Cayenne Pepper
- Oil
Directions:
- First marinate the chicken. To marinate, make a mixture of buttermilk and hot sauce. Place the chicken into the mixture and put it into the refrigerator.
- There is no specified length of time to follow.
- Fetch a bowl, put in the all-purpose flour, garlic powder, onion powder, salt cayenne pepper, and Italian seasoning. Whisk them all together and then keep aside.
- Line the air fryer basket with some parchment liner. When you bring out the chicken from the refrigerator, dip into the flour mix-

ture, making sure that the entirety of the chicken is submerged and coated on all sides. Place the chicken in a single layer on the air fryer basket. Make sure they are not jam-packed.
- The air fryer should be set to about 390 degrees F before you start cooking.
- Set the timer for 25 minutes, then you can start cooking.
- Halfway into cooking, open the air fryer and spray on the chicken. Flip to the other side and spray with oil as well; make sure to cover every flour spot.
- When the time is up, use a thermometer to ensure that the internal temperature of the chicken has reached 165 degrees F.

130.Crispy Pizza

Prep time: 10 mins
Cook time: 15 mins
Servings: 4
Ingredients
- 1 teaspoon of Parsley
- (Optional) Bread Seeds
- 25 grams of Cheddar Cheese
- 1 teaspoon of Garlic Puree
- Salt & Pepper
- 2 tablespoon of Desiccated Coconut
- 1/3 Homemade Pizza Dough
Directions
- In a small pan, melt the coconut oil over medium heat. In a small bowl, add the melted butter, garlic puree and seasoning and mix well.
- Lay out pizza dough on a smooth work surface and form into thick rectangle.
- Brush garlic oil evenly over the pizza dough until well coated. Sprinkle top with the desiccated coconut until no more traces of the garlic oil. Top layer with a sprinkle of cheddar cheese. Lastly, top with bread seeds.
- Cook at 360 F for 10 minutes in the Air fryer, then cook at 400 F for another 5 minutes or until nice and crispy on the outside. Chop and serve.

131.Salmon Main Quiche

Prep time: 15 mins
Cook time: 20 mins
Servings: 2
Ingredients
- 1 green onion, sliced into 1 cm pieces
- 3 tbsp of whipping cream

- 2 eggs + 1 egg yolk
- 1.7 ounces of cold butter, in cubes
- 3.5 ounces of flour
- Freshly ground black pepper
- ½ tbsp of lemon juice
- 5.2 ounces of salmon fillet, cut into small cubes

Directions
- Heat up your Air fryer to 180°C. In a bowl, mix together the lemon juice,
- salmon pieces, salt and pepper. Let rest for a few minutes.
- Mix together the egg yolk, butter with flour, and ½-1 tbsp of cold water in a different bowl; knead mixture into a smooth ball.
- Working on a floured surface, roll dough into an 18 cm circle. Transfer into a quiche pan and firmly press along the edges. Trim the dough close to the pan along the edge to let dough stick out roughly on the pan edges.
- Lightly beat the eggs with the mustard, cream, pepper and salt. Fill the quiche pan with the mixture and then layer with the salmon pieces and evenly divide the green onion on top. Transfer the pan into the Air fryer basket and bake for 20 minutes until golden brown and done.

132.Tuna and Zucchini Tortillas

Preparation time: 10 mins Cooking time: 10 mins

Ingredients:
- 4 corn tortillas
- 4 tablespoons butter, soft
- 6 ounces canned tuna, drained
- 1 cup zucchini, shredded
- 1/3 cup mayonnaise
- 2 tablespoons mustard
- 1 cup cheddar cheese, grated

Instructions:
- Spread butter on tortillas, place them in your air fryer's basket and cook them at 400 degrees F for 3 minutes.
- Meanwhile, in a bowl, mix tuna with zucchini, mayo and mustard and stir.
- Divide this mix on each tortilla, top with cheese, roll tortillas, place them in your air fryer's basket again and cook them at 400 degrees F for 4 mins more.

133.Squash Fritters

Preparation time: 10 mins Cooking

time: 7 mins
Ingredients:
- 3 ounces cream cheese
- 1 egg, whisked
- ½ teaspoon oregano, dried

- A pinch of salt and black pepper
- 1 yellow summer squash, grated
- 1/3 cup carrot, grated
- 2/3 cup bread crumbs
- 2 tablespoons olive oil

Instructions:
- In a bowl, mix cream cheese with salt, pepper, oregano, egg, breadcrumbs, carrot and squash and stir well.
- Shape medium patties out of this mix and brush them with the oil.
- Place squash patties in your air fryer and cook them at 400 degrees F for 7 minutes.

134.Lunch Shrimp Croquettes

Preparation time: 10 mins Cooking time: 8 mins
Ingredients:
- 2/3 pound shrimp, cooked, peeled, deveined and chopped
- 1 and ½ cups bread crumbs
- 1 egg, whisked
- 2 tablespoons lemon juice
- 3 green onions, chopped
- ½ teaspoon basil, dried
- Salt and black pepper to the taste
- 2 tablespoons olive oil

Instructions:
- In a bowl, mix half of the bread crumbs with egg and lemon juice and stir well.
- Add green onions, basil, salt, pepper and shrimp and stir really well.
- In a separate bowl, mix the rest of the bread crumbs with the oil and toss well.
- Shape round balls out of shrimp mix, dredge them in bread crumbs, place them in preheated air fryer and cook the for 8 mins at 400 degrees F.

135.Lunch Special Pancake

Preparation time: 10 mins Cooking time: 10 mins
Ingredients:
- 1 tablespoon butter
- 3 eggs, whisked
- ½ cup flour
- ½ cup milk

- 1 cup salsa
- 1 cup small shrimp, peeled and deveined

Instructions:
- Preheat your air fryer at 400 degrees F, add fryer's pan, add 1 tablespoon butter and melt it.
- In a bowl, mix eggs with flour and milk, whisk well and pour into air fryer's pan, spread, cook at 350 degrees for 12 mins and transfer to a plate.
- In a bowl, mix shrimp with salsa, stir and serve your pancake with this on the side.

136.Scallops and Dill

Preparation time: 10 mins Cooking time: 5 mins
Ingredients:
- 1 pound sea scallops, debearded
- 1 tablespoon lemon juice
- 1 teaspoon dill, chopped
- 2 teaspoons olive oil
- Salt and black pepper to the taste

Instructions:
- In your air fryer, mix scallops with dill, oil, salt, pepper and lemon juice, cover and cook at 360 degrees F for 5 minutes.
- Discard unopened ones, divide scallops and dill sauce on plates and serve for lunch.

137.Chicken Sandwiches

Preparation time: 10 mins Cooking time: 10 mins
Ingredients:
- 2 chicken breasts, skinless, boneless and cubed
- 1 red onion, chopped
- 1 red bell pepper, sliced
- ½ cup Italian seasoning
- ½ teaspoon thyme, dried
- 2 cups butter lettuce, torn
- 4 pita pockets
- 1 cup cherry tomatoes, halved
- 1 tablespoon olive oil

Instructions:
- In your air fryer, mix chicken with onion, bell pepper, Italian seasoning and oil, toss and cook at 380 degrees F for 10 minutes.
- Transfer chicken mix to a bowl, add thyme, butter lettuce and cherry tomatoes, toss well, stuff pita pockets

with this mix and serve for lunch.

138. Mac and Cheese

Prep Time: 15 minutes

Ingredients
- 1 cup cooked macaroni
- 1 cup grated cheddar cheese
- ½ cup warm milk
- 1 tbsp. Parmesan cheese
- Salt and pepper, to taste

Instructions
- Preheat the air fryer to 350 degrees F.Add the macaroni to an ovenproof baking dish.Stir in the cheddar and milk.Season with some salt and pepper, to taste.Place the dish in the air fryer and cook for 10 minutes.Sprinkle with Parmesan cheese just before serving.

139. Air Fried Calzone

Prep Time: 20 minutes

Ingredients
- Pizza dough, preferably homemade
- 4 oz. cheddar cheese, grated
- 1 oz. mozzarella cheese
- 1 oz. bacon, diced
- 2 cups cooked and shredded turkey
- 1 egg, beaten
- 1 tsp. thyme4 tbsp. tomato paste
- 1 tsp. basil
- 1 tsp. oregano
- Salt and pepper, to taste

Instructions
- Preheat the air fryer to 350 degrees F.Divide the pizza dough into 4 equal pieces so you have dough for 4 small pizza crusts.
- Combine the tomato paste, basil, oregano, and thyme, in a small bowl.
- Brush the mixture onto the crusts just make sure not to go all the way and avoid brushing near the edges.
- On one half of each crust, place ½ turkey, and season the meat with some salt and pepper.
- Top the meat with some bacon.
- Combine the cheddar and mozzarella and divide it between the pizzas, making sure that you layer only one half of the dough.
- Brush the edges of the crust with the beaten egg.
- Fold the crust and seal with a fork.Cook for 10 minutes

140. Roasted Radish and Onion Cheesy Salad

Prep Time: 35 minute

Ingredients
1 lb. radishes, green parts too
- 1 large red onion, sliced
- ½ lb. mozzarella, sliced
- 2 tbsp. olive oil, plus more for drizzling
- 2 tbsp. balsamic glaze
- 1 tsp. dried basil
- 1 tsp. dried parsley
- 1 tsp. salt

Instructions
- Preheat the air fryer to 350 degrees F.Wash the radishes well and dry them by patting with paper towels.
- Cut them in half and place in a large bowl.Add the onion slices in.
- Stir in salt, basil, parsley and olive oil.Place in the basket of the air fryer.
- Cook for 30 minutes.
- Make sure to toss them twice while cooking.Stir in the mozzarella immediately so that it begins to melt.Stir in the balsamic glaze.Drizzle with olive oil

141. Mock Stir Fry

Prep Time: 25 minutes

Ingredients
- 4 boneless and skinless chicken breasts cut into cubes
- 2 carrots, sliced
- 1 red bell pepper, cut into strips
- 1 yellow bell pepper, cut into strips
- 1 cup snow peas
- 15 oz. broccoli florets
- 1 scallion, slicedSauce:
- 3 tbsp. soy sauce
- 2 tbsp. oyster sauce
- 1 tbsp. brown sugar
- 1 tsp. sesame oil
- 1 tsp. cornstarch
- 1 tsp. sriracha
- 2 garlic cloves, minced
- 1 tbsp. grated ginger
- 1 tbsp. rice wine vinegar

Instructions
- Preheat the air fryer to 370 degrees F.
- Place the chicken, bell peppers, and carrot, in a bowl.In a small bowl, combine the sauce **Ingredients**.
- Coat the chicken mixture with the

sauce. Place on a lined baking sheet and cook for 5 minutes.
- Add snow peas and broccoli and cook for additional 8 to10 minutes.Serve garnished with scallion

142. Potato and Bacon Salad

Prep Time: 10 minutes

Ingredients
- 4 lb. boiled and cubed potatoes
- 15 bacon slices, chopped
- 2 cups shredded cheddar cheese
- 15 oz. sour cream
- 2 tbsp. mayonnaise
- 1 tsp. salt
- 1 tsp. pepper
- 1 tsp. dried herbs by choice

Instructions
- Preheat the air fryer to 350 degrees F.
- Combine the potatoes, bacon, salt, pepper, and herbs, in a large bowl.
- Transfer to a baking dish.Cook for about 7 minutes.
- Stir in sour cream and mayonnaise.

143. Carbonara and Mushroom Spaghetti

Prep Time: 30 - 35 minutes

Ingredients
- ½ lb. white button mushrooms, sliced
- ½ cup of water
- 1 tsp. butter
- 2 garlic cloves, chopped
- 12 oz. spaghetti, cooked
- 14 oz. carbonara mushroom sauce (store bought)Salt and pepper, to taste

Instructions
- Preheat the air fryer to 300 degrees F.
- Add the butter and garlic and cook for 3 minutes.
- Add the mushrooms and cook for 5 more minutes.
- Stir in mushroom carbonara sauce and water.
- Season with salt and pepper.
- Cook for 18 minutes.Stir in the spaghetti and cook for 1 minute more.

144. Ham and Mozzarella Eggplant Boats

Prep Time: 17 minutes

Ingredients
- 1 eggplant
- 4 ham slices, chopped
- 1 cup shredded mozzarella cheese, divided

- 1 tsp. dried parsley
- Salt and pepper, to taste

Instructions
- Preheat the air fryer to 330 degrees.
- Peel the eggplant and cut it lengthwise in half. Scoop some of the flash out. Season with salt and pepper.
- Divide half the mozzarella cheese between the eggplants.
- Place the ham on top of the mozzarella.
- Top with the remaining mozzarella cheese.
- Sprinkle with parsley. Cook 12 minutes

145. Leftover Turkey and Mushroom Sandwich

Prep Time: 15 MInutes

Ingredients
- 1/3 cup shredded leftover turkey
- 1/3 cup sliced mushrooms
- 1 tbsp. butter, divided
- 2 tomato slices
- ½ tsp. red pepper flakes
- ¼ tsp. salt
- ¼ tsp. black pepper
- 1 hamburger bun

Instructions
- Preheat the air fryer to 350 degrees F.
- Melt half of the butter and add the mushrooms.
- Cook for about 4 minutes.
- Meanwhile, cut the bun in half and spread the remaining butter on the outside of the bun.
- Place the turkey on one half of the bun. Arrange the mushroom slices on top of the turkey. Place the tomato slices on top of the mushrooms.
- Sprinkle with salt pepper and red pepper flakes. Top with the other bun half. Cook for 5 minutes.

146. Italian Sausage Patties

Prep Time: 20 Minutes

Ingredients
- 1 lb. ground Italian sausage
- ¼ cup breadcrumbs
- 1 tsp. dried parsley
- 1 tsp. red pepper Flakes
- ½ tsp. salt
- ¼ tsp. black peppe
- r¼ tsp. garlic powder
- 1 egg, beaten

Instructions

- Preheat the air fryer to 350 degrees F.
- Combine all of the **Ingredients** in a large bowl. Line a baking sheet with parchment paper.
- Make patties out of the sausage mixture and arrange them on the baking sheet. Cook for about 15 minutes.
- Serve as desired (they are amazing with tzatziki sauce)

147. Popcorn Chicken Gizzards

Prep Time: 10 mins
Cook Time: 45 mins
Additional Time: 5 mins
Total Time: 1 hr

Ingredient
- 1 pound chicken gizzards
- ⅓ cup all-purpose flour
- 1 ½ Tsp. seasoned salt
- ½ Tsp. ground black pepper
- ½ Tsp. garlic powder
- ½ Tsp. paprika
- 1 pinch cayenne pepper (optional)
- 1 large egg, beaten
- Cooking spray

Instructions
- Bring a large pot of water to a boil. Cut gizzards into bite-sized pieces and add to the boiling water. Boil for 30 min.. Drain.
- Combine flour, seasoned salt, pepper, garlic powder, paprika, and cayenne in a flat plastic container. Snap the lid on and shake until combined.
- Add gizzards to the seasoned flour. Snap the lid back on and shake until evenly coated.
- Place beaten egg in a separate bowl. Dip each gizzard piece into the beaten egg and then place it back in the seasoned flour. Snap the lid on and shake one last time. Let sit for 5 mins while the air fryer preheats.
- Preheat the air fryer to 400 degrees F (200 degrees C).
- Place gizzards in the basket and spray the tops with cooking spray. Cook for 4 min.. Shake the basket and spray any chalky spots with more cooking spray. Cook for 4 mins more.

148. Air Fryer Crab Rangoon

Prep Time: 15 mins Cook Time: 20 mins
Total Time: 35 mins

Ingredient

- 1 (8 ounces) package cream cheese, softened
- 4 ounces lump crab meat
- 2 Tbsp chopped scallions
- 1 Tsp. soy sauce
- 1 Tsp. Worcestershire sauce
- 1 serving nonstick cooking spray
- 24 each wonton wrappers
- 2 Tbsps Asian sweet chili sauce, for dipping

Instructions
- Combine cream cheese, crab meat, scallions, soy sauce, and Worcestershire sauce in a bowl; stir until evenly combined.
- Preheat an air fryer to 350 degrees F (175 degrees C). Spray the basket of the air fryer with cooking spray. Fill a small bowl with warm water.
- Place 12 wonton wrappers on a clean work surface. Spoon 1 Tsp. of cream cheese mixture into the center of each wonton wrapper. Dip index finger into the warm water and wet around the sides of each wonton wrapper. Crimp wrapper corners upwards to meet in the center to form dumplings.
- Place dumplings in the prepared basket and spray the tops with cooking spray.
- Cook dumplings until desired crispness, about 8 to 10 min.. Transfer to a paper towel-lined plate.
- While the first batch is cooking, assemble the remaining dumplings with the remaining wrappers and filling.
- Serve with sweet chili sauce for dipping.

149. Air Fryer Cauliflower Fried Rice

Prep Time: 5 mins Cook Time: 10 mins
Total Time: 15 mins

Ingredient
- 1 (12 ounces) package frozen cauliflower rice
- 2 large eggs
- 2 slices deli ham
- ¼ cup chopped green onions
- 2 Tbsps soy sauce

Instructions
- Cook cauliflower rice in the microwave for 5 to 6 min.. Let stand for 1 minute before carefully opening the bag.
- Preheat the air fryer to 400 degrees F

(200 degrees C). Cover the bottom and 1/2 inch of the basket sides with aluminum foil.

• Mix cauliflower rice, eggs, ham, green onions, and soy sauce in a bowl until well combined.

• Air fry for 5 minutes. Remove the basket and stir the cauliflower mixture. Return to air fryer and cook for an additional 5 min..

150. Air Fryer Wiener Schnitzel

Prep Time: 10 mins Cook Time: 20 mins
Total Time: 30 mins

Ingredient

• 1 pound veal, scallopini cut
• 2 Tbsps lemon juice
• salt and ground black pepper to taste
• ¼ cup all-purpose flour
• 1 egg
• 1 Tbsp chopped fresh parsley
• 1 cup panko bread crumbs
• nonstick cooking spray
• 1 lemon, cut into wedges

Instructions

• Preheat an air fryer to 400 degrees F (200 degrees C).

• Place veal on a clean work surface and sprinkle with lemon juice, salt, and pepper.

• Place flour in a flat dish. Beat egg and parsley together in a second dish. Place bread crumbs in a third dish. Dredge each veal cutlet first in flour, then in the egg-parsley mixture, followed by bread crumbs, pressing down so that bread crumbs adhere.

• Spray the basket of the air fryer with nonstick cooking spray. Place breaded veal cutlets into the basket, making sure not to overcrowd. Spray the tops with nonstick cooking spray.

• Cook for 5 minutes. Flip, spray any chalky spots with nonstick cooking spray and cook for 5 mins longer. Repeat with remaining veal. Serve with lemon wedges.

151. Air Fryer Steak And Cheese Melts

Prep Time: 10 mins
Cook Time: 25 mins
Additional Time: 4 hrs 30 mins
Total Time: 5 hrs 5 mins

Ingredient

• 1 pound beef rib-eye steak, thinly sliced

• 2 Tbsps Worcestershire sauce
• 1 Tbsp reduced-sodium soy sauce
• 1 medium onion, sliced into petals
• 4 ounces sliced baby portobello mushrooms
• ½ green bell pepper, thinly sliced
• 1 Tbsp olive oil
• ½ Tsp. salt
• ½ Tsp. ground mustard
• ¼ Tsp. ground black pepper
• 4 hoagie rolls
• 4 slices Provolone cheese

Instructions

• Place steak in a bowl and add Worcestershire and soy sauce. Cover and refrigerate 4 hours to overnight. Remove from the refrigerator and let come to room temperature, about 30 min..

• Preheat the air fryer to 380 degrees F (190 degrees C).

• Combine onion, mushrooms, and bell pepper in a large bowl. Add olive oil, salt, ground mustard, and pepper; stir to coat.

• Place hoagie rolls in the basket of the air fryer and cook until toasted, about 2 minutes. Transfer rolls to a plate.

• Place steak in the basket of the air fryer and cook for 3 minutes. Stir and cook for 1 more minute. Transfer to a plate.

• Add vegetable mix to the basket of the air fryer and cook for 5 min.. Stir and cook until softened, about 5 more minutes.

• Stir steak into the vegetable mixture. Place cheese slices on top, slightly overlapping. Cook until cheese is melted and bubbly, about 3 min.. Spoon mixture onto toasted rolls and serve immediately.

152. Air Fryer Salmon For One

Prep Time: 5 mins Cook Time: 15 mins
Total Time: 20 mins

Ingredient

• 1 (6 ounces) salmon fillet
• ½ Tsp. salt
• ½ Tsp. Greek seasoning (such as Cavender's®)
• ¼ Tsp. ground black pepper
• 1 pinch dried dill weed

Instructions

• Preheat the air fryer to 370 degrees F

(190 degrees C) for 5 minutes.

• Meanwhile, season salmon fillet with salt, Greek seasoning, pepper, and dill.

• Line the inner basket of the air fryer with a perforated parchment round. Place salmon onto the parchment, skin side down.

• Air fry salmon until salmon is cooked through, about 15 minutes.

153. Easy Air Fryer French Toast Sticks

Prep Time: 10 mins Cook Time: 10 mins
Total Time: 20 mins

Ingredient

• 4 slices of slightly stale thick bread, such as Texas toast
• Parchment paper
• 2 eggs, lightly beaten
• ¼ cup milk
• 1 Tsp. vanilla extract
• 1 Tsp. cinnamon
• 1 pinch ground nutmeg (optional)

Instructions

• Cut each slice of bread into thirds to make sticks. Cut a piece of parchment paper to fit the bottom of the air fryer basket.

• Preheat air fryer to 360 degrees F (180 degrees C).

• Stir together eggs, milk, vanilla extract, cinnamon, and nutmeg in a bowl until well combined. Dip each piece of bread into the egg mixture, making sure each piece is well submerged. Shake each breadstick to remove excess liquid and place it in a single layer in the air fryer basket. Cook in batches, if necessary, to avoid overcrowding the fryer.

• Cook for 5 min., turn bread pieces and cook for an additional 5 min..

154. Air Fryer Fish Sticks

Prep Time: 10 mins Cook Time: 10 mins
Total Time: 20 mins

Ingredient

• 1 pound cod fillets
• ¼ cup all-purpose flour
• 1 egg
• ½ cup panko bread crumbs
• ¼ cup grated parmesan cheese
• 1 Tbsp parsley flakes
• 1 Tsp. paprika
• ½ Tsp. black pepper
• Cooking spray

Instructions

- Preheat an air fryer to 400 degrees F (200 degrees C).
- Pat fish dry with paper towels and cut into 1x3-inch sticks.
- Place flour in a shallow dish. Beat egg in a separate shallow dish. Combine panko, Parmesan cheese, parsley, paprika, and pepper in a third shallow dish.
- Coat each fish stick in flour, then dip in beaten egg, and finally coat in seasoned panko mixture.
- Spray the basket of the air fryer with nonstick cooking spray. Arrange 1/2 the sticks in the basket, making sure none are touching. Spray the top of each stick with cooking spray.
- Cook in the preheated air fryer for 5 min.. Flip fish sticks and cook for an additional 5 min.. Repeat with remaining fish sticks.

155.ir Fryer Keto Chicken Wings

Prep Time: 5 mins Cook Time: 15 mins
Total Time: 20 mins
Ingredient
- 3 pounds chicken wings
- 1 Tbsp taco seasoning mix
- 2 teaspoons olive oil
Instructions
- Combine chicken wings, taco seasoning, and oil in a resealable plastic bag. Shake to coat.
- Preheat the air fryer to 350 degrees F (175 degrees C) for 2 min..
- Place wings in the air fryer and cook for 12 min., turning after 6 minutes. Serve immediately.

156.Sexy Air-Fried Meatloaf

Prep Time: 10 mins Cook Time: 45 mins
Additional Time: 1 day Total Time: 1 day
Ingredient
- ½ pound ground pork
- ½ pound ground veal
- 1 large egg
- ¼ cup chopped fresh cilantro
- ¼ cup gluten-free bread crumbs
- 2 medium spring onions, diced
- ½ Tsp. ground black pepper
- ½ Tsp. Sriracha salt
- ½ cup ketchup
- 2 teaspoons gluten-free chipotle chili sauce

- 1 Tsp. olive oil
- 1 Tsp. blackstrap molasses
Instructions
- Preheat the air fryer to 400 degrees F (200 degrees C).
- Combine pork and veal in a nonstick baking dish that fits inside the air fryer basket. Make a well and add egg, cilantro, bread crumbs, spring onions, black pepper, and 1/2 Tsp. of Sriracha salt. Mix well using your hands. Form a loaf inside the baking dish.
- Combine ketchup, chipotle chili sauce, olive oil, and molasses in a small bowl and whisk well. Set aside, but do not refrigerate.
- Cook meatloaf in the air fryer for 25 mins without opening the basket. Remove meatloaf and top with ketchup mixture, covering the top completely. Return meatloaf to air fryer and bake until internal temperature reaches 160 degrees F (71 degrees C), about 7 mins more.
- Turn off the air fryer and let the meatloaf rest inside for 5 minutes. Take the meatloaf out and let rest 5 mins more before slicing and serving.

157.Air-Fried Crumbed Fish

Prep Time: 10 mins
Cook Time: 12 mins
Total Time: 22 mins
Ingredient
- 1 cup dry bread crumbs
- ¼ cup vegetable oil
- 4 flounder fillets
- 1 egg, beaten
- 1 lemon, sliced
Instructions
- Preheat an air fryer to 350 degrees F (180 degrees C).
- Mix bread crumbs and oil in a bowl. Stir until the mixture becomes loose and crumbly.
- Dip fish fillets into the egg; shake off any excess. Dip fillets into the bread crumb mixture; coat evenly and fully.
- Lay coated fillets gently in the preheated air fryer. Cook until fish flakes easily with a fork, about 12 minutes. Garnish with lemon slices.

158.Air Fryer Ranch Pork Chops

Prep Time: 5 mins Cook Time: 10 mins
Additional Time: 10 mins Total Time: 25

mins
Ingredient
- 4 boneless, center-cut pork chops, 1-inch thick
- cooking spray
- 2 teaspoons dry ranch salad dressing mix
- Aluminum foil
Instructions
- Place pork chops on a plate and lightly spray both sides with cooking spray. Sprinkle both sides with ranch seasoning mix and let sit at room temperature for 10 minutes.
- Spray the basket of an air fryer with cooking spray and preheat the air fryer to 390 degrees F (200 degrees C).
- Place chops in the preheated air fryer, working in batches if necessary, to ensure the fryer is not overcrowded.
- Cook for 5 min.. Flip chops and cook 5 mins more. Let rest on a foil-covered plate for 5 mins before serving.

159.Air Fryer Rib-Eye Steak

Prep Time: 5 mins Cook Time: 15 mins
Additional Time: 2 hrs 5 mins
Total Time: 2 hrs 25 mins
Ingredient
- 2 rib-eye steaks, cut 1 1/2- inch thick
- 4 teaspoons grill seasoning (such as Montreal Steak Seasoning®)
- ¼ cup olive oil
- ½ cup reduced-sodium soy sauce
Instructions
- Combine steaks, soy sauce, olive oil, and seasoning in a large resealable bag. Marinate meat for at least 2 hours.
- Remove steaks from bag and discard the marinade. Pat excess oil off the steaks.
- Add about 1 Tbsp water to the bottom of the air fryer pan to prevent it from smoking during the cooking process.
- Preheat the air fryer to 400 degrees F (200 degrees C).
- Add steaks to air fryer and cook for 7 min.. Turn steaks and cook for another 7 mins until steak is medium-rare. For a medium steak, increase the total cook time to 16 min., flipping steak after 8 min..
- Remove steaks, keep warm, and let sit for about 4 mins before serving.

160. Air-Fried Sesame-Crusted Cod With Snap Peas

Prep Time: 10 mins Cook Time: 20 mins Total Time: 30 mins

Ingredient
- 4 (5 ounces) cod fillets
- salt and ground black pepper to taste
- 3 Tbsps butter, melted
- 2 Tbsp sesame seeds
- Vegetable oil
- 2 (6 ounce) packages sugar snap peas
- 3 cloves garlic, thinly sliced
- 1 medium orange, cut into wedges

Instructions
- Brush the air fryer basket with vegetable oil and preheat to 400 degrees F (200 degrees C).
- Thaw fish if frozen; blot dry with paper towels, and sprinkle lightly with salt and pepper.
- Stir together butter and sesame seeds in a small bowl. Set aside 2 Tbsps of the butter mixture for the fish. Toss peas and garlic with the remaining butter mixture and place in the air fryer basket.
- Cook peas in the preheated air fryer in batches, if needed, until just tender, tossing once, about 10 min.. Remove and keep warm while cooking fish.
- Brush fish with 1/2 of the remaining butter mixture. Place fillets in an air fryer basket. Cook 4 min.; turn fish. Brush with the remaining butter mixture. Cook 5 to 6 mins more or until fish begins to flake when tested with a fork. Serve with snap peas and orange wedges.

161. Breaded Air Fryer Pork Chops

Prep Time: 10 mins Cook Time: 10 mins Total Time: 20 mins

Ingredient
- 4 boneless, center-cut pork chops, 1-inch thick
- 1 Tsp. cajun seasoning
- 1 ½ cups cheese and garlic-flavored croutons
- 2 eggs
- Cooking spray

Instructions
- Preheat the air fryer to 390 degrees F (200 degrees C).
- Place pork chops on a plate and season both sides with Cajun seasoning.
- Pulse croutons in a small food processor until they have a fine consistency; transfer to a shallow dish. Lightly beat eggs in a separate shallow dish. Dip pork chops into eggs, letting excess drip off. Coat chops in crouton breading and set on a plate. Mist chops with cooking spray.
- Spray basket of the air fryer with cooking spray and place chops inside, making sure to not overcrowd the fryer. You may have to do two batches depending on the size of your air fryer.
- Cook for 5 min.. Flip chops and mist again with cooking spray if there are dry or powdery areas. Cook 5 mins more. Repeat with remaining chops.

162. Air Fryer Meatballs

Prep Time: 10 mins **Cook Time: 20 mins Additional Time: 5 mins Total Time: 35 mins Servings: 16**

Ingredient
- 16 ounces lean ground beef
- 4 ounces ground pork
- 1 Tsp. Italian seasoning
- ½ Tsp. salt
- 2 cloves garlic, minced
- 1 egg
- ½ cup grated Parmesan cheese
- ⅓ cup Italian seasoned bread crumbs

Instructions
- Preheat the air fryer to 350 degrees F (175 degrees C).
- Combine beef, pork, Italian seasoning, salt, garlic, egg, Parmesan cheese, and bread crumbs in a large bowl. Mix well until evenly combined. Form into 16 equally-sized meatballs using an ice cream scoop and place on a baking sheet.
- Place 1/2 of the meatballs in the basket of the air fryer and cook for 8 minutes. Shake the basket and cook 2 mins more. Transfer to a serving plate and let rest for 5 min.. Repeat with remaining meatballs.

163. Basic Air Fryer Hot Dogs

Prep Time: 5 mins Cook Time: 5 mins Total Time: 10 mins Servings: 4

Ingredient
- 4 hot dog buns
- 4 hot dogs

Instructions
- Preheat air fryer to 390 degrees F (200 degrees C).
- Place buns in the basket of the air fryer and cook for 2 min.. Remove buns to a plate.
- Place hot dogs in the basket of the air fryer and cook for 3 min.. Transfer hot dogs to buns.

164. Air Fryer Baked Potatoes

Prep Time: 5 mins Cook Time: 1 hr Total Time: 1 hr 5 mins Servings: 2

Ingredient
- 2 large russet potatoes, scrubbed
- 1 Tbsp peanut oil
- ½ Tsp. coarse sea salt

Instructions
- Preheat air fryer to 400 degrees F (200 degrees C).
- Brush potatoes with peanut oil and sprinkle with salt. Place them in the air fryer basket and place the basket in the air fryer.
- Cook potatoes until done, about 1 hour. Test for doneness by piercing them with a fork.

165. Air Fryer Baked Potatoes

Prep Time: 5 mins Cook Time: 1 hr Total Time: 1 hr 5 mins Servings: 2

Ingredient
- 2 large russet potatoes, scrubbed
- 1 Tbsp peanut oil
- ½ Tsp. coarse sea salt

Instructions
- Preheat air fryer to 400 degrees F (200 degrees C).
- Brush potatoes with peanut oil and sprinkle with salt. Place them in the air fryer basket and place the basket in the air fryer.
- Cook potatoes until done, about 1 hour. Test for doneness by piercing them with a fork.

166. Air Fryer Meatloaf

Prep Time: 10 mins Cook Time: 25 mins Additional Time: 10 mins Total: 45 mins Servings: 4

Ingredient
- 1 pound lean ground beef
- 1 egg, lightly beaten
- 3 Tbsp dry bread crumbs
- 1 small onion, finely chopped
- 1 Tbsp chopped fresh thyme

- 1 Tsp. salt
- Ground black pepper to taste
- 2 mushrooms, thickly sliced
- 1 Tbsp olive oil, or as needed

Instructions

- Preheat an air fryer to 392 degrees F
- Combine ground beef, egg, bread crumbs, onion, thyme, salt, and pepper in a bowl. Knead and mix thoroughly.
- Transfer beef mixture to a baking pan and smooth the top. Press mushrooms into the top and coat with olive oil.
- Place the pan into the air fryer basket and slide it into the air fryer.
- Set air fryer timer for 25 mins and roast meatloaf until nicely browned.
- Let meatloaf rest at least 10 mins before slicing into wedges and serving.

167. Crumbed Chicken Tenderloins

Prep: 15 mins Cook: 12 mins
Total: 27 mins
Servings: 4

Ingredient

- 1 egg
- ½ cup dry bread crumbs
- 2 Tbsps vegetable oil
- 8 chicken tenderloins

Instructions

- Preheat an air fryer to 350 degrees F (175 degrees C).
- Whisk egg in a small bowl.
- Mix bread crumbs and oil in a second bowl until the mixture becomes loose and crumbly.
- Dip each chicken tenderloin into the bowl of an egg; shake off any residual egg. Dip chicken into the crumb mixture, making sure it is evenly and fully covered. Lay chicken tenderloins into the basket of the air fryer. Cook until no longer pink in the center, about 12 minutes. An instant-read thermometer inserted into the center should read at least 165 degrees F

168. Air Fryer Chicken Taquitos

Prep Time: 15 mins Cook Time: 20 mins
Total Time: 35 mins Servings: 6

Ingredient

- 1 Tsp. vegetable oil
- 2 Tbsp diced onion
- 1 clove garlic, minced
- 2 Tbsp chopped green chiles (such as Ortega®)

- 2 Tbsps Mexican-style hot tomato sauce (such as El Pato®)
- 1 cup shredded rotisserie chicken
- 2 Tbsps Neufchatel cheese
- ½ cup shredded Mexican cheese blend
- 1 pinch salt and ground black pepper to taste
- 6 each corn tortillas
- 1 serving avocado oil cooking spray

Instructions

- Heat oil in a skillet. Add onion and cook until soft and translucent, 3 to 5 min..
- Add garlic and cook until fragrant, about 1 minute. Add green chiles and Mexican tomato sauce; stir to combine.
- Add chicken, Neufchatel cheese, and Mexican cheese blend.
- Cook and stir until cheeses have melted and the mixture is completely warmed for about 3 minutes. Season with salt and pepper.
- Heat tortillas in a skillet or directly on the grates of a gas stove until soft and pliable.
- Place 3 Tbsp of chicken mixture down the center of each tortilla. Fold over and roll into taquitos.
- Preheat an air fryer to 400 degrees F (200 degrees C).
- Place taquitos in the air fryer basket, making sure they are not touching, and mist with avocado oil. Cook in batches if necessary.
- Cook until golden brown and crispy, 6 to 9 min..
- Turn taquitos over, mist with avocado oil, and air fry for an additional 3 to 5 minutes.

169. Air Fryer Chicken Katsu With Homemade Katsu Sauce

Prep Time: 20 mins Cook Time: 20 mins
Total Time: 40 mins Servings: 4

Ingredients

Katsu Sauce:

- ½ cup ketchup
- 2 Tbsps soy sauce
- 1 Tbsp brown sugar
- 1 Tbsp sherry
- 2 teaspoons Worcestershire sauce
- 1 Tsp. minced garlic

Chicken:

- 1 pound boneless skinless chicken

breast, sliced in half horizontally
- 1 pinch salt and ground black pepper to taste
- 2 large eggs, beaten
- 1 ½ cups panko bread crumbs
- 1 serving cooking spray

Instructions

- Whisk ketchup, soy sauce, brown sugar, sherry, Worcestershire sauce, and garlic together in a bowl until sugar has dissolved. Set katsu sauce aside.
- Preheat an air fryer to 350 degrees F (175 degrees C).
- Meanwhile, lay chicken pieces on a clean work surface. Season with salt and pepper.
- Place beaten eggs in a flat dish. Pour bread crumbs into a second flat dish. Dredge chicken pieces in egg and then in bread crumbs. Repeat by dredging the chicken in egg and then bread crumbs again, pressing down so that the bread crumbs stick to the chicken.
- Place chicken pieces in the basket of the preheated air fryer. Spray the tops with nonstick cooking spray.
- Air fry for 10 min.. Flip chicken pieces over using a spatula and spray the tops with nonstick cooking spray. Cook for 8 mins more. Transfer chicken to a cutting board and slice. Serve with katsu sauce.

170. Air Fryer Lemon Pepper Shrimp

Prep Time: 5 mins Cook Time: 10 mins
Total Time: 15 mins Servings: 2

Ingredient

- 1 Tbsp olive oil
- 1 lemon, juiced
- 1 Tsp. lemon pepper
- ¼ Tsp. paprika
- ¼ Tsp. garlic powder
- 12 ounces uncooked medium shrimp, peeled and deveined
- 1 lemon, sliced

Instructions

- Preheat an air fryer to 400 degrees F (200 degrees C).
- Combine olive oil, lemon juice, lemon pepper, paprika, and garlic powder in a bowl. Add shrimp and toss until coated.
- Place shrimp in the air fryer and cook until pink and firm, 6 to 8 min.. Serve with lemon slices.

171. Dry-Rub Air-Fried Chicken Wings

Prep Time: 10 mins Cook Time: 35 mins

Total Time: 45 mins Servings: 2

Ingredient

- 1 Tbsp dark brown sugar
- 1 Tbsp sweet paprika
- ½ Tbsp kosher salt
- 1 Tsp. garlic powder
- 1 Tsp. onion powder
- 1 Tsp. poultry seasoning
- ½ Tsp. mustard powder
- ½ Tsp. freshly ground black pepper
- 8 chicken wings, or more as needed

Instructions

- Preheat air fryer to 350 degrees F (175 degrees C).
- Whisk together brown sugar, paprika, salt, garlic powder, onion powder, poultry seasoning, mustard powder, and pepper in a large bowl. Toss in chicken wings and rub the seasonings into them with your hands until fully coated.
- Arrange wings in the basket of the preheated air fryer, standing up on their ends and leaning against each other and the wall of the basket.
- Cook until wings are tender inside and golden brown and crisp on the outside, about 35 min.. Transfer wings to a plate and serve hot.

172.Air Fryer Chicken Cordon Bleu

Prep Time: 15 mins Cook Time: 20 mins Additional Time: 5 mins Total Time: 40 mins Servings: 2

Ingredient

- 2 boneless, skinless chicken breasts
- Salt and ground black pepper to taste
- 1 Tbsp dijon mustard
- 4 slices deli swiss cheese
- 4 slices of deli ham
- 2 toothpicks
- ¼ cup all-purpose flour
- 1 egg, beaten
- 1 cup panko bread crumbs
- ⅓ cup grated parmesan cheese
- Cooking spray

Instructions

- Set 1 chicken breast on a cutting board. Hold a sharp knife parallel to the cutting board and along one long side of the breast; cut chicken breast almost in half, leaving breast attached at one side.
- Open breast so it lies flat like a book

and covers with plastic wrap.

- Lightly pound with the flat side of a meat mallet to 1/4-inch thickness. Repeat with the remaining chicken breast.
- Season each chicken breast with salt and pepper. Spread Dijon mustard on top.
- Place 1 slice of cheese on each breast. Top each with 2 slices of ham and 1 slice of cheese. Roll each breast up and secure it with a toothpick.
- Place flour in a shallow bowl. Place egg in a second bowl. Mix panko bread crumbs and grated Parmesan in a third bowl.
- Preheat an air fryer to 350 degrees F (175 degrees C).
- Dip chicken first in flour, followed by the egg, and finally, roll in the bread crumb mixture. Spray chicken rolls with nonstick spray and let sit for 5 mins while the air fryer preheats.
- Place chicken in the basket of the preheated air fryer and cook for 10 min.. Spray any chalky spots with nonstick spray again. Cook until chicken is no longer pink in the center, 8 mins more.

173.Cajun Air Fryer Salmon

Prep Time: 10 mins Cook Time: 10 mins Total Time: 20 mins Servings: 2

Ingredient

- 2 (6 ounces) skin-on salmon fillets
- Cooking spray
- 1 Tbsp cajun seasoning
- 1 Tsp. brown sugar

Instructions

- Preheat the air fryer to 390 degrees F (200 degrees C).
- Rinse and dry salmon fillets with a paper towel. Mist fillets with cooking spray. Combine Cajun seasoning and brown sugar in a small bowl. Sprinkle onto a plate. Press the flesh sides of fillets into the seasoning mixture.
- Spray the basket of the air fryer with cooking spray and place salmon fillets skin-side down. Mist salmon again lightly with cooking spray.
- Cook for 8 minutes. Remove from air fryer and let rest for 2 mins before serving.

174.Easy Air Fryer Pork Chops

Prep Time: 10 mins Cook Time: 20 mins Additional Time: 5 mins Total Time: 35 mins Servings: 4

Ingredient

- ½ cup grated Parmesan cheese
- 1 Tsp. paprika
- 1 Tsp. garlic powder
- 1 Tsp. kosher salt
- 1 Tsp. dried parsley
- ½ Tsp. ground black pepper
- 4 (5 ounces) center-cut pork chops
- 2 Tbsps extra virgin olive oil

Instructions

- Preheat the air fryer to 380 degrees F
- Combine Parmesan cheese, paprika, garlic powder, salt, parsley, and pepper in a flat shallow dish; mix well.
- Coat each pork chop with olive oil. Dredge both sides of each chop in the Parmesan mixture and set on a plate.
- Place 2 chops in the basket of the air fryer and cook for 10 min.; flipping halfway through cook time.
- Transfer to a cutting board and let rest for 5 minutes. Repeat with remaining chops.

175.Lumpia In The Air Fryer

Prep Time: 15 mins Cook Time: 20 mins Total: 35 mins Servings: 16

Ingredient

- 1 pound Italian hot sausage links
- ½ cup finely sliced green onions
- ¼ cup diced onions
- ½ cup finely chopped carrots
- ½ cup finely chopped water chestnuts
- 2 cloves garlic, minced
- 2 Tbsps soy sauce
- ½ Tsp. salt
- ¼ Tsp. ground ginger
- 16 spring roll wrappers
- Avocado oil cooking spray

Instructions

- Remove casing from sausage and cook in a skillet over medium heat until slightly browned 4 to 5 min..
- Add green onions, onions, carrots, and water chestnuts. Cook and stir until onions are soft and translucent, 5 to 7 minutes.
- Add garlic and cook for 1 to 2 minutes. Season with soy sauce, salt, and ginger. Stir until filling is well combined and remove from heat.

- Lay a spring roll wrapper at an angle. Place a scant 1/4 cup filling in the center of the wrapper. Fold bottom corner over filling and tuck in the sides to form a roll.
- Use your finger to lightly moisten edges with water.
- Repeat with remaining wrappers and filling. Mist each roll with avocado oil spray.
- Preheat an air fryer to 390 degrees F
- Place lumpia rolls in the basket, making sure they are not touching; cook in batches if necessary. Fry for 4 min.; flip and cook until skins are crispy, about 4 mins more.

176. Air Fryer Buttermilk Fried Chicken

Prep Time: 5 mins Cook Time: 30 mins Additional Time: 4 hrs Total Time: 4 hrs 35 mins Servings: 6

Ingredient

- 1 ½ pound boneless, skinless chicken thighs
- 2 cups buttermilk
- 1 cup all-purpose flour
- 1 Tbsp seasoned salt
- ½ Tbsp ground black pepper
- 1 cup panko bread crumbs
- 1 serving cooking spray

Instructions

- Place chicken thighs in a shallow casserole dish. Pour buttermilk over chicken and refrigerate for 4 hours, or overnight.
- Preheat an air fryer to 380 degrees F (190 degrees C).
- Mix flour, seasoned salt, and pepper in a large gallon-sized resealable bag. Dredge chicken thighs in seasoned flour. Dip back into the buttermilk, then coat with panko bread crumbs.
- Spray the basket of the air fryer with nonstick cooking spray. Arrange 1/2 of the chicken thighs in the basket, making sure none are touching. Spray the top of each chicken thigh with cooking spray.
- Cook in the preheated air fryer for 15 min.. Flip. Spray tops of chicken again. Cook until chicken is no longer pink in the center and the juices run clear for about 10 more min.. An instant-read thermometer inserted into the center should read at least 165 degrees F (74 degrees C). Repeat with the remaining

chicken.

177. Air Fryer Potstickers

Prep Time: 10 mins Cook Time: 25 mins Total Time: 35 mins Servings: 24

Ingredient

- ½ pound ground pork
- 1 (4 ounces) can water chestnuts, drained and chopped
- 1 (4 ounces) can shiitake mushrooms, drained and chopped
- 2 Tbsps soy sauce
- 2 Tbsps sesame oil
- 1 Tbsp Sriracha sauce
- 1 (12 ounces) package round dumpling wrappers

Instructions

- Preheat an air fryer to 400 degrees F (200 degrees C).
- Combine ground pork, water chestnuts, shiitake mushrooms, sesame oil, soy sauce, and Sriracha in a large skillet over medium-high heat. Cook until pork is no longer pink, about 6 min.. Remove from heat and let sit until cool enough to handle.
- Layout 8 dumpling wrappers on a clean work surface. Place a heaping teaspoonful of pork mixture in the middle of each wrapper. Pull both sides up like a taco and pinch the tops until sealed.
- Cook in batches in the preheated air fryer for 3 minutes. Use tongs to flip the potstickers and cook 3 mins more. Transfer to a paper-towel-lined plate. Repeat with remaining dumpling wrappers and filling.

178. Mexican-Style Stuffed Chicken Breasts

Prep Time: 20 mins Cook Time: 10 mins Total Time: 30 mins Servings: 2

Ingredient

- 4 extra-long toothpicks
- 4 teaspoons chili powder, divided
- 4 teaspoons ground cumin, divided
- 1 skinless, boneless chicken breast
- 2 teaspoons chipotle flakes
- 2 teaspoons mexican oregano
- Salt and ground black pepper to taste
- ½ red bell pepper, sliced into thin strips
- ½ onion, sliced into thin strips
- 1 fresh jalapeno pepper, sliced into

thin strips
- 2 teaspoons corn oil
- ½ lime, juiced

Instructions

- Place toothpicks in a small bowl and cover with water; let them soak to keep them from burning while cooking.
- Mix 2 teaspoons chili powder and 2 teaspoons cumin in a shallow dish.
- Preheat an air fryer to 400 degrees F (200 degrees C).
- Place chicken breast on a flat work surface. Slice horizontally through the middle. Pound each half using a kitchen mallet or rolling pin until about 1/4-inch thick.
- Sprinkle each breast half equally with remaining chili powder, remaining cumin, chipotle flakes, oregano, salt, and pepper.
- Place 1/2 the bell pepper, onion, and jalapeno in the center of 1 breast half. Roll the chicken from the tapered end upward and use 2 toothpicks to secure it. Repeat with other breast, spices, and vegetables and secure with remaining toothpicks. Roll each roll-up in the chili-cumin mixture in the shallow dish while drizzling with olive oil until evenly covered.
- Place roll-ups in the air-fryer basket with the toothpick side facing up. Set timer for 6 minutes.
- Turn roll-ups over. Continue cooking in the air fryer until juices run clear and an instant-read thermometer inserted into the center reads at least 165 degrees F (74 degrees C), about 5 mins more.
- Drizzle lime juice evenly on roll-ups before serving.

179. Air Fryer Chimichangas

Prep Time: 15 mins Cook Time: 20 mins Total Time: 35 mins Servings: 6

Ingredient

- 1 Tbsp vegetable oil
- ½ cup diced onion
- 2 cups shredded cooked chicken
- ½ (8 ounces) package Neufchatel cheese, softened
- 1 (4 ounces) can hot fire-roasted diced green chiles (such as Ortega®)
- ¼ cup chicken broth
- 1 ½ Tbsps chicken taco seasoning mix

(such as McCormick®)

- ½ Tsp. salt
- ¼ Tsp. ground black pepper
- 6 (10 inches) flour tortillas
- 1 cup shredded Mexican cheese blend, or to taste
- Avocado oil cooking spray

Instructions

- Heat oil in a medium skillet. Add onion and cook until soft and translucent, 4 to 6 min.. Add chicken, Neufchatel cheese, diced chiles, chicken broth, taco seasoning, salt, and pepper. Cook and stir until mixture is well combined and Neufchatel has softened been incorporated.
- Heat tortillas in a large skillet or directly on the grates of a gas stove until soft and pliable. Place 1/3 cup chicken mixture down the center of each tortilla and top with a heaping Tbsp of Mexican cheese. Fold top and bottom of tortillas over the filling, then roll each into a burrito shape. Mist with cooking spray and place in the basket of an air fryer.
- Air fry at 400 degrees F (200 degrees C) for 4 to 6 min.. Flip each chimichanga over, mist with cooking spray, and air fry until lightly browned, 2 to 4 mins more.

180. Breaded Air Fryer Pork Chops

Prep Time: 10 mins Cook Time: 10 mins Total Time: 20 mins Servings: 4

Ingredient

- 4 boneless, center-cut pork chops, 1-inch thick
- 1 Tsp. Cajun seasoning
- 1 ½ cups cheese and garlic-flavored croutons
- 2 eggs

Instructions

- Preheat the air fryer to 390 degrees F (200 degrees C).
- Place pork chops on a plate and season both sides with Cajun seasoning.
- Pulse croutons in a small food processor until they have a fine consistency; transfer to a shallow dish. Lightly beat eggs in a separate shallow dish. Dip pork chops into eggs, letting excess drip off. Coat chops in crouton breading and set on a plate. Mist chops with cooking spray.
- Spray basket of the air fryer with

cooking spray and place chops inside, making sure to not overcrowd the fryer. You may have to do two batches depending on the size of your air fryer.
- Cook for 5 min.. Flip chops and mist again with cooking spray if there are dry or powdery areas. Cook 5 mins more. Repeat with remaining chops.

181. Air Fryer Crab Rangoon

Prep Time: 15 mins Cook Time: 20 mins Total Time: 35 mins Servings: 12

Ingredient

- 1 (8 ounces) package cream cheese, softened
- 4 ounces lump crab meat
- 2 Tbsp chopped scallions
- 1 Tsp. soy sauce
- 1 Tsp. Worcestershire sauce
- 1 serving nonstick cooking spray
- 24 each wonton wrappers
- 2 Tbsp Asian sweet chili sauce, for dipping

Instructions

- Combine cream cheese, crab meat, scallions, soy sauce, and Worcestershire sauce in a bowl; stir until evenly combined.
- Preheat an air fryer to 350 degrees F (175 degrees C). Spray the basket of the air fryer with cooking spray. Fill a small bowl with warm water.
- Place 12 wonton wrappers on a clean work surface. Spoon 1 Tsp. of cream cheese mixture into the center of each wonton wrapper. Dip index finger into the warm water and wet around the sides of each wonton wrapper. Crimp wrapper corners upwards to meet in the center to form dumplings.
- Place dumplings in the prepared basket and spray the tops with cooking spray.
- Cook dumplings until desired crispness, about 8 to 10 minutes. Transfer to a paper towel-lined plate.
- While the first batch is cooking, assemble the remaining dumplings with the remaining wrappers and filling.
- Serve with sweet chili sauce for dipping.

182. Lemon-Garlic Air Fryer Salmon

Prep Time: 10 mins Cook Time: 10 mins Additional Time: 5 mins Total Time: 25 mins

Ingredient

- 1 Tbsp melted butter
- ½ Tsp. minced garlic
- 2 (6 ounce) fillets center-cut salmon fillets with skin
- ¼ Tsp. lemon-pepper seasoning
- ⅛ Tsp. dried parsley
- Cooking spray
- 3 thin slices lemon, cut in half

Instructions

- Preheat the air fryer to 390 degrees F (200 degrees C).
- Combine melted butter and minced garlic in a small bowl.
- Rinse salmon fillets and dry with a paper towel. Brush with butter mixture and sprinkle with lemon-pepper seasoning and parsley.
- Spray the basket of the air fryer with cooking spray. Place salmon fillets in the basket, skin-side down, and top each with 3 lemon halves.
- Cook in the preheated air fryer for 8 to 10 min.. Remove from the air fryer and let rest for 2 mins before serving.

183. Air Fryer Ranch Pork Chops

Prep Time: 5 mins Cook Time: 10 mins Additional Time: 10 mins Total Time: 25 mins

Ingredient

- 4 boneless, center-cut pork chops, 1-inch thick
- Cooking spray
- 2 teaspoons dry ranch salad dressing mix
- Aluminum foil

Instructions

- Place pork chops on a plate and lightly spray both sides with cooking spray. Sprinkle both sides with ranch seasoning mix and let sit at room temperature for 10 minutes.
- Spray the basket of an air fryer with cooking spray and preheat the air fryer to 390 degrees F (200 degrees C).
- Place chops in the preheated air fryer, working in batches if necessary, to ensure the fryer is not overcrowded.
- Cook for 5 minutes. Flip chops and cook 5 mins more. Let rest on a foil-covered plate for 5 mins before serving.

184. Air Fryer Tacos De Papa

Cook Time: 25 mins Additional Time: 5 mins Total Time: 30 mins

Ingredient

- 2 cups water
- 1 (4 ounces) package instant mashed potatoes
- ½ cup shredded cheddar cheese
- 1 green onion, chopped
- ½ Tsp. ground cumin
- 10 corn tortillas
- 1 serving nonstick cooking spray
- ½ cup salsa verde
- ¼ cup crumbled cotija cheese

Instructions

- Heat water in a medium saucepan to boiling. Remove from the heat and stir in instant mashed potatoes. Mix thoroughly with a fork to moisten all potatoes and let stand 5 min.. Stir in Cheddar cheese, green onion, and cumin.
- Preheat an air fryer to 400 degrees F (200 degrees C).
- Wrap tortillas in a damp paper towel and microwave on high until warm, about 20 seconds.
- Spread 1 Tbsp potato mixture in the center of a tortilla and fold over to make a taco. Repeat with remaining tortillas.
- Working in batches, place tacos in the basket of an air fryer. Spray the tops with cooking spray and cook until crispy, about 5 min.. Transfer to a serving platter and repeat to cook remaining tacos.
- Drizzle salsa verde over tacos and top with cotija cheese.

Side Dishes & Dinner

185.Shrimp Po' Boy Sandwich

Prep Time: 20 mins Cook Time: 10 mins
Total Time: 30 mins

Ingredients

- 1 pound shrimp, deveined
- 1 Tsp. creole seasoning i used tony chachere
- 1/4 cup buttermilk
- 1/2 cup louisiana fish fry coating
- Cooking oil spray (if air frying) i use olive oil
- Canola or vegetable oil (if pan-frying)

you will need enough oil to fill 2 inches of height in your frying pan.

- 4 french bread hoagie rolls i used 2 loaves, cut each in half
- 2 cups shredded iceberg lettuce
- 8 tomato slices

Remoulade Sauce

- 1/2 cup mayo I used reduced-fat
- 1 tsp minced garlic
- 1/2 lemon juice of
- 1 tsp Worcestershire
- 1/2 tsp Creole Seasoning I used Tony Chachere
- 1 tsp Dijon mustard
- 1 tsp hot sauce
- 1 green onion chopped

Instructions

Remoulade Sauce

- Combine all of the ingredients in a small bowl. Refrigerate before serving while the shrimp cooks.

Shrimp And Breading

- Marinate the shrimp in the Creole seasoning and buttermilk for 30 min.. I like to use a sealable plastic bag to do this.
- Add the fish fry to a bowl. Remove the shrimp from the bags and dip each into the fish fry. Add the shrimp to the air fryer basket.

Pan Fry

- Heat a frying pan with 2 inches of oil to 350 degrees. Use a thermometer to test the heat.
- Fry the shrimp on both sides for 3-4 mins until crisp.
- Remove the shrimp from the pan and drain the excess grease using paper towels.

Air Fryer

- Spray the air fryer basket with cooking oil. Add the shrimp to the air fryer basket.
- Spritz the shrimp with cooking oil.
- Cook the shrimp for 5 mins at 400 degrees. Open the basket and flip the shrimp to the other side. Cook for an additional 3-5 mins or until crisp.
- Assemble the Po Boy
- Spread the remoulade sauce on the French bread.
- Add the sliced tomato and lettuce, and then the shrimp.

186.Air Fryer Beef Taco Fried Egg Rolls

Prep Time: 15 mins Cook Time: 25 mins
Total Time: 40 mins
Servings: 8

Ingredients

- 1 pound ground beef
- 16 egg roll wrappers i used wing hing brand
- 1/2 cup chopped onion i used red onion.
- 2 garlic cloves minced
- 16 oz can diced tomatoes and chilies i used mexican rotel.
- 8 oz refried black beans i used fat-free and 1/2 of a 16oz can.
- 1 cup shredded mexican cheese
- 1/2 cup whole kernel corn i used frozen
- Cooking oil spray
- Homemade taco seasoning
- 1 Tbsp chili powder
- 1 Tsp. cumin
- 1 Tsp. smoked paprika
- Salt and pepper to taste

Instructions

- Add the ground beef to a skillet on medium-high heat along with the salt, pepper, and taco seasoning. Cook until browned while breaking the beef into smaller chunks.
- Once the meat has started to brown add the chopped onions and garlic. Cook until the onions become fragrant.
- Add the diced tomatoes and chilis, Mexican cheese, beans, and corn. Stir to ensure the mixture is combined.
- Lay the egg roll wrappers on a flat surface. Dip a cooking brush in water. Glaze each of the egg roll wrappers with the wet brush along the edges. This will soften the crust and make it easier to roll.
- Load 2 Tbsp of the mixture into each of the wrappers. Do not overstuff. Depending on the brand of egg roll wrappers you use, you may need to double wrap the egg rolls.
- Fold the wrappers diagonally to close. Press firmly on the area with the filling, cup it to secure it in place. Fold in the left and right sides as triangles. Fold the final layer over the top to close. Use the cooking brush to wet the area and secure it in place.
- Spray the air fryer basket with cooking

oil.

- Load the egg rolls into the basket of the Air Fryer. Spray each egg roll with cooking oil.
- Cook for 8 mins at 400 degrees. Flip the egg rolls. Cook for an additional 4 mins or until browned and crisp.

187. Air Fryer Beef Taco Fried Egg Rolls

Prep Time: 15 mins Cook Time: 25 mins
Total Time: 40 mins
Servings: 8

Ingredients

- 1 pound ground beef
- 16 egg roll wrappers i used wing hing brand
- 1/2 cup chopped onion i used red onion.
- 2 garlic cloves minced
- 16 oz can diced tomatoes and chilies i used mexican rotel.
- 8 oz refried black beans i used fat-free and 1/2 of a 16oz can.
- 1 cup shredded mexican cheese
- 1/2 cup whole kernel corn i used frozen
- Cooking oil spray

Homemade Taco Seasoning

- 1 Tbsp chili powder
- 1 Tsp. cumin
- 1 Tsp. smoked paprika
- Salt and pepper to taste

Instructions

- Add the ground beef to a skillet on medium-high heat along with the salt, pepper, and taco seasoning. Cook until browned while breaking the beef into smaller chunks.
- Once the meat has started to brown add the chopped onions and garlic. Cook until the onions become fragrant.
- Add the diced tomatoes and chilis, Mexican cheese, beans, and corn. Stir to ensure the mixture is combined.
- Lay the egg roll wrappers on a flat surface. Dip a cooking brush in water. Glaze each of the egg roll wrappers with the wet brush along the edges. This will soften the crust and make it easier to roll.
- Load 2 Tbsps of the mixture into each of the wrappers. Do not overstuff. Depending on the brand of egg roll wrappers you use, you may need to double wrap the egg rolls.

- Fold the wrappers diagonally to close. Press firmly on the area with the filling, cup it to secure it in place. Fold in the left and right sides as triangles. Fold the final layer over the top to close. Use the cooking brush to wet the area and secure it in place.
- Spray the air fryer basket with cooking oil.
- Load the egg rolls into the basket of the Air Fryer. Spray each egg roll with cooking oil.
- Cook for 8 mins at 400 degrees. Flip the egg rolls. Cook for an additional 4 mins or until browned and crisp.

188. Potato Wedges

Prep time: 10 mins Cook time: 25 mins

Ingredients

- Potatoes – 2, cut into wedges
- Olive oil – 1 tbsp.
- Salt and black pepper to taste
- Sour cream – 3 tbsp.
- Sweet chili sauce – 2 tbsp.

Directions:

- In a bowl, mix potato wedges with oil, salt and pepper. Toss well.
- Place into the air fryer basket and cook at 360F for 25 minutes. Flip once.
- Arrange potato wedges on plates.
- Drizzle with chili sauce and sour cream all over and serve them as a side
- dish.

189. Mushroom Side Dish

Prep time: 10 mins Cook time: 8 mins

Ingredients

- Button mushrooms – 10, stems removed
- Italian seasoning – 1 tbsp.
- Salt and black pepper to taste
- Cheddar cheese – 2 tbsp., grated
- Olive oil – 1 tbsp.
- Mozzarella – 2 tbsp., grated
- Dill – 1 tbsp., chopped

Directions:

- In a bowl, combine mushrooms with oil, seasoning, dill, salt and pepper.
- Mix well.
- Arrange mushrooms in the air fryer basket, sprinkle mozzarella and cheddar on each and cook them at 360F for 8 minutes.
- Divide among plates and serve.

190. Corn with Lime and Cheese

Prep time: 10 mins Cook time: 15 mins

Ingredients

- Corns on the cob – 2, husks removed
- A drizzle of olive oil
- Feta cheese – ½ cup, grated
- Sweet paprika – 2 tsp.
- Juice from 2 limes

Directions:

- Rub corn with oil and paprika.
- Place in the air fryer basket and cook at 400F for 15 minutes. Flip once.
- Divide corn among plates, sprinkle cheese on top.
- Drizzle with lime juice and serve.

191. Creamy Potato

Prep time: 10 mins Cook time: 1 hour 20 mins

Ingredients

- Big potato – 1
- Bacon strips – 2, cooked and chopped
- Olive oil – 1 tsp.
- Cheddar cheese – 1/3 cup, shredded
- Green onions – 1 tbsp. chopped
- Salt and black pepper to taste
- Butter – 1 tbsp.
- Heavy cream – 2 tbsp.

Directions:

- Rub potato with oil, season with salt and pepper.
- Place in the preheated air fryer and cook at 400F for 30 minutes.
- Flip potato and cook for 30 minsmore.
- Transfer to a cutting board. Cool and slice in half lengthwise and scoop pulp into a bowl.
- Add salt, pepper, green onions, heavy cream, butter, cheese and bacon. Stir well and stuff potato skins with this mixture.
- Return potato to the air fryer and cook them at 400F for 20 minutes.

192. Green Beans

Prep time: 10 mins Cook time: 25 mins

Ingredients

- Green beans – 1 ½ pounds, trimmed and steamed for 2 mins
- Salt and black pepper to taste
- Shallots – ½ pound, chopped
- Almonds – ¼ cup, toasted
- Olive oil – 2 tbsp.

Directions:

- Mix green beans with oil, almonds, shallots, salt and pepper in the air fryer basket.
- Toss well and cook at 400F for 25

minutes.

- Divide among plates and serve.

193. Parmesan Mushrooms

Prep time: 10 mins Cook time: 15 mins

Ingredients

- Button mushroom caps – 9
- Cream cracker slices – 3, crumbled
- Egg white – 1
- Parmesan – 2 tbsp., grated
- Italian seasoning – 1 tsp.
- Salt and black pepper
- Butter – 1 tbsp., melted

Directions:

Mix crackers with butter, Parmesan, salt, pepper, seasoning and egg white. Stir well and stuff mushrooms with this mixture.

Arrange mushrooms in the air fryer basket and cook them at 360F for 15 minutes.

Divide among plates and serve

194. Eggplant Side Dish

Prep time: 10 mins Cook time: 10 mins

Ingredients

- Baby eggplants – 8, scooped in the center and pulp reserved
- Salt and black pepper to taste
- A pinch of oregano, dried
- Green bell pepper – 1, chopped
- Tomato paste – 1 tbsp.
- Coriander – 1 bunch, chopped
- Garlic powder – ½ tsp.
- Olive oil – 1 tbsp.
- Yellow onion – 1, chopped
- Tomato – 1, chopped

Directions:

- Heat oil in a pan and add the onion. Stir-fry for 1 minute.
- Add tomato, coriander, garlic powder, tomato paste, green bell pepper, oregano, eggplant pulp, salt and pepper.
- Stir-fry for 2 minsmore. Remove from heat and cool.
- Stuff eggplants with this mixture; place them in the air fryer basket.
- Cook at 360F for 8 minutes.
- Divide eggplants among plates and serve.

195. Zucchini Fries

Prep time: 10 mins Cook time: 12 mins

Ingredients

- Zucchini – 1, cut into medium sticks
- Olive oil – 1 drizzle

- Salt and black pepper to taste
- Eggs – 2, whisked
- Bread crumbs – 1 cup
- Flour – ½ cup

Directions:

- In a bowl, add flour and mix with salt and pepper.
- Put breadcrumbs in another bowl.
- In a third bowl, mix the egg with salt and pepper.
- Dredge zucchini fries in flour, then in eggs and in bread crumbs.
- Grease the air fryer with olive oil.
- Heat up at 400F. Add zucchini fries and cook them for 12 minutes.
- Serve.

196. Herbed Tomatoes

Prep time: 10 mins

Cook time: 15 mins

Servings: 4

Ingredients

- Big tomatoes – 4, halved and inside scooped out
- Salt and black pepper to taste
- Olive oil – 1 tbsp.
- Garlic – 2 cloves, minced
- Thyme – ½ tsp., chopped

Directions:

In the air fryer, mix tomatoes with thyme, garlic, oil, salt and pepper. Mix and cook at 390F for 15 minutes. Serve.

197. Creamy Endives

Prep time: 10 mins

Cook time: 10 mins

Ingredients

- Endives – 6, trimmed and halved
- Garlic powder – 1 tsp.
- Greek yogurt – ½ cup
- Curry powder – ½ tsp.
- Salt and black pepper to taste
- Lemon juice – 3 tbsp.

Directions:

- In a bowl, mix endives with lemon juice, salt, pepper, curry powder, yogurt and garlic powder. Coat well and set aside for 10 minutes.
- Cook in the preheated 350F air fryer for 10 minutes.
- Serve.

198. Easy Polenta Pie

Prep. time: 10 min

Cook Time: 55 min

Ingredients :

- Egg, slightly beaten (1 piece)
- Water (2 cups)
- Monterey Jack cheese, w/ jalapeno peppers, shredded (3/4 cup)
- Cornmeal (3/4 cup)
- Salt (1/4 teaspoon)
- Chili beans, drained (15 ounces)
- Tortilla chips/crushed corn (1/3 cup)

Directions:

- Preheat air fryer at 350 degrees Fahrenheit.
- Mist cooking spray onto a pie plate.
- In saucepan heated on medium-high, combine water, salt, and cornmeal.
- Let mixture boil, then cook on medium heat for six minutes. Stir in egg and let sit for five minutes.
- Pour cornmeal mixture into pie plate and spread evenly.
- Air-fry for fifteen minsand top with beans, corn chips, and cheese.
- Air-fry for another twenty minutes.

199. Bean and Rice Dish

Prep. time: 10 min

Cook Time: 1 hr 5 min

Ingredients :

- Boiling water (1 ½ cups)
- Kidney beans, dark red, undrained (15 ounces)
- Marjoram leaves, dried (1/2 teaspoon)
- Cheddar cheese, shredded (1/2 cup)
- White rice, long grain, uncooked (1 cup)
- Bouillon, chicken/vegetable, granulated (1 tablespoon)
- Onion, medium, chopped (1 piece)
- Baby lima beans, frozen, thawed, drained (9 ounces)

Directions:

- Preheat air fryer at 325 degrees Fahrenheit.
- Combine all **Ingredients** , save for cheese, in casserole.
- Cover and air-fry for one hour and fifteen minutes. Give dish a stir before topping with cheese.

200. Squash Casserole

Prep. time: 20 min

Cook Time: 40 min

Ingredients :

- Yellow summer squash, medium,

sliced thinly (1 piece)
- Thyme leaves, fresh, chopped (1 tablespoon)
- Salt (1/2 teaspoon)
- Italian cheese blend, gluten free, shredded (1/2 cup)
- Olive oil, extra virgin (1 tablespoon)
- Zucchini, medium, sliced thinly (1 piece)
- Onion, diced (1/2 cup)
- Brown rice, cooked (1 cup)
- Plum tomato, diced (1 piece)
- Pepper (1/8 teaspoon)

Directions:
- Preheat air fryer to 375 degrees Fahrenheit.
- Mist cooking spray onto a gratin dish.
- Combine rice, onion, tomato, pepper, salt (1/4 teaspoon), oil, and ½ thyme leaves. Spread evenly into gratin dish and layer on top with squash and zucchini.
- Sprinkle with remaining salt (1/4 teaspoon) and thyme.
- Cover and air-fry for twenty minutes. Top with cheese and air-fry for another ten to twelve minutes.

201.Broccoli Pasta

Prep. time: 10 mins
Cook Time: 4 mins

Ingredients :
- 2 cups water
- ½ pound pasta
- 8 ounces cheddar cheese, grated
- ½ cup broccoli
- ½ cup half and half

Directions:
- Put the water and the pasta in your pressure cooker.
- Add the steamer basket, add the broccoli, cover the cooker and cook on High for 4 minutes.
- Drain pasta, transfer it as well as the broccoli, and clean the pot.
- Set it on sauté mode, add pasta and broccoli, cheese and half and half, stir well, cook for 2 minutes, divide between plates and serve as a side dish for chicken.

202.Refried Beans

Prep. time: 10 mins
Cook Time: 35 mins

Ingredients :
- 1 pound pinto beans, soaked for 20 minsand drained
- 1 cup onion, chopped
- 2 garlic cloves, minced
- 1 teaspoon oregano, dried
- ½ jalapeno, chopped
- 1 teaspoon cumin, ground
- A pinch of salt and black pepper
- 1 and ½ tablespoon olive oil
- 2 cups chicken stock

Directions :
- In your pressure cooker, mix oil with onion, jalapeno, garlic, oregano, cumin, salt, pepper, stock and beans, stir, cover and cook on Manual for 30 minutes.
- Stir beans one more time, divide them between 2 plates and serve as a side dish.

203.Roasted Potatoes

Prep. time: 10 mins Cook Time: 15 mins

Ingredients:
- ½pound potatoes, cut into wedges
- ¼ teaspoon onion powder
- ½ teaspoon garlic powder
- 2 tablespoons avocado oil
- A pinch of salt and black pepper
- ½ cup chicken stock

Directions:
- Set your pressure cooker on sauté mode, add the oil and heat it up.
- Add potatoes, onion powder, garlic powder, salt and pepper, stir and sauté for 8 minutes.
- Add stock, cover and cook on High for 7 minsmore.
- Divide between 2 plates and serve as a side dish.

204.Squash Risotto

Prep. time: 10 mins
Cook Time: 13 mins

Ingredients :
- 1 small yellow onion, chopped
- A drizzle of olive oil
- 1 garlic clove, minced
- ½ red bell pepper, chopped
- 1 cup butternut squash, chopped
- 1 cup Arborio rice
- 1 and ½ cups veggie stock
- 3 tablespoons dry white wine
- 4 ounces mushrooms, chopped
- A pinch of salt and black pepper
- A pinch of oregano, dried

- ¼ teaspoon coriander, ground
- 1 and ½ cups mixed kale and spinach
- 1 tablespoon nutritional yeast

Directions:
- Set your pressure cooker on sauté mode, add the oil and heat it up.
- Add onion, bell pepper, squash and garlic, stir and cook for 5 minutes.
- Add rice, stock, wine, salt, pepper, mushrooms, oregano and coriander, stir, cover and cook on High for 5 minutes.
- Add mixed kale and spinach, parsley and yeast, stir and leave aside for 5 minutes.
- Divide between 2 plates and serve as a side dish.

205.Beans and Chorizo

Prep. time: 10 mins Cook Time: 42 mins

Ingredients:
- ½ tablespoon vegetable oil
- 3 ounces chorizo, chopped
- ½ pound black beans
- ½ yellow onion, chopped
- 3 garlic cloves, minced
- ½ orange
- 1 bay leaf
- 1 quart chicken stock
- A pinch of salt and black pepper
- 1 tablespoon cilantro, chopped

Directions:
- Set your pressure cooker on sauté mode, add the oil and heat it up.
- Add chorizo, stir and cook for 2 minutes.
- Add garlic, onion, beans, orange, bay leaf, salt, pepper and stock, stir, cover and cook on High for 40 minutes.
- Discard bay leaf and orange, add cilantro, stir, divide between plates and serve as a side dish.

206.Spaghetti Squash Delight

Prep. time: 10 mins
Cook Time: 33 mins
Servings: 2

Ingredients :
- 1 cup water
- 1 small spaghetti squash
- ½ cup apple juice
- 1 tablespoon duck fat
- A pinch of salt and black pepper

Directions:

- Put the water in your pressure cooker, add the steamer basket, add the squash inside, cover and cook on High for 30 minutes.
- Cut squash in half, scoop seeds and take out squash spaghetti.
- Clean the pressure cooker, set it on sauté mode, add duck fat and heat it up.
- Add apple juice, salt and pepper, stir and simmer for 3 minutes.
- Divide squash spaghetti between 2 plates, drizzle the sauce all over, toss a bit and serve as a side dish

207.Artichokes Side Dish

Prep. time: 10 mins Cook Time: 20 mins

Ingredients :
- 2 artichokes, trimmed and tops cut off
- 1 cup water
- 1 lemon wedges

Directions:
- Rub artichokes with the lemon wedge.
- Add the water to your pressure cooker, add the steamer basket, place artichokes inside, cover and cook on High for 20 minutes.
- Divide between 2 plates and serve as a side dish.

208.Beets Side Dish

Prep. time: 10 mins
Cook Time: 25 mins

Ingredients :
- 2 beets
- 1 tablespoon balsamic vinegar
- ½ bunch parsley, chopped
- A pinch of salt and black pepper
- 1 small garlic clove, minced
- ½ tablespoon olive oil
- 1 tablespoon capers
- 1 cup water

Directions:
- Put the water in your pressure cooker, add the steamer basket, add beets inside, cover and cook on High for 25 minutes.
- Transfer beets to a cutting board, leave aside to cool down, peel, slice and transfer to a bowl.
- In another bowl, mix parsley with salt, pepper, garlic, oil and capers and whisk really well.
- Divide beets on plates, drizzle vinegar

all over, add parsley dressing and serve
- as a side dish.

209.Marinated Air Fryer Vegetables:

Prep time: 30 mins Cook Time: 15 mins

Ingredients:
For the Marinade:
- 1 tablespoon Olive Oil
- 2 tablespoons Lemon Juice
- 1 teaspoon Italian Seasoning
- 1 teaspoon Garlic Powder
- 1/2 teaspoon Onion Powder
- Salt and Pepper – to taste
For the Veggies:
- 2 Medium Zucchinis
- 1 cup Grape Tomatoes
- 1/2 of a Sweet Onion
- 4 ounces Button Mushrooms
- 1 tablespoon Lemon Juice

Directions:
- Put all of the **Ingredients** together in a bowl and marinade.
- You should make use of only dry ingredients so that it will be easy to whisk together and form
- the marinade. Set aside.
- Chop up the veggies. The time should not be more than 10 minsfor this, depending on how fast you are on the chopping board.
- Put the veggies into the marinade and toss. This will take 15 minutes, but you can allow 30 minsso that the veggies can soak in the flavor really well.
- Put the veggies into the air fryer basket using a slotted spoon.
- Cooking time should be 15 minutes. Midway into the cooking, you can dribble the leftover marinade over the veggies.
- When you do this, shake the veggies very well before placing them back into the air fryer to cook.
- Serve.

210.Air Fryer Chickpeas Recipe:

Prep time: 5 mins Cook Time: 20 mins

Ingredients:
- 1 can of 15.5 ounce Chickpeas, low sodium or no salt
- 1/4 tsp Cayenne Pepper Powder
- 1/4 tsp Cumin Powder
- 1 tsp Salt
- Few Sprays of Cooking Oil or Olive Oil
Directions:
- Take the chickpeas out from the can

and drain with a colander before you wash.
- Keep aside so that the water can be drained from the chickpeas completely.
- Place the chickpeas into the air fryer basket.
- Set the temperature to about 300 degrees F. Also set the cooking time, which should be 20 minutes.
- Fetch a bowl and put in the cumin powder, cayenne pepper, and salt. Toss until they are all combined.
- When 5 minshave elapsed, bring out the basket and spray some oil on the chickpeas. The reason for this is that the chickpeas would have gotten really dry at this point and so the oil spray is necessary.
- Spray a third of the seasoning.
- Use a spoon to stir the seasonings into the chickpeas before placing back into the air fryer basket.
- After every five minutes, bring out the air fryer basket and toss the ingredients.
- Cooking time should be 15 minutes. It may be more depending on the type of chickpeas that you are making use of and the kind of weather prevalent at the moment.
- The chickpeas are done when they become crispy.
- When the chickpeas are cooked, put them into the leftover seasoning. You can taste to know if more salt should be added to make the entire mix tastier.
- Serve.

211.Air Fryer Tacos

Prep time: 5 mins
Cook Time: 20 mins

Ingredients:
- 400 g (1 x 400g/15oz can) Cooked Kidney Beans, drained and rinsed
- 2 Onions, peeled and thinly sliced
- 2 cloves Garlic, peeled and finely chopped
- 300 ml (15 oz) can of Crushed/Chopped Tomatoes
- 1 spoonful of Ground Cumin
- 1/2 spoonful of Sweet or Hot Chili Powder

- 1/2 ActiFry spoonful of Ground Coriander Seeds
- 100 g Crumbled Feta Cheese (optional)
- 1/2 Red Onion, peeled and thinly sliced
- Handful Fresh Coriander/Cilantro, roughly chopped
- 2 Limes, quartered
- 4 Taco Shells or Tortillas
- Salt and Pepper

Directions:

- Put the kidney beans, garlic and onions into the air fryer basket. Also add in the tinned tomatoes with salt and pepper.
- Cooking time should be for 20 minsand the air fryer should be set for 400 degrees F.
- Using the bean mixture, fill in the tortillas. Red onion rings, crumbled feta, and chopped coriander can be added as a garnish.

212. Air Fryer Prepared Tofu

Prep time: 10 mins
Cook Time: 20 mins

Ingredients:

- 15 ounces Extra-firm Tofu
- 2 teaspoons Olive Oil
- 1/4 teaspoon Salt

Directions:

- Begin by preheating the air fryer to 375 degrees F. Set the timer for 20 minutes. Let the air fryer heat up while you carry out some other actions.
- Pull out the air fryer basket and also spread some olive oil on it.
- Take out the tofu from its container and wrap with a paper towel. Squeeze out all of the excess liquids from the tofu and then start cutting.
- Do not forget to be gentle while squeezing the tofu and also make sure to cut into halves.
- 5.Spray some olive oil on the tofu cubes and place them into the air fryer basket.
- Open the air fryer basket and stir every few minsuntil you make sure the tofu has been well cooked. Each cube should brown nicely.
- The tofu can be served with rice. Steamed veggies can also be added to the mix.

213. Prepared Buffalo Cauliflower

Prep time: 5 mins Cooking: 20 mins

Ingredients:

- 1 Large Head of Cauliflower
- 1 cup Unbleached All-purpose Flour
- 1 teaspoon Vegan Chicken Bouillon Granules
- 1/4 teaspoon Cayenne Pepper
- 1/4 teaspoon Chili Powder
- ¼ teaspoon Paprika
- 1/4 teaspoon Dried Chipotle Chili Flakes
- 1 cup Soy Milk
- Canola Oil Spray
- 2 tablespoons Non Dairy Butter
- ½ cup Cayenne Pepper
- 2 cloves Garlic, minced

Directions:

- Start by preheating the air fryer to 390 degrees F. Set the timer for 10 minutes. Pull out the air fryer basket and spray with some olive oil.
- Chop up the cauliflower into bits that can be easily eaten. Wash and drain.
- Fetch a bowl and put in the bouillon granules, flour, chili powder, cayenne,
- paprika, and chipotle flakes and mix thoroughly. Put some milk into the mix and whisk.
- Put the cauliflower into the batter and mix. Then turn the cauliflower into the air fryer basket. Cooking time is 10 minutes. Do not forget to turn the cauliflower every few minsto make sure it cooks properly.
- While the cauliflower is cooking, grab a small pan and put in the butter, hot sauce and garlic. Let it boil for a few minsover low heat. Once the mixture is boiled, you can reduce the heat and just let it simmer.
- Bring out the cauliflower from the air fryer and put it into a large bowl. Pour the sauce in the pan into the bowl containing the cauliflower. Turn the mixture around for a few minsthen serve.

214. Air Fryer Brussel Sprouts:

Prep Time: 10 mins Cook Time: 10 mins

Ingredients:

- 1 pound Brussels Sprouts
- 2 teaspoons Olive Oil
- 1/4 teaspoon Salt
- 1/4 teaspoon Garlic Powder

Directions:

- Clean the Brussel sprouts by washing under running water and picking out the dead leaves. When done, put it into a small bowl.
- Into the bowl, put in salt, olive oil and garlic powder. Make sure it mixes very well. You can decide to put the sprouts into the efrigerator and allow them to marinate.
- The air fryer should be set to 370 degrees F. Place the Brussels sprouts into the air fryer basket and allow it to cook. Remove the air fryer basket and shake every 6 minutes.
- The sprouts are done when they get tender and turn a shade of brown. Do not overcook.
- At the end of the cooking time, remove from the air fryer and serve.

215. Crispy Crab Rangoon

Prep Time: 15 mins Cook Time: 15 mins
Total Time: 30 mins

Ingredients

- 4 or 6 oz cream cheese, softened If you prefer creamy crab rangoon use 6 oz
- 4 or 6 oz lump crab meat If you prefer your crab rangoon to have more cream cheese and less crab, use 4 oz. Seafood lovers may want to go for 6 oz
- 2 green onions, chopped
- 21 wonton wrappers
- 2 garlic cloves, minced
- 1 Tsp. Worcestershire sauce
- Salt and pepper to taste
- Cooking oil I use olive oil.

Instructions

- You can soften your cream cheese by heating it in the microwave for 20 seconds.
- Combine the cream cheese, green onions, crab meat, Worcestershire sauce, salt, pepper, and garlic in a small bowl. Stir to mix well.
- Layout the wonton wrappers on a working surface. I used a large, bamboo cutting board. Moisten each of the wrappers with water. I use a cooking brush, and brush it along all of the edges.
- Load about a Tsp. and a half of filling onto each wrapper. Be careful not to overfill.

- Fold each wrapper diagonally across to form a triangle. From there bring up the two opposite corners toward each other. Don't close the wrapper yet. Bring up the other two opposite sides, pushing out any air. Squeeze each of the edges together. Be sure to check out the recipe video above for illustration.
- Spritz the air fryer basket with cooking oil.
- Load the crab rangoon into the air fryer basket. Do not stack or overfill. Cook in batches if needed.
- Spritz with oil.
- Place the Air Fryer at 370 degrees. Cook for 10 min..
- Open and flip the crab rangoon. Cook for an additional 2-5 mins until they have reached your desired level of golden brown and crisp.
- Remove the crab rangoon from the air fryer and serve with your desired dipping sauce.

216. 3 Ingredient Fried Catfish

Prep Time5 mins Cook Time: 20 mins Total Time: 25 mins

Ingredients
- 4 catfish fillets
- 1/4 cup Louisiana Fish Fry Coating
- 1 tbsp olive oil
- 1 tbsp chopped parsley optional

Instructions
- Pat the catfish dry.
- Sprinkle the fish fry onto both sides of each fillet. Ensure the entire filet is coated with seasoning.
- Spritz olive oil on the top of each filet.
- Place the filet in the Air Fryer basket. Do not stack the fish and do not overcrowd the basket. Cook in batches if needed. Close and cook for 10 mins at 400 degrees.
- Open the air fryer and flip the fish. Cook for an additional 10 min..
- Open and flip the fish.
- Cook for an additional 2-3 mins or until desired crispness.
- Top with optional parsley.

217. Air Fryer Bang Bang Fried Shrimp

Prep Time: 10 mins Cook Time: 20 mins Total Time: 30 mins

Ingredients
- 1 pound raw shrimp peeled and deveined

- 1 egg white 3 tbsp
- 1/2 cup all-purpose flour
- 3/4 cup panko bread crumbs
- 1 tsp paprika
- Mccormick's grill mates montreal chicken seasoning to taste
- Salt and pepper to taste
- Cooking oil

Bang Bang Sauce
- 1/3 cup plain, non-fat Greek yogurt
- 2 tbsp Sriracha
- 1/4 cup sweet chili sauce

Instructions
- Preheat Air Fryer to 400 degrees.
- Season the shrimp with the seasonings.
- Place the flour, egg whites, and panko bread crumbs in three separate bowls.
- Create a cooking station. Dip the shrimp in the flour, then the egg whites, and the panko bread crumbs last.
- When dipping the shrimp in the egg whites, you do not need to submerge the shrimp. Do a light dab so that most of the flour stays on the shrimp. You want the egg white to adhere to the panko crumbs.
- Spray the shrimp with cooking oil.
- Add the shrimp to the Air Fryer basket. Cook for 4 min.. Open the basket and flip the shrimp to the other side. Cook for an additional 4 mins or until crisp.

Bang Bang Sauce
- Combine all of the ingredients in a small bowl. Mix thoroughly to combine.

218. Parmesan Truffle Oil Fries

Prep Time10 mins Cook Time40 mins Total Time50 mins

Ingredients
- 3 large russet potatoes peeled and cut lengthwise
- 2 tbsp white truffle oil
- 2 tbsp parmesan shredded
- 1 tsp paprika
- salt and pepper to taste
- 1 tbsp parsley chopped

Instructions
- Place the sliced potatoes in a large bowl with cold water.
- Allow the potatoes to soak in the water for at least 30 minutes, preferably an hour.

- Spread the fries onto a flat surface and dry them completely with paper towels. Coat them with 1 tbsp of the white truffle oil and seasonings.
- Add half of the fries to the Air Fryer basket. Adjust the temperature to 380 degrees and cook for 15-20 min.. Set a timer for 10 mins and stop and shake the basket at the 10-minute mark (once).
- Use your judgment. If the fries need to be crisper, allow them to cook for additional time. If the fries look crisp before 15 min., remove them. I cooked both of my batches for almost 20 minutes.
- When the first half finishes, cook the remaining half.
- Add the remaining truffle oil and parmesan to the fries immediately upon removing them from the Air Fryer.
- Top with shredded parsley. Serve!

219. Low-Fat Mozzarella Cheese Sticks

Prep Time: 10 mins
Cook Time: 16 mins
Total Time: 26 mins

Ingredients
- 10 pieces mozzarella string cheese
- 1 cup Italian breadcrumbs
- 1 egg
- 1/2 cup flour
- 1 cup marinara sauce
- Salt and pepper to taste

Instructions
- Season the breadcrumbs with salt and pepper.
- Create a workstation by adding the flour, bread crumbs, and eggs to separate bowls.
- Dip each string of cheese in flour, then egg, and last the breadcrumbs.
- Freeze the sticks for one hour so that they harden. This will help the cheese maintain the stick shape while frying.
- Season your Air Fryer basket before each use so that items do not stick. I like to glaze the basket with coconut oil using a cooking brush.
- Turn the Air Fryer on 400 degrees. Add the sticks to the fryer.
- Cook for 8 min.. Remove the basket. Flip each stick. You can use tongs, but be careful not to manipulate the shape. I used my hands to flip them. They

weren't too hot. Cook for an additional 8 minutes.

- Allow the sticks to cool for 5 mins before removing them from the pan. Some of the sticks may leak cheese on the outside. Allow the sticks to cool, and then use your hands to correct the shape.

220. Air Fryer Carrots (Three Ways)

Prep Time: 5 mins Cook Time: 20 mins Total Time: 25 mins

Ingredients
- 4 cups sliced carrots (1/4-inch thick), washed and patted dry
- 2 Tbsps extra virgin olive oil

Savory Version
- 1/2 Tsp. garlic powder
- 1/2 Tsp. dried basil
- 1/2 Tsp. dried oregano
- 1/2 Tsp. dried parsley
- 1/2 Tsp. kosher salt
- 1/4 Tsp. ground black pepper

Sweet Version
- 1 Tbsp coconut sugar
- 1/2 Tbsp maple syrup
- 1/4 Tsp. kosher salt
- 1/8 Tsp. crushed red pepper flakes

Spicy Version
- 1 Tsp. ground cumin
- 1 Tsp. smoked paprika
- 1/2 Tsp. kosher salt
- 1/8 Tsp. cayenne pepper
- 1/8 Tsp. ground black pepper

Instructions
- Add the sliced carrots to a large bowl and evenly coat with oil. Add your choice of seasonings and toss to coat.
- Place carrots in the air fryer basket and air fry on 400F for 18-20 min., or until fork-tender. Shake or stir the carrots after about 10 minutes. Serve immediately.

221. Butternut Squash

Prep Time: 10 mins Cook Time: 20 mins Total Time: 30 mins

Ingredients
- 4 cups chopped butternut squash, 1-inch cubes (see cutting tips above)
- 2 Tbsps extra virgin olive oil
- 1 Tbsp maple syrup
- 1 Tsp. dried oregano
- 1/2 Tsp. garlic powder
- 1/2 Tsp. smoked paprika

- 1/2 Tsp. kosher salt
- 1/4 Tsp. ground chipotle chili pepper

Instructions
- In a large bowl, add the squash cubes along with the other ingredients. Toss until the cubes are well coated.
- Arrange the cubes in a single layer in the air fryer basket and air fry on 400F for 15-20 min., or until the squash is fork-tender and a little crispy on the outside. Shake or stir the cubes at the mid-way point.
- Carefully remove from the air fryer and serve immediately.

222. Air Fryer Mushrooms

Prep Time: 5 mins Cook Time: 15 mins

Ingredients
- 7 oz 200 grams chestnut mushrooms
- 2 tsp vegetable oil
- 2 tsp low sodium soy sauce or tamari sauce
- 1 sprig rosemary
- ½ tsp salt and pepper

Instructions
- Cut the mushrooms into thick slices, I usually cut each into 2 halves but if it's too big then I cut into smaller pieces. Try to make the size of the slices even so everything cooks evenly.
- In a white bowl, toss the mushrooms with the rest of the ingredients so everything is well coated in soy, oil, and seasonings.
- No need to preheat the Air Fryer. Place the mushrooms directly into the Air Fryer basket, and cook at 356f (180) for about 15 mins flipping halfway through.
- Open the Air Fryer basket and check every 5 minutes, shake the basket and decide how much longer you would like to cook the mushrooms for.
- The mushrooms should be cooked well, but not dried out or burnt. So make sure not to overcook them.
- Serve with some extra sea salt flakes, and red chili flakes if desired.

223. Baked Potatoes

Prep Time: 5 mins Cook Time: 35 mins Total Time: 40 mins

Ingredients
- 4 medium russet potatoes scrubbed and dried
- 4 teaspoons olive oil

- 1 Tsp. kosher sea salt plus more for serving if desired

Instructions
- Preheat the air fryer to 375°F for about 10 minutes.
- Wash, dry, and prick each potato
- Drizzle each potato with oil and sprinkle with salt.
- Place 2 to 4 potatoes in your air fryer, depending on size.
- Set air fryer to cook at 375° for 35 min., or until potatoes are fork-tender.
- Use tongs to remove potatoes from the air fryer basket then carefully cut a slit in the top of each one.
- Add desired toppings & enjoy!

224. Crispy Spicy Air Fryer Okra

Prep Time: 10 Mins Cook Time: 10 Mins Total Time: 20 Mins

Ingredients
- 1 1/4 lb fresh okra
- For the egg wash:
- 1 egg
- 1/2 tsp coriander
- 1/2 tsp smoked paprika
- 1/2 tsp chili powder (optional)
- Pinch of salt
- For the panko breading:
- 1 cup gluten-free flaked panko breading
- 1 tsp coriander
- 1 tsp smoked paprika
- 1/2 tsp chili powder (optional)
- 1/2 tsp garlic powder
- 2 tbsp parsley
- 1/4 tsp each salt and pepper

Instructions
- Rinse okra and dry thoroughly - I used paper towels to do so.
- Prepare egg wash by mixing the egg with coriander, smoked paprika, chili powder (if using), and salt in a bowl.
- Prepare to bread by mixing panko bread flakes with coriander, smoked paprika, chili powder (if using), garlic powder, parsley, salt, and pepper.
- Then, using one hand, dip the dried okra in the spiced egg wash and drop it onto the plate with the breading.
- Then, using the other hand, coat the okra well with the spiced panko breading. Repeat this with all the okra.
- When the okra is all breaded, place

them in a single layer at the bottom of your air fryer basket and spray them with your favorite cooking spray.

- For best results, preheat the air fryer to 400 degrees for 2-3 min..
- Set the air fryer to air fry the okra at 400 degrees for 4-5 min.. Then open the air fryer, and using tongs, flip the okra over and air fry for 4-5 mins at 400 degrees. Repeat if you have any more breaded okra (depending on the size of your air fryer, this might take 2- 3 batches to cook - but the result works it.
- Enjoy with your favorite sauces!

225. Air Fryer Radishes (Healthy Side Dish)

Prep Time: 10 mins Cook Time: 15 mins Total Time: 25 mins

Ingredients

- 1 pound (or 454 gram packages) fresh radishes or about 3 cups halved
- 1 Tbsp extra virgin olive oil
- 1/2 Tsp. dried oregano
- 1/2 Tsp. kosher salt
- 1/4 Tsp. garlic powder
- 1/4 Tsp. onion powder
- Dash of ground black pepper

Instructions

- Wash and trim the radishes, scrubbing off any dirt and cutting off any dark spots. Pat dry with a paper towel.
- Slice the radishes in half so they are roughly 1-inch pieces (it doesn't need to be exact), or quarter them if they are larger.
- Place the radishes in a large bowl and evenly coat with oil. Add the seasonings and toss to combine.
- Place radishes in the air fryer basket and air fry on 400F for 15-17 min., or until fork-tender. Shake or stir the radishes after about 10 min.. Serve immediately.

226. Air Fryer Zucchini And Onions

Total Time: 30 mins

Ingredients

- 2-3 zucchini small-medium sized
- 1 red onion
- 2 tbsp olive oil or avocado oil
- 1/2 tsp dried basil
- 1/2 tsp salt
- 1/2 tsp dried oregano
- 1/2 tsp garlic powder
- 1/4 tsp black pepper

Instructions

- Do the Prep Work
- Preheat your Air Fryer to 400F.
- Meanwhile, wash and dice the zucchini and onions, at least twice the size of the holes in your air fryer basket.
- In a bowl, toss the vegetables, oil, and all the Italian seasonings together.
- Cook the Dish
- Pour the vegetable mixture into the heated air fryer, then shake or spread the vegetables so they're evenly spaced out in the basket. Close and set the timer for 20 min..
- Halfway through cook time, open the air fryer and shake the basket or turn the vegetables with a spoon or spatula. Close and allow to finish cooking, then season to taste if needed and serve. Note: Sometime in the final two to three minutes, open the air fryer to make sure the vegetables aren't beginning to burn.

227. Baby Potatoes

Prep Time: 5 mins Cook Time: 18 mins Total Time: 23 mins

Ingredients

- 4 cups baby potatoes, skin on, pre-washed, and halved
- 1 lime, juiced
- 1 Tbsp extra virgin olive oil
- 1 Tbsp chili powder
- 1/2 Tsp. sea salt

Instructions

- Place potatoes in a large bowl and coat them with lime juice. Drain any excess juice.
- Add the oil, chili powder, and sea salt and stir until potatoes are well coated.
- Arrange the potatoes in a single layer in the air fryer basket. Roast on 400F for 15-18 min., or until the potatoes are tender with crispy edges. You can check on them after 7-8 mins and give them a shake or stir.
- Serve immediately (while hot and crispy).

228. Air Fryer Broccoli Cheese Bites

Prep Time: 50 mins Active Time: 20 mins Total Time: 1 hr 10 mins

Ingredients

- 10 oz. fresh broccoli florets
- 1/4 cup water
- 1 large egg
- 1 1/2 cups shredded cheddar cheese
- 3/4 cup bread crumbs (panko or traditional)
- 1/2 tsp. kosher salt
- 1/2 tsp. black pepper

Instructions

- Place broccoli and water in a microwave-safe container with a microwave-safe lid (if you don't have a lid you can use plastic wrap). Place lid lightly on top or cover tightly with plastic wrap. Microwave for 4 minutes.
- Remove from microwave and allow to cool enough to handle. Chop very finely then place in a bowl. Add egg, cheese, bread crumbs, salt, and pepper to the broccoli and mix well. Grab a rimmed baking sheet.
- Scoop out 1 1/2 Tbsps of the broccoli mixture and squeeze and form into a ball. Set on a baking sheet. Continue until you've used all the mixture. Place in the freezer for 30 min..
- Place broccoli bites in an air fryer in a single layer and cook at 350 degrees F for 5-10 mins depending on your air fryer. You may need to do this in batches (I did). Cover lightly with foil to keep warm while others are baking.

229. Healthy Air Fryer Eggplant

Prep Time: 35 mins Cook Time: 15 mins Total Time: 50 mins

Ingredients

- 1.5 lb eggplant cut into half-inch pieces (approx 1 medium-sized)
- 2 tbsp low sodium vegetable broth
- 1 tsp garlic powder
- 1 tsp paprika
- 1/2 tsp dried oregano
- 1/4 tsp dried thyme
- 1/4 tsp black pepper optional

Instructions

- Wash and dice your eggplant into half-inch pieces. (See step by step photos above if needed.)
- Now place your cut up eggplant in a large colander and place the colander inside a bowl. Generously sprinkle with salt and let it sit for 30 minutes. Then transfer to a clean, dry dishtowel, and using another dish towel, or paper towels, press and pat them dry.

- Now, wipe out the bowl that was sitting under your colander and place the dry eggplant inside. Add the broth and all the seasoning to the bowl and mix well to evenly coat the pieces.
- Place in your air fryer basket, set to 380 degrees, and cook for 15-20 min., tossing once at the halfway point. Cook until nicely golden, and fork-tender, then serve warm with a sprinkle of fresh parsley or chives and sriracha mayo for dipping.

230. Air Fryer Tortilla Chips

Prep Time: 10 mins Cook Time: 9 mins
Total Time: 19 mins
Ingredients
Salt And Vinegar
- 6 corn tortillas
- 1 Tbsp extra virgin olive oil
- 1/2 Tbsp white vinegar
- 1 Tsp. kosher salt

Zesty Cheese
- 6 corn tortillas
- 2 Tbsps extra virgin olive oil
- 2 teaspoons **Nutrition Facts**al yeast
- 1/2 Tsp. smoked paprika
- 1/4 Tsp. kosher salt

Spicy Chipotle
- 6 corn tortillas
- 1 Tbsp extra virgin olive oil
- 1/2 Tsp. ground chipotle chili pepper
- 1/4 Tsp. kosher salt

Chili Lime
- 6 corn tortillas
- 1 Tbsp extra virgin olive oil
- 1/2 Tbsp lime juice
- 1 Tsp. chili powder
- 1/4 Tsp. kosher salt

Maple Cinnamon
- 6 corn tortillas
- 1 Tbsp extra virgin olive oil
- 1/2 Tbsp maple syrup
- 1/2 Tsp. ground cinnamon
- 1/2 Tsp. coconut sugar

Instructions
- In a small bowl, whisk together the oil with the ingredients for your flavor choice. Brush a light coating of the mixture on both sides of the tortillas.
- Cut each tortilla into quarters to form triangles.
- Arrange the tortilla triangles in a single layer in your air fryer basket. (You will need to do this in batches).
- Air fry on 350F for about 7-9 min., or until they start to brown around the edges. (Note: the maple cinnamon chips will take 5-7 min.).
- Let the chips cool enough to handle and then transfer them to a wire rack to cool completely. They will get crunchier as they cool.
- Store in an airtight container at room temperature and enjoy within 5 days.

231. Air Fryer Asparagus

Prep Time: 5 mins Cook Time: 6 mins
Total Time: 11 mins
Ingredients
- 1 lb fresh asparagus (16 oz.)
- 2 tsp extra virgin olive oil
- Sea salt to taste

Instructions
- Wash the asparagus spears and pat them dry. Trim the ends enough so that they fit in the air fryer basket (about 1 to 1 ½ inches up from the bottom).
- Add the asparagus to a rectangular container with a tight-fitting lid or a zip-top bag along with the olive oil and salt. Shake until asparagus is well-coated.
- If your air fryer has a separate elevated crisping tray or plate, be sure to insert it. Add the asparagus to the air fryer basket and air fry at 400° F for 6-9 minutes, shaking the basket every few min.. Thinner spears will take less time to cook while thicker spears will take longer. Asparagus should be tender with a slight crisp. Add more sea salt to taste before serving, if desired.

232. Pumpkin Fries

Prep Time: 15 mins Cook Time: 15 mins
Total Time: 30 mins
Ingredients
- 2 mini pumpkins, peeled, seeded, and cut into 1/2-inch slices (see cutting tips above)
- 2 teaspoons extra virgin olive oil
- 1/2 Tsp. garlic powder
- 1/2 Tsp. smoked paprika
- 1/2 Tsp. kosher salt

Instructions
- Quicker version – air fry in one large batch:
- Add the pumpkin slices to a large bowl and toss with oil and seasonings.
- Place all the pumpkin in the air fryer basket and air fry on 400F for about 15 min., or until fork-tender. Shake or stir them at the mid-way point.

233. Lemon Garlic Air Fryer Roasted Potatoes

Prep Time: 10 Mins Cook Time: 30 Mins
Air Fryer Preheating Time: 5 Mins
Total Time: 45 Mins
Ingredients
- 900 g / 2 lb potatoes
- 2 Tbsp oil of choice, avocado, olive, vegetable, sunflower are all fine
- 1 Tsp. salt
- 1 Tsp. freshly ground black pepper
- 2 lemons
- 1 entire head of garlic
- 4 big fresh rosemary stems

Instructions
- Peel the potatoes and cut them into large pieces. With a large potato, I generally get 5 pieces.
- Put the cut potatoes in a bowl and cover with cold water. Leave to soak for 15 min., then drain and pour the potatoes onto a clean dish towel. Bundle it up around them and rub them dry.
- Dry the bowl you had them in and return them, then pour in the oil and sprinkle in the salt and pepper. Stir to coat them all evenly.
- Preheat your Air Fryer if it has a preheat function, then add the potatoes carefully to the hot basket and cook on 350°F (175 °C) for 15 min..
- While they are cooking, break up the head of garlic into individual cloves and remove any skin that is loose and papery. Leave the rest of the skin intact.
- Cut the 2 lemons in half lengthways. Save one half for juicing, then cut the other halves into 3 wedges each.
- Once the 15 mins is up, open the Air Fryer and squeeze the juice from the half of lemon over the potatoes. Throw in the garlic cloves and the lemon wedges and give it all a really good toss together. Tuck in the rosemary stalks amongst the potatoes.
- Return the basket to the Air Fryer and cook for a further 15 min.. Check. They should be done, but if you prefer them a little more golden, put them back on for 5 min..

- Pick out the woody rosemary sticks and serve the potatoes with the garlic cloves and the lemon wedges. Guests can squeeze the soft, sweet cloves of garlic out of their skins and eat it with the potatoes and the caramelized lemon.

234. Air Fryer Broccoli

Prep Time: 5 mins Cook Time: 15 mins
Total Time: 20 mins

Ingredients

- 1 pound (450 grams) broccoli cut into florets
- 1 Tbsp olive oil
- ½ Tsp. salt
- ¼ Tsp. ground black pepper
- ¼ Tsp. chili flakes optional

Instructions

- Wash the broccoli head, and cut it into florets.
- In a mixing bowl, toss the broccoli florets with olive oil, salt, pepper, and chili flakes.
- Add to the Air Fryer basket, and cook at 390°F (200°C) for 15 mins flipping at least twice while cooking.
- Serve with lemon wedges.

235. Air Fryer Green Beans

Prep Time: 5 mins Cook Time: 10 mins
Total Time: 15 mins

Ingredients

- 12 ounces (or 340 grams) fresh green beans, washed, trimmed, and dried
- 1 Tbsp extra virgin olive oil
- 1/2 Tsp. dried basil
- 1/2 Tsp. dried oregano
- 1/4 Tsp. garlic powder
- 1/4 Tsp. kosher salt
- Fresh lemon wedges (optional)

Instructions

- Place the green beans in a large bowl and add the oil and seasoning. Toss until well coated.
- Arrange the beans in the air fryer basket and air fry on 400F for 7-10 mins (see note).
- Squeeze some fresh lemon juice over top (optional) and serve immediately.

236. Air Fryer Cauliflower

Prep Time: 8 mins Cook Time: 12 mins
Total Time: 20 mins

Ingredients

- 1 head cauliflower

- 2 tbsp olive oil
- 1 tsp salt
- 2 tsp onion powder
- **To Top:** lime wedge and parmesan

Instructions

- Cut your cauliflower into florets.
- Toss the cauliflower in olive oil, salt, and onion salt.
- Add the cauliflower into the air fryer basket (try to have it in a single layer if possible, cook in two batches if too many overlap).
- Cook for 12-15 mins on 375F.
- When done, serve with parmesan shaved on top and some lime squeezed on top.

237. Air Fryer Tater Tots

Prep Time: 15 mins Cook Time: 20 mins
Total Time: 35 mins

Ingredients

- 6 large potatoes or 8 medium, peeled
- 2 tbsp corn starch (cornflour)
- 1 1/2 tsp dried oregano
- 1 tsp garlic powder
- Salt

Instructions

- Preheat the air fryer to 350 F / 180C.
- Boil the potatoes till they are about half cooked and then plunge them into a cold water bath to stop the cooking process and cool them down.
- Using a box shredder, shred the cooled potatoes into a large bowl, then squeeze out any excess water.
- Add in the rest of the ingredients and combine. Then form the mixture into individual tater tots (I was able to make about 20).
- Place half of the homemade tater tots into the air fryer basket (making sure they don't touch) and cook for 18-20 mins till golden brown. Turn the tots twice during cooking so that they brown evenly.
- Remove the tater tots and keep warm, then repeat steps to make the remaining air fryer tater tots.
- Serve your air fryer tater tots with a side of vegan ranch dressing or tomato sauce for dipping.

238. Air Fryer Beets (Easy Roasted Beets)

Prep Time: 10 mins Cook Time: 20 mins

Total Time: 30 mins

Ingredients

- 3 cups fresh beets, peeled and cut into 1-inch pieces (see note)
- 1 Tbsp extra virgin olive oil
- 1/2 Tsp. kosher salt
- Pinch of ground black pepper

Instructions

- Add the beets, oil, salt, and pepper to a large bowl and toss to combine.
- Place the beets in the air fryer basket and air fry on 400F for 18-20 minutes, or until fork-tender. Stir or shake them a few times while air frying.

239. Crispy Air Fryer Brussels Sprouts

Prep Time: 5 mins Cook Time: 10 mins
Total Time: 15 mins

Ingredients

- 340 grams Brussels sprouts
- 1-2 tbsp olive oil
- Salt, to taste
- Pepper, to taste
- Garlic powder, to taste

Instructions

- Trim and half your Brussels sprouts and lightly coat them with olive oil.
- Coat with a mixture of salt, pepper, and garlic powder.
- Place the Brussels sprouts in the air fryer at 350F for 10 min.. Shaking the basket once or twice during the cooking time.
- Serve immediately or warm.

240. Air-Fried Cauliflower With Almonds And Parmesan

Prep: 10 mins Cook: 15 mins
Total: 25 mins Servings: 4

Ingredient

- 3 cups cauliflower florets
- 3 teaspoons vegetable oil, divided
- 1 clove garlic, minced
- ⅓ cup finely shredded Parmesan cheese
- ¼ cup chopped almonds
- ¼ cup panko bread crumbs
- ½ Tsp. dried thyme, crushed

Instructions

- Place cauliflower florets, 2 teaspoons oil, and garlic in a medium bowl; toss to coat. Place in a single layer in an air fryer basket.
- Cook in the air fryer at 360 degrees F (180 degrees C), for 10 min., shaking the

basket halfway through.

- Return cauliflower to the bowl and toss with the remaining 1 Tsp. oil. Add Parmesan cheese, almonds, bread crumbs, and thyme; toss to coat. Return cauliflower mixture to the air fryer basket and cook until mixture is crisp and browned about 5 min..

241.Air Fryer Falafel

Prep Time: 20 mins Cook: 20 mins
Additional: 1 day Total: 1 day

Ingredient

- 1 cup dry garbanzo beans
- 1 ½ cups fresh cilantro, stems removed
- ¾ cup fresh flat-leafed parsley stems removed
- 1 small red onion, quartered
- 1 clove garlic
- 2 Tbsps chickpea flour
- 1 Tbsp ground coriander
- 1 Tbsp ground cumin
- 1 Tbsp sriracha sauce
- salt and ground black pepper to taste
- ½ Tsp. baking powder
- ¼ Tsp. baking soda
- cooking spray

Instructions

- Soak chickpeas in a large amount of cool water for 24 hours. Rub the soaked chickpeas with your fingers to help loosen and remove skins. Rinse and drain well. Spread chickpeas on a large clean dish towel to dry.
- Blend chickpeas, cilantro, parsley, onion, and garlic in a food processor until rough paste forms. Transfer mixture to a large bowl. Add chickpea flour, coriander, cumin, sriracha, salt, and pepper and mix well. Cover bowl and let the mixture rest for 1 hour.
- Preheat an air fryer to 375 degrees F (190 degrees C).
- Add baking powder and baking soda to the chickpea mixture. Mix using your hands until just combined. Form 15 equal-sized balls and press slightly to form patties. Spray falafel patties with cooking spray.
- Place 7 falafel patties in the preheated air fryer and cook for 10 min.. Transfer cooked falafel to a plate and repeat with the remaining 8 falafel, cooking for 10 to 12 min..

242.Carrots With Balsamic Glaze

Prep Time: 10 mins Cook Time: 10 mins
Total Time: 20 mins

Ingredient

- Olive oil for brushing
- 1 Tbsp olive oil
- 1 Tsp. honey
- ¼ Tsp. kosher salt
- ¼ Tsp. ground black pepper
- 1 pound tri-colored baby carrots
- 1 Tbsp balsamic glaze
- 1 Tbsp butter
- 2 teaspoons chopped fresh chives

Instructions

- Brush an air fryer basket with olive oil.
- Whisk together 1 Tbsp olive oil, honey, salt, and pepper in a large bowl. Add carrots and toss to coat. Place carrots in the air fryer basket in a single layer, in batches, if needed.
- Cook in the air fryer at 390 degrees F (200 degrees C), stirring once, until tender, about 10 min.. Transfer warm cooked carrots to a large bowl, add balsamic glaze and butter and toss to coat. Sprinkle with chives and serve.

243.Simple Air Fryer Brussels Sprouts

Prep Time: 5 mins Cook Time: 30 mins
Total Time: 35 mins

Ingredient

- 1 ½ pound Brussels sprouts
- 2 Tbsp olive oil
- 1 Tsp. garlic powder
- 1 Tsp. salt
- ½ Tsp. ground black pepper

Instructions

- Preheat the air fryer to 390 degrees F (200 degrees C) for 15 min..
- Place Brussels sprouts, olive oil, garlic powder, salt, and pepper in a bowl and mix well. Spread evenly in the air fryer basket. Cook for 15 min., shaking the basket halfway through the cycle.

244.Air Fryer Potato Wedges

Prep Time: 5 mins Cook Time: 30 mins
Total Time: 35 mins

Ingredient

- 2 medium Russet potatoes, cut into wedges
- 1 ½ Tbsp olive oil
- ½ Tsp. paprika
- ½ Tsp. parsley flakes
- ½ Tsp. chili powder

- ½ Tsp. sea salt
- ⅛ Tsp. ground black pepper

Instructions

- Preheat air fryer to 400 degrees F (200 degrees C).
- Place potato wedges in a large bowl. Add olive oil, paprika, parsley, chili, salt, and pepper, and mix well to combine.
- Place 8 wedges in the basket of the air fryer and cook for 10 min..
- Flip wedges with tongs and cook for an additional 5 minutes. Repeat with the remaining 8 wedges.

245.Air-Fryer Roasted Veggies

Prep Time: 20 mins Cook Time: 10 mins
Total Time: 30 mins

Ingredient

- ½ cup diced zucchini
- ½ cup diced summer squash
- ½ cup diced mushrooms
- ½ cup diced cauliflower
- ½ cup diced asparagus
- ½ cup diced sweet red pepper
- 2 teaspoons vegetable oil
- ¼ Tsp. salt
- ¼ Tsp. ground black pepper
- 1/4 Tsp. seasoning, or more to taste

Instructions

- Preheat the air fryer to 360 degrees F (180 degrees C).
- Add vegetables, oil, salt, pepper, and desired seasoning to a bowl. Toss to coat; arrange in the fryer basket.
- Cook vegetables for 10 min., stirring after 5 min..

246.Air Fryer Roasted Asparagus

Prep Time: 10 mins Cook Time: 10 mins
Total Time: 20 mins

Ingredient

- 1 bunch fresh asparagus, trimmed
- Avocado oil cooking spray
- ½ Tsp. garlic powder
- ½ Tsp. himalayan pink salt
- ¼ Tsp. ground multi-colored peppercorns
- ¼ Tsp. red pepper flakes
- ¼ cup freshly grated parmesan cheese

Instructions

- Preheat the air fryer to 375 degrees F (190 degrees C). Line the basket with parchment paper.
- Place asparagus spears in the air fryer basket and mist with avocado oil.

Sprinkle with garlic powder, pink Himalayan salt, pepper, and red pepper flakes. Top with Parmesan cheese.

• Air fry until asparagus spears start to char, 7 to 9 min..

247.Sweet And Spicy Roasted Carrots

Prep Time: 5 mins Cook Time: 20 mins Total: 25 mins

Ingredient

• 1 serving cooking spray
• 1 Tbsp butter, melted
• 1 Tbsp hot honey (such as Mike's Hot Honey®)
• 1 Tsp. grated orange zest
• ½ Tsp. ground cardamom
• ½ pound baby carrots
• 1 Tbsp freshly squeezed orange juice
• 1 pinch salt and ground black pepper to taste

Instructions

• Preheat an air fryer to 400 degrees F (200 degrees C). Spray the basket with nonstick cooking spray.

• Combine butter, honey, orange zest, and cardamom in a bowl. Remove 1 Tbsp of the sauce to a separate bowl and set aside. Add carrots to the remaining sauce and toss until all are well coated. Transfer carrots to the air fryer basket.

• Air fry until carrots are roasted and fork-tender, tossing every 7 min., for 15 to 22 min.. Mix orange juice with reserved honey-butter sauce. Toss with carrots until well combined. Season with salt and pepper.

248.Air Fryer One-Bite Roasted Potatoes

Prep Time: 5 mins Cook Time: 10 mins Total Time: 15 mins

Ingredient

• ½ Pound mini potatoes
• 2 teaspoons extra-virgin olive oil
• 2 teaspoons dry italian-style salad dressing mix
• Salt and ground black pepper to taste

Instructions

• Preheat the air fryer to 400 degrees F (200 degrees C).

• Wash and dry potatoes. Trim edges to make a flat surface on both ends.

• Combine extra-virgin olive oil and salad dressing mix in a large bowl. Add potatoes and toss until potatoes are well coated. Place in a single layer into the air fryer basket. Cook in batches if necessary.

• Air fry until potatoes are golden brown, 5 to 7 minutes. Flip potatoes and air fry for an additional 2 to 3 min.. Season with salt and pepper.

249.Air Fryer Cauliflower Tots

Prep Time: 5 mins Cook Time: 10 mins Total Time: 15 mins

Ingredient

• 1 serving nonstick cooking spray
• 1 (16 ounces) package frozen cauliflower tots (such as Green Giant® Cauliflower Veggie Tots)

Instructions

• Preheat air fryer to 400 degrees F (200 degrees C). Spray the air fryer basket with nonstick cooking spray.

• Place as many cauliflower tots in the basket as you can, making sure they do not touch, cooking in batches if necessary.

• Cook in the preheated air fryer for 6 min.. Pull the basket out, turn tots over, and cook until browned and cooked through, about 3 mins more.

250.Air Fryer Sweet Potato Tots

Prep Time: 15 mins Cook Time: 35 mins Additional Time: 10 mins Total Time: 1 hr

Ingredient

• 2 sweet potatoes, peeled
• ½ Tsp. cajun seasoning
• Olive oil cooking spray
• Sea salt to taste

Instructions

• Bring a pot of water to a boil and add sweet potatoes. Boil until potatoes can be pierced with a fork but are still firm for about 15 minutes. Do not over-boil, or they will be messy to grate. Drain and let cool.

• Grate sweet potatoes into a bowl using a box grater. Carefully mix in Cajun seasoning. Form mixture into tot-shaped cylinders.

• Spray the air fryer basket with olive oil spray. Place tots in the basket in a single row without touching each other or the sides of the basket. Spray tots with olive oil spray and sprinkle with sea salt.

• Heat air fryer to 400 degrees F (200 degrees C) and cook tots for 8 minutes.

Turn, spray with more olive oil spray, and sprinkle with more sea salt. Cook for 8 mins more.

251.Air Fryer Fried Green Tomatoes

Prep Time: 15 mins Cook Time: 20 mins Total Time: 35 mins

Ingredient

• 2 green tomatoes, cut into 1/4-inch slices
• Salt and freshly ground black pepper to taste
• ⅓ cup all-purpose flour
• ½ cup buttermilk
• 2 eggs, lightly beaten
• 1 cup plain panko bread crumbs
• 1 cup yellow cornmeal
• 1 Tsp. garlic powder
• ½ Tsp. paprika
• 1 Tbsp olive oil, or as needed

Instructions

• Season tomato slices with salt and pepper.

• Set up a breading station in 3 shallow dishes: pour flour into the first dish; stir together buttermilk and eggs in the second dish; and mix breadcrumbs, cornmeal, garlic powder, and paprika in the third dish.

• Dredge tomato slices in flour, shaking off the excess. Dip tomatoes into the egg mixture, and then into the bread crumb mixture, making sure to coat both sides.

• Preheat the air fryer to 400 degrees F (200 degrees C). Brush the fryer basket with olive oil. Place breaded tomato slices in the fryer basket, making sure they do not touch each other; cook in batches if necessary. Brush the tops of tomatoes with olive oil.

• Cook for 12 min., then flip the tomatoes and brush again with olive oil. Cook until crisp and golden brown, 3 to 5 mins more. Remove tomatoes to a paper towel-lined rack to keep crisp. Repeat with the remaining tomatoes.

252.Air Fryer Latkes

Prep Time: 20 mins Cook Time: 20 mins Total Time: 40 mins

Ingredient

• 1 (16 ounces) package frozen shredded hash brown potatoes, thawed
• ½ cup shredded onion
• 1 egg

- Kosher salt and ground black pepper to taste
- 2 Tbsps matzo meal
- Avocado oil cooking spray

Instructions

- Preheat an air fryer to 375 degrees F (190 degrees C) according to the manufacturer's instructions. Layout a sheet of parchment or waxed paper.
- Place thawed potatoes and shredded onion on several layers of paper towels. Cover with more paper towels and press to squeeze out most of the liquid.
- Whisk together egg, salt, and pepper in a large bowl. Stir in potatoes and onion with a fork. Sprinkle matzo meal on top and stir until ingredients are evenly distributed. Use your hands to form the mixture into ten 3- to 4-inch wide patties. Place patties on the parchment or waxed paper.
- Spray the air fryer basket with cooking spray. Carefully place half of the patties in the basket and spray generously with cooking spray.
- Air-fry until crispy and dark golden brown on the outside, 10 to 12 minutes. (Check for doneness at 8 mins if you prefer a softer latke.) Remove latkes to a plate. Repeat with remaining patties, spraying them with cooking spray before cooking.

253. Air Fryer Truffle Fries

Prep Time: 10 mins Cook Time: 20 mins
Additional Time: 30 mins
Total Time: 1 hr

Ingredient

- 1 ¾ pounds russet potatoes, peeled and cut into fries
- 2 Tbsps truffle-infused olive oil
- ½ Tsp. paprika
- 1 Tbsp grated Parmesan cheese
- 2 teaspoons chopped fresh parsley
- 1 Tsp. black truffle sea salt

Instructions

- Place fries in a bowl. Cover with water and let soak for 30 min.. Drain and pat dry.
- Preheat the air fryer to 400 degrees F (200 degrees C) according to the manufacturer's **Instructions**.
- Place drained fries into a large bowl. Add truffle olive oil and paprika; stir until evenly combined. Transfer fries to

the air fryer basket.
- Air fry for 20 minutes, shaking every 5 min.. Transfer fries to a bowl. Add Parmesan cheese, parsley, and truffle salt. Toss to coat.

254. Air Fryer Spaghetti Squash

Prep Time: 5 mins Cook Time: 25 mins
Total Time: 30 mins

Ingredient

- 1 (3 pounds) spaghetti squash
- 1 Tsp. olive oil
- ¼ Tsp. sea salt
- ⅛ Tsp. ground black pepper
- ⅛ Tsp. smoked paprika

Instructions

- Using a sharp knife, make a dotted line lengthwise around the entire squash.
- Place whole squash in the microwave and cook on full power for 5 min..
- Transfer to a cutting board and cut the squash in half lengthwise, using the dotted line as a guide.
- Wrap one half in plastic wrap and refrigerate for another use.
- Spoon pulp and seeds out of the remaining half and discard.
- Brush olive oil over all of the flesh and sprinkle with salt, pepper, and paprika.
- Preheat an air fryer to 360 degrees F (180 degrees C). Place spaghetti squash half skin-side-down in the basket. Cook for 20 min..
- Transfer to a dish and fluff with a fork to create 'noodles'.

255. Roasted Brussels Sprouts With Maple-Mustard Mayo

Prep Time: 5 mins Cook Time: 10 mins
Total Time: 15 mins

Ingredient

- 2 Tbsps maple syrup, divided
- 1 Tbsp olive oil
- ¼ Tsp. kosher salt
- ¼ Tsp. ground black pepper
- 1 pound Brussels sprouts, trimmed and halved
- ⅓ cup mayonnaise
- 1 Tbsp stone-ground mustard

Instructions

- Preheat the air fryer to 400 degrees F (200 degrees C).
- Whisk together 1 Tbsp maple syrup, olive oil, salt, and pepper in a large

bowl. Add Brussels sprouts and toss to coat. Arrange Brussels sprouts in a single layer in an air fryer basket without overcrowding; work in batches, if necessary. Cook for 4 min.. Shake basket and cook until sprouts are deep golden brown and tender, 4 to 6 mins more.
- Meanwhile, whisk together mayonnaise, remaining 1 Tbsp maple syrup, and mustard in a small bowl. Toss sprouts in some of the sauce mixtures and/or serve as a dipping sauce. .

256. Air Fryer Peri Peri Fries

Prep Time: 10 mins Cook Time: 25 mins
Additional Time: 15 mins Total Time: 50 mins

Ingredient

- 2 pounds russet potatoes
- ¼ Tsp. smoked paprika
- ¼ Tsp. chile powder
- ¼ Tsp. garlic granules
- ⅛ Tsp. ground white pepper
- ½ Tsp. salt
- 2 Tbsp grapeseed oil

Instructions

- Peel and cut potatoes into 3/8-inch slices. Place into a bowl of water for 15 mins to remove most of the starch. Transfer onto a clean kitchen towel and dry.
- Preheat the air fryer to 350 degrees F (180 degrees C) for 5 min..
- Mix paprika, chile powder, garlic. white pepper, and salt together in a small bowl.
- Place the potatoes into a medium bowl and add grapeseed oil; mix well. Pour into the air fryer basket.
- Air fry for 10 min., shaking occasionally. Increase the temperature to 400 degrees F (200 degrees C) and air fry until golden brown, 12 to 15 more minutes.
- Pour fries into a bowl, sprinkle with the seasoning mix, and shake the bowl to ensure fries are evenly covered. Taste and adjust salt, if necessary. Serve immediately.

257. Air Fryer Fish And Chips

Prep Time: 20 mins Cook Time: 30 mins
Additional Time: 1 hr 10 mins
Total Time: 2 hrs

Ingredients

Chips:
- 1 russet potato
- 2 teaspoons vegetable oil
- 1 pinch salt and ground black pepper to taste

Fish:
- ¾ cup all-purpose flour
- 2 Tbsps cornstarch
- ½ Tsp. salt
- ½ Tsp. garlic powder
- ¼ Tsp. baking soda
- ¼ Tsp. baking powder
- ¾ cup malt beer
- 4 (3 ounces) fillets cod fillets

Instructions
- Peel the russet potato and cut it into 12 wedges. Pour 3 cups water into a medium bowl and submerge potato wedges for 15 min.. Drain off water and replace it with fresh water. Soak wedges for 15 more min..
- Meanwhile, mix flour, cornstarch, salt, garlic powder, baking soda, and baking powder in a bowl. Pour in 1/2 cup malt beer and stir to combine. If batter seems too thick, add remaining beer 1 Tbsp at a time.
- Place cod fillets on a rimmed baking sheet lined with a drip rack. Spoon 1/2 of the batter over the fillets. Place rack in the freezer to allow the batter to solidify, about 35 min.. Flip fillets over and coat the remaining side with the batter. Return to the freezer for an additional 35 min..
- Preheat the air fryer to 400 degrees F (200 degrees C) for 8 min..
- Cook frozen fish fillets for 15 min., flipping at the halfway point.
- Meanwhile, drain off water from potato wedges and blot dry with a paper towel. Toss with oil, salt, and pepper. Air fry for 15 min..

258. "Everything" Seasoning Asparagus
Prep Time: 5 mins Cook Time: 5 mins
Total Time: 10 mins

Ingredient
- 1 pound thin asparagus
- 1 Tbsp olive oil
- 1 Tbsp everything bagel seasoning
- 1 pinch salt to taste
- 4 wedge (blank)s lemon wedges

Instructions
- Rinse and trim asparagus, cutting off any woody ends. Place asparagus on a plate and drizzle with olive oil. Toss with bagel seasoning until evenly combined. Place asparagus in the air fryer basket in a single layer. Work in batches if needed.
- Heat the air fryer to 390 degrees F (200 degrees C).
- Air fry until slightly soft, tossing with tongs halfway through, 5 to 6 min.. Taste and season with salt if needed. Serve with lemon wedges.

259. Air Fryer Tajin Sweet Potato Fries
Prep Time: 10 mins Cook Time: 10 mins
Total Time: 20 mins

Ingredient
- Cooking spray
- 2 medium sweet potatoes, cut into 1/2-inch-thick fries
- 3 teaspoons avocado oil
- 1 ½ Tsp. chili-lime seasoning (such as tajin)

Dipping Sauce:
- ¼ cup mayonnaise
- 1 Tbsp freshly squeezed lime juice
- 1 Tsp. chili-lime seasoning
- 4 lime wedges

Instructions
- Preheat the air fryer to 400 degrees F (200 degrees C) for 5 min.. Lightly spray the fryer basket with cooking spray.
- Place sweet potato fries in a large bowl, drizzle with avocado oil, and stir. Sprinkle with 1 1/2 teaspoons chili-lime seasoning and toss well. Transfer to the air fryer basket, working in batches if necessary.
- Cook sweet potato fries until brown and crispy, 8 to 9 minutes, shaking and turning the fries after 4 min..
- While sweet potatoes are cooking, whisk together mayonnaise, lime juice, and chili-lime seasoning for the dipping sauce in a small bowl. Serve sweet potato fries with dipping sauce and lime wedges.

260. Air Fryer Fingerling Potatoes
Prep Time: 10 mins Cook Time: 15 mins
Total Time: 25 mins

Ingredient
- 1 pound fingerling potatoes, halved lengthwise
- 1 Tbsp olive oil
- ½ Tsp. ground paprika
- ½ Tsp. parsley flakes
- ½ Tsp. garlic powder
- Salt and ground black pepper to taste

Instructions
- Preheat an air fryer to 400 degrees F (200 degrees C).
- Place potato halves in a large bowl. Add olive oil, paprika, parsley, garlic powder, salt, and pepper and stir until evenly coated.
- Place potatoes in the basket of the preheated air fryer and cook for 10 min.. Stir and cook until desired crispness is reached, about 5 more minutes.

261. Sweet and Spicy Air Fried Sweet Potatoes
Prep Time: 10 mins Cook Time: 15 mins
Total Time: 25 mins

Ingredient
- 1 large sweet potato, cut into 1/2-inch pieces
- 1 Tbsp olive oil
- 1 Tbsp packed light brown sugar
- ¼ Tsp. sea salt
- ¼ Tsp. chili powder
- ¼ Tsp. ground paprika
- ¼ Tsp. cayenne pepper
- ⅛ Tsp. onion powder
- Ground black pepper to taste

Instructions
- Preheat an air fryer to 400 degrees F (200 degrees C) according to the manufacturer's **Instructions**.
- Place sweet potato in a large bowl. Drizzle with olive oil, then add brown sugar, salt, chili powder, paprika, cayenne pepper, onion powder, and pepper. Stir until potatoes are evenly coated and spread out onto the air fryer rack.
- Cook on the upper rack of the preheated air fryer until browned and crispy, 15 to 20 min..

262. Rosemary Potato Wedges
Prep Time: 10 mins Cook Time: 20 mins
Total Time: 30 mins

Ingredient
- 2 russet potatoes, sliced into 12 wedges each with skin on
- 1 Tbsp extra-virgin olive oil
- 2 teaspoons seasoned salt
- 1 Tbsp finely chopped fresh rosemary

Instructions
- Preheat an air fryer to 380 degrees F (190 degrees C).
- Place potatoes in a large bowl and toss with olive oil. Sprinkle with seasoned salt and rosemary and toss to combine.
- Place potatoes in an even layer in a fryer basket once the air fryer is hot; you may need to cook them in batches.
- Air fry potatoes for 10 minutes, then flip wedges with tongs. Continue air frying until potato wedges reach the desired doneness, about 10 mins more.

263. Air Fryer Roasted Cauliflower
Prep Time: 10 mins Cook Time: 15 mins
Total Time: 25 mins
Ingredient
- 3 cloves garlic
- 1 Tbsp peanut oil
- ½ Tsp. salt
- ½ Tsp. smoked paprika
- 4 cups cauliflower florets

Instructions
- Preheat an air fryer to 400 degrees F
- Cut garlic in half and smash with the blade of a knife. Place in a bowl with oil, salt, and paprika. Add cauliflower and turn to coat.
- Place the coated cauliflower in the bowl of the air fryer and cook to desired crispiness, shaking every 5 min., about 15 mins total.

264. Air-Fried Ratatouille, Italian-Style
Prep Time: 25 mins Cook Time: 25 mins
Additional Time: 5 mins
Total Time: 55 mins
Ingredient
- ½ small eggplant, cut into cubes
- 1 zucchini, cut into cubes
- 1 medium tomato, cut into cubes
- ½ large yellow bell pepper, cut into cubes
- ½ large red bell pepper, cut into cubes
- ½ onion, cut into cubes
- 1 fresh cayenne pepper, diced
- 5 sprigs fresh basil, stemmed and chopped
- 2 sprigs of fresh oregano, stemmed and chopped
- 1 clove garlic, crushed
- salt and ground black pepper to taste
- 1 Tbsp olive oil
- 1 Tbsp white wine
- 1 Tsp. vinegar

Instructions
- Preheat an air fryer to 400 degrees F (200 degrees C).
- Place eggplant, zucchini, tomato, bell peppers, and onion in a bowl. Add cayenne pepper, basil, oregano, garlic, salt, and pepper. Mix well to distribute everything evenly. Drizzle in oil, wine, and vinegar, mixing to coat all the vegetables.
- Pour vegetable mixture into a baking dish and insert it into the basket of the air fryer. Cook for 8 min.. Stir; cook for another 8 min.. Stir again and continue cooking until tender, stirring every 5 min., 10 to 15 mins more. Turn off the air fryer, leaving the dish inside. Let rest for 5 mins before serving.

265. Air Fryer Spicy Green Beans
Prep Time: 10 mins Cook Time: 25 mins
Additional Time: 5 mins
Total Time: 40 mins
Ingredient
- 12 ounces fresh green beans, trimmed
- 1 Tbsp sesame oil
- 1 Tsp. soy sauce
- 1 Tsp. rice wine vinegar
- 1 clove garlic, minced
- ½ Tsp. red pepper flakes

Instructions
- Preheat an air fryer to 400 degrees F
- Place green beans in a bowl. Whisk together sesame oil, soy sauce, rice wine vinegar, garlic, and red pepper flakes in a separate bowl and pour over green beans. Toss to coat and let marinate for 5 minutes.
- Place half the green beans in the air fryer basket. Cook 12 minutes, shaking the basket halfway through cooking time. Repeat with remaining green beans.

266. Five-Spice Butternut Squash Fries
Prep Time: 15 mins Cook Time: 15 mins
Total Time: 30 mins
Ingredient
- 1 large butternut squash, peeled and cut into "fries"
- 2 Tbsp olive oil
- 1 Tbsp Chinese five-spice powder
- 1 Tbsp minced garlic
- 2 teaspoons sea salt
- 2 teaspoons black pepper

Instructions
- Preheat the air fryer to 400 degrees F (200 degrees C).
- Place cut the squash in a large bowl. Add oil, five-spice powder, garlic, salt, and black pepper, and toss to coat.
- Cook butternut squash fries in the preheated air fryer, shaking every 5 min., until crisp, 15 to 20 mins total. Remove fries and season with additional sea salt.

267. Air Fryer Brussels Sprouts
Prep Time: 5 mins Cook Time: 10 mins
Total Time: 15 mins
Ingredient
- 1 Tsp. avocado oil
- ½ Tsp. salt
- ½ Tsp. ground black pepper
- 10 ounces Brussels sprouts, trimmed and halved lengthwise
- 1 Tsp. balsamic vinegar
- 2 teaspoons crumbled cooked bacon (optional)

Instructions
- Preheat an air fryer to 350 degrees F (175 degrees C).
- Combine oil, salt, and pepper in a bowl and mix well. Add Brussels sprouts and turn to coat.
- Air fry for 5 min., shake the sprouts and cook for an additional 5 minutes.
- Transfer sprouts to a serving dish and sprinkles with balsamic vinegar; turn to coat. Sprinkle with bacon.

268. Root Vegetables With Vegan Aioli
Prep Time: 30 mins Cook Time: 30 mins
Total Time: 1 hr
Ingredients
Garlic Aioli:
- ½ cup vegan mayonnaise
- 1 clove garlic, minced
- ½ Tsp. fresh lemon juice
- Salt and ground black pepper to taste
Root Vegetables:
- 4 Tbsp extra virgin olive oil
- 1 Tbsp minced fresh rosemary
- 3 cloves garlic, finely minced
- 1 Tsp. kosher salt, or to taste
- ½ Tsp. ground black pepper, or to taste
- 1 pound parsnips, peeled and cut

vertically into uniform pieces

• 1 pound baby red potatoes, cut lengthwise into 4 or 6 pieces

• ½ pound baby carrots split lengthwise

• ½ red onion cut lengthwise into 1/2-inch slices

• ½ Tsp. grated lemon zest, or to taste (Optional)

Instructions

• Combine mayonnaise, garlic, lemon juice, salt, and pepper in a small bowl for the garlic aioli; place in the refrigerator until ready to serve.

• Preheat the air fryer to 400 degrees F (200 degrees C) if your air fryer manufacturer recommends preheating.

• Combine olive oil, rosemary, garlic, salt, and pepper in a small bowl; set aside to allow the flavors to mingle. Combine parsnips, potatoes, carrots, and onion in a large bowl. Add olive oil-rosemary mixture and stir until vegetables are evenly coated. Place a portion of vegetables in a single layer in the basket of the air fryer, then add a rack and another layer of vegetables.

• Air fry for 15 min..

• When the timer sounds, you may plate the veggies and keep warm, or continue cooking in 5-minute intervals until the vegetables reach desired doneness and browning.

• Place remaining vegetables in the bottom of the air fryer basket and air fry for 15 min., checking for doneness, as needed. Use the rack again, if you have more vegetables then fit in a single layer. When all the vegetables have cooked, serve with garlic aioli and garnish with lemon zest.

269.Roasted Broccoli And Cauliflower

Prep Time: 10 mins Cook Time: 15 mins
Total Time: 25 mins

Ingredient

• 3 cups broccoli florets

• 3 cups cauliflower florets

• 2 Tbsps olive oil

• ½ Tsp. garlic powder

• ¼ Tsp. sea salt

• ¼ Tsp. paprika

• ⅛ Tsp. ground black pepper

Instructions

• Heat an air fryer to 400 degrees F (200 degrees C) following the

manufacturer's instructions.

• Place broccoli florets in a large, microwave-safe bowl. Cook in the microwave on high power for 3 min.. Drain any accumulated liquid.

• Add cauliflower, olive oil, garlic powder, sea salt, paprika, and black pepper to the bowl with the broccoli. Mix well to combine. Pour mixture into the air fryer basket. Cook for 12 min., tossing vegetables halfway through cooking time for even browning.

Poultry Recipes

270.Ranch-Seasoned Roast Turkey

Prep time: 10mins Cook. time: 3 hours

Ingredients: :

• 1 Whole Turkey, thawed

• 2 sticks Butter

• 2 packets Ranch Seasoning Mix

Directions:

• Begin by preheating the air fryer. The air fryer should be set to about 370 degrees F. Then drain the turkey of any fluids. Dry with a paper towel and set in a pan.

• In a bowl, mix the butter and the ranch seasoning. Keep stirring until a paste is formed. The paste should be thick and even. Smear the paste all over the turkey.

• Do not overlook any side - smear below as well as on top of the turkey, as much as you can.

• Turn the turkey upside down so that the breast is facing upwards, wrap the turkey in a thin foil and insert a thermometer into its thighs. Place the turkey inside the basket. Remember to remove the foil thirty mins before you are done cooking so that the turkey can be cooked evenly.

• Depending on how heavy the turkey is, you may have to cook for thirty mins or more. (As a rule of thumb, twenty mins should be enough to cook a pound of turkey. You can measure the length of time it will take depending on the weight of the turkey.)

• Wait for fifteen to twenty mins before you go ahead to serve.

271.Creamy Coconut Chicken

Prep time: 2 hours Cook time: 25 mins

Ingredients:

• Big chicken legs – 4

• Turmeric powder – 5 tsp.

• Ginger – 2 tbsp., grated

• Salt and black pepper to taste

• Coconut cream – 4 tbsp.

Directions:

• In a bowl, mix salt, pepper, ginger, turmeric and cream. Whisk. Add chicken pieces, coat and marinate for 2 hours.

• Transfer chicken to the preheated air fryer and cook at 370F for 25 mins.

• Serve.

272.Chinese Chicken Wings

Prep time: 2 hours Cook time: 15 mins

Ingredients:

• Chicken wings – 16

• Honey – 2 tbsp.

• Soy sauce – 2 tbsp.

• Salt and black pepper to taste

• White pepper – ¼ tsp.

• Lime juice – 3 tbsp.

Directions:

• In a bowl, mix soy sauce, honey, salt, black pepper, lime juice and white pepper. Whisk well.

• Add chicken pieces and coat well. Marinate in the refrigerator for 2 hours.

• Cook in the air fryer at 370F for 6 mins on each side.

• Increase heat to 400F and cook for 3 mins more.

• Serve.

273.Chicken Parmesan

Prep time: 10 mins Cook time: 15 mins

Ingredients:

• Panko bread crumbs – 2 cups

• Parmesan – ¼ cup, grated

• Garlic powder – ½ tsp.

• White flour – 2 cups

• Egg – 1, whisked

• Chicken cutlets – 1 ½ pounds, skinless and boneless

• Salt and pepper to taste

• Mozzarella - 1 cup, grated

• Tomato sauce – 2 cups

• Basil – 3 tbsp., chopped

Directions:

• In a bowl, mix garlic powder and parmesan, and stir.

• Put flour in a second bowl and the egg in a third.

• Season chicken with salt and pepper.

• Dip chicken in flour, then in the egg

mix and in panko.
- Cook chicken pieces in the air fryer at 360F for 3 mins on each side.
- Transfer chicken to a baking dish.
- Add tomato sauce and top with mozzarella.
- Cook in the air fryer at 375F for 7 mins.
- Divide among plates, sprinkle basil on top and serve.

274.Chicken with Rice
Prep time: 10 mins Cook time: 30 mins
Ingredients:
- Chicken breasts – 1 pound, skinless, boneless and cut into quarters
- White rice – 1 cup, cooked
- Salt and black pepper to taste
- Olive oil – 1 tbsp.
- Garlic – 3 cloves, minced
- Yellow onion – 1, chopped
- White wine – ½ cup
- Heavy cream – ¼ cup
- Chicken stock – 1 cup
- Parsley – ¼ cup, chopped
- Peas – 2 cups, frozen
- Parmesan - 1 ½ cups, grated
Directions:
- Season chicken with salt and pepper. Drizzle half of the oil and rub well.
- Place in the air fryer basket and cook at 360F for 6 mins.
- Heat the rest of the oil in a pan. Add garlic, wine, onion, stock, heavy cream,
- salt and pepper, and stir.
- Bring to a simmer and cook for 9 mins.
- Transfer chicken breasts to a dish and add peas, rice and cream mixture over them. Sprinkle with parsley and parmesan.
- Place in the air fryer and cook at 420F for 10 mins.
- Serve.

275.Healthy Chicken And Veggies
Prep Time: 5 minutes Cook Time: 15 minutes Total Time: 20 minutes
Ingredients
- 1 pound chicken breast, chopped into bite-size pieces (2-3 medium chicken breasts)
- 1 cup broccoli florets (fresh or frozen)
- One zucchini chopped
- 1 cup bell pepper chopped (any colors you like)
- 1/2 onion chopped

- Two cloves garlic minced or crushed
- Two tablespoons olive oil
- 1/2 teaspoon EACH garlic powder, chili powder, salt, pepper
- One tablespoon Italian seasoning
Instructions
- Preheat air fryer to 400F.
- Chop the veggies and chicken into small bite-size pieces and transfer to a large mixing bowl.
- Add the oil and seasoning to the bowl and toss to combine.
- Add the chicken and veggies to the preheated air fryer and cook for 10 minutes, shaking halfway, or until the chicken and veggies are charred, and chicken is cooked through. If your air fryer is small, you may have to cook them in 2-3 batches.

276.Honey Duck Breasts
Prep time: 10 mins Cook time: 22 mins
Ingredients:
- Smoked duck breast – 1, halved
- Honey – 1 tsp.
- Tomato paste – 1 tsp.
- Mustard – 1 tbsp.
- Apple vinegar – ½ tsp.
Directions:
- Mix tomato paste, honey, mustard and vinegar in a bowl. Whisk well.
- Add duck breast pieces and coat well.
- Cook in the air fryer at 370F for 15 mins.
- Remove the duck breast from the air fryer and add to the honey mixture.
- Coat again.
- Cook again at 370F for 6 mins.
- Serve.

277.Duck and Plum Sauce
Prep time: 10 mins Cook time: 32 mins
Ingredients:
- Duck breasts – 2
- Butter – 1 tbsp., melted
- Star anise – 1
- Olive oil – 1 tbsp.
- Shallot – 1, chopped
- Red plumps – 9 ounces, stoned, cut into small wedges
- Sugar – 2 tbsp.
- Red wine – 2 tbsp.
- Beef stock – 1 cup
Directions:
- In a pan, heat olive oil over medium

heat. Add shallot. Stir-fry for 5 mins.
- Add plums and sugar, stir and cook until sugar dissolves.
- Add wine and stock. Stir and cook for 15 mins. Remove from heat and keep warm.
- Score duck breasts, season with salt and pepper. Rub with melted butter, transfer to a heatproof dish. Add plum sauce and star anise.
- Place in the air fryer and cook at 360F for 12 mins.
- Serve.

278.Japanese Duck Breasts
Prep time: 10 mins Cook time: 20 mins
Ingredients:
- Duck breasts – 6, boneless
- Soy sauce – 4 tbsp.
- Five-spice powder – 1 ½ tsp.
- Honey – 2 tbsp.
- Salt and black pepper to taste
- Chicken stock – 20 ounces
- Ginger – 4 slices
- Hoisin sauce – 4 tbsp.
- Sesame oil – 1 tsp.
Directions:
- In a bowl, mix the five-spice powder with honey, salt, pepper and soy sauce.
- Whisk, add duck breasts and coat well. Set aside.
- Heat up the chicken stock, hoisin sauce, ginger and sesame oil in a pan over medium-high heat. Stir well and cook for 3 mins. Remove from the heat and set aside.
- Cook duck breasts in the air fryer at 400F for 15 mins.
- Divide among plates, drizzle with hoisin and ginger sauce mixture, and serve.

279.Duck Breasts with Endives
Prep time: 10 mins
Cook time: 25 mins
Servings: 4
Ingredients:
- Duck breasts – 2
- Salt and black pepper to taste
- Sugar – 1 tbsp.
- Olive oil – 1 tbsp.
- Endives – 6, julienned
- Cranberries – 2 tbsp.
- White wine – 8 ounces
- Garlic – 1 tbsp., minced
- Heavy cream – 2 tbsp.

Directions:

- Score duck breasts and season with salt and pepper.
- Cook in the air fryer at 350F for 20 mins. Flip once.
- Meanwhile, heat up a pan with oil over medium heat. Add endives and sugar.
- Stir and cook for 2 mins.
- Add salt, pepper, wine, garlic, cream and cranberries. Stir fry for 3 mins.
- Divide duck breasts among plates. Drizzle with the endives sauce and serve.

280. Chicken Salad

Prep time: 10 mins Cook time: 10 mins

Ingredients:

- Chicken breast – 1 pound, boneless, skinless and halved
- Cooking spray
- Salt and black pepper to tray
- Feta cheese – ½ cup, cubed
- Lemon juice – 2 tbsp.
- Mustard – 1 ½ tsp.
- Olive oil – 1 tbsp.
- Red wine vinegar – 1 ½ tsp.
- Anchovies – ½ tsp. minced
- Garlic – ¾ tsp. minced
- Water – 1 tbsp.
- Lettuce leaves – 8 cups, cut into strips
- Parmesan – 4 tbsp., grated

Directions:

- Spray chicken breasts with cooking oil. Season with salt and pepper.
- Place in the air fryer and cook at 370F for 10 mins. Flip once.
- Shred the chicken with 2 forks. Put in a salad bowl and mix with lettuce
- leaves.
- In a blender, mix feta cheese with lemon juice, olive oil, mustard, vinegar, garlic, anchovies, water and half of the parmesan, and blend very well.
- Add this over the chicken mixture. Toss and sprinkle with the remaining parmesan then serve.

281. Italian Chicken

Prep. time: 10 mins Cook. time: 16 mins

Ingredients:

- 5 chicken thighs
- 1 tablespoon olive oil
- 2 garlic cloves, minced
- 1 tablespoon thyme, chopped

- ½ cup heavy cream
- ¾ cup chicken stock
- 1 teaspoon red pepper flakes, crushed
- ¼ cup parmesan, grated
- ½ cup sun dried tomatoes
- 2 tablespoons basil, chopped
- Salt and black pepper to the taste

Directions:

- Season the chicken with salt and hu season, rub with half of the oil and cook in a 350 ° F preheated air fryer for 4 mins.
- Meanwhile, heat the pot with the remaining oil over medium high heat, add thyme garlic, pepper flakes, sun dried tomatoes, heavy cream, stock, parmesan, salt and pepper, stir, bring to a simmer, take off heat and transfer to a dish that fits your air fryer.
- Add chicken thighs on top, introduce in your air fryer and cook at 320 degrees F for 12 mins.
- Divide among plates and serve with basil sprinkled on top.
- Enjoy!

282. Honey Duck Breast

Prep. time: 10 mins Cook. time: 22 mins

Ingredients:

- 1 smoked duck breast, halved
- 1 teaspoon honey
- 1 teaspoon tomato paste
- 1 tablespoon mustard
- ½ teaspoon apple vinegar

Directions:

- In a bowl, mix honey with tomato paste, mustard and vinegar, whisk well, add duck breast pieces, toss to coat well, transfer to your air fryer and cook at 370 degrees F for 15 mins.
- Take duck breast out of the fryer, add to honey mix, toss again, return to air fryer and for a duration of 6 mins boil at 370 degrees.
- Divide among plates and serve with a side salad.
- Enjoy!

283. Stuffed Chicken

Prep time: 10 mins Cook time: 35 mins

Ingredients:

- 1 whole chicken
- 10 wolfberries

- 2 red chilies, chopped
- 4 ginger slices
- 1 yam, cubed
- 1 teaspoon soy sauce
- Salt and white pepper to the taste
- 3 teaspoons sesame oil

Directions:

- Season chicken with salt, pepper, rub with soy sauce and sesame oil and stuff with wolfberries, yam cubes, chilies and ginger.
- Place in your air fryer, cook at 400 degrees F for 20 mins and then at 360 degrees F for 15 mins.
- Carve chicken, divide among plates and serve.

284. Mexican Chicken Breast

Prep. time: 10 mins Cook. time: 20 mins

Ingredients:

- 8 ounces salsa verde
- ½ tablespoon olive oil
- Salt and black pepper, to taste
- ½ pound boneless, skinless chicken breast
- ¾ cup Monetary Jack cheese, grated
- 2 tablespoons cilantro, chopped
- ½ teaspoon garlic powder

Directions:

- Pour salsa verde into a baking dish.
- Season chicken with salt, pepper, garlic powder, and brush with olive oil.
- Place over the salsa verde.
- Place baking dish in the air fryer and cook at 380F for 20 mins.
- Sprinkle cheese over the top and cook 2 more mins.

285. Chicken Wings

Prep. time: 10 mins Cook. time: 25 mins

Ingredients:

- 10 chicken wings (about 700g)
- Oil in spay
- 1 tbsp soy sauce
- ½ tbsp cornstarch
- 2 tbsp honey
- 1 tbsp ground fresh chili paste
- 1 tbsp minced garlic
- ½ tsp chopped fresh ginger
- 1 tbsp lime sumo
- ½ tbsp salt
- 2 tbsp chives

Directions:

- Dry the chicken with a tea towel.
- Cover the chicken with the oil spray.
- Place the chicken inside the hot air electric fryer, separating the wings towards the edge so that it is not on top of each other. Cook at 200ºC until the skin is crispy for about 25 min. Turn them around half the time.
- Mix the soy sauce with cornstarch in a small pan. Add honey, chili paste, garlic, ginger, and lime sumo.
- Simmer until it boils and thickens.
- Place the chicken in a bowl, add the sauce and cover all the chicken. Sprinkle with chives.

286.Cordon Bleu Chicken Breast
Prep. time: 10 mins Cook. time: 40 mins

Ingredients: :
- 4 flattened chicken breasts
- 8 slices of ham
- 16 slices of Swiss cheese
- 2 tsp fresh thyme
- ¼ cup flour
- 1 cup of ground bread
- 2 tsp melted butter
- 2 eggs
- 1 clove garlic finely chopped
- pam cooking spray

Directions:
- Preheat the air fryer to 350 degrees Fahrenheit (180 °C), set timer to 5 mins.
- Then, flatten chicken breasts.
- Fill the chicken breasts with two slices of cheese, then 2 slices of ham and finally 2 slices of cheese and roll up. Use a stick if necessary, to save the shape.
- Mix the ground bread with the thyme, the garlic finely chopped, with the melted butter and with salt and pepper. Beat the eggs. Season the flour with salt and pepper.
- Pass the chicken rolls first through the flour, then through the egg and finally through the breadcrumbs.
- Bake until the breasts are cooked, about 20 mins.
- Alternatively, before putting the chicken breasts in the air fryer you can fry them in a little butter and then finish cooking in the air fryer for 13-15 mins

287.Chicken Flutes with Sour Sauce and Guacamole

Prep. time: 15 mins Cook. time: 25 mins

Ingredients: :
- 8 wheat cakes
- 1 large roasted breast
- Grated cheese
- Sour sauce
- Guacamole
- Extra virgin olive oil

Directions:
- Extend the wheat cakes.
- Stuffed with grated cheese and well-roasted chicken breast.
- Form the flues and paint with extra virgin olive oil.
- Place in batches in the air fryer and select 180 degrees, 5 mins on each side or until you see the flutes golden.
- Serve with sour sauce and guacamole.

288.Spinach Stuffed Chicken Breasts
Prep. time: 15 mins Cook. time: 30 mins

Ingredients:
- 1 tablespoon olive oil
- 1¾ ounces fresh spinach
- ¼ cup ricotta cheese, shredded
- 2, 4-ouncesskinless, boneless chicken breasts
- Salt and ground black pepper, as required
- 2 tablespoons cheddar cheese, grated
- ¼ teaspoon paprika
Instructions
- In a medium skillet, add the oil over medium heat and cook until heated.
- Add the spinach and cook for about 3-4 mins.
- Stir in the ricotta and cook for about 40-60 seconds.
- Remove the skillet from heat and set aside to cool.
- Cut slits into the chicken breasts about ¼-inch apart but not all the way through.
- Stuff each chicken breast with the spinach mixture.
- Sprinkle each chicken breast evenly with salt and black pepper and then with cheddar cheese and paprika.
- Set the temperature of Air Fryer to 390 degrees F. Grease an Air Fryer basket.
- Arrange chicken breasts into the

prepared basket in a single layer.
- Air Fry for about 20-25 mins.
- Remove from Air Fryer and transfer the chicken breasts onto a serving platter.
- Serve hot.

289.Bacon Wrapped Chicken Breasts
Prep. time: 20 mins Cook. time: 23 mins

Ingredients:
- 1 tablespoon palm sugar
- 6-7 Fresh basil leaves
- 2 tablespoons fish sauce
- 2 tablespoons water
- 2, 8-ounceschicken breasts, cut each breast in half horizontally
- Salt and ground black pepper, as required
- 12 bacon strips
- 1½ teaspoon honey

Instructions
- In a small heavy-bottomed pan, add palm sugar over medium-low heat and cook for about 2-3 mins or until caramelized, stirring continuously.
- Add the basil, fish sauce and water and stir to combine.
- Remove from heat and transfer the sugar mixture into a large bowl.
- Sprinkle each chicken breast with salt and black pepper.
- Add the chicken pieces in sugar mixture and coat generously.
- Refrigerate to marinate for about 4-6 hours.
- Set the temperature of Air Fryer to 365 degrees F. Grease an Air Fryer basket.
- Wrap each chicken piece with 3 bacon strips.
- Coat each piece slightly with honey.
- Arrange chicken pieces into the prepared Air Fryer basket.
- Air Fry for about 20 mins, flipping once halfway through.
- Remove from Air Fryer and transfer the chicken pieces onto a serving platter.
- Serve hot.

290.Simple Chicken Wings
Prep. time: 10 mins Cook. time: 25 mins

Ingredients:

- 1 pound chicken wings
- Salt and ground black pepper, as required

Instructions

- Set the temperature of Air Fryer to 380 degrees F. Generously, grease an Air Fryer basket.
- Sprinkle the chicken wings evenly with salt and black pepper.
- Arrange chicken wings into the prepared Air Fryer basket in a single layer.
- Air Fry for about 25 mins, flip the wings once halfway through.
- Remove from Air Fryer and transfer the chicken wings onto a serving platter.
- Serve hot.

291.BBQ Chicken Wings

Prep. time: 10 mins
Cook. time: 30 mins

Ingredients:

- 2 pounds chicken wings, cut into drumettes and flats
- ½ cup BBQ sauce

Instructions

- Set the temperature of Air Fryer to 380 degrees F. Grease an Air Fryer basket.
- Arrange chicken wings into the prepared Air Fryer basket in a single layer.
- Air Fry for about 24 mins, flipping once halfway through.
- Now, set the temperature of Air Fryer to 400 degrees F.
- Air Fry for about 6 mins.
- Remove from Air Fryer and transfer the chicken wings into a bowl.
- Drizzle with the BBQ sauce and toss to coat well.
- Serve immediately.

292.Sweet Chicken Kabobs

Prep. time: 20 mins
Cook. time: 14 mins

Ingredients:

- 4 scallions, chopped
- 1 tablespoon fresh ginger, finely grated
- 4 garlic cloves, minced
- ½ cup pineapple juice
- ½ cup soy sauce
- ¼ cup sesame oil

- 2 teaspoons sesame seeds, toasted
- A pinch of black pepper
- 1 pound chicken tenders

Instructions

- In a large baking dish, mix together the scallion, ginger, garlic, pineapple juice,
- soy sauce, oil, sesame seeds, and black pepper.
- Thread chicken tenders onto the pre-soaked wooden skewers.
- Add the skewers into the baking dish and evenly coat with marinade.
- Cover and refrigerate for about 2 hours or overnight.
- Set the temperature of Air Fryer to 390 degrees F. Grease an Air Fryer basket.
- Place chicken skewers into the prepared Air Fryer basket in 2 batches.
- Air Fry for about 5-7 mins.
- Remove from Air Fryer and transfer the chicken skewers onto a serving platter.
- Serve hot.

293.Chicken & Veggie Kabobs

Prep. time: 20 mins
Cook. time: 30 mins

Ingredients:

- 1 lb. skinless, boneless chicken thighs, cut into cubes
- ½ cup plain Greek yogurt
- 1 tablespoon olive oil
- 2 teaspoons curry powder
- ½ teaspoon smoked paprika
- ¼ teaspoon cayenne pepper
- Salt, to taste
- 2 small bell peppers, seeded and cut into large chunks
- 1 large red onion, cut into large chunks

Instructions

- In a bowl, add the chicken, oil, yogurt, and spices and mix until well combined.
- Refrigerate to marinate for about 2 hours.
- Thread the chicken cubes, bell pepper and onion onto pre-soaked wooden skewers.
- Set the temperature of Air Fryer to 360 degrees F. Grease an Air Fryer basket.
- Arrange chicken skewers into the

prepared Air Fryer basket in 2 batches.
- Air Fry for about 15 mins.
- Remove from Air Fryer and transfer the chicken skewers onto a serving platter.
- Serve hot.

294.Chicken with Apple

Prep. time: 20 mins
Cook. time: 20 mins

Ingredients:

- 1 shallot, thinly sliced
- 1 tablespoon fresh ginger, finely grated
- 1 teaspoon fresh thyme, minced
- ½ cup apple cider
- 2 tablespoons maple syrup
- Salt and ground black pepper, as required
- 2, 4-ouncesboneless, skinless chicken thighs, sliced into chunks
- 1 large apple, cored and cubed

Instructions

- In a bowl, mix together the shallot, ginger, thyme, apple cider, maple syrup, salt, and black pepper.
- Add the chicken pieces and generously mix with the marinade.
- Refrigerate to marinate for about 6-8 hours.
- Set the temperature of Air Fryer to 390 degrees F. Grease an Air Fryer basket.
- Place the chicken pieces and cubed apple into the prepared Air Fryer basket.
- Air Fry for about 20 mins, flipping once halfway.
- Remove from Air Fryer and transfer the chicken mixture onto a serving platter.
- Serve hot.

295.Chicken with Veggies

Prep. time: 20 mins
Cook. time: 45 mins

Ingredients:

- 2 garlic cloves, minced
- 2 tablespoons chicken broth
- 2 tablespoons red wine vinegar
- 2 tablespoons olive oil
- 1 tablespoon Dijon mustard
- 1/8 teaspoon dried thyme
- 1/8 teaspoon dried basil
- 4 small artichoke hearts, quartered

- 4 fresh large button mushrooms, quartered
- ½ small onion, cut in large chunks
- Salt and ground black pepper, as required
- 2 skinless, boneless chicken breasts
- 2 tablespoons fresh parsley, chopped

Instructions

- Grease a small baking dish that will fit in the cooking basket of Air Fryer.
- In a small bowl, mix together the garlic, broth, vinegar, olive oil, mustard, thyme, and basil.
- In the prepared baking dish, add the artichokes, mushrooms, onions, salt, and black pepper and mix well
- Now, place the chicken breasts on top of veggie mixture in a single layer.
- Spread half of the mustard mixture evenly over chicken breasts.
- Set the temperature of Air Fryer to 350 degrees F.
- Arrange the baking dish into an Air Fryer cooking basket.
- Air Fry for about 23 mins.
- Coat the chicken breasts with the remaining mustard mixture and flip the side.
- Air Fry for about 22 mins.
- Remove from Air Fryer and transfer the chicken mixture onto a serving platter.
- Garnish with parsley and serve hot.

296.Chicken with Veggies & Rice

Prep. time: 15 mins
Cook. time: 20 mins

Ingredients:

- 3 cups cold boiled white rice
- 6 tablespoons soy sauce
- 1 tablespoon vegetable oil
- 1 cup cooked chicken, diced
- ½ cup frozen carrots
- ½ cup frozen peas
- ½ cup onion, chopped

Instructions

- In a large bowl, add the rice, soy sauce, and oil and mix thoroughly.
- Add the remaining **Ingredients:** and mix until well combined.
- Transfer the rice mixture into a 7" nonstick pan.
- Arrange the pan into an Air Fryer basket.

- Set the temperature of Air Fryer to 360 degrees F.
- Air Fry for about 20 mins.
- Remove the pan from Air Fryer and transfer the rice mixture onto serving
- plates.
- Serve immediately.

297.Seasoned Turkey Breast

Prep time: 15mins
Cook. time: 1hr

Ingredients: :

- 1 Bone-in, Skin-on Turkey Breast, room temperature
- 2 tbsp Packed Light Brown Sugar
- 1 tbsp Chili Powder
- 1 tbsp Smoked Paprika
- 1 tsp Garlic Powder
- Kosher Salt
- Freshly Ground Black Pepper
- 1/2 cup Low-sodium Chicken Broth
- 2 tbsp Honey
- 1/4 cup Soy Sauce
- 2 tbsp Freshly Chopped Parsley

Directions:

- Bring out the turkey from inside the refrigerator and pat dry. Then add seasonings to the turkey, to taste.
- Fetch a small bowl and put in the brown sugar, chili powder, paprika, and garlic powder. Whisk them together thoroughly. Apply the mixture all over
- the turkey. When this is done, place the turkey inside the air fryer and proceed to cook.
- In another bowl, put in the chicken broth, honey and soy sauce, whisk them together and further smear the turkey with it, then cook.
- Cooking should take between 4 to 5 hours and should be slow.

298.Duck in Orange Sauce

Cook. time: 30 mins
Servings: 4

Ingredients: :

- ¾ cup Orange Juice, plus 2 tablespoons
- ¾ cup Chicken Broth
- 1 cup Orange Marmalade
- 1 tablespoon Cornstarch
- 4 Duck Breast
- 1 tablespoon Paprika

Directions

- The first step will be the making of the sauce.

- To do that you have to fetch a saucepan, pour in the chicken broth and the orange marmalade and bring to a boil.
- Make sure that the heat is turned on very high. When it has boiled for about 10 mins, you can reduce the heat and let the pot simmer.
- At the point where it is simmering, you have to check whether the mixture is thick enough. If it isn't, you can pour out two tablespoons of orange juice and add some cornstarch to it. It will form a slurry that you can add to the sauce to act as a thickener. Bring to a boil.
- Heat up a grill to medium heat. Then grill the duck on both sides. Before then, you may want to sprinkle some paprika on both sides of the duck.
- When the duck is grilled, you can then pour the sauce over it and serve.

299.Air Fried Chicken Tenderloins

Prep: 15mins Cook. time: 12mins

Ingredients: :

- 1 Egg
- ½ cup Dry Breadcrumbs
- 2 tablespoons Vegetable Oil
- 8 Chicken Tenderloins

Directions:

- Begin by preheating the air fryer. You should get the temperature to about 350 degrees F.
- Fetch a bowl and whisk an egg in it.
- In another bowl, mix some breadcrumbs and oil together. The mixture should be loose.
- Dip each chicken into the bowl containing the whisked egg, making sure the residue of the egg is not dripping. Next, dip the chicken into the crumb mixture, make sure that the chicken is covered thoroughly by the mixture.
- Place the chicken tenderloins into the air fryer. Cook. time is normally 12 mins and at that time, the chicken will no longer be pink. Alternatively, you can also insert a thermometer into the chicken to determine when the
- temperature has gotten high enough for the chicken to be done. The temperature should be about 165 degrees F for it to have been well

cooked.

300. Buttermilk Chicken

Prep time: 5 mins
Cook. time: 30mins
Servings: 6
Ingredients: :
- 1 cup Buttermilk
- 1 teaspoon Hot Sauce
- 1/3 cup Tapioca Flour
- ½ teaspoon Garlic Salt
- 1/8 teaspoon Ground Black Pepper
- 1 Egg
- ½ cup All-purpose Flour
- 2 teaspoons Salt
- 1 1/2 teaspoons Brown Sugar
- 1 teaspoon Garlic Powder
- ½ teaspoon Paprika
- ½ teaspoon Onion Powder
- ¼ teaspoon Oregano
- ¼ teaspoon Black Pepper
- 1 pound Skinless, Boneless Chicken Thighs

Directions:
- Preheat the air fryer. The temperature should be set to about 380 degrees F.
- Also use some parchment paper to line the air fryer basket.
- Grab two bowls. In one, mix the buttermilk and hot sauce in it and mix well.
- In the other, put in the tapioca flour, 1/8 teaspoon black pepper, and garlic salt and shake in order to mix well.
- Whisk the egg in another bowl.
- In a resealable bag, put in the flour, brown sugar, salt, garlic powder, onion powder, paprika, oregano and ¼ teaspoon black pepper. Shake very well to ensure that the **Ingredients:** mix thoroughly.
- You can begin dipping the chicken thighs into the mixed **Ingredients:** . The first should be the buttermilk mixture, next should be the tapioca mixture, and finally the flour mixture. You should make sure that you shake the chicken after every dipping to ensure that the extras get removed.
- Place the chicken into the air fryer and cook for 10 mins. Flip to the other side and cook for an extra 10 mins. You can remove it when the chicken no longer has a pink sheen.

301. Air Fried Buffalo Chicken:

Ingredients: :
- ½ cup Plain Fat-free Greek Yogurt
- ¼ cup Egg Substitute
- 1 tablespoon hot sauce
- 1 teaspoon Hot Sauce
- 1 cup Panko Bread Crumbs
- 1 tablespoon Sweet Paprika
- 1 tablespoon Garlic Pepper Seasoning
- 1 tablespoon Cayenne Pepper
- 1 pound Skinless Chicken Breasts, cut into 1 inch strips

Directions:
- Put the Greek yogurt, egg substitute, 1 tablespoon, and 1 teaspoon hot sauce and place into a bowl.
- In another bowl, place the panko breadcrumbs, paprika, garlic pepper and cayenne pepper and shake until all the **Ingredients:** mix thoroughly.
- Dunk the chicken strips into the yogurt mixture. After that, smear the panko bread mixture over the chicken strips.
- Place the chicken strips on the air fryer, making sure to place in a level, even pattern. Cooking should take 10 mins for each side of the chicken strip.
- Serve.

302. Chicken Wings

Prep time: 10 mins Cook time: 30 mins
Ingredients:
- 10 (about 1 1/2 pounds) chicken drumettes, pat dry
- Cooking spray
- 1 tbsp of lower-sodium soy sauce
- 1/2 tsp of cornstarch
- 2 tsp of honey
- 1 tsp of sambal oelek (ground fresh chili paste)
- 1 tsp of garlic, finely chopped
- 1/2 tsp of fresh ginger, finely chopped
- 1 tsp of fresh lime juice)
- 1/8 tsp of kosher salt
- 2 tbsp of chopped scallions

Directions
- Spray the chicken evenly with cooking spray.
- Arrange the chicken drumettes on their sides in the Air fryer basket to avoid overcrowding.
- Cook for 25 mins at 400°F, turning halfway through cooking until very crispy,

- While the chicken is cooking, in a small skillet, Whisk together cornstarch and soy sauce. Whisk in lime juice, ginger, garlic, sambal, honey, and salt over medium-high. Simmer until mixture is thickened and just begin to bubble.
- Toss the chicken and sauce in a bowl. Sprinkle with scallions.

303. Air fryer Chicken Meal

Prep time: 15 mins Cook time: 20 mins
Ingredients:
- 1 (3 to 4 pounds) broiler chicken, cut up
- 1 beaten large egg
- 1/4 tsp of rubbed sage
- 1/4 tsp of ground cumin
- 1/2 tsp of pepper
- 1 tsp of paprika
- 1 tsp of garlic salt
- 1 tbsp of minced fresh parsley
- 2 cups of crushed Ritz crackers

Directions
- Heat up the Air fryer to 375 Degrees and spray basket with cooking spray.
- Stir the third to ninth **Ingredients:** in a shallow bowl. In a different shallow bowl, place beaten egg. Dip the chicken in egg, allow to drip and then coat in garlic/crack- mixture, pat to make coating stay.
- Place coated chicken (in batches) in the Air fryer basket, in a single layer.
- Spray with cooking spray.
- Cook chicken for ten mins, flip and spray with more cooking spray; cook for 10-20 mins more until juices run clear and chicken is golden brown. Repeat steps to cook the remaining chicken.

304. Spicy Marinated Drumsticks

Prep time: 25 mins Cook time: 20 mins
Ingredients:
- 4 drumsticks
- 1 tbsp of olive oil
- Freshly ground black pepper
- 1 tsp of chili powder
- 2 tsp of brown sugar
- ½ tbsp of mustard
- 1 crushed clove garlic

Directions
- Preheat the Air fryer to 200°C.
- Mix the chili powder, brown sugar, mustard, garlic, freshly ground pepper

and a pinch of salt to taste. Mix with the olive oil. Add drumsticks and rub into the marinade, allow to marinate for 20 mins.

• Transfer the drumsticks into the Air fryer basket and roast for 10 mins at 200c until brown. Reduce the Air fryer temperature to 150°C and keep roasting for

• an additional 10 mins until its set. Serve the drumsticks with French bread and corn salad.

305. Crispy Chicken Wing Drumettes

Prep time: 10 mins Cook time: 15 mins
Ingredients:
• 1 tbsp of toasted sesame oil
• 1 tbsp of lower-sodium soy sauce
• Cooking spray
• 2 tbsp of chopped unsalted roasted peanuts
• 3 tbsp of honey
• 1 tbsp of chopped fresh chives
• 1/4 cup of rice vinegar
• 1 finely chopped garlic clove
• 3/8 tsp of crushed red pepper
• 10 large chicken drumettes
• 2 tbsp of unsalted chicken stock
Directions
• Arrange drumettes in Air fryer basket, in single layer; Spray generously with cooking spray.
• Cook for 30 mins at 400°F turning halfway through cooking until very crispy
• While the chicken is cooking, in a small skillet over medium-high, stir together garlic, crushed red pepper, oil, soy sauce, stock, honey and vinegar. Bring to a simmer and cook about 6 mins until almost syrupy and slightly thickened.
• Arrange chicken in a medium bowl, pour in the mixture, and toss to coat.
• Sprinkle with chives and peanuts.

306. Crispy Buttered Chicken Wings

Prep time: 10 mins Cook time: 45 mins
Ingredients:
• Fresh Lemons
• 1 tsp of True Lemon
• 3/4 cup of Potato Starch
• 1/2 cup of melted Butter
• 1 tbsp of Homemade Old Bay Seasoning Recipe

• 3 lbs of Chicken Wing, pat dry
Directions
• In a bowl, combine Old Bay Seasoning and Potato Starch.
• Add chicken and toss to coat. Shake chicken to drop excess seasoning/ starch
• Arrange in the Air fryer Basket and cook for 35 mins at 360 degrees, shaking constantly as you cook.
• Turn up the temperature to 400 F and continue cooking for 10 mins more, shaking constantly.
• Mix True Lemon with butter, add chicken wings and toss to coat. Serve with more Butter Lemon for dipping and squeeze of Lemons.

307. Yogurt Mix Buffalo Chicken

Prep time: 20 mins Cook time: 16 mins
Ingredients:
• 1 cup of panko bread crumbs
• 1 tbsp hot sauce plus 1 tsp of hot sauce
• 1/4 cup of egg substitute
• 1/2 cup of plain fat-free Greek yogurt
Directions
• Beat, egg substitute, Greek yogurt and hot sauce in a bowl.
• In a separate bowl, mix together the bread crumbs, cayenne pepper, garlic pepper, and paprika.
• In the bowl of yogurt mixture, dip the chicken strips; dredge in bread crumb mixture.
• Place the chicken strips in an Air fryer in a single layer. Cook for additional 8 mins until evenly browned per side.

308. Fresh Herb Turkey Breast

Prep time: 15 mins Cook time: 1 hr 3 mins
Ingredients:
• 1/4 tsp of ground pepper
• 1/2 tsp of fresh sage leaves, chopped or 1/4 teaspoon dried
• 1/2 tsp of fresh thyme leaves, chopped or 1/4 teaspoon dried
• 1 tsp of salt
• Cooking spray
• 1 (2 to 2 1/2 lb) of turkey breast half, (bone-in skin-on) patted dry
• 1 tbsp of softened butter
Directions
• Arrange 8" round parchment paper in

base of your Air fryer basket. Spritz
• with the cooking spray.
• Rub the turkey breast on all sides with softened butter; season with pepper, herbs and salt.
• Place the turkey breast in the Air fryer basket with the skin side facing up.
• Cook at 325°F for 30 mins.
• Carefully flip over using tongs and cook for extra 27 to 32 mins or until it reads at least 165°F at the thickest centre part and juice runs clear.
• Let stand out of the basket for 10 mins before slicing.

309. Tasty Air fryer Chicken Wings

Prep time: 10 mins Cook time: 20 mins
Ingredients:
• 2 pounds of chicken wings split and remove tips, Pat dry
• 1 1/2 tbsp of flour
• 2 tsp of baking powder
• 1/2 tsp of seasoned salt
• 1/2 tsp of black pepper
Directions
• Heat up the Air fryer to 400°F.
• Combine together the, baking powder, flour, pepper and salt, add the chicken wings and toss together. Shake any excess off.
• Arrange coated chicken wings in a single layer in the basket of the Air fryer and cook at 400°F for 20-22 mins shaking every 6 mins until crispy.
• If desired season more with pepper and salt and desired sauce.

310. Chicken Tenderloins

Prep time: 15 mins Cook time: 12 mins
Ingredients:
• 8 chicken tenderloins
• 2 tbsp of vegetable oil
• 1/2 cup of dry bread crumbs
• 1 egg
Directions
• Heat up your Air fryer to 350 F.
• Beat the egg in a mixing bowl. In a second bowl, mix together vegetable oil with the bread until mixture it's loose and crumbly.
• Dip chicken one by one into egg; shake any excess off, dredge chicken in the bread crumb mixture, press to adhere.
• Place the chicken tenderloins in the

Air fryer basket. Cook about 12 mins at 350 F until it reads at least 165°F at the thickest center part and juice runs clear.

311. Garlic Chicken Breasts

Prep time: 10 mins Cook time: 35 mins
Ingredients:
- 4 (6 oz each) skinless, boneless chicken breasts
- 1/4 tsp of black pepper
- 1/4 tsp of smoked paprika
- 1/4 tsp of garlic powder
- 1/2 tsp of salt
- 2 tbsp of melted butter

Directions
- Mix together the butter, smoked paprika, garlic powder, salt and pepper in small bowl.
- Brush the butter mixture on chicken breasts on both sides.
- Transfer the chicken into the Air fryer basket and cook for 15 mins at350 F.
- If you can, stand the chicken breast against sides of basket.
- Flip the chicken and cook for an additional 5 to 8 mins or until it reads at least 165°F at the thickest center part and juice runs clear.

312. Spicy AirFried Drumsticks

Prep time: 20 mins Cook time: 10 mins
Ingredients:
Pepper & Salt
- 1 teaspoon of Olive Oil
- 1 teaspoon of Chili Powder
- 2 teaspoon of Brown Sugar
- 1/2 tablespoon of Mustard
- 1 crushed garlic Clove
- 6 Chicken Drumsticks, skin on

Directions
- In a mixing bowl, mix together the olive oil, garlic, mustard, sugar, and chili powder. Season with salt and pepper.
- Place the drumsticks in the mixture, rub all over the marinade and leave for 20 mins or overnight.
- Heat-up your Air fryer at 200°C.
- Arrange the drumsticks in the basket of the Air fryer and roast for 10 mins.
- Flip and roast for another 10 mins with a temperature of 150°C until the drumsticks are cooked through.

313. Pickle Chicken Nugget

Prep time: 15 mins Cook time: 8 mins
Ingredients:

- Olive oil spraying
- ½ teaspoon of paprika
- 1½ teaspoon of pepper
- 2 teaspoon of salt
- 3 tablespoon of powdered sugar
- 1½ cups of flour
- 1 cup of milk
- 1 egg
- 1 pound skinless, boneless chicken breasts, cut into about 1 inch pieces
- 1 cup of dill pickle juice

Directions
- Marinate chicken chunks in the pickle juice and place about 30 mins in the refrigerator.
- Whisk together egg and milk in a bowl, set aside. In a separate bowl, combine together the dry **Ingredients:** .
- Heat up the Air fryer to 370 F. Remove the chicken and drain the pickle juice.
- Coat each chicken into the dry ingredients , shake off any excess.
- Dip coated chicken in the egg mixture and lastly, coat in the dry ingredient to coat well, shake off any excess.
- Spray coated chicken with olive oil and cook for 8 mins in the Air fryer in a single layer or until golden brown, flip and spray with additional oil just halfway through cooking.
- Serve over your desired dipping sauce.

314. Chicken Thai Peanut Egg Rolls

Prep time: 15 mins Cook time: 8 mins
Ingredients:
- Cooking spray
- 1/4 red bell pepper julienned
- 3 chopped green onions
- 1 very thinly sliced medium carrot or ribboned
- 1/4 cup of Thai peanut sauce
- 2 cups of shredded rotisserie chicken
- 4 egg roll wrappers

Directions
- Heat up the Air fryer to 390 degrees. Toss Thai peanut sauce with the chicken in a small bowl.
- Arrange each wrapper on a dry and clean surface. Layer 1/4 carrot, onions and bell pepper over the third bottom of the egg roll; wrapper and top with half cup of the chicken mixture.
- Gently moisten the outer wrapper

edges with water and fold Wrap edges toward the middle and roll firm.
- Do the same with the remaining wrappers.
- Sprits both sides of the prepared egg rolls with the spray.
- Transfer into the Air fryer for 6-8 mins at 390° or until outside of the egg rolls and golden brown and crispy.
- Half the egg roll and serve with extra Thai Peanut Sauce

315. Air fryer Popcorn Chicken

Prep time: 10 mins Cook time: 12 mins
Ingredients:
- Salt & Pepper
- 50 grams of Plain Flour
- 1 Small Egg beaten
- 1/4 cup of Bread Crumbs
- 2 ml of Spice Blend
- 1 Chicken Breast

Directions
- Blend the chicken in the food processor until it looks like minced chicken.
- In separate bowls, add flour, beaten egg and the last bowl mix pepper, spice blend, bread crumbs and salt.
- Shape chicken into balls, coat in the flour, and shake off any excess. Dip in egg and lastly coat the bread crumbs mixture.
- Arrange coated chicken balls in the Air fryer basket and cook for 10-12 mins at 180c or until cooked in the center.

316. Lemon Pepper Chicken

Prep time: 15 mins Cook time: 15 mins
Ingredients:
- Salt & Pepper
- 1 boneless Chicken Breast, trim of excess fat
- Handful of Black Peppercorns
- 1 teaspoon of Garlic Puree
- 1 Tbsp of Chicken Seasoning
- 2 Lemons rind and juice

Directions
- Heat up the Air fryer to 360 F. Layer a large sheet of silver foil on a work surface and add lemon rind seasonings to it.
- Season both sides of the chicken with salt and pepper and rub evenly with the chicken seasoning. The color will change slightly.

- Transfer unto the silver foil sheet; rub every part of the chicken well with the seasoning. Place in a zillop bag to get the season into it. Pat hard with a rolling pin to release more flavor and flatten out.
- Arrange in the Air fryer basket and cook at 360 F for 15 mins or until it's cooked through in the middle.
- Serve.

317. Old Bay Fried Chicken

Prep time: 4 mins Cook time: 25 mins
Ingredients:
- (Optional) cooking spray
- 1 teaspoon of seasoning salt
- 1 1/2 tablespoon of Old Bay Cajun Seasoning
- 4 small chicken thighs skin on
- 1 egg beaten
- 1/2 cup of all-purpose flour
Directions
- Preheat your Air fryer to 390 F. In a bowl, whisk together the Old Bay, flour and salt.
- Dip chicken in flour mixture, shake off excess, then dip in the egg, allow to drip and lastly dip again in the flour mixture. Shake any excess off. Lightly spray the chicken with cooking spray.
- Transfer into the Air fryer and cook at 180 degrees for 25 mins until the chicken is cooked through. Remove and serve.

318. Seasoned Air Fried Whole Chicken

Prep time: 5 mins Cook time: 50 mins
Ingredients:
- Dry rub recipe **Ingredients:** or your own seasonings
- 4.25 lbs of whole chicken, pat dry
Directions
- Sprinkle chicken very well with own seasonings or dry rub.
- Spritz the Air fryer tray with cooking spray, then arrange in the basket, legs facing down.
- Roast for 30 mins at 330 degrees F. Turnover and roast for 20 mins more at 330 or until cooked through.

319. Chicken With Fried Rice

Prep time: 10 mins Cook time: 20 mins
Ingredients:
- 1/2 cup of diced onion
- 1 tablespoon of vegetable oil
- 6 tablespoon of soy sauce
- 1 cup of carrots and peas, frozen
- 1 cup of diced cooked chicken
- 3 cups of cooked white rice cold
Directions
- In a mixing bowl, place the white rice and add soy sauce and vegetable oil.
- Mix thoroughly. Add the carrots, peas, onion and chicken. Mix well.
- Transfer the chicken/rice mixture into the nonstick cooking pan. Transfer the pan to the Air fryer and cook for 20 minute at 360 F. Once the time completes, withdraw from the Air fryer.
- Serve and enjoy!

320. Hearty Chicken Tenders

Prep time: 10 mins Cook time: 10 mins
Ingredients:
- 35 grams of Panko Bread Crumbs
- 1/8 Cup of Flour
- 1 Egg White
- Salt and Pepper
- 12 ounces of Chicken Breasts, trim excess fat and cut into tenders
Directions
- Season chicken tenders with salt and pepper on each side.
- Place the flour, egg whites and panko bread crumb in three different bowls.
- Dredge chicken in flour, shake off excess, then dip coated chicken in egg whites, and lastly dip in panko bread crumbs, shaking off any excess.
- Spritz the Air fryer basket with olive spray and cook for 10 mins at 350 degrees or until cooked through

321. Spring Rolls with Leftover Turkey

Prep time: 33 mins Cook time: 5 mins
Ingredients:
- 1 tablespoon of Chinese Five Spice
- 1 tsp of Coriander
- 1 tsp of Worcester sauce
- 1 tablespoon ofSoy Sauce
- 1 tablespoon of Honey
- Salt & Pepper
- 2 Large beaten eggs
- 30 grams of shredded leftover Turkey Breast
- 2 Tortilla Wraps
Directions
- Combine the leftover turkey with the seasonings in a mixing bowl, mix until well coated.

- Straighten tortilla wraps on a smooth surface without them breaking, then brush both sides of the tortilla with a little water, then brush with the egg. Place tortilla in the fridge for 1/2 hour for proper absorption.
- Remove tortilla and cut into eight equal spring roll sheets.
- Fill each spring roll sheet with the turkey filling and roll up in spring roll style.
- Brush once again with egg and transfer into the Air fryer. Air fry for 5 mins at 360 F. Serve.

322. Chicken Quesadilla With Green Peppers

Prep time: 15 mins Cook time: 10 mins
Ingredients:
- (Optional)Sour Cream for servings
- (Optional) Salsa for servings
- Shredded Mexican Cheese
- 1/2 cup of sliced onions
- Vegetable oil for spraying
- 1/2 cup of sliced green peppers
- Chicken Fajita Strips
- Soft Taco Shells
Directions
- Heat up the Air fryer at 370 degrees. Lightly Spritz Air fryer basket with vegetable oil and add one soft taco shell in basket. Layer the cheese, as you desire on shell.
- Place chicken strips on then in a single layer.
- Top with green peppers, onions and more shredded cheese.
- Layer top with another taco shell and lightly spritz with vegetable oil.
- 3. Cook for 4 mins then turn over gently using a large spatula. Lightly spritz with vegetable oil and cook for another 4 mins, place rack on the shells to prevent falling.
- For a more crispy chicken, leave for few more mins.
Remove and slice into 4 or 6 slices. If desired, serve with sour cream and Salsa.

Snacks And Appetizers

323. Pita Pizza

Preparation Time: 5 mins
Ingredients:
- ¼ cup pizza sauce

- 1 large thin pita bread
- ¼ cup sliced mushrooms
- 10 black olives
- ¼ cup green pepper
- ½ cup fat free mozzarella
- Pinch of pizza seasoning
- 2 teaspoon parmesan

Instructions:
- Preheat oven to broil.
- Spread the pita with pizza sauce.
- Layer on the vegetables and the top with the cheese and seasoning.
- Spray with cooking spray.
- Broil for 2 minutes.

324. Vegan Bacon Wrapped Mini Breakfast Burritos

Preparation time: 20 mins

Ingredients
- 2 tablespoons cashew butter
- 6-8 stalks fresh asparagus
- handful spinach, kale, other greens
- 2 – 3 tablespoons tamari
- 2 servings Vegan Egg scramble or Tofu Scramble
- veggie add-ins:
- ⅓ cup roasted sweet potato cubes
- 1 – 2 tablespoons liquid smoke
- 1-2 tablespoons water
- 4 pieces of rice paper
- 8 strips roasted red pepper
- 1 small tree broccoli, sautéed

Instructions
- Preheat Air Fryer to 350 °F.
- In a small shallow bowl, whisk together cashew butter, tamari, liquid smoke, and water. Set aside.
- Prepare all fillings to assemble rolls.
- Rice Paper Hydrating Technique: have a large plate/surface ready to fill/roll wrapper.
- Hold one rice paper under water faucet running cool water, getting both sides of wrapper wet, for just a few seconds.
- Remove from water and while still firm, place on a plate to fill – rice paper will soften as it sits, but will not be so soft that it sticks to the surface or rips when handling.
- Fill by placing ingredients just off from the middle, leaving sides of rice paper free.
- Fold two sides in like a burrito, roll

from ingredient side to other side, and seal.
- Dip each roll into cashew - liquid smoke mixture, coating completely. Arrange rolls on parchment
- Air fryer.
- Cook at 350 °F for 8-10 minutes, or until crisp.
- Serve warm

325. Baked Thai Peanut Chicken Egg Rolls

Preparation time: 18 mins

Ingredients
- 1 medium carrot, very thinly sliced or ribboned
- 3 green onions, chopped
- 4 egg roll wrappers
- 2 c. rotisserie chicken, shredded
- ¼ c. Thai peanut sauce
- ¼ red bell pepper, julienned
- non-stick cooking spray or sesame oil

Instructions
- Preheat Air fryer to 390° or oven to 425°.
- In a small bowl, toss the chicken with the Thai peanut sauce.
- Lay the egg roll wrappers out on a clean dry surface. Over the bottom third of an egg roll wrapper, arrange ¼ the carrot, bell pepper, and onions. Spoon ½ cup of the chicken mixture over the vegetables.
- Moisten the outside edges of the wrapper with water. Fold the sides of the wrapper toward the center and roll tightly.
- Repeat with remaining wrappers. (Keep remaining wrappers covered with a damp paper towel until ready to use.)
- Spray the assembled egg rolls with non-stick cooking spray. Turn them over and spray the backsides as well.
- Place the egg rolls in the Air fryer and bake at 390° for 6-8 mins or until they are crispy and golden brown.
- (If you are baking the egg rolls in an oven, place the seam side down on a baking sheet coated with cooking spray. Bake at 425° for 45-20 minutes.)
- Slice in half and serve with additional Thai Peanut Sauce for dipping.

326. Coconut Chicken Bites

Prep time: 10 mins

Cook time: 13 mins

Ingredients
- Garlic powder – 2 tsp.
- Eggs – 2
- Salt and black pepper to taste
- Panko bread crumbs – ¾ cup
- Coconut – ¾ cup, shredded
- Cooking spray
- Chicken tenders – 8

Directions:
- In a bowl, mix eggs with garlic powder, salt and pepper, and whisk well.
- In another bowl, mix coconut with panko and stir well.
- Dip chicken tenders in the egg mixture and then coat well with coconut mix-
- ture.
- Spray chicken bits with cooking spray.
- Place them in the air fryer basket and cook at 350F for 10 minutes.
- Serve.

327. Cauliflower Snack

Prep time: 10 mins

Cook time: 15 mins

Ingredients
- Cauliflower florets – 4 cups
- Panko bread crumbs – 1 cup
- Butter – ¼ cup, melted
- Buffalo sauce – ¼ cup
- Mayonnaise for serving

Directions:
- In a bowl, mix butter and buffalo sauce, and whisk well.
- Dip cauliflower florets in the mixture and coat them in panko bread crumbs.
- Place them in the air fryer basket and cook at 350F for 15 minutes.
- Serve.

328. Apple Snack

Prep time: 10 mins

Cook time: 5 mins

Ingredients
- Big apples – 3, cored, peeled and cubed
- Lemon juice – 2 tsp.
- Pecans – ¼ cup, chopped
- Dark chocolate chips – ½ cup
- Clean caramel sauce – ½ cup

Directions:
- Mix apples and lemon juice in a bowl.
- Place in a dish that fits in the air fryer.
- Add pecans and chocolate chips, then drizzle with caramel sauce. Toss to coat.

- Cook at 320F for 5 minsin the air fryer.
- Serve.

329. Zucchini Cakes

Prep time: 10 mins
Cook time: 12 mins
Ingredients
- Cooking spray
- Dill – ½ cup, chopped
- Egg – 1
- Whole wheat flour – ½ cup
- Salt and black pepper to taste
- Yellow onion – 1, chopped
- Garlic cloves – 2, minced
- Zucchinis – 3, grated

Directions:
- In a bowl, combine zucchinis with dill, egg, salt, pepper, flour, onion and
- garlic. Mix well.
- Make small patties with the mixture and spray them with cooking spray.
- Place them in the air fryer basket and cook at 370F for 6 minson each side.
- Serve.

330. Pesto Crackers

Prep time: 10 mins Cook time: 17 mins
Ingredients
- Baking powder – ½ tsp.
- Salt and black pepper to taste
- Flour – 1 ¼ cups
- Basil – ¼ tsp., dried
- Garlic – 1 clove, minced
- Basil pesto - 2 tbsp.
- Butter – 3 tbsp.

Directions:
- Mix butter, pesto, basil, cayenne, garlic, flour, baking powder, salt and pepper in a bowl and make a dough.
- Spread the dough on a lined baking sheet.
- Bake in the air fryer at 325F for 17 minutes.
- Cool and cut into crackers. Serve.

331. Pumpkin Muffins

Prep time: 10 mins Cook time: 15 mins
Ingredients
- Butter – ¼ cup
- Pumpkin puree – ¾ cup
- Flaxseed meal – 2 tbsp.
- Flour – ¼ cup
- Sugar – ½ cup
- Nutmeg – ½ tsp., ground
- Cinnamon powder – 1 tsp.
- Baking powder – ½ tsp.
- Egg – 1

- Baking powder – ½ tsp.

Directions:
- Mix butter, pumpkin puree and egg in a bowl, and blend well.
- Add cinnamon, nutmeg, baking powder, baking soda, sugar, flour and
- flaxseed meal.
- Spoon this into a muffin pan.
- Bake in the air fryer at 350F for 15 minutes.
- Serve.

332. Zucchini Chips

Prep time: 10 mins Cook time: 1 hour
Ingredients
- Zucchinis – 3, thinly sliced
- Salt and black pepper to taste
- Olive oil – 2 tbsp.
- Balsamic vinegar – 2 tbsp.

Directions:
- Mix vinegar, oil, salt and pepper, and whisk well.
- Add zucchini slices and toss to coat.
- Cook in the air fryer at 200F for 1 hour. Shake once.
- Serve.

333. Salmon Party Patties

Prep time: 10 mins Cook time: 22 mins
Ingredients
- Big potatoes – 3, boiled, drained and mashed
- Big salmon fillet – 1, skinless, boneless
- Parsley – 2 tbsp., chopped
- Dill – 2 tbsp., chopped
- Salt and black pepper to taste
- Egg – 1
- Bread crumbs – 2 tbsp.
- Cooking spray

Directions:
- Cook salmon in the air fryer basket at 360F for 10 minutes.
- Transfer salmon to a cutting board. Cool, flake it and put it in a bowl.
- Add bread crumbs, egg, parsley, dill, salt, pepper and mashed potatoes. Mix
- and shape 8 patties.
- Place salmon patties in the air fryer basket and spray with cooking oil.
- Cook at 360F for 12 minutes. Flip once at the halfway mark.
- Serve.

334. Spring Rolls

Prep time: 10 mins
Cook time: 25 mins
Servings: 8
Ingredients
- Green cabbage – 2 cups, shredded
- Yellow onions – 2, chopped
- Carrot – 1 grated
- Chili pepper – ½, minced
- Ginger – 1 tbsp.
- Garlic – 3 cloves, minced
- Sugar – 1 tsp.
- Salt and black pepper to taste
- Soy sauce – 1 tsp.
- Olive oil – 2 tbsp.
- Spring roll sheets – 10
- Corn flour – 2 tbsp.
- Water – 2 tbsp.

Directions:
- Heat oil in a pan over medium heat.
- Add soy sauce, pepper, salt, sugar, garlic, ginger, chili pepper, carrots, onions and cabbage.
- Stir-fry for 2 to 3 minutes.
- Remove from heat and let it cool down.
- Cut spring roll sheets in squares, distribute cabbage mixture on each and roll them.
- In a bowl, mix corn flour with water, stir well and seal spring rolls with this
- mixture.
- Place spring rolls in the air fryer basket and cook at 360F for 10 minutes.
- Flip roll and cook them for 10 minsmore.
- Serve.

335. Chickpeas Snack

Prep time: 10 mins Cook time: 10 mins
Ingredients
- Canned chickpeas – 15 ounces, drained
- Cumin – ½ tsp. ground
- Olive oil – 1 tbsp.
- Smoked paprika – 1 tsp.
- Salt and black pepper to taste

Directions:
- In a bowl, mix chickpeas with oil, salt, pepper, paprika and cumin. Toss to
- coat and place in the air fryer basket.
- Cook at 390F for 10 minutes.
- Serve.

336. Cheddar Bacon Croquettes

Active: 40 minstotal: 50 min
Ingredients :

•1 pound of sharp cheddar cheese,
•1 pound of bacon, thinly cut, room temperature
For the breading
•Four spoons full of olive oil
•1 cup of all-purpose flour
•Two eggs
•1 cup of seasoned breadcrumbs

Directions:

• Break the cheddar cheese block into six pieces of similar thickness, around 1-inch x 13⁄4- inch each.

• Take 2 slices of bacon and wrap them around each slab of cheddar, with the cheese fully enclosed.

• Take off some extra fat. Place the bacon cheddar bits in the freezer to firm for 5 minutes. Freeze not.

• Air fryer preheat to 390 ° F. Mix the oil than breadcrumbs, then whisk until

• the mixture is crumbly and loose. Place each block of cheddar in the flour, then put the eggs, then the breadcrumbs.

• Push the croquettes on paint and make sure it adheres.

• Place the croquettes in the basket and cook for 7-8 minsor until they are golden brown.

337. Feta Triangles

Active: 20 min total: 30 min serves: five

Ingredients :

•One egg yolk
•4 ounces of feta cheese
•Two tablespoons of flat-leafed parsley, finely chopped
•One scallion, finely chopped
•Two sheets of frozen filo pastry, defrosted
•Two tablespoons of olive oil.

Directions:

• In a pot, smash the egg yolk and blend in the feta, parsley, and scallion; sauté with pepper to taste. Cut into three strips each layer of filo dough.

• Scoop a full feta combination teaspoon at the underside of a pastry sheet.

• Fold over the tip of the pastry to shape a rectangle, fold the strip in a zigzag fashion until the filling is rolled into a rectangle. Repeat before both of the filo and feta is used.

• Air fryer preheat to 390 ° F. Brush the filo with a little oil and put three triangles in the basket for frying. Slide into the Air fryer basket and steam for 3 minutes.

• Change the temperature to 360 ° F, then cook until golden brown for 2 minutes.

• Repeat it with the remaining feta triangles.

338. Jerk Chicken Wings

Active: 15 minstotal: 45 min serves: 6

Ingredients :

•four pounds of chicken wings
•Two tablespoons of olive oil
•Two tablespoons of soy sauce
•Six cloves of garlic, finely chopped
•One habanero pepper, seeds and ribs cut, finely chopped
•One tablespoon of allspice
•One teaspoon of cinnamon
•One teaspoon of white pepper
•One teaspoon of salt
•Two tablespoons of brown sugar
•One tablespoon of fresh thyme, finely chopped
•One teaspoon of white pepper

Directions:

• Add all the ingredients in a mixing pot, completely coating the chicken with the seasonings and marinade.

• Switch to a 1-gallon jar, then efrigerate for up to 24 hours for 2 hours.

• Air fryer preheat to 390 ° F. Cut the wings and remove all liquid from the bag.

• Fully dry Pat wings with a paper towel. Place half the wings in the basket and cook for 14-16 minsevery pan, shaking halfway through.

• Serve with dipping sauce or ranch dressing in blue cheese.

339. Pigs in a Blanket

Active: fifteen min total: thirty min serves: four

Ingredients :

•12-ounce cocktail franks
•8-ounce crescent can of rolls

Directions:

• Remove from the box the cocktail franks, and drain; pat dry on paper towels.

• Cut the dough into triangular lines, around 1-inch x 1.5 inches.

• Roll the strips along with the franks, such that the ends are visible. Place it in the freezer to firm for 5 mins

• Air fryer preheat to 330 ° F. Take the franks from the fridge, then put half of them in the basket.

• Cook for 6-8 minsevery pan, or until golden brown.

340. Buffalo Cauliflower Bites

Ingredients :

•1 cup of all-purpose flour
•One teaspoon of kosher salt
•One teaspoon of garlic powder
•One teaspoon of onion powder
•Two eggs
•1/2 cup of whole milk
•2 cups Panko breadcrumbs
•One large head of cauliflower, sliced into florets
•1 1/2 cup of ranch dressing
•1 cup of hot sauce
•Chopped parsley, for garnishing

Directions:

• In a small dish, mix the flour, salt, garlic powder, and onion. In a second

• cup, whisk the egg and milk together. Place the Breadcrumbs in a separate bowl.

• Dip one flower of cauliflower into the flour mixture, then apply the mixture of eggs and then the breadcrumbs. Repeat before you bread all of the cauliflower.

• Without overcrowding, add some of the cauliflower to the fry basket.

• Pick the Fry configuration (8 minsto 400F degrees).

• Halfway swirl the tub. When time is up, cut the cauliflower with caution.

• Cook another 2-3 minsif the larger parts aren't fork-tender. Repeat until the entire cauliflower is baked.

• Meanwhile, whisk together the ranch and hot sauce in a large saucepan.

• Heat to dry, over low altitude. Put the cauliflower into the warm sauce and eat right away.

• Garnish with peregrinate.

341. Cheddar Scallion Biscuits

Ingredients

•2 cups of all-purpose flour
•Two tablespoons of baking powder
•1/2 teaspoon salt

•1/2 cup (4 ounces or eight tablespoons) cold unsalted butter, sliced into
eight parts
•1 cup shredded cheddar cheese
•1/4 cup crumbled bacon
•One scallion, minced
•1 cup cold strong whipping cream
Instructions
• Add the baking powder, flour, and salt in a bowl, using a pastry knife to remove the butter or use the fingers until the paste is crumbly and looks like little pebbles.
• Add the cheese, ham, scallion, and cream and stir until it is moistened and a dough forms.
• Knead the dough gently on a finely floured surface, about 3-4 times. Roll the dough to a thickness of ¾.
• Cut about nine biscuits (you would need to pick the scraps and roll them out again) using a two 1/2-inch diameter cookie cutter.
• Without overcrowding, add some of the biscuits to the fry bowl.
• Choose the environment for the bake, increase the temperature to 350 degrees F, and change the time to 20 minsor to a golden brown.
• Take off the biscuits gently until the time is over.
• Repeat until the biscuits are all baked.

342. Air Fryer Goat Cheese Balls

Prep Time: 10 mins
Cooking Time: 7 mins

Ingredients:
•8 oz. log Soft Goat Cheese
•2 tbsp Flour
•1 Egg, beaten
•½ cup Panko Breadcrumbs
•¼ cup Bee Harmony Honey

Directions:
• Cut the goat cheese into pieces (24 or more) and make them into balls. Put
• the balls onto a plate and place them into the refrigerator.
• After the balls are frozen, remove them from the refrigerator and coat them lightly with flour. When that is done, also dip the balls into the beaten egg.
• Use the Panko breadcrumbs to coat the cheese balls.

• There are two options available when you have breaded the goat cheese balls; you can either decide to cook them immediately or you could just put them into the refrigerator for 12 more hours.
• Whenever you decide to cook, whether immediately or after the 12 hours, arrange the goat cheese balls on the air fryer basket.
• You can spray the cheese balls with non-stick cooking spray or with olive oil to make sure that they do not stick to the frying basket.
• Set the air fryer to 390 degrees F and cook for 9 minutes. The cheese balls
• should be golden brown when they are done.
• Serve, with honey drizzled over them

343. Egg Rolls

Prep time: 30 mins Cooking time: 15 mins

Ingredients:
•2 cups Frozen Corn, thawed
•1 (15 ounce) can Black Beans, drained and rinsed
•1 (13.5 ounce) can Spinach, drained
•1 ½ cups Shredded Jalapeno Jack Cheese
•1 cup Sharp Cheddar Cheese, shredded
•1 (4 ounce) can Diced Green Chilies, drained
•4 Green Onions, sliced
•1 teaspoon Salt
•1 teaspoon Ground Cumin
•1 teaspoon Chili Powder
•1 (16 ounce) package Egg Roll Wrappers
•Cooking Spray

Directions:
• Start by preheating the air fryer to about 390 degrees F.
• Get a bowl and put in the beans, mix corn, spinach, jalapeno, cheddar
• cheese, jack cheese, green onions, green chilies, cumin, salt, and chili powder. Mix them together and put the bowl aside, the mixture will be used for the egg roll filling.
• Lay out the egg roll wrapper flat on the working table. Dip your finger into water and make use of the mixture to moisten all of the edges of the wrapper. Take a quarter of the filling and place it

at the center of the wrapper. Roll the wrapper to form a normal egg roll and set aside. Do the same until all of the filling is finished. Then spray all of the egg rolls.
• Place the egg rolls into the air fryer basket. Be careful to make sure that there is some space between the egg rolls. You do not have to cook everything at once.
• The cooking time should be 4 minutes. After that, the meal will be ready.

344. Energy Bites:

Prep time: 15 mins Servings: 6
Ingredients:
•1 cup Rolled Oats
•½ cup Mini, Semi-sweet Chocolate Chips
•½ cup Ground Flax Seed
•½ cup Crunchy Peanut Butter
•1/3 cup Honey
•1 teaspoon Vanilla Extract
Directions:
• Place the oats, chocolate chips, flaxseed, peanut butter, honey, and vanilla extract into a bowl and mix perfectly. Form them into balls using your hands.
• When they are formed into balls, arrange on a baking sheet and freeze.
• This should take about an hour after which it will be ready to be served.

345. Best Air fryer Fries

Prep time: 5 mins Cook time: 25 mins
Ingredients
• Salt & Pepper
• 4 tablespoon of Olive Oil
• 4 Medium peeled Potatoes, cut into fries
Directions
• Heat up the Air fryer to 360 F. Place the Potatoes fries in the Air fryer, add the olive oil and cook for 2 minutes. Shake well.
• Cook for another eight minutes, shake again.
• Cook more for additional 15 minutes.(If you prefer it golden fries, add additional 5 minsto the cooking time at 400 F).
• Season with salt and pepper.

346. Air fryer Crinkle Cut Chips

Prep time: 2 mins Cook time: 15 mins

Ingredients:
- 1 tablespoon of Olive Oil
- 1 Large Potato, peel and cut into crinkle (use a crinkle knife)
- Salt & Pepper to taste

Directions
- Season the crinkle cut chips with pepper and salt and then toss in the olive oil.
- Transfer to your Air fryer and cook for 15 mins at 400 Degrees, tossing midway through the cooking time.
- Best served with homemade tomato ketchup.

347. Air Fried Cashews

Prep time: 5 mins Cook time: 10 mins

Ingredients
- 2 tbsp of blackstrap molasses
- 3 tbsp of liquid smoke
- 2 tsp of salt
- 3 cups of whole raw cashews or halves and pieces

Directions
- Toss all of the ingredients together in a large bowl until evenly and well coated.
- In the Air fryer basket, place the cashews and cook for 8-10 mins at 350F, shaking regularly within 2 mins intervals to make sure the cashews are evenly cooked.
- Towards the final two mins of cooking, shake every minute and keep a close eye on the cashew to avoid burning.
- The cashew should be darken a bit.
- Allow cooling at room temperature for 10 to 15 minutes, will get crunchier once they're cooled.
- Store in an airtight container.

348. Potatoes Rösti With Salmon

Prep time: 10 mins Cook time: 15 mins

Ingredients
- 100 grams of smoked salmon
- 2 tbsp of sour cream
- Freshly ground black pepper
- 1 tbsp of finely chopped chives
- 250 grams of waxy potatoes, peeled and grate coarsely

Directions
- Heat up your Air fryer to 180°C. In a bowl, Place the potatoes, add 3/4 of the chives and season with salt and pepper.
- Mix well.

- Brush oil on a pizza pan and evenly share the potato mixture into the pan.
- Press potatoes into the pizza pan and brush with olive oil over the top.
- Transfer the pan into the Air fryer basket and slide in the basket and roast 15 mins until soft and the outside is nicely browned and set on the inside.
- Divide rösti into four equal portions and share among four plates.
- Serve aside slices of salmon on a plate and garnish with a spoonful of sour cream.
- Sprinkle sour cream with the remaining chives add a little ground pepper.

349. Ranch Seasoned Chickpeas

Prep time: 5 mins Cook time: 20 mins

Ingredients
- 2 tbsp of lemon juice
- 1 tsp of sea salt
- 1 batch of Homemade Ranch Seasoning
- 2 tbsp of olive oil - divided
- 1 15 oz can of chickpeas - drained, do not rinse

Directions
- Toss the chickpeas with 1 tbsp of the olive oil together in a small bowl.
- Place in the Air fryer and air fry for 15 mins at 400F.
- Remove chickpeas and transfer into the small bowl, add the remaining olive oil and toss with the lemon juice, salt and Ranch Seasoning until well coated.
- Place the coated chickpeas in the Air fryer basket and cook for additional 5 mins at 350F.
- Serve immediately or cool and store in an airtight container.

350. Fried Corn Tortilla Chips

Prep time: 1 mins Cook time: 3 mins

Ingredients
- Salt to season
- 1 tablespoon of olive oil
- 8 Corn Tortillas, Cut into triangles

Directions
- Heat up your Air fryer to 200C.
- Brush the triangles with olive oil.
- Do this in batches.
- Place tortilla triangles in the Air fryer basket and cook for three minutes.
- Repeat steps with the remaining

tortillas.
- Season with salt and serve.

351. Cinnamon Apple Chips

Prep time: 5 mins
Cook time: 8 mins
Servings: 1

Ingredients
- ¼ teaspoon of nutmeg
- ¼ teaspoon of cinnamon
- 1 medium thinly slice apple

Directions
- Heat up your Air fryer to 375° F.
- Mix cinnamon, apple slices, and nutmeg together in a bowl.
- Place in a single layer in the Air fryer basket and bake for 8 minutes, flipping midway through baking time.

352. Mini Frankfurters

Prep time: 10 mins Cook time: 20 mins

Ingredients
- 1 tbsp of fine mustard
- 100 grams of ready-made puff pastry, chilled or frozen, thwart (cut into 5 x 1½
- cm strips)
- 1 tin (about 20 frankfurters) of mini frankfurters (drained weight 220 g)

Directions
- Heat up your Air fryer to 400 F. Drain the sausages thoroughly on a paper
- towel and pat dry.
- Coat the puff pastry strips with a little layer of mustard. Roll strip of pastry
- around each sausage spirally.
- Transfer half of the pastry/sausages into the Air fryer basket and bake for 10 mins until golden brown.
- Repeat with the remaining pastry/sausages.
- Serve with a small dish of mustard.

353. Peppers With Goat Cheese

Prep time: 10 mins Cook time: 8 mins

Ingredients
- 100 grams of soft goat cheese, in 8 pieces
- 1 tsp of freshly ground black pepper
- ½ tbsp of olive oil
- 8 mini peppers or snack peppers, Cut and remove the seeds and membrane

Directions
- Heat up your Air fryer to 400 F.
- In a dip bowl, mix together the Italian herb, olive oil and pepper. Add the
- goat cheese and toss to coat.

- Press each goat cheese into each mini pepper. In the Air fryer basket, place each of the mini peppers beside each other and bake for 8 minsuntil the cheese melts.

354. Roasted Potatoes Paprika with Greek Yoghurt

Prep time: 10 mins Cook time: 20 mins

Ingredients
- 800 grams of waxy potatoes, peel and cut into 3 cm cubes
- 2 tbsp of olive oil
- 1 tbsp of spicy paprika
- Freshly ground black pepper
- 150 ml Greek yoghurt

Directions
- Heat up your Air fryer to 180°C.
- Soak potatoes cubes in water, about 30 minutes.
- Drain well and pat dry using a kitchen paper.
- Mix the paprika, 1 tbsp of olive oil with pepper in a medium-sized bowl. Add
- the potatoes, toss to coat well in the spicy oil.
- Cook in the Air fryer basket for 20 minutes, turning every now and then until they are golden brown and cooked through.
- Mix the remaining olive oil, Greek yoghurt, salt and pepper in a small bowl.
- Add a sprinkle of paprika. Serve potatoes in a platter with a sprinkle of salt and the yoghurt as a dip.
- Lovely with kebabs or with rib eye.

355. Mini Turkey Pies

Prep time: 2 mins Cook time: 10 mins

Ingredients
- 1 tablespoon of Coriander
- 1 teaspoon of Oregano
- 20 millimeter of Turkey Stock
- 200 millimeter of Homemade Tomato Sauce
- 50 millimeter of Whole Milk
- 50 millimeter of Coconut Milk
- 1 Small Egg beaten
- 50 grams of Shredded Turkey
- 8 Filo Pastry Slices
- Salt & Pepper

Directions
- In a mixing bowl, combine the wet ingredients with the exemption of egg and mix well. Add in the seasoning and turkey and mix well.
- Apply little flour on mini pie pot to prevent them from sticking and then line each with one sheet of filo pastry if possible.
- Fill each mini pie pot with the mixture, about ¾ full. Add the remaining pastry on top to cover, then brush with the egg.

356. Coated Pickles

Prep time: 20 mins Cook time: 15 mins

Ingredients
- (Optional) Ranch salad dressing
- Cooking spray
- 2 tbsp ofsnipped fresh dill
- 2 cups of panko (Japanese-style bread crumbs)
- 1/2 tsp of garlic powder
- 1/2 tsp of cayenne pepper
- 2 tbsp of dill pickle juice
- 3 lightly beaten large eggs
- 1/2 tsp of salt
- 1/2 cup of all-purpose flour
- 32 slices of dill pickle

Directions
- Heat up the Air fryer to 425 Degrees. Allow pickles stand about 15 minson a paper towel to drain liquid.
- Mix salt and flour in a bowl. Whisk pickle juice, eggs, cayenne and garlic powder in a separate bowl. In a third bowl, mix together the dill and panko.
- Coat pickles on both sides in flour mixture, shaking any excess off.
- Dip coated pickles in egg mixture, allow to drip, and then coat in the panko mixture, making sure it's well coated.
- Spray fryer basket with cooking spray, then the pickles.
- Place well coated pickles in basket, in a single layer, working in batches if needed.
- Cook about 7-10 minsuntil crispy and golden brown.
- Flip and spray with more cooking spray. Keep cooking about 7-10 minsuntil golden brown and crispy.
- Serve with ranch dressing if desired.

357. Garlic Cheese Pull Apart Bread

Prep time: 15 mins Cook time: 4 mins

Ingredients
- 2 teaspoon of Chives
- 30 grams of Edam Cheese
- 30 grams of Soft Cheese
- 30 grams of Mozzarella Cheese
- 30 grams of Goats Cheese
- 30 grams of grated Cheddar Cheese, four piles
- Salt & Pepper
- 2 teaspoon of Garlic Puree
- 100 grams of melted Butter
- 1 Large Bread Loaf

Directions
- Add the melted butter, garlic, chives, pepper and salt in a sauce pan 2 min-
- utes, mixing well.
- Create little slits with a bread knife into bread. Add garlic butter in each of the slit, then cover with soft cheese, it gives fine creamy taste.
- In some of the slits, fill with a little goats and cheddar cheese, then add mozzarella and Edam cheese to the ones that have not been filled.
- Transfer into the Air fryer and air fry for 4 minsor until the cheese melts

358. Skewer Yakitori

Prep time: mins Cook time: mins

Ingredients
- 8 skewer sitcks
- 1 tsp of garlic salt
- 1 tbsp of mirin
- 1 tsp of sugar
- 1/4 cup of dark or light soy sauce
- 5 green spring onions, cut into 1" length
- 4 pieces of chicken thigh, cut into 1" square

Directions
- Heat up the Air fryer to 180c.
- In a bowl of water, soak the skewer for 15 mins
- Alternately pierce skewer through the chicken and onion.
- To make the marinade, mix sugar, mirin, garlic salt, and soy sauce
- Place the chicken skewers into the marinade, let it marinate for a few hours.
- Transfer the chicken skewer into Air fryer and air fry at 180°c for 10 to 12 minsuntil chicken is cooked through.

359. Sausage Stuffed in Chicken

Prep time: 2 mins Cook time: 15 mins
Ingredients
- 8 skewer or toothpicks
- 4 chicken breast or thigh filet
- 4 favorite sausages

Directions
- Heat up the Air fryer to 375 °F
- Push the filets and roll for few minsusing a rolling pin.
- Arrange the chicken filets and place your sausage meat over the fillet. Fold filets over the sausage meat in half.
- Secure chicken/sausage by threading 2 skewer or toothpicks into each filet.
- Place chicken/sausage skewer in the Air fryer and cook for 15 mins at 375 °F

360. Flourless Crispy Calamari Rings

Prep time: 5 mins Cook time: 8 mins
Ingredients
- Salt & Pepper
- 1 teaspoon of Parsley
- 1 tablespoon of Paprika
- 1 Small Lemon juice and rind
- 1 Large Egg beaten
- 30 grams Calamari, slice into small rings
- 1 Cup of Gluten Free Oats

Directions
- Heat up the Air fryer to 360 F. Blitz the oats using a blender or food processor into breadcrumbs.
- In a bowl, add the beaten egg. In another bowl, place the oats and stir in the seasoning.
- Coat the calamari rings with lemon, pepper and salt on your chopping board.
- Coat the calamari rings in oats, dip in eggs and lastly coat in oats until well coated.
- Shake off excess oats.
- Transfer in the Air fryer basket and cook at 360 F for 8 minutes.

361. Peach Pies

Prep time: 20 mins Cook time: 1 hr
Ingredients
- Cooking spray
- 1 (14.1-ounces) package refrigerated pie crusts
- 1 tsp of cornstarch
- 1/4 tsp of table salt
- 1 tsp of vanilla extract
- 3 tbsp of granulated sugar
- 1 tbsp of fresh lemon juice
- 2 (5-oz.) of fresh peaches, peeled and chopped

Directions
- In a medium bowl, Mix together vanilla, sugar, lemon juice, peaches and salt. Let mixture stand for 15 minutes, stirring not too often.
- Drain the peaches, but reserve 1 tbsp.
- Whisk the reserved liquid with cornstarch and then mix into drained peaches.
- Slice piecrusts into 8 circles of about (4-inch). Add 1 tbsp of the filling in the
- middle of each.
- Brush dough edges with water; fold and crimp edges to seal; cut three small slits on the pies top and smear with cooking spray.
- Arrange three pies in Air fryer basket in single layer and cook for 12 to 14 minsat 350°F until golden brown.
- Repeat steps to cook the remaining pies.

362. Air Fryer Cheese Sticks Recipe

Preparation time: 22 mins
Ingredients
- 1/4 cup grated parmesan cheese
- 1 tsp. Italian Seasoning
- 1 tsp. garlic powder
- 6 snack-size cheese sticks (the individual ones you buy for kids)
- 2 large eggs
- 1/4 cup whole wheat flour (any type - pastry or white whole wheat work well)
- 1/4 tsp. ground rosemary

Instructions
- Unwrap your cheese sticks and set aside.
- Crack and beat your eggs with a fork a shallow bowl that is wide enough to fit the length of the cheese sticks.
- In another bowl (or plate), mix the flour, cheese, and seasonings.
- Roll the cheese sticks in the egg, then in the batter. Repeat until the cheese sticks are well coated.
- Place them in the basket of your air fryer, ensuring they don't touch.
- Cook to your air fryer's **Instructions**.

On mine, the temperature was 370 F. for 6-7 minutes.
- Serve with a clean marinara or ketchup

363. Healthy Air Fried Chicken Meatballs

Prep Time: 20 mins Total Time: 25 mins
Ingredients
- 1 Pound of ground chicken
- 2 Finely chopped green onions
- ½ Cup of chopped cilantro
- 1 Tbsp of Hoisin Sauce
- 1 Tbsp of soy sauce
- 1 tsp of Sriracha
- 1 tsp of sesame oil
- ¼ Cup of unsweetened shredded coconut
- 1 Pinch of salt
- 1 Pinch of ground black pepper

Instructions:
- Heat your Air Fryer to a temperature of about 350°F.
- Mix all your **Ingredients** in a large bowl. Line your Air Fryer baking pan with a paper sheet. With spoon, scoop the mixture into small rounds.
- Place the baking pan in your Air Fryer; then lock the lid of your Air Fryer. Set the timer to about 10 to 12 mins and the temperature to about 380° F
- When the timer beeps; turn off your Air Fryer; then remove the pan from the air fryer and set it aside to cool for about 5 minutes.
- Serve and enjoy your appetizing chicken balls!

364. Mexican Empanada

Preparation time: 40 mins
Ingredients
- 1 shallot, chopped
- 7 ounces store-bought pizza dough
- ¼ red bell pepper, diced
- 4 ½ ounces chorizo, cubed
- 2 tbsp. parsley

Instructions:
In a pan over medium heat, sauté the pepper, shallots, and chorizo together for 3-5 minutes.
Turn the heat off before adding in the parsley.
Take 20 small rounds from the dough. You may use a cookie cutter if you want.
Scoop out some of the chorizo mixture

and place it on the center of each round of dough. Fold and secure the edges. Do the same for the rest of the ingredients. Cook the empanadas in the air fryer at 390°F for 10-12 minutes.

365. Mushroom-Salami Pizza

Preparation time: 30mins

Ingredients

- 1 tsp. butter, melted
- ¼ cup tomato sauce
- 1 small, store-bought
- 8-in pizza dough
- ½ ball of mozzarella sliced thinly
- ½ tbsp. olive oil
- 3 mushrooms, sliced
- 1 ½ ounces salami, cut into strips
- Pepper to taste
- 2 tsp. dried oregano
- 2 tbsp. Parmesan cheese, grated

Instructions:

- Press and pat the dough on a well-greased pizza pan.
- Use the butter to grease the pan.
- Spread the sauce all over the dough then top it all with cheese.
- Now, sprinkle the mushrooms and salami over the pizza base.
- Season it with oregano, pepper, and cheese.
- Cook it in a preheated air-fryer at 390°F for 12 minutes.

366. Lemony Roasted Bell Peppers

Preparation time: 10mins

Ingredients

- 4 Bell Peppers
- 1 tsp. chopped Parsley
- ¼ tsp. minced garlic
- 1 tsp. Olive Oil
- Pinch of Sea Salt
- 1 tbsp. Lemon Juice
- Pinch of Pepper

Instructions

- Preheat your Air Fryer to 390 degrees
- Arrange the bell peppers in the Air Fryer and drizzle with the olive oil.
- Air Fry for 5 minutes. Transfer to a serving plate.
- In a small bowl, combine the lemon juice, garlic, parsley, salt, and pepper. Drizzle this mixture over the peppers.
- Serve and enjoy!

367. Crunchy Onion Rings

Preparation time: 10mins

Ingredients

- ¾ cup Breadcrumbs
- ¼ tsp. Salt
- ¾ Cup Milk
- 1 Large Onion 1 cup Flour
- 1 tbsp. Baking Powder
- 1 Egg
- ¼ tsp. Paprika

Instructions:

- Preheat your Air Fryer to 340°F.
- Whisk together the milk, eggs, flour, salt, and paprika in a bowl.
- Peel and slice the onion. Separate into rings.
- grease the Air Fryer with some cooking spray. Dip each onion ring into the batter and then coat with breadcrumbs.
- Arrange in the Air Fryer. Cook for 10 minutes.

Serve and enjoy!

368. Crispy Kale

Preparation time: 10 mins

Ingredients

- 1 tsp. soy sauce
- 1 tbsp. olive oil
- 4 cups kale leaves, torn into 1 ½ pieces

Instructions:

- Preheat the air fryer to 390°F.
- Season the kale with soy sauce and some olive oil.
- Cook it for 3-5 minutes.

369. Roasted Mushrooms

Preparation time: 40 mins

Ingredients

- 2 teaspoons of herbes de Provence
- 2 tbsp. of white (French) vermouth
- 2 pounds of mushrooms
- 1 tbsp. of duck fat
- ½ tsp. of garlic powder

Instructions

- Wash mushrooms and spin dry in a salad spinner, quarter them and set aside.
- Put duck fat, garlic and the herbes de Provence in the pan of your paddle type air fryer.
- Heat for 2 minutes. Stir with a wooden spoon if it clumped.
- Include mushrooms, cook for 25 mins Include vermouth and cook for an additional 5 minutes.

370. Crispy Kale Chips

Preparation time: 10 mins

Ingredients

- 1 head of kale
- 1 tbsp. of Olive oil
- 1 tsp. of soya sauce

Instructions

- Remove the center stem of the kale
- Tear the kale up into 1½" pieces.
- Wash clean and dry thoroughly.
- Toss with the olive oil and soya sauce.
- Fry in the air fryer at 200oC for 2 to 3 minutes, tossing the leaves halfway through.

371. Air Fried Vegetable Spring Rolls

Preparation time: 40 mins

Ingredients

- 10 spring roll sheets
- 5-6 mushrooms, sliced
- 1 clove garlic, smashed
- 1/4 yellow bell pepper, thinly sliced
- 1/4 red bell pepper, thinly sliced
- 1 tsp. galangal/ginger, minced
- 1 green onion, finely chopped
- 1/2 cup carrot, thinly sliced
- 1/2 cup cabbage, thinly sliced
- 2 birds eye chilies, finely chopped
- 1 tbsp. soya sauce
- 1 tbsp. vegetarian oyster sauce (optional)

To serve

- 2 tbsp. sweet chili sauce
- 2 tbsp. soya sauce

Instructions

- In a small saucepan, sauté the green onion, ginger, and garlic until soft and fragrant.
- Mix in the carrot and after a few mins the rest of the vegetables (except the chilies). The pan may seem overcrowded but in a few mins the vegetables will release their juices and it will cook down noticeably.
- Add the soy sauce and the oyster sauce and cook for 10-12 minutes, stirring occasionally.
- Once the pan seems dry (no liquid is visible when you move the vegetables around), take off the heat, add the chilies to taste, and leave to cool completely.
- Remove the spring roll sheets from the freezer and cover with a cloth, for approx. 30 mins until the vegetables

cool.

- Preheat the air fryer to 200*.
- Place a single sheet on a clean surface/plate in a diamond shape (as pictured above). Place a tablespoon full on the mixture once inch from the triangle closest to you.
- Roll tightly halfway, tuck on the left and right corners and continue rolling. It's actually really easy.
- Place on the rack of the air fryer and brush with a little bit of vegetable oil. Air fry, shaking every few mins and brushing with oil if it looks very dry. Your perfect golden brown and super crisp spring rolls will be ready in under 10 minutes.
- Enjoy served with 2 dipping sauces - soy and sweet chili.

372.Parsley Flakes Onion Chips

Prep Time: 9 mins
Total Time: 10 mins
Ingredients
- 1 Onion
- 1 Large egg
- 2 Tbsp of coconut flour
- 2 Tbsp of grated parmesan cheese
- 1/8 tsp of garlic powder
- ¼ tsp of parsley flakes
- 1/8 tsp of cayenne pepper
- 1 Pinch of salt
- 1 Tbsp of olive oil
Instructions:
- Preheat your Air Fryer to a temperature of 360° F
- Crack the egg and beat it a shallow bowl
- Mix the parmesan with the coconut flour, the garlic powder, the parsley flakes, the cayenne and the salt in a shallow bowl
- Slice the onion into rings of about ½ inch of thickness
- Add the onion rings to the egg wash for about 1 minute; then coat very well
- Remove the onion rings from the egg wash; then coat it in the shallow dish of the flour
- Arrange the onion rings in the Air Fryer basket; then drizzle with 1 tbsp of oil
- Lock the lid of your Air Fryer
- Set the timer for about 9 to 10 mins and set the temperature to about

200°C/ 390° F
- When the timer beeps; turn off your Air Fryer
- Serve and enjoy your delicious appetizer!

373.Air Fried Shrimp Tails

Prep Time: 15 mins Total Time: 20 mins
Ingredients
- 1 lb of peeled and deveined raw Shrimp
- 1 Cup of almond flour
- 1 tbsp of pepper to taste
- 1 tbsp of salt
- 1 tsp of cayenne pepper
- 1 tsp of cumin
- 1 tsp of garlic powder
- 1 tbsp of paprika
- 1 tbsp of onion powder
Instructions:
- Preheat your Air Fryer to a temperature of 390° F
- Peel the shrimp and devein it
- Dip in the shrimp into the heavy cream
- Dredge the shrimp into the mixture of the almond flour
- Shake off any excess of flour
- Put the shrimp in the Air Fryer basket and
- Lock the lid of your Air Fryer and set the timer to about 15 mins and the temperature to 200° C/400° F
- You can check your appetizer after about 6 mins and you can flip the shrimp if needed
- When the timer beeps; turn off your Air Fryer
- Serve and enjoy your shrimps!

374. Air fried Radish with Coconut Oil

Prep Time: 12 mins Total Time: 15 mins
Ingredients
- 16 Ounces of fresh radishes
- 2 tbsp of melted coconut oil
- ½ tsp of sea salt
- ½ tsp of pepper
Instructions:
- Preheat your Air Fryer to a temperature of about 400 degrees F.
- Slice the radishes into thin slices
- Place the radish slices in a bowl and toss it with oil
- Lay the radishes in the Air Fryer basket

- Whisk the pepper and the salt together; then sprinkle it over the radishes
- Lock the lid of your Air Fryer and set the timer for about 12 mins
- Set the temperature to about 200° C/400° F
- When the timer beeps; turn off your Air Fryer
- Remove the pan from the air fryer
- Serve and enjoy your air fried radishes!

375.Air fried Okra with Parmesan Cheese

Prep Time: 25 mins Total Time: 10 mins
Ingredients
- 1 Pound of fresh okra
- 1 tsp of sea salt
- 2 tbsp of almond flour
- ¼ Cup of finely grated Parmesan cheese
- ½ tsp of pepper
- 1 Pinch of sea salt
Instructions:
- Preheat your Air Fryer to a temperature of about 390° F
- Wash the okra; then chop it into small pieces
- Toss the chopped okra with the salt and a little bit of ground pepper; then set it aside for about 3 mins
- In a bowl; mix the almond flour with Parmesan cheese, the pepper, and the salt
- Coat the okra pieces into the mixture and place it in your Air Fryer basket
- Lock the lid and set the timer to about 25 mins and the temperature to 390° F
- When the timer beeps; turn off your Air Fryer
- Remove the pan; then serve and enjoy your okras!

376.Chicken Nuggets with Almond Flour

Prep Time: 15 mins Total Time: 18 mins
Ingredients
- 1 Whisked egg
- 4 tbsp of oil
- 2 lbs of chicken breast
- 1 Cup of almond flour
- ½ tsp of salt
- ½ tsp of garlic powder
- 1 tsp of onion flakes

Instructions

- Combine the egg and the oil and whisk very well
- In a separate bowl; combine the almond flour, the salt, the garlic and the onion
- Cut the chicken breast meat into thin strips; then dip each of the strips into the egg mixture and coat very well
- Arrange the chicken nuggets in the Air Fryer basket and spray with a little bit of oil
- Lock the lid of the Air Fryer and set the timer for about 15 mins and set the temperature for about 180° C/350° F
- When the timer beeps; turn off your Air Fryer
- Serve and enjoy the chicken nuggets!

377. Easy Crab Sticks

Preparation time: 15 mins

Ingredients

- 20 ounces crabsticks, sliced into thin strips
- 2 tsps. sesame oil
- 1 tsp. Cajun seasoning

Instructions:

- Season the crabsticks with some Cajun seasoning and sesame oil.
- Cook it in the air fryer at 320°F for 10-12 minutes

378. Sausage Balls

Preparation time: 30 mins

Ingredients

- 1 tsp. sage
- 3 tbsp. breadcrumbs
- ¼ tsp. salt
- 3 ½ ounces sausage meat
- 1 onion, diced
- ½ tsp. garlic powder
- 1/8 tsp. black pepper

Instructions:

- Mix all the **Ingredients** in the bowl.
- Take about 2-3 tbsp. of the mixture and roll it into a ball in between your palms.
- Do the same for the rest of the mixture.
- Cook the meatballs in a preheated air fryer at 350°F for 15-20 minutes.

379. Cajun Salmon

Preparation time: 10 mins

Ingredients

- 0.44lbs/1 piece of fresh salmon fillet

- Cajun seasoning
- Juice from ¼ of lemon to serve

Direction

- Preheat Air Fryer to 180oC for 5 minutes.
- Clean the salmon and pat dry.
- In a plate, sprinkle Cajun seasoning all over and ensure all sides are coated.
- Air fry for a salmon fillet about ¾ of an inch thick, air fry for 7 minutes, skin side upon the grill pan.
- Serve hot or immediately with a squeeze of lemon.

SEAFOODS

380. Cheesy Bacon Wrapped Shrimp

Preparation time: 20mins

Ingredients

- 16 extra-large raw shrimp, peeled, deveined, and butterflied
- 16 (1 in) cubes cheddar jack cheese
- 16 slices of bacon, cooked half way
- ¼ cup BBQ sauce

Instructions

- Preheat the air fryer to 350 degrees F.
- Stuff each shrimp with a cheese cube and wrap with a slice of bacon.
- Secure the bacon to the shrimp with a toothpick.
- Brush the wrapped shrimp with BBQ sauce and place in the air fryer.
- Cook for 6 minutes.
- Remove and brush with additional BBQ sauce.

381. Salmon Quiche

Preparation time: 60mins

Ingredients

- 2 cups salmon, skinless and cubed
- 1 tsp. salt
- ¼ tsp. ground black pepper
- 1 (9 in) premade pie crust
- 3 large eggs
- 1 tbsp. Dijon mustard
- ¼ cup green onion, chopped
- ½ cup shredded mozzarella cheese
- 4 tbsp. heavy cream

Instructions

- Preheat the air fryer to a temperature of 350 degrees F
- Then, Season the salmon with salt and pepper to your taste. Set aside. Place the pre-made pie crust into individual quiche pans and press into the sides of the pans.

- Trim off any overhanging crust. Trim the dough onto the edges of the pan you intend to use or just let it stick out.
- Place the cubed salmon into the crust and top with the green onion and mozzarella. In a mixing bowl, combine the heavy cream, eggs, and mustard.
- Carefully pour over the salmon, being careful not cause the mixture to overflow.
- Carefully slide the quiche into the fryer basket and cook for 20 minutes.
- Let rest for 10 mins before serving.

382. Frozen sesame Fish Fillets

Prep Time: 20 minutes

Ingredients:

- 5 frozen fish fillets
- 5 biscuits, crumbled
- 3 tbsp. flour
- 1 egg, beaten
- Pinch of salt
- Pinch of black pepper
- ¼ tsp. rosemary
- 3 tbsp. olive oil divided
- A handful of sesame seeds

Instructions:

- Preheat the air fryer to 390 degrees F.
- Combine the flour, pepper and salt, in a shallow bowl. In another shallow bowl, combine the sesame seeds, crumbled biscuits, oil, and rosemary.
- Dip the fish fillets into the flour mixture first, then into the beaten egg, and finally, coat them with the sesame mixture. Arrange them inside the air fryer on a sheet of aluminum foil. Cook the fish for 8 minutes.
- Flip the fillets over and cook for additional 4 minutes.

383. Fish Tacos

Prep Time: 15 minutes

Ingredients:

- 4 corn tortillas
- 1 halibut fillet
- 2 tbsp. olive oil1
- ½ cup flour, divided
- 1 can of beer
- 1 tsp. salt
- 4 tbsp. peach salsa
- 4 tsp. chopped cilantro1 tsp. baking powder

Instructions:

- Preheat the air fryer to 390 degrees F.

- Combine 1 cup of flour, baking, powder and salt.
- Pour in some of the beer, enough to form a batter-like consistency. Save the rest of the beer to gulp with the taco.
- Slice the fillet into 4 strips and toss them in half cup of flour. Dip them into the beer batter and arrange on a lined baking sheet.
- Place in the air fryer and cook for 8 minutes.
- Meanwhile, spread the peach salsa on the tortillas.Top each tortilla with one fish strip and 1 tsp. chopped cilantro.

384.Peppery and Lemony Haddock

Prep Time: 15 minutes
Ingredients:
- 4 haddock fillets
- 1 cup breadcrumbs
- 2 tbsp. lemon juice
- ½ tsp. black pepper
- ¼ cup dry instant potato flakes1 egg, beaten¼ cup Parmesan cheese
- 3 tbsp. flour
- ¼ tsp. salt

Instructions:
- Combine the flour, pepper and salt, in a small shallow bowl. In another bowl, combine the lemon, breadcrumbs, Parmesan, and potato flakes.
- Dip the fillets in the flour first, then in the beaten egg, and coat them with the lemony crumbs.
- Arrange on a lined sheet and place in the air fryer.
- Air fry for about 8 to 10 mins at 370 degrees F.

385.Soy Sauce Glazed Cod

Prep Time: 15 minutes
Ingredients:
- 1 cod fillet1 tsp. olive oil
- Pinch of sea salt
- Pinch of pepper
- 1 tbsp. soy sauce
- Dash of sesame oil
- ¼ tsp. ginger powder
- ¼ tsp. honey

Instructions:
- Preheat the air fryer to 370 degrees F.
- Combine the olive oil, salt and pepper, and brush that mixture over the cod.
- Place the cod onto an aluminum sheet

and into the air fryer.Cook for about 6 minutes.
- Meanwhile, combine the soy sauce, ginger, honey, and sesame oil.Brush the glaze over the cod.
- Flip the fillet over and cook for additional 3 minutes.

386.Salmon Cakes

Prep Time: 1 hour and 15 minutes
Ingredients:
- 10 oz. cooked salmon
- 14 oz. boiled and mashed potatoes
- 2 oz. flour
- Handful capers
- Handful chopped parsley
- 1 tsp. olive oil
- Zest of 1 lemon

Instructions:
- Place the mashed potatoes in a large bowl and flake the salmon over.
- Stir in capers, parsley, and lemon zest.Shape small cakes out of the mixture.
- Dust them with flour and place in the fridge to set, for about 1 hour.Preheat the air fryer to 350 degrees F.Brush the olive oil over the basket's bottom and add the cakes.Cook for about 7 minutes.

387.Tasty Cod

Prep time: 10 minsCook time: 12 mins
Ingredients
- Cod fillets – 2 (7-ounces each)
- Sesame oil – 1 drizzle
- Salt and black pepper to taste
- Water – 1 cup
- Dark soy sauce – 1 tsp.
- Light soy sauce – 4 tbsp.
- Sugar – 1 tbsp.
- Olive oil – 3 tbsp.
- Ginger – 4 slices
- Spring onions – 3, chopped
- Coriander – 2 tbsp., chopped

Directions: :
- Season fish with sesame oil, salt and pepper. Rub well and set aside for 10
- minutes.
- Cook in the air fryer at 356F for 12 minutes.
- Meanwhile, heat up a pot with water over medium heat.
- Add both soy sauces and sugar, stir and bring to a simmer. Remove from
- heat.

- Heat olive oil in a pan over medium heat. Add green onions and ginger, stir
- and cook for a few minsthen remove from heat.
- Divide fish among plates, top with green onions and ginger.
- Drizzle with soy sauce mix and sprinkle with coriander.
- Serve.

388.Tasty Cod

Prep time: 10 mins Cook time: 12 mins
Servings: 4
- Cod fillets – 2 (7-ounces each)
- Sesame oil – 1 drizzle
- Salt and black pepper to taste
- Water – 1 cup
- Dark soy sauce – 1 tsp.
- Light soy sauce – 4 tbsp.
- Sugar – 1 tbsp.
- Olive oil – 3 tbsp.
- Ginger – 4 slices
- Spring onions – 3, chopped
- Coriander – 2 tbsp., chopped

Directions: :
- Season fish with sesame oil, salt and pepper. Rub well and set aside for 10
- minutes.
- Cook in the air fryer at 356F for 12 minutes.
- Meanwhile, heat up a pot with water over medium heat.
- Add both soy sauces and sugar, stir and bring to a simmer. Remove from
- heat.
- Heat olive oil in a pan over medium heat. Add green onions and ginger, stir
- and cook for a few minsthen remove from heat.
- Divide fish among plates, top with green onions and ginger.
- Drizzle with soy sauce mix and sprinkle with coriander.
- Serve.

389.Buttered Shrimp Skewers

Prep time: 10 mins Cook time: 6 mins
Ingredients
- Shrimps – 8, peeled and deveined
- Garlic – 4 cloves, minced
- Salt and black pepper to taste
- Green bell pepper slices – 8
- Rosemary – 1 tbsp., chopped
- Butter – 1 tbsp., melted

Directions: :
- In a bowl, mix bell pepper slices,

rosemary, pepper, salt, butter, garlic and shrimp.

• Toss to coat and marinate for 10 minutes.

• Arrange 2 bell pepper slices and 2 shrimps on a skewer and repeat with the rest of the shrimp and bell pepper pieces.

• Cook them at 360F for 6 minutes.

• Serve.

390. Tasty Salmon

Prep time: 1 hour Cook time: 8 mins

Ingredients

• Salmon fillets – 2
• Lemon juice – 2 tbsp.
• Salt and black pepper to taste
• Garlic powder – ½ tsp.
• Water – 1/3 cup
• Soy sauce – 1/3 cup
• Scallions – 3, chopped
• Brown sugar – 1/3 cup
• Olive oil – 2 tbsp.

Directions: :

• In a bowl, mix water, sugar, garlic powder, soy sauce, salt, pepper, oil and lemon juice. Whisk well and add salmon fillets.

• Coat well and marinate in the refrigerator for 1 hour.

• Cook salmon in the air fryer at 360F for 8 minutes. Flip once.

• Divide salmon among plates. Sprinkle scallions on top and serve.

391. Asian Halibut

Prep time: 30 mins Cook time: 10 mins

Ingredients

• Halibut steaks – 1 pound
• Soy sauce – 2/3 cup
• Sugar – ¼ cup
• Lime juice – 2 tbsp.
• Mirin – ½ cup
• Red pepper flakes – ¼ tsp., crushed
• Orange juice – ¼ cup
• Ginger – ¼ tsp., grated
• Garlic – 1 clove, minced

Directions: :

• Pour soy sauce in a pan and heat over medium heat.

• Add garlic, ginger, pepper flakes, orange juice, lime, sugar and mirin.

• Stir well, bring to a boil and remove from heat.

• Transfer half of the marinade to a bowl, add halibut, toss to coat and mari-

nate in the refrigerator for 30 minutes.

• Cook halibut in the air fryer at 390F for 10 minutes. Flip once.

• Divide halibut steaks among plates, drizzle the rest of the marinade all over and serve.

392. Seafood Casserole

Prep time: 10 mins Cook time: 40 mins

Ingredients

• Butter – 6 tbsp.
• Mushrooms – 2 ounces, chopped
• Green bell pepper – 1 small, chopped
• Celery – 1 stalk, chopped
• Garlic – 2 cloves, minced
• Small yellow onion – 1, chopped
• Salt and black pepper to taste
• Flour – 4 tbsp.
• White wine – ½ cup
• Milk – 1 ½ cups
• Heavy cream – ½ cup
• Sea scallops – 4, sliced
• Haddock – 4 ounces, skinless, boneless and cut into small pieces
• Lobster meat – 4 ounces, cooked and cut into small pieces
• Mustard powder – ½ tsp.
• Lemon juice – 1 tbsp.
• Bread crumbs – 1/3 cup
• Salt and black pepper to taste
• Cheddar cheese – 3 tbsp., grated
• Handful parsley, chopped
• Sweet paprika – 1 tsp.

Directions: :

• Heat 4 tbsp. butter in a pan over medium-high heat.

• Add wine, onion, garlic, celery, mushrooms and bell pepper, and cook for 10 minutes.

• Add milk, cream and flour, stir well and cook for 6 minutes.

• Add haddock, lobster meat, scallops, mustard powder, salt, pepper and lemon juice, and stir well. Remove from heat and place in a pan.

• In a bowl, mix the rest of the butter with cheese, paprika and bread crumbs, and sprinkle over seafood mix.

• Transfer the pan to the air fryer and cook at 360F for 16 minutes.

• Serve garnished with parsley.

393. Creamy Salmon

Prep time: 10 mins Cook time: 10 mins

Ingredients

• Salmon – 4 fillets, boneless
• Olive oil – 1 tbsp.
• Salt and black pepper to taste
• Cheddar cheese – 1/3 cup, grated
• Mustard – 1 ½ tsp.
• Coconut cream – ½ cup

Directions: :

• Season salmon with salt and pepper. Drizzle with oil and rub well.

• In a bowl, mix cheddar, coconut cream, mustard, salt and pepper, and stir well.

• Transfer salmon to a pan and add coconut cream mixture.

• Cook in the air fryer at 320F for 10 minutes.

• Serve.

394. Creamy Shrimp and Veggies

Prep time: 10 mins Cook time: 30 mins

Ingredients

• Mushrooms – 8 ounces, chopped
• Asparagus – 1 bunch, cut into medium pieces
• Shrimp – 1 pound, peeled and deveined
• Salt and black pepper to taste
• Spaghetti squash – 1, cut into halves
• Olive oil – 2 tbsp.
• Italian seasoning – 2 tsp.
• Yellow onion – 1, chopped
• Red pepper flakes -1 tsp., crushed
• Butter – ¼ cup, melted
• Parmesan cheese – 1 cup, grated
• Garlic – 2 cloves, minced
• Heavy cream – 1 cup

Directions: :

• Cook squash halves in the air fryer at 390F for 17 minutes. Transfer to a cut-
• ting board, scoop insides and transfer to a bowl.

• Bring a pot of lightly salted water to boil. Add asparagus and steam for a
• couple of minutes. Then remove and place in ice water, drain and set aside.

• In a pan, heat up oil over medium heat. Add mushrooms and onions, and stir-fry for 7 minutes.

• Add garlic, parmesan, cream, melted butter, shrimp, asparagus, squash, salt, pepper, seasoning and pepper flakes. Toss and cook in the air fryer at 360F for 6 minutes.

• Serve.

395. Cajun Style Shrimp

Preparation time: 3 mins
Cooking time: 10 mins
Ingredients :
- 6g of salt
- 2g smoked paprika
- 2g garlic powder
- 2g Italian seasoning
- 2g chili powder
- 1g onion powder
- 1g cayenne pepper
- 1g black pepper
- 1g dried thyme
- 454g large shrimp, peeled and unveiled
- 30 ml of olive oil
- Lime wedges, to serve

Directions: :
- Select Preheat, in the air fryer, set the temperature to 190°C and press Start/ Pause.
- Combine all seasonings in a large bowl. Set aside
- Mix the shrimp with olive oil until they are evenly coated.
- Sprinkle the dressing mixture over the shrimp and stir until well coated.
- Place the shrimp in the preheated air fryer.
- Select Shrimp set the time to 5 minsand press Start/Pause.
- Shake the baskets in the middle of cooking.
- Serve with pieces of lime.

396.Tuna Pie

Preparation time: 10 mins
Cooking time: 30 mins
Ingredients :
- 2 hard-boiled eggs
- 2 tuna cans
- 200 ml fried tomato
- 1 sheet of broken dough.

Directions: :
- Cut the eggs into small pieces and mix with the tuna and tomato.
- Spread the sheet of broken dough and cut into two equal squares.
- Put the mixture of tuna, eggs, and tomato on one of the squares.
- Cover with the other, join at the ends and decorate with leftover little pieces.
- Preheat the air fryer a few minsat 1800C.
- Enter in the air fryer basket and set

the timer for 15 mins at 180

397.Cajun Style Catfish

Preparation time: 3 mins
Cooking time: 7 mins
Ingredients :
- 5g of paprika
- 3g garlic powder
- 2g onion powder
- 2g ground dried thyme
- 1g ground black pepper
- 1g cayenne pepper
- 1g dried basil
- 1g dried oregano
- 2 catfish fillets (6 oz)
- Nonstick Spray Oil

Directions: :
- Preheat the air fryer for a few minutes. Set the temperature to 175°C.
- Mix all seasonings in a bowl.
- Cover the fish generously on each side with the dressing mixture.
- Spray each side of the fish with oil spray and place it in the preheated air fryer.
- Select Marine Food and press Start /Pause.
- Remove carefully when you finish cooking and serve on semolina

398.Fish Tacos

Preparation time: 10 mins
Cooking time: 7 mins
Ingredients :
- 454g of tilapia, cut into strips of
- 38 mm thick
- 52g yellow cornmeal
- 1g ground cumin
- 1g chili powder
- 2g garlic powder
- 1g onion powder
- 3g of salt
- 1g black pepper
- Nonstick Spray Oil
- Corn tortillas, to serve
- Tartar sauce, to serve
- Lime wedges, to serve

Directions: :
- Cut the tilapia into strips 38 mm thick.
- Mix cornmeal and seasonings in a shallow dish.
- Cover the fish strips with seasoned cornmeal. Set aside in the fridge.
- Preheat the air fryer for 5 minutes. Set the temperature to 170°C.

- Sprinkle the fish coated with oil spray and place it in the preheated air fryer.
- Put the fish in the air fryer, set the timer to 7 minutes.
- Turn the fish halfway through cooking.
- Serve the fish in corn tortillas with tartar sauce and a splash of lemon

399.Salmon and Veggie Patties

Preparation time: 15 mins
Cooking time: 7 mins
Ingredients :
- 3 large russet potatoes, boiled and mashed
- 1 (6-ounce) salmon fillet
- 1 egg
- ¾ cup frozen vegetables, parboiled and drained
- 1 cup breadcrumbs
- 2 tablespoons dried parsley, chopped
- 1 teaspoon dried dill, chopped
- Salt and freshly ground pepper, to taste
- ¼ cup olive oil

Directions: :
- Preheat the Air fryer to 355 o F and line a pan with foil paper.
- Place salmon in the Air fryer basket and cook for about 5 minutes.
- Dish out the salmon in a large bowl and flake with a fork.
- Mix potatoes, egg, parboiled vegetables, parsley, dill, salt and black pepper until well combined.
- Make 6 equal sized patties from the mixture and coat the patties evenly with breadcrumbs.
- Drizzle with the olive oil and arrange the patties in the pan.
- Transfer into the Air fryer basket and cook for about 12 minutes, flipping once in between.

400.Ham-Wrapped Prawns with Roasted Pepper Chutney

Preparation time: 15 mins
Cooking time: 13 mins
Ingredients :
- 1 large red bell pepper
- 8 king prawns, peeled and deveined
- 4 ham slices, halved
- 1 garlic clove, minced
- 1 tablespoon olive oil
- ½ tablespoon paprika

- Salt and freshly ground black pepper, to taste

Directions: :

- Preheat the Air fryer to 375 o F and grease an Air fryer basket.
- Place the bell pepper in the Air fryer basket and cook for about 10 minutes.
- Dish out the bell pepper into a bowl and keep aside, covered for about 15 minutes.
- Now, peel the bell pepper and remove the stems and seeds and chop it.
- Put the chopped bell pepper, garlic, paprika and olive oil in a blender and pulse until a puree is formed.
- Wrap each ham slice around each prawn and transfer to the Air fryer basket.
- Cook for about 3 minsand serve with roasted pepper chutney.

401.Tuna Patties

Preparation time: 15 mins
Cooking time: 10 mins
Ingredients :

- 2 (6-ounce) cans tuna, drained
- ½ cup panko bread crumbs
- 1 egg
- 2 tablespoons fresh parsley, chopped
- 2 teaspoons Dijon mustard
- Dash of Tabasco sauce
- Salt and black pepper, to taste
- 1 tablespoon fresh lemon juice
- 1 tablespoon olive oil

Directions: :

- Preheat the Air fryer to 355 o F and line a baking tray with foil paper.
- Mix all the ingredients in a large bowl until well combined.
- Make equal sized patties from the mixture and refrigerate overnight.
- Arrange the patties on the baking tray and transfer to an Air fryer basket.
- Cook for about 10 mins and dish out to serve warm.

402.Quick and Easy Shrimp

Preparation time: 10 mins
Cooking time: 5 mins
Ingredients :

- ½ pound tiger shrimp
- 1 tablespoon olive oil
- ½ teaspoon old bay seasoning
- ¼ teaspoon smoked paprika

- ¼ teaspoon cayenne pepper
- Salt, to taste

Directions: :

- Preheat the Air fryer to 390 o F and grease an Air fryer basket.
- Mix all the ingredients in a large bowl until well combined.
- Place the shrimps in the Air fryer basket and cook for about 5 minutes.
- Dish out and serve warm.

403.Tuna-Stuffed Potato Boats

Preparation time: 10 mins
Cooking time: 16 mins
Ingredients :

- 4 starchy potatoes, soaked for about 30 minsand drain
- 1 (6-ounce) can tuna, drained
- 2 tablespoons plain Greek yogurt
- 1 scallion, chopped and divided
- 1 tablespoon capers
- ½ tablespoon olive oil
- 1 teaspoon red chili powder
- Salt and black pepper, to taste

Directions: :

- Preheat the Air fryer to 355 o F and grease an Air fryer basket.
- Arrange the potatoes in the Air fryer basket and cook for about 30 minutes.
- Meanwhile, mix tuna, yogurt, red chili powder, salt, black pepper and half of scallion in a bowl and mash the mixture well.
- Remove the potatoes from the Air fryer and halve the potatoes lengthwise carefully.
- Stuff in the tuna mixture in the potatoes and top with capers and remaining scallion.
- Dish out in a platter and serve immediately

404.Salmon Fillets

Preparation time: 5 mins
Cooking time: 7 mins
Ingredients :

- 2 (7-ounce) (¾-inch thick) salmon fillets
- 1 tablespoon Italian seasoning
- 1 tablespoon fresh lemon juice

Directions: :

- Preheat the Air fryer to 355 o F and grease an Air fryer grill pan.
- Rub the salmon evenly with Italian seasoning and transfer into the Air fryer

grill pan, skin-side up.

- Cook for about 7 minsand squeeze lemon juice on it to serve

405.Glazed Halibut Steak

Preparation time: 30 mins
Cooking time: 11 mins
Ingredients :

- 1 pound haddock steak
- 1 garlic clove, minced
- ¼ teaspoon fresh ginger, grated finely
- ½ cup low-sodium soy sauce
- ¼ cup fresh orange juice
- 2 tablespoons lime juice
- ½ cup cooking wine
- ¼ cup sugar
- ¼ teaspoon red pepper flakes, crushed

Directions: :

- Preheat the Air fryer to 390 o F and grease an Air fryer basket.
- Put all the ingredients except haddock steak in a pan and bring to a boil.
- Cook for about 4 minutes, stirring continuously and remove from the heat.
- Put the haddock steak and half of the marinade in a resealable bag and shake
- well.
- Refrigerate for about 1 hour and reserve the remaining marinade.
- Place the haddock steak in the Air fryer basket and cook for about 11 minutes.
- Coat with the remaining glaze and serve hot.

406.Fish Cakes:

Prep time: 15mins
Cooking time: 15mins
Ingredients:

- 10 ounces Finely-chopped White Fish (you should consider using either grouper, cod or even catfish)
- 2/3 cup Whole-wheat Panko Breadcrumbs
- 3 tablespoons Finely-chopped Fresh Cilantro
- 2 tablespoons Thai Sweet Chili Sauce
- 2 tablespoons Canola Mayonnaise
- 1 Large Egg
- 1/8 teaspoon Salt
- ¼ teaspoon Ground Pepper
- 2 Lime Wedges

Directions: :

- Use the cooking spray on the basket of the air fryer. This should help it not to stick during the frying.
- Fetch a medium bowl and put in the fish, panko, cilantro, chili sauce, egg, mayonnaise, salt, and pepper. Stir all of the mixture until they are all combined well and form a nice paste. Form the paste into round cakes. They should be about 3 inches in diameter.
- Preheat the oven to about 400 degrees F.
- Use some of the cooking spray on the cakes before placing them into the basket to fry.
- You should leave the cakes there until they turn a golden-brown, that will be when you will be sure that the cakes are well cooked.
- Cooking should take no more than 10 minutes.
- Bring out and leave to cool before serving

407. Air Fryer Fish

Prep time: 10mins Cooking time: 20mins

Ingredients:

- 1 lb. Cod, cut into 4 strips
- Kosher Salt
- Freshly Ground Black Pepper
- 1/2 cup All-purpose Flour
- 1 Large Egg, beaten
- 2 cups Panko Breadcrumbs
- 1 tsp Old Bay Seasoning
- Lemon Wedges, for serving
- Tartar Sauce, for serving

Directions: :

- Remove the fish from the refrigerator and wipe down with some paper nap
- kins until they are dry. Then proceed to add some seasonings to the fish.
- You can make use of pepper and salt for seasoning.
- Fetch three bowls and put in the flour, egg and panko in each of them separately.
- Add some Old Bay to the bowl containing the panko.
- Dip the fish in the bowl containing the flour, then remove and do the same for the egg, finally ending with the panko.
- Use fingers to press down on the fish to make sure it absorbs the ingredients.

- Set the temperature of the air fryer to 400 degrees F and place the fish into the air fryer's basket.
- Cooking time is usually slated for just 10 minutes, after which the fish would have been thoroughly cooked. You should be on the lookout for when the fish is golden or the flakes start falling off.
- That is an indication that it is done.
- The lemon wedges or tartar sauce can be used to serve with the dish.

408. Fish Fillets

Prep time: 5mins
Cooking time: 15mins

Ingredients:

- 8 (800 grams) Fish Fillets
- 1 tbsp Olive Oil
- 1 cup 50 grams Breadcrumbs.
- 1/2 tsp Paprika
- 1/4 tsp Dried Chili Powder
- 1/4 tsp Ground Black Pepper
- 1/4 tsp Garlic Powder
- 1/4 tsp Onion Powder
- 1/2 tsp Salt

Directions: :

- Defrost the fish first. That is, if it is frozen fish that you are making use of for the fillets.
- Afterward, smear some olive oil on the fish. You can turn the fish on their sides to make sure that the olive oil gets to every part of the fish.
- Get a small shallow dish and put in the breadcrumbs.
- Then add paprika, chili powder, garlic, black pepper, salt and onion powder to the breadcrumbs.
- For each fish fillet that you get, coat in breadcrumbs. Do that for each of the filets and then transfer to the air fryer.
- Heat up the air fryer to 390 degrees F and place the basket into the air fryer.
- The cooking time should generally be for 15 minutes.
- However, when the first 10 minshave elapsed, you can flip the fish fillets onto their other side and proceed with the cooking.
- After 15 minutes, bring out the fillet and let it cool. Then they will be ready to serve.

409. Crumbed Fish

Prep time: 10mins Cooking time: 12mins

Ingredients:

- 1 cup Dry Breadcrumbs
- 1/4 cup Vegetable Oil
- 4 Flounder Fillets
- 1 Egg, beaten
- 1 Lemon

Directions: :

- Begin by preheating the air fryer. The ideal temperature should be 350 de-
- grees F, although it is possible to set it higher.
- Put the breadcrumbs and the oil into a bowl. Mix them thoroughly until they
- are well mixed. Fetch another bowl and put in the eggs
- Put the fillets into the eggs first. Make sure they are thoroughly coated with the egg, then proceed to dip into the crumb mixture.
- Make sure that they are well coated.
- Place the fillets into the air fryer basket. Cook. Cooking time should be at
- least 12 minutes. The fish is ready when the flakes begin to fall off or when it turns golden.
- Remove the fillets from the air fryer and serve with the lemon slices.

410. Air Fryer Fish Cod

Prep time: 5 mins
Cooking time: 12 mins

Ingredients:

- 1 lb Cod Fillet
- 1 Lemon
- 1/4 cup Butter
- 1 tsp Salt
- 1 tsp Seasoning Salt

Directions: :

- Start the preparation for the cod fillets. Add some seasonings to the fillets and coat very well.
- Use a brush and spread some olive oil on the air fryer basket. The oil should be minimal.
- Then place the fillets into the air fryer basket.
- Add some butter and some slices of lemon into the mix.
- Keep the temperature at about 400 degrees F and cook for 10 minutes. You may have to cook for longer depending on the size of your fillets.
- Use the thermometer to check the

internal temperature of the fish. When it reaches 145 degrees F, you can be sure it is cooked.

- Serve.

411. Tasty Salmon Patties

Prep time: 5 mins
Cook Time: 8 mins

Ingredients:

- 14 ounces (400g) Fresh Salmon
- 3 tbsp Cilantro (Coriander) chopped
- 3 Green Onions
- 1 tsp Paprika
- 1 Egg

Directions: :

- Start by preheating the air fryer. It should be set to about 360 degrees F.
- Mince the fresh salmon you'll be using. After mincing, remove the bones from the fish and drain all of the fluids.
- You can mince by hand since you are making use of fresh salmon.
- Get a bowl and add all of the ingredients. Toss until they are well combined.
- Use the minced salmon to form patties. The ideal number is 6 and they should all be of the same size.
- Spray the patties with cooking spray and put them into the air fryer basket.
- The cooking time is 8 minsat most. Do not forget to flip the patties midway into the cooking to make sure that they cook properly.

412. Crumbed Fish

Prep time: 15 mins Cook time: 12 mins

Ingredients

- 1 sliced lemon
- 1 beaten egg
- 4 flounder fillets
- 1/4 cup of vegetable oil
- 1 cup of dry bread crumbs

Directions:

- Heat up the Air fryer to 356 F.
- In a bowl, mix together the oil with bread crumbs, stirring until crumbly.
- Dip fillets in the beaten egg; let any excess drip off, you can also shake.
- Dredge fillets in bread crumb to coat evenly.
- Gently arrange the finely coated fillets in the Air fryer. Cook about 12 mins until fish easily flakes with a fork.
- Garnish with slices of lemon.

413. Bang Bang Fried Shrimp

Prep time: 10 mins Cook time: 20 mins

Ingredients

- Bang Bang Sauce
- 1/4 cup sweet chili sauce
- 2 tbsp Sriracha
- 1/3 cup plain, non-fat Greek yogurt
- Cooking spray
- McCormick's Grill Mates Montreal Chicken Seasoning to taste
- Salt and pepper to taste
- 1 teaspoon of paprika
- 3/4 cup of panko bread crumbs
- 1/2 cup of all-purpose flour
- 1 egg white, 3 tbsp
- 1 pound of raw shrimp peeled and deveined

Directions:

- Heat up the Air fryer to 400 F.
- Season all sides of the shrimp with the Chicken seasonings.
- In three different bowls, Place the panko bread crumbs, flour and egg whites.
- Dredge the shrimp in the bowl containing flour, dip coated shrimp lightly the egg whites, and allow excess to drip and lastly coat in the panko bread crumbs.
- Sprits with cooking spray at a distance. If the spraying is too direct, the panko may not stay.
- Place coated shrimp in the Air fryer basket and cook at 400 F for 8-10 minutes, flipping the shrimp half way through the cooking time until crisp.

Bang Bang Sauce

- In a small bowl, Combine together all of the ingredients until well mixed.

414. Fish Finger With Pea Puree Sandwich

Prep time: 5 mins Cook time: 15 mins

Ingredients

- 8 small slices of bread or 4 bread rolls
- Squeeze of lemon juice
- 10–12 capers
- 1 tablespoon of creme fraiche or greek yogurt
- 250 grams of frozen peas
- Spray oil
- 40 grams of dried breadcrumbs
- 2 tablespoon of flour
- Salt and pepper

- 4 small skinless cod fillets

Directions:

- Heat up your Air fryer to 200c.
- Season the cod fillets with pepper and salt and dust lightly with the flour. Next; roll cod fillets in breadcrumbs lightly.
- Spritz the bottom of the fryer basket with oil spray. Add fish and cook at 200c for 15 minutes.
- Meanwhile, cook the peas for few minsin boiling water in a microwave.
- Drain peas well and place into the blender along the capers, lemon juice and crème fraiche.
- Pulse until combined.
- To serve, layer sandwich with fish and puree pea.

415. Chili Lime Tilapia

Prep time: 10 mins Cook time: 15 mins

Ingredients

- Salt & Pepper to taste
- 1 Juice of lime
- 1 tablespoon of chili powder or less
- 1 -2 eggs
- 1/2 cup of flour
- 1 cup of panko crumbs
- 1 pounds of tilapia

Directions:

- Arrange a wide plate, enough to contain the tilapia. In a bowls, mix together the chili powder, panko, pepper and salt.
- Place flour in a second bowl and egg in a last bowl.
- Spritz your Air fryer lightly with cooking spray. Coat the tilapia on both sides in flour, then dip tilapia in the egg and lastly coat in the panko mix, pressing to coat well.
- Transfer the coated tilapia into your Air fryer and spray the top with cooking spray (You can do it batches if you have a small Air fryer).
- Cook for 7-8 minsat 37Turn over and cook for extra 7-8 minsor until cooked through.
- To serve, add a squeeze of lime juice over the tilapia with avocado, pico de gallo and lime wedges.

416. Lobster Tails with Garlic Lemon Butter

Prep time: 15 mins Cook time: 5 mins

Ingredients

- Vegetable oil
- ½ lemon, sliced
- ½ cup of white wine
- Salt and freshly ground black pepper
- 2 (6-oz) of lobster tails
- 1 thinly sliced clove garlic
- 1 tbsp of finely chopped lemon zest
- 4 oz of unsalted butter

Directions:
- In a small saucepan, mix together the butter, garlic and lemon zest over low heat.
- Cut the center top of the lobster shell down.
- To crack the bottom shell, squeeze the lobster sides together to give you access to the meat inside. Draw out the tail of the shell, leaving it connected at the tail's bottom.
- Arrange the meat over the shell top, season with pepper and salt. Add a bit of butter mixture over the lobster meat
- Refrigerate the lobster to solidify the butter a bit.
- In the Air fryer drawer, add white wine and lemon slices. Heat up your Air fryer to 200c for 5 minutes.
- Place lobster tails to the basket of the Air fryer and cook for 5 minsat 370º, brush with additional butter midway through cooking.
- Serve with extra butter for drizzling.

417. Grilled Air fryer Cajun Salmon With Fries

Prep time: 10 mins Cook time: 20 mins
Ingredients
- Cooking Spray
- Salt to taste
- 2 tablespoon of Cajun Seasoning
- 100 grams of Frozen Fries
- 2 Salmon Steak

Directions:
- Pat the salmon steak dry and rub with the Cajun seasoning all over. Leave to marinate for about ten minutes.
- Heat up your Air fryer at 200°C. Arrange salmon steaks over Air fryer grill pan and grill for 8 minutes, turning over midway through the cooking. Keep warm while you make the fries
- Spritz your grill pan with the cooking oil and arrange your fries over the grill and grill for 12 minutes, shaking halfway through cooking until golden

brown.
- Sprinkle with salt and serve.

418. Fish and Chips

Prep time: 15 mins Cook time: 12 mins
Ingredients
- ½ tbsp of lemon juice
- 1 tbsp of vegetable oil
- 300 grams of (red) potatoes, scrub clean and cut lengthwise into thin strips
- 1 egg
- 30 grams of tortilla chips
- 200 grams of white fish filet (cut into 4 equal parts)

Directions:
- Heat up your Air fryer to 180°C.
- Rub fish pieces with pepper, lemon juice and salt and allow to rest for five minutes.
- In the food processor, grind the tortilla chips finely and place the grounded
- tortilla unto a bowl. In a deep dish, beat the egg. Dip fish pieces in the egg one after another, allowing excess to drip off and then roll the fish in the ground tortilla until well coated.
- Pour water in a bowl and soak the potato strips for at least 30 mins in water. Drain potatoes well and pat them dry. Coat potatoes strips with oill.
- Insert Air fryer basket divider. Arrange the pieces of fish on one side and the potato strips on the other. Cook for 12 minsuntil potatoes are crispy brown and fish is done.

419. Air fryer Cornmeal Fish

Prep time: 10 mins Cook time: 17 mins
Ingredients
- ½ teaspoon of black pepper
- ½ teaspoon of garlic powder
- 1 teaspoon of paprika
- 1 ½ teaspoon of salt
- 2 teaspoon of old bay
- ¼ cup of flour
- ¾ cup of fine cornmeal
- Oil to mist
- 4-6 White Fish fillets cut in half, rinse and pat dry

Directions:
- Combine fine cornmeal, flour, old bay, black pepper, garlic powder, paprika and salt in a Ziploc bag and shake.

420. Place fish fillets into the mixture Tortilla Crusted Tilapia Salad

Prep time: 15 mins Cook time: 15 mins
Ingredients
- 1/2 cup of Chipotle Lime Dressing
- 2 Tortilla Crusted frozen Tilapia fillets
- 1 avocado
- 1/3 cup of diced red onion
- 1 cup of cherry tomatoes
- 6 cup of mixed greens

Directions:
- Spritz both sides of the tilapia fillets with spray. Arrange in the basket of your Air fryer and cook at 390° for 15-18 minsuntil crispy.
- Meanwhile, in 2 bowls, pour 1/2 of the mixed greens, red onion and tomatoes.
- Add Chipotle Lime Dressing, toss together.
- Serve baked fish with greens and sliced avocado.and shake to cover the fillets with seasoning.
- Transfer the fillets onto a rack to enable excess flour mixture fall off.
- Grease the basket of your Air fryer with oil, add the coated fillets and cook filets for 10 minute on 400 F.
- Open and spritz fish (the side facing up) before turning, make sure the fish is well coated.
- Turnover and cook for seven more minutes.
- Serve.

421. Cheesy Parmesan Shrimp

Prep time: 10 mins Cook time: 8-10 mins
Ingredients
- Lemon, quartered
- 2 tbsp of olive oil
- 1 tsp of onion powder
- 1 tsp basil
- 1/2 tsp oregano
- 1 tsp of pepper
- 2/3 cup of grated parmesan cheese
- 4 minced cloves garlic
- 2 lbs of jumbo cooked shrimp, peeled and deveined

Directions:
- Mix together the onion powder, olive oil, oregano, pepper, basil, garlic and parmesan cheese in a large bowl.
- Toss the shrimp gently in mixture

until finely coated. Spritz a non-stick spray on Air fryer basket.

- Arrange Shrimp in the Air fryer basket and cook for 8-10 minsat 350 degrees or until browned and crispy. Serve with a squeeze of lemon over shrimp.

422. Air fryer Fish Sticks

Prep time: 10 mins Cook time: 10 mins

Ingredients

- Salt and pepper to taste
- 3/4 teaspoon of cajun seasoning
- 1 1/2 cups of pork rind panko
- 2 tablespoon of water
- Avocado oil spray
- 2 tablespoon of Dijon mustard
- 1/4 cup of mayonnaise
- 1 pound of white fish, pat dry and cut into 1 by 2 inches wide stick

Directions:

- Spritz oil spray on the rack of your Air fryer.
- Whisk the mustard, mayo, and water together in a small shallow bowl.
- Whisk the Cajun seasoning with pork rinds together in another shallow bowl.
- Add pepper and salt to taste
- Dip each fish one by one into the mayo mixture, let excess drip off.
- Coat fish in the pork rind mixture until well coated.
- Arrange onto the rack of the Air fryer and cook

423. Baked Salmon

Prep time: 5 mins Cook time: 10 mins

Ingredients

- Black pepper, to taste
- Kosher salt to taste
- 1 tsp of olive oil
- 2 (6 ounce) skinless, boneless salmon fillets
- 1 pound of white

Directions:

- Coat salmon on both sides with olive oil and then season all sides with pepper and salt.
- Arrange the salmon fillets in the basket of your Air fryer and cook for about 10 minsat 360°F until cooked through.

424. Cajun Salmon

Prep time: 5 mins Cook time: 7 mins

Ingredients

- Juice from a 1/4 of lemon, to serve
- (Optional) sprinkle of sugar
- Cajun seasoning, enough to coat
- 1 (about 200g) fresh salmon fillet, pat dry

Directions:

- Heat up the Air fryer to 350 F for 5 minutes.
- Sprinkle the salmon fillet with Cajun seasoning on all sides in a plate to evenly coat. If using, add a light sprinkle of sugar for a tad of sweetness.
- Place skin side up in the Air fryer grill pan and air fry for 7 minsor until cooked through.
- Cooking time depends on the thickness.
- Serve with a squeeze of lemon.

425. Coconut Shrimp In Marmalade Sauce

Prep time: 10 mins Cook time: 20 mins

Ingredients

- 1/4 tsp of hot sauce
- 1 tsp of mustard
- 1 tbsp of honey
- 1/2 cup of orange marmalade
- 1/4 tsp of fresh ground pepper
- 1/4 tsp of kosher salt
- 1/2 tsp of cayenner pepper
- 1/2 cup of panko bread
- 1/2 cup of sweetened coconut, shredded
- 8 oz of coconut milk
- 8 large shrimp shelled and deveined

Directions:

- Whisk together the coconut milk, salt and pepper with the season in a small bowl.
- Whisk together the panko, cayenne pepper, coconut, salt and pepper in a separate small bowl.
- Dip each shrimp one by one in the coconut milk mixture, then the panko mixture.
- Place coated shrimp in the Air fryer basket and cook for 20 minsat 350 F or until cooked through.
- Meanwhile, whisk the mustard, honey, marmalade and hot sauce.
- Pour sauce over the shrimp and serve immediately.

426. Fish Cakes with Mango Salsa

Prep time: 20 mins Cook time: 14 mins

Ingredients

- 50 grams of ground coconut
- 1 finely chopped green onion
- 1 egg
- 500 grams of white fish fillet (pollack,pangasius, tilapia, cod or halibut)
- 1 zest and Juice of lime
- 3 tbsp of fresh coriander or flat leaf parsley
- 1½ tsp of red chili paste
- 1 ripe mango, peel and chop into small size cubes

Directions:

- In a mixing bowl, combine together the mango cubes, half lime zest and
- juice, 1 tbsp of coriander and ½ teaspoon red chili paste.
- Purée fish in a blender or food processor and then mix with remaining of the lime zest, 1 egg, red chili paste, remaining juice and 1 teaspoon salt. Stir in the remaining coriander, 2 tbsp of coconut and green onion.
- Pour the remaining coconut onto a soup plate. Shape the fish mixture evenly into 12 round cakes, and coat in the coconut.
- Cook in batches, arrange 6 fish cakes in the Air fryer basket and cook for 7 mins until they are golden brown. Repeat with the remaining fish cakes.
- Pour mango salsa over fish cakes and serve.

427. Grilled Fish & Pesto Sauce

Prep time: 10 mins Cook time: 8 mins

Ingredients

- 250 ml of extra virgin olive oil
- 1 tablespoon of grated parmesan cheese
- 2 tablespoon of pine nuts
- 2 garlic cloves
- 1 (15 g) bunch of fresh basil
- Pepper & salt
- 1 tablespoon of olive oil
- 3 (200 g each) white fish fillets (pollack, pangasius, tilapia, cod or halibut)

Directions:

- Heat up your Air fryer to 180°C.
- Brush both sides of the fillets with olive oil and a sprinkle of salt and pepper to taste.
- Transfer fillet in the Air fryer basket and cook for 8 minutes.

- Puree the basil leaves along with the parmesan cheese, pine nuts, garlic and oil in a food processor until smooth. Season with salt to taste.
- Drizzle pesto sauce over fish fillets on a serving plate.

428. Air Friyer Crumbed Fish

Prep time: 10 mins Cook time: 12 mins
Ingredients
- 1 lemon, to serve
- 4 fish fillets
- 1 egg, whisked
- 1/2 cup of breadcrumbs
- 4 tbsp of vegetable oil

Directions:
- Heat up the Air fryer to 350 F.
- Mix together the breadcrumbs and vegetable oil in a bowl, stirring until you have a crumbly and loose mixture. In another bowl, whisk the egg.
- Dip fish in the egg, allow excess to drip, then Dredge the in the breadcrumbs mixture until well coated.
- Arrange in the Air fryer, cook at 350 F for 12 minutes. (Cooking time depends on the thickness). Serve hot with lemon.

429. Spicy Catfish Fries

Prep time: 10 mins Cook time: 3 mins
Ingredients
- 1 quart of oil for frying
- Salt and pepper to taste
- 1/2 cup of corn flour
- 1 tsp of cayenne pepper, or to taste
- 1 (10 ounce) fillet catfish, frozen for easy cutting

Directions:
- Arrange the catfish on cutting board horizontally. Cut into 1/4" wide strips at a 45 degree angle.
- Sprinkle cayenne pepper moderately on fish strips, and carefully rub together to coat all strips evenly; should look pink when you are finished.
- Arrange strips on pan to thaw as you set aside for a few minutes.
- Add corn flour in a bowl and season with black pepper and salt.
- Dredge thawed catfish in the corn flour until all strips are coated evenly.
- Place coated catfish strips in the Air fryer and cook for 8 minsat 400ºF or until slightly crisp outside, golden brown and flakes easily.

430. Easy Salmon Croquettes

Prep time: 10 mins Cook time: 10 mins
Ingredients
- 3 tbsp of olive oil
- 5 tbsp of wheat germ
- 1/2 tsp of garlic granules
- 1 tbsp of chopped fresh dill
- 4 tbsp of sliced spring onion
- 4 tbsp of finely chopped celery
- 1 egg
- 1 (180 grams) tin of salmon, drained and flaked

Directions:
- Heat up your Air fryer to 370 F.
- Mix together the egg, celery, salmon, green onion, garlic granules and dill in a medium bowl.
- Shape mixture into small sized golf balls, and dredge to coat in wheat germ.
- Slightly flatten into patties, place in the Air fryer and cook for 10 minsat 370 degrees F, flipping half way through the cooking time.

431. Spicy Prawns with cocktail sauce

Prep time: 10 mins Cook time: 6 mins
Ingredients
- 1 tablespoon of cider or wine vinegar
- 1 tablespoon of ketchup
- 8-12 fresh king prawns
- ½ teaspoon of freshly ground black pepper
- ½ teaspoon of sea salt
- 3 tablespoon of mayonnaise
- 1 teaspoon of chilli powder
- 1 teaspoon of chilli flakes

Directions:
- Preheat your Air fryer to 180c.
- In a bowl, mix together all the spices. Toss prawns in the spice until well coated.
- Transfer prawns to the Air fryer basket and cook for 6 to 8 minutes. Cooking time vary based on size of the prawns.
- In a bowl, mix together the sauce ingredients.
- Serve prawns with the sauce.

432. Coconut Shrimp

Prep time: 15 mins Cook time: 30 mins
Ingredients
- 1/2 cup of all-purpose flour
- 1 1/2 tsp of black pepper
- 2 large eggs

- 2/3 cup of unsweetened flaked coconut
- 1/3 cup of panko (Japanese breadcrumbs)
- 12 oz. (about 24 shrimp) medium peeled, deveined, tail-on
- Cooking spray
- 1/2 tsp of kosher salt
- 1/4 cup of honey
- 1/4 cup of lime juice
- 1 thinly sliced serrano chile
- 2 tsp of chopped fresh cilantro

Directions:
- In a shallow dish, stir together pepper and flour. In a separate shallow dish, lightly beat the eggs. Stir panko and coconut together in a third shallow dish.
- Coat each shrimp in flour mixture, holding by the tail. (No need to coat the
- tail) shake any excess flour off, then Dip in egg, hold out to allow any excess drip off.
- Coat in coconut mixture, tumble to coat well then spray with cooking spray.
- To avoid overcrowding, you have to cook in batches.
- Place the first batch of shrimp in Air fryer basket and cook for 6 to 8 minsat 400°F, turning halfway through cooking until golden.
- Season with half of the salt and season the other batch with the remaining sail.
- Whisk Serrano Chile, lime juice, and honey together in small bowl.
- Sprinkle cilantro over the cooked shrimp and Serve with sauce, if desired.

433. Rosemary Garlicky Prawns

Prep Time: 1 h 15 minutes
Ingredients:
- 8 large prawns
- 3 garlic cloves, minced
- 1 rosemary sprig, chopped
- ½ tbsp. melted butter
- Salt and pepper, to taste

Instructions:
- Combine the garlic, butter, rosemary, and some salt and pepper, in a bowl.
- Add the prawns to the bowl and mix to coat them well.
- Cover the bowl and refrigerate for about an hour.Preheat the air fryer to

350 degrees F.
- Cook for about 6 minutes.
- Increase the temperature to 390 degrees, and cook for one more minute.

434. Parmesan Tilapia

Prep Time: 15 minutes
Ingredients:
- ¾ cup grated Parmesan cheese
- 1 tbsp. olive oil
- 2 tsp. paprika
- 1 tbsp. chopped parsley
- ¼ tsp. garlic powder¼ tsp. salt4 tilapia fillets

Instructions:
- Preheat the air fryer to 350 degrees F.
- Mix parsley, Parmesan, garlic, salt, and paprika in a shallow bowl.Brush the olive oil over the fillets, and then coat them with the Parmesan mixture.
- Place the tilapia onto a lined baking sheet, and then into the air fryer.
- Cook for about 4 to 5 mins on all sides.

435. Fish Finger Sandwich

Prep Time: 20 minutes
Ingredients:
- 4 cod fillets
- 2 tbsp. flour10 capers
- 4 bread rolls
- 2 oz. breadcrumbs
- 4 tbsp. pesto sauce
- 4 lettuce leaves
- Salt and pepper, to taste

Instructions:
- Preheat the air fryer to 370 degrees F.
- Season the fillets with some salt and pepper, and coat them with the flour, and then dip in the breadcrumbs.
- You should get a really thin layer of breadcrumbs, that's why we don't use eggs for this recipe.
- Arrange the fillets onto a baking mat.
- Air fry for about 10 to 15 minutes.Cut the bread rolls in half.
- Place a lettuce leaf on top of the bottom halves.Place the fillets over.
- Spread a tablespoon of pesto sauce on top of each fillet.
- Top with the remaining halves.

436. Quick and Easy Air Fried Salmon

Prep Time: 13 minutes
Ingredients:
- 1 salmon fillet

- 1 tbsp. soy sauce
- ¼ tsp. garlic powder
- Salt and pepper

Instructions:
- Preheat the air fryer to 350 degrees F.
- Combine the soy sauce with the garlic powder and some salt and pepper.
- Brush the mixture over the salmon.
- Place the salmon onto a sheet of parchment paper and into the air fryer.Cook for 10 minutes.

437. Delicious Coconut Shrimp

Prep Time: 30 minutes
Ingredients:
- 8 large shrimp
- ½ cup breadcrumbs
- 8 oz. coconut milk
- ½ cup shredded coconut
- ¼ tsp. salt¼ tsp. pepper
- ½ cup orange jam
- 1 tsp. mustard1 tbsp. honey
- ½ tsp. cayenne pepper
- ¼ tsp. hot sauce
- **Instructions:**
- Preheat the air fryer to 350 degrees F.
- Combine the breadcrumbs, cayenne pepper, shredded coconut, salt, and pepper in a small bowl.
- Dip the shrimp in the coconut milk, first, and then in the coconut crumbs.Arrange on a lined sheet, and air fry for 20 minutes.
- Meanwhile whisk the jam, honey, hot sauce, and mustard.
- Serve the shrimp with the sauce.

438. Crab Cakes

Prep Time: 55 minutes
Ingredients:
- ½ cup cooked crab meat
- ¼ cup chopped red onion
- 1 tbsp. chopped basil¼ cup chopped celery
- ¼ cup chopped red pepper
- 3 tbsp. mayonnaise
- Zest of half a lemon
- ¼ cup breadcrumbs
- 2 tbsp. chopped parsley
- Old Bay seasoning, as desired
- Cooking spray

Instructions:
- Preheat the air fryer to 390 degrees F.Place all of the ingredients in a large bowl and mix well until completely

incorporated.
- Make 4 large crab cakes from the mixture and place them on a lined sheet.
- Refrigerate for about 30 minutes, to set. Spay the air basket with cooking spray and arrange the crab cakes in it.
- Cook for about 7 mins on each side.

439. Cajun Lemony Salmon

Prep Time: 10 minutes
Ingredients:
- 1 salmon fillet
- ¼ tsp. brown sugar
- Juice of ½ lemon
- 1 tbsp. Cajun seasoning
- 2 lemon wedges, for serving
- 1 tbsp. chopped parsley, for garnishing

Instructions:
- Preheat the air fryer to 350 degrees F.
- Meanwhile, Combine the sugar and lemon and coat the salmon with this mixture completely.
- Coat the salmon with the Cajun seasoning as well.
- Place a parchment paper into your air fryer and cook the salmon for 7 minutes.
- Remember if using a thicker fillet, cook no more than 6 minutes.
- Serve with lemon wedges and chopped parsley.

440. Cod Cornflakes Nuggets

Prep Time: 25 minutes
Ingredients:
- 1-¼ lb. cod fillets, cut into 4 to 6 chunks each
- ½ cup flour
- 1 egg
- 1 tbsp. water
- 1 cup (use more if needed) cornflakes
- 1 tbsp. olive oil salt and pepper, to taste

Instructions:
- Place the oil and cornflakes in a food processor and process until crumbed.
- Season the fish chunks with some salt and pepper.
- Beat the egg along with 1 tbsp. water.
- Dredge the chunks in flour first, then dip in the egg, and coat with cornflakes.
- Arrange on a lined sheet.
- Air fry at 350 degrees for about 15

minutes.

441.Tuna Patties Servings:

Time: 50 minutes

Ingredients:
- 5 oz. of canned tuna
- 1 tsp. lime juice
- 1 tsp. paprika
- ¼ cup flour
- ½ cup milk
- 1 small onion, diced
- 2 eggs
- 1 tsp. chili powder, optional
- ½ tsp. salt

Instructions:
- Place all of the ingredients in a bowl and mix well to combine.
- Make two large patties, or a few smaller ones, out of the mixture.
- Place them on a lined sheet and refrigerate for 30 minutes.
- Preheat the air fryer to 350 degrees F.
- Air fry the patties for about 6 mins on each side.

442.Pistachio Crusted Salmon

Prep Time: 15 - 20 minutes

Ingredients:
- 1 salmon fillet
- 1 tsp. mustard
- 3 tbsp. pistachios
- Pinch of sea salt
- Pinch of garlic powder
- Pinch of black pepper
- 1 tsp. lemon juice1 tsp. grated Parmesan cheese1 tsp. olive oil

Instructions:
- Preheat the air fryer to 350 degrees F.
- Whisk the mustard and lemon juice together.
- Season the salmon with salt, pepper, and garlic powder.Brush the olive oil on all sides.
- Brush the mustard/lemon mixture on top of the salmon.
- Chop the pistachios finely and combine them with the Parmesan cheese.Sprinkle them on top of the salmon.
- Place the salmon in the air fryer basket with the skin side down.
- Cook for about 10 minutes, or to your liking.

443.Cedar Plank Salmon

Preparation time: 30mins

Ingredients
- 4 untreated cedar planks
- 1½ tbsp. of rice vinegar
- 2 tbsp. sesame oil
- ½ cup soy sauce
- ¼ cup green onions, chopped
- 3 cloves garlic, minced
- 1 tbsp. fresh ginger grated
- 2 lb. of salmon fillets, skin removed

Instructions
- Submerge the cedar planks in water and soak for 2 hours.
- In a shallow dish, combine all ingredients except salmon and mix well.
- Add the salmon to the marinade and coat each side.
- Marinate, refrigerated, for 30minutes.
- Preheat fryer to 350 degrees F.
- Remove the cedar planks from the water and pat dry.
- Place on the fryer basket and place the salmon on top.
- Cook for 15 minutes. Serve and enjoy

444.Chinese Mushroom Tilapia

Preparation time: 20mins

Ingredients
- ½ cup yellow onion, sliced thin
- 2 cloves garlic, minced
- 4 (8oz) fillets tilapia
- 2½ tsps. of salt
- 2 tbsp. olive oil
- 2 cups sliced mushrooms
- 4 tbsp. soy sauce
- 1 tsp. red chili flakes
- 1 tbsp. honey 2 tbsp. rice vinegar

Instructions
- Preheat the fryer to 350 degrees F.
- Season the fish with half the salt and drizzle with half the oil. Cook for 15 minutes.
- Meanwhile, heat the remaining oil in a large skillet.
- Once hot add the mushroom onion and garlic.
- Cook until onions are soft. Stir in the soy sauce, chili flakes, honey, and vinegar. Simmer for 1 minute.
- Remove fish from the fryer and top with mushroom sauce.
- Serve and enjoy!

445.Air Fried Spinach Fish

Preparation time: 20mins

Ingredients
- 1 cup spinach leaves, wilted
- 2 cups flour
- 1 tsp. salt
- ½ tsp. ground black pepper
- 2 tbsp. olive oil
- 1 large egg
- 4 (6oz) filets perch
- 1 tbsp. lemon juice

Instructions
- Preheat the fryer to 370 degrees F.
- In a bowl, combine the spinach, flour, salt, pepper, and egg.
- Dip each filet in the batter and place on the fryer tray.
- Drizzle with olive oil. Cook for 12 minutes.
- Remove and drizzle with lemon juice.

446.Air Fryer Fried Louisiana Shrimp Po Boy with Remoulade Sauce

Preparation time: 30mins

Ingredients
- 4 French bread hoagie rolls I used 2 loaves, cut each in half
- 2 cups shredded lettuce
- 1 pound shrimp, deveined
- 1/2 cup Louisiana Fish Fry
- 1/4 cup buttermilk
- 8 tomato slices
- 1 tsps. Creole Seasoning
- 1 tsps. butter optional Remoulade Sauce
- 1/2 cup mayo I used reduced-fat
- 1 tsp. minced garlic
- 1/2 lemon juice of
- 1 tsp. Worcestershire
- 1/2 tsp. Creole Seasoning
- 1 tsp. Dijon mustard
- 1 tsp. hot sauce
- 1 green onion chopped

Instructions
Remoulade Sauce
- Combine all of the ingredients in a small bowl. Refrigerate prior to serving while the shrimp cooks.

Shrimp Po Boy
- Season the shrimp with the seasonings.
- Pour the buttermilk in a bowl. Dip each of the shrimp in the buttermilk. Place the shrimp in a Ziploc bag and in

the fridge to marinate. Marinate for at least 30 minutes. I prefer overnight.

• Add the fish fry to a bowl. Remove the shrimp from the bags and dip each into the fish fry. Add the shrimp to Air Fryer basket.

• Preheat Air Fryer to 400 degrees.

• Spray the shrimp with olive oil. Do not spray directly on the shrimp. The fish fry will go flying. Keep a nice distance.

• Cook the shrimp for 5 minutes. Open the basket and flip the shrimp to the other side. Cook for an additional 5 mins or until crisp.

• Preheat oven to 325 degrees. Place the sliced bread on a sheet pan.

• Allow the bread to toast for a couple of minutes.

• Optional step if you prefer butter: Melt the butter in the microwave. Using a cooking brush, spread the butter over the bottom of the French bread.

• Assemble the po boy. Spread the remoulade sauce on the French bread. Add the sliced tomato and lettuce, and then the shrimp.

447. 3 Ingredient Fried Catfish

Preparation time: 65mins

Ingredients

• 4 catfish fillets
• 1/4 cup seasoned fish fry I used Louisiana
• 1 tbsp. olive oil
• 1 tbsp. chopped parsley optional

Instructions

• Preheat Air Fryer to 400 degrees.
• Rinse the catfish and pat dry.
• Pour the fish fry seasoning in a large Ziploc bag.
• Add the catfish to the bag, one at a time. Seal the bag and shake. Ensure the entire filet is coated with seasoning.
• Spray olive oil on the top of each filet.
• Place the filet in the Air Fryer basket. (Due to the size of my fillets, I cooked each one at a time). Close and cook for 10 minutes.
• Flip the fish. Cook for an additional 10 minutes.
• Flip the fish.
• Cook for an additional 2-3 mins or until desired crispness.
• Top with parsley

448. Air Fried Dragon Shrimp

Preparation time: 15mins

Ingredients

• 1 lb. raw shrimp, peeled and deveined
• 2 eggs 2 tbsp. olive oil
• ½ cup soy sauce
• 1 cup yellow onion, diced
• ½ tsps. ground ginger
• ½ tsps. salt
• ¼ cup flour
• ½ tsps. ground red pepper

Instructions

• Preheat air fryer to 350 degrees F.
• Combine all ingredients, except for the shrimp, and create a batter. Let sit for 10 minutes.
• Dip the shrimp into the batter to coat all sides and place in the fryer basket.
• Cook for 10 mins and serve.

449. Keto Shrimp Scampi

Preparation time: 15mins

Ingredients

• 1 tablespoon chopped chives or 1 teaspoon dried chives
• 1 tablespoon minced basil leaves plus more for sprinkling or 1 teaspoon dried basil
• 2 tablespoons chicken stock (or white wine)
• 4 tablespoons butter
• 1 tablespoon lemon juice
• 1 tablespoon minced garlic
• 2 teaspoons red pepper flakes
• 1 lb. defrosted shrimp (21-25 count)

Instructions

• Turn your air fryer to 330F. Place a 6 x 3 metal pan in it and allow the oven to start heating while you gather your **Ingredients**.
• Place the butter, garlic, and red pepper flakes into the hot 6-inch pan.
• Allow it to cook for 2 minutes, stirring once, until the butter has melted. Do not skip this step. This is what infuses garlic into the butter, which is what makes it all taste so good.
• Open the air fryer, add all **Ingredients** to the pan in the order listed, stirring gently.
• Allow shrimp to cook for 5 minutes, stirring once. At this point, the butter should be well-melted and liquid,

bathing the shrimp in spiced goodness.

• Mix very well, remove the 6-inch pan using silicone mitts, and let it rest for 1 minute on the counter. You're doing this so that you let the shrimp cook in the residual heat, rather than letting it accidentally overcook and get rubbery.

• Stir at the end of the minute. The shrimp should be well-cooked at this point.

• Sprinkle additional fresh basil leaves and enjoy.

450. Fish Lettuce Wraps

Preparation time: 20mins

Ingredients

• 6 iceberg lettuce leaves
• 6 small filets of tilapia
• 1 tsp. salt
• ½ tsp. ground black pepper
• 2 tsp. Cajun seasoning
• 1 tbsp. olive oil
• ½ cup shredded purple cabbage
• ½ cup shredded carrot
• 1 tbsp. lemon juice

Instructions

• Preheat the air fryer to 390 degrees F.
• Season tilapia with salt, pepper and Cajun seasoning.
• Drizzle with olive oil and place in the air fryer.
• Cook for 10 minutes.
• Remove fish from the fryer and place the fish on each lettuce leaf.
• Top with carrots and cabbage.
• Drizzle lemon juice on top

451. Tuna Risotto

Preparation time: 35mins

Serves: 6

Ingredients

• 4 cups chicken broth, warm
• ¼ cup grated parmesan cheese
• 1 tbsp. olive oil
• 2 cups Arborio rice
• ½ cup yellow onion, minced
• 1 cup peas 2 (4oz) cans tuna, drained
• 1 tsp. ground black pepper

Instructions

• Preheat air fryer to 320.
• Season the tuna and peas with black pepper.
• Place in the air fryer and cook for 10 minutes.
• Meanwhile, heat the oil and add the

onion and rice. Cook until lightly browned.

• Add 1 cup of the warm broth, and cook until absorbed.

• Repeat until all the broth is used. Stir in the parmesan, tuna, and peas.

452. Tandoori Fish

Preparation time: 25mins

Ingredients

• 1 whole fish, such as trout
• 1 tbsp. garam Masala seasoning
• 3 tbsp. olive oil
• 8 cloves garlic, minced
• 1 cup papaya, mashed
• 1 tsp. ground turmeric
• ½ tsp. ground cumin
• 1 tbsp. chili powder
• 1 tsp. salt ½ tsp. ground black pepper

Instructions

• Preheat the air fryer to 340 degrees F.
• Slash slits into the sides of the fish.
• Combine all remaining **Ingredients** and coat all sides of the fish with the mixture.
• Place the coated fish into the fryer basket and cook for 20 minutes.

453. Pecan Crusted Salmon

Preparation time: 20mins

Ingredients

• ½ cup pecans
• 3 tbsp. fresh chopped parsley
• 1 tsp. salt
• ½ tsp. ground black pepper
• 3 tbsp. Dijon mustard
• 3 tbsp. olive oil
• 1 tbsp. honey
• ½ cup Panko breadcrumbs
• 4 salmon filets 1 tbsp. lemon juice

Instructions

• Preheat air fryer to 390 degrees F.
• In a small bowl combine the mustard, oil, and honey. Combine the Panko, pecans, parsley, salt, and pepper in a food processor and process until crumbs are fine.
• Dip the salmon in the mustard mixture then dip the salmon into the pecan mixture, pressing the pecans into all sides of the fish.
• Place the coated salmon in the fryer basket and cook for 10 minutes.
• Drizzle with lemon juice.

454. Broiled Tilapia Done

Preparation time: 9mins

Ingredients

• 1 to 1 1/2 lb. tilapia fillets
• molly mcbutter or butter buds
• light spritz of canola oil from an oil spritzer
• Old Bay seasoning,
• lemon pepper
• salt

Instructions

• Thaw fillets, if frozen. Spray the basket of your air fryer with cooking spray.
• Place fillets in the basket (do not stack them) and season to taste with the spices. Spray lightly with oil.
• Set temperature at 400 degrees and set timer for 7 minutes.
• When the timer goes off, check for doneness. Fish should flake easily with a fork.
• Serve and enjoy with your favorite veggies.

455. Prawn Curry

Preparation time: 15mins

Ingredients

• 2 tbsp. curry powder
• 1 medium finely chopped onion
• 1½ cup chicken broth
• ½ tsp. of coriander
• 6 king prawns
• 1 tsp. salt
• ½ tsp. ground black pepper
• 1 tbsp. olive oil
• 1 tbsp. tomato paste

Instructions

• Preheat the air fryer to 370 degrees F. Season the prawns with salt and pepper.
• Cook for 7 minutes. Meanwhile, heat the olive oil in a large skillet. Once hot add the onion.
• Cook until soft. Sit in the curry, tomato paste, and coriander.
• Cook, stirring, for 1 minute.
• Add the chicken broth and stir until smooth.
• Remove prawns from the fryer and add to the sauce.

456. Crusted Halibut

Preparation time: 30mins

Ingredients

• 2 tsp. lemon zest
• 1 tsp. salt
• ½ tsp. ground black pepper
• ¾ cup Panko bread crumbs
• ½ cup fresh parsley, chopped
• ¼ cup fresh dill, chopped
• 4 halibut filets
• 1 tbsp. olive oil

Instructions

• Preheat the air fryer to 390 degrees F.
• Combine all ingredients except halibut and olive oil in a food processor and pulse until the mixture is a fine crumb. Gently coat the halibut in the mixture and place inside the fryer basket.
• Drizzle with olive oil and cook for 25 minutes.

457. Shrimp and Mushroom Risotto

Preparation time: 30mins

Ingredients

• 4 Chicken Legs
• 2 tbsp. Olive Oil
• 4 tsp. dried Basil
• 2 tsp. minced garlic
• Pinch of Pepper
• Pinch of Salt
• 1 Lemon, sliced

Instructions

• Preheat your Air Fryer to 350 degrees F.
• Brush the chicken with the oil and sprinkle with the remaining **Ingredients**.
• Place in the Air Fryer and arrange the lemon slices around the chicken legs.
• Close the lid and cook for 20 minutes.

458. Halibut Sitka

Preparation time: 20mins

Ingredients

• ½ cup green onion, chopped
• ½ cup mayonnaise
• ½ cup sour cream
• 6 (8 oz.) skinless halibut filets
• 1 tsp. salt
• ½ tsp. ground black pepper
• 1 tsp. dry dill

Instructions

• Preheat the air fryer to 390 degrees F
• Season the halibut with salt and pepper, place on the fryer plate.

- In a small bowl, combine the remaining **Ingredients**.
- Mix well then spread over the top of the halibut. Cook for 15 minutes.

459.Calamari and Tomato Pasta

Preparation time: 25mins

Ingredients

- 2 cloves garlic, minced
- 1 lb. sliced calamari, cut into rings
- 1 egg 1 cup Italian bread crumbs
- 1 tbsp. of olive oil
- ½ cup diced onion
- 2 tsps. Italian seasoning
- 2 (15 oz.) cans diced tomatoes, drained
- 1 lb. dry angel hair pasta
- ½ cup grated parmesan

Instructions

- Preheat fryer to 360 degrees.
- Dip the calamari into the egg and then into the breadcrumbs. Coating all sides. Place in the air fryer basket and drizzle with olive oil. Cook for 15 minutes. Meanwhile, bring a large pot of water to a boil.
- Add the pasta and cook for 10 mins or until tender. Drain. Combine the pasta, garlic, onion, Italian seasoning, and diced tomatoes. Heat just until hot. Spoon on to a serving plate. Remove calamari from air fryer and place on top of pasta. Sprinkle with Parmesan

460.Pork Chop Perfection

Preparation time: 35mins

Ingredients

- ½ cup Dijon mustard
- ½ cup bread crumbs, seasoned
- ½ tsp. cayenne pepper
- 4 pork chops, lean, bone-in or boneless
- 1 tsp. salt
- 1 tsp. pepper
- 1 tbsp. canola or sunflower oil

Instructions

- Coat each pork chop with Dijon mustard.
- In a shallow bowl, combine bread crumbs, salt, pepper, and cayenne pepper.
- Dredge pork chops in breadcrumb mixture, coating evenly.
- Brush or spray thin coating of oil on each pork chop.

- Air fry at 400°F for 10 minutes.
- Remove air fryer basket, flip chops.
- Air fry at 400°F for an additional 10 minutes.
- Allow to cool five mins before serving.

461.Almond, and Poppy Seed Cabbage Salad

Preparation time: 15mins

Ingredients

- ½ cup diced green Pepper
- 1 cup of Mayonnaise
- 2 tbsp. minced Chives
- 1 tbsp. Poppy Seeds
- ½ cup Slivered Almonds
- 5 cups Shredded Cabbage
- ½ cup chopped Celery
- 2 tbsp. Mustard
- 1 tbsp. Honey
- ¼ tsp. Salt Pinch of Black Pepper
- 1 tbsp. Lemon Juice

Instructions

- Preheat your Air Fryer to 340 degrees F. Place the cabbage and almonds, in the air dryer. Drizzle with olive oil and cook for 5 minutes. ransfer to a bowl.
- Add the green peppers, chives, and celery, and toss to combine. In a small bowl, whisk together the rest of the **Ingredients**. Pour the mixture over the salad.
- Toss to coat well.

462.Easy Eggplant Parmesan

Preparation time: 140mins

Ingredients

- 1 lb. fresh mozzarella cheese, sliced into rounds
- 1 medium eggplant
- 1 tsp. salt
- ½ cup all-purpose flour
- 2 eggs, beaten
- 1 cup seasoned breadcrumbs
- ¼ cup olive oil
- 16 oz. jar marinara sauce

Instructions

- Peel and slice eggplant into ½" slices.
- Place the eggplant rounds in a colander and toss them with 1 teaspoon of salt. Let them drain in the colander over a bowl in the sink for 45 mins to remove excess moisture. Mix breadcrumbs and olive oil in a medium bowl. Bread the eggplant rounds in batches by coating them in the flour,

then the eggs and then the breadcrumbs. Preheat air fryer to 390 F.

- Place 4-5 slices of breaded eggplant into the fryer and air fry for 8 minutes. Transfer fried eggplant to a non-stick cookie sheet and top with one tablespoon of marinara sauce and one slice of mozzarella cheese.
- Broil eggplant until cheese bubbles and browns lightly.
- Allow five mins to cool before serving.

463.Rib Eye Steak

Preparation time: 35mins

Ingredients

- 1 tbsp. onion powder
- 1 tbsp. garlic powder
- 1 tbsp. oregano
- 2 tsp. ground cumin
- 2 lb. ribeye steak
- 4 ½ tsp. salt
- 2 tbsp. ground black pepper
- 2 tbsp. paprika
- 1 tbsp. high-heat cooking

Instructions

- In a small bowl, mix all the seasonings to create a dry rub. Rub seasoning into the surface of the entire ribeye.
- Brush oil over the seasoned ribeye. Preheat air fryer to 400°F .Place rib eye into fryer basket and air fry at 400°F for 7 minutes. gently flip rib eye with tongs.
- Air fry at 400°F for an additional 7 to 10 minutes.
- Allow to cool at least five minutes.

464.Philly Cheese Steak Stromboli

Preparation time: 45mins

Ingredients

- 1½ cup grated Cheddar cheese
- ½ onion, sliced
- ½ cup jarred cheese sauce
- ¼ tsp. salt
- ¼ tsp. ground black pepper
- 1 lb. strip loin steak, trimmed and thinly sliced
- 14 ounces pizza dough store-bought or homemade
- 1 tbsp. Worcestershire sauce
- 2 tsp. high-heat cooking oil
- 1 cup marinara sauce

Instructions

- Mix 1 tsp. oil and onion in air fry basket and air fry for 8 minutes, stirring once at 4 minutes. Add the sliced beef,

Worcestershire sauce, salt and pepper, and mix well. Air fry for 8 mins at 400ºF, stirring occasionally.

• Remove the chicken and onion from the air fryer and allow to cool. On a lightly floured surface, roll the pizza dough into a 13x11" rectangle.

• Sprinkle half of the Cheddar cheese over the dough leaving an empty 1" border on one side. Evenly top the cheese with the beef mixture. Warm the jarred cheese sauce and drizzle over the meat.

• Sprinkle the remaining Cheddar cheese on top. Roll the Stromboli toward the empty border, keeping the filling tightly tucked inside the roll. Tuck the ends of the dough in and pinch the seam shut.

• Cut 4 small slits evenly in the top of the dough and brush with remaining oil.

• Place the seam side down and shape the Stromboli into a U-shape to fit in the air fry basket.

• Air fry at 370°F 6 minutes. gently flip the Stromboli, apply additional oil, and air fry for an additional 6 to 8 mins until the dough becomes golden brown.

• Allow to cool 10 mins before serving. Service with marinara sauce.

465. Baked Marinarah Eggs

Preparation time: 25mins

Ingredients

• 2 tsps. parmesan cheese
• 1 tsp. salt
• 1 tsp. pepper
• 4 eggs
• ½ cup whole milk or heavy cream
• 1 cup spinach
• 2 tsps. marinara sauce

Instructions

• In a medium saucepan, stir spinach with ¼ cup of milk or cream over medium heat for 3 mins or until spinach wilts and absorbs milk. Divide spinach equally between four small baking dishes Crack an egg into each ramekin. Add one tablespoon of milk to each egg to the side of the yolk. prinkle salt and pepper on each egg.

• Add an equal dollop of marinara to each ramekin.

• Sprinkle parmesan cheese over each

ramekin.Air fry at 350°F for seven minutes.

• Remove from air fryer and check yoke consistency. If too runny, air fry for an additional 3-5 mins until desired yoke consistency.

• Allow to cool for 2-3 mins before serving.

466. Beefalo Burgers

Preparation time: 25mins

Ingredients

• 1 tsp. garlic powder
• ½ tsp. celery salt
• ½ tsp. oregano
• 1 lb. lean ground beef
• 3 tbsp. buffalo wing sauce
• 4 slices blue cheese

Instructions

• In a medium bowl, gently mix together ground beef and seasonings.

• Shape ground beef into four ¼ lb. patties. Preheat air fryer to 350°F

• Air fry at 350°F for 10 minutes.

• Remove and place a single blue cheese slice on each patty. Return patties to hot air fryer and allow the cheese to melt slightly without additional frying.

• Allow to cool five mins before serving.

467. Beef Goulash with Sour Cream

Total Time: 40mins

Ingredients

• 2 tbsp of Olive oil
• 1 and ½ pounds of chopped stewing steak
• ½ Cup of almond flour
• 1 Large, thinly sliced onion
• 2 Finely chopped garlic clove
• 1 Deseeded and thinly sliced green pepper
• 1 Thinly sliced red pepper
• 2 tbsp of tomato puree
• 2 tbsp of Paprika
• 2 large diced Tomatoes
• 3 tbsp of beef stock
• 2 tbsp of chopped leaf parsley
• 1 Pinch of black pepper
• 1 cup of low fat sour cream

Instructions:

• Preheat your air fryer to 390° F .Place 1 tablespoon oil in your air fryer pan .

• Sprinkle the beef steak with the almond flour and add it to the pan .

• Add the onion, the garlic, the green pepper and the red pepper .

• Add the tomato puree and the paprika.

• Place the pan in your air fryer and lock the lid .

• Set your timer to 35 mins and the temperature to 35 mins .When the timer beeps; turn off your air fryer .

468. Chicken Kebobs with Cilantro

Total Time: 15mins

Ingredients

• 1 and ¼ pounds of cubed beef sirloin
• 1 Pinch of fresh ground pepper
• 1 and ¼ tsp of kosher salt
• 1 large; diced red onion
• 17 to 18 cherry tomatoes
• Soaked bamboo skewers

To make the Chimichurri sauce:

• 2 tbsp of finely chopped parsley
• 2 tbsp of chopped cilantro
• 2 tbsp of finely chopped red onion
• 1 Minced garlic clove
• 2 tbsp of extra virgin olive oil
• 2 tbsp of apple cider vinegar
• 1 tbsp of water
• ¼ tsp of kosher salt
• 1/8 tsp of fresh black pepper
• 1/8 tsp of crushed red pepper flakes

Instructions

• Season your meat with 1 pinch of salt and 1 pinch of pepper.

• To make the chimichurri, combine the vinegar, the red onion, the salt and the olive oil and set it aside for about 5 minutes.Put the onions, the beef and the tomatoes into the skewers.

• Place the skewers in the air fryer basket and lock the lid.

• Set the timer to about 10 mins and the temperature to about 375 degrees.

• When the timer beeps, turn off your air fryer.

• Serve and enjoy your kabobs with the chimichurri sauce!

469. Juicy Sweet Chili Chicken Fillets

Preparation Time: 35 mins

Ingredients

• 2 Chicken Fillets
• Salt and Pepper to taste
• 1 cup Almond Flour
• 3 Eggs
• ½ cup Apple Cider Vinegar

- ½ tsp ginger Paste
- ½ tsp garlic Paste
- 1 tbsp Swerve Sweetener
- 2 Red Chilies, minced
- 2 tsp Tomato Puree
- 1 Red Pepper
- 1 green Pepper
- 1 tsp Paprika
- 4 tbsp Water Cooking Spray

Instructions

- Preheat the Air Fryer to 350 F.
- Put the chicken breasts on a clean flat surface.
- Cut them in cubes. Pour the almond flour in a bowl, crack the eggs into it, add the salt and pepper.
- Whisk it using a fork or whisk.
- Put the chicken in the flour mixture.
- Mix to coat the chicken with it using a wooden spatula. Place the chicken in the fryer basket, spray them with cooking spray, and fry them for 8 minutes.
- Pull out the fryer basket, shake it to toss the chicken, and spray again with cooking spray.
- Keeping cooking for 7 mins or until golden and crispy.
- Remove the chicken into a plate and set aside. Put the red, yellow, and green peppers on a chopping board. Using a knife, cut them open and deseed them.
- Cut the flesh in long strips.
- In a bowl, add the water, apple cider vinegar, swerve sweetener, ginger and garlic puree, red chili, tomato puree, and smoked paprika. Mix with a fork.
- Place a skillet over medium heat on a stove top and spray it with cooking spray.
- Add the chicken to it and the pepper strips. Stir and cook until the peppers are sweaty but still crunchy.
- Pour the chili mixture on the chicken, stir, and bring it to simmer for 10 minutes. Turn off the heat.

Dish the chicken chili sauce into a serving bowl and serve with a side of steamed cauli rice

470. Chicken Lollipop

Preparation Time: 20 mins

Ingredients

- 1 lb mini Chicken Drumsticks
- ½ tsp Soy Sauce

- 1 tsp Lime Juice Salt and Pepper to taste
- 1 tsp Arrowroot Starch
- ½ tsp Minced garlic
- ½ tsp Chili Powder
- ½ tsp chopped Coriander
- ½ tsp garlic ginger Paste
- 1 tsp Plain Vinegar
- 1 tsp Chili Paste
- ½ tsp Beaten Egg
- 1 tsp Paprika
- 1 tsp Almond Flour
- 2 tsp Monk Fruit Syrup

Instructions

- Mix the garlic ginger paste, chili powder, monk fruit syrup, paprika powder, chopped coriander, plain vinegar, egg, garlic, and salt in a bowl.
- Add the chicken drumsticks and toss to coat completely.
- Stir in the arrowroot starch, almond flour, and lime juice.
- Preheat the Air Fryer to 350 F.
- Remove each drumstick, shake off the excess marinade, and place them in a single layer in the fryer basket.
- Cook them for 5 minutes. Slide out the fryer basket, spray the chicken with cooking spray and continue cooking for 5 minutes.
- Remove them onto a serving platter and serve with a tomato dip and a side of steamed asparagus.

471. Chicken Cheesy Divan Casserole

Preparation Time: 53 mins

Ingredients

- 3 Chicken Breasts
- Salt and Pepper to taste
- 1 cup shredded Cheddar Cheese
- 1 Broccoli Head
- ½ cup Mushroom Soup Cream
- ½ cup Keto Croutons
- Cooking Spray

Instructions

- Preheat the Air Fryer to 390 F.
- Place the chicken breasts on a clean flat surface and season with salt and pepper.
- Grease with cooking spray and place them in the fryer basket.
- Close the Air Fryer and cook for 13 minutes.
- Meanwhile, place the broccoli on the

chopping board and use a knife to chop.
- Remove them onto the chopping board, let cool, and cut into bite-size pieces. In a bowl, add the chicken, broccoli, cheddar cheese, and mushroom soup cream and mix well.
- Scoop the mixture into a 3 X 3cm casserole dish, add the keto croutons on top and spray with cooking spray.
- Put the dish in the fryer basket and cook for 10 minutes. Serve with a side of steamed greens.

472. Chipotle Steak with Avocado-Lime Salsa

Preparation Time: 32 mins

Ingredients:

- 1 ½ lb Rib Eye Steak
- 2 tsp Olive Oil
- 1 tbsp Chipotle Chili Pepper
- Salt and Black pepper to taste
- 1 Avocado, diced
- Juice from ½ Lime

Instructions:

- Place the steak on a chopping board.
- Pour the olive oil over it and sprinkle with the chipotle pepper, salt, and black pepper. Use your hands to rub the spices on the meat. Leave it to sit and marinate for 10 minutes. Preheat the Air Fryer to 400 F.
- Pull out the fryer basket and place the meat in it. Slide it back into the Air Fryer and cook for 14 minutes.
- Turn the steak and continue cooking for 6 minutes.
- Remove the steak, cover with foil, and let it sit for 5 mins before slicing. Meanwhile, prepare the avocado salsa by mashing the avocado with potato mash.
- Add in the lime juice and mix until smooth. Taste, adjust the seasoning.
- Slice and serve the steak with salsa.

473. Air Fried Stuffed Pizza Pastries

Preparation time: 25mins

Ingredients

- 1 (13.5-ounce) readymade pizza crust
- 6-ounces of sliced pepperoni
- 1 tbsp. of melted butter
- 1 tsp. of black pepper
- 1 tsp. of garlic powder
- 3 tbsp. of Parmesan cheese, grated
- 1 tsp. of salt

- 1 tsp. of Italian seasoning
- 12-ounces of mozzarella cheese, shredded

Instructions

- Preheat the air fryer to 390 degrees Fahrenheit. In a bowl combine the butter, salt, garlic powder, Italian seasoning, and black pepper.
- Cut the pizza crust into 4-inch squares. Fill the middle of each square using the pepperoni.
- Add cheese on top. Take one edge of each square and bring it to another end. Seal using a fork.
- Brush the pastries using the butter mixture. Air fry for about 15 minutes.
- Serve hot.

474. Royal Meatball Sub

Preparation time: 30mins

Ingredients

- 3 baguettes
- 1 onion, peeled and chopped
- 1 (15-ounce) can of tomato sauce
- ½ cup of cheddar cheese, shredded
- 1 pound of ground beef
- ¼ cup of panko breadcrumbs
- 1 egg
- 4 slices of provolone cheese
- 1 tbsp. of olive oil
- 1 tsp. of black pepper
- 1 tbsp. of dried parsley
- 1 tbsp. of dried oregano
- 1 tsp. of salt

Instructions

- Preheat the air fryer to 360 degrees Fahrenheit. Combine the ground beef, egg, seasonings, breadcrumbs, and onion in a bowl.
- Mix well and create meatballs using the hands.
- Fry them in the air fryer for 15 minutes.
- Put egg and stir until it is properly mixed Cut the baguettes into small pieces and drizzle some olive oil.
- Toast them in the air fryer for a minute or two.
- In a pan add the tomato sauce and add to the air fryer.
- Cook for about 5 minutes. Brush the baguettes with the tomato sauce, add the meatballs and cheese.
- Add to the air fryer one more time

and wait for the cheese to melt.
- Serve hot.

475. Spinach Stuffed Cannelloni

Preparation time: 25mins

Ingredients

- 2 tbsp. Parmesan cheese
- 1 egg 1 cup spinach, cooked
- 9 cannelloni shells, cooked
- 3 cups Tomato Sauce
- 2 cups alfredo sauce
- 1 cup ricotta cheese
- 1 cup shredded mozzarella

Instructions

- Preheat the fryer to 380 degrees F .Combine the spinach, ricotta, parmesan, garlic, and egg. Mix well.
- Place the spinach mixture into a piping bag and fill the cannelloni shells. Place the filled shells on to the fryer try. Top with the alfredo and tomato sauce. Sprinkle mozzarella on top. Bake for 15 minutes.

476. Cheesy Stuffed Manicotti

Preparation time: 25mins

Ingredients

- 1 tbsp. dried parsley
- 8 Manicotti Shells, cooked
- 1 large egg
- 1 cups ricotta cheese
- 2 cups shredded mozzarella
- 1 cup grated Parmesan cheese
- 3 cups alfredo sauce

Instructions

- Preheat the air fryer to 350 degrees F.
- Combine the egg, ricotta, one cup of the mozzarella, and parmesan cheese. Mix well. Place the filling into a piping bag and fill the manicotti shells with the mixture. Place the filled shells on the fryer tray. Top with Alfredo sauce and sprinkle the last cup of mozzarella on top.
- Bake for 15 minutes. Remove and sprinkle parsley on top.

477. Air Fryer Coconut Shrimp

Prep Time: 30 mins
Cook Time: 15 mins
Total Time: 45 mins

Ingredient

- ½ cup all-purpose flour
- 1 ½ Tsp. ground black pepper
- 2 large eggs
- ⅔ cup unsweetened flaked coconut

- ⅓ cup panko bread crumbs
- 12 ounces uncooked medium shrimp, peeled and deveined
- cooking spray
- ½ Tsp. kosher salt, divided
- ¼ cup honey
- ¼ cup lime juice
- 1 serrano chile, thinly sliced
- 2 teaspoons chopped fresh cilantro

Instructions

- Stir together flour and pepper in a shallow dish. Lightly beat eggs in a second shallow dish.
- Stir together coconut and panko in a third shallow dish. Hold each shrimp by the tail, dredge in flour mixture, and shake off excess.
- Then dip floured shrimp in egg, and allow any excess to drip off.
- Finally, dredge in coconut mixture, pressing to adhere. Place on a plate.
- Coat shrimp well with cooking spray.
- Preheat air fryer to 400 degrees F (200 degrees C).
- Place 1/2 the shrimp in the air fryer and cook for about 3 minutes.
- Turn shrimp over and continue cooking until golden, about 3 mins more. Season with 1/4 Tsp. salt.
- Repeat with remaining shrimp.
- Meanwhile, whisk together honey, lime juice, and serrano chile in a small bowl for the dip.
- Sprinkle fried shrimp with cilantro and serve with dip.

478. Air-Fried Shrimp

Prep Time: 5 mins Cook Time: 10 mins
Total Time: 15 mins Servings: 4

Ingredient

- 1 Tbsp butter, melted
- 1 Tsp. lemon juice
- ½ Tsp. garlic granules
- ⅛ Tsp. salt
- 1 pound large shrimp - peeled, deveined, and tails removed
- Perforated parchment paper
- ⅛ cup freshly grated parmesan cheese

Instructions

- Place melted butter in a medium bowl. Mix in lemon juice, garlic granules, and salt. Add shrimp and toss to coat.
- Line air fryer basket with perforated

parchment paper. Place shrimp in the air fryer basket and sprinkle with Parmesan cheese.

• Cook shrimp in the air fryer at 400 degrees F (200 degrees C) until shrimp are bright pink on the outside and the meat is opaque for about 8 minutes.

479.Chef John's Baked Lemon Pepper Salmon

Prep Time: 10 mins Cook Time: 15 mins Additional Time: 30 mins Total Time: 55 mins Servings: 2

Ingredient

• 2 Tbsps lemon juice
• 1 Tbsp ground black pepper
• 1 ½ Tbsp mayonnaise
• 1 Tbsp yellow miso paste
• 2 teaspoons dijon mustard
• 1 pinch cayenne pepper, or to taste
• 2 (8 ounces) center-cut salmon fillets, boned, skin on
• Sea salt to taste

Instructions

• Whisk together lemon juice and black pepper in a small bowl. Add mayonnaise, miso paste, Dijon mustard, and cayenne pepper to lemon-pepper mixture; whisk together.

• Spread the lemon-pepper mixture over salmon fillets. Reserve about a Tbsp for later use.

• Cover salmon with plastic wrap and refrigerate for 30 min..

• Preheat oven to 450 degrees F (230 degrees C). Line a baking sheet with parchment paper or a silicone baking mat.

• Place fillets on the prepared baking sheet. Spread the remaining lemon-pepper mixture on fillets without letting it pool around the base. Sprinkle with a pinch more black pepper and a generous amount of sea salt.

• Bake in the preheated oven until the fish flakes easily with a fork, 10 to 15 minutes.

480.Rockin' Oysters Rockefeller

Prep Time: 30 mins Cook Time: 30 mins Total Time: 1 hr Servings: 16

Ingredient

• 48 fresh, unopened oysters
• 1 ½ cups beer
• 2 cloves garlic
• seasoned salt to taste

• 7 black peppercorns
• ½ cup butter
• 1 onion, chopped
• 1 clove garlic, crushed
• 1 (10 ounces) package frozen chopped spinach, thawed and drained
• 8 ounces Monterey Jack cheese, shredded
• 8 ounces fontina cheese, shredded
• 8 ounces mozzarella cheese, shredded
• ½ cup milk
• 2 teaspoons salt, or to taste
• 1 Tsp. ground black pepper
• 2 Tbsp fine bread crumbs

Instructions

• Clean oysters, and place them in a large stockpot. Pour in beer and enough water to cover oysters; add 2 cloves garlic, seasoned salt, and peppercorns. Bring to a boil. Remove from heat, drain, and cool.

• Once oysters are cooled, break off and discard the top shell. Arrange the oysters on a baking sheet. Preheat oven to 425 degrees F (220 degrees C.)

• Melt butter in a saucepan over medium heat. Cook onion and garlic in butter until soft. Reduce heat to low, and stir in spinach, Monterey Jack, fontina, and mozzarella. Cook until cheese melts, stirring frequently. Stir in the milk, and season with salt and pepper. Spoon sauce over each oyster, just filling the shell. Sprinkle with bread crumbs.

• Bake until golden and bubbly, approximately 8 to 10 min.

481.Dinah's Baked Scallops

Prep Time: 20 mins Cook Time: 15 mins Total Time: 35 mins Servings: 4

Ingredient

• 20 buttery round crackers, crushed
• black pepper to taste
• 1 Tsp. garlic powder
• 1 pound sea scallops, rinsed and drained
• ½ cup butter, melted
• ¼ cup dry white wine
• ½ lemon, juiced
• 1 Tbsp chopped fresh parsley, for garnish

Instructions

• Preheat oven to 350 degrees F (175

degrees C). Lightly grease an 8x8 inch baking dish.

• Combine crushed crackers, black pepper, and garlic powder in a small bowl. Press scallops into the mixture so that they are evenly coated, and place them in the greased baking dish.

• In a separate bowl, mix melted butter, wine, and lemon juice; drizzle mixture over scallops.

• Bake in the preheated oven until scallops are lightly browned, about 15 min.. Garnish with chopped parsley.

482.Easy-Bake Fish

Prep Time: 15 mins Cook Time: 20 mins Total Time: 35 mins Servings: 4

Ingredient

• 3 Tbsp honey
• 3 Tbsps Dijon mustard
• 1 Tsp. lemon juice
• 4 (6 ounces) salmon steaks
• ½ Tsp. pepper

Instructions

• Preheat oven to 325 degrees F (165 degrees C).

• In a small bowl, mix honey, mustard, and lemon juice. Spread the mixture over the salmon steaks. Season with pepper. Arrange in a medium baking dish.

• Bake 20 mins in the preheated oven, or until fish easily flakes with a fork.

483.Hudson's Baked Tilapia With Dill Sauce

Prep Time: 10 mins Cook Time: 20 mins Total Time: 30 mins Servings: 4

Ingredient

• 4 (4 ounce) fillets tilapia
• Salt and pepper to taste
• 1 Tbsp cajun seasoning, or to taste
• 1 lemon, thinly sliced
• ¼ cup mayonnaise
• ½ cup sour cream
• ⅛ Tsp. garlic powder
• 1 Tsp. fresh lemon juice
• 2 Tbsps chopped fresh dill

Instructions

• Preheat the oven to 350 degrees F (175 degrees C). Lightly grease a 9x13 inch baking dish.

• Season the tilapia fillets with salt, pepper, and Cajun seasoning on both sides. Arrange the seasoned fillets in a single layer in the baking dish. Place a layer of lemon slices over the fish fillets. I usually use about 2 slices on each piece so that it covers most of the surface of the fish.

- Bake uncovered for 15 to 20 mins in the preheated oven, or until fish flakes easily with a fork.
- While the fish is baking, mix the mayonnaise, sour cream, garlic powder, lemon juice, and dill in a small bowl. Serve with tilapia.

484.Best Tuna Casserole

Prep Time: 15 mins Cook Time: 20 mins
Total Time: 35 mins Servings: 6
Ingredient
- 1 (12 ounces) package egg noodles
- ¼ cup chopped onion
- 2 cups shredded Cheddar cheese
- 1 cup frozen green peas
- 2 (5 ounce) cans tuna, drained
- 2 (10.75 ounces) cans condensed cream of mushroom soup
- ½ (4.5 ounces) can sliced mushrooms
- 1 cup crushed potato chips
Instructions
- Bring a large pot of lightly salted water to a boil. Cook pasta in boiling water for 8 to 10 min., or until al dente; drain.
- Preheat oven to 425 degrees F (220 degrees C).
- In a large bowl, thoroughly mix noodles, onion, 1 cup cheese, peas, tuna, soup, and mushrooms. Transfer to a 9x13 inch baking dish, and top with potato chip crumbs and remaining 1 cup cheese.
- Bake for 15 to 20 mins in the preheated oven, or until cheese is bubbly.

485.Perfect Ten Baked Cod

Prep Time: 10 mins Cook Time: 25 mins
Total Time: 35 mins Servings: 4
Ingredient
- 2 Tbsp butter
- ½ sleeve buttery round crackers (such as Ritz®), crushed
- 2 Tbsp butter
- 1 pound thick-cut cod loin
- ½ lemon, juiced
- ¼ cup dry white wine
- 1 Tbsp chopped fresh parsley

- 1 Tbsp chopped green onion
- 1 lemon, cut into wedges
Instructions
- Preheat oven to 400 degrees F
- Place 2 Tbsp butter in a microwave-safe bowl; melt in the microwave on high, about 30 seconds. Stir buttery round crackers into melted butter.
- Place remaining 2 Tbsps butter in a 7x11-inch baking dish. Melt in the preheated oven, 1 to 3 minutes. Remove dish from oven.
- Coat both sides of cod in melted butter in the baking dish.
- Bake cod in the preheated oven for 10 min.. Remove from oven; top with lemon juice, wine, and cracker mixture. Place back in the oven and bake until fish is opaque and flakes easily with a fork, about 10 more minutes.
- Garnish baked cod with parsley and green onion. Serve with lemon wedges.

Meat Recipes

486.Air Fryer Steak

Prep Time: 5 mins Cook Time: 25 mins
Total Time: 30 mins
Ingredients
- 2 (6 oz.) steaks, 3/4" thick rinsed and patted dry
- 1 Tsp. (5 ml) olive oil, to coat
- 1/2 Tsp. (0.5) garlic powder (optional)
- Salt, to taste
- Pepper, to taste
- Butter
Instructions
- Lightly coat steaks with olive oil. Season both sides of steaks with garlic powder (optional), salt, and pepper (we'll usually season liberally with salt & pepper).
- Preheat the Air Fryer at 400°F for 4 min..
- Air Fry for 400°F for 10-18 minutes, flipping halfway through (cooking time depends on how thick and cold the steaks are plus how do you prefer your steaks).
- If you want steaks to be cooked more, add additional 3-6 mins of cooking time.
- Add a pat of butter on top of the steak, cover with foil, and allow the steak to rest for 5 min..

- Season with additional salt and pepper, if needed. Serve immediately.

487.Steak Bites & Mushrooms

Prep Time: 10 mins Cook Time: 18 mins
Total Time: 28 mins
Ingredients
- 1 lb. (454 g) steaks, cut into 1/2" cubes (ribeye, sirloin, tri-tip, or what you prefer)
- 8 oz. (227 g) mushrooms (cleaned, washed, and halved)
- 2 Tbsps (30 ml) butter, melted (or olive oil)
- 1 Tsp. (5 ml) worcestershire sauce
- 1/2 Tsp. (2.5 ml) garlic powder, optional
- Flakey salt, to taste
- Fresh cracked black pepper, to taste
- Minced parsley, garnish
- Melted butter, for finishing - optional
- Chili flakes, for finishing - optional
Instructions
- Rinse and thoroughly pat dry the steak cubes. Combine the steak cubes and mushrooms. Coat with the melted butter and then season with Worcestershire sauce, optional garlic powder, and a generous seasoning of salt and pepper.
- Preheat the Air Fryer at 400°F for 4 min..
- Spread the steak and mushrooms in an even layer in the air fryer basket. Air fry at 400°F for 10-18 minutes, shaking and flipping and the steak and mushrooms 2 times through the cooking process (time depends on your preferred doneness, the thickness of the steak, size of air fryer).
- Check the steak to see how well done it is cooked. If you want the steak more done, add an extra 2-5 mins of cooking time.
- Garnish with parsley and drizzle with optional melted butter and/or optional chili flakes. Season with additional salt & pepper if desired. Serve warm.

488.Air fryer Steak Tips

Prep Time: 5 mins Cook Time: 9 mins
Total Time: 14 mins
Servings: 3
Ingredients
- 1.5 lb steak or beef chuck for a cheaper version cut to 3/4 inch cubes

- Air Fryer Steak Marinade
- 1 tsp oil
- 1/4 tsp salt
- 1/2 tsp black pepper, freshly ground
- 1/2 tsp dried garlic powder
- 1/2 tsp dried onion powder
- 1 tsp Montreal Steak Seasoning
- 1/8 tsp cayenne pepper
- Air Fryer Asparagus
- 1 lb Asparagus, tough ends trimmed
- 1/4 tsp salt
- 1/2 tsp oil (optional)

Instructions

- Preheat the air fryer at 400F for about 5 min..
- Meanwhile, trim the steak of any fat and cut it into cubes. Then, toss with the ingredients for the marinade (oil, salt, black pepper, Montreal seasoning, onion and garlic powder & the cayenne pepper) and massage the spices into the meat to coat evenly. Do this in a ziplock bag for easier cleanup.
- Spray the bottom of the air fryer basket with nonstick spray if you have any and spread the prepared meat along the bottom of it. Cook the beef steak tips for about 4-6 mins and check for doneness.
- Toss the asparagus with 1/2 tsp oil and 1/4 tsp salt until evenly coated.
- Once the steak bites are browned to your liking, toss them around and move to one side. Add the asparagus to the other side of the air fryer basket and cook for another 3 minutes.
- Remove the steak tips and the asparagus to a serving plate and serve while hot.

489. Easy Air Fryer Steak Bites

Prep Time: 5 mins Cook Time: 9 mins
Total Time: 14 mins
Yield: 2-4 servings

Ingredients

- Sirloin Steak Bites or a 1lb. sirloin steak cut into bite-size pieces
- Steak seasoning or salt and pepper
- Olive oil

Instructions

- Start by preheating your air fryer to 390° or 400°.
- Place the steak bites in a bowl and add about a Tbsp of steak seasoning or season with salt and pepper.

- Pour in a Tbsp of olive oil and toss to coat all of the steak bites.
- Place the steak bites in a single layer in your air fryer basket and cook for 5 min..
- Turn the steak bites over and cook for an additional 4 mins for a medium steak. Cook for an additional 2-3 mins for medium-well and a couple of mins less for medium-rare.
- Remove from the air fryer and allow them to rest for 5-10 mins so the meat will retain its juices.
- Enjoy a salad or with your favorite veggies for lunch or dinner!

490. Air Fryer Steak Bites (With Or Without Potatoes)

Prep Time: 10 mins Cook Time: 20 mins
Total Time: 30 mins Servings: 4 Servings

Ingredients

- 1 lb. steaks, cut into 1/2" cubes & patted dry
- 1/2 lb. (227 g) potatoes (optional), cut into 1/2" pieces
- 2 Tbsp (30 ml) butter, melted (or oil)
- 1 Tsp. (5 ml) worcestershire sauce
- 1/2 Tsp. (2.5 ml) garlic powder
- Salt, to taste
- Black pepper, to taste
- Minced parsley, garnish
- Melted butter for finishing, optional
- Chili flakes, for finishing, optional

Instructions

- Heat a large pot of water to a boil and then add the potatoes. Cook for about 5 minutes, or until nearly tender, and then drain.
- Combine the steak cubes and blanched potatoes. Coat with the melted butter and then season with Worcestershire sauce, garlic powder, salt, and pepper.
- Preheat the Air Fryer at 400°F for 4 min..
- Spread the steak and potatoes in an even layer in an air fryer basket. Air fry at 400°F for 10-18 min., shaking and flipping and the steak and potatoes about 3 times through the cooking process (time depends on your preferred doneness, the thickness of the steak, and size of air fryer).
- Check the steak to see how well done

it is cooked. If you want the steak more done, add an extra 2-5 mins of cooking time.
- Garnish with parsley and drizzle with optional melted butter and/or optional chili flakes. Season with additional salt & pepper if desired. Serve warm

491. Perfect Air Fryer Steak

Prep Time: 20 mins Cook Time: 12 mins
Resting Time: 5 mins
Total Time: 32 mins Servings: 2

Ingredients

- 2 8 oz Ribeye steak
- Salt
- Freshly cracked black pepper
- Olive oil
- Garlic Butter
- 1 stick unsalted butter softened
- 2 tbsp fresh parsley chopped
- 2 tsp garlic minced
- 1 tsp Worcestershire Sauce
- 1/2 tsp salt

Instructions

- Prepare Garlic Butter by mixing butter, parsley garlic, Worcestershire sauce, and salt until thoroughly combined.
- Place in parchment paper and roll into a log. Refrigerate until ready to use.
- Remove steak from the fridge and allow to sit at room temperature for 20 minutes. Rub a little bit of olive oil on both sides of the steak and season with salt and freshly cracked black pepper.
- Grease your Air Fryer basket by rubbing a little bit of oil on the basket. Preheat Air Fryer to 400 degrees Fahrenheit. Once preheated, place steaks in the air fryer and cook for 12 min., flipping halfway through.
- Remove from air fryer and allow to rest for 5 min.. Top with garlic butter.

492. Air Fryer Steak

Prep Time: 5 min Cook Time: 12 min
Total Time: 12 min Yield: 2

Ingredients

- 2 (1 in thick) Steaks Rib Eye, or Tri-Tip), 4 to 6 oz each
- Salt and Pepper to taste
- 2 Tbsps of butter (optional)

Instructions

- If your air fryer requires preheating, preheat your air fryer.

- Set the temperature to 400 degrees Fahrenheit.
- Season your steak with salt and pepper on each side.
- Place the steak in your air fryer basket. Do not overlap the steaks.
- **Medium Steak:** Set the time to 12 mins and flip the steak at 6.
- **Medium Rare:** For a medium-rare steak, cook the steak for 10 mins and flip it at 5 min..

493.Air Fryer Steak

Prep Time: 5 Mins Cook Time: 8 Mins
Rest Time: 5 Mins
Total Time: 18 Mins Servings: 2 Steaks
Ingredients
- 2 steaks 1" thick, ribeye, sirloin, or striploin
- 1 Tbsp olive oil
- 1 Tbsp salted butter melted
- Steak seasoning to taste
Instructions
- Remove steaks from the fridge at least 30 mins before cooking.
- Preheat air fryer to 400°F.
- Rub the steaks with olive oil and melted butter. Generously season on each side.
- Add the steaks to the air fryer basket and cook for 8-12 mins (flipping after 4 min.) or until steaks reach desired doneness.
- Remove steaks from the air fryer and transfer them to a plate. Rest at least 5 mins before serving.
- Top with additional butter if desired and serve.

494.Air Fryer Roast Beef With Herb Crust

Prep Time: 5 mins Cook Time: 1 hour
RestingTime: 10 mins
Total Time: 1 hour 15 mins
Servings: 6 people
Ingredients
- 2- 2-pound beef roast
- 2 teaspoons garlic powder
- 2 teaspoons onion salt
- 2 teaspoons parsley
- 2 teaspoons thyme
- 2 teaspoons basil
- 1/2 Tbsp salt
- 1 Tsp. pepper
- 1 Tbsp olive oil

Instructions
- Preheat the air fryer for 15 mins at 390 degrees.
- Combine the garlic powder, onion salt, parsley, thyme, and basil, salt, and pepper.
- Rub the roast with olive oil then rub the herb mixture over the entire roast.
- Place the roast in the preheated air fryer. Set timer for 15 minutes.
- After 15 min., remove the basket and turn the roast over.
- Reduce the temperature to 360 degrees on the air fryer and return the roast. Cook for another 60 min., or until the thermometer reaches desired degree of doneness.
- Let roast rest for 15 mins before slicing.

495.Air Fryer Garlic Steak Bites

Prep Time: 10 Mins Cook Time: 15 Mins
Total Time: 25 Mins
Servings: 4 People
Ingredients
- 1 pound New York steak or sirloin steak cut into one inch cubes
- 2 Tbsp olive oil
- 1/2 Tsp. salt
- 1/4 Tsp. pepper
- 1 Tsp. Italian seasoning
- 3 cloves garlic minced
Herb Butter:
- 1/4 cup butter melted
- 1/2 Tsp. thyme
- 1/2 Tsp. rosemary minced
- 1 Tsp. parsley minced
Instructions
- In a medium-sized bowl add the steak bites, olive oil, salt, pepper, Italian seasoning, and garlic. Add to the basket of the air fryer.
- Cook at 400 degrees for 10-12 minutes. Once cooked toss to coat with the garlic herb butter.

496.Best Air Fryer Steak Recipe

Prep Time: 15 mins Cook Time: 10 mins
Total Time: 25 mins
Servings: 2
Ingredients
- 2 Steak Ribeye, New York, Sirloin, or any steak of choice.
- 1 Tsp. Paprika
- 1/2 Tsp. Oregano

- 1/2 Tsp. Black pepper or to taste
- Salt
- For the Garlic Herb Butter
- 2 Tbsps Butter
- 1 Tsp. garlic granules
- 1 Tbsp freshly chopped Parsley
Instructions
- Add the paprika, oregano, black pepper, salt to a bowl and mix.
- Add the garlic granules and freshly chopped parsley in the butter, mix well and store in the fridge till it's time to use.
- Garlic herb butter displayed.
- Pat steak dry and season both sides with the seasoning mix. Leave to marinate for 10-15 min..
- Seasoned steaks.
- Arrange the side of the steak by side in the air fryer basket and air fry at a temperature of 195C for 10 mins (well done). After half of the time, bring the air fryer basket out and turn the steak to the other side.
- Steaks displayed in the air fryer basket.
- After the 5 mins cycle is done, bring the steaks out, serve and immediately add the garlic butter to the steaks.
- Enjoy air fryer garlic butter steak.
- Air fryer steak topped with garlic butter.

497.Perfect Air Fryer Steak: Paleo, Whole30, Keto, Easy!

Prep Time: 5 MinsCook Time: 12 Mins
Total Time: 17 Mins
Ingredients
- 2 sirloin steaks
- 2–3 tbsp steak seasoning
- Spray oil or cooking fat of choice (I prefer avocado oil)
Instructions
- First, pat the steak dry and let come to room temperature
- Spray (or brush) oil lightly on the steak and season liberally
- Spray or coat the bottom of the air fryer basket with oil and place the steaks into the air fryer. The steaks can be touching or sort of "smooshed" in the basket.
- Cook at 400 degrees F. for 6 minutes, flip the steaks, and cook for another 6 min.. If you want your steak more well-

done, add 2-3 minutes. Let rest before serving.

498. How To Make Steak In The Air Fryer

Prep Time: 5 Mins Cook Time: 15 Mins
Total Time: 20 Mins

Ingredients

- 2 Pounds Steak (I Used Delmonico)
- Salt
- Pepper
- Garlic Powder
- 2 Tbs Butter

Instructions

- Preheat your air fryer to 400 for about 5 mins
- Salt and pepper both sides of the steak
- Place a pad of butter on top of each steak
- Place on the top rack of your air fryer
- Cook on-air fry for 15 mins for medium-well
- Flip over after 7 mins
- For Medium-rare cook for 10 mins flipping after 5
- For well-done cook for 20 mins flipping after 10 mins
- Remove steak and let rest for 5 mins and serve

499. Air Fryer Steak Bites With Mushrooms

Prep Time: 10 mins Cook Time: 15 mins
Total Time: 25 mins

Ingredients

- 2 lb beef
- 2 lb mushrooms
- 2 tbsp Worcester sauce
- 1 tbsp salt
- 1 tbsp pepper

Instructions

- Preheat an Air Fryer for 3 mins at 400 °F. Cut beef into bite-size pieces and mushrooms into halves.
- Mushrooms and steak in a bowl
- Add Worchester sauce, salt, and pepper to the mixture. Let it sit for a few minutes.
- Steak and mushrooms withs seasoning
- Add beef and mushrooms to the air fryer basket. Air-dry it for 5 min..
- Uncooked steak and mushrooms in a basket

- Remove the basket and toss the steak bites to ensure all the sides are getting nice and crispy.
- Basket with steak and mushrooms
- Air fry for another 5-7 min.. Once complete, check to make sure the temperature of the beef reached 145F.
- Steak bites with mushrooms in an air fryer basket

500. Air Fryer Steak

Ready In: 49min
Prep Time: 15min
Cook Time: 9min

Ingredients

- 2 boneless ribeye steaks
- 1 Tbsp steak rub
- 1 Tsp. kosher salt
- 1 Tbsp unsalted butter

Directions

- Rub steaks with steak rub and salt. Allow resting at room temperature for 15 to 30 minutes. The longer you allow them to rest with the rub on, the more flavorful they will be!
- Preheat air fryer for 5 mins at 400°F (200°C).
- Arrange steaks in a single layer in an air fryer basket, work in batches as needed and cook about 9 mins for medium-rare. The internal temperature should read at least 145°F (63°C).
- Transfer steak to a cutting board and put half the butter on each steak. Allow resting for at least 5 mins before slicing into 1/2-inch thick slices.

501. Air Fryer Italian-Style Meatballs

Active Time: 10 Mins Total Time: 45 Mins Yield: Serves 12 (2 meatballs)

Ingredients

- 2 Tbsps olive oil 1 medium shallot, minced (about 2 Tbsp.) 3 cloves garlic, minced (about 1 Tbsp.) 1/4 cup whole-wheat panko crumbs 2 Tbsps whole milk 2/3 pound lean ground beef 1/3 pound bulk turkey sausage 1 large egg, lightly beaten 1/4 cup finely chopped fresh flat-leaf parsley 1 Tbsp chopped fresh rosemary 1 Tbsp finely chopped fresh thyme 1 Tbsp Dijon mustard 1/2 Tsp. kosher salt

How To Make It

- Preheat air-fryer to 400°F. Heat oil in a medium nonstick pan over medium-high heat. Add shallot and cook until

softened, 1 to 2 min.. Add garlic and cook just until fragrant, 1 minute. Remove from heat.

- In a large bowl, combine panko and milk. Let stand 5 min..
- Add cooked shallot and garlic to the panko mixture, along with beef, turkey sausage egg, parsley, rosemary, thyme, mustard, and salt. Stir to gently combine.
- Gently shape mixture into 1 1/2-inch ball. Place shaped balls in a single-layer in the air-fryer basket. Cook half the meatballs at 400°F until lightly browned and cooked for 10 to 11 minutes. Remove and keep warm. Repeat with remaining meatballs.
- Serve warm meatballs with toothpicks as an appetizer or serve over pasta, rice, or spiralized zoodles for a main dish.

502. Air Fryer Marinated Steak

Prep Time: 5 mins Cook Time: 10 mins
Total Time: 15 mins
Servings: 2

Ingredients

- 2 New York Strip Steaks (mine were about 6-8 oz each) You can use any cut of steak
- 1 Tbsp low-sodium soy sauce This is used to provide liquid to marinate the meat and make it juicy.
- 1 Tsp. liquid smoke or a cap full
- 1 Tbsp mccormick's Grill Mates Montreal Steak Seasoning or Steak Rub (or season to taste) See recipe notes for instructions on how to create your steak rub
- 1/2 Tbsp unsweetened cocoa powder
- Salt and pepper to taste
- Melted butter (optional)

Instructions

- Drizzle the steak with soy sauce and liquid smoke. You can do this inside Ziploc bags if you wish.
- Season the steak with the seasonings.
- Refrigerate for at least a couple of hours, preferably overnight.
- Place the steak in the air fryer. I did not use any oil. Cook two steaks at a time (if the air fryer is the standard size). You can use an accessory grill pan, a layer rack, or the standard air fryer basket.

- Cook for 5 mins at 370 degrees. After 5 min., open the air fryer and examine your steak. Cook time will vary depending on your desired doneness. Use a meat thermometer and cook to 125° F for rare, 135° F for medium-rare, 145° F for medium, 155° F for medium-well, and 160° F for well done.
- I cooked the steak for an additional 2 mins for medium-done steak.
- Remove the steak from the air fryer and drizzle with melted butter.

503. Air Fryer Steak Bites And Mushrooms

Prep Time: 1 hour 5 mins
Cook Time: 15 mins
Total Time: 1 hour 20 mins
Servings: 2

Ingredients
- 1 Tsp. kosher salt
- 1/2 Tsp. garlic powder
- 1/4 Tsp. black pepper
- 2 Tbsps Worcestershire Sauce
- 2 Tbsp avocado oil (Click here for my favorite brand on Amazon)
- 8 oz Baby Bella Mushrooms, sliced
- 1 pound Top Sirloin steak, cut into 1.5 inch cubes

Instructions
- Combine all your ingredients for the marinade into a large mixing bowl.
- Add your steak cubes and sliced mushrooms into your mixing bowl with the marinade and toss to coat.
- Let the steak and mushrooms marinate for 1 hour.
- Preheat your Air Fryer to 400F for 5 minutes.
- Make sure you spray the inside of your air fryer will a cooking spray and pour your steak and mushrooms into the air fryer basket.
- Cook the steak and mushrooms in the Air Fryer for 5 mins at 400F. Open the basket and shake the steak and mushrooms so they cook evenly. Continue to cook for 5 mins more.
- Check the steak using an internal meat thermometer. If the steak has not reached your desired doneness, continue to cook in 3-minute intervals until the thermometer placed in the center of 1 steak bite reaches the desired temperature. (Rare=125F,

Medium-rare=130F, Medium=140F, Medium-well=150F, well-done=160F)
- Serve

504. Air Fryer Beef Tips

Prep Time 2 mins Cook Time 12 mins
Marinate Time 5 mins
Total Time 14 mins
Servings: 4

Ingredients
- 1 pound ribeye or New York steak, cut into 1-inch cubes
- 2 tsp sea salt
- 1 tsp black pepper
- 1 tsp garlic powder
- 2 tsp onion powder
- 1 tsp paprika
- 2 tsp rosemary crushed
- 2 tbsp coconut aminos

Instructions
- Place steak cubes in a medium sized bowl.
- In a small bowl, combine the salt, pepper, garlic powder, onion powder, paprika, and rosemary. Mix well.
- Sprinkle the mixed dry seasoning on the steak cubes. Mix to evenly distribute the seasoning.
- Sprinkle the coconut aminos all over the seasoned steak. Mix well.
- Let it sit for 5 minutes.
- Place the steak in a single layer in the air fryer basket.
- Cook at 380F for 12 min..
- Shake the basket halfway to ensure that the steak cooks evenly.
- Remove from the air fryer and let it cool for a few mins before serving.

505. Air Fryer Beef Kabobs

Prep Time: 30 mins Cook Time: 8 mins
Servings: 4 servings

Ingredients
- 1.5 pounds sirloin steak cut into 1-inch chunks
- 1 large bell pepper color of choice
- 1 large red onion or onion of choice

For The Marinade:
- 4 Tbsps olive oil
- 2 cloves garlic minced
- 1 Tbsp lemon juice
- 1/2 Tsp.
- 1/2 Tsp.
- Salt and pepper pinch

Instructions

- In a large bowl, combine the beef and ingredients for the marinade until fully combined. Cover and marinate in the fridge for 30 mins or up to 24 hours.
- When ready to cook, preheat the air fryer to 400F. Thread the beef, pepper, and onion onto skewers.
- Place skewers into the preheated air fryer and the air fryer for 8-10 min., turning halfway through until charred on the outside and tender on the inside.

506. Air Fryer Corned Beef

Total Time: 2 hours

Ingredients
- Corned Beef, 3-4 pounds
- 1/2 Cup Brown Sugar
- 1/4 cup Dijon Mustard
- 1 TBSP Apple Cider Vinegar

Instructions
- Mix brown sugar, Dijon mustard, & apple cider vinegar together.
- Baste corned beef with glaze and tightly wrap it in aluminum foil.
- Air Fry at 360 degrees for 1 hour.
- Unwrap aluminum foil, baste again, and loosely wrap with aluminum foil.
- Air Fry at 360 degrees for 40 minutes.
- Remove foil, baste one last time. Air Fry at 400 degrees for 10 min..

507. Air Fryer Ground Beef

Prep Time: 2 mins Cook Time: 10 mins
Yield: 6 servings

Ingredients
- 1 to 1 and 1/2 lbs. ground beef
- 1 tsp. salt
- 1/2 tsp. pepper
- 1/2 tsp. garlic powder

Instructions
- Put the ground beef into the basket of the air fryer.
- Season the beef with salt, pepper, and garlic powder. Stir it a bit with a wooden spoon.
- Cook in the air fryer at 400°F for 5 minutes. Stir it around.
- Continue to cook until cooked through and no longer pink, 3-5 more minutes.
- Crumble the beef up using a wooden spoon. Remove the basket and discard any fat and liquid left behind. Use the beef in your favorite ground beef recipe.

508. Steak With Easy Herb Butter

Prep Time: 6 Mins Cook Time: 9 Mins
Total Time: 15 Mins

Ingredients

- 2 medium steaks about 8 ounces each
- 2 Tsp. salt
- Herb butter
- 1/4 cup butter softened
- 1 clove garlic
- 1/4 Tsp. salt minced
- 1 Tbsp parsley chopped
- Pepper lots, to taste
- Wine pairings
- 2018 adelante pinot noir
- 2017 hushkeeper zinfandel
- 2018 middle jane cabernet sauvignon reserve

Instructions

- Mix butter, garlic, salt, parsley, and pepper together for herb butter.
- Shape into a log. Chill in the fridge. (See notes.)
- Preheat the air fryer for 5 mins at 400º F. Liberally salt both sides of the steak. Add the steaks and cook for 7-9 mins for medium-rare.
- Immediately remove from air fryer. Rest 5 min..

509. Air Fryer Roast Beef

Prep Time: 5 Mins Cook Time: 45 Mins
Inactive Time: 10 Mins
Total Time: 1 Hour

Ingredients

- 2 lb beef roast
- 1 tbsp olive oil
- 1 medium onion, (optional)
- 1 tsp salt
- 2 tsp rosemary and thyme, (fresh or dried)

Instructions

- Preheat air fryer to 390°F (200°C).
- Mix sea salt, rosemary, and oil on a plate.
- Pat the beef roast dry with paper towels. Place beef roast on a plate and turn so that the oil-herb mix coats the outside of the beef.
- Seasoned beef roast on a white plate
- If using, peel the onion and cut it in half, place onion halves in the air fryer basket.
- Place beef roast in the air fryer basket.
- Beef roast in the air fryer basket

- Set to air fry beef for 15 min..
- When the time is up, change the temperature to 360°F (180°C). Some air fryers require you to turn food during cooking, so check your manual and turn the beef roast over if required (my Philips Viva air fryer doesn't need food to be turned).
- Set the beef to cook for an additional 30 min.. This should give you medium-rare beef. Though is best to monitor the temperature with a meat thermometer to ensure that it is cooked to your liking. Cook for additional 5-minute intervals if you prefer it more well done.
- Remove roast beef from the air fryer, cover with kitchen foil and leave to rest for at least ten mins before serving. This allows the meat to finish cooking and the juices to reabsorb into the meat.
- Carve the roast beef thinly against the grain and serve with roasted or steamed vegetables, wholegrain mustard, and gravy.

510. Air Fryer Chicken Fried Steak

Prep Time: 20 mins Cook Time: 8 mins
Total Time: 28 mins

Ingredients

For The Steaks

- 2 cube steaks, 5-6 ounces each
- 3/4 cup All-Purpose Flour
- 1 Tsp. Ground Black Pepper
- 1 Tsp. Kosher Salt
- 1/2 Tsp. smoked paprika
- 1/2 Tsp. Onion Powder
- 1/2 Tsp. garlic powder
- 1/4 Tsp. Cayenne Pepper
- 2 teaspoons crumbled dried sage
- 3/4 cup buttermilk
- 1 Tsp. hot pepper sauce
- 1 Egg
- Non-Stick Cooking Spray

For The Gravy

- 4 Tbsps butter
- 2 Tbsp All-Purpose Flour
- 1 Tsp. Cracked Black Pepper
- 1/2 Tsp. Kosher Salt
- 1/4 Tsp. garlic salt
- 1/2 cup Whole Milk
- 1/2 cup Heavy Cream

Instructions

Steaks

- For the flour dredge, mix together in a

shallow bowl, whisk the flour, 1 Tsp. pepper, 1 Tsp. salt, paprika, onion powder, garlic powder, cayenne, and sage.

- In a separate shallow bowl, whisk the buttermilk, hot pepper sauce, and egg.
- Pat the steaks dry with a paper towel. Season to taste with salt and pepper. Allow standing for 5 min., then pat dry again with a paper towel.
- Dredge the steaks in the seasoned flour mixture, shaking off any excess. Then dredge in the buttermilk mixture, allowing excess to drip off. Dredge in the flour mixture again, shaking off excess. Place the breaded steaks on a sheet pan and press any remaining flour mixture onto the steaks, making sure that each steak is completely coated. Let stand for 10 min..
- Place steaks in the air fryer basket. Lightly coat with vegetable oil spray. Set the air fryer to 400°F for 8 min., carefully turning steaks and coating the other side with vegetable oil spray halfway through the cooking time.

Gravy

- Meanwhile, for the gravy: In a small saucepan, melt the butter over low heat. Whisk in the flour, pepper, salt, and garlic salt, continually whisking.
- Slowly add the milk and cream mixture, whisking constantly. Turn the heat to medium and cook, whisking occasionally, until thickened.
- Use a meat thermometer to ensure the steaks have reached an internal temperature of 145°F. Serve the steaks topped with the gravy.

511. Air Fryer Korean BBQ Beef

Prep Time: 15 Mins Cook Time: 30 Mins
Total Time: 45 Mins

Ingredients

Meat

- 1 Pound Flank Steak or Thinly Sliced Steak
- 1/4 Cup Corn Starch
- Pompeian Oils Coconut Spray

Sauce

- 1/2 Cup Soy Sauce or Gluten-Free Soy Sauce
- 1/2 Cup Brown Sugar
- 2 Tbsp Pompeian White Wine Vinegar
- 1 Clove Garlic, Crushed

- 1 Tbsp Hot Chili Sauce
- 1 Tsp Ground Ginger
- 1/2 Tsp Sesame Seeds
- 1 Tbsp Cornstarch
- 1 Tbsp Water

Instructions

- Begin by preparing the steak. Thinly slice it then toss in the cornstarch.
- Spray the basket or line it with foil in the air fryer with coconut oil spray.
- Add the steak and spray another coat of spray on top.
- Cook in the air fryer for 10 mins at 390*, turn the steak, and cook for an additional 10 minutes.
- While the steak is cooking add the sauce ingredients EXCEPT for the cornstarch and water to a medium saucepan.
- Warm it up to a low boil, then whisk in the cornstarch and water.
- Carefully remove the steak and pour the sauce over the steak, mix well.
- Serve topped with sliced green onions, cooked rice, and green beans.

512. Air Fryer Mongolian Beef

Prep Time: 20 Mins
Cook Time: 20 Mins
Total Time: 40 Mins

Ingredients

Meat

- 1 Lb Flank Steak
- 1/4 Cup Corn Starch

Sauce

- 2 Tsp Vegetable Oil
- 1/2 Tsp Ginger
- 1 Tbsp Minced Garlic
- 1/2 Cup Soy Sauce or Gluten Free Soy Sauce
- 1/2 Cup Water
- 3/4 Cup Brown Sugar Packed

Extras

- Cooked Rice
- Green Beans
- Green Onions

Instructions

- Thinly slice the steak into long pieces, then coat with the corn starch.
- Place in the Air Fryer and cook on 390* for 5 mins on each side. (Start with 5 mins and add more time if needed. I cook this for 10 mins on each side; however, others have suggested that

was too long for theirs.)

- While the steak cooks, warm up all sauce ingredients in a medium sized saucepan on medium-high heat.
- Whisk the ingredients together until it gets to a low boil.
- Once both the steak and sauce are cooked, place the steak in a bowl with the sauce and let it soak in for about 5-10 min..
- When ready to serve, use tongs to remove the steak and let the excess sauce drip off.
- Place steak on cooked rice and green beans, top with additional sauce if you prefer.

513. Air Fryer Beef And Bean Taquitos

Prep Time: 10 Mins Cook Time: 15 Mins
Total Time: 25 Mins

Ingredients

- 1 Pound Ground Beef
- 1 Package Gluten-Free or Regular Taco Seasoning
- 1 Can of Refried Beans
- 1 Cup Shredded Sharp Cheddar
- 20 White Corn Tortillas

Instructions

- Begin by preparing the ground beef if it isn't already.
- Brown the meat on medium-high heat and add in the taco seasoning per the instructions on the package.
- Once you are done with the meat, heat up the corn tortillas for about 30 seconds.
- Spray the air fryer basket with non-stick cooking spray or add a sheet of foil and spray.
- Add ground beef, beans, and a bit of cheese to each tortilla.
- Wrap them tightly and place seam side down in the air fryer.
- Add a quick spray of cooking oil spray, such as olive oil cooking spray.
- Cook at 390 degrees for 12 min..
- Repeat for any additional tortillas.

514. Steak Fajitas With Onions And Peppers

Prep Time: 10 Mins Cook Time: 15 Mins
Total Time: 25 Mins

Ingredients

- 1 lb Thin Cut Steak
- 1 Green Bell Pepper Sliced

- 1 Yellow Bell Pepper Sliced
- 1 Red Bell Pepper Sliced
- 1/2 Cup White Onions Sliced
- 1 Packet Gluten Free Fajita Seasoning
- Olive Oil Spray
- Gluten-Free Corn Tortillas or Flour Tortillas

Instructions

- Line the basket of the air fryer with foil and coat with spray.
- Thinly slice the steak against the grain, this should be about 1/4 inch slices.
- Mix the steak with peppers and onions.
- Add to the air fryer.
- Evenly coat with the fajita seasoning.
- Cook for 5 mins on 390*.
- Mix up the steak mixture.
- Continue cooking for an additional 5-10 mins until your desired doneness.
- Serve in warm tortillas.

515. Air Fryer Meatballs (Low Carb)

Prep Time: 10 mins Cook Time: 14 mins
Total Time: 24 mins
Servings: 3 -4

Ingredients

- 1 lb Lean Ground Beef
- 1/4 Cup Marinara Sauce
- 1 Tbsp Dried Minced Onion or Freeze Dried Shallots
- 1 Tsp. Minced Garlic I used freeze-dried
- 1 Tsp. Pizza Seasoning or Italian Seasoning
- 1/3 Cup Shredded Parmesan
- 1 Egg
- Salt and Pepper to taste
- Shredded Mozzarella Cheese optional
- 1 1/4 cups Marinara Sauce optional

Instructions

- Mix together all ingredients except reserve 1 1/4 cup of the marinara sauce and the mozzarella cheese.
- Form mixture into 12 meatballs and place in a single layer in the air fryer basket.
- Cook in the air fryer at 350 for 11 min..
- Optional: Place meatballs in an air fryer pan, toss in remaining marinara sauce, and top with mozzarella cheese. Place air fryer pan into the basket and cook at 350 for 3 min..

516. Air Fryer Roast Beef

Prep Time: 5 mins Cook Time: 35 mins
Total Time: 40 mins

Ingredients

- 2 lb beef roast top round or eye of round is best
- Oil for spraying
- Rub
- 1 tbs kosher salt
- 1 tsp black pepper
- 2 tsp garlic powder
- 1 tsp summer savory or thyme

Instructions

- Mix all rub ingredients and rub into the roast.
- Place fat side down in the basket of the air fryer (or set up for rotisserie if your air fryer is so equipped)
- Lightly spray with oil.
- Set fryer to 400 degrees F and air fry for 20 minutes; turn fat-side up and spray lightly with oil. Continue cooking for 15 additional mins at 400 degrees F.
- Remove the roast from the fryer, tent with foil, and let the meat rest for 10 minutes.
- The time given should produce a rare roast which should be 125 degrees F on a meat thermometer. Additional time will be needed for medium, medium-well, and well. Always use a meat thermometer to test the temperature.
- Approximate times for medium and well respectively are 40 mins and 45 minutes. Remember to always use a meat thermometer as times are approximate and fryers differ by wattage.

517. Air Fryer Stuffed Peppers

Prep Time: 15 Mins Cook Time: 15 Mins
Total Time: 30 Mins

Ingredients

- 6 Green Bell Peppers
- 1 Lb Lean Ground Beef
- 1 Tbsp Olive Oil
- 1/4 Cup Green Onion Diced
- 1/4 Cup Fresh Parsley
- 1/2 Tsp Ground Sage
- 1/2 Tsp Garlic Salt
- 1 Cup Cooked Rice
- 1 Cup Marinara Sauce More to Taste
- 1/4 Cup Shredded Mozzarella Cheese

Instructions

- Warm-up a medium-sized skillet with the ground beef and cook until well done.
- Drain the beef and return to the pan.
- Add in the olive oil, green onion, parsley, sage, and salt. Mix this well.
- Add in the cooked rice and marinara, mix well.
- Cut the top off of each pepper and clean the seeds out.
- Scoop the mixture into each of the peppers and place it in the basket of the air fryer. (I did 4 the first round, 2 the second to make them fit.)
- Cook for 10 mins at 355*, carefully open and add cheese.
- Cook for an additional 5 mins or until peppers are slightly soft and cheese is melted.
- Serve.

518. Air Fryer Steak

Prep Time: 10 mins Cook Time: 15 mins
Resting Time: 8 mins Total Time: 30 mins

Ingredients

- 2 (10 to 12 ounces EACH) sirloin steaks, about one inch thick, and at room temperature which is important for proper and even cooking.
- ½ Tbsp olive oil OR olive oil cooking spray, for the steaks
- 1 Tbsp kosher salt
- 1 Tbsp garlic powder
- 1 Tbsp onion powder
- ½ Tbsp paprika, sweet or smoked
- ½ Tbsp freshly ground black pepper
- 2 teaspoons dried herbs of choice

Instructions

- Preheat Air Fryer to 400°F.
- Rub both steaks with olive oil, or spray with cooking spray, and set aside.
- In a small mixing bowl combine salt, garlic powder, onion powder, paprika, pepper, and dried herbs. This makes enough seasoning for about 4 large steaks.
- Rub preferred amount of seasoning all over the steaks. Store leftover seasoning blends in a small airtight container and keeps it in a cool, dry place.
- Place 1 steak in the Air Fryer basket and cook for 6 mins at 400°F.
- If you have a bigger Air Fryer, both steaks can fit in at the same time, but just make sure they aren't one on top of the other. You want a little space between the two.
- Flip over the steak and continue to cook for 4 to 5 more min., or until cooked through.
- Please use an Instant Read Thermometer to check for doneness; for a RARE steak, the temperature should register at 125°F to 130°F. For Medium-Rare, you want an internal temperature of 135°F.
- IF the steak isn't cooked through, it may be too thick and you'll want to return the steak to the air fryer and give it a minute or two to finish cooking.
- Repeat the cooking method with the other steak.
- Remove from air fryer and let rest for 5 to 8 mins before cutting.
- Serve with a pat of butter and garnish with chopped parsley.

519. Air Fryer Steak Fajitas

Prep Time: 10 mins Cook Time: 10 mins
Total Time: 20 mins

Ingredients

- 2 pounds flank steak strips
- 1 packet taco seasoning
- 1/2 red bell pepper, seeded, cored, and sliced
- 1/2 yellow bell pepper, seeded, cored, and sliced
- 1 onion, peeled and sliced
- 2 Tbsps freshly squeezed lime juice
- Cooking spray
- Flour tortillas
- Cilantro, chopped

Instructions

- Season steak with taco seasoning. Marinate for about 20 to 30 min..
- Preheat your air fryer to 400 degrees. Spray the air fryer tray with cooking spray,
- Arrange the seasoned beef on the air fryer tray, cooking in batches depending on the size of the air fryer.
- Add a layer of the sliced onions and a layer of bell peppers on top of the meat.
- Place in the air fryer for 10 min.. Toss halfway through cooking to ensure the steak is cooked evenly.
- Remove from the air fryer and drizzle with lime juice.

- Serve in warm tortillas with fresh cilantro.

520. Air Fryer Taco Calzones

Prep Time: 10 Mins
Cook Time: 10 Mins
Total Time: 20 Mins

Ingredients

- 1 tube Pillsbury thin crust pizza dough
- 1 cup taco meat
- 1 cup shredded cheddar

Instructions

- Spread out your sheet of pizza dough on a clean surface. Using a pizza cutter, cut the dough into 4 even squares.
- Cut each square into a large circle using the pizza cutter. Set the dough scraps aside to make cinnamon sugar bites.
- Top one half of each circle of dough with 1/4 cup taco meat and 1/4 cup shredded cheese.
- Fold the empty half over the meat and cheese and press the edges of the dough together with a fork to seal it tightly. Repeat with all four calzones.
- Gently pick up each calzone and spray it with pan spray or olive oil. Arrange them in your Air Fryer basket.
- Cook the calzones at 325° for 8-10 min.. Watch them closely at the 8-minute mark so you don't overcook them.
- Serve with salsa and sour cream.
- To make cinnamon sugar bites, cut the scraps of dough into even-sized pieces, about 2 inches long. Add them to the Air Fryer basket and cook at 325° for 5 minutes. Immediately toss with a 1:4 cinnamon-sugar mixture.

521. Jalapeno Lime Air Fryer Steak

Prep Time: 5 mins Cook Time: 10 mins
Marinate Time: 30 mins Total Time: 45 mins Servings: 4

Ingredients

- 1 lb flank steak used flat iron – check keywords
- 1 lime juice and zest
- 1 jalapeno, sliced
- 3 cloves of garlic, minced
- 1/2 cup fresh cilantro, roughly chopped
- 2 Tbsps light brown sugar
- 1/2 Tsp. paprika
- 1/2 Tsp. fresh cracked pepper

- 1/4 cup avocado oil
- Salt

Instructions

- Preheat the air fryer to 400F.
- Season the steak with salt and pepper. In a large mixing bowl, combine the avocado oil, paprika, pepper, brown sugar, cilantro, garlic, jalapeño, and lime zest from 1 lime. Add the steak and toss to coat. Marinate for 30 min..
- Air fry for 10 mins for medium-rare, flipping the steak halfway through. When the steak is finished cooking, squeeze lime juice from half a lime over it. Allow it to rest with the air fryer lid open for 10 mins before slicing. Serve the steak with steamed veggies, over a salad, or in a taco.

Oven Instructions

- To make the steak in the oven, preheat the broiler on high and cook for 6 mins for medium-rare. Squeeze lime juice from half a lime over the steak and allow it to rest for 10 mins before slicing. Serve the steak with steamed veggies, over a salad, or in a taco.

522. Ribeye Steak (Frozen + Fresh)

Prep Time: 5 Mins Cook Time: 10 Mins
Additional Time: 30 Mins
Total Time: 45 Mins

Ingredients

- 8-ounce ribeye steak, about 1-inch thick
- 1 Tbsp McCormick Montreal Steak Seasoning

Instructions

- Remove the ribeye steak from the fridge and season with the Montreal Steak seasoning. Let steak rest for about 20 mins to come to room temperature (to get a more tender juicy steak).
- Preheat your air fryer to 400 degrees.
- Place the ribeye steak in the air fryer and cook for 10-12 min., until it reaches 130-135 degrees for medium-rare. Cook for an additional 5 mins for medium-well.
- Remove the steak from the air fryer and let rest at least 5 mins before cutting to keep the juices inside the steak then enjoy!

523. Air Fryer Beef Chips

Prep Time: 1 minute Cook Time: 1 hour

Cooling Time: 5 mins Total Time: 1 hour 6 mins Servings: 2

Ingredients

- 1/2 lb Thinly Sliced Beef we recommend leaner cuts like sirloin
- 1/4 tsp Salt
- 1/4 tsp Black Pepper
- 1/4 tsp Garlic Powder

Instructions

- Gather all the ingredients.
- In a small mixing bowl, combine salt, black pepper, garlic powder and mix well to create the seasoning.
- Lay the beef slices flat and sprinkle seasoning on both sides.
- Transfer beef into the air fryer tray single stacked (very important each slice is single stacked, otherwise they will not get crispy) and air fry for 45-60 mins at 200F. Once done, let beef slices cool for 5 mins before enjoying. Note - the time is going to vary greatly depending on thickness.

524. Meatloaf With Tangy Sauce

Prep Time: 9 Mins Cook Time: 20 Mins
Resting Time: 5 Mins Total Time: 34 Mins

Ingredients

- 1 large egg
- 2 pounds ground chuck or a combination of ground beef and venison or ground sirloin
- 1/2 cup quick-cooking oats
- 3/4 Tsp. salt or garlic salt
- 1/4 Tsp. ground black pepper
- Tangy sauce
- 3/4 cup ketchup
- 2 Tbsps light brown sugar
- 1 Tbsp apple cider vinegar or white vinegar or rice vinegar
- 1 Tsp. worcestershire sauce or soy sauce or liquid amino liquid aminos are gluten-free

Instructions

- To save washing another bowl, start by beating the egg in a large bowl with a fork.
- Break up the ground meat in the bowl. There's no getting around using your hands here. I usually use a pair of nylon/rubber gloves simply for easy cleanup. Gloves may be a luxury this day, though.
- Add quick-cooking oats, salt, and

pepper.

- With your hands, gently mix in the egg, oats, salt, and pepper with the ground meat. Overworking the meat will make it tough. Under mixing may leave patches of oats or eggs not evenly incorporated.
- Shape the mixture into 2 free-form loaves, roughly 3 x 5.5 inches. The size will depend on what will fit into your air fryer. (For conventional oven method, see the size in recipe notes) Carefully place the loaves side by side in the preheated air fryer basket or tray.
- Air fry or Roast for about 19 mins or until meatloaves are done in the middle-firm when pressed in the middle of temperature on an instant-read thermometer reads 155°.
- It's a good idea to check at 17 mins to make sure they aren't getting too brown. All air fryers are not alike.
- Prepare Tangy Sauce and Spread on Meatloaf
- Stir or whisk together ketchup, brown sugar, vinegar, and Worcestershire sauce.
- When meat waves are 155° or no pink shows in the center, evenly spread the Tangy Sauce over both meatloaves. Cook an additional 1 minute on Air Fry to set the sauce.
- Remove the meatloaves with silicone coated tongs if the air fryer basket is coated with a nonstick surface. Let the meatloaf stand on a cutting board or plate 5 mins before slicing.

525.Air Fryer Asian Beef & Veggies

Prep Time: 10 mins Cook Time: 8 mins
Total Time: 18 mins
Servings: 4 people
Ingredients
- 1 lb sirloin steak cut into strips
- 2 Tbsp cornstarch (or arrowroot powder)
- 1/2 medium yellow onion, sliced
- 1 medium red pepper, sliced into strips
- 3 cloves garlic, minced
- 2 Tbsps grated ginger do not sub dry ground ginger
- 1/4 Tsp. red chili flakes
- 1/2 cup low sodium soy sauce
- 1/4 cup rice vinegar

- 1 tsp sesame oil
- 1/3 cup brown sugar
- 1 Tsp. chinese 5 spice optional
- 1/4 cup water
Instructions
For Freezer Prep
- Add all ingredients to a gallon-sized zip bag. Ensure all of the ingredients are combined.
- Label and freeze for up to 4 months.
To Cook
- Thaw zip bag in the fridge overnight.
- Using tongs, remove the steak and veggies, and transfer to the Air Fryer. Discard the marinade.
- Set the Air Fryer to 400F and the timer to 8 minutes. I like to shake the basket halfway through, but I don't think it is necessary.
- Serve with rice, and garnish with sesame seeds and scallions.

526.Kofta Kebabs

Prep Time: 45 mins Cook Time: 5 mins
Additional Time: 30 mins Total Time: 1 hr 20 mins Servings: 28
Ingredient
- 4 cloves garlic, minced
- 1 Tsp. kosher salt
- 1 pound ground lamb
- 3 Tbsps grated onion
- 3 Tbsp chopped fresh parsley
- 1 Tbsp ground coriander
- 1 Tsp. ground cumin
- ½ Tbsp ground cinnamon
- ½ Tsp. ground allspice
- ¼ Tsp. cayenne pepper
- ¼ Tsp. ground ginger
- ¼ Tsp. ground black pepper
- 28 bamboo skewers, soaked in water for 30 mins
Instructions
- Mash the garlic into a paste with the salt using a mortar and pestle or the flat side of a chef's knife on your cutting board.
- Mix the garlic into the lamb along with the onion, parsley, coriander, cumin, cinnamon, allspice, cayenne pepper, ginger, and pepper in a mixing bowl until well blended.
- Form the mixture into 28 balls. Form each ball around the tip of a skewer, flattening into a 2-inch oval; repeat with

the remaining skewers.
- Place the kebabs onto a baking sheet, cover, and refrigerate for at least 30 mins or up to 12 hours.
- Preheat an outdoor grill for medium heat, and lightly oil grate.
- Cook the skewers on the preheated grill, turning occasionally, until the lamb has cooked to your desired degree of doneness, about 6 mins for medium.

527.Simple Grilled Lamb Chops

Prep Time: 10 mins Cook Time: 6 mins
Additional Time: 2 hrs Total Time: 2 hrs 16 mins Servings: 6
Ingredient
- ¼ cup distilled white vinegar
- 2 teaspoons salt
- ½ Tsp. black pepper
- 1 Tbsp minced garlic
- 1 onion, thinly sliced
- 2 Tbsps olive oil
- 2 pounds lamb chops
Instructions
- Mix together the vinegar, salt, pepper, garlic, onion, and olive oil in a large resealable bag until the salt has dissolved. Add lamb, toss until coated, and marinate in the refrigerator for 2 hours.
- Preheat an outdoor grill for medium-high heat.
- Remove lamb from the marinade and leave any onions on that stick to the meat. Discard any remaining marinade. Wrap the exposed ends of the bones with aluminum foil to keep them from burning. Grill to desired doneness, about 3 mins per side for medium. The chops may also be broiled in the oven for about 5 mins per side for medium.

528.Roast Leg Of Lamb

Prep Time: 15 mins Cook Time: 1 hr 45 mins Additional Time: 10 mins Total Time: 2 hrs 10 mins Servings: 12
Ingredient
- 4 cloves garlic, sliced
- 2 Tbsp fresh rosemary
- Salt to taste
- Ground black pepper to taste
- 5 pounds leg of lamb
Instructions
- Preheat oven to 350 degrees F
- Cut slits in the top of the leg of lamb every 3 to 4 inches, deep enough to

push slices of garlic down into the meat.

- Salt and pepper generously all over the top of the lamb, place several sprigs of fresh rosemary under and on top of the lamb. Place lamb on roasting pan.
- Roast in the preheated oven until the lamb is cooked to your desired doneness, about 1 3/4 to 2 hours. Do not overcook the lamb, the flavor is best if the meat is still slightly pink. Let rest at least 10 mins before carving.

529.Roasted Lamb Breast

Prep Time: 30 mins Cook Time: 2 hrs 25 mins Total Time: 2 hrs 55 mins
Servings: 4
Ingredient
- 2 Tbsp olive oil
- 2 teaspoons salt
- 2 teaspoons ground cumin
- 1 Tsp. freshly ground black pepper
- 1 Tsp. dried Italian herb seasoning
- 1 Tsp. ground cinnamon
- 1 Tsp. ground coriander
- 1 Tsp. paprika
- 4 pounds lamb breast, separated into two pieces
- ½ cup chopped Italian flat-leaf parsley
- ⅓ cup white wine vinegar, more as needed
- 1 lemon, juiced
- 2 cloves garlic, crushed
- 1 Tsp. honey
- ½ Tsp. red pepper flakes
- 1 pinch salt

Instructions
- Preheat oven to 300 degrees F (150 degrees C).
- Combine chopped parsley, vinegar, fresh lemon juice, garlic, honey, red pepper flakes, and salt in a large bowl. Mix well and set aside.
- Whisk olive oil, salt, cumin, black pepper, dried Italian herbs, cinnamon, coriander, and paprika in a large bowl until combined.
- Coat each lamb breast in the olive oil and spice mixture and transfer to a roasting pan, fat side up.
- Tightly cover the roasting pan with aluminum foil and bake in the preheated oven until the meat is tender when pierced with a fork, about 2 hours.
- Remove lamb from the oven and cut

into four pieces.
- Increase oven temperature to 450 degrees F (230 degrees C).
- Line a baking sheet with aluminum foil and place lamb pieces on it. Brush the tops of each piece with fat drippings from the roasting pan.
- Bake lamb until meat is browned and edges are crispy about 20 min..
- Increase the oven's broiler to high and brown lamb for 4 min.. Remove from oven.
- Serve lamb topped with parsley and vinegar sauce.

530.Moroccan Lamb Stew With Apricots

Prep Time: 30 mins Cook Time: 1 hr 55 mins Total Time: 2 hrs 25 mins
Servings: 4
Ingredient
- 2 pounds boneless leg of lamb, cut into 1-inch cubes
- 2 teaspoons ground coriander
- 1 Tsp. ground cumin
- 1 Tsp. sweet paprika
- ½ Tsp. cayenne pepper
- ½ Tsp. ground cardamom
- ½ Tsp. ground turmeric
- 2 teaspoons kosher salt
- 2 Tbsp olive oil
- 2 cups finely chopped onion
- 4 cloves garlic, minced
- 1 Tbsp minced fresh ginger root
- 2 (3 inches) cinnamon sticks
- 2 cups low-sodium chicken stock
- 1 cup dried apricots, halved
- 2 (3 inches) orange peel strips
- 1 Tbsp honey
- ¼ cup chopped fresh cilantro
- ¼ cup toasted pine nuts

Instructions
- Combine lamb, coriander, cumin, paprika, cayenne, cardamom, turmeric, and salt in a large bowl; toss together until lamb is evenly coated.
- Heat oil in a large Dutch oven or tagine over medium heat. Add onions; cook, stirring occasionally until soft and translucent, about 5 minutes. Stir in garlic, ginger, and cinnamon; cook, stirring frequently, until fragrant, about 1 minute.
- Add seasoned lamb; cook, stirring

frequently until light brown, being careful not to caramelize, about 2 minutes.
- Add chicken stock and bring to a gentle boil over medium heat. Reduce heat to low and simmer, covered, until the lamb is just tender, about 1 hour and 15 minutes.
- Stir in apricots, orange peels, and honey; continue to simmer over low heat, uncovered, until the liquid has thickened slightly and lamb is fork-tender, about 30 minutes.
- Remove from the heat, discard cinnamon sticks and orange peels.
- Divide evenly among 4 bowls. Garnish each bowl with a Tbsp each of cilantro and pine nuts.

531.Slow Cooker Lamb Chops

Prep Time: 15 mins Cook Time: 4 hrs 30 mins Additional Time: 5 mins
Total Time: 4 hrs 50 mins
Servings: 6
Ingredient
- ½ cup red wine
- ½ sweet onion, roughly chopped
- 3 Tbsps honey
- 2 Tbsps Dijon mustard
- 2 Tbsp lemon juice
- 4 garlic cloves, minced
- 1 Tbsp ground thyme
- 1 Tbsp dried rosemary
- 2 teaspoons ground basil
- 1 Tsp. salt
- 1 Tsp. coarse ground black pepper
- ¼ cup tapioca starch
- 1 ½ pound sirloin lamb chops, room temperature

Instructions
- Combine red wine and onion in a slow cooker.
- Whisk honey, mustard, lemon juice, garlic, thyme, rosemary, basil, salt, and pepper together in a small bowl until well blended. Add tapioca starch and whisk until well combined. Let sit until the mixture is thickened, at least 5 min..
- Dip lamb chops in the mustard mixture and massage until fully coated.
- Place chops in a single layer over the red wine and onion mixture in the slow cooker. Pour the remaining mustard mixture on top.
- Cover slow cooker and cook on Low

until an instant-read thermometer inserted into the center of a chop reads at least 130 degrees F (54 degrees C), about 4 1/2 hours.

532.Grilled Leg Of Lamb Steaks

Prep Time: 10 mins Cook Time: 10 mins
Additional Time: 30 mins Total: 50 mins
Servings: 4

Ingredient
- 4 bone-in lamb steaks
- ¼ cup olive oil
- 4 large cloves garlic, minced
- 1 Tbsp chopped fresh rosemary
- Salt and ground black pepper to taste

Instructions
- Place lamb steaks in a single layer in a shallow dish. Cover with olive oil, garlic, rosemary, salt, and pepper. Flip steaks to coat both sides. Let sit until steaks absorb flavors, about 30 min..
- Preheat an outdoor grill for high heat and lightly oil the grate. Cook steaks until browned on the outside and slightly pink in the center, about 5 mins per side for medium. An instant-read thermometer inserted into the center should read at least 140 degrees F (60 degrees C).

533.Easy Meatloaf

Prep Time: 10 mins Cook Time: 1 hr
Total Time: 1 hr 10 mins Servings: 8

Ingredient
- 1 ½ pounds ground beef
- 1 egg
- 1 onion, chopped
- 1 cup milk
- 1 cup dried bread crumbs
- Salt and pepper to taste
- 2 Tbsp brown sugar
- 2 Tbsp prepared mustard
- ⅓ cup ketchup

Instructions
- Preheat oven to 350 degrees F (175 degrees C).
- In a large bowl, combine the beef, egg, onion, milk, and bread OR cracker crumbs. Season with salt and pepper to taste and place in a lightly greased 9x5-inch loaf pan, or form into a loaf and place in a lightly greased 9x13-inch baking dish.
- In a separate small bowl, combine the brown sugar, mustard, and ketchup. Mix well and pour over the meatloaf.

- Bake at 350 degrees F (175 degrees C) for 1 hour.

534.Classic Meatloaf

Prep: 30 mins Cook: 45 mins
Total: 1 hr 15 mins Servings: 10

Meatloaf Ingredients:
- 1 carrot, coarsely chopped
- 1 rib celery, coarsely chopped
- ½ onion, coarsely chopped
- ½ red bell pepper, coarsely chopped
- 4 white mushrooms, coarsely chopped
- 3 cloves garlic, coarsely chopped
- 2 ½ pounds ground chuck
- 1 Tbsp Worcestershire sauce
- 1 egg, beaten
- 1 Tsp. dried Italian herbs
- 2 teaspoons salt
- 1 Tsp. ground black pepper
- ½ Tsp. cayenne pepper
- 1 cup plain bread crumbs
- 1 Tsp. olive oil

Glaze Ingredients:
- 2 Tbsps brown sugar
- 2 Tbsps ketchup
- 2 Tbsp dijon mustard
- Hot pepper sauce to taste

Instructions
- Preheat the oven to 325 degrees F.
- Place the carrot, celery, onion, red bell pepper, mushrooms, and garlic in a food processor, and pulse until very finely chopped, almost to a puree. Place the minced vegetables into a large mixing bowl, and mix in ground chuck, Worcestershire sauce, and egg. Add Italian herbs, salt, black pepper, and cayenne pepper. Mix gently with a wooden spoon to incorporate vegetables and egg into the meat. Pour in bread crumbs. With your hand, gently mix in the crumbs with your fingertips just until combined, about 1 minute.
- Form the meatloaf into a ball. Pour olive oil into a baking dish and place the ball of meat into the dish. Shape the ball into a loaf, about 4 inches high by 6 inches across.
- Bake in the preheated oven just until the meatloaf is hot, about 15 min..
- Meanwhile, in a small bowl, mix together brown sugar, ketchup, Dijon mustard, and hot sauce. Stir until the

brown sugar has dissolved.
- Remove the meatloaf from the oven. With the back of a spoon, smooth the glaze onto the top of the meatloaf, then pull a little bit of glaze down the sides of the meatloaf with the back of the spoon.
- Return meatloaf to the oven, and bake until the loaf is no longer pink inside and the glaze has baked onto the loaf, 30 to 40 more minutes. An instant-read thermometer inserted into the thickest part of the loaf should read at least 160 degrees F (70 degrees C). Cooking time will depend on the shape and thickness of the meatloaf.

535.Salisbury Steak

Prep Time: 20 mins Cook Time: 20 mins
Total Time: 40 mins Servings: 6

Ingredient
- 1 (10.5 ounces) can condense French onion soup
- 1 ½ pounds ground beef
- ½ cup dry bread crumbs
- 1 egg
- ¼ Tsp. salt
- ⅛ Tsp. ground black pepper
- 1 Tbsp all-purpose flour
- ¼ cup ketchup
- ¼ cup water
- 1 Tbsp Worcestershire sauce
- ½ Tsp. mustard powder

Instructions
- In a large bowl, mix together 1/3 cup condensed French onion soup with ground beef, bread crumbs, egg, salt, and black pepper. Shape into 6 oval patties.
- In a large skillet over medium-high heat, brown both sides of patties. Pour off excess fat.
- In a small bowl, blend flour and remaining soup until smooth. Mix in ketchup, water, Worcestershire sauce, and mustard powder. Pour over meat in skillet. Cover, and cook for 20 min., stirring occasionally.

Vegetables Recipes

536.Nutty Pumpkin with Blue Cheese

Prep Time :30 minutes
Ingredients:
- ½ small pumpkin
- 2 oz. blue cheese, cubed

- 2 tbsp. pine nuts1 tbsp. olive oil½ cup baby spinach, packed
- 1 spring onion, sliced
- 1 radish, thinly sliced
- 1 tsp. vinegar

Instructions:
- Preheat the air fryer to 330 degrees F.
- Place the pine nuts in a baking dish and toast them for 5 minutes. Set aside. Peel the pumpkin and chop it into small pieces.
- Place in the baking dish and toss with the olive oil. I
- ncrease the temperature to 390 degrees and cook the pumpkin for about 20 minutes.
- Make sure to toss every 5 mins or so. Place the pumpkin in a serving bowl.
- Add baby spinach, radish and spring onion. Toss with the vinegar.
- Stir in the cubed blue cheese. Top with the toasted pine nuts.

537. Eggplant Cheeseburger
Prep Time: 10 minutes
Ingredients:
- 1 hamburger bun
- 1 2-inch eggplant slice, cut along the round axis
- 1 mozzarella sliceRed onion cut into 3 rings
- 1 lettuce leaf
- ½ tbsp. tomato sauce
- 1 pickle, sliced

Instructions:
- Preheat the air fryer to 330 degrees F.
- Place the eggplant slice and roast for 6 minutes.
- Place the mozzarella slice on top of the eggplant and cook for 30 more seconds.
- Spread the tomato sauce on one half of the bun.
- Place the lettuce leaf on top of the sauce.
- Place the cheesy eggplant on top of the lettuce.
- Top with onion rings and pickles.
- Top with the other bun half and enjoy.

538. Veggie Meatballs
Prep Time: 30 minutes
Ingredients:
- 2 tbsp. olive oil
- 2 tbsp. soy sauce

- 1 tbsp. flax meal
- 2 cups cooked chickpeas
- ½ cup sweet onion, diced
- ½ cup grated carrots
- ½ cup roasted cashewsJuice of 1 lemon
- ½ tsp. turmeric1 tsp. cumin
- 1 tsp. garlic powder
- 1 cup rolled oats

Instructions:
- Preheat the air fryer to 350 degrees F.
- Combine the oil, onions, and carrots into a baking dish and cook them in the air fryer for 5 minutes.
- Meanwhile, ground the oats and cashews in a food processor. Place them in a large bowl. Process the chickpeas with the lemon juice and soy sauce, until smooth. Add them to the bowl as well.
- Add the onions and carrots to the bowl with the chickpeas.
- Stir in all of the remaining ingredients, and mix until fully incorporated. Make 12 meatballs out of the mixture.
- Increase the temperature to 370 degrees. Cook the meatballs for about 12 minutes..

539. Crunchy Parmesan Zucchini
Prep Time: 40 minutes
Ingredients:
- 4 small zucchini cut lengthwise
- ½ cup grated Parmesan cheese
- ½ cup breadcrumbs
- ¼ cup melted butter
- ¼ cup chopped parsley
- 4 garlic cloves, minced
- Salt and pepper, to taste

Instructions:
- Preheat the air fryer to 350 degrees F. In a bowl, mix the breadcrumbs, Parmesan, garlic, and parsley. Season with some salt and pepper, to taste.
- Stir in the melted butter. Arrange the zucchinis with the cut side up. Spread the mixture onto the zucchini evenly.
- Place half of the zucchinis in your air fryer and cook for 13 minutes.
- Increase the temperature to 370 degrees F and cook for 3 more mins for extra crunchiness. Repeat with the other batch.

540. Chili Bean Burritos
Prep Time: 30 minutes
Ingredients:
- 6 tortillas
- 1 cup grated cheddar cheese
- 1 can (8 oz.) beans
- 1 tsp. seasoning, by choice

Instructions:
- Preheat the air fryer to 350 degrees F.
- Mix the beans with the seasoning.
- Divide the bean mixture between the tortillas. Top the beans with cheddar cheese.
- Roll the burritos and arrange them on a lined baking dish.
- Place in the air fryer and cook for 5 minutes, or to your liking. Serve as desired (I recommend salsa dipping)

541. Spinach and Feta Crescent Triangles
Prep Time: 20 minutes
Ingredients:
- 14 oz. store-bought crescent dough
- 1 cup steamed spinach
- 1 cup crumbled feta cheese
- ¼ tsp. garlic powder
- 1 tsp. chopped oregano
- ¼ tsp. salt

Instructions:
- Preheat the air fryer to 350 degrees F.
- Roll the dough onto a lightly floured flat surface.
- Combine the feta, spinach, oregano, salt, and garlic powder together in a bowl.
- Cut the dough into 4 equal pieces.
- Divide the spinach/feta mixture between the dough pieces.
- Make sure to place the filling in the center. Fold the dough and secure with a fork.
- Place onto a lined baking dish, and then in the air fryer.
- Cook for about 12 minutes, or until lightly browned.

542. Ratatouille
Prep Time: 30 minutes
Ingredients:
- 1 tbsp. olive oil
- 3 roma tomatoes, thinly sliced
- 2 garlic cloves, minced
- 1 zucchini, thinly sliced
- 2 yellow bell peppers, sliced

- 1 tbsp. vinegar
- 2 tbsp. Herbs de Provence
- Salt and pepper, to taste

Instructions:
- Preheat the air fryer to 390 degrees F.
- Place all of the ingredients in a bowl.
- Season with some salt and pepper, and stir until the veggies are well coated.
- Arrange the vegetable in a round baking dish and place in the air fryer.
- Cook for about 15 minutes, shaking occasionally.
- Let sit for 5 more mins after the time goes off.

543. Cabbage Steaks

Prep Time: 25 minutes
Ingredients:
- 1 cabbage head
- 1 tbsp. garlic stir-in paste
- 1 tsp. salt
- 2 tbsp. olive oil
- ½ tsp. black pepper
- 2 tsp. fennel seeds

Instructions:
- Preheat the air fryer to 350 degrees F.
- Slice the cabbage into 1-½ inch slices.
- In a small bowl combine all of the other ingredients.
- Brush the cabbage with the mixture.
- Arrange the cabbage steaks in your air fryer and cook for 15 minutes.

544. Vegetable Spring Rolls

Prep Time: 15 mins
Ingredients:
- ½ cabbage, grated
- 2 carrots, grated
- 1 tsp. minced ginger
- 1 tsp. minced garlic
- 1 tsp. sesame oil1 tsp. soy sauce
- 1 tsp. sesame seeds½ tsp. salt
- 1 tsp. olive oil
- 1 package spring roll wrappers

Instructions:
- Preheat the air fryer to 370 degrees F.
- Combine all of the ingredients in a large bowl.
- Divide the mixture between the spring roll sheets, and roll them up.
- Arrange on the baking mat. Cook in the air fryer for about 5 minutes.
- Serve with your favorite dipping sauce.

545. Stuffed Mushrooms

Prep Time: 15 minutes
Ingredients:
- 3 Portobello mushrooms
- 1 tomato, diced
- 1 small red onion, diced
- 1 green bell pepper, diced
- ½ cup grated mozzarella cheese
- ½ tsp. garlic powder
- ¼ tsp. pepper
- ¼ tsp. salt

Instructions:
- Preheat the air fryer to 330 degrees F.
- Wash the mushrooms, remove the stems, and pat them dry.
- Coat them with the olive oil.
- Combine all of the remaining ingredients, except the mozzarella, in a small bowl.
- Divide the filling between the mushrooms. Top the mushrooms with mozzarella.
- Place in the air fryer and cook for 8 minutes.

546. Cauliflower Rice

Prep Time: 30 minutes
Ingredients:
- Tofu:½ block tofu
- ½ cup diced onion
- 2 tbsp. soy sauce
- 1 tsp. turmeric
- 1 cup diced carrot
- Cauliflower:3 cups cauliflower rice
- 2 tbsp. soy sauce
- ½ cup chopped broccoli
- 2 garlic cloves, minces
- 1-½ tsp. toasted sesame oil
- 1 tbsp. minced ginger
- ½ cup frozen peas
- 1 tbsp. rice vinegar

Instructions:
- Preheat the air fryer to 370 degrees F.
- Crumble the tofu and combine it with all of the tofu ingredients .
- Place in a baking dish and air fry for 10 minutes.
- Meanwhile, place all of the cauliflower ingredients in a large bowl.
- Mix to combine well.
- Add the cauliflower mixture to the tofu and stir to combine. Cook for 12 minutes.

547. Pasta with Roasted Veggies

Prep Time: 25 minutes
Ingredients:
- 1 lb. penne, cooked
- 1 zucchini, sliced
- 1 pepper, sliced
- 1 acorn squash, sliced
- 4 oz. mushrooms, sliced
- ½ cup kalamata olives, pitted and halved
- ¼ cup olive oil
- 1 tsp. Italian seasoning
- 1 cup grape tomatoes, halved
- 3 tbsp. balsamic vinegar
- 2 tbsp. chopped basil
- Salt and pepper, to taste

Instructions:
- Preheat the air fryer to 380 degrees F.
- Combine the pepper, zucchini, squash, mushrooms, and olive oil, in a large bowl. Season with some salt and pepper.
- Air fry the veggies for 15 minutes. In a large bowl, combine the penne, roasted vegetables, olives, tomatoes, Italian seasoning, and vinegar.
- Divide between 6 serving bowls and sprinkle basil.

548. Poblano and Tomato Stuffed Squash

Prep Time: 50 minutes
Ingredients:
- ½ butternut squash
- 6 grape tomatoes, halved
- 1 poblano pepper, cut into strips
- ¼ cup grated mozzarella, optional
- 2 tsp. olive oil divided
- Salt and pepper, to taste

Instructions:
- Preheat the air fryer to 350 degrees F. Meanwhile, cut trim the ends and cut the squash lengthwise.
- You will only need one half for this recipe. Scoop the flash out, so you make room for the filling.
- Brush 1 tsp. oil over the squash.Place in the air fryer and roast for 30 minutes.
- Combine the other teaspoon of olive oil with the tomatoes and poblanos.Season with salt and pepper, to taste.
- Place the peppers and tomatoes into the squash.
- Cook for 15 more minutes.

- If using mozzarella, add it on top of the squash, two mins before the end.

549. Spicy Pepper, Sweet Potato Skewers

Prep Time: 20 minutes
4.9 g
Ingredients:
- 1 large sweet potato
- 1 beetroot
- 1 green bell pepper
- 1 tsp. chili flakes
- ¼ tsp. black pepper
- ½ tsp. turmeric
- ¼ tsp. garlic powder
- ¼ tsp. paprika1 tbsp. olive oil

Instructions:
- Soak 3 to 4 skewers until ready to use.
- Preheat the air fryer to 350 degrees F.
- Peel the veggies and cut them into bite-sized chunks.
- Place the chunks in a bowl along with the remaining ingredients.
- Mix until fully coated. Thread the veggies in this order: potato, pepper, beetroot.
- Place in the air fryer and cook for 15 minutes.

550. Grilled Tofu Sandwich

Prep Time: 20 minutes
Ingredients:
- 2 slices of bread
- 1 1-inch thick Tofu slice
- ¼ cup red cabbage, shredded
- 2 tsp. olive oil divided¼ tsp. vinegar Salt and pepper, to taste

Instructions:
- Preheat the air fryer to 350 degrees F.
- Place the bread slices and toast for 3 minutes.Set aside.
- Brush the tofu with 1 tsp. oil and place in the basket of your air fryer.grill for 5 mins on each side.
- Combine the cabbage, remaining oil, and vinegar, and season with salt and pepper.
- Place the tofu on top of one bread slice, place the cabbage over, and top with the other bread slice.

551. Quinoa and Veggie Stuffed Peppers

Prep Time: 16 minutes
Ingredients:
- ¼ cup cooked quinoa

- 1 bell pepper
- ½ tbsp. diced onion
- ½ diced tomato, plus one tomato slice
- ¼ tsp. smoked paprika
- Salt and pepper, to taste1 tsp. olive oil
- ¼ tsp. dried basil

Instructions:
- Preheat the air fryer to 350 degrees F.
- Core and clean the bell pepper to prepare it for stuffing.
- Brush the pepper with half of the olive oil on the outside.In a small bowl, combine all of the other ingredients, except the tomato slice and reserved half-teaspoon olive oil.
- Stuff the pepper with the filling.Top with the tomato slice.
- Brush the tomato slice with the remaining half-teaspoon of olive oil and sprinkle with basil.
- Air fry for 10 minutes.

552. Avocado Rolls

Prep Time: 15 minutes
Ingredients:
- 3 ripe avocados, pitted and peeled
- 10 egg roll wrappers
- 1 tomato, diced
- ¼ tsp. pepper
- ½ tsp. salt

Instructions:
- Place all of the filling ingredients in a bowl.
- Mash with a fork until somewhat smooth. There should be chunks left.
- Divide the feeling between the egg wrappers.
- Wet your finger and brush along the edges, so the wrappers can seal well. Roll and seal the wrappers.
- Arrange them on a baking sheet lined dish, and place in the air fryer.
- Air fry at 350 degrees F, for 5 minutes. Serve with favorite dipping (I recommend a chili one)

553. Simple Air Fried Ravioli

Prep Time: 15 minutes
Ingredients:
- 1 package cheese ravioli
- 2 cup Italian breadcrumbs
- ¼ cup Parmesan cheese
- 1 cup buttermilk
- 1 tsp. olive oil
- ¼ tsp. garlic powder

Instructions:
- Preheat the air fryer to 390 degrees F.
- In a small bowl, combine the breadcrumbs, Parmesan cheese, garlic powder, and olive oil.
- Dip the ravioli in the buttermilk and then coat them with the breadcrumb mixture.
- Line a baking sheet with parchment paper and arrange the ravioli on it.
- Place in the air fryer and cook for 5 minutes.
- Serve the air-fried ravioli with favorite sauce (I used simple marinara jar sauce)

554. Veggie Kebab

Prep Time: 20 minutes
Ingredients:
- 2 tbsp. corn flour
- 2/3 cup canned beans
- 1/3 cup grated carrots
- 2 boiled and mashed potatoes
- ¼ cup chopped fresh mint leaves½ tsp. garam masala powder
- ½ cup paneer
- 1 green chili1-inch piece of fresh ginger
- 3 garlic clovesSalt, to taste

Instructions:
- Soak 12 skewers until ready to use.
- Preheat the air fryer to 390 degrees F.
- Place the beans, carrots, garlic, ginger, chili, paneer, and mint, in a food processor and process until smooth.
- Transfer to a bowl. Add the mashed potatoes, corn flour, some salt, and garam masala powder to the bowl.
- Mix until fully incorporate. Divide the mixture into 12 equal pieces. (Mine were lemon-sized.)Shape each of the pieces around a skewer.
- Air fry the skewers for 10 minutes.

555. Roasted Vegetable Salad

Prep Time: 25 minutes
Ingredients:
- 1 potato, peeled and chopped
- ¼ onion, sliced
- 1 carrot, sliced diagonally
- ½ small beetroot, sliced
- 1 cup cherry tomatoes
- Juice of 1 lemon
- Handful of rocket salad
- Handful of baby spinach
- 3 tbsp. canned chickpeas

- ½ tsp. cumin
- ½ tsp. turmeric
- ¼ tsp. sea salt
- 2 tbsp. olive oil
- Parmesan shavings

Instructions:
- Preheat the air fryer to 370 degrees F.
- Combine the onion, potato, cherry tomatoes, carrot, beetroot, cumin, seas salt, turmeric, and 1 tbsp. olive oil, in a bowl.
- Place in the air fryer and cook for 20 minutes.Let cool for 2 minutes.Place the rocket, salad, spinach, lemon juice, and 1 tbsp. olive oil, into a serving bowl.
- Mix to combine.Stir in the roasted veggies.
- Top with chickpeas and Parmesan shavings.

556.Stuffed Meatballs

Preparation time: 10 mins Cooking time: 10 mins

Ingredients:
- 1/3 cup bread crumbs
- 3 tablespoons milk
- 1 tablespoon ketchup
- 1 egg
- ½ teaspoon marjoram, dried
- Salt and black pepper to the taste
- 1 pound lean beef, ground
- 20 cheddar cheese cubes
- 1 tablespoon olive oil

Instructions:
- In a bowl, mix bread crumbs with ketchup, milk, marjoram, salt, pepper and egg and whisk well.
- Add beef, stir and shape 20 meatballs out of this mix.
- Shape each meatball around a cheese cube, drizzle the oil over them and rub.
- Place all meatballs in your preheated air fryer and cook at 390 degrees F for 10 minutes.
- Serve them for lunch with a side salad.

557.Steaks and Cabbage

Preparation time: 10 mins Cooking time: 10 mins

Ingredients:
- ½ pound sirloin steak, cut into strips
- 2 teaspoons cornstarch
- 1 tablespoon peanut oil
- 2 cups green cabbage, chopped
- 1 yellow bell pepper, chopped
- 2 green onions, chopped
- 2 garlic cloves, minced
- Salt and black pepper to the taste

Instructions:
- In a bowl, mix cabbage with salt, pepper and peanut oil, toss, transfer to air fryer's basket, cook at 370 degrees F for 4 mins and transfer to a bowl.
- Add steak strips to your air fryer, also add green onions, bell pepper, garlic, salt and pepper, toss and cook for 5 minutes.
- Add over cabbage, toss, divide among plates and serve for lunch.

558.Succulent Lunch Turkey Breast

Preparation time: 10 mins Cooking time: 47 mins

Ingredients:
- 1 big turkey breast
- 2 teaspoons olive oil
- ½ teaspoon smoked paprika
- 1 teaspoon thyme, dried
- ½ teaspoon sage, dried
- Salt and black pepper to the taste
- 2 tablespoons mustard
- ¼ cup maple syrup
- 1 tablespoon butter, soft

Instructions:
- Brush turkey breast with the olive oil, season with salt, pepper, thyme, paprika and sage, rub, place in your air fryer's basket and fry at 350 degrees F for 25 minutes.
- Flip turkey, cook for 10 mins more, flip one more time and cook for another 10 minutes.
- Meanwhile, heat up a pan with the butter over medium heat, add mustard and maple syrup, stir well, cook for a couple of mins and take off heat.
- Slice turkey breast, divide among plates and serve with the maple glaze drizzled on top.

559.Italian Eggplant Sandwich

Preparation time: 10 mins Cooking time: 16 mins

Ingredients:
- 1 eggplant, sliced
- 2 teaspoons parsley, dried
- Salt and black pepper to the taste
- ½ cup breadcrumbs
- ½ teaspoon Italian seasoning
- ½ teaspoon garlic powder
- ½ teaspoon onion powder
- 2 tablespoons milk
- 4 bread slices
- ½ cup mayonnaise
- ¾ cup tomato sauce
- 2 cups mozzarella cheese, grated

Instructions:
- Season eggplant slices with salt and pepper, leave aside for 10 mins and then pat dry them well.
- In a bowl, mix parsley with breadcrumbs, Italian seasoning, onion and garlic powder, salt and black pepper and stir.
- In another bowl, mix milk with mayo and whisk well.
- Brush eggplant slices with mayo mix, dip them in breadcrumbs, place them in your air fryer's basket, spray with cooking oil and cook them at 400 degrees F for 15 minutes, flipping them after 8 minutes.
- Brush each bread slice with olive oil and arrange 2 on a working surface.
- Add mozzarella and parmesan on each, add baked eggplant slices, spread tomato sauce and basil and top with the other bread slices, greased side down.
- Divide sandwiches on plates, cut them in halves and serve for lunch.

560.Creamy Chicken Stew

Preparation time: 10 mins Cooking time: 25 mins

Ingredients:
- 1 and ½ cups canned cream of celery soup
- 6 chicken tenders
- Salt and black pepper to the taste
- 2 potatoes, chopped
- 1 bay leaf
- 1 thyme spring, chopped
- 1 tablespoon milk
- 1 egg yolk
- ½ cup heavy cream

Instructions:
- In a bowl, mix chicken with cream of celery, potatoes, heavy cream, bay leaf, thyme, salt and pepper, toss, pour into your air fryer's pan and cook at 320 degrees F for 25 minutes.
- Leave your stew to cool down a bit, discard bay leaf, divide among plates and serve right away.

561. Lunch Pork and Potatoes

Preparation time: 10 mins Cooking time: 25 mins

Ingredients:
- 2 pounds pork loin
- Salt and black pepper to the taste
- 2 red potatoes, cut into medium wedges
- ½ teaspoon garlic powder
- ½ teaspoon red pepper flakes
- 1 teaspoon parsley, dried
- A drizzle of balsamic vinegar

Instructions:
- In your air fryer's pan, mix pork with potatoes, salt, pepper, garlic powder, pepper flakes, parsley and vinegar, toss and cook at 390 degrees F for 25 minutes.
- Slice pork, divide it and potatoes on plates and serve for lunch.

562. Turkey Cakes

Preparation time: 10 mins Cooking time: 10 mins

Ingredients:
- 6 mushrooms, chopped
- 1 teaspoon garlic powder
- 1 teaspoon onion powder
- Salt and black pepper to the taste
- 1 and ¼ pounds turkey meat, ground
- Cooking spray
- Tomato sauce for serving

Instructions:
- In your blender, mix mushrooms with salt and pepper, pulse well and transfer to a bowl.
- Add turkey, onion powder, garlic powder, salt and pepper, stir and shape cakes out of this mix.
- Spray them with cooking spray, transfer them to your air fryer and cook at 320 degrees F for 10 minutes.
- Serve them with tomato sauce on the side and a tasty side salad.

563. Cheese Ravioli and Marinara Sauce

Preparation time: 10 mins Cooking time: 8 mins

Ingredients:
- 20 ounces cheese ravioli
- 10 ounces marinara sauce
- 1 tablespoon olive oil
- 1 cup buttermilk
- 2 cups bread crumbs
- ¼ cup parmesan, grated

Instructions:
- Put buttermilk in a bowl and breadcrumbs in another bowl.
- Dip ravioli in buttermilk, then in breadcrumbs and place them in your air fryer on a baking sheet.
- Drizzle olive oil over them, cook at 400 degrees F for 5 minutes, divide them on plates, sprinkle parmesan on top and serve for lunch

564. Beef Stew

Preparation time: 10 mins Cooking time: 20 mins

Ingredients:
- 2 pounds beef meat, cut into medium chunks
- 2 carrots, chopped
- 4 potatoes, chopped
- Salt and black pepper to the taste
- 1 quart veggie stock
- ½ teaspoon smoked paprika
- A handful thyme, chopped

Instructions:
- In a dish that fits your air fryer, mix beef with carrots, potatoes, stock, salt, pepper, paprika and thyme, stir, place in air fryer's basket and cook at 375 degrees F for 20 minutes.
- Divide into bowls and serve right away for lunch.

565. Meatballs Sandwich

Preparation time: 10 mins Cooking time: 22 mins

Ingredients:
- 3 baguettes, sliced more than halfway through
- 14 ounces beef, ground
- 7 ounces tomato sauce
- 1 small onion, chopped
- 1 egg, whisked
- 1 tablespoon bread crumbs
- 2 tablespoons cheddar cheese, grated
- 1 tablespoon oregano, chopped
- 1 tablespoon olive oil
- Salt and black pepper to the taste
- 1 teaspoon thyme, dried
- 1 teaspoon basil, dried

Instructions:
- In a bowl, combine meat with salt, pepper, onion, breadcrumbs, egg, cheese, oregano, thyme and basil, stir, shape medium meatballs and add them

to your air fryer after you've greased it with the oil.
- Cook them at 375 degrees F for 12 minutes, flipping them halfway.
- Add tomato sauce, cook meatballs for 10 mins more and arrange them on sliced baguettes.
- Serve them right away.

566. Marinated Air Fryer Vegetables

Prep Time: 10 mins Cook Time: 15 mins
Marinading time: 20 mins
Total Time: 25 mins Servings: 4 servings

Ingredients
- Vegetables
- 2 green zucchini cut into ½ inch pieces
- 1 yellow squash cut into ½ inch pieces
- 4 oz button mushrooms cut in half
- 1 red onion cut into ½ inch pieces
- 1 red bell pepper cut into ½ inch pieces
- Marinade
- 4 Tbsp Olive Oil
- 2 Tbsp Balsamic Vinegar
- 1 Tbsp Honey
- 1 ½ tsp salt
- ½ tsp dried thyme
- ½ tsp dried oregano
- ¼ tsp garlic powder
- A few drops of liquid smoke optional
- Salt to taste

Instructions
- Place marinade ingredients in a large bowl and whisk until combined. Place chopped vegetables in a bowl and stir until all vegetables are fully covered.
- Allow vegetables to marinate for 20-30 minutes.
- Place marinated vegetables in an air fryer basket and cook at 400 degrees Fahrenheit for 15-18 minutes, stirring every 5 min., until tender. Salt to taste.

567. Airfried Vegetables

Prep time: 10 min Cook time: 20 min
Total time: 30 min Serves: 4

Ingredients
- 1 lb / 0.5kg of vegetables (broccoli, brussels sprouts, carrots, cauliflower, parsnips, potatoes, sweet potatoes, zucchini will all work), chopped evenly
- 1 Tbsp / 30 mL of cooking oil
- Some salt and pepper

Instructions
Prep

- Preheat air fryer for about 5 mins at 360F / 182C degrees.
- Evenly chop veggies and toss with oil and some salt and pepper. If making potato or sweet potato fries, soak them in water for ~30 mins to draw out excess starch for crispier results, and then pat dry thoroughly with paper towels before tossing with oil.

Make

- Transfer veggies into frying compartment and fry for 15 to 20 minutes, stirring veggies every 5 to 8 mins or so. Some veggies might need longer and some will need less – just use your judgment when you open the compartment to stir the veggies. You want the outside to be golden and crispy and the inside to be tender.
- Enjoy or toss with your favorite dipping sauce when done! If you need sauce ideas, check out 5 of our favorites.

568.Air Fryer Vegetables

Prep Time: 10 mins Cook Time: 15 mins
Total Time: 25 mins
Servings: 4

Ingredients

- 380 g Broccoli
- 250 g Carrots
- 1 Large Bell pepper
- 1 Large Onion
- 1/2 Tsp. Black pepper
- 1 Tbsp Olive oil
- 1 Tsp. Seasoning vegetable, chicken, turkey seasoning, or any of choice.
- Salt to taste

Instructions

- Wash and cut the vegetables into bite-size.
- Cut veggies on a white flat plate.
- Add them to a bowl and season with salt, black pepper, or any seasoning of choice, and olive oil. Mix so that the veggies are covered in the seasoning.
- Seasoning and olive oil added to the veggies.
- Add the seasoned veggies into the air fryer basket and air fry at a temperature of 175c for 15 minutes.
- Air fryer roasted vegetables in the air fryer basket.
- Toss the veggies in the basket halfway through cooking so that all sides are

crisp.
- When done, take out the basket and serve.
- The finished dish displayed.

569.Roasted Air Fryer Vegetables

Prep Time: 5 mins Cook Time: 12 mins
Total Time: 17 mins
Servings: 4

Ingredients

- 1 red bell pepper
- 1-2 yellow squash
- 1 zucchini
- 1/4 medium red onion
- 1 cup broccoli
- 1 tbsp olive oil
- 1/2 Tsp. salt
- 1/2 Tsp. garlic powder
- 1/8 Tsp. black pepper

Instructions

- Cut up 1 red bell pepper, 2 small yellow zucchini squash, 1 zucchini, 1/2 a medium onion, and 1 cup of broccoli into similar sized chunks.
- Add the sliced vegetables into a large bowl and toss them with 1 Tbsp of olive oil, 1/2 Tsp. salt, 1/2 Tsp. garlic powder, and 1/8 Tsp. black pepper.
- Once the veggies a coated in the oil and seasoning, place them onto the bottom of your air fryer basket and roast for 10-12 mins at 400 degrees Fahrenheit.

570.Air Fryer Roast Vegetables

Prep Time: 5 Mins Cook Time: 10 Mins
Total Time: 15 Mins

Ingredients

- 1 large sweet potato
- 1 large potato
- 1 large carrot
- ¼ small pumpkin
- ½ tsp spice or herb mix, optional

Instructions

- Wash the vegetables or peel if preferred, and cut into chunks no thicker than 1 inch (they can be as long as you like). Pat vegetables dry.
- Place vegetable pieces in an air fryer basket and spray with olive oil. Add spice if desired. Shake and spray with oil again.
- Cook in the air fryer at 360°F (180°C) for 5 min.. Remove the basket and shake.

- Return to the air fryer and cook for a further 5-10 mins until golden brown.

571.Air Fryer Veggies

Prep Time: 5 mins Cook Time: 20 mins
Total Time: 25 mins

Ingredients

- 3 cups mixed vegetables, cut into 1-inch pieces (cauliflower, broccoli, squash, carrots, beets, etc)
- 1 Tbsp olive oil
- 1/2 Tsp. kosher salt

Preparation

- Place the vegetables in a bowl and toss to coat with the oil and salt.
- Place the vegetables in the air fryer basket and cook at 375F degrees for 15-20 mins or until golden and fork-tender.

572.Air Fryer "Roasted" Asparagus

Prep Time: 3 mins Cook Time: 7 mins
Total Time: 10 mins Servings: 4 servings

Ingredients

- 1 pound fresh asparagus, ends trimmed
- Oil spray or olive oil
- Salt, to taste
- Black pepper, to taste

Instructions

- Coat the asparagus with oil spray or olive oil and season with salt and pepper. Lay the asparagus evenly in the air fryer basket.
- Make sure to coat the asparagus tips so they don't burn or dry out too fast. It is best to season before you put it in the air fryer basket.
- Too much excess salt in the air fryer baskets will often start to break down with coating.
- Air Fry at 380°F for 7-10 min., depending on thickness, shake, and turn asparagus halfway through cooking.
- Taste for seasoning & tenderness, then serve.

573.Air Fryer Vegetables

Prep Time: 10 mins Cook Time: 10 mins
Servings: 6

Ingredients

- 2 zucchini cut into dials
- 2 yellow squash cut into dials
- 1 container mushrooms cut in half
- 1/2 c olive oil
- 1/2 onion sliced

- 3/4 tsp Italian seasoning
- 1/2 tsp garlic salt
- 1/4 tsp Lawry's seasoned salt

Instructions

- Slice zucchini and yellow squash into dials. The thinner they are the softer they will get. I would recommend 3/4" thick so they all are the same consistency when done.
- Slice mushrooms in half. Put all vegetables in a bowl and toss together gently. (if you want to add 1/2-1 full precooked sausage link diced into bite-size pcs., add that now too)
- Pour olive oil on top and toss gently, then sprinkle in all seasonings in a bowl and gently toss one more time.
- Add half of your vegetables into your air fryer, close, and set to 400 degrees for 10 min.. I did not bother shaking or tossing halfway through and they came out amazing.
- Remove, enjoy, and add another half at 400 degrees for 10 mins to finish the cooking batch.

574. Air Fryer Frozen Broccoli, Carrots, And Cauliflower

Prep time: 5 min Cook time: 10 min
Total time: 15 min Serves: 3 people

Ingredients:

- 3 cups frozen mixed broccoli, carrots, and cauliflower
- 1 TBS extra virgin olive oil
- 1 tsp Italian seasoning blend (or basil, oregano, rosemary, and thyme)
- 1/2 tsp **Nutrition Facts**al yeast (optional)
- 1/2 tsp sea salt
- 1/4 tsp freshly cracked pepper

Directions:

- Preheat the air fryer to 375°F for 5 minutes.
- Place the frozen vegetables in a large mixing bowl. Pour the olive oil over the vegetables and toss to coat. Sprinkle the herbs, salt, pepper, and nutritional yeast over the vegetables and toss again.
- Add the vegetables to the crisper plate or basket of the air fryer in an even layer. Cook for 5 min.. Shake the bucket, or rotate the vegetables. Continue to cook for an additional 4 to 6 mins until the vegetables are tender

and cooked through to a warm temperature. Taste one to test for doneness.

- Place the cooked vegetables on a serving platter. You can top with more

575. Healthy Air Fryer Chicken And Veggies

Prep Time: 5 mins Cook Time: 15 mins
Total Time: 20 mins
Servings: 4 servings

Ingredients

- 1 pound chicken breast, chopped into bite-size pieces (2-3 medium chicken breasts)
- 1 cup broccoli florets (fresh or frozen)
- 1 zucchini chopped
- 1 cup bell pepper chopped (any colors you like)
- 1/2 onion chopped
- 2 cloves garlic minced or crushed
- 2 Tbsps olive oil
- 1/2 Tsp. EACH garlic powder, chili powder, salt, pepper
- 1 Tbsp Italian seasoning (or spice blend of choice)

Instructions

- Preheat air fryer to 400F.
- Chop the veggies and chicken into small bite-size pieces and transfer to a large mixing bowl.
- Add the oil and seasoning to the bowl and toss to combine.
- Add the chicken and veggies to the preheated air fryer and cook for 10 minutes, shaking halfway, or until the chicken and veggies are charred and chicken is cooked through. If your air fryer is small, you may have to cook them in 2-3 batches.

576. Air Fryer Vegetable "Stir-Fry"

Prep Time: 5 mins Cook Time: 7 mins
Total Time: 12 mins

Ingredients

- 50 grams extra firm tofu, cut into strips (about 1 cup)
- 4 stalks asparagus, ends trimmed and cut in half
- 4 brussels sprouts, halved
- 3 brown mushrooms, sliced
- 2 cloves garlic, minced
- 1 Tsp. italiano seasoning
- ½ Tsp. sesame oil (or olive oil)
- ¼ Tsp. soy sauce

- Salt and pepper, to taste
- Roasted white sesame seeds

Instructions

- Combine all ingredients into a large mixing bowl, and toss to combine.
- Transfer into air fryer basket and air fry at 350 F for 7-8 minutes, depending on how well done you would like the vegetables. Give the basket a shake halfway through.
- Remove from air fryer basket, sprinkle some roasted white sesame seeds on top, and serve with a side of rice.

577. Air Fryer Roasted Vegetables

Prep Time: 5 mins Cook Time: 20 mins
Total Time: 25 mins
Servings: 4

Ingredients

- 2 Tbsps olive oil
- 1 medium zucchini sliced
- 8 oz fresh mushrooms sliced
- 1 Tbsp minced garlic
- Garlic powder to taste
- Onion powder to taste
- Salt and pepper to taste

Instructions

- Preheat air fryer to 390.
- Combine all ingredients in a bowl and toss well to coat in oil.
- Spread out in a single layer in your air fryer basket (in batches if needed).
- Cook for 10 mins and stir.
- Cook for an additional 5 to 10 mins until vegetables reach your desired texture.

578. Air Fryer vegetables

Prep Time: 10 mins Cook Time: 10 mins
Total Time: 20 mins

Ingredients

- 2 zucchini
- 1-2 yellow squash
- 1/2 sweet onion
- 1 8 oz container mushrooms
- 1 bell pepper
- 1/4 cup olive oil
- 1 Tsp. Italian seasoning
- 1/2 Tsp. salt
- 1/4 Tsp. ground black pepper

Instructions

- Cut squash, zucchini, pepper, onion, and mushrooms into bite-sized pieces. Place in a large bowl.
- Pour olive oil over vegetables.

Sprinkle Italian seasoning, salt, and pepper over vegetables. Toss to coat.
- Pour vegetables into an air fryer basket. Spread out for one layer. (You might need to cook in 2 batches.)
- Cook at 400 degrees F for 10-12 minutes.
- Serve warm.

579.Air Fryer Garlic Zucchini

Prep Time: 5 mins Cook Time: 15 mins
Total Time: 20 mins Servings: 2 servings

Ingredients
- 2 zucchini (1 lb. Or 455g total)
- Olive oil or cooking spray
- 1/2 Tsp. garlic powder
- Salt, to taste
- Black pepper, to taste

Instructions
- Trim the ends of the zucchini, if desired. Cut the zucchini into 1/2" thick slices (either into lengthwise slices or into coins). If cutting into lengthwise slices, cut to length to fit the width of your air fryer basket if needed.
- Lightly oil or spray the zucchini slices on both sides and then season with garlic powder, salt, and pepper.
- Air Fry at 400°F for 8-14 mins or until browned and cooked through.

580.Healthy Air Fryer Chicken And Veggies

Prep Time: 5 mins Cook Time: 15 mins
Total Time: 20 mins
Servings: 4 servings

Ingredients
- 1 pound chicken breast, chopped into bite-size pieces (2-3 medium chicken breasts)
- 1 cup broccoli florets (fresh or frozen)
- 1 zucchini chopped
- 1 cup bell pepper chopped (any colors you like)
- 1/2 onion chopped
- 2 cloves garlic minced or crushed
- 2 Tbsps olive oil
- 1/2 Tsp. EACH garlic powder, chili powder, salt, pepper
- 1 Tbsp Italian seasoning (or spice blend of choice)

Instructions
- Preheat air fryer to 400F.
- Chop the veggies and chicken into small bite-size pieces and transfer to a large mixing bowl.
- Add the oil and seasoning to the bowl and toss to combine.
- Add the chicken and veggies to the preheated air fryer and cook for 10 min., shaking halfway, or until the chicken and veggies are charred and chicken is cooked through. If your air fryer is small, you may have to cook them in 2-3 batches.

581.Air Fryer Veggie Tots

Prep Time: 10 mins Cook Time: 12 mins
Servings: 20 tots

Ingredients
- 1 cup sweet potato (baked in the oven until soft and skin removed)
- 1 ½ cups kale
- 1 egg
- ½ cup rice crumbs I grab my rice crumbs at Trader Joe's. These are a great gluten-free option. Panko bread crumbs can be substituted.
- ½ tsp garlic powder
- ½ tsp paprika
- ¼ tsp salt
- ¼ tsp pepper
- 2 tsp olive oil

Instructions
- Spray or drizzle 1/2 tsp olive oil in the air fryer. Place the tots into the air fryer. Do not stack them on top of each other to ensure they become crispy. Spray or drizzle 1 tsp olive oil over the top of the tots and cook at 400 degrees for 10-15 min.. Repeat if needed (depending on the size of your air fryer.)
- Pulse kale in a food processor into small flakes.

Air Fryer Veggie Tots
- Mash the cooked sweet potato with a fork. If you just cooked the sweet potato, allow it to cool completely. Mix in the kale, egg, and rice crumbs and spices until combined.
- Form into "tot-like" shapes with a 1 tbsp scoop or just create small round shapes. They don't have to be perfect!
- Spray or drizzle ½ tsp olive oil into the air fryer. Place the tots into the air fryer. Do not stack them on top of each other to ensure they become crispy. Spray or drizzle 1 tsp olive oil over the top of the tots and air fry at 400 degrees for 10-15

minutes. Repeat if needed, depending on the size of your air fryer.
- Serve with a dipping sauce! I made an easy 3 ingredient sauce with Wunder Creamery Quark, Primal Kitchen Dairy-Free Mayo, and Primal Kitchen Ketchup.
- Enjoy!

582.Asian-Style Air Fryer Green Beans

Prep Time: 5 Mins Cook Time: 5 Mins
Total Time: 10 Mins

Ingredients
- 1 lb green beans, washed and trimmed
- 2 teaspoons sesame oil
- 1 Tsp. garlic salt
- Pepper to taste

Instructions
- Preheat your air fryer to 400 degrees.
- Place the trimmed green beans, sesame oil, garlic salt, and pepper into a bowl and mix to evenly coat green beans.
- Put green beans into your preheated air fryer for 5-7 mins shaking the basket halfway through. You can check the tenderness with a fork to test if the green beans are done.
- Remove green beans from the air fryer and enjoy!

583.Air Fryer Broccoli

Prep Time: 5 min Cook Time: 6 min
Total Time: 11 mins

Ingredients
- 12 oz fresh broccoli florets, cut/torn into toughly even, very-small pieces
- 2 Tbsps extra virgin olive oil
- 1/4 tsp garlic powder
- 1/4 tsp onion powder
- 1/8 tsp kosher salt
- 1/8 tsp freshly ground black pepper

Instructions
- Combine all ingredients in a bowl; toss well to fully incorporate seasonings into the broccoli florets
- Pour 1 TB water into the bottom of the air fryer pan (this helps prevent contents from smoking.)
- Add broccoli mixture evenly into the air fryer basket. Set to 400F for 6 min.. Once the timer goes off, immediately remove the basket and serve.

584.Instant Pot Vortex Air Fryer Vegetables

Prep Time: 5 Mins Cook Time: 18 Mins
Total Time: 23 Mins

Ingredients

Vegetables Of Choice. Used Here Are:

- 1 cup broccoli
- 1 cup cauliflower
- 1 cup carrots
- 1 Tbsp Olive oil or oil of choice

Instructions

- Place the vegetables in a bowl and toss with the oil
- Add seasoning and toss
- Add the vegetable to the Vortex rotisserie basket (or your air fryer basket with other brands)
- Air fry on 380 or 18 mins or until vegetables are roasted with golden brown parts
- Carefully remove the basket using the removal tool, serve, and enjoy!

585."Fried" Tempura Veggies

Hands-On: 15 mins Total Time: 25 mins
Servings: 4

Ingredients

- ½ Cup flour
- ½ Tsp. salt, plus more to taste
- ½ Tsp. black pepper
- 2 eggs
- 2 water
- 1 cup panko bread crumbs
- 2 teaspoons vegetable oil
- ¼ Tsp. seasoning to taste
- 2 – 3 cups vegetable pieces (whole green beans, sweet pepper rings, zucchini slices, whole asparagus spears, red onion rings, or avocado wedges), cut 1/2 inch thick

Instructions

- Mix together flour, 1/4 tsp. salt, and the pepper in a shallow dish. Whisk together eggs and water in another shallow dish. Stir together panko and oil in a third shallow dish. Add the desired Seasoning to either panko and/or flour mixture.
- Sprinkle vegetables with remaining 1/4 tsp. salt. Dip in flour mixture, then in egg mixture, and finally in panko mixture to coat.
- Preheat air fryer to 400°F and oven to 200°F. Arrange half of the vegetables in a single layer in a fryer basket. Cook until golden brown, about 10 min.. Sprinkle with additional salt, if desired.

Transfer vegetables to the oven to keep warm. Repeat with remaining vegetables. Serve with dipping sauce.

586.Air Fryer Roasted Potatoes

Prep Time: 5 mins Cook Time: 22 mins
Total Time: 27 mins
Servings 4

Ingredients

- 1.5 pounds potatoes (diced into 1-inch pieces - gold, red, or russets)
- 1/2 Tsp. garlic powder or granulated garlic
- 1/2 Tsp. salt or more, to taste
- 1/4 Tsp. pepper
- 1/2 Tsp. oregano dried
- 1/2 Tsp. basil dried
- Cooking spray (i am using avocado oil cooking spray)

Instructions

- Spray the air fryer cooking basket with the cooking spray.
- Add diced potatoes to the basket, and give the potatoes a spray.
- Add salt, pepper, garlic powder, oregano, and basil, and toss to combine and evenly coat the potatoes.
- Cook at 400 degrees (not preheated) until brown and crispy, about 20 to 24 min..
- Toss them halfway through with a flipper, and shake the basket once more to ensure even cooking.

587.Cauliflower & Broccoli Bites

Total Time: 1 hour SERVES: 6 servings

Ingredients

- Cooking spray
- 1 cup panko bread crumbs
- ¼ cup grated Parmesan
- 1 Tbsp. Creole seasoning
- 2 cups cauliflower florets
- 2 cups broccoli florets
- ½ cup whole wheat flour
- 2 large eggs
- 1 Tbsp. Fresh parsley, finely chopped, optional
- Marinara sauce for serving, optional

Directions

- Preheat air fryer to 400°F.
- Lightly spray the fryer basket with oil.
- In a large bowl, combine panko, Parmesan, and creole seasoning. Set aside.
- Place flour in a shallow dish and set

aside. In a separate dish, whisk 2 eggs and set aside.

- Working in small batches, dip cauliflower and broccoli florets into flour and gently shake off excess. Dip into egg and then press into breadcrumb mixture.
- Place florets in the basket and cook until golden and crispy, about 5-6 minutes. Remove from fryer basket and sprinkle with parsley.
- Serve immediately with marinara sauce.

588.Air Fryer Vegetable And Cheese Quesadillas

Servings: 2 Ready In: 18min
Prep Time: 10min Cook Time: 8min

Ingredients

- 2 (6 inches) flour tortillas
- Cooking spray
- 1/2 cup shredded cheddar cheese
- 1/2 red bell pepper, sliced
- 1/2 zucchini, sliced

Directions

- Preheat air fryer to 400°F (200°C).
- Spray 1 side of a single tortilla generously with cooking spray and place flat in an air fryer basket.
- Spread half the Cheddar cheese over tortilla. Top cheese layer with bell pepper and zucchini. Spread remaining Cheddar cheese over top.
- Place the second tortilla over fillings and spray the top with cooking spray.
- Air fry until cheese is melted and tortillas are crisp, 8 to 9 min..

589.Air Fryer Veggie Fajitas

Yield: 2-3 Servings Prep Time: 10 Mins
Cook Time: 15 Mins Total Time: 25 Mins

Ingredients

- 4 portobello mushrooms, sliced into strips
- 2 sweet peppers (red or yellow), sliced into strips
- 1 large onion, sliced into strips
- Fajita sauce
- 3 tbsp sweet chili sauce
- 1 tbsp soy sauce
- 1 tsp smoked paprika
- 1/8 tsp chili powder (more if you want it spicy)
- 1/2 tsp cumin
- 1/4 tsp ground coriander

- To serve
- 8 tortillas
- Toppings of your choice - guacamole, salsa, sour cream or vegan cream, chopped fresh cilantro (coriander)

Instructions
- Make the fajita sauce by whisking all ingredients together.
- Place the sliced vegetables in a large bowl and coat with the fajita sauce. Allow marinating for a little while in the fridge if you have the time. If you don't, that's OK too - you can go ahead and put them in straight away.
- Heat the air fryer to 200C / 390F.
- Coat the marinated vegetables with a spray of oil and place them in the fry basket.
- Cook for 15 min., opening the fryer up to mix the vegetables halfway through.
- They're ready when the vegetables are juicy and a little bit charred. You may want to cook for another 5 mins if they're not yet charred to your liking.
- Serve immediately with warmed tortillas and your toppings of choice.

590. Roasted Winter Vegetables

Servings: 6 Persons Prep Time: 5 Mins
Cooking Time: 20 Mins
Total Time: 25 Mins

Ingredients
- 300 g parsnips
- 300 g celeriac
- 2 red onions
- 300 g 'butternut squash'
- 1 tbsp fresh thyme needles
- 1 tbsp olive oil
- pepper & salt

Directions
- Preheat the Airfryer to 200°C.
- Peel the parsnips, celeriac, and onions. Cut the parsnips and celeriac into 2 cm cubes and the onions into wedges. Halve the 'butternut squash', remove the seeds and cut into cubes. (There's no need to peel it.)
- Mix the cut vegetables with thyme and olive oil. Season to taste.
- Place the vegetables into the basket and slide the basket into the Airfryer. Set the timer for 20 mins and roast the vegetables until the timer rings and the vegetables are nicely brown and done. Stir the vegetables once while roasting.

591. Roast Potatoes In A Basket Air Fryer

Prep Time: 5 mins Cook Time: 40 mins
Total Time: 45 mins
Servings: 4 servings

Ingredients
- 1.25 kg potato (3 lbs)
- 1 Tsp. oil

Instructions
- Wash potato, peel, cut into large chunks, adding chunks to a large bowl.
- Add 1 Tsp. of oil to the bowl of potato chunks and just using your clean hands, toss well until all surfaces are coated. (Tip! first, have the air basket pulled out and beside you, ready to receive the potatoes because your hands will be oily.)
- Cook (no need to pre-heat) at 160 C (320 F) for 25 min..
- Take out the potatoes and tip them back into the bowl you have been using. Toss them in there briefly and gently using a large spoon.
- Transfer potato chunks back into fryer basket. Place back into the machine, raise the temperature on the machine to 180 C (350 F), and cook for another 7 minutes.
- Take out the potatoes and tip them back into the bowl you have been using. Toss them in there using a large spoon. (At this point, a few might look just about done, but once you toss them you'll see that there are loads that aren't quite as far along.)
- Transfer potato chunks back into fryer basket. Leave temperature unchanged. Roast for a final 7 min..
- Serve piping hot.

592. Crispy Air Fryer Broccoli

Prep Time: 5 mins Cook Time: 8 mins
Total Time: 13 mins

Ingredients
- 4-6 cups broccoli florets
- 1 Tbsp olive oil
- 1 Tbsp balsamic vinegar
- 1/8 Tsp. salt

Instructions
- Heat air fryer to 200°C/390°F.
- Chop broccoli into equal-sized 1 to 1.5-inch florets and place in a bowl.
- Toss broccoli florets with olive oil, balsamic vinegar, and salt.

- Add broccoli to the basket. Cook for 7-8 min., shaking up the basket every 2-3 min.. When broccoli florets start to become golden and brown, broccoli is done.
- Enjoy!

593. Keto Air Fryer Chicken & Veggies

Prep time: 15 mins Cook time: 15 mins
Total time: 30 mins
Serves: 4

Ingredients
- 1 lb boneless, skinless chicken breast, cut into bite-sized pieces
- 2.5 cups broccoli florets
- 1 medium red bell pepper, chopped
- 1/2 medium onion, chopped
- 1 tbsp olive oil
- 1.5 tsp italian seasoning
- 1 tsp garlic powder
- 1/2 tsp paprika
- 1/2 tsp chili powder
- 1/2 tsp salt
- 1/4 tsp black pepper
- 1/4 tsp onion powder

Direction
- Preheat the air fryer to 400 degrees F (if your air fryer allows).
- Add chicken breast, broccoli, bell pepper, and onion to a large mixing bowl. Coat with olive oil and seasonings, toss to combine.
- Place in air fryer basket and cook for 12-15 minutes, or until chicken is completely cooked through. Stir halfway through cooking time. Serve hot.

594. Veg Cutlet Recipe

Prep Time: 15 Mins Cook Time: 40 Mins
Total Time: 55 Mins

Ingredients For Cutlets
- 2 cups Sweet Potatoes (Boiled, Peeled and Mashed) 1 cup is 250 ml
- 3/4 cup Carrot (finely grated)
- 1/2 cup Sweet Corn (steamed)
- 1/2 cup Capsicum (finely chopped)
- 1/3 cup Green Peas (Steamed)
- 1/2 cup Quick Cooking Oats Or Instant Oats
- 1 tbsp Ginger Paste
- 1 & 1/2 tbsp Oil For Cooking cutlets (1 tbsp oil is 15 ml)
- Salt to taste
- 2 to 3 tbsp Coriander Leaves (finely

chopped)
- Spices
- 1 tsp Kashmiri Red chili powder 1 tsp is 5 ml
- 1 & 1/2 tsp Garam Masala Powder
- 1/2 tsp Turmeric Powder
- 1/4 tsp Chaat Masala Powder
- 1/2 tsp Amchur Powder or Dry Mango Powder

Instructions
- In a wide bowl, add boiled and mashed sweet potatoes, cooked peas, steamed sweet corn, grated carrots, and finely chopped capsicum.
- Add all the spices, ginger paste, quick-cooking oats, and salt to taste.
- Now add the finely chopped coriander leaves (I have used stems as well).
- Mix everything together.
- Divide and take an equal portion of the cutlet mixture and shape them into an "oval" shape. Once the cutlets are shaped, preheat the Air Fryer at 200 Degrees C for 5 mins
- Place around 12 cutlets, brush or spray oil and cook them for 15 mins at 200 Degree C.
- Turn them after 8 to 10 mins of cooking, repeat the process of spraying oil or brushing and air fry them until they are golden brown. Serve with the accompaniment of your choice.

595. Air-Fried Crispy Vegetables

Prep Time: 10 Mins Cook Time: 15 Mins
Ingredients
- 2 cups mixed vegetables(bell peppers, cauliflower, mushrooms, zucchini, baby corn)
- For batter
- 1/4 cup cornstarch(cornflour in india)
- 1/4 cup all-purpose flour/maida
- ½ tsp garlic powder
- ½-1 tsp red chilli powder
- ½-1 tsp black pepper powder
- 1 tsp salt or as per taste
- 1 tsp oil

For Sauce Mix
- 2 tbsp soy sauce
- 1 tbsp chilli sauce/
- 1 tbsp tomato ketchup
- 1 tbsp vinegar(rice/synthetic or apple cider)

- 1 tsp brown sugar/coconut sugar

Other
- 1 tbsp sesame oil or any plant-based oil
- 1 tsp sesame seeds
- Spring onion greens for garnish

Instructions
- Cut Cauliflower in small florets, cubed bell peppers, cut mushrooms in half, and carrots and zucchini in circles. Do not cut very thin strips.
- Make a batter with all-purpose flour, cornstarch(sold as cornflour in India), garlic powder, bell pepper powder, red chili powder, and salt.
- Add a tsp of oil and make a smooth lump-free batter. Add and coat all the vegetables nicely in the batter.
- Preheat the air fryer at 350F, then add the veggies when indicated. Air fry the veggies, it takes about 10 minutes.
- Make the sauce mix. In a heavy-bottomed pan, heat a tbsp of oil, add finely chopped garlic, sauté till it gives aroma, and then add the sauce mix and freshly ground black pepper.
- Cook for a minute then add the air fried vegetables and mix well with light hands. Coat all the veggies nicely in sauce.
- Sprinkle Sesame Seeds and finely chopped spring onion greens and serve hot.
- For Sauce Mix.
- Mix all the ingredients together listed under the Sauce section.
- For the deep-fried version.
- Coat vegetables in batter nicely and then deep fry in hot oil, till light brown in color. Oil should be hot enough so that the veggies remain crispy. Take out and cool down and then add to the sauce mix.

596. Air Fryer Roasted Brussels Sprouts

Prep Time: 5 Mins Cook Time: 18 Mins
Total Time: 23 Mins
Ingredients
- 1 pound Brussels sprouts
- 1 ½ Tbsp olive oil
- ½ Tsp. salt
- ½ Tsp. black pepper

Instructions
- Preheat the air fryer to 390 degrees.
- Wash Brussels sprouts and pat dry.

- Remove any loose leaves.
- If the sprouts are larger cut them in half.
- Place Brussels sprouts into a bowl.
- Drizzle olive oil over the vegetables.
- Stir to make sure the Brussels sprouts are fully coated. Place the Brussels sprouts in the basket.
- Season with salt and pepper.
- Cook for 15 to 18 mins or until the Brussels sprouts soften and begin to brown.
- Serve immediately.

597. Air Fryer Roasted Broccoli (Low Carb + Keto)

Yield: 4 Cook Time: 8 Mins
Total Time: 8 Mins
Ingredients
- 5 cups broccoli florets
- 2 Tbsps butter
- 2 teaspoons minced garlic
- 1/3 cup shredded parmesan cheese
- Salt and pepper to taste
- Lemon slices (optional)

Instructions
- Melt the butter and combine with the minced garlic, set aside for later.
- Preheat your air fryer according to the manufactures directions at a temperature of 350 degrees.
- Add the chopped broccoli florets to the basket of the air fryer and spray very lightly with cooking oil.
- Roast the broccoli for 8 mins total. I remove the basket after 4 mins and shake or toss with tongs to make sure everything is cooking evenly, then cook for 4 more min..
- At this point, the broccoli should be fork tender at the thickest part of the stem and slightly crispy on the outside.
- Remove the broccoli from the basket and toss with the garlic butter, parmesan and add salt and pepper to taste.

598. Air-Fryer Roasted Veggies

Prep Time: 20 mins Cook Time: 10 mins
Total Time: 30 mins Servings: 4
Ingredient
- ½ cup diced zucchini
- ½ cup diced summer squash
- ½ cup diced mushrooms
- ½ cup diced cauliflower

- ½ cup diced asparagus
- ½ cup diced sweet red pepper
- 2 teaspoons vegetable oil
- ¼ Tsp. salt
- ¼ Tsp. ground black pepper
- 1/4 Tsp. seasoning, or more to taste

Instructions
- Preheat the air fryer to 360 degrees F (180 degrees C).
- Add vegetables, oil, salt, pepper, and desired seasoning to a bowl. Toss to coat; arrange in the fryer basket.
- Cook vegetables for 10 min., stirring after 5 min..

599.Buttery Garlic Green Beans
Prep Time: 10 mins Cook Time: 10 mins Total Time: 20 mins Servings: 4

Ingredient
- 1 pound fresh green beans, trimmed and snapped in half
- 3 Tbsps butter
- 3 cloves garlic, minced
- 2 pinches lemon pepper
- Salt to taste

Instructions
- Place green beans into a large skillet and cover with water; bring to a boil. Reduce heat to medium-low and simmer until beans start to soften about 5 min.. Drain water. Add butter to green beans; cook and stir until butter is melted 2 to 3 min..
- Cook and stir garlic with green beans until garlic is tender and fragrant for 3 to 4 min.. Season with lemon pepper and salt.

600.Superb Sauteed Mushrooms
Prep Time: 10 mins Cook Time: 15 mins Total Time: 25 mins Servings: 4

Ingredient
- 3 Tbsps olive oil
- 3 Tbsp butter
- 1 pound button mushrooms, sliced
- 1 clove garlic, thinly sliced
- 1 Tbsp red cooking wine
- 1 Tbsp teriyaki sauce, or more to taste
- ¼ Tsp. garlic salt, or to taste
- Freshly ground black pepper to taste

Instructions
- Heat olive oil and butter in a large saucepan over medium heat. Cook and stir mushrooms, garlic, cooking wine, teriyaki sauce, garlic salt, and black

pepper in the hot oil and butter until mushrooms are lightly browned, about 5 minutes. Reduce heat to low and simmer until mushrooms are tender, 5 to 8 more minutes.

601.Pan-Fried Asparagus
Prep Time: 5 mins Cook Time: 15 mins Additional Time: 5 mins Total Time: 25 mins Servings: 4

Ingredient
- ¼ cup butter
- 2 Tbsps olive oil
- 1 Tsp. coarse salt
- ¼ Tsp. ground black pepper
- 3 cloves garlic, minced
- 1 pound fresh asparagus spears, trimmed

Instructions
- Melt butter in a skillet over medium-high heat. Stir in the olive oil, salt, and pepper. Cook garlic in butter for a minute, but do not brown. Add asparagus, and cook for 10 minutes, turning asparagus to ensure even cooking.

602.Easy Roasted Broccoli
Prep Time: 10 mins Cook Time: 20 mins Total Time: 30 mins Servings: 4

Ingredient
- 14 ounces broccoli
- 1 Tbsp olive oil
- Salt and ground black pepper to taste

Instructions
- Preheat oven to 400 degrees F (200 degrees C).
- Cut broccoli florets from the stalk. Peel the stalk and slice into 1/4-inch slices. Mix florets and stem pieces with olive oil in a bowl and transfer to a baking sheet; season with salt and pepper.
- Roast in the preheated oven until broccoli is tender and lightly browned, about 18 min..

603.Fried Broccoli
Prep Time: 5 mins Cook Time: 5 mins Total Time: 10 mins Servings: 4

Ingredient
- 1 (16 ounces) package frozen broccoli, thawed
- 1 Tbsp olive oil
- ½ Tsp. crushed red pepper flakes
- Salt, to taste

Instructions
- Rinse and pat dry the broccoli.
- Heat the olive oil in a large skillet over medium heat, add the crushed red pepper, and heat for 1 minute. Cook and stir the broccoli in the skillet until it begins to get crispy, 5 to 7 minutes. Season with salt to serve.

604.Roasted Garlic Lemon Broccoli
Prep Time: 10 mins Cook Time: 15 mins Total Time: 25 mins Servings: 6

Ingredient
- 2 heads of broccoli, separated into florets
- 2 teaspoons extra-virgin olive oil
- 1 Tsp. sea salt
- ½ Tsp. ground black pepper
- 1 clove garlic, minced
- ½ Tsp. lemon juice

Instructions
- Preheat the oven to 400 degrees F (200 degrees C).
- In a large bowl, toss broccoli florets with extra virgin olive oil, sea salt, pepper, and garlic. Spread the broccoli out in an even layer on a baking sheet.
- Bake in the preheated oven until florets are tender enough to pierce the stems with a fork, 15 to 20 min.. Remove and transfer to a serving platter. Squeeze lemon juice liberally over the broccoli before serving for a refreshing, tangy finish.

605.Vegetables And Cabbage Stir-Fry With Oyster Sauce
Prep Time: 15 mins Cook Time: 5 mins Total Time: 20 mins Servings: 6

Ingredient
- 2 Tbsps olive oil
- 1 pound broccoli florets
- 1 pound cauliflower florets
- ½ head cabbage, cut into bite-size pieces
- 2 cloves garlic, minced
- 2 Tbsp oyster sauce

Instructions
- Heat olive oil in a large skillet or wok over medium-high heat; saute broccoli, cauliflower, cabbage, and garlic in the hot oil until tender-crisp, about 5 min..
- Remove pan from heat and drizzle oyster sauce over the vegetable mix and toss to coat.

606. Bright And Zesty Broccoli

Prep Time: 15 mins Cook Time: 10 mins Total Time: 25 mins Servings: 4

Ingredient

- 1 Tbsp extra-virgin olive oil
- 1 ½ Tbsp grated orange zest
- ½ Tsp. red pepper flakes
- 1 head broccoli, cut into small pieces with stalks peeled
- ¼ Tsp. sea salt
- ¼ Tsp. freshly ground black pepper
- 2 Tbsps freshly squeezed orange juice

Instructions

- Heat the olive oil in a large skillet over medium heat; add the orange zest and red pepper flakes and allow to heat briefly for about 1 minute.
- Stir the broccoli into the mixture; season with salt and pepper.
- Continue cooking about 5 mins more; transfer to a serving bowl. Pour the orange juice over the broccoli and toss to coat.
- Serve hot.

607. Spinach & Mushroom Quiche

Active Time: 25 mins Total Time: 1 hr 5 mins Servings: 6

Ingredient

- 2 Tbsps extra-virgin olive oil
- 8 ounces sliced fresh mixed wild mushrooms such as cremini, shiitake, button, and/or oyster mushrooms
- 1 ½ cups thinly sliced sweet onion
- 1 Tbsp thinly sliced garlic
- 5 ounces fresh baby spinach (about 8 cups), coarsely chopped
- 6 large eggs
- ¼ cup whole milk
- ¼ cup half-and-half
- 1 Tbsp Dijon mustard
- 1 Tbsp fresh thyme leaves, plus more for garnish
- ¼ Tsp. salt
- ¼ Tsp. ground pepper
- 1 ½ cups shredded Gruyère cheese

Instructions

- Preheat oven to 375 degrees F. Coat a 9-inch pie pan with cooking spray; set aside.
- Heat oil in a large nonstick skillet over medium-high heat; swirl to coat the pan. Add mushrooms; cook, stirring occasionally until browned and tender, about 8 min.. Add onion and garlic; cook, stirring often, until softened and tender, about 5 min.. Add spinach; cook, tossing constantly, until wilted, 1 to 2 min.. Remove from heat.
- Whisk eggs, milk, half-and-half, mustard, thyme, salt, and pepper in a medium bowl. Fold in the mushroom mixture and cheese. Spoon into the prepared pie pan. Bake until set and golden brown, about 30 min.. Let stand for 10 min.; slice. Garnish with thyme and serve.

608. Cabbage Diet Soup

Active Time: 35 mins
Total Time: 55 mins
Servings: 6

Ingredient

- 2 Tbsp extra-virgin olive oil
- 1 medium onion, chopped
- 2 medium carrots, chopped
- 2 stalks celery, chopped
- 1 medium red bell pepper, chopped
- 2 cloves garlic, minced
- 1 ½ Tsp. Italian seasoning
- ½ Tsp. ground pepper
- ¼ Tsp. salt
- 8 cups low-sodium vegetable broth
- 1 medium head green cabbage, halved and sliced
- 1 large tomato, chopped
- 2 teaspoons white-wine vinegar

Instructions

- Heat oil in a large pot over medium heat. Add onion, carrots, and celery. Cook, stirring until the vegetables begin to soften, 6 to 8 minutes. Add bell pepper, garlic, Italian seasoning, pepper, and salt and cook, stirring, for 2 minutes.
- Add broth, cabbage, and tomato; increase the heat to medium-high and bring to a boil. Reduce heat to maintain a simmer, partially cover, and cook until all the vegetables are tender, 15 to 20 mins more. Remove from heat and stir in vinegar.

609. Mexican Cabbage Soup

Total Time: 20 mins
Servings: 8

Ingredient

- 2 Tbsps extra-virgin olive oil
- 2 cups chopped onions
- 1 cup chopped carrot
- 1 cup chopped celery
- 1 cup chopped poblano or green bell pepper
- 4 large cloves garlic, minced
- 8 cups sliced cabbage
- 1 Tbsp tomato paste
- 1 Tbsp minced chipotle chiles in adobo sauce
- 1 Tsp. ground cumin
- ½ Tsp. ground coriander
- 4 cups low-sodium vegetable broth or chicken broth
- 4 cups water
- 2 (15 ounces) cans of low-sodium pinto or black beans, rinsed
- ¾ Tsp. salt
- ½ cup chopped fresh cilantro, plus more for serving
- 2 Tbsps lime juice

Instructions

- Heat oil in a large soup pot (8-quart or larger) over medium heat. Add onions, carrot, celery, poblano (or bell pepper), and garlic; cook, stirring frequently, until softened, 10 to 12 min.. Add cabbage; cook, stirring occasionally until slightly softened, about 10 mins more. Add tomato paste, chipotle, cumin, and coriander; cook, stirring, for 1 minute more.
- Add broth, water, beans, and salt. Cover and bring to a boil over high heat. Reduce heat and simmer, partially covered, until the vegetables are tender about 10 minutes. Remove from heat and stir in cilantro and lime juice. Serve garnished with cheese, yogurt, and/or avocado, if desired.

610. Everything Bagel Avocado Toast

Active Time: 5 mins Total Time: 5 mins Servings: 1

Ingredient

- ¼ medium avocado, mashed
- 1 slice whole-grain bread, toasted
- 2 teaspoons everything bagel seasoning
- Pinch of flaky sea salt (such as Maldon)

Instructions

- Spread avocado on toast. Top with seasoning and salt.

611. Quick Vegetable Saute

Total Time: 15 mins

Servings: 4

Ingredient

- 1 Tbsp extra-virgin olive oil
- 1 small shallot, minced
- 4 cups mixed frozen vegetables, such as corn, carrots, and green beans
- ½ Tsp. dried dill or tarragon
- ¼ Tsp. salt
- ¼ Tsp. freshly ground pepper

Instructions

- Heat oil in a large skillet over medium heat.
- Add shallot and cook, stirring, until softened, about 1 minute. Stir in frozen vegetables.
- Cover and cook, stirring occasionally, until the vegetables are tender, 4 to 6 min.. Stir in dill (or tarragon), salt, and pepper.

Salad Recipes

612. Air Fryer Healthy Southwestern Salad

Prep Time: 5 mins Cook Time: 8 mins
Total Time: 13 mins

Ingredients

Kitchen Gadgets:

- Air Fryer
- Air Fryer Grill Pan
- Salad Bowl
- Southwestern Salad Recipe Ingredients:
- 600 g Chickpeas
- 1 Medium Red Pepper
- 200 g Frozen Sweetcorn
- 2 Celery Sticks
- ¼ Medium Cucumber
- ½ Small Red Onion
- 2 Tbsp Extra Virgin Olive Oil
- 1 Tsp Grainy Mustard
- ¼ Tsp Garlic Powder
- 1 Tsp Basil
- 2 Tsp Mexican Seasoning
- Salt & Pepper

Instructions

- Drain and rinse your chickpeas. Chop your red pepper into bite-size cubes. Load into the air fryer basket with the grill attachment the chickpeas, sweetcorn, and pepper. Sprinkle with Mexican seasoning and salt and pepper and cook for 8 mins at 180c/360f.
- While the air fryer is in action, prep

the rest of your salad. Peel and thinly slice your red onion. Clean and thinly dice your cucumber and celery. Load all three into a salad bowl.

- Mix extra virgin olive oil, basil, grainy mustard, and garlic powder. Pour into your salad bowl and mix.
- When the air fryer beeps, load in the ingredients and mix a little more.
- Serve or store into containers for later.

613. Kale Salad with Air Fryer Herb Chicken Breast

Prep Time: 20 mins Cook Time: 20 mins
Total Time: 40 mins

Ingredients

- 1 Tbsp Panko (Bread Crumbs)
- 2 Tbsps Mixed Dry Herbs Use your favorite blend
- 1 Tsp. Smoked Paprika
- 1 Tsp. Salt
- 1 Tbsp Olive Oil
- 1.5 Pounds Chicken Breast Pounded Evenly
- 1 Cup Corn Kernels From about 2 years, if fresh
- 8 Strawberries, Sliced & Quartered
- 1/2 Ounce Goat Cheese
- 2 Avocados, halved and sliced
- 2 Hard Boiled Eggs, sliced
- 2 Tbsps Extra Virgin Olive Oil
- 16 Ounce Bag Baby Kale Greens (Washed & Ready)

Instructions

- Combine panko, herbs, smoked paprika, salt, and olive oil in a small bowl to make a paste. Apply this evenly to the chicken breast.
- Cook the chicken in a preheated air fryer for 20 mins at 370 degrees. Let it rest outside of the air fryer for 5 mins before slicing for the salad
- In a large salad bowl or serving plate, place your bed of salad greens and then add the corn, strawberries, goat cheese, avocado, hard-boiled eggs, and chicken
- Drizzle the extra virgin olive oil over the top and then season lightly with salt and pepper

614. Easy Air Fryer Broccoli

Prep Time: 5 Mins Cook Time: 6 Mins
Total Time: 11 Mins

Ingredients

- 2 heads of broccoli, cut into bite-sized pieces
- 2 Tbsps olive oil
- Sea salt, to taste
- Fresh cracked black pepper, to taste

Instructions

- 2 heads of broccoli, cut into bite-sized pieces
- 2 Tbsps olive oil
- Sea salt, to taste
- Fresh cracked black pepper, to taste

615. Roasted Vegetable Pasta Salad

Prep Time: 40 mins
Cook Time: 1 hour 45 mins
Total Time: 2 hours 25 mins

Ingredients

- 3 eggplant (small)
- 1 Tbsp olive oil
- 3 zucchini (medium-sized. Aka courgette.
- 1 Tbsp olive oil
- 4 tomatoes (medium. Cut in eighths)
- 300 g pasta (large, shaped pasta. 4 cups)
- 2 bell peppers (any color)
- 175 g cherry tomatoes (sliced. Or tomatoes cut into small chunks. 1 cup)
- 2 teaspoons salt (or salt sub)
- 8 Tbsp parmesan cheese (grated)
- 125 ml italian dressing (bottled, fat free/ 1/2 cup / 4 oz)
- Basil (few leaves of fresh)

Instructions

- Wash eggplant, slice off and discard the green end. Do not peel. Slice the eggplant into 1 cm (1/2 inch) thick rounds. If using a paddle-type air fryer such as an Actifry™, put in a pan with 1 Tbsp of olive oil. If using a basket-type such as an AirFryer™, toss with 1 Tbsp of olive oil and put in the basket. Cook for about 40 mins until quite soft and no raw taste left. Set aside.
- Wash zucchini/courgette, slice off and discard the green end. Do not peel. Slice into 1 cm (1/2 inch) thick rounds. If using a paddle-type air fryer such as an Actifry™, put in a pan with 1 Tbsp of olive oil. If using a basket-type such as an AirFryer™, toss with 1 Tbsp of olive oil and put in the basket. Cook for about 25 mins until quite soft and no raw taste left. Set aside.
- Wash and chunk the tomatoes. If

using an Actifry 2 in 1, arranged in a top grill pan. If using a basket-type air fryer, arrange it in the basket. Spray lightly with cooking spray. Roast for about 30 mins until reduced in size and starting to brown. Set aside.

• Cook the pasta according to pasta directions, empty into a colander, run cold water over it to wash some starch off, drain, set aside to cool.

• Wash, seed, and chop the bell pepper; put into a large bowl. Wash and slice the cherry tomatoes (or small-chunk the regular tomato); add to that bowl. Add the roast veggies, the pasta, the salt, the dressing, the chopped basil, and the parm, and toss all with your (clean) hands to mix well.

• Set in fridge to chill and marinate.

• Serve chilled or room temperature.

616. Air Fryer Buffalo Chicken Salad

Prep Time: 15 Mins Cook Time: 15 Mins Total Time: 30 Mins

Ingredients

• 1 pound boneless, skinless chicken breasts, thick sides pounded to make an even thickness
• 1/2 cup WHOLE30 Buffalo Vinaigrette
• 6 cups chopped romaine lettuce
• 1 cup thinly sliced celery
• 1/2 cup shredded carrot
• 3-4 tbsp WHOLE30 Ranch Dressing
• 1 small ripe avocado, peeled, pitted, and sliced
• 1 cup cherry tomatoes, halved
• Freshly ground black pepper
• 2 tsp finely chopped chives

Instructions

• IN a large resealable plastic bag, combine chicken and WHOLE30 Buffalo Vinaigrette. Massage to coat. Seal bag and marinate in the refrigerator for at least 2 hours and up to 4 hours.

• PREHEAT air fryer* to 375°F. Remove chicken from bag; discard marinade. Add the chicken to the air fryer. Cook until chicken is no longer pink and the internal temperature is 170°F, turning once about 15 min.. Let stand while making the salad.

• IN a large bowl, combine the romaine, celery, and carrot. Add the WHOLE30 Ranch Dressing; toss to combine. Divide salad among four serving plates.

• SLICE the chicken. Top the salads with sliced chicken, avocado, and cherry tomatoes. Season to taste with black pepper. Sprinkle with chives.

617. Cajun Potato Salad Recipe

Prep Time: 10 Mins Cook Time: 20 Mins Total Time: 30 Mins

Ingredients

• 2 1/2 lb red potatoes, quartered
• 2 Tbsp avocado oil (or grapeseed, coconut, or vegetable)
• 3 Tbsp The Fit Cook Southern Creole
• pinch of sea salt & pepper
• 2 slices cooked bacon, chopped and crumbled

Salad Sauce

• 2/3 cup light mayo (I used olive oil mayo)
• 7oz 2% Greek yogurt
• 1/8 cup Dijon mustard (or more to taste)
• 5 BOILED eggs, chopped
• 1 cup diced Dill pickles (OR sweet if you prefer)
• 1/2 medium red onion, diced
• Sea salt & pepper to taste

Steps

• Set the air-fryer to 400F (or oven to 420F).

• In a large bowl, toss the sliced potatoes with oil and seasoning. Add the potatoes to the air-fryer basket. Air-fry for about 20 min., or until the potatoes are cooked through and the edges are crispy.

• Air-fried Cajun Potato Salad

• Mix the ingredients for the sauce.

• Cook up some bacon in a skillet until crispy.

• Allow the pieces to cool on a paper towel, then chop into pieces.

• Once the potatoes have finished air-frying, LIGHTLY mash about 40-50% of the potatoes in a bowl, then fold in the remaining potatoes and mix. Add the sauce and the remaining ingredients and fold everything together.

• Season to taste using salt & pepper, dill (or sweet) pickles, mustard, or Greek yogurt. Cover with plastic and store in the fridge for at least 20 minutes, but it's much better overnight.

618. Fried Chickpeas In The Air Fryer

Prep Time: 2 mins Cook Time: 12 mins Total Time: 14 mins

Ingredients

• 1 1/2 cups chickpeas 1 15 ounces can drain & rinse
• Spritz cooking spray
• 2 teaspoons yeast flakes
• 1/2 Tsp. granulated onion
• Pinch salt

Instructions

• Put the drained chickpeas into the air fryer basket. Set the air fryer for 400 degrees and 12 minutes.

• Cook the plain chickpeas for the first 5 minutes. This will dry them out.

• Then open the basket, spritz the chickpeas with oil, give a shake, and spritz them again. Sprinkle on **Nutrition Facts**al yeast flakes, granulated onion, and a pinch of salt.

• Return the basket to the air fryer and cook for the remaining 7 min..

• Test a chickpea to see if it's done enough for you. Depending on your air fryer, the softness of your chickpeas, and your personal preferences, you may want to cook them for an additional 3 to 5 minutes. If desired, add another pinch of salt before serving.

619. Air Fryer Buffalo Chicken Tenders Salad

Prep Time: 15 mins Cook Time: 25 mins Total Time: 40 mins

Ingredients

Chicken Tenders:

• ½ cup blanched almond flour
• 1 tsp sea salt
• 1 tsp paprika
• ¼ tsp ground black pepper
• 2 large chicken breasts, sliced lengthwise into ½" strips
• ¼ cup tapioca flour
• 2 tbsp garlic-infused olive oil
• Avocado oil cooking spray

Salad:

• 2 hearts of romaine, chopped
• 1 cup carrots, coarsely-shredded
• 1 cup grape tomatoes, halved
• 1 bunch scallions, green tops only, chopped
• 1 red pepper, diced

- Your other favorite salad ingredients

Ranch Dressing:
- ½ Batch of my dairy-free homemade ranch dressing recipe (paleo, whole30, low fodmap)

Buffalo Sauce:
- ⅓ cup Paleo Low-FODMAP hot sauce
- 3 tbsp ghee, melted
- 1 tbsp garlic-infused olive oil
- ½ tbsp coconut aminos

Instructions
- Preheat the air fryer to 370° F for 10 min.. While your air fryer preheats, combine almond flour, sea salt, paprika, and pepper in a large bowl, whisk to combine, and set aside. Place chicken strips in another large bowl. Add tapioca flour to the bowl and toss with your hands to coat the strips evenly. Add the garlic-infused oil and toss again to coat. Dredge each strip in the almond flour mixture, shaking off the excess, and set on a plate.
- Once your air fryer has preheated, spray the pan with cooking spray. Using tongs, place half of the breaded chicken strips in the pan in one layer, ideally not touching one another. Spray the strips lightly with cooking spray. Air fry for 12 minutes, flipping halfway through.
- Once the first batch has cooked, place it on a clean plate using a clean set of tongs and set aside. Using tongs, take one of the thickest strips out of the air fryer and check its temperature using an instant-read thermometer.
- The temperature of cooked chicken should be at least 165° F (75° C) to be safely consumed.
- Once the first batch is at the proper temperature, repeat these steps for the second half of the strips.
- While the chicken strips are frying, prepare a half-batch of my dairy-free homemade ranch dressing recipe, cover, and refrigerate until ready to serve.
- Chop the ingredients under "salad," place in a large serving bowl, and refrigerate.
- A minute or two before the chicken strips are done, in a large bowl, add the ingredients under "buffalo sauce," whisk to combine, and set aside until all the chicken strips are cooked.
- If the sauce solidifies, microwave it (covered) for about 20 seconds and whisk again.
- Once the second batch of strips has finished cooking, if desired, place the first batch back in the air fryer on top of the second batch and air fry at 370° F for a minute or so until heated (I typically skip this step as they're going on a cold salad anyway). Using tongs, take each strip out of the air fryer, dip in the buffalo sauce until fully-coated, and place it on a plate. Chop strips horizontally into small pieces if desired and serve on top of the salad with the ranch dressing.

---

620. Roasted Salmon With Fennel Salad In An Air Fryer

Active Time: 15 Mins Total Time: 25 Mins

Ingredients
- 2 teaspoons chopped fresh flat-leaf parsley
- 1 Tsp. finely chopped fresh thyme
- 1 Tsp. kosher salt, divided 4 (6-oz.) skinless center-cut salmon fillets
- 2 Tbsps olive oil
- 4 cups thinly sliced fennel
- 2/3 cup 2% reduced-fat Greek yogurt 1 garlic clove, grated
- 2 Tbsps fresh orange juice
- 1 Tsp. fresh lemon juice
- 2 Tbsps chopped fresh dill

How To Make It
- Your air fryer has more up its sleeve than the expected crispy tricks—it's also a fantastic oven for roasting meaty fish fillets like salmon.
- This recipe serves four, but you can easily cut it in half to make a date night dinner for two.
- Everything comes together so easily—while the salmon cooks, whip up the quick and tangy fennel slaw. By the time you're finished, the salmon will be hot and ready to plate up. For a little extra heft, serve this meal with a side of your favorite quick-cooking brown rice.
- Try it with the air-fryer broccoli with cheese sauce, also pictured.

621. Air Fryer Taco Salad Bowls

Prep Time: 1 Minute Cook Time: 7 Mins
Total Time: 8 Mins

Ingredients
- 1 burrito sized flour tortilla
- Cooking spray

Instructions
- Spray both sides of the tortilla with cooking spray.
- Fold a piece of foil double thickness the size of the tortilla.
- Fold into the basket of your air fryer.
- Place a larger ramekin (or something similar) into the middle of the shell.
- Air fry for 5 mins at 400 degrees.
- Carefully remove ramekin (it's HOT!!) and foil. Place ramekin back into the center, air fry 2 mins more.

---

622. Air Fryer, Grilled Chicken Caesar Salad

Prep Time: 5 Mins Cook Time: 10 Mins
Additional Time: 5 Mins
Total Time: 20 Mins

Ingredients
Grilled Chicken:
- 2 boneless skinless chicken breast, about 5 ounces each
- 2 Tbsps chicken seasoning (i used lawry's)
- Olive oil spray

Salad:
- 1/2 cup garlic croutons
- 1/4 cup caesar salad dressing
- 2 cups shredded romaine lettuce
- 1/3 cup shredded Parmesan cheese

Instructions
- Rub the chicken seasoning all over the chicken
- As you coat them place them in either a greased air fryer basket or on a greased air fryer tray. Once you are all done coating your chicken, spray them with olive oil spray (the entire chicken breast, otherwise you will get white spots on your chicken)
- Set the temperature to 350 degrees F, for 5-10 minutes. (air fryer setting)
- When the time is up, make sure that the internal temperature reads at least: 165 degrees F.
- In a large mixing bowl, add the lettuce, shredded parmesan cheese, and salad dressing.
- Mix well.
- Cut up the chicken and add it on top.

- Plate, serve, and enjoy!

623. Air Fryer Brussel Sprout Caesar Salad

PREP TIME: 2 mins COOK TIME: 15 mins

Ingredients

- 10 oz Brussel sprouts, cut the ends off
- 4 tbsp Caesar dressing, storebought or homemade
- 2 tbsp shaved parmesan
- 1/4 cup garlic croutons

Instructions

- Cut the ends off of the Brussel sprouts and with your hands flake them apart. The more loose pieces, the more crispy crunchy pieces!
- Add to the air fryer basket and drizzle with olive oil, season with salt and pepper.
- Air fry for 15 mins at 375 until many of the edges and pieces are brown and crispy
- Transfer to a salad bowl, drizzle with caesar dressing, top with parmesan and croutons.

624. Crispy Chicken Cobb Salad

Prep Time: 15 mins
Total Time: 15 mins

Ingredients

- 3 oz of cooked chicken strips (I like Tyson)
- hard-boiled
- 10 cherry tomatoes, cut in half
- to 3 green onions
- 1/2 cup of cucumbers
- cups of lettuce
- 2 Tbsps of reduced-fat cheese
- Ranch Dressing or Catalina Dressing

Instructions

- Place 3 oz of frozen chicken breast strips in the air fryer basket and cook the chicken breast for 12 mins at 350.
- While the chicken is cooking slice the cucumbers and cherry tomatoes.
- To make the salad place 2 cups of lettuce, cucumbers, cherry tomatoes, hard-boiled eggs, (optional) cheese, and chopped chicken on top of the lettuce.
- The salad with Catalina or Ranch dressing on top. I typically don't count dressings for points and that is just what works for me.

625. Egg Salad Poppers Recipe

Prep time: 20mins

Ingredients

- ¼ cup eggs, hard-boiled (chopped)
- 4 ounces Neufchatel cheese
- 2 Tbsps Mayonnaise
- 2 Tbsp spinach leaf (chopped)
- 2 Tbsps green onion (minced)
- For the coating
- 2 Tbsp THM Oat Fiber
- ¼ cup egg white
- 2 each Low Carb Whole Wheat Tortilla (toasted and crushed)

Instructions

- In a medium bowl mix eggs, cheese, mayonnaise, spinach, and onion together.
- Scoop mixture into 1 TBS mounds on a parchment-lined sheet and freeze for 30 min..
- Preheat Air Fryer to 350° F
- Remove egg mounds from the freezer and roll in oat fiber, dip each one into the egg whites, and roll in the crushed low carb tortillas.
- Place coated egg salad balls onto your air fryer rack and bake for 6-8 min..
- Be careful when removing from your air fryer as these are delicate and the shell will break easily when they are hot.
- Allow cooling for a few mins before eating. Can also be eaten cold when stored in the fridge.

626. Gluten Free Buffalo Cauliflower Salad

Serves: 4 Salads Prep Time: 15 Mins
Cook Time: 20 Min Total Time: 35 Min

Ingredients

- 1/2 cup Frank's red hot sauce
- 1 Tbsp coconut oil (or butter)
- Florets from 1 medium head of cauliflower
- 1/2 cup almond milk
- 1/2 cup water
- 3/4 cup almond flour
- 2 teaspoons garlic powder
- 2 teaspoons onion powder
- 1 Tsp. paprika
- salt and pepper
- 2 celery ribs
- 1 cup halved cherry tomatoes (you can do this while you wait for the cauliflower to cook)

- 1 ripe large avocado
- 2 romaine hearts, chopped
- 1 cup shredded carrots
- to drizzle: ½ cup Ranch dressing

Instructions

- Preheat an air fryer to 400 degrees.
- Place two large bowls next to each other on your workspace. In one bowl, whisk together the hot sauce and coconut oil. In the other bowl, whisk together almond milk, water, flour, garlic powder, onion powder, paprika, salt, and pepper. Add the cauliflower to the bowl. Dredge the cauliflower florets through the mixture and coat them well, patting the mixture into the crevices of the cauliflower. Using tongs (or your hands), transfer the dredged cauliflower into the hot sauce bowl and toss well to coat.
- Add the cauliflower in an even layer in the basket of the air fryer. Set for 10 mins and halfway through, flip the cauliflower and let cook for an additional 5 minutes.
- While cauliflower cooks, prepare the rest of the recipe. Pour the hot sauce into a large bowl and set aside. Dice the celery, halve the cherry tomatoes, and peel, pit, and slice the avocado. Set everything aside.
- After you're done prepping the salad ingredients, prepare the salads. Divide the romaine lettuce into bowls and drizzle each with 1 Tbsp of Ranch dressing. Divide the toppings onto the bowls (the celery, tomatoes, avocado, carrots) and once the cauliflower is done cooking, add that to the salad bowls. Drizzle with another Tbsp of Ranch dressing. Serve.

627. Air Fryer Coconut Shrimp Salad

Prep Time: 30 mins Cook Time: 30 mins
Servings: 6 servings

Ingredients

Coconut Shrimp

- 2 lbs extra-large shrimp (13-15 per lb), peeled, tail-on
- 1 cup panko bread crumbs* (56 grams)
- 1/2 cup finely shredded sweetened coconut* (40 grams)
- 1/2 cup white whole wheat flour* (60 grams)

- 2 eggs
- 1/2 tsp each: salt and pepper

Salad
- 10 cups baby spinach (325 grams)
- 2 medium mangos, peeled and chopped (650 grams)
- 2 small avocados, peeled and chopped (225 grams)
- 1 1/2 cups cherry tomatoes, halved (225 grams)
- 1/3 cup pickled red onion – recipe below (45 grams)
- 1/4 cup cilantro, chopped (5 grams)

Sweet Chili Dressing
- 1/4 cup sweet Thai chili sauce (2 oz)
- 2 tbsp lime juice (1 oz)
- 2 tbsp coconut milk (1 oz)

Instructions
- Whisk dressing ingredients until combined, set aside.
- Assemble the base of salad with spinach, mango, avocado, tomatoes, pickled red onion, and cilantro. Set aside in the refrigerator while prepping the shrimp.
- Add coconut and breadcrumbs to a bowl and mix until combined. Set aside.
- Add flour, salt, and pepper to a separate bowl and mix. Set aside.
- Add eggs to a third bowl and whisk. Set aside.
- Rinse and dry shrimp on a paper towel, then dip them one at a time into flour, then eggs, then breadcrumb mixture, coating the shrimp completely.
- Air fry shrimp at 380 degrees for 7-8 mins or until breading is golden brown and shrimp is cooked through.
- Top salad base with shrimp and dressing and serve.

628. Crispy Keto Air Fryer Pork Chops

Prep Time: 15 mins Cook Time: 10 mins
Total Time: 25 mins

Ingredients
- Boneless Pork Chops
- 4–6 center-cut boneless pork chops (4–6 oz each, ~ ¾ inch thick)
- Keto Pork Chops Coating
- ⅓ cup almond flour
- ⅓ cup grated parmesan (or sub additional almond flour)
- 1 tsp garlic powder
- 1 tsp paprika

- ½ tsp onion powder
- ½ tsp salt
- ½ tsp black pepper
- 2 eggs

Instructions

How To Air Fry Pork Chops
- Preheat air fryer to 400°F (200°C).
- Mix almond flour, grated parmesan, and seasonings in a shallow dish.
- In a separate dish, beat eggs.
- Coat pork chops in egg, and then coating mixture. Transfer coated chops to a plate.
- Spray both sides of coated chops with cooking spray, then add to the air fryer. Cook 3-4 at a time only. (Don't overcrowd your air fryer!)
- Cook boneless pork chops for 10 minutes, flipping halfway through. (Thicker chops and bone-in chops may need to cook for longer, 12-20 minutes.)
- After flipping, check the internal temperature of the pork every 1-2 minutes, until it reaches 145°F (63°C). To check the internal temperature, insert a meat thermometer straight into the side of the pork chop.
- Allow resting 3 mins before slicing to reveal a perfect blush pink center.

How To Oven Fry Pork Chops
- Preheat oven to 425°F (210°C).
- Prepare and coat keto pork chops as described above.
- Spray both sides of coated pork chops with cooking spray and add to a baking rack on top of a lined baking sheet.
- Bake for 20 min., flipping halfway through. (May need to bake longer for thicker chops or bone-in chops.)
- Near the end of cook time, check oven fried pork chops temperature as explained above.

629. Air Fryer Buffalo Salmon Salad

Total Time: 30 mins

Ingredients
- 4 Tbsp. unsalted butter
- ¼ cup hot sauce
- 4 Verlasso salmon fillets (about 1 lb.)
- Cooking spray
- 1 large head romaine lettuce, chopped (about 8 cups)
- 1 ear of corn, kernels removed (or ½ cup frozen corn, thawed)

- ½ cup matchstick carrots
- 1 small red onion, thinly sliced
- 1 bell pepper, thinly sliced
- 3 stalks celery, chopped
- ¼ cup blue cheese crumbles
- Ranch or blue cheese dressing for serving, optional
- Additional hot sauce for serving, optional

Directions
- Melt butter in a small saucepan over medium heat. Remove pan from heat and stir in hot sauce.
- Place salmon in a baking pan and pour the sauce over salmon. Let marinate for 20-30 min., turning once halfway through.
- Preheat air fryer to 400°F. Lightly spray the fryer basket with cooking spray. Remove salmon from marinade and pat bottom (skin) dry. Place salmon in basket, skin side down, and cook for 7-10 min., or until salmon is cooked to desired doneness.
- While salmon is cooking, assemble the salad. Divide the lettuce among four bowls. Top each bowl with corn, carrots, onion, bell pepper, celery, and blue cheese. Place a salmon fillet on top of each salad.
- Drizzle with dressing and additional hot sauce if desired. Enjoy!

630. Air Fryer Sesame Ginger Salmon With Spicy Cucumber Salad

Prep time: 10mins Cook time: 8mins

Ingredients
- 1/ 3 cup Annie's Organic Sesame Ginger Vinaigrette
- 1 pound salmon, cut into 4 portions
- 2 hothouse cucumbers, thinly sliced
- 1 jalapeño, thinly sliced
- A handful of fresh mint leaves, chopped
- 1/ 2 cup seasoned rice vinegar
- 1/ 2 Tsp. salt
- 1 Tsp. sugar

Method
- Pour ¼ cup Annie's Sesame Ginger Vinaigrette into the bottom of a medium bowl or baking dish
- Marinate salmon portions skin side facing up in dish for 5 mins
- Mix cucumber slices, hot pepper, mint, vinegar, salt, + sugar in a large

mason jar or medium bowl. Chill cucumber salad in the refrigerator, stirring every 5 mins while salmon is cooking.

• After salmon has marinated for 5 min., place skin side down in air fryer

• Air Fry at 400°F for 8 mins

• Drizzle salmon with remaining vinaigrette and air fry an additional 1-2 mins until cooked through, browned, and crispy on the edges

• Using a slotted spoon to eliminate excess pickling juices, place ¼ cucumber salad topped with 1 salmon portion on each plate. Serve immediately!

631. Citrus & Avocado Salad

Prep Time: 10 Mins Total Time: 10 mins

Ingredients

• 1/2 red grapefruit
• 1 blood orange
• 1 Navel orange
• 1/2 avocado
• 1/4 cup chopped roasted pistachios
• 2 Tbsp. chives
• 1 Tbsp. blood orange infused olive oil
• Sea salt & black pepper to taste!

Instructions

• Slice all citrus in whole circular thin slices.

• Arrange citrus on a large plate and top with avocado slices.

• Garnish with chopped chives, pistachios, blood orange olive oil, sea salt, and pepper.

632. Air Fryer Croutons

Total Time: 30 mins

Ingredients

• 4 slices bread
• 2 Tbsps melted butter
• 1 Tsp. parsley
• 1/2 Tsp. onion powder
• 1/2 Tsp. seasoned salt
• 1/2 Tsp. garlic salt

Instructions

• Preheat the air fryer to 390 degrees.

• Cut 4 slices of bread into bite-sized pieces.

• Melt butter, and place butter into a medium-sized bowl.

• Add 1 Tsp. parsley, 1/2 Tsp. seasoned salt, 1/2 Tsp. garlic salt, 1/2 Tsp. of onion powder to the melted butter. Stir well.

• Add bread to the bowl and carefully stir to coat the bread so that it is coated by the seasoned butter.

• Place buttered bread into the air fryer basket.

• Cook for 5 to 7 mins or until the bread is toasted.

• Serve immediately.

633. Instant Pot Southern-Style Potato Salad

Prep Time: 15 mins Cook Time: 4 mins Chill Time: 1 hour

Total Time1 hour 19 mins

Ingredients

• 1 1/2 cups water
• 5 (about 2 pounds total) russet potatoes peeled and sliced into 1 1/2 inch cubes
• 4 eggs
• 1 large bowl of cold water ice added to the water is optional
• 1 cup mayo
• 1/2 cup white onions chopped
• 1/4 cup pickle relish
• 1 Tbsp yellow mustard
• salt and pepper to taste
• Lawry's seasoning salt to taste optional
• 1 Tsp. paprika

Instructions

• Add the water to the Instant Pot. Place the Instant Pot on the saute' function. This will allow the water to warm so that it comes to pressure sooner.

• While the water heats up slice the potatoes.

• Add the steamer basket to the pot. Place the potatoes on top of the basket. Season the potatoes with about 1/4 Tsp. of salt.

• Place the eggs on the very top of the potatoes.

• Close the pot and seal. Cook for 4 mins on Manual > High-Pressure Cooking.

• When the Instant Pot indicates it has finished cooking, quick release the steam.

• Remove the eggs and place them in the bowl of cold water for 5 min..

• Remove the potatoes and transfer to a large bowl.

• Peel the eggs and slice them into small cubes.

• Add the cooked eggs, mayo, mustard, relish, white onions, paprika, and salt and pepper to taste to the mixture. Taste repeatedly. You may need to add additional salt and pepper.

• (If you prefer sweet potato salad add a little more relish and maybe sugar.)

• Stir to combine.

• Cover and chill for at least an hour to two hours before serving.

634. Grilled Romaine Salad

Prep Time: 10 Mins Cook Time: 2 Mins Total Time: 12 Mins

Ingredients

• 2 heads of romaine lettuce
• 6 slices of bacon
• 6 oz. pomegranate seeds
• 6 oz. of blue cheese crumbles
• 12 oz. of blue cheese dressing (see recipe card below)
• 4 tbsp of olive oil
• 1 tbsp balsamic glaze

Instructions

• Cook the bacon in an air fryer at 370°F for 8-12 mins until crispy and slice into crumbles. Check out the recipe for the best air fryer bacon.

• Slice the heads of romaine in half, lengthwise.

• Brush the romaine lettuce with olive oil.

• Place the romaine cut side down on the medium-hot grill.

• Flip the heads of romaine after 1-2 mins and cook on for equal time on the other side.

• Transfer the romaine cut side up to a serving platter and pile on the bacon, pomegranate seeds, and blue cheese crumbles.

• Finish by drizzling the amazing blue cheese salad dressing over the grilled romaine (see recipe below)

• Drizzle with a sweet balsamic glaze, and serve.

635. Air Fryer Kale

Prep Time: 5 mins Cook Time: 3 mins

Ingredients

• 3.5 ounces kale leaves 100 grams or 2-3 cups
• Oil spray
• Salt to taste optional

Instructions

- Preheat air fryer to 350 degrees F (175 C) for at least 5 mins
- While the air fryer preheats, wash and dry the kale leaves thoroughly. Remove the stems from the leaves if desired (see note). Slice the leaves into very thin strips.
- When the air fryer has finished preheating, add the sliced kale into the basket. Spray the leaves with oil as you shake the basket. Season lightly with salt (if using). Make sure the leaves are spread evenly across the basket before you put the basket back in the fryer.
- Air fry for 3 minutes, pausing briefly after 1.5 or 2 mins to shake and agitate the kale. Serve immediately.

636. Chopped Salad With Japanese Sweet Potato Croutons

Total Time: 30 mins

Ingredients

- 1 pound salad mixture including greens and vegetables of your choice
- 1 each crisp sweet apple, cored and diced
- 2 each mandarin oranges, peeled, segmented & cut in half
- 1/3 cup pomegranate seeds
- 1 8-12 ounce baked Japanese Sweet Potato cold, cut into pieces with skin on
- 2 tbsp Sweet Balsamic Vinegar 4% acidity Nappa Valley Naturals Grand Reserve or California Balsamic Simply Lemon are two of my favorites for this salad.

Instructions

- To make the JSP croutons, place the cold diced sweet potato pieces in a cold air fryer set to 400 degrees. Air fry for about 20 mins or until golden brown. If You don't have an air fryer you can crisp them up under the broiler. Watch them carefully as they go from lightly brown to burnt in a hurry.
- While the croutons are in the air fryer, chop the salad with a mezzaluna knife in a wood bowl or you can use a large knife and a large cutting board or one of the other methods I show in my video on how to chop a salad without a wood bowl.
- Add the diced apple, mandarin oranges, pomegranate seeds, JSP

croutons, and the balsamic vinegar of your choice. Gently stir all of the ingredients together and place it in a pretty bowl to serve. Many different flavors would work well with this salad. Don't add the vinegar until you are ready to serve the salad as it is best served freshly tossed.

637. Chicken Cordon Bleu Salad

Prep Time: 10 Mins Cook Time: 12 Mins Total Time: 22 Mins

Ingredients

- 2 boneless, skinless chicken breasts
- 2 Tbsps flour
- 1 egg, beaten
- 1/4 cup seasoned bread crumbs
- 4 Tbsps white wine vinegar
- 2 Tbsp nonfat plain Greek yogurt
- 2 Tbsps Dijon mustard
- 2 Tbsps honey
- 4 Tbsps olive oil
- 8 slices deli ham
- 4 slices Swiss cheese, cut in half
- 12 cups lettuce
- 1 seedless cucumber, chopped
- 1 cup tomatoes, halved
- 1/4 cup thinly sliced red onion

Instructions

- Lightly coat the chicken with flour, then dip it into the egg. Dredge in bread crumbs to coat. Spritz with oil.
- Air fry at 400 degrees for 12 minutes, or until cooked through. Slice into bite-sized pieces.
- Meanwhile, make the dressing by whisking together the vinegar, yogurt, mustard, and honey until smooth. Drizzle in the olive oil. Season with salt and pepper.
- Layer together one piece of ham and one piece of cheese. Roll together, then slice into 4 pinwheels. Repeat with remaining ham and cheese.
- Pile the lettuce onto a platter. Top with cucumber, tomatoes, onion, chicken, and ham and cheese pinwheels. Drizzle with dressing.

638. Southwest Tortilla Crusted Tilapia Salad

Cook Time: 15 mins Total Time: 15 mins

Ingredients

- 6 c. mixed greens
- 1 c. cherry tomatoes

- 1/3 c. diced red onion
- 1 avocado
- 2 Tortilla Crusted Tilapia fillets I used Sea Cuisine frozen fillets
- 1/2 c. Chipotle Lime Dressing

Instructions

- Spray your frozen tilapia fillets with cooking spray on both sides. Place in your Airfryer and cook for 15-18 mins at 390° until crispy. (If you don't have an air fryer, you can bake the fillets in the oven according to the directions.)
- While the fish is baking, in two bowls, add half of the greens, tomatoes, and red onion. Toss the mixture with the Chipotle Lime Dressing.
- Top the greens with the baked fish and sliced avocado. Serve immediately.

639. Pecan Chicken Salad Sandwiches

Prep Time: 15 mins Cook Time: 15 mins

Ingredients

- 1 pound Chicken Breasts Boneless/Skinless Air Fried or Poached
- sprinkling Salt & Pepper
- 1/2 cup Red Grapes diced
- 1/2 cup Apples peeled and diced
- 1/4 cup Celery Stalks strings peeled away and diced
- 1/4 cup Whole Pecans chopped
- 1/2 cup Olive Oil Mayonnaise Light or Regular
- 1/2 Tsp. Sea Salt
- Romaine Lettuce
- 8 slices Honey Wheat Bread
- 1 Avocado sliced into 8 slices

Instructions

- Air Fryer - Season Chicken Breasts with Salt and Pepper and place into Air Fryer.
- Cook at 340 degrees for 15 min.. When time is up, wait 5 mins and then remove Chicken from the Basket. OR
- Allow Chicken to fully cool and then dice into cubes.
- Remove the threads from the Celery and then dice.
- Dice up the Grapes, Apples, and Pecans and add to a Bowl.
- Add Salt and Mayonnaise and combine.
- Add diced chicken and combine. Taste and add more Mayonnaise or Salt, as needed.

- Place in refrigerator for one hour.
- Lightly toast bread and pile on Pecan Chicken Salad.
- Top with sliced Avocados and place top slice of Bread

Meatless Recipes

640.Korean BBQ Chickpeas

Prep Time: 5 mins Cook Time: 25 mins
Ingredients
- 1 can of garbanzo (chickpeas) beans drained
- 2 Tbsp Korean BBQ sauce
- 1/2 Tsp. gochujang Korean hot pepper paste or to taste
- 1/2 Tsp. honey

Instructions
- Line the fryer basket with a sheet of lightly greased aluminum foil.
- In a medium-sized bowl, mix the Korean BBQ sauce, gochujang, and honey until homogenous.
- Add in the garbanzo beans. Gently mix everything until all the beans are coated with the sauce.
- Transfer all the garbanzo beans and the sauce in the bowl to the fryer basket. Spread the beans out so they are not stacked on top of each other.
- Air fry at 320F (160C) for 23-25 min., string a few times in the middle until the sauce on the bean's surface caramelized.
- Let cool for about 5 mins before serving.

641.Blueberry Cream Cheese Croissant Bake

Prep Time: 10 mins Cook Time: 20 mins
Ingredients
- 1/2 tube crescent dough (4 crescents) (or puff pastry sheets)
- 1/2 cup blueberry
- 4 oz cream cheese (約 113g)
- 1/3 cup sugar
- 1 egg
- 1/2 Tsp. vanilla
- 2 Tbsp milk

Instructions
- Roll the crescent dough into the shape of a crescent and set it aside.
- Lightly grease a shallow baking dish and set it aside.
- In an electric mixer, cream together cream cheese and sugar until fluffy.

- Add in milk, egg, and vanilla and mix until well combined and pour the mixture into the baking dish.
- Place the crescents on top and sprinkle the blueberries into the dish.
- Air fry at 280F (140C) for 18-20 mins until the egg is set and the crescent rolls are golden brown.

642.Garlic And Herb Artisan Bread

Prep Time: 2 hrs Cook Time: 20 mins
Ingredients
- 1 cup water about 95F (35C)
- 1/2 Tbsp instant dry yeast
- 1/2 Tbsp salt
- 2 1/4 cup all-purpose flour
- 2 Tsp. garlic powder or to taste
- 1/2 Tsp. onion powder
- 1 Tsp. thyme
- 1/2 Tsp. dried parsley

Instructions
- In a medium bowl, gently stir the water and yeast.
- In a large mixing bowl, combine all dry ingredients and mix well.
- Pour the yeast and water mixture into the mixing bowl containing the dry ingredients and mix well. Cover the mixing bowl with a damp towel and let rise for about 2 hours or until the dough rose and double in size.
- Line a 7-inch cake barrel with parchment paper. Sprinkle a little flour onto the parchment paper.
- Use a spatula to punch down the dough then transfer the dough to the cake barrel. Sprinkle some flour on top and let it rise for about 30 minutes.
- If the air fryer you use has a detachable basket, pour about 3 Tbsps of water into the bottom of the outer basket. Preheat the air fryer at 400F (200C) for about 4 minutes.
- Put the cake barrel inside the fryer basket and air fryer at 400F (200C) for about 10-12 mins until the bread has a nice golden-brown crust.
- Turn the bread over and air fry again at 400F (200C) for another 4-6 mins until the crust is golden brown. Try knocking on the bread, if it sounds hollow then it is cooked through on the inside.
- Let cool on a wired rack for about 10-15 mins before slicing.

643.Hilton DoubleTree Hotel Chocolate Chip Cookies

Prep Time: 10 mins Cook Time: 1 hr
Ingredients
- 1/2 cup butter softened
- 1/3 cup granulated sugar
- 1/4 cup packed brown sugar
- 1 egg
- 1/2 teaspoons vanilla extract
- 1/8 Tsp. lemon juice
- 1 cup and 2 Tbsps all-purpose flour
- 1/4 cup rolled oats
- 1/2 Tsp. baking soda
- 1/2 Tsp. salt
- Pinch cinnamon
- 1 1/4 cup semi-sweet chocolate chips
- 1 cup chopped walnuts

Instructions
- Cream butter, sugar, and brown sugar in the bowl of a stand mixer on medium speed for about 2 min..
- Add eggs, vanilla, and lemon juice, blending with mixer on low speed for 30 seconds, then medium speed for about 2 min., or until light and fluffy, scraping down bowl.
- With the mixer on low speed, add flour, oats, baking soda, salt, and cinnamon, blending for about 45 seconds. Don't overmix.
- Remove bowl from mixer and stir in chocolate chips and walnuts.
- Line the fryer basket with a grill mat or a sheet of parchment paper.
- Scoop about one Tbsp of dough onto a baking sheet lined with parchment paper about 2 inches apart.
- Air fry at 260F (130C) for 18-20 minutes.
- Remove from the air fryer and cool on a wired rack for about 1/2 hour.

644.Korean Air Fried Green Beans

Prep Time: 5 mins Cook Time: 15 mins
Ingredients
- 1 pound green beans (about 500g) washed and dried in a colander
- 1/3 cup Korean BBQ sauce
- 1/2 Tsp. black pepper or to taste
- 2 Tsp. toasted sesame seeds

Instructions
- Line the fryer basket with a grill mat or a sheet of lightly greased aluminum foil.

- In a mixing bowl, mix and coat the green beans with the seasoning ingredients.
- Transfer all contents in the mixing bowl into the fryer basket.
- Air fry at 400F (200C) for 14-16 min., stirring a few times in between until the surface is slightly caramelized. When you see the BBQ sauce starts drying up, keep an eye on it, as you don't want the beans to get charred. Therefore, check more frequently towards the end.
- Sprinkle some sesame seeds to serve.

645.General Tso Tofu

Prep Time: 2 hrs Cook Time: 15 mins
Ingredients
- 10 oz firm tofu (about 285g)
- 2 Tbsp thinly sliced green onion
- 1 Tsp. sesame seeds
- Ingredients for the sauce:
- 1 Tbsp chili oil
- 2 Tbsp minced garlic
- 1 Tbsp grated ginger
- 2 Tbsp soy sauce
- 1 Tbsp vinegar
- 1 1/2 Tbsp sugar
- 2 Tsp. corn starch mix with 4 Tsp. water

Instructions
- Place a kitchen towel on the counter and place the tofu on top. Put a heavy item, such as a small pot, on top of the tofu for one hour to squeeze out excess water.
- Line the fryer basket with a grill mat or a sheet of lightly greased aluminum foil.
- Cut tofu into bite-size pieces and put them in a fryer basket without stacking. Spritz them with some oil and air fry at 400F (200C) for about 10-12 minutes, flip them once in the middle.
- In the meantime, prepare the sauce by mixing chili oil, minced garlic, grated ginger, soy sauce, vinegar, and sugar.
- Heat the sauce in a wok and bring it to a boil. Mix corn starch with water and add it to the sauce in the wok. Stir constantly until the sauce thickens.
- When the tofu is done, toss them in the wok to coat.
- Sprinkle some sesame seeds and green onion to serve.

646.Roasted Barley Tea

Prep Time: 5 mins Cook Time: 35 mins
Ingredients
1/2 cup round or pressed barley
Instructions
- Rinse the barley, drain and let dry a bit in a colander.
- Put barley in a cake barrel and air fry at 400F (175C) for 30-35 min., stirring 3-4 times in the middle, until the color turns dark brown.
- Let cool completely before use.
- In a teapot put one Tbsp of roasted barley with one cup of boiling water. Let sit for at least 10 mins for it to become fragrant and flavorful.

647.Roasted Cinnamon Sugar Orange

Prep Time: 5 mins Cook Time: 5 mins
Ingredients
- 4 Oranges
- 1/2 tsp cinnamon
- 2 tsp brown sugar
- Instructions
- Mix cinnamon and sugar and set aside.
- Cut each half of the orange in half. Then, take a serrated knife to cut along the inner edges of the orange rind.
- Sprinkle the cinnamon sugar the orange.
- Air fry at 400F (200C) for about 4-5 minutes.
- Serve warm by itself or over ice cream.

648.Air Fryer Sweet Potato Fries

Prep Time: 5 mins Cook Time: 15 mins
Ingredients
- 1 pound sweet potatoes peeled (about 500g)
- 1 Tbsp olive oil
- 1/2 Tsp. garlic powder
- 1/2 Tsp. onion powder
- 1/2 Tsp. paprika
- 1/2 Tsp. salt or to taste
- 1/4 Tsp. white pepper powder
- 1/2 Tsp. dried basil flakes to garnish
Instructions
- Line the fryer basket with a grill mat or a sheet of lightly greased aluminum foil.
- Cut the sweet potato into 1/4 inch sticks.
- In a large mixing bowl, toss the sweet potato sticks with all other ingredients, except dried basil flakes.
- Place the sweet potato sticks inside the fryer basket without stacking, if possible. Air fry at 380F (190C) for 14-16 min., stirring once in the middle until the edges look nice and crisp.
- Sprinkle some dried basil to serve.

649.Blueberry Cream Cheese Muffins

Prep Time: 10 mins Cook Time: 10 mins
Ingredients
- 1 1/2 cups all-purpose flour
- 1/2 cup white sugar
- 1/2 Tsp. salt
- 2 teaspoons baking powder
- 1/4 cup vegetable oil
- 8 oz cream cheese (about 225g) softened at room temperature
- 1 egg
- 1/2 Tsp. vanilla extract
- 1/3 cup milk
- 1 cup fresh blueberries
Instructions
- Grease muffin cups or line with muffin liners.
- In a large bowl, combine flour, sugar, salt, and baking powder.
- In a large mixing bowl, cream together vegetable oil, cream cheese, egg, and vanilla extract. Then, add in milk and all the dried ingredients and mix until well combined.
- Fold in blueberries. Scoop the mixture into the muffin tins, about 3/4 full.
- Air fry at 320F (160C) for about 12-14 mins until done, and the toothpick comes out clean.

650.Air Fryer BBQ Brussels Sprouts

Prep Time: 5 mins Cook Time: 25 mins
Ingredients
- 1 pound Brussels sprouts about 500g
- 2 tsp olive oil
- 1/8 tsp black pepper or to taste
- 1/4 cup BBQ sauce American-style BBQ sauce (such as the Sweet Baby Ray's BBQ sauce)
- 1/4 cup Parmesan cheese or to taste
Instructions
- Rinse the Brussels sprouts with cold water and let dry in a colander. Trim off the ends and cut them in half.
- In a large mixing bowl, toss the Brussels sprouts, olive oil, and black

pepper. Then, wrap them in aluminum foil and air fry at 380F (190C) for about about 16 min..

• Mix in the BBQ sauce and air fry again at 360F (180C) for 5-6 minutes, stirring once in the middle until the surface is slightly caramelized.

• Sprinkle some Parmesan cheese to serve.

651. Hotteok Korean Sweet Pancakes

Prep Time: 2 hrs 30 mins
Cook Time: 10 mins
Ingredients
Ingredients For The Dough:
• 1 1/4 cup all-purpose flour
• 1/2 tsp salt
• 1 tsp white sugar
• 1 tsp instant dry yeast
• 1/2 cup lukewarm milk
• Ingredients for the filling:
• 1/4 cup brown sugar
• 1/4 tsp cinnamon powder
• 1/4 cup chopped walnuts
Instructions

• In a mixing bowl, mix all the dough ingredients with a spatula.

• Lightly cover the bowl with saran wrap and let the dough rise for about 1-2 hours or until the dough doubles in size.

• Punch the dough down several times to release the air in the dough. Then, cover with saran wrap again and let it rest for about 20 minutes.

• In the meantime, mix all the filling ingredients in a bowl and set aside.

• Line the fryer basket with a grill mat or a sheet of lightly greased aluminum foil.

• Rub some cooking oil in your hands and take the dough out from the bowl. Roll the dough into a cylinder shape on the counter surface then cut it into six equal pieces. Roll each piece into a ball.

• Take one ball of dough and flatten it between the palms of your hand. Scoop about 1 Tbsp of filling and wrap it inside the dough. Place the dough inside the fryer basket, leaving about 2 inches between the balls. Repeat until done.

• Press the balls down with the palm of your hand. Spritz some oil on top and air fry at 300F (150C) for 8-10 minutes, flip once in the middle until the surface is

golden brown.

652. Parmesan Sugar Snap Peas

Prep Time: 5 mins Cook Time: 10 mins
Ingredients
• 1/2 pound sugar snap peas)
• 1 tsp olive oil
• 1/4 cup panko breadcrumbs
• 1/4 cup parmesan cheese
• Salt and pepper to taste
• 2 tbsp minced garlic
Instructions

• Remove and discard the stem end and string from each pea pod. Then, rinse and drained in a colander.

• Line the fryer basket with a grill mat or a sheet of lightly greased aluminum foil.

• In a large mixing bowl, toss the snap peans with olive oil, panko breadcrumbs, half of the parmesan cheese, and salt and pepper.

• Put the snap pea mixture into the fryer basket and air fry at 360F for about 4 min..

• Stir in the minced garlic then air fry again at 360F (180C) for another 4-5 minutes.

• Sprinkle the rest of the parmesan cheese to serve.

653. Air Fryer Roasted Almonds

Prep Time: 1 min Cook Time: 15 mins
Ingredients
• 1 cup raw almonds
Instructions

• Put raw almonds in bakeware, air fry at 320F for 10-12 minutes, stirring twice in the middle to ensure they roast evenly.

• Let cool completely before serving.

654. Gochujang Lotus Root

Prep Time: 10 mins Cook Time: 10 mins
Ingredients
• 1/2 pound lotus root sliced about 1/4 inch thick (about 250g)
• 1 Tbsp Gochujang Korean hot pepper paste
• 1 Tbsp soy sauce
• 4 Tbsp honey
• 2 Tsp. apple cider vinegar
• 1 Tsp. sesame seed
Instructions

• In a Ziploc bag, mix Gochujang, soy sauce, honey, and apple cider vinegar.

Add lotus roots to the bag and mix. Seal the bag and marinate for at least one hour or best overnight.

• Line the fryer basket with a grill mat or a sheet of lightly greased aluminum foil.

• Put the lotus root slices in the fryer basket without stacking. Air fry at 380F (190C) for about 10 min., flip once in the middle until the surface looks slightly caramelized.

• In the meantime, transfer the marinade from the bag to a wok or saucepan and bring it to a boil. Stir constantly until the sauce thickens.

• Toss the lotus root with the sauce. Then, sprinkle some sesame seeds and scallion to serve.

655. Korean BBQ Lotus Root

Prep Time: 5 mins Cook Time: 10 mins
Ingredients
• 1/3 cup Korean BBQ Sauce
• 1/2 pound Lotus root cut into 1/4 inch slices (about 250g)
• 1 Tsp. sesame seeds
• 2 Tbsp scallion
Instructions

• Marinate lotus in Korean BBQ sauce for at least 1 hour or best overnight.

• Line the fryer basket with a grill mat or a sheet of lightly greased aluminum foil.

• Put the lotus root slices in the fryer basket without stacking. Air fry at 380F (190C) for about 6-8 min., flip once in the middle until the surface looks slightly caramelized.

• In the meantime, transfer the marinade from the bag to a wok or saucepan and bring it to a boil. Stir constantly until the sauce thickens.

• Toss the lotus root with the sauce. Then, sprinkle some sesame seeds and scallion to serve.

656. Honey Sesame Tofu

Prep Time: 1 hr Cook Time: 30 mins
Ingredients
• 1 box firm tofu about 1 pound or 500g
• 1/3 cup honey
• 1/3 cup soy sauce
• 1/4 cup ketchup
• 1/4 cup brown sugar
• 1/4 cup rice vinegar
• 1 tsp sesame oil

- 2 Tbsp minced garlic
- 1 Tbsp sesame seeds for garnish
- 1/4 cup scallions for garnish

Instructions
- Wrap the tofu in a cheesecloth. Place a heavy pan on top for about 30 min..
- Then, place the tofu in the freezer for at least 6 hours.
- Remove the tofu from the freezer and use the defrost function of the microwave for about 10 minutes. After that, repeat step one to squeeze out excess water.
- In the meantime, take a large bowl to mix and combine honey, soy sauce, ketchup, brown sugar, vinegar, sesame oil, and garlic. Scoop about 1/2 cup of the marinade and set aside.
- Use hands to break the tofu into bite-size pieces and put them inside the large bowl containing the marinade. Stir and let the tofu marinate for at least 30 min..
- Line the fryer basket with a grill mat or sheet of lightly greased aluminum foil.
- Put the tofu pieces inside the fryer basket without stacking and air fry at 400F (200C) for 14-16 minutes, stir once in the middle until the edges of tofu looks a bit caramelized.
- While air frying, use a wok or a frying pan to bring the sauce to a boil. Stir constantly until the sauce thickens.
- When the tofu is done, toss in the wok to coat. Sprinkle some sesame seeds and scallions to serve.

657.Raspberry Nutella Toast Cups
Prep Time: 5 mins Cook Time: 10 mins

Ingredients
- 6 pieces of bread
- 2 tbsp unsalted butter melted
- 1/4 cup Nutella or to taste
- 1/2 cup Raspberry or to taste
- 2 tbsp powdered sugar optional

Instructions
- Trim off the sides of the toast and save for them for other uses such as croutons or bread pudding. Flatten the toast with a rolling pin and brush a thin layer of butter to both sides.
- Place each of the toast inside a muffin tin and press down against the walls of the tin. Air fry at 320F (160C) for about

7-8 mins until the toast becomes golden brown.
- Spoon some Nutella into the bread cup and spread it inside of the cup. Finally, place the raspberries inside the cup. Dust the cups with powdered sugar if desired.

658.Turnip Fries
Prep Time: 30 mins Cook Time: 15 mins

Ingredients
- 1/2 pound turnip peeled and cut into sticks
- 1/4 tsp salt
- 2 Tsp. olive oil
- 1/4 tsp paprika
- 1/4 tsp onion powder
- 1/8 tsp white pepper powder or to taste
- 1/8 tsp cayenne pepper or to taste

Instructions
- In a mixing bowl, toss the turnip sticks with salt. Let it rest for about 20 mins to draw some of the water out. Discard the excess water in the bowl.
- Toss the turnips sticks in olive oil to coat. Then, add in the rest of the ingredients and toss. Put the turnip sticks into the fryer basket and try to spread them out as much as possible.
- Air fry at 380F (190C) for 10-12 minutes, shake basket a couple of times in between until the surface looks crisp and golden brown.
- Serve immediately. Sprinkle some dried basil if desired.

659.Home Fries
Prep Time: 5 mins Cook Time: 10 mins

Ingredients
- 1 russet potato
- 1 tbsp olive oil
- 1/2 tsp salt or to taste
- 1/2 tsp paprika
- 1/4 tsp black pepper
- 1/4 tsp cayenne pepper (optional)

Instructions
- Peel and dice the potato into 1/2 inch pieces. Soak the potato in cold water for about 10-15 minutes. Drain.
- Toss the potato in olive oil. Then, add the remaining ingredients and toss.
- Line the fryer basket with a grill mat or a sheet of lightly greased aluminum foil.

- Spread the diced potato inside the fryer basket. Air fry at 380F (190C) for about 10-12 min., stir twice in the middle until the surface is crispy and golden brown.

660.BBQ Baby Corn
Prep Time: 5 mins Cook Time: 10 mins

Ingredients
- 1 can baby corn drained and rinse with cold water
- 1/4 cup Korean BBQ sauce or to taste
- 1/2 tsp Sriracha or to taste optional

Instructions
- Line the fryer basket with a grill mat or a sheet of lightly greased aluminum foil.
- In a large bowl, mix the Korean BBQ sauce and Sriracha. Roll the baby corn in the sauce and place them inside the fryer basket without stacking.
- Air fry at 400F (200C) for about 8-10 min., brush some more sauce onto baby corn if necessary until the sauce on the surface is slightly caramelized.

661.Air Fried Banana
Prep Time: 5 mins Cook Time: 10 mins

Ingredients
- 1 ripe banana cut into 1/2 inch slices
- 1/4 tsp cinnamon
- 1/2 tsp brown sugar
- 1 tbsp Granola to taste
- 1 tbsp Chopped toasted nuts to taste

Instructions
- In a small bowl, mix the cinnamon and brown sugar and set aside.
- Lightly grease a shallow baking pan. Place the banana slices into the pan. Spray some oil onto the banana and sprinkle some cinnamon sugar. Air fry at 400F (200C) for about 4-5 min..
- Sprinkle some granola and nuts over the banana to serve.

662.Mozzarella Stuffed Mushrooms
Prep Time: 5 mins Cook Time: 10 mins

Ingredients
- 8 medium to large button mushrooms wiped clean and stem removed
- 3-4 tbsp Korean BBQ sauce
- 1/3 cup mozzarella cheese
- Olive oil spray
- 1/2 tsp basil flakes

Instructions
- Line the fryer basket with a grill mat

or a sheet of lightly greased aluminum foil.

- Scoop about 1/2 Tsp. of Korean BBQ sauce into the mushroom. Then, stuff the mushroom with the desired amount of mozzarella cheese.
- Place the mushrooms inside the fryer basket. Spray the mushrooms with some olive oil and air fry at 380F (190C) for about 4-5 mins until the cheese is golden brown.
- Sprinkle some basil flakes to serve if desired.

663. Vietnamese Vegetarian Egg Meatloaf

Prep Time: 30 mins Cook Time: 20 mins
Ingredients
- 15 g wood ear mushrooms
- 20 g dried shiitake mushrooms
- 4 eggs
- 1/4 cup milk
- small carrot shredded or grated
- 1 Tbsp minced garlic
- 60 g mung bean noodles glass noodles
- Tbsp fish sauce
- 1/4 Tsp. sugar
- 1/4 Tsp. salt
- 1/4 Tsp. black pepper

Instructions
- Soak the shiitake mushrooms and wood ear mushrooms in warm water for about 20 min.. Once they are softened, squeeze out excess water in the shiitake mushrooms and thinly slice both mushrooms.
- Soak mung bean noodles in cold water for about 15 mins then cut them into 2-inch sections.
- Crack 2 whole eggs and 2 egg whites into a large bowl and save the 2 egg yolks in a small bowl for later use.
- Add milk into the large bowl and use a whisk to mix until homogenous. Add all the ingredients, except for the egg yolks, into the large bowl and mix.
- Spray some oil in a mini loaf pan and pour the egg mixture into the pan. Smooth out the top surface as much as possible since anything that sticks out of the surface will likely be charred during the air frying process.
- Air fry at 280F (140C) for 16-18 mins until the egg is set.

- In the meantime, add a pinch of salt into the small bowl containing the egg yolks and mix.
- When the egg loaf is done, pour the egg yolk on top and spread it evenly over the egg loaf. Air fry again at 400F (200C) for about 2 mins until the egg yolks are hardened.
- When cool enough to handle, remove the egg loaf from the pan and cut them into 3/4 inch thick slices. Spoon some sauce over it to serve.

664. Taro Balls With Salted Egg Yolks

Prep Time: 20 mins Cook Time: 10 mins
Ingredients
- 6 salted egg yolk
- 1 Tsp. rice wine
- 500 g taro steamed
- 50 g corn starch
- 80 g sugar
- 1/4 Tsp. salt
- 2 Tbsp coconut oil

Instructions
- Coat the egg yolk with rice wine and let sit for 10 min.. Put the egg yolks in shallow bakeware and air fry at 380F (190C) for about 3-4 min..
- Put all other ingredients in a mixing bowl. Mush and mix all ingredients until the texture is dough-like and without lumps. Alternatively, a food processor can be used as well.
- When done, divide this taro dough into 6 equal portions and roll them into round balls. Flatten each ball and put an egg yolk in the middle. Wrap the dough around the egg yolk and roll it into a ball again, making sure there are no cracks or openings.
- Line the fryer basket with a grill mat or lightly greased aluminum foil.
- Place the taro balls inside the fryer basket. Air fry at 380F (190C) for 8-10 min., shake the basket once in the middle until the surface is golden brown.

665. Black Pepper Mushroom

Prep Time: 5 mins Cook Time: 10 mins
Ingredients
- 8 oz button mushrooms (about 250g) wiped clean, halved, or quartered
- 1 Tbsp butter melted
- 2 cloves of garlic thinly sliced
- 1 Tbsp oyster sauce or to taste

- 3/4 Tsp. black pepper or to taste
- 1/4 cup green onion finely sliced

Instructions
- Put melted butter and garlic in a cake pan and air fry at 380F (190C) for 2 minutes.
- Add the mushroom into the pan and stir. Air fry at 360F (180C) for 3 minutes. Stir in the oyster sauce and black pepper. Air fry again at 360F (180C) for 2-3 min..
- Sprinkle some green onion to serve.

666. Vegetarian Grilled Unagi

Prep Time: 10 mins Cook Time: 5 mins
Ingredients
- 1 Chinese eggplant cut in half
- 2 Tbsp Unagi sauce or Teriyaki sauce or to taste
- 1 Tsp. toasted sesame seeds
- 2 Tbsp thinly sliced green onion

Instructions
- Steam the eggplants until tender.
- When cool enough to handle, cut the eggplant vertically without cutting through. Then, score the flesh of the eggplants so they look like tiny squares or rectangles.
- Line the fryer basket with a grill mat or lightly greased aluminum foil.
- Brush both sides of the eggplants with Unagi sauce (or Teriyaki sauce). Place the eggplant into the fryer basket skin side down and air fry at 400F (200C) for about 4-5 minutes.
- Sprinkle some sesame seeds and green onion to serve.

667. Air Fried Button Mushrooms

Prep Time: 5 mins Cook Time: 10 mins
Ingredients
- 10 medium button mushrooms wiped clean with a paper towel and quartered
- 1 egg beaten
- 1/2 cup breadcrumbs
- 1/2 Tsp. garlic powder
- 1/2 Tsp. onion powder
- 1/4 Tsp. dried basil
- 1/4 Tsp. black pepper
- 1/4 Tsp. salt
- Ranch dressing optional

Instructions
- Put all the dry ingredients in a large Ziploc bag and shake well.
- Dip the mushroom pieces in the egg

then drop them into the Ziploc bag. Shake the bag to coat the mushroom pieces with bread crumb mixture.

• Shake off excess bread crumbs from the mushroom and place them in the fryer basket. Spray some oil onto the mushrooms and air fry at 400F (200C) for about 3 min.. Flip the mushrooms and spray some oil again. Air fry at 400F (200C) for another 2-3 min..

• Serve immediately with ranch dressing or the sauce of your choice.

668. Marinated Korean BBQ Tofu

Prep Time: 2 hrs Cook Time: 15 mins

Ingredients

• 8 oz firm tofu cut into bite-size cubes
• 1 cup Korean BBQ Sauce
• 2-3 Tbsp minced garlic
• Thinly sliced scallions and sesame optional

Instructions

• In a Ziploc bag or a container with a lid, marinate the tofu with Korean BBQ sauce and grated garlic for at least 2 hours.

• Line the fryer basket with a Grill mat or a sheet of lightly greased aluminum foil.

• Place the tofu cube inside the fryer basket and air fry at 400F (200C) for 10-12 min., flip once in the middle, until the surface is caramelized.

• Garnish with scallions and sesame seeds to serve if desired.

669. Buttered Green Beans

Prep Time: 5 mins Cook Time: 10 mins

Ingredients

• 1 pound green beans (about 500g) rinsed and dried
• 1 1/2 Tbsp unsalted butter melted
• 1/2 Tsp. sea salt
• 1/4 Tsp. black pepper
• 2 Tbsp chopped garlic

Instructions

• Toss the green beans with melted butter, salt, and pepper. Air fry at 350F (175C) for about 4 min..

• Add in the garlic, stir, and air fry again at 350F (175C) for another 3-4 min..

670. Matcha Red Bean Toast

Prep Time: 5 mins Cook Time: 10 mins

Ingredients

• 4 pieces of bread

• 1 Tbsp unsalted butter softened
• Canned Japanese sweetened red bean (mashed), to taste
• 3 Tbsp matcha green tea powder
• 1 1/4 Tbsp water

Instructions

• In a small bowl, matcha mixes green tea powder with water until it forms a thickened paste. Spread the paste on one piece of bread and the mashed red bean on the other piece (one side only).

• Put the two pieces together to make a sandwich.

• Spread the softened butter onto the outside of the sandwich on both sides. Stick one toothpick through the sandwich to prevent the displacement of bread during the air frying process.

• Air fry at 400F (200C) for about 7-8 min., flip once until the surface is golden brown.

671. Cumin Spiced Tofu Skewers

Prep Time: 1 hr 10 mins Cook Time: 15 mins

Ingredients

• 8 oz firm tofu
• 2 Tbsp soy paste
• 1 Tbsp olive oil
• 1 Tbsp cumin
• 1 Tsp. brown sugar
• 1/4 Tsp. cayenne pepper or to taste
• 1/4 Sichuan peppercorn powder or to taste
• 2 Tbsp thinly sliced green onion
• 1 Tsp. toasted sesame seeds

Instructions

• Place a kitchen towel on the counter and place the tofu on top.

• Put a heavy item, such as a small pot, on top of the tofu for one hour to squeeze out excess water.

• Soak bamboo skewers in water for at least 10 minutes. Take a metal steamer rack and brush olive oil onto the surface of the rack and put it inside the fryer basket.

• In a small bowl, prepare the sauce by mixing all the seasoning ingredients and set aside.

• Cut tofu into bite-size pieces and thread them on 2 skewers parallel to each other. Generously brush both sides of the tofu with a layer of the seasoning mixture and place the

skewers on top of the steamer rack.

• Air fry at 400F (200C) for about 10-12 min., brushing more sauce in the middle if necessary, until the surface of the tofu is slightly caramelized.

• Sprinkle some sesame seeds and green onion to serve.

672. Maple Banana French Toast Bake

Prep Time: 5 mins Cook Time: 20 mins

Ingredients

• Makes two loaves using 5.75 in x 3 in mini loaf pans
• 2 eggs beaten
• 1/4 cups milk
• 1 Tbsp brown sugar
• 3 Tbsp maple syrup
• 1 Tbsp butter melted
• 1 Tsp. vanilla extract
• 1/4 Tsp. ground cinnamon
• 1 small banana sliced
• 4 slices of bread cubed
• 1/3 cup raw walnut chopped
• Raw chop walnuts to top

Instructions

• In a large mixing bowl, mix the eggs, milk, brown sugar, maple syrup, butter, vanilla extract, and cinnamon. When the mixture is well combined, gently stir in bread cubes, banana, and chopped pecans.

• Scoop the mixture into a lightly greased mini loaf pan and top it with the whole pecan.

• Air fry at 280F (140C) for about 12 min.. Then, carefully remove the loaf from the pan, flip, and place the bread loaf directly on parchment paper (now bottom side up). Air fry at 280F (140C) again for about 6 mins more.

673. Wasabi Avocado Fries

Prep Time: 5 mins Cook Time: 10 mins

Ingredients

• 1 avocado pitted and diced
• 1 egg
• 1 1/2 Tbsp wasabi paste or to taste
• 1/2 Tsp. salt
• 1/2 cup breadcrumbs or Japanese panko
• Lime wedges optional

Instructions

• Put the breadcrumbs in a Ziploc bag and set them aside.

• In a medium bowl, use a whisk to mix

the egg, wasabi paste, and salt until homogenous.

- Put all the avocado chunks in the egg mixture to coat.
- Carefully transfer the avocado into the bag. Shake the bag to coat the avocado with breadcrumbs.
- Place the avocado pieces into the fryer basket, spray them with some oil, and air fry at 400F (200C) for about 3 min..
- Squeeze some lime juice to serve.

674. Roasted Garlic

Prep Time: 5 mins Cook Time: 30 mins
Ingredients
- 3-4 head of garlic
- 2 tbsp Olive oil
- A pinch of salt

Instructions
- Slice off the top of garlic. Drizzle some olive oil over it and sprinkle with some salt and pepper.
- Wrap the garlic with aluminum foil and air fry at 400F (200C) for 25-30 mins until the garlic is tender and slightly golden brown.

675. Tofu with Bamboo Shoots

Prep Time: 10 mins Cook Time: 15 mins
Ingredients
Ingredients For Tofu:
- 1 1/4 cup bean curd cut into 1/4 inch thick strips
- 1 Tsp. olive oil

Other Ingredients:
- 2 cups bamboo shoots
- 2 Tbsp garlic minced
- 2 Tbsp oyster sauce
- 2 Tbsp soy sauce
- 1 Tbsp rice wine
- 1 Tbsp brown sugar
- 1/2 Tsp. Sriracha optional
- 2 green onions cut into one-inch pieces.

Instructions
- Line the fryer basket with lightly greased aluminum foil. Toss tofu strips with olive oil then put them into the basket. Air fry at 380F (190C) for about 5 min.. Add in the bamboo shoots, stir, and air fry again at 380F (190C) for another 3 min..
- In a frying pan or wok, stir fry the garlic in olive oil. Then, add in all other

ingredients (except green onions) and continue to stir until the sauce thickens a little.
- Add in the tofu strips, bamboo shoots, and green onion and toss. Enjoy!

676. Oyster Sauce Mushroom

Prep Time: 5 mins Cook Time: 10 mins
Ingredients
- 8 ounces large button mushrooms cleaned and quartered. For smaller ones, keep whole or cut in half
- 1 Tbsp melted butter
- 1 Tbsp oyster sauce
- 1/4 Tsp. black pepper or to taste
- 1 Tbsp green onion thinly sliced optional

Instructions
- In a large bowl, toss the mushroom with melted butter, oyster sauce, and black pepper.
- Put the mushroom in a lightly greased cake pan, ait fry the mushroom at 380F (190C) for about 6-7 minutes, stir once in between.
- Garnish with some green onion to serve.

677. Fried Okra With Sriracha Mayo

Prep Time: 5 mins Cook Time: 10 mins
Ingredients
- 15 okra
- 1 egg beaten
- 1/2 cup Japanese panko
- 3 Tbsp freshly chopped Thai basil
- 1/4 cup mayonnaise
- 1 Tbsp Sriracha or to taste
- 2-3 Tbsp Mirin

Instructions
- Mix chopped basil with panko and set aside.
- Line the fryer basket with lightly greased aluminum foil. Dip the okra in the egg wash, roll them in panko mix, and put them in the fryer basket without stacking. Air fry at 380F (190C) for about 8 minutes, shake the basket once in between.
- In the meantime, mix the mayo, sriracha, and mirin and set aside.
- Serve the fried okra with sriracha mayo when done.

678. Miso Tofu

Prep Time: 10 mins Cook Time: 20 mins
Ingredients

- 1 box firm tofu
- 2 Tbsp miso paste
- 1 Tsp. Sriracha Hot Sauce optional
- 4 Tsp. brown sugar
- 2 Tsp. sesame oil
- 2 Tsp. soy sauce
- 1 green onion thinly sliced
- 1 Tbsp sesame seeds

Instructions
- Place a kitchen towel on the counter and place the tofu on top. Put a heavy item, such as a small pot, on top of the tofu for one hour to squeeze out excess water.
- In the meantime, prepare the sauce by mixing miso, Sriracha, brown sugar, sesame oil, and soy sauce.
- Cut tofu into 1/2-3/4 inches thick slices then cut the surface of the tofu in a crisscrossed fashion without cutting through.
- Carefully put the tofu pieces into the parchment-lined fryer basket. Brush a thick layer of sauce onto the tofu and lightly dab the surface so the sauce can get into the crevices. Air fry at 400F (200C) for 10-12 min., brushing a layer of the sauce every 3-4 mins until the sauce is caramelized.
- Sprinkle some green onion and sesame seeds to serve.

679. Maple Walnut Biscotti

Prep Time: 10 mins Cook Time: 40 mins
Ingredients
- 1 cup all-purpose flour
- 1/3 cup packed brown sugar
- 1 1/4 teaspoons baking powder
- 1/4 Tsp. salt
- 1 egg
- 2 Tbsp maple syrup
- 2 Tbsp melted unsalted butter
- 1 cups coarsely chopped walnuts

Instructions
- In a parchment-lined fryer basket, air fry the walnuts at 300F (150C) for 6 min.
- In the meantime, take a large and bowl and mix all the dry ingredients. Then, add in the wet ingredients until everything is well combined. Finally, fold in the chopped walnuts and form the batter into a ball shape.
- Place the ball-shaped dough on parchment paper and press it down with the palm of your hand to mold the

dough into a rectangular shape with a thickness of about 1/2 inch. Air fry at 360F (180C) for 15 min..

• Remove the rectangular cookie along with the parchment paper from the fryer basket and let cool for a few min.. When cool enough to handle, cut it into 3/4 inch wide pieces.

• Place all the pieces back into the fryer basket with the cut side up and air fry at 360 for about 10 min., flipping once in between with the other cut side facing up.

• When done, carefully remove the biscotti from the fryer basket and let them cool completely on a cooling rack before serving.

680.Kimchi Tofu Stir Fry

Prep Time: 5 mins Cook Time: 10 mins

Ingredients

• 8 oz firm tofu (about 250g) cut into cubes
• 4 Tbsp honey
• 2 Tbsp Korean hot pepper paste Gochujang or to taste
• 2 Tbsp soy sauce
• 1 Tbsp oyster sauce
• 1 Tbsp sesame oil
• 2 Tbsp minced garlic
• 1/2 cup kimchi chopped
• 2 green onions cut into one-inch pieces
• 1 Tsp. sesame seeds

Instructions

• Line the fryer basket with parchment paper and place the tofu cubes inside the basket without stacking. Spray the surface of the tofu with some oil and air fry at 400F (200C) for 10 min., flipping once in the middle.

• In the meantime, in a saucepan, saute the minced garlic with sesame oil. Then, add honey, soy sauce, oyster sauce, and kimchi into the sauce to the pan and bring to boil, stirring frequently until the sauce thickens a bit.

• When the tofu is done, toss the tofu in the sauce along with the green onion for about a minute. Sprinkle some sesame seeds over the tofu to serve.

681.Cheesy Roasted Potatoes

Prep Time: 20 mins Cook Time: 20 mins

Ingredients

• 1 potato peeled and cubed
• 2 Tbsp olive oil
• 1/2 Tsp. garlic powder
• 1/2 Tsp. paprika
• 1/4 Tsp. salt
• 1/2 Tsp. dried parsley flakes
• 1/3 cup shredded cheese

Instructions

• Soak the potato cubes in cold water for at least 15 mins then drained.

• Combine all ingredients, except parsley flakes and cheese, and toss. Air fry, without stacking, in a lightly greased aluminum foil-lined fryer basket at 360F (180C) for 15-17 min.. Stir a couple of times in between until the potato cubes are tender.

• Pull the fryer basket out, sprinkle the parsley flakes and mix. Top the potato with cheese and push the basket into the air fryer unit for about a minute for the cheese to melt. Serve immediately.

Pork And Beef Recipes

682.Leek And Pork Stir Fry

Total Time: 40 mins

Ingredients

• 1 pound pork shoulder thinly sliced (about 500g)
• 2 Tbsp oyster sauce
• 2 Tbsp soy sauce
• 1 Tbsp sesame oil
• 1 Tsp. garlic powder
• 1 Tsp. onion powder
• 1 Tsp. corn starch
• 1/2 Tsp. black pepper
• 1 cup of leek cleaned and sliced diagonally about 1/2 inch wide

Instructions

• In a large bowl, mix the pork slices with all the seasoning ingredients. Marinate for at least 30 min..

• Lightly grease the inside of the cake barrel.

• Put the marinated pork sliced inside the cake barrel. Air fry at 380F (190C) for about 8 min., stirring once in the middle

• Add the leek to the pork and mix. Air fry again at 380F (190C) for another 4-5 mins until the pork is cooked through.

683.Hearty Meatball Soup

Prep Time: 10 mins Cook Time: 45 mins

Ingredients

Meatball Ingredients:
• 1 pound ground meat I used ground turkey, about 500g
• 1/4 cup yellow onion finely chopped
• 1/2 cup Panko breadcrumb
• 1/2 Tbsp Italian seasoning
• 2 Tbsp grated Parmesan cheese
• 1 Tbsp soy sauce
• 2 Tsp. corn starch
• 1 Tsp. garlic powder
• 1 Tsp. onion powder
• 1/4 Tsp. black pepper or to taste

Soup Ingredients:
• 2 Tbsp olive oil
• 1 stalk celery diced
• 2 Tbsp garlic chopped
• 1/4 cup yellow onion diced
• 1/4 cup tomato ketchup
• 1/2 cup carrot diced
• 1 large zucchini diced
• 1/4 cup wine I used rice wine
• 1 can crushed tomatoes
• 1/2 can corn kernels
• 2 cup broth I used chicken
• 1 Tbsp Italian seasoning
• 2 Tsp. garlic powder
• Salt and pepper to taste

Instructions

• Line the fryer basket with a grill mat or a sheet of lightly greased aluminum foil.

• In a large bowl, combine all the meatball ingredients. Take about 1 Tbspful of the mixture and roll it into a ball. Place the meatballs into the fryer basket. Spritz the meatballs with oil and air fry at 380F (190C) for about 8 minutes, shake the basket once in the middle.

• In the meantime, pour olive oil into a pot and saute garlic, celery, and onion until fragrant. Add in the rest of the soup ingredient and bring it to boil.

• When the meatballs are done, transfer them to the pot. Fill the pot with water just enough to cover all the ingredients. Let it simmer for about 30 minutes.

• Serve on its own or with pasta or bread.

684.Easy Swedish Meatballs

Prep Time: 15 mins Cook Time: 25 mins

Ingredients

• Ingredients for meatballs: (makes

about 30 meatballs)
- 1 1/2 pound ground meat or ground meat mixtures (about 750g) I used ground turkey
- 1/3 cup Panko breadcrumbs
- 1/2 cup milk
- 1/2 of an onion finely chopped
- 1 large egg
- 2 Tbsp parsley dried or fresh
- 2 Tbsp minced garlic
- 1/3 Tsp. salt
- 1/4 Tsp. black pepper or to taste
- 1/4 Tsp. paprika
- 1/4 Tsp. onion powder

Ingredients For Sauce:
- 1/3 cup butter
- 1/4 cup all-purpose flour
- 2 cups broth I used chicken broth
- 1/2 cup milk
- 1 Tbsp soy sauce
- Salt and pepper to taste

Instructions
- Line the fryer basket with a grill mat or a sheet of lightly greased aluminum foil.
- In a large bowl, combine all the meatball ingredients and let it rest for 5-10 min..
- Using the palm of your hands, roll the meat mixture into balls of the desired size. Place them in the fryer basket and air fry at 380F (190C) for 8-12 mins (depending on the size of the meatballs) until they are cooked through and internal temperature exceeds 165F or 74C)
- In the meantime, melt the butter in a wok or a pan. Whisk in flour until it turns brown. Pour in the broth, milk, and soy sauce and bring it to a simmer. Season with salt and pepper to taste. Stir constantly until the sauce thickens.
- Serve meatballs and sauce over pasta or mashed potato. Sprinkle some parsley if desired.

685. Garlicky Honey Sesame Ribs

Prep Time: 3 hrs Cook Time: 15 mins
Ingredients
- 2 pounds pork ribs about 1000g
- 1/3 cup honey
- 1/4 cup soy sauce
- 1/4 cup ketchup
- 1/4 cup brown sugar

- 2 tbsp rice vinegar
- 2 tbsp lemon juice
- 2 tsp sesame oil
- 2 Tbsp minced garlic
- 1 Tbsp sesame seeds for garnish or to taste
- 1/4 cup scallions for garnish or to taste

Instructions
- In a medium-size bowl, prepare the marinade by mixing honey, soy sauce, ketchup, brown sugar, vinegar, and lemon juice.
- Take a Ziploc bag, put the ribs in the bag. Pour about 2/3 of the marinade into the bag, mix with the ribs, and marinate in the refrigerator for at least 3 hours or best overnight. Save the rest of the marinade for later use.
- Take the pork ribs out from the refrigerator 30 mins before air frying.
- Line the fryer basket with a grill mat or a sheet of lightly greased aluminum foil.
- Put the ribs inside the fryer basket without stacking. Air fry at 380F (190C) for about 10-12 min., flip once in the middle until the edges are slightly caramelized.
- In the meantime, use a wok to saute garlic in sesame oil until fragrant, about one minute. Then, add in the rest of the marinade. Stir constantly until the sauce thickens.
- When the ribs are done, toss the ribs in the wok along with sesame seeds. Sprinkle some scallions on top to serve.

686. Chinese BBQ Pork Pastry

Prep Time: 20 mins Cook Time: 10 mins
Ingredients
- 1/2 pound char siu Chinese BBQ pork diced (about 250g)
- 2 tsp olive oil
- 1/4 onion diced
- 1 1/2 tbsp ketchup
- 1/2 tbsp oyster sauce
- 1 tbsp sugar
- 1 tbsp honey
- 1/4 cup water
- 1 1/2 tbsp corn starch
- 1 1/2 tbsp water
- 1 roll of store-bought pie crust thawed according to package instruction

- 1 egg beaten

Instructions
- In a wok or frying pan, saute diced onion in olive oil until translucent. Then, add in ketchup, oyster sauce, sugar, honey, and 1/4 cup water. Stir and bring to boil
- In the meantime, take a small bowl and mix the corn starch with 1 1/2 Tbsp of water. Add the mixture to the wok and stir constantly until the sauce thickens.
- Add the diced BBQ pork and stir. Wait for it to cool, then put it in the refrigerator for at least 30 min.. The refrigeration will cause the mixture to harden and will make it easier to handle later.
- Line the fryer basket with a grill mat or lightly greased aluminum foil.
- Roll out pie crusts. Use a bowl size of your choice to trace circles onto the pie crust and cut them into circular pieces. Mix the leftover pie crust, use a rolling pin to roll them out. Repeat the above process to get as many circular crusts as you can.
- Lay the circular pieces of pie crust on the counter and put the desired amount of BBQ pork filling in the center. Fold pie crust in half and keep the fillings inside. Use the back of a fork to press down on the edges of the pie crust to seal.
- Carefully transfer the pork pastry into the fryer basket. Brush the top surface with egg and air fry at 340F (170C) for about 5-6 minutes. Flip the pastries over and brush the top side with egg. Air fry again at 340F (170C) for another 5-6 mins until the surface is golden brown.

687. Vietnamese Style Pork Chops

Prep Time: 2 hrs Cook Time: 10 mins
Ingredients
- 1 pound pork shoulder blade steak (about 500g)
- 3 tbsp dark soy sauce
- 3 tbsp fish sauce
- 2 tbsp minced garlic
- 2 tbsp grated ginger
- 2 tbsp brown sugar
- 1 Lime juice and zest
- 1 tbsp olive oil
- Chopped cilantro to garnish optional

Instructions

• Mix the pork with all the pork ingredients, except olive oil and cilantro, and marinate in the refrigerator for at least 2 hours or best overnight. Take the meat out of the refrigerator 30 mins before air frying.

• Pat dry the pork steaks with a paper towel. Brush both sides of the meat with olive oil and place them in the fryer basket without stacking. Air fry at 400F (200C) for 8-10 min., flip once in the middle until the pork is cooked through when the temperature exceeds 145F or 63C.

• Garnish with chopped cilantro if desired.

688. Meatballs With Gochujang Mayo

Prep Time: 15 mins Cook Time: 10 mins

Ingredients

Ingredients For Meatballs:

• 1 pound ground pork (about 500g) or meat of your choice
• 1/4 cup onion finely chopped
• 2 Tbsp soy sauce
• 2 Tsp. corn starch
• 1 Tsp. dried basil
• 1 Tsp. garlic powder
• 1 Tsp. onion powder
• 1/4 Tsp. white pepper powder

Ingredients For Sauce:

• 1 Tsp. Gochujang (Korean hot pepper paste)
• 2 Tbsp Mayonnaise
• 2 Tbsp mirin

Instructions

• Line the fryer basket with a grill mat or a sheet of lightly greased aluminum foil.

• Mix all the meatball ingredients then form them into about 1 inch balls. Put the meatballs in the fryer basket without stacking. Spray some oil onto the meatballs and air fry at 380F (190C) for 8-10 mins until the meat is cooked through at its proper temperature.

• In the meantime, take a small bowl and mix all the sauce ingredients.

• Dip the meatballs in the Gochujang mayo to serve.

689. Five Spices Salt And Pepper Pork

Prep Time: 1 hr 15 mins Cook Time: 15 mins

Ingredients

Ingredients For Pork:

• 1/2 pound pork shoulder cut into thick slices (about 250g)
• 2 Tbsp soy sauce
• 1/2 Tbsp rice wine
• 1 Tsp. corn starch
• 1 Tbsp minced garlic
• 1 Tsp. sesame oil
• 1/2 Tsp. sugar
• 1/2 Tsp. Chinese five spices powder
• 1/4 cup tapioca starch

Instructions

• Marinate the meat with all the pork ingredients, except tapioca flour, for at least 1 hour.

• Dredge the pork slices in tapioca flour, shake off excess, and let sit for about 5-10 mins until you don't see dry flour.

• Place the meat in the fryer basket and spray some oil. Air Fry at 380F for 12-14 min., flip once in the middle until the surface appears to be nice and crisp.

• Toss in the pork slices with chili pepper and chopped cilantro. Then, sprinkle some salt and pepper to serve.

690. Seasoned Pork Chops With Avocado Salsa

Prep Time: 5 mins Cook Time: 15 mins

Ingredients

• 2 pork chops or pork shoulder blade steaks
• 2 Tbsp olive oil
• 1 Tsp. sea salt
• 1 Tsp. black pepper
• 1/2 Tsp. paprika
• 1/2 Tsp. garlic powder
• 1/2 Tsp. cumin

Ingredients For Salsa:

• 1 avocado pitted and diced
• 1 large tomato seeded and diced
• 1/3 cup cilantro chopped
• 1 lime juiced
• 1/4 yellow onion finely chopped
• Pickled or fresh jalapeno to taste chopped (optional)
• Salt to taste

Instructions

• In a small bowl, mix all the dry seasonings in the pork ingredients and set them aside.

• Use a paper towel to pat dry the pork chop then rub both sides with olive oil.

Generously season both sides of the meat and air fry at 380F (190C) for 10-12 min., flip once in the middle until the internal temperature exceeds 145F (63C).

• In the meantime, combine all the ingredients for the salsa in a large bowl.

• When the pork chops are done, let them rest for a few min.. Scoop some salsa over the pork chops to serve.

691. Chinese Style Ground Meat Patties

Prep Time: 5 mins Cook Time: 10 mins

Ingredients

• 1 pound ground pork about 500g
• 1 egg
• 1 Tsp. corn starch
• 1/3 cup green onion chopped
• 1/4 cup cilantro stems chopped
• 1/4 cup yellow onion finely diced
• 2 1/2 Tbsp oyster sauce
• 2 Tbsp minced garlic
• 1/4 Tsp. black pepper

Instructions

• Mix all the ingredients and making sure everything is well combined.

• Line the fryer basket with lightly greased aluminum foil. Form patties of equal size and place them into the fryer basket. Air fry at 380F (190C) for 8-10 mins until fully cooked when the internal temperature exceeds 160F (72C).

692. Pork Satay Skewers

Prep Time: 1 hr Cook Time: 15 mins

Ingredients

Ingredients For Pork:

• 1 pound pork shoulder (about 500g) cut into 1/2 inch cubes
• 1/4 cup soy sauce
• 2 Tbsps brown sugar
• 2 Tbsps Thai sweet chili sauce
• 1 Tbsp sesame oil
• 1 Tbsp minced garlic
• 1 Tbsp fish sauce

Ingredients For The Sauce:

• 1/3 cup peanut butter
• 3 Tbsp coconut milk or milk or water
• 2 Tbsp Thai Sweet Chili Sauce
• 2 Tsp. minced garlic
• 2 Tsp. brown sugar
• 1 Tsp. fish sauce

Instructions

• Combine all the ingredients for the

pork and marinate for at least 1 hour or overnight.

- In the meantime, soak the wooden skewers in water for at least 15 min.. Also, combine all the ingredients for the dipping sauce and set aside.
- Thread the pork cubes onto skewers and place them in the fryer basket. Air fry at 380F (190C) for about 8-10 min., flip once in between until the meat is cooked through.

693. Pork Chop Marinated With Fermented Bean Curd

Prep Time: 2 hrs Cook Time: 15 mins
Ingredients
Ingredients For Pork:
- 1 pound pork shoulder cut into chunks.
- 1-2 pieces fermented bean curd chunk
- 2 Tsp. rice wine
- 1 Tbsp dark soy sauce
- 1 Tbsp brown sugar
- 2 Tbsp garlic minced
- Other ingredients:
- Fried garlic chips to taste
- Thinly sliced green onions to taste
Instructions
- Marinate the pork with all the pork ingredients for at least 2 hours or best overnight in the refrigerator.
- Leave the pork out at room temperature 30 mins before air frying.
- Line the fryer basket with a sheet of lightly greased aluminum foil. Put the pork inside without stacking and air fry at 380F (190C) for about 10-12 mins until the temperature exceeds 160F (71C).
- Sprinkle some fried garlic and green onion to serve.

694. Pork And Bean Curd Strips

Prep Time: 1 hr Cook Time: 15 mins
Ingredients
Ingredients For Pork:
- 1/2 pound pork shoulder cut into strips (about 250g)
- 2 Tsp. sesame oil
- 2 Tsp. corn starch
- 1 Tsp. sugar
- 1 Tbsp rice wine
- Other ingredients:
- 8 ounces bean curd cut into strips

- 1 Tsp. olive oil
- 4-5 cloves of garlic
- 1/4 cup chicken broth
- 3-4 green onion cut into thin slices
- 1 Tsp. black vinegar optional
Instructions
- Marinate the pork strips with all the pork ingredients for at least one hour or overnight.
- In the meantime, mix 1 Tsp. of olive oil with bean curd strips. In a lightly greased cake pan, air fry the bean curd at 380F (190C) for 6 min., stir once in between. Remove and set aside when done.
- Put the garlic on the bottom of the cake pan put pork strips over it. Air fry at 380F (190C) for about 8 minutes, stir once in between.
- Add in the chicken broth, bean curd strips, and half of the green onion and mix. Air fry at 380F (190C) for 4-5 mins until the pork is cooked through.
- Mix in the remaining green onion and black vinegar to serve.

695. Marinated Korean Style Pork With Mushroom

Prep Time: 35 mins Cook Time: 15 mins
Ingredients
Ingredients For The Pork:
- 1/2 pound pork shoulder (about 250g) cut into thin slices
- 1/4 cup Korean BBQ sauce
Other Ingredients:
- 1 Tbsp garlic minced
- 1/2 cup button mushroom cut into slices
- 1/3 cup carrots sliced
- 1 Tbsp Korean BBQ sauce
- 1 Tsp. corn starch
- 1/3 cup green onion cut into 1-inch pieces
Instructions
- Marinate the pork with Korean BBQ sauce and set aside for 30 min..
- In a lightly greased cake barrel, put the garlic and carrots on the bottom then put pork slices on top. Air fry at 380F (190C) for about 8-9 min., stir once in between.
- Mix the rest of the ingredients into the cake pan and air fry again 380F (190C) for 3-4 mins until pork is cooked through.

696. Cilantro Lime Spiced Pork

Prep Time: 1 hr 10 mins Cook Time: 15 mins
Ingredient:
- 12 Ounces pork shoulder thinly sliced
- 1 Tbsp soy sauce
- 1/4 Tsp. cumin
- 1/2 Tsp. curry
- 1/4 Tsp. salt
Other Ingredients:
- 1/4 cup cilantro chopped
- 3-4 Tbsp of lime juice or to taste
Instructions
- Marinate the pork slices with all the ingredients for at least 1 hour.
- Line the fryer basket with lightly greased aluminum foil. Place the pork slices in the basket and air fry at 380F (190C) for 10-12 mins until the pork is cooked through.
- When done, mix in cilantro and lime juice to serve.

697. Chinese Style Meatloaf With Pickled Cucumber

Prep Time: 5 mins Cook Time: 20 mins
Ingredients For Pork:
- 1 pound ground pork about 500g
- 1 egg
- 1/4 cup pickled cucumber chopped
- 1 Tbsp minced garlic
- 1 Tbsp soy sauce
- 3 Tbsp juice from pickled cucumber
- 2 Tsp. of rice wine
- 1 Tsp. sesame oil
- 1 Tsp. sugar
- 2 Tsp. corn starch
- White pepper powder to taste
Other Ingredients:
- Chicken or beef stock
- 1/4 cup thinly sliced scallions to garnish.
Instructions
- Mix all the pork ingredients and scoop the meatloaf into each ramekin and put them inside the fryer basket.
- Fill the stock up to almost to the rim of the ramekins as the fluid may dry up during the air frying process. Put a sheet of aluminum foil over the ramekins and place a steamer rack on top. Air fry at 360F (170C) for about 15-18 mins until the meat temperature exceeds 160F (72C).

- Sprinkle some green onion on top to serve.

698. Honey Garlic Pork

Prep Time: 35 mins Cook Time: 15 mins

Ingredients For Pork:
- 1/2 pound pork shoulder thinly sliced
- 1 Tbsp soy sauce
- 1 Tsp. garlic powder
- 1 Tsp. corn starch
- 1 Tsp. rice wine
- 3 Tbsp tapioca starch

Ingredients For Sauce:
- 1 Tbsp sesame oil
- 3 Tbsp minced garlic
- 2 Tbsp honey
- 2 Tbsp Chinese black vinegar
- 1 Tbsp soy sauce

Instructions

- In a Ziploc bag, combine all the ingredients for the pork, except for tapioca starch, and marinate for 30 minutes. Before air frying, add tapioca starch to the bag and shake well. The goal is to have all the pork slices coat with some tapioca starch.
- Place a sheet of lightly greased aluminum foil in the fryer basket. Put the pork slices in and try to separate them as much as possible. Air fry at 400F (200C) for about 15 min., stir 2-3 times in between until the edges are crispy.
- In the meantime, saute garlic with sesame oil in a saucepan for about one minute. Then combine the rest of the ingredients and stir constantly until the sauce thickens.
- When the pork is done, toss the pork slices in the sauce to serve.

699. General Tso's Pork

Prep Time: 15 mins Cook Time: 20 mins

Ingredients For Pork:
- 1 pound pork shoulder cut into slices
- 1 egg beaten
- 2 Tbsp soy sauce
- 1/4 Tsp. salt
- 1/4 Tsp. black pepper
- 1 Tsp. corn starch
- 1/4 cup tapioca starch
- Ingredients for sauce:
- 1 1/2 Tbsp chili oil
- 2-3 Tbsp minced garlic
- 1 Tbsp grated ginger

- 2 Tbsp soy sauce
- 2 Tbsp vinegar
- 2 Tbsp sugar
- 2 Tsp. corn starch mix with 4 Tsp. water

Instructions

- In a Ziploc bag, mix all the ingredients for the pork, except tapioca starch, and marinate in the refrigerator for at least one hour. Add the tapioca starch into the bag. Shake the bag or mix gently.
- Line the fryer basket with lightly greased aluminum foil. Put the pork slices in and spread them out as much as possible. Air fry at 400F (200C) for 15-17 mins until the outside is crispy and the meat is cooked through, stir 2-3 times in between.
- In the meantime, use a saucepan to saute the garlic and ginger in chili oil for one minute. Add in the rest of the ingredients and bring them to a boil. Add in the corn starch and water mixture, stir until the sauce thickens.
- When the pork is done, toss in the sauce to coat. Sprinkle some chopped green onion to serve.

700. Korean Marinated Pork Belly

Prep Time: 35 mins Cook Time: 15 mins

Ingredients
- 1 pound pork belly with or without skin, (about 500g) cut into thin slices
- 2 Tbsp minced garlic
- 2 Tbsp minced ginger
- 1/2 Tbsp Korean hot pepper paste Gochujang, or to taste
- 3 Tbsp honey
- 3 Tbsp soy sauce
- 1 Tbsp sesame oil
- 1/2 Tbsp apple cider vinegar
- 3 Tbsp toasted white sesame seeds

Instructions

- Prepare the marinade by mixing all other ingredients. Use 3/4 of the marinade to marinate the pork belly for at least 30 mins and save the rest for later use.
- On a lightly greased aluminum foil, air fry the pork belly slices at 380F (190C) for about 12 minutes, stir about 2 times in between, until the meat is cooked through.
- In the meantime, use a saucepan to heat the remaining marinade on the

stovetop. Stir constantly until the sauce thickens. When the pork is done, toss with the sauce.
- To serve, sprinkle some sesame seeds and garnish with cilantro leaves or chopped green onion.

701. Korean Style Pork Chops

Prep Time: 3 hrs Cook Time: 15 mins

Ingredients
- 1 pound pork chops (about 500g)
- 1/2 cup soy sauce
- 1/3 cup brown sugar
- 1/3 cup onion thinly sliced
- 2 Tbsp grated ginger
- 2 Tbsp minced garlic
- 2 Tsp. sesame oil
- 1 Tsp. black pepper
- 1-2 Tsp. Sriracha hot sauce optional
- 3 Tbsp sliced green onions
- 1 Tbsp toasted sesame seeds

Instructions

- Marinate the pork chops in all the ingredients (except sesame seeds and green onion) in the refrigerator for at least 3 hours. Take the pork chops out of the refrigerator about 30 mins before air frying.
- Put the pork chops in the parchment paper-lined fryer basket without stacking. Air fry at 380F (190C) for about 15 mins until the meat temperature is at least 165F (64C).
- Sprinkle some green onion and sesame seeds to serve.

702. Char Siu Pork Chops

Prep Time: 3 hrs Cook Time: 15 mins

Ingredients
- 1 pound pork chop about 500g
- 1/3 cup of store-bought char siu sauce see notes for substitution
- 2 Tbsp soy sauce

Instructions

- Marinate the pork chops in all the ingredients. Refrigerate for at least 3 hours. Take the pork chops out of the refrigerator 30 mins before air frying.
- Place the pork chops in the parchment paper-lined fryer basket and air fry at 380F (190C) for about 15 mins until the meat temperature is at least 165F (64C).

703. Wasabi Lime Steak

Prep Time: 1 hr 15 mins Cook Time: 15

mins

Ingredients for the steak:
- 1 pound flank steak (about 500g) thinly sliced
- 1 Tbsp wasabi paste
- 2 Tbsp soy sauce
- 2 Tbsp lime juice
- 1/2 Tbsp Sesame oil
- 1 Tbsp grated ginger

Wasabi Mayonnaise:
- 1/4 cup mayonnaise
- 1 Tbsp water
- 1 Tbsp mirin non-alcohol
- 1 Tbsp lime juice
- 1 Tsp. wasabi paste
- Other ingredients:
- 1/3 cup cilantro chopped

Instructions
- Combine all the ingredients for the steak and mix well. Marinate for at least one hour or overnight in the refrigerator.
- Line the fryer basket with a sheet of lightly greased aluminum foil. Spread the beef slices out as much as possible and air fry at 380F (190C) for about 8-10 min., stir 1-2 times in between.
- In the meantime, mix the mayonnaise, water, mirin, lime juice, and wasabi paste in a medium bowl.
- Drizzle the wasabi mayo over the steak and garnish with some cilantro to serve.

704.Korean Beef With Veggie
Prep Time: 40 mins Cook Time:15 mins
Ingredients For Beef:
- 12 ounces flank steak cut into thin slices
- 1 Tsp. corn starch
- 1/4 cup Korean BBQ sauce

Other Ingredients:
- 2 cups mung bean sprouts
- 3 cups baby spinach or spinach cut into 2-inch length
- 1 Tbsp sesame oil
- 1 Tbsp minced garlic
- 1 Tbsp freshly grated ginger
- 1 Tbsp rice wine
- 2-3 Tbsp Korean BBQ sauce
- 1 Tsp. jalapeno pepper sliced (optional)
- 1 Tsp. toasted sesame seeds

Instructions
- In a large bowl, marinate the beef with Korean BBQ sauce and corn starch for about 30 minutes.
- In a small pot, boil the mung bean sprouts until tender. Remove and set aside. Then, boil the spinach for about one minute and set aside.
- In a lightly greased cake pan, air fry the marinated beef at 380F (190C) for about 7-8 min., stir once in between.
- In the meantime, stir fry the garlic, grated ginger, and jalapeno pepper with sesame oil in a wok for about 1-2 mins until fragrant. Add in the Korean BBQ sauce and rice wine and bring to a boil then turn the stove off.
- Toss the spinach, bean sprouts, and beef slices in the sauce. Sprinkle some sesame seeds over the dish to serve.

705.Mongolian Beef
Prep Time: 15 mins Cook Time: 10 mins
Ingredients For The Beef:
- 1 pound flank steak cut into 1/4 inch thick pieces (about 500g)
- 2 Tsp. soy sauce
- 1 Tsp. sesame oil
- 2 Tsp. cornstarch
- 1/4 cup tapioca starch

Ingredients For The Sauce:
- 2 Tbsp olive oil
- 1 Tbsp grated ginger
- 1 Tbsp minced garlic
- 2 Tbsp soy sauce
- 3 Tbsp brown sugar
- 3-4 green onion green parts only, cut into 1-2 inch pieces
- 1-2 Tsp. sesame seeds optional

Instructions
- In a Ziploc back, marinate the steak pieces with soy sauce, sesame oil, and corn starch for at least 15 min.. Add in the tapioca starch and shake, making sure all the pieces are coated.
- Line the fryer basket with a sheet of lightly greased aluminum foil. Put the steak pieces in, preferably without stacking, and air fry at 400F (200C) for about 8 minutes, flip once until the edges look slightly crispy.
- In the meantime, in a frying pan or a wok, saute the garlic and grated ginger in olive oil for about 1-2 mins until fragrant. Add in the soy sauce and brown sugar and stir constantly until

the sauce thickens.
- When the beef is done, toss the beef in the sauce, followed by the green onion. To serve, sprinkle the dish with sesame seeds if desired.

706.Beef Wrapped Cheesy Mushroom
Prep Time: 10 mins Cook Time: 10 mins
Ingredients
- 12 pieces of thinly sliced beef
- 12 button mushrooms
- 1/3 cup cheddar cheese
- 1/4 cup Korean BBQ sauce
- 2 Tbsp sesame seeds optional
- 6 pieces of pickled jalapeno peppers chopped (optional)

Instructions
- Marinate the beef with Korean BBQ sauce for 15 min..
- Use a paper towel to wipe the button mushroom clean and remove the stems. Fill the mushroom with cheese and some chopped jalapeno pepper.
- Take a slice of beef and wrap it around the mushroom. Air fry at 380F (190C) for about 5 mins (depending on the thickness of the meat).
- Sprinkle some sesame seeds to serve.

707.Cumin Beef
Prep Time: 3 hrs Cook Time:15 mins
Ingredients
- 1 pound beef flank steak thinly sliced
- 3 Tbsp Soy sauce
- 2 Tbsp chopped garlic
- 1 Tbsp Shaoxing wine
- 1 1/2 Tbsp cumin
- 1 Tbsp paprika
- 1 1/2 Tsp. corn starch
- 1/4 Tsp. salt
- 1/2 Tsp. black pepper
- 1/2 Tsp. hot pepper flakes optional
- 1/3 cup chopped cilantro
- 1/2 cup chopped green onion

Instructions
- Marinate the beef slices with all of the ingredients, except cilantro and green onion, in the refrigerator for at least 3 hours. Remove from the refrigerator about 30 mins before air frying.
- In a lightly greased foiled lined fryer basket, air fry the beef slices at 380F (190C), stir 2-3 times in between, about 10-12 min., or until the desired degree of doneness is reached.

- When done, toss the beef with cilantro and green onion to serve.

708.Meatballs With Gochujang Mayo

Prep Time: 15 mins Cook Time: 10 mins
Ingredients For Meatballs:
- 1 pound ground pork
- 1/4 cup onion finely chopped
- 2 Tbsp soy sauce
- 2 Tsp. corn starch
- 1 Tsp. dried basil
- 1 Tsp. garlic powder
- 1 Tsp. onion powder
- 1/4 Tsp. white pepper powder
- Ingredients for sauce:
- 1 Tsp. Gochujang
- 2 Tbsp Mayonnaise
- 2 Tbsp mirin

Instructions
- Line the fryer basket with a grill mat or a sheet of lightly greased aluminum foil.
- Mix all the meatball ingredients then form them into about 1 inch balls. Put the meatballs in the fryer basket without stacking. Spray some oil onto the meatballs and air fry at 380F (190C) for 8-10 mins until the meat is cooked through at its proper temperature.
- In the meantime, take a small bowl and mix all the sauce ingredients.
- Dip the meatballs in the Gochujang mayo to serve.

709.Pie Crust Beef Empanadas

Prep Time: 30 mins Cook Time: 15 mins
Ingredients
- 1 pound ground beef
- 1-2 Tbsp pickled jalapeno chopped (optional)
- 1 Tsp. corn starch
- 1 Tsp. cumin
- 1 Tsp. chili powder
- 1/4 Tsp. salt or to taste
- 1/4 Tsp. pepper or to taste
- 1 Tsp. olive oil
- 2 Tbsp minced garlic
- 1/4 cup diced onions
- 2 rolls of pie crust thawed according to package instruction
- 1 cup Mexican blend cheese or to taste
- 1 egg beaten

Instructions
- In a large bowl, mix the ground beef with jalapeno (optional), corn starch, cumin, chili powder, salt, and pepper, and let it sit for about 5-10 minutes.
- Line the fryer basket with a grill mat or lightly greased aluminum foil.
- In a large skillet, saute garlic and onion for about 1 minute until fragrant. Add in the ground beef and stir fry until beef is cooked through and the onion is translucent.
- Roll out pie crusts. Use a bowl size of your choice to trace circles onto the piecrust and cut them into circular pieces. Mix the leftover pie crust, use a rolling pin to roll them out. Repeat the above process to get as many circular crusts as you can.
- Lay the circular pieces of pie crust on the counter and put the desired amount of filling and cheese in the center. Fold pie crust in half and keep the fillings inside. Use the back of a fork to press down on the edges of the pie crust.
- Carefully transfer the empanadas into the fryer basket. Brush the top surface with egg and air fry at 350F (175C) for about 4-5 minutes. Flip the empanadas over and brush the top side with egg. Air fry again at 350F (175C) for another 3-4 mins until the surface is golden brown.

710.Tri-tip Roast

Prep Time: 1 hr 10 mins Cook Time: 30 mins
Ingredients
- 2 pound tri-tip roast excess fat trimmed
- 6-8 garlic cloves
- 1/4 cup olive oil
- 2 1/2 tsp salt
- 1 tsp garlic powder
- 1/2 tsp black pepper

Instructions
- In a food processor or a blender, pulse the seasoning ingredient several times.
- Pat dry the tri-tip roast with a paper towel and put it inside a large Ziploc bag.
- Put the seasoning mixture inside the bag, squeeze out as much air as possible and seal the bag. Spread the seasoning and massage the meat at the same time, making sure all surfaces are covered with the mixture. Leave it at room temperature for about one hour.
- Insert a meat thermometer into the center of the roast. Air fry at 400F (200C) for about 20-25 mins until the desired temperature is reached, 125F (52C) for rare, 135F (57C) for medium-rare and 145F (63C) for medium.
- Let the roast rest for about 10 mins before serving.

711.Cheese Stuffed Meatballs

Prep Time: 10 mins Cook Time: 15 mins
Ingredients
- 1 lb ground beef (about 500g)
- 3/4 cup crushed saltine crackers or breadcrumb
- 1/4 cup onion chopped
- 1/4 cup Parmesan cheese
- 1 tsp onion powder
- 1 tsp garlic powder
- 1 tsp parsley
- 1/2 tsp salt
- 1/4 tsp pepper
- 2 eggs
- 3 sticks mozzarella cheese cut into 4-5 pieces each

Other Ingredients:
- Spaghetti sauce

Instructions
- Line the fryer basket with a grill mat or lightly greased aluminum foil.
- Mix all the ingredients, except mozzarella cheese. Scoop about 2 Tbsps of the meat mixture and wrap one piece of the cheese in the middle to form a ball. Place the meatballs inside the air fryer.
- Spray the meatballs with some oil. Air fry at 380F (190C) for about 6 min.. Flip, spray some oil again, and air fry at 380F (190C) for another 4-5 min..
- Take a pot to heat the spaghetti sauce. When the meatballs are done, simmer the meatballs in the sauce for a few min..
- Serve the meatballs and sauce with your favorite pasta.

712.Asian Meatball Stuffed Zucchini

Prep Time: 15 mins Cook Time: 15 mins
Ingredients
- 1 pound ground beef (about 500g)
- 1 egg beaten
- 1/4 cup minced onion
- 2 tbsp chopped basil

- 2 tbsp oyster sauce
- 1 tsp corn starch
- 1/4 tsp black pepper or to taste
- 2 large zucchinis peeled

Instructions

- Combine all the ingredients, except zucchini, and let it marinate at room temperature for about 15 min..
- Line the fryer basket with a large sheet of aluminum and spray it with some oil.
- Cut zucchini into 1-inch sections and hollow out the center with a sharp knife. Then, fill the zucchini with the beef mixture and put them into the fryer basket without stacking.
- Air fry at 360F (180C) for 10-12 minutes. Flip sides about halfway through and continue to air fry until the ground meat is cooked through when then internal temperature exceeds 160F (72C).

713. Air Fried Bulgogi

Prep Time: 30 mins Cook Time: 10 mins

Ingredients

- 1 pound thinly sliced beef rib-eye
- 1/4 cup thinly sliced onion
- 1/3 cup Korean BBQ Sauce or to taste
- 2 tbsp grated ginger
- 1/4 cup thinly sliced green onion
- 2 tsp sesame seed

Instructions

- In a large Ziploc bag, combine the meat, onion, Korean BBQ sauce, and ginger and mix well. Marinate for at least 30 minutes.
- Lin the fryer basket with a grill mat or a sheet of lightly greased aluminum foil.
- Spread the beef out inside the basket as much as possible and air fry at 380F (190C) for 8-10 min., stir once in the middle until the meat is cooked through.
- Sprinkle with sesame seeds and green onion to serve.

714. Black Pepper Steak And Mushroom

Prep Time: 1 hr 15 mins Cook Time: 15 mins

Ingredients For Steak:

- 1 pound rib eye steak about 500g, cubed (about 1/2 inch pieces)
- 1 tsp cornstarch

- 1 tbsp rice wine
- 1 tbsp lime juice
- 2 tsp light soy sauce
- 2 tsp dark soy sauce
- 2 tbsp grated ginger
- 1/4 tsp black pepper or to taste

Other Ingredients:

- 8 button mushrooms thinly sliced
- 1 tbsp garlic finely chopped
- 1 tbsp oyster sauce

Instructions

- In a Ziploc bag, mix all the ingredients for the steak and marinate for about one hour.
- Line the fryer basket with a sheet of lightly greased aluminum foil.
- Put the steak inside the fryer basket and air fry at 380F (190C) for about 5 min..
- Add all other ingredients to the steak and stir. Air fry at 380F (190C) for another 4-5 mins or until the desired doneness is reached.
- Carefully pour the drippings from aluminum foil into a wok and bring it to a boil. Stir constantly until the sauce thickens.
- Toss the steak cubes in the wok to coat. Serve immediately.

715. Marinated Rib-Eye Steak

Prep Time: 2 hrs Cook Time: 10 mins

Ingredients

- 1 pound rib-eye steak (or any cut you prefer) 500g
- 2 Tbsp grated Ginger
- 2 Tbsp Honey
- 1 Tbsp minced garlic
- 1 Tbsp sesame oil
- 2 Tsp. apple cider vinegar
- 1/4 cup soy sauce
- 1 Tsp. scallion optional
- 1 Tsp. dried minced garlic optional

Instructions

- Combine all the seasoning ingredients, except scallions and fried minced garlic, and marinate the steak in a Ziploc bag for at least 2 hours or best overnight in the refrigerator.
- If refrigerated, remove from the fridge about 30 mins before air frying.
- Preheat air fryer for 400F (200C) for 3-4 minutes.
- Place the steak in the preheated air

fryer and air fry at 400F (200C) for 6-8 min., flip once in the middle, until the desired doneness is reached.

- Let the steak rest for about 10 mins before cutting. Sprinkle some fried minced garlic and scallions to serve if desired.

716. Asian Flavored Ribs

Prep Time: 2 hrs 15 mins Cook Time: 10 mins

Ingredients

- 1 pound beef short ribs about 500g
- 1/3 cup brown sugar
- 1/4 cup oyster sauce
- 1/4 cup soy sauce
- 2 tbsp rice wine
- 3 cloves garlic minced
- 1 tbsp fresh grated ginger
- 1 tbsp scallions

Instructions

- Put the short ribs in a large Ziploc bag.
- In a large bowl, mix all other ingredients, except scallions. Pour the mixture into the Ziploc bag and mix it with the ribs. Marinate the ribs for about 2 hours.
- Line the fryer basket with a sheet of lightly greased aluminum foil.
- Place the ribs inside the fryer basket, without stacking. Air fry at 380F (190C) for 8-10 min., flip once in the middle until the surface is slightly caramelized.
- Sprinkle some scallions to garnish.

717. Ground Beef Stir Fry

Prep Time: 5 mins Cook Time: 10 mins

Ingredients

- 1/2 pound ground beef (or ground meat of your choice) about 500g
- 1 Tsp. corn starch
- 1/4 cup Korean BBQ sauce to taste
- 1/4 cup zucchini julienned
- 1/4 cup steamed carrots julienned
- 1 Tbsp sesame seeds
- 1/4 cup scallions

Instructions

- In a large bowl, mix the ground beef, corn starch, and Korean BBQ sauce. Marinate for about 5 min..
- Add the carrots and zucchini to the bowl, and gently mix.
- Transfer the mixture to a lightly greased cake barrel and use a spatula to spread them out a bit. Air fry at 380F

(190C) for 8-10 minutes, stirring twice in the middle until the ground beef is cooked through.

- Sprinkle some sesame seeds and scallions to serve.

718.Easy Swedish Meatballs

Prep Time: 15 mins Cook Time: 25 mins

Ingredients For Meatballs: (Makes About 30 Meatballs)

- 1 1/2 pound ground meat or ground meat mixtures (about 750g) I used ground turkey
- 1/3 cup Panko breadcrumbs
- 1/2 cup milk
- 1/2 of an onion finely chopped
- 1 large egg
- 2 Tbsp parsley dried or fresh
- 2 Tbsp minced garlic
- 1/3 Tsp. salt
- 1/4 Tsp. black pepper or to taste
- 1/4 Tsp. paprika
- 1/4 Tsp. onion powder

Ingredients For Sauce:

- 1/3 cup butter
- 1/4 cup all-purpose flour
- 2 cups broth I used chicken broth
- 1/2 cup milk
- 1 Tbsp soy sauce
- Salt and pepper to taste

Instructions

- Line the fryer basket with a grill mat or a sheet of lightly greased aluminum foil.
- In a large bowl, combine all the meatball ingredients and let it rest for 5-10 min..
- Using the palm of your hands, roll the meat mixture into balls of the desired size. Place them in the fryer basket and air fry at 380F (190C) for 8-12 mins (depending on the size of the meatballs) until they are cooked through and internal temperature exceeds 165F or 74C)
- In the meantime, melt the butter in a wok or a pan. Whisk in flour until it turns brown. Pour in the broth, milk, and soy sauce and bring it to a simmer. Season with salt and pepper to taste. Stir constantly until the sauce thickens.
- Serve meatballs and sauce over pasta or mashed potato. Sprinkle some parsley if desired.

719.Kimchi Beef

Prep Time: 30 mins Cook Time: 10 mins

Ingredients For Beef:

- 1 pound tri-tip strip about 500g, thinly sliced
- 1/4 cup kimchi juice
- 1 Tbsp oyster sauce
- 1 Tbsp soy sauce
- 1 Tbsp freshly grated ginger
- 1 Tsp. sesame oil
- 1 Tsp. corn starch

Other Ingredients:

- 1/2 cup kimchi or to taste
- 1/4 cup thinly sliced green onion
- 1 Tsp. sesame seeds optional

Instructions

- In a large bowl, combine all the beef ingredients and marinate for at least 30 min..
- Line the fryer basket with a sheet of lightly greased aluminum foil.
- Transfer the content of the bowl to the fryer basket and air fry at 380F (190C) for 5 minutes. Stir once in the middle.
- Add the kimchi and green onion to the beef and stir. Air fry again at 380F (190C) for about 3 minutes.
- Sprinkle some toasted sesame seeds to serve if desired.

720. A Minnesotan's Beef And Macaroni Hotdish

Prep: 15 mins Cook: 25 mins Total: 40 mins

Ingredient

- 1 pound ground beef
- 2 cups elbow macaroni
- ½ large green bell pepper, coarsely chopped
- ½ large onion, chopped
- 1 (16 ounces) can tomato sauce
- 1 pound tomatoes, coarsely chopped
- 2 teaspoons Worcestershire sauce
- 1 Tsp. soy sauce
- 1 Tsp. salt
- ¾ Tsp. dried basil
- ¾ Tsp. dried oregano
- ½ Tsp. ground black pepper
- ½ Tsp. chili powder
- ¼ Tsp. garlic powder
- ⅛ Tsp. hot pepper sauce (such as Tabasco®)
- 1 cup beef broth

Instructions

- Cook beef in a large skillet over medium heat, stirring occasionally, until browned, about 5 min.. Transfer beef to a bowl.
- Cook macaroni, bell pepper, and onion in the same skillet over medium heat for 3 min.. Add cooked beef, tomato sauce, tomatoes, Worcestershire sauce, soy sauce, salt, basil, oregano, ground black pepper, chili powder, garlic powder, and hot pepper sauce. Pour in beef broth. Cover skillet and simmer until macaroni is tender about 15 minutes. Remove lid and simmer, stirring occasionally, until thickened, 5 to 10 min..

721.Tennessee Meatloaf

Prep Time: 40 mins Cook Time: 1 hr Additional Time: 15 mins Total Time: 1 hr 55 mins

Ingredients

Brown Sugar Glaze:

- ½ cup ketchup
- ¼ cup brown sugar
- 2 Tbsps cider vinegar

Meatloaf:

- Cooking spray
- 1 onion, chopped
- ½ green bell pepper, chopped
- 2 cloves garlic, minced
- 2 large eggs, lightly beaten
- 1 Tsp. dried thyme
- 1 Tsp. seasoned salt
- ½ Tsp. ground black pepper
- 2 teaspoons prepared mustard
- 2 teaspoons worcestershire sauce
- ½ Tsp. hot pepper sauce (such as tabasco®)
- ½ cup milk
- ⅔ cup quick-cooking oats
- 1 pound ground beef
- ½ pound ground pork
- ½ pound ground veal

Instructions

- Combine ketchup, brown sugar, and cider vinegar in a bowl; mix well.
- Preheat oven to 350 degrees F (175 degrees C). Spray two 9x5-inch loaf pans with cooking spray or line with aluminum foil for easier cleanup (see Cook's Note).
- Place onion and green pepper in a covered microwave container and cook

until softened, 1 to 2 minutes. Set aside to cool.

• In a large mixing bowl, combine garlic, eggs, thyme, seasoned salt, black pepper, mustard, Worcestershire sauce, hot sauce, milk, and oats. Mix well. Stir in cooked onion and green pepper. Add ground beef, pork, and veal. With gloved hands, work all ingredients together until completely mixed and uniform.

• Divide meatloaf mixture in half and pat half of mixture into each prepared loaf pan. Brush loaves with half of the glaze; set the remainder of glaze aside.

• Bake in preheated oven for 50 min.. Remove pans from oven; carefully drain fat. Brush loaves with remaining glaze. Return to oven and bake for 10 mins more. Remove pans from the oven and allow the meatloaf to stand for 15 mins before slicing.

Soup And Stew Recipes

722.Peruvian Roast Chicken With Green Sauce

Prep Time: 8 hrs Cook Time: 20 mins
Ingredients
For The Chicken
• 4 pieces of skin-on chicken thighs
• 3 Tbsp olive oil
• 1/4 cup lime juice
• 4 garlic cloves chopped
• 1 Tbsp salt
• 2 Tsp. paprika
• 1 Tsp. black pepper
• 1 Tbsp cumin
• 1 Tsp. dried oregano
• 2 teaspoons sugar
• 1 Tsp. black pepper
For The Green Sauce
• 3 jalapeno peppers seeded and chopped
• 1 cup cilantro leaves
• 2 cloves garlic chopped
• 1/2 cup mayonnaise
• 1/4 cup sour cream
• 1 Tbsp lime juice
• 1/2 Tsp. salt
• 1/8 Tsp. black pepper
• 2 Tbsp olive oil
Instructions
• Blend all the seasoning ingredients for the chicken in the food processor until

smooth to make the marinade.

• Put the chicken thighs in a large Ziploc bag and pour in the marinade. Marinate the thighs in the refrigerator overnight.

• Air fry at 380F (190C) skin side down for about 8-10 min.. Turn the thighs over and air fry again at 380F (190C) for another 6-8 mins until temp at 165F (74C).

• To make the green sauce, first, blend everything (except olive oil) until smooth. Then, drizzle olive oil slowly and blend to thicken. Refrigerate until ready to serve.

• Drizzle the sauce over the chicken or serve it on the side.

723.Chicken Pasta In Creamy Chimichurri Sauce

Prep Time: 1 hr 30 mins Cook Time: 15 mins
Ingredients
• 4 pieces of skinless boneless chicken thighs
• 1/4 cup bacon bits
• 2 tbsp butter bacon grease, or olive oil
• 1 tbsp all-purpose flour
• 2/3 cup milk or heavy creamer
• 1 pound cooked spaghetti about 500g or to taste
For The Chimichurri Sauce:
• 1 1/2 cup cilantro minced
• 1/4 cup thinly sliced chives or green onions
• 2 Tbsp minced garlic
• 2 limes zested and juiced
• 1/2 cup olive oil
• 3 Tbsp chopped pickled jalapenos
• 1/2 Tsp. sea salt
• 1/4 Tsp. black pepper
Instructions
• Use the food processor or a blender to mix all the ingredients for chimichurri sauce for about 10 seconds. Pour about 3/4 cup out and set aside.

• In a Ziploc bag, put the chicken pieces in the bag along with the rest of the sauce. Seal the bag, mix, and let them marinate in the refrigerator for at least one hour.

• Take the chicken out of the refrigerator 30 mins before air frying.

• Line the fryer basket with a grill mat or a sheet of lightly greased aluminum foil.

• Place the chicken inside the fryer basket without stacking. Air fry at 380F (190C) for 10-12 mins until fully cooked through when the internal temperature exceeds 165F (74C)

• In the meantime, heat butter in a wok or a frying pan. Add in flour and stir constantly until it bubbles and thickens. Then, add in milk and 3/4 cup of chimichurri sauce and stir until thickens.

• When done, stir in the chicken and serve over pasta.

• Sprinkle some bacon bits to serve.

724.Air Fryer Cashew Chicken

Prep Time: 40 mins Cook Time: 10 mins
Ingredients
• 1 lb boneless and skinless chicken thigh or breast (about 500g) cut into bite-size pieces
Ingredients For Marinade:
• 1/4 cup hoisin sauce
• 1/4 cup soy sauce
• 1 Tbsp white vinegar
• 1 Tbsp sugar
• 2 Tbsp freshly grated ginger
• 1 Tsp. corn starch
• Other ingredients:
• 1 Tsp. olive oil
• 2 Tbsp minced garlic
• 1/4 cup steamed carrots diced
• 2 Tbsp scallions
• 1/3 cup roasted cashew halves
Instructions
• Mix all the marinade ingredients.

• Put the chicken pieces in a Ziploc bag along with 2/3 of the sauce and mix. Marinade the chicken for about 30 min.. If longer, refrigerate it until cooking.

• Line the fryer basket with a grill mat or a sheet of lightly greased aluminum foil.

• Spread the chicken out in the fryer basket and air fry at 380F (190C) for 10-12 mins until cooked through.

• In the meantime, use a wok or a frying pan to saute garlic in olive oil until fragrant, about 1 minute.

• Add the remaining 1/3 of the marinade and stir constantly until the sauce thickens.

• Toss the chicken, carrots, and cashew in the wok to coat. Then, sprinkle some scallions to serve.

725. Air Fryer Roasted Curry Chicken

Prep Time: 2 hrs Cook Time: 20 mins
Ingredients For Chicken:
• 5 pieces skin-on bone-in chicken thighs
• 1/4 cup mayonnaise
• 1 Tbsp brown sugar
• 1 Tbsp garlic minced
• 2 Tbsp soy sauce
• 2 Tbsp grated ginger
• 1 Tsp. curry powder
• 1/4 Tsp. paprika
• 1/4 Tsp. cumin
• Other ingredients:
• 1/2 Tsp. curry powder
• 1/4 Tsp. cumin
• 1/4 Tsp. paprika
• 1/4 cup scallion
Instructions
• Mix all the ingredients for chicken. Marinate the chicken in this marinade for at least 2 hours or overnight in the refrigerator.
• Mix 1/2 Tsp. of curry, 1/4 Tsp. of cumin, and 1/4 Tsp. of paprika and set aside for later.
• Take the chicken out of the refrigerator 30 mins before air frying.
• Line the fryer basket with a grill mat or a sheet of lightly greased aluminum foil.
• Put the chicken thighs into the basket skin side down, without stacking, and air fry at 380F (190C) for 10 minutes.
• Flip the chicken thigh over, now ski side up, and sprinkle some dry seasoning mix over the skin.
• Air fry at 380F (190C) for another 6-7 mins until the meat is cooked through, internal temperature exceeds 170F (77C).
• Sprinkle some scallion to serve

726. Yakitori Japanese Skewered Chicken

Prep Time: 1 hr 10 mins Cook Time: 10 mins
Ingredients
• 1 pound skinless and boneless chicken thigh (about 500g) cut into 1 inch cubes
• 1/4 cup dark soy sauce
• 1/4 cup mirin
• 2 tbsp rice wine
• 2 tbsp brown sugar
• 2 tbsp minced garlic
• 2 tbsp freshly grated ginger
• 1/4 cup scallions for garnish
Instructions
• In a large bowl, mix dark soy sauce, mirin, rice wine, brown sugar, garlic, and ginger. Save about 1/3 of the sauce in a small bowl and set aside for later.
• Put the chicken thigh cubes in the bowl and mix. Marinate for about 1 hour.
• Soak the bamboo skewers in water for at least 15 min..
• Line the fryer basket with a grill mat or a sheet of lightly greased aluminum foil.
• Thread the skewers through the chicken pieces then put the skewers in the fryer basket. Spritz some oil over the skewers and air fry at 380F (190C) for 10-12 minutes, flip once in the middle, until the surface is slightly caramelized and the meat is cooked through.
• In the meantime, use a saucepan to bring the previously set-aside sauce to boil. Stir constantly until the sauce thickens. Put the sauce in a small bowl to be used for dipping.
• Sprinkle the yakitori with scallions and serve with dipping sauce on the side.

727. Chicken With Scallion And Ginger Sauce

Prep Time: 5 mins
Marinate At Least One Hour: 20 mins
Ingredients
• 4 pieces of skinless boneless thighs
• 1/2 tsp salt
• 2 tbsp rice wine
• 3 tbsp olive oil
• 1/4 cup dripping from the chicken
• 1/4 cup scallions
• 2 tbsp freshly grated ginger
• 1 tbsp minced garlic
• Salt to taste
Instructions
• Marinate the chicken with 1/2 Tsp. of salt and rice wine for at least one hour.
• Wrap the thighs in a large, lightly greased aluminum foil (without stacking) and air fry at 380F (190C) for about 15 mins until the internal temperature exceeds 165F (74C).
• When the chicken is done, pour about

1/4 cup of drippings from the foil into a saucepan. Combine it with the rest of the ingredients and bring it to a boil.
• Pour the sauce over the chicken to serve.

728. Chicken And Kimchi Fritters

Prep Time: 10 mins Cook Time: 10 mins
Ingredients For Chicken:
• 2 cups of chicken fully cooked and shredded
• 1/3 cup kimchi finely shopped
• 1/3 cup Japanese Panko
• 1/4 cup shredded cheese I used Mexican blend
• 2 Tbsp green onion finely chopped
• 1 Egg beaten
• Other ingredients:
• Mayonnaise to taste
• Thinly sliced green onions to taste
• Kimchi to taste
Instructions
• Line the fryer basket with a grill mat or a sheet of lightly greased aluminum foil.
• Combine all the ingredients. Then, form them into round patties and place them in the fryer basket without stacking.
• Air fry at 380F (190C) for about 7-8 min., flip once in the middle until the surface is slightly golden brown.

729. Thai Chicken Drumsticks

Prep Time: 10 mins Cook Time: 20 mins
Ingredients For Chicken:
• 8 chicken drumsticks
• 2-3 Tbsp minced garlic
• 3 Tbsp fish sauce
• 2 Tbsp rice wine
• 1 Tsp. sesame oil
• 1 Tsp. black pepper or to taste
• 1/2 Tsp. sriracha hot sauce optional
• 1/4 cup brown sugar
• Juice of one lime
Instructions
• Marinate the chicken drumsticks with all the chicken ingredients in a Ziploc bag and refrigerate for at least 3-4 hours, preferably overnight.
• Remove the chicken from the refrigerator 30 mins before air frying.
• Line the fryer basket with a grill mat or a sheet of lightly greased aluminum foil.

- Air fry at 360F (180C) for about 18-20 mins until the chicken is cooked through when the internal temperature exceeds 170F (77C).
- Drizzle some Thai sweet chili sauce over drumsticks and sprinkle some chopped cilantro to serve.

730. Curry Chicken Tenderloins

Prep Time: 5 mins Cook Time: 15 mins
Ingredients
- 4 pieces of chicken tenderloin
- 2 Tsp. coconut oil melted
- 1/2 Tsp. curry powder
- 1/4 Tsp. paprika
- 1/4 Tsp. garlic powder
- 1/4 Tsp. sea salt

Instructions
- In a small bowl, mix all the dry ingredients.
- Dap dry the tenderloins with a paper towel. Brush coconut oil to both sides of tenderloins. Then, sprinkle the dry ingredients to both sides of the chicken.
- Place the tenderloins in the fryer basket. Air fry at 380F (190C) for 10-12 min., flip once in the middle until the meat is cooked through when internal temperature exceeds 165F (74C).
- Serve the chicken over a bed of greens or rice.

731. Keto Chicken And Kimchi Rice Bake

Prep Time: 10 mins Cook Time: 10 mins
Ingredients
- 1 small head of cauliflower
- 2 cups chicken cooked and chopped
- 1 cup kimchi chopped, or to taste
- 2/3 cup juice from kimchi jar or to taste
- 1 cup shredded mozzarella cheese divided, or to taste
- 1 green onion cut into 1/2 inch pieces
- 1/4 cup green onion thinly sliced to garnish (optional)

Instructions
- Put the cauliflower into a food processor and pulse it a few times so the cauliflower becomes the size of a grain of rice. Transfer it to a large microwavable bowl and microwave for about 4-5 min..
- In the meantime, lightly grease a cake pan and set it aside.

- When the cauliflower is done, stir in chicken, kimchi, kimchi juice, 2/3 cup of mozzarella cheese, and large green onion pieces. Then, transfer the mixture to the cake pan.
- Put the cake pan in the fryer basket and air fry at 360F (180C) for about 4 min.. Then, sprinkle the rest of the mozzarella cheese over the top and air fry again at 360F (180C) for 3-4 mins until the cheese melts.
- Sprinkle some green onion on to serve.

732. Roast Chicken Stuffed Avocados

Prep Time: 5 mins Cook Time: 10 mins
Ingredients
- 2 avocados pitted
- 2 cups roast chicken shredded
- 1/3 cup tomato seeded and diced
- 1/4 cup shredded cheese Mexican blend
- 1/4 cup cilantro stems chopped
- 2 Tbsp mayonnaise
- 1 Tbsp Sriracha optional
- Mozzarella cheese to top

Instructions
- Preheat the air fryer at 400F (200C) for 2 min..
- Mix all the ingredients, except Mozzarella cheese, and them on top of avocados. Place them inside the fryer basket.
- Sprinkle some mozzarella cheese over the chicken mixture and let the cheese melt for 1 minute in the preheated air fryer.
- Air fry at 360F (180C) for 4-5 mins until the cheese is slightly golden brown.

733. Kimchi Chicken

Prep Time: 35 mins Cook Time: 15 mins
Ingredients
- 1/2 pound of chicken thigh cut into thin slices
- 1/3 cup kimchi juice from kimchi jar
- 2 Tbsp of grated ginger
- 1 Tsp. soy sauce
- 1/2 Tsp. corn starch
- 1/4 cup kimchi sliced or to taste
- 1 green onion thinly sliced

Instructions
- Mix the chicken slices with corn starch, kimchi sauce, grated ginger, and

soy sauce. Marinate for at least 30 min..
- In a lightly greased cake pan, air fry the chicken at 380F (190C) for about 10-12 mins until the meat is cooked through. When done, add in chopped kimchi and stir. Air fry at 380F (190C) for 2 more min..
- Garnish with green onion to serve.

734. Garlic Parmesan Chicken Tenderloins

Prep Time: 10 mins Cook Time: 15 mins
Ingredients
- 4-6 pieces of chicken tenderloins defrosted and pat dry
- 1 egg beaten
- 1 Tbsp Italian seasoning
- 1/2 cup shredded Parmesan cheese
- 1 Tsp. garlic powder
- 1/2 Tsp. paprika
- 1/4 Tsp. cayenne pepper or to taste

Instructions
- In a shallow plate, mix all the dry ingredients and set aside.
- Dip the tenderloins into egg then dredge them in seasoning mix.
- Place the tenderloins in the fryer basket and air fry at 380F (190C) for 10-12 minutes, flip once in the middle, until the chicken is cooked through at 165F (74C) and the surface is golden brown.

735. Easy Chicken With Creamed Spinach

Prep Time: 5 mins Cook Time: 15 mins
Ingredients For Chicken:
- 4 boneless skinless chicken (thighs, breasts, or tenderloins)
- 1 Tbsp olive oil
- 1/2 Tsp. paprika
- 1/2 Tsp. garlic powder
- 1/2 Tsp. onion powder
- 1/2 Tsp. dried basil
- Salt and pepper to taste

Ingredients For Creamed Spinach:
- 2 cans of Campbell Cream of Chicken Soup
- 1 can of water using the soup cans
- 1 Tbsp olive oil
- 1/2 yellow onion diced
- 4 garlic cloves minced
- 8 ounces baby spinach or chopped spinach
- 1/3 cup grated Parmesan cheese or to taste

Instructions

- In a small bowl, mix all the dry ingredients for the chicken and set aside.
- Use a paper towel to pat dry the chicken pieces and rub them with olive oil. Season both sides of the chicken with the seasoning mixture and place them inside the fryer basket. Air fry at 380F (190C) for 10-12 minutes, flip once in the middle until the chicken is fully cooked and the internal meat temperature exceeds 165F (74C).
- In the meantime, use a skillet to saute the onion and garlic in olive oil until the onion is translucent. Stir in two cans of soup and one can of water and bring it to boil. Then, turn the heat to low and stir in the cheese.
- When the chicken is done, transfer the chicken to the skillet and add in the spinach. Let it simmer for 2-3 mins until the spinach wilts.

736.Easy Dry Rub Chicken

Prep Time: 5 mins Cook Time: 15 mins
Ingredients
- 4 skin-on boneless chicken thighs
- 2 Tbsp olive oil
- 1 Tbsp Italian seasoning
- 2 teaspoons paprika
- 2 teaspoons garlic powder
- 2 teaspoons onion powder
- 1/2 Tsp. salt
- 1/2 Tsp. black pepper

Instructions
- Mix all the dry ingredients and set aside.
- Make a few slices on the flesh part of the chicken thigh without cutting through. Use a paper towel to pat dry the thighs.
- Rub both sides of the chicken with olive oil. Then, rub both sides of the chicken generously with the dry mix.
- Line the fryer basket with lightly greased aluminum foil. Put the chicken thighs into the basket without stacking. Air fry at 360F (180C) for about 8 min.. Then, air fry again at 400F (200C) for about 4 mins until cooked through at 165F (74C).

737.Breaded Parmesan Chicken

Prep Time: 10 mins Cook Time: 15 mins
Ingredients

- 4 boneless skinless chicken thighs
- 1 egg
- 2 Tbsp milk
- Salt and pepper to taste
- 3/4 cups Italian breadcrumbs. If using regular breadcrumbs, add 2 teaspoons of Italian seasoning to the bread crumbs.
- 1/3 cup freshly grated Parmesan cheese
- 1 1/2 Tsp. garlic powder
- Olive oil in a spritzer

Instructions
- Mix egg and milk in a shallow dish and season with salt and pepper.
- In a shallow dish, mix bread crumbs, Parmesan cheese, and garlic powder.
- Dab dry the chicken thighs with paper towels. Dip chicken thighs in the egg mixture and dredge both sides with bread crumbs mix.
- Place thighs inside the fryer basket without stacking and spray some olive oil on chicken thighs.
- Air fry at 380F (190C) for 10-12 mins until the thighs are fully cooked through when the internal temperature exceeds 165F (74C).

738.Fusion Chicken Wrap

Prep Time: 5 mins Cook Time: 15 mins
Ingredients For Chicken:
- 3 pieces of skinless boneless chicken thighs or breast, thinly sliced
- 3 Tbsp soy sauce
- 1 Tbsp garlic powder
- 1 Tsp. corn starch
- 1 Tsp. Chinese five spices powder
- 1/4 Tsp. black pepper

Other Ingredients:
- 4 Tortillas
- 1/3 cup Hoisin sauce or to taste
- 1/2 cup thinly sliced green onion
- Green salad optional

Instructions
- Mix all the ingredients for the chicken and marinate for at least one hour in the refrigerator. Air fry at 380F (190C) for 10-12 min., stir 1-2 times in between until chicken is fully cooked through.
- To assemble, spread some Hoisin sauce onto a piece of tortilla. Put some green onion, chicken, and come green salad (optional) on the tortilla and wrap it up.

739.Honey Ginger Chicken

Prep Time: 3 hrs Cook Time: 15 mins
Ingredients For Chicken:
- 4 pieces skin-on boneless chicken thighs
- 2 Tbsp minced garlic
- 2 Tbsps soy sauce
- 2 Tbsp rice wine
- 2 Tbsp honey
- 2 Tbsp grated ginger

Instructions
- In a Ziploc bag, combine all the ingredients for the chicken and marinate in the refrigerator for at least 3 hours or overnight. Remove from the refrigerator 30 mins before air frying.
- Line the fryer basket with a sheet of lightly greased aluminum foil. Put the chicken thighs in the basket skin side down without stacking. Air fry at 380F (190C) for about 7 min..
- Turn the chicken thighs over so they are skin side up. Air fry again at 380F (190C) for 5-6 mins until the chicken is cooked through when the internal temperature exceeds 165F (74C). Save the juices on the foil to drizzle over rice if desired.
- Sprinkle some green onion and sesame seeds to serve.

740.Three Cup Chicken

Prep Time: 40 mins Cook Time: 20 mins
Ingredients For The Chicken:
- 1 pound boneless skinless thighs (about 500g) cut into one inch pieces
- 2 Tbsp sesame oil
- 4 Tbsp soy paste
- 3 Tbsp rice wine
- 2 Tbsp mirin
- 2 Tbsp grated ginger

Other Ingredients:
- 2 Tsp. olive oil
- 5 cloves of garlic
- 6-7 slices of ginger
- Red chili pepper optional
- 1 Tsp. sesame oil
- 1 bunch of basil
- 2 green onion cut into one-inch pieces

Instructions
- Mix all of the seasonings in the chicken ingredients and marinate the chicken with half of the marinade for about 30 mins

- Put the garlic cloves and ginger slices into the cake pan and drizzle them with 2 teaspoons of olive oil. Air fry at 400F (200C) for about 2-3 min..
- Add in the chicken along with its marinade and air fry at 380F (190C) for 10 minutes, stir two times in between. Add the rest of the marinade, 3/4 of the green onion, 3/4 of the basil, and chili pepper (optional), and stir. Air fry at 380F (190C) for 6-7 mins stirring once in between until the chicken is cooked through.
- When done, mix the rest of the basil and green onion and drizzle 1 Tsp. of sesame oil to serve.

741.Mushroom Chicken
Prep Time: 35 mins Cook Time: 15 mins
Ingredients For Chicken:
- 1 Tbsp soy sauce
- 1 Tbsp Shaoxing wine
- 1 Tbsp corn starch
- Ingredients for the sauce:
- 3 Tbsp oyster sauce
- 1 Tbsp Shaoxing wine
- 1 Tbsp soy sauce
- 2 Tbsp chicken stock
- 2 Tsp. grated ginger
- 1 Tsp. sugar
- 1/4 Tsp. black pepper
Other Ingredients:
- 1/4 lbs button mushroom
- 3 cloves garlic chopped
- 1 green onion cut into 1-inch pieces
- 1 Tsp. sesame oil
Instructions
- Marinate the chicken with soy sauce, Shaoxing wine, and corn starch for at least 30 min..
- In a small bowl, mix all the ingredients for the sauce,
- In a lightly greased cake, pan put garlic on the bottom of the pan then put in the marinated chicken. Air fry at 380F (190C) for 10 mins stirring once in the middle.
- Stir in the sauce and air and mushroom and air fry at 380F (190C) for about 4 mins until the chicken is cooked through.
- When done, stir in the sesame oil and green onion to serve.

742.Thai Basil Chicken

Prep Time: 45 mins Cook Time: 15 mins
Ingredients For Chicken:
- 1/2 pound boneless skinless chicken thighs thinly sliced
- 3 Tbsps minced garlic
- 1 Tbsp fish sauce
- 1/2 Tbsp olive oil
- 1 Tsp. sugar or to taste
- 1 Tsp. corn starch
- 1/2 Tbsp dark soy sauce
- 1/2 Tsp. light soy sauce
- 1/2 Tbsp oyster sauce
- 1/4 Tsp. white pepper powder
Instructions
- Marinate the chicken in all the meat ingredients for about 30 min..
- In a lightly greased cake pan, air fry the onion at 320F (160C) for about 3-4 min.. Put the marinated chicken over the onion and air fry at 380F (190C) for about 10 mins until the meat is cooked through, stirring twice in between.
- Finally, stir in the basil leaves, jalapeno, and chicken broth into the cake pan. Air fry again at 380F (190C) for 2 min..
- Serve over rice or when done.

743.Salt And Pepper Wings
Prep Time: 30 mins Cook Time: 25 mins
Ingredients For The Wings:
- 18 chicken wings
- 3 Tbsp soy sauce
- 1 Tbsp minced garlic
- 2 Tsp. sugar
- 2 Tsp. rice wine
- 1 Tsp. sesame oil
- 2 egg yolks
- Other ingredients:
- 1/2 cup tapioca starch
- Thinly sliced red chili pepper or jalapeno optional
- 2 Tbsp thinly sliced green onion
- Salt to taste
- White pepper powder to taste
- Chopped cilantro for garnish
Instructions
- In a Ziploc bag, marinate the wings with all the other wing ingredients combined for at least 30 mins in the refrigerator.
- Add the tapioca starch into the bag and shake. Let the bag sit at room temperature. When you see the tapioca

starch appears to be moist (no longer white), put them in the fryer basket. Air fry at 380F (190C) for 20-22 minutes, turn the wings twice in between. During the second turn, put in the hot chili peppers and continue to air fry until the wings exceed 165F (74C) and the skin is crispy.
- Place the wings in a large mixing bowl and toss with the salt, pepper, green onion, and cilantro. Serve the wings while still hot.

744.Roasted Cornish Hen
Prep Time: 5 mins Cook Time: 40 mins
Ingredients
- 1 Cornish hen completely defrosted and pat dry
- 1/2 Tsp. salt
- 1/2 Tsp. Italian seasoning
- 1/2 Tsp. paprika
- 1/2 Tsp. garlic powder
- 1/4 Tsp. black pepper
Instructions
- Combine all the dried ingredients and set them aside. Put a steamer rack inside an aluminum lined fryer basket.
- Generously rub the surface of the Cornish hen with seasoning mix and place the Cornish hen on the rack with the breast side facing up. Spray some oil on the Cornish hen. Stick the thermometer probe inside the breast and covered the hen with a sheet of aluminum foil. If possible, use another steamer rack to hold the foil down.
- Air fry at 390F (195C) for about 30 minutes. Remove the foil and air fry again at 390F (195C) for another 7-8 mins until the temperature of the breast exceeds 170F (77C).
- Leave the Cornish hen in the air fryer for 10 mins before serving.

745.Miso Marinated Chicken
Prep Time: 3 hrs Total Time: 20 mins
Ingredients
- 3 boneless chicken thighs
- 3 Tbsp miso
- 1 Tbsp soy sauce
- 1 Tbsp mirin
- 1 Tbsp rice wine
Instructions
- Combine miso, soy sauce, mirin, and rice wine and mix well. Marinate the chicken with the sauce mixture in the

refrigerator for at least 3 hours or overnight.

- Take the chicken out of the refrigerator 30 minute before air frying.
- Place the chicken thighs skin-side down in the fryer basket lined with lightly greased aluminum foil. Air fry at 380F (190C) for about 12 minutes. Flip, then air fry again at 380F (190C) for 6-7 mins or until the meat temperature exceeds 165 (74C).

746. Black Bean Sauce Marinated Chicken

Prep Time: 4 mins Cook Time: 20 mins
Ingredients
- 3 boneless chicken thighs
- 1 Tbsp Black Bean Sauce
- 1 Tbsp oyster sauce
- 1 Tbsp mirin
- 1 Tbsp rice wine
- Thinly sliced green onion to garnish

Instructions
- Combine the black bean sauce, oyster sauce, mirin, and rice wine. Marinate the chicken with the sauce mixture and refrigerate for at least 3 hours or overnight.
- Take the chicken out of the refrigerator 30 minute before air frying. Line the fryer basket with lightly greased aluminum foil.
- Place the chicken thighs in the fryer basket skin side down and air fry at 380F (190C) for about 12 minutes. Flip, then air fry again at 380F (190C) for 6-7 mins or until the meat temperature exceeds 165 (74C). Save the drippings.
- Thinly slice the chicken, garnish with green onion, and drizzle with some drippings to serve.

747. Tomato And Pesto Chicken

Prep Time: 5 mins Cook Time: 20 mins
Ingredients
- 2 skinless and boneless chicken thighs
- 1-2 Roma tomatoes cut into 1/4 inch slices
- 1/4 cup pesto sauce
- 1/3 cup shredded Mozzarella cheese
- black pepper to taste
- 1/2 Tsp. parsley flakes

Instructions
- Cover the chicken thighs with a large piece of saran wrap. Use a heavy object or a rolling pin to lightly pound the chicken so the thighs are somewhat flattened and even in thickness throughout.
- Line the fryer basket with a sheet of lightly greased aluminum foil. Place the thighs in the basket and sprinkle with some black pepper.
- Scoop and spread about 2 Tbsps of pesto sauce onto the chicken thighs and top them with a layer of tomato slices. Air fry at 360F (180C) for 14 min..
- Sprinkle Mozzarella cheese over the tomato slices and air fry at 380F (190C) for about 4-5 mins until meat temperature exceeds 165F (74C).
- Garnish with some parsley to serve.

748. Chicken Fajitas

Prep Time: 45 mins Cook Time: 20 mins
Ingredients For The Chicken:
- 1 1/2 pound skinless boneless chicken thighs (about 750g) cut into strips
- 1/2 cup chopped onion
- 1 Tbsp olive oil
- 1 lime juiced
- 1 Tsp. salt
- 1 1/2 Tsp. ground cumin
- 1 1/2 Tsp. garlic powder
- 1 Tsp. chili powder
- 1/2 Tsp. paprika

Instructions
- Combine all the ingredients for the chicken and marinate it in the refrigerator for at least 30 min..
- Cut the bell peppers into thin slices and microwave for about 2-3 min..
- Air fry chicken strips on a lightly greased aluminum foil or a baking pan at 320F (160C) for about 16-18 mins until all the meat is cooked through, stirring every 3-4 min.. During the last stir, mix in the bell pepper and continue to air fry until completion.
- To serve, wrap the chicken with tortilla and top it with chopped green onion, cilantro, cheese, and sour cream if desired.

749. Keto Muffins

Prep Time: 5 mins Cook Time: 15 mins
Ingredients
- 8 oz ground turkey or chicken
- 1 Tsp. garlic powder
- 1/4 cup shredded cheese
- 1/4 Tsp. black pepper
- 1 egg beaten
- 1/4 cup chopped basil
- 1/4 cup chopped green onion
- 2 Tbsp chopped pickled jalapeno optional
- 1/4 Tsp. salt

Instructions
- In a large bowl, mix the ground turkey, garlic powder, shredded cheese, and black pepper. Divide the ground meat mixture into four portions.
- Lightly grease the muffin cups. Scoop one portion of the ground meat into each cup then press it against the walls and form it into a cup shape. Air fry at 380F (190C) for 6 min..
- In the meantime, mix the egg with basil, green onion, and salt. Then, scoop the egg mixture into each cup and air fry again at 380F (190C) for another 6-7 mins until the egg is cook through.

750. Basil Chicken Zucchini Wrap

Prep Time: 10 mins Cook Time: 15 mins
Ingredients
- 1 large chicken breast butterflied
- 1 medium zucchini cut into 1/4 inch thick slices
- 7-8 basil leaves
- 1/4 Tsp. black pepper
- 4 strips of bacon

Instructions
- On a cutting board, cover the butterflied chicken breast with a large sheet of saran wrap. Use a rolling pin or a heavy object to pound the chicken so the thickness is even throughout. Then, cut the chicken into 4 pieces.
- Sprinkle some black pepper onto the chicken. Then, put the zucchini slice and 1 or 2 basil leaves on top of each chicken and roll it up. Finally, take one strip of bacon and wrap it around the chicken roll. Secure it with toothpicks if necessary.
- Place a metal steamer rack inside the fryer basket and place the wraps on the rack. Air fry at 400F (200C) for 10-12 mins or until the internal meat temp exceeds 165F (74C).

751. Garlic Chicken Roll

Prep Time: 45 mins Cook Time: 20 mins
Ingredients
- 4 pieces of chicken breast or thigh
- 1/4 cup of minced garlic divided

- 4 Tsp. of rice wine divided
- 1 Tsp. of pink Himalayan salt divided
- white pepper powder to taste
- 2 Tbsp of chopped fresh Thai basil optional

Instructions
- Butterfly the chicken breast to make the breast into one large thinner piece and cover it with saran wrap. Use a rolling pin or a heavy pan to pound the meat so the chicken is uniform in thickness. Sprinkle 1 Tsp. rice wine, 1/4 Tsp. salt, 1 Tbsp minced garlic, and some white pepper powder over each piece of chicken.
- Roll the chicken up. Then, use a sheet of aluminum foil to wrap the chicken tightly the way one would wrap a candy (like Tootsie Roll). Refrigerate for at least 30 minutes.
- Place the foil-wrapped chicken rolls in the fryer basket and air fry at 320F (160C) for 18-20 minutes. Check the internal meat temperature by inserting a food thermometer directly through the aluminum foil. The chicken is done when the temperature exceeds 165F (74C). Let cool before cutting it into slices.
- This dish is usually served chilled. Sprinkle some chopped fresh Thai basil to serve.

752.Cheesy Chicken Balls

Prep Time: 10 mins Cook Time: 15 mins
Ingredients
- 10 oz Ground chicken or turkey 300g
- 1 egg
- 1/4 cup minced yellow onion
- 1/2 Tsp. garlic powder
- 1/2 Tsp. parsley flakes
- 1/4 Tsp. salt
- 1/4 Tsp. black pepper
- Cheddar cheese cubes or take the slices of cheese together
- 1/4 cup Japanese Panko about 14g carbs (Optional)
- 1/4 cup mayo
- 2 Tbsp Sriracha hot sauce or to taste
- 1-2 Tbsp honey optional

Instructions
- Mix ground chicken, egg, onion, garlic powder, parsley flakes, salt, and black pepper together.
- Take a cube of cheddar and wrap the

ground meat around it. Roll it in the Panko and place it inside the parchment-lined fryer basket. Air fry at 360F (180C) for 12-14 min., turn the chicken cheese balls once in the middle until the meat is cooked through.
- in the meantime, mix the mayo, Sriracha, and honey. To serve, drizzle the sriracha mayo over the chicken cheese balls or use it as a dip.

753.Chicken Zucchini Boats

Prep Time: 30 mins Cook Time: 15 mins
Ingredients
- 3 Medium Zucchini
- 8 oz ground or finely chopped chicken (about 250g)
- 1/4 cup finely chopped kimchi optional
- 1 Tbsp oyster sauce
- 1 Tsp. Gochujang Korean hot pepper sauce
- 1 Tsp. sesame seeds
- 1 Tsp. sesame oil
- 1/2 Tsp. corn starch
- 1/3 cup Mozzarella cheese
- 2-3 Tbsp thinly sliced fresh basil

Instructions
- Marinate the chicken with all the ingredients, except Mozzarella cheese and basil, for at least 30 min..
- Line the fryer basket with a grill mat or a sheet of lightly greased aluminum foil. Cut zucchini lengthwise to about 1/4-1/2 inch thickness and put them side by side inside the fryer basket. Top the zucchini slices with ground meat mixture and air fry at 360F (180C) for about 8 min..
- Sprinkle cheese over ground chicken and let it melt in the air fryer unit for about 1 minute. Then, air fry at 380F (190C) for about 3 mins until the cheese is lightly golden brown.
- Sprinkle with some thinly sliced fresh basil leaves to serve.

754.Air Fryer Chicken Tenders

Prep Time: 5 Mins Cook Time: 30 Mins
Total Time: 35 Mins Yield: 4 Servings
Ingredients
- 12 chicken tenders, (1 1/4 lbs)
- 2 large eggs, beaten
- 1 Tsp. kosher salt
- Black pepper, to taste
- 1/2 cup seasoned breadcrumbs

- 1/2 cup seasoned panko
- Olive oil spray
- Lemon wedges, for serving

Instructions
- Season chicken with salt and pepper.
- Place egg in a shallow bowl. In a second shallow bowl, combine the bread crumbs and panko.
- Dip chicken in the egg, then into the breadcrumb mixture and shake off excess, and place on a large dish or cutting board. Spray both sides of the chicken generously with oil.
- Preheat air fryer to 400F.
- In batches, cook the chicken 5 to 6 mins on each side, until the chicken is cooked through and crispy and golden on the outside. Serve with lemon wedges.

755.Air Fryer Fried Chicken

Prep Time: 10 mins Cook Time: 25 mins
Total Time: 35 mins
Ingredients
- Marinade
- ½ whole chicken cut into separate pieces (breast, thigh, wing, and leg)
- ½ cup hot sauce
- ½ cup buttermilk
- Seasoning
- ¾ cup All-Purpose Flour
- 2 tsp seasoning salt
- 1 tsp garlic powder
- 1 tsp onion powder
- 1 tsp Italian seasoning
- ½ tsp cayenne pepper
- Oil for spraying Canola or Vegetable

Instructions
- Place chicken pieces in buttermilk and hot sauce. Place in refrigerator and allow to marinate anytime from 1-24 hours.
- Whisk together all-purpose flour, seasoning salt, garlic powder, onion powder, Italian seasoning, and cayenne pepper in a bowl. Set aside.
- Place a parchment liner in the Air Fryer basket.
- Remove a piece of chicken from the buttermilk mixture and place in the flour mixture, coating all sides of the chicken and shaking off any excess flour. Place the chicken pieces in the basket in a single layer.
- Close the Air Fryer basket and set the

temperature to 390 degrees Fahrenheit and the timer to 25 min.. Start the Air Fryer.

- After 13 minutes, open the air fryer and spray any flour spots on the chicken. Flip the chicken and spray the other side with oil, ensuring all the flour spots are covered. Close the air fryer and cook for 12 more min..

- Once the timer is up, open the Air Fryer and check chicken pieces with a quick read thermometer. Chicken is done when it reaches an internal temperature of 165 degrees at the thickest part of the chicken.

756. Crispy Air Fryer Chicken Breast

American Prep Time: 10 mins
Cook Time: 10 mins Total Time: 20 mins
Servings: 4

Ingredients

- 2 large boneless skinless chicken breasts sliced into cutlets
- 1 Tbsp oil olive oil, canola, or vegetable oil
- ½ cup (25g) dried bread crumbs
- ½ Tsp. paprika
- ¼ Tsp. dried chili powder
- ¼ Tsp. ground black pepper
- ¼ Tsp. garlic powder
- ¼ Tsp. onion powder
- ¼ Tsp. cayenne pepper
- ½ Tsp. salt

Instructions

Breaded Version:

- Put the chicken breasts in a bowl and drizzle with oil. Make sure that they're well coated.

- In a shallow dish, mix the dried bread crumbs with the spices until well combined.

- Coat each chicken breast in bread crumbs, and transfer to your air fryer basket.

- Air fry in the air fryer at 390°F or 200°C for 10-12 minutes. After the first 7 min., open the air fryer and flip the chicken on the other side then continue cooking (cook for 3 min., depending on the size of the chicken breast used).

Unbreaded Version:

- Drizzle oil over your boneless skinless chicken breasts, and season with your favorite seasonings.

- Place the seasoned chicken breasts in

the Air Fryer basket breast side down, and air fry for 12-15 mins flipping halfway through using kitchen tongs.

- When the cooking time is up, remove from the Air Fryer immediately so that the chicken does not dry out. Allow resting for 5 mins before serving.

757. Air Fryer Chicken & Broccoli

Prep Time: 10 mins Cook Time: 15 mins
Total Time: 25 mins Servings: 4 Servings

Ingredients

- 1 pound (454 g) boneless skinless chicken breast, cut into bite-sized pieces
- 1/4-1/2 pound (113-226 g) broccoli, cut into florets (1-2 cups)
- 1/2 medium (0.5 medium) onion, sliced thick
- 2 Tbsps (30 ml) olive oil or grapeseed oil
- 1/2 Tsp. (2.5 ml) garlic powder
- 1 Tbsp (15 ml) fresh minced ginger
- 1 Tbsp (15 ml) low sodium soy sauce, or to taste (use tamari for gluten free)
- 1 Tsp. (5 ml) sesame seed oil
- 2 teaspoons (10 ml) rice vinegar (use distilled white vinegar for gluten free)
- 2 teaspoons (10 ml) hot sauce (optional)
- Additional salt, to taste
- Additional black pepper, to taste
- Serve with lemon wedges

Instructions

- In a large bowl, combine chicken breast, broccoli, and onion. Toss ingredients together.

Make The Marinade:

- In a bowl, combine oil, garlic powder, ginger, soy sauce, sesame oil, rice vinegar, and hot sauce. Add the chicken, broccoli, and onions to the marinade. Stir thoroughly to combine the marinade with chicken, broccoli, and onions.

- Air Fry: Add ingredients to the air fry basket. Air fry 380°F for 16-20 min., shaking and gently tossing halfway through cooking. Make sure to toss so that everything cooks evenly.

- Check chicken to make sure it's cooked through. If not, cook for additional 3-5 minutes.

- Add additional salt and pepper, to taste. Squeeze fresh lemon juice on top

and serve warm.

758. Air-fried General Tso's Chicken

Active Time: 20 Mins Total Time: 35 Mins

Ingredients

- 1 large egg
- 1 pound boneless, skinless chicken thighs, patted dry and cut into1 to 1
- 1/4-inch chunk
- 1/3 cup plus
- 2 tsp. cornstarch, divided
- 1/4 Tsp. kosher salt
- 1/4 Tsp. ground white pepper
- 7 Tbsp lower-sodium chicken broth
- 2 Tbsps lower-sodium soy sauce
- 2 Tbsp ketchup
- 2 teaspoons sugar
- 2 teaspoons unseasoned rice vinegar
- 1 1/2 Tbsps canola oil
- 3 to 4 chiles de árbol, chopped and seeds discarded
- 1 Tbsp finely chopped fresh ginger
- 1 Tbsp finely chopped garlic
- 2 Tbsps thinly sliced green onion, divided
- 1 Tsp. toasted sesame oil
- 1/2 Tsp. toasted sesame seeds

Ingredients

- Beat egg in a large bowl, add chicken, and coat well. In another bowl, combine 1/3 cup cornstarch with salt and pepper. Transfer chicken with a fork to cornstarch mixture, and stir with a spatula to coat every piece.

- Transfer chicken to air-fryer oven racks (or fryer basket, in batches), leaving a little space between pieces. Preheat the air-fryer at 400°F for 3 minutes. Add the battered chicken; cook for 12 to 16 min., giving things a shake midway. Let dry for 3 to 5 min.. If chicken is still damp on one side, cook for 1 to 2 mins more.

- Whisk together the remaining 2 teaspoons cornstarch with broth, soy sauce, ketchup, sugar, and rice vinegar. Heat canola oil and chiles in a large skillet over medium heat. When gently sizzling, add the ginger and garlic; cook until fragrant, about 30 seconds.

- Re-whisk cornstarch mixture; stir into mixture in skillet. Increase heat to medium-high. When sauce begins to bubble, add chicken. Stir to coat; cook until sauce thickens and nicely clings to chicken, about 1 1/2 min.. Turn off heat; stir in 1 Tbsp green onion and sesame oil. Transfer to a serving plate, and top with sesame seeds and remaining 1 Tbsp green onion.

759.Air Fryer Chicken Wings

Prep Time: 10 Mins Cook Time: 30 Mins
Total Time: 40 Mins

Ingredients

- 2 pounds chicken wings
- Kosher salt, or sea salt, to taste
- Black pepper, to taste
- Garlic powder, optional

Instructions

- If needed, pat dries the chicken wings. Season with salt, pepper, and optional garlic powder.
- For an oil-free version, place an even layer in the air fryer basket/tray. Follow the air fry instructions below.

Air Fry

- Air Fry wings at 400°F/205°C for 30-35 mins or until crispy and cooked through. You must flip the wings over after the first 20 mins of cooking. Or you might need an extra flip to get the wings crispy to your personal preference.
- If using a sauce, toss with a little sauce, then air fry for another 2-4 minutes. Or you can just toss or dip the wings in the sauce after they are finished cooking.

760.Air Fryer Nashville Hot Chicken Tender

Prep Time: 10 mins Cook Time: 30 mins
Total Time: 40 mins

Ingredients

- 1 lb chicken tenders
- ¾ cup milk
- 2 tbsp hot sauce
- ¾ cup panko bread crumbs
- 1 tsp paprika
- ½ tsp italian seasoning
- ½ tsp salt
- ½ garlic powder
- ½ onion powder
- ¼ tsp black pepper
- Salt and pepper to taste
- Oil for spraying canola, olive oil
- Hot paste
- ½ cup peanut oil
- 2 tbsp brown sugar

- 1 ½ tbsp cayenne pepper
- 1 tsp paprika
- 1 tsp dry mustard
- 1 tsp garlic powder
- ½ tsp salt

Instructions

- Season tenders with a little salt and pepper. Set aside. Create a dredging station by whisking milk and hot sauce in one bowl. In a separate bowl, mix panko bread crumbs, paprika, Italian seasoning, salt, garlic powder, onion powder, and black pepper.
- Preheat your air fryer to 375 degrees Fahrenheit.
- Start by coating chicken tenders with milk mixture and drain off excess milk, then coat chicken in panko bread crumbs mixture, ensuring all of the chicken is coated.
- Place chicken in greased air fryer basket or use a parchment sheet liner. Cook on 375 degrees for 14-16 minutes, flipping and spraying chicken halfway through cooking, until chicken is fully cooked and has reached a temperature of at least 165 degrees Fahrenheit.
- Meanwhile, when there are about 5 mins left on the chicken, create the hot paste. Add peanut oil, brown sugar, cayenne pepper, paprika, dry mustard, garlic powder, and salt to a medium-sized saucepan over medium heat and whisk to combine. Once your mixture starts to bubble and simmer, remove from heat.
- Once chicken tenders are done, remove from air fryer and add them to a large bowl. Pour the hot paste over the chicken and toss to combine, making sure hot sauce covers all of the chicken. Serve and enjoy.

761.Air Fryer Sesame Chicken

Prep Time: 10 Mins Cook Time: 25 Mins
Total Time: 35 Mins

Ingredients

Chicken

- 6 Boneless, Skinless Chicken Thighs
- 1/2 Cup Cornstarch
- Olive Oil Spray

Sauce

- 1/4 Cup Soy Sauce or Gluten-Free Soy Sauce
- 2 Tbsp Brown Sugar

- 2 Tbsp Orange Juice
- 5 Tsp Hoisin Sauce or Gluten-Free Sauce
- 1/2 Tsp Ground Ginger
- 1 Garlic Clove, Crushed
- 1 Tbsp Cold Water
- 1 Tbsp Cornstarch
- 2 Tsp Sesame Seeds

Instructions

- Cut the chicken into cubed chunks, then toss in a bowl with Cornstarch or Potato Starch. Use enough to coat the chicken evenly.
- Place in the Air Fryer and cook according to your Air Fryer Manual for chicken. (Note - I cooked ours on 390* for 24 min., 12 mins on each side.)When the chicken is in the air fryer, add a nice even coat of olive oil cooking spray, once it's in the air fryer, it works best to mix it up halfway through cook time and add a coat of spray.
- While the chicken is cooking, in a small saucepan, begin to make the sauce.
- Add the soy sauce, brown sugar, orange juice, hoisin sauce, ground ginger, and garlic to the saucepan on medium-high heat. Whisk this up until well combined.
- Once the sugar has fully dissolved and a low boil is reached, whisk in the water and cornstarch.
- Mix in the sesame seeds. (The sauce should only take about 5 mins or less to make on the stove and then an additional 5 mins to thicken up.)
- Remove the sauce from the heat and set aside for 5 mins to thicken.
- Once the chicken is done, remove it from the air fryer and place it in a bowl, and then coat it with the sauce.
- Serve topped over rice and beans.

762.Air Fryer Chicken Parmesan

Prep Time: 10 min Cook Time: 20 min
Ready in 30 min

Ingredients

Chicken

- 4 boneless skinless chicken breasts (4 oz./125 g each)
- ¼ tsp (2 ml) salt
- ½ cup (125 ml) all-purpose flour
- 2 eggs
- 2 tbsp (30 ml) milk

- 1½ oz. (45 g) fresh parmesan cheese (⅓ cup/75 ml grated)
- ⅔ cup (150 ml) panko breadcrumbs
- 1 tbsp (15 ml) italian seasoning mix
- 8 oz. (250 g) fresh mozzarella cheese
- Pasta
- 3 cups (750 ml) cherry tomatoes
- 1 pkg (9 oz./275 g) refrigerated cheese-filled tortellini
- 1 oz. (30 g) fresh parmesan cheese (¼ cup/60 ml grated)
- ½ cup (125 ml) fresh basil leaves, loosely packed
- 1 tbsp (15 ml) olive oil
- 1 tbsp (15 ml) balsamic vinegar
- ¼ tsp (1 ml) salt

Directions

- Season the chicken with salt. Add the flour to one Coating Tray. Whisk the eggs and milk together in a second coating tray. Grate the Parmesan with the Microplane Adjustable Coarse Grater and combine with the panko and seasoning in the third coating tray.
- Coat each chicken breast in flour first, then the eggs, then the panko mixture.
- Divide the chicken onto two cooking trays of the Deluxe Air Fryer. Place the trays on the top and middle racks.
- Cut the tomatoes in half with the Close & Cut; place them on the drip tray of the air fryer. Turn the wheel to select the setting; press the wheel to select AIR FRY. Turn the wheel to adjust the time to 18 minutes. Press the wheel to start. Switch the trays with the chicken halfway through cooking (you'll hear beeps as a reminder). Cook until the internal temperature reaches 165°F (74°C).
- Slice the mozzarella with the Quick Slice. When the chicken is halfway through cooking, add the tortellini to the 3-qt. (3-L) Micro-Cooker Plus with enough water to cover the pasta. Microwave, covered, on HIGH, for 8 min..
- Drain the pasta and transfer it to a medium mixing bowl. Grate the Parmesan cheese into the bowl with the Microplane® Adjustable Fine Grater. Grate the basil into the bowl with the Herb Mill. Add the remaining pasta ingredients and toss to combine.

- When the timer is up, top each chicken breast with the mozzarella. Turn the wheel to select the AIR FRY setting; press the wheel to select. Turn the wheel to adjust the time to 2 min.. Press the wheel to start.
- Add the tomatoes to the pasta mixture and serve with the chicken.

763. Air Fryer Chicken Breast

Prep Time: 5 mins Cook Time: 20 mins Resting Time: 5 mins Total Time: 30 mins

Ingredients

- 1.5 tbsp cornstarch
- 1.5 tsp garlic powder
- 1 tsp smoked paprika
- 1.5 tsp dried oregano
- 4 chicken breasts boneless
- Oil

Instructions

- Prepare the chicken breasts by trimming off any excess fat and unwanted pieces.
- Mix the spices and cornstarch in a bowl.
- Coat the chicken breasts with oil or cooking spray.
- Sprinkle the spice & cornstarch mixture on the chicken.
- Place a piece of parchment or foil in the bottom of your air fryer basket. Place the chicken on top of that.
- Air fry the chicken for 16-18 mins at 350 degrees F, flipping the chicken breasts halfway through. Cook until the internal temperature in the thickest part of the chicken reaches a minimum of 165 degrees F.
- Let the chicken rest for 5 mins before slicing & plating.

764. Garlic Parmesan Chicken Wings

Prep Time: 5 min Cook Time: 20 min Total Time: 25 min

Ingredients

- 2 pounds chicken wings (or drumsticks)
- 3/4 cup grated Parmesan cheese
- 2 teaspoons minced garlic
- 2 teaspoons fresh parsley (chopped)
- 1 Tsp. salt
- 1 Tsp. pepper

Instructions

- Preheat your air fryer to 400 degrees

for 3-4 mins

- Pat chicken pieces dry with a paper towel.
- Mix Parmesan cheese, garlic, parsley, salt, and pepper together in a bowl.
- Toss chicken pieces in cheese mixture until coated.
- Place chicken in the bottom of the air fryer basket and set the timer to 10-12 min..
- After 12 minutes, use tongs to flip the chicken.
- Fry again for 12 min..
- Remove chicken from the basket with tongs and sprinkle with more Parmesan cheese and parsley.
- Serve with your favorite dipping sauce. We like ranch and buffalo.

765. Marinated chicken breasts

Total Time: 5 Hours

Ingredients

- Chicken marinade
- ¼ cup olive oil
- ¼ cup freshly squeezed lemon juice
- 3 tbsp worcestershire sauce
- 3 medium cloves garlic minced
- ½ tsp salt
- ½ tsp black pepper
- 2 tbsp fresh oregano minced or 2 teaspoons dried oregano
- ¼ cup fresh parsley minced and lightly packed or 4 teaspoons dried parsley
- ¼ cup fresh basil minced and lightly packed or 4 teaspoons dried basil
- Chicken
- 4 8 oz boneless, skinless chicken breasts
- Olive oil cooking spray

Instructions

- In a large bowl, whisk together ingredients for the marinade. Add chicken breast to a large container or resealable bag, pour marinade over chicken, seal, or cover.
- Chill in the refrigerator for up to 4 hours.
- Remove from the refrigerator and let your chicken reach room temperature. (20-30 min.)
- Preheat your air fryer to 370° F for 5 minutes.
- Remove the air fryer basket and place chicken breasts inside, leaving room

between the breasts, so they cook evenly.

• Spray each chicken breast with olive oil.

• Place back into the preheated air fryer and cook for 10 mins

• Remove the basket and flip breasts over, spray again with olive oil and cook for another 6-8 min.; chicken is done when the internal temperature reaches 160° F when checked with an instant-read thermometer.

• Remove your chicken from the air fryer basket and allow it to rest for 5 mins before serving!

• Garnish chicken with fresh oregano, parsley, and/or basil.

766. Amazing Buttermilk Chicken

Prep Time:15 mins Cook Time: 20 mins
Total Time:35 mins

Ingredient
• 1 cup buttermilk
• ½ Tsp. hot sauce
• ⅓ cup tapioca flour
• ½ Tsp. garlic salt
• ⅛ Tsp. ground black pepper
• 1 egg
• ½ cup all-purpose flour
• 2 teaspoons salt
• 1 ½ teaspoons brown sugar
• 1 Tsp. garlic powder
• ½ Tsp. paprika
• ½ Tsp. onion powder
• ¼ Tsp. oregano
• ¼ Tsp. black pepper
• 1 pound skinless, boneless chicken thighs

Instructions
• Combine buttermilk and hot sauce in a shallow dish; mix to combine.

• Combine tapioca flour, garlic salt, and 1/8 Tsp. black pepper in a resealable plastic bag and shake to combine.

• Beat egg in a shallow bowl.

• Mix flour, salt, brown sugar, garlic powder, paprika, onion powder, oregano, and 1/4 Tsp. black pepper in a gallon-sized resealable bag and shake to combine.

• Dip chicken thighs into the prepared ingredients in the following order: buttermilk mixture, tapioca mixture, egg, and flour mixture, shaking off excess after each dipping.

• Preheat an air fryer to 380 degrees F (190 degrees C). Line the air fryer basket with parchment paper.

• Place coated chicken thighs in batches into the air fryer basket and fry for 10 min.. Turn chicken thighs and fry until chicken is no longer pink in the center and the juices run clear for an additional 10 minutes.

767. Crumbed Chicken Tenderloins

Prep Time: 15 mins Cook Time: 12 mins
Total Time: 27 mins

Ingredient
• 1 egg
• ½ cup dry bread crumbs
• 2 Tbsps vegetable oil
• 8 chicken tenderloins

Instructions
• Preheat an air fryer to 350 degrees F (175 degrees C).

• Whisk egg in a small bowl.

• Mix bread crumbs and oil in a second bowl until the mixture becomes loose and crumbly.

• Dip each chicken tenderloin into the bowl of an egg; shake off any residual egg. Dip chicken into the crumb mixture, making sure it is evenly and fully covered. Lay chicken tenderloins into the basket of the air fryer. Cook until no longer pink in the center, about 12 min.. An instant-read thermometer inserted into the center should read at least 165 degrees F (74 degrees C).

768. Air Fryer Blackened Chicken Breast

Prep Time: 10 mins Cook Time: 20 mins
Additional Time: 10 mins
Total Time: 40 mins

Ingredient
• 2 teaspoons paprika
• 1 Tsp. ground thyme
• 1 Tsp. cumin
• ½ Tsp. cayenne pepper
• ½ Tsp. onion powder
• ½ Tsp. black pepper
• ¼ Tsp. salt
• 2 teaspoons vegetable oil
• 2 (12 ounces) skinless, boneless chicken breast halves

Instructions
• Combine paprika, thyme, cumin, cayenne pepper, onion powder, black pepper, and salt in a bowl. Transfer

spice mixture to a flat plate.

• Rub oil over each chicken breast until fully coated. Roll each piece of chicken in a blackening spice mixture, making sure to press down so spice sticks on all sides. Let sit for 5 mins while you preheat the air fryer.

• Preheat an air fryer to 360 degrees F (175 degrees C) for 5 min..

• Place chicken in the basket of the air fryer and cook for 10 minutes. Flip and cook for an additional 10 min.. Transfer chicken to a plate and let rest for 5 mins before serving.

769. Air Fryer BBQ Cheddar-Stuffed Chicken Breasts

Prep Time:10 mins Cook Time: 25 mins
Total Time: 35 mins

Ingredients
• 3 strips bacon, divided
• 2 ounces cheddar cheese, cubed, divided
• ¼ cup barbeque sauce, divided
• 2 (4 ounces) skinless, boneless chicken breasts
• Salt and ground black pepper to taste

Instructions
• Preheat an air fryer to 380 degrees F (190 degrees C). Cook 1 strip of bacon in the air fryer for 2 min.. Remove from air fryer and cut into small pieces. Line the air fryer basket with parchment paper and increase the temperature to 400 degrees F (200 degrees C).

• Combine cooked bacon, Cheddar cheese, and 1 Tbsp barbeque sauce in a bowl.

• Use a long, sharp knife to make a horizontal 1-inch cut at the top of each chicken breast, creating a small internal pouch. Stuff each breast equally with the bacon-cheese mixture. Wrap remaining strips of bacon around each chicken breast. Coat chicken breast with remaining barbecue sauce and place into the prepared air fryer basket.

• Cook for 10 mins in the air fryer, turn and continue cooking until chicken is no longer pink in the center and the juices run clear about 10 more min.. An instant-read thermometer inserted into the center should read at least 165 degrees F (74 degrees C).

770. Air-Fried Buffalo Chicken

Prep Time: 20 mins Cook Time: 16 mins
Total Time: 36 mins

Ingredients

- ½ cup plain fat-free Greek yogurt
- ¼ cup egg substitute
- 1 Tbsp hot sauce (such as Frank's®)
- 1 Tsp. hot sauce (such as Frank's®)
- 1 cup panko bread crumbs
- 1 Tbsp sweet paprika
- 1 Tbsp garlic pepper seasoning
- 1 Tbsp cayenne pepper
- 1 pound skinless, boneless chicken breasts, cut into 1-inch strips

Instructions

- Whisk Greek yogurt, egg substitute, and 1 Tbsp plus 1 Tsp. hot sauce in a bowl.
- Mix panko bread crumbs, paprika, garlic pepper, and cayenne pepper in a separate bowl.
- Dip chicken strips into yogurt mixture; coat with panko bread crumb mixture.
- Arrange coated chicken strips in a single layer in an air fryer. Cook until evenly browned, about 8 mins per side.

771.Crispy Ranch Air Fryer Nuggets

Prep Time: 15 mins Cook Time: 10 mins
Additional Time: 15 mins Total Time: 40 mins

Ingredients

- 1 pound chicken tenders, cut into 1.5 to 2-inch pieces
- 1 (1 ounce) package dry ranch salad dressing mix
- 2 Tbsp flour
- 1 egg, lightly beaten
- 1 cup panko bread crumbs
- 1 serving olive oil cooking spray

Instructions

- Place chicken in a bowl, sprinkle with ranch seasoning and toss to combine. Let sit for 5-10 minutes.
- Place flour in a resealable bag. Place egg in a small bowl and panko bread crumbs on a plate. Preheat air fryer to 390 degrees F (200 degrees C).
- Place chicken into the bag and toss to coat. Lightly dip chicken into the egg mixture, letting excess drip off. Roll chicken pieces in panko, pressing crumbs into the chicken.
- Spray basket of the air fryer with oil and place chicken pieces inside, making sure not to overlap. You may have to do

two batches, depending on the size of your air fryer. Lightly mist chicken with cooking spray.

- Cook for 4 minutes. Turn chicken pieces and cook until chicken is no longer pink on the inside, about 4 more min.. Serve immediately.

Dessert And Snack Recipes

772.Chocolate Chip Cookies

Prep Time: 10 mins Cook Time: 1 hr

Ingredients

- 1/2 cup butter softened
- 1/3 cup granulated sugar
- 1/4 cup packed brown sugar
- 1 egg
- 1/2 teaspoons vanilla extract
- 1/8 Tsp. lemon juice
- 1 cup and 2 Tbsp all-purpose flour
- 1/4 cup rolled oats
- 1/2 Tsp. baking soda
- 1/2 Tsp. salt
- Pinch cinnamon
- 1 1/4 cup semi-sweet chocolate chips
- 1 cup chopped walnuts

Instructions

- Cream butter, sugar, and brown sugar in the bowl of a stand mixer on medium speed for about 2 min..
- Add eggs, vanilla, and lemon juice, blending with mixer on low speed for 30 seconds, then medium speed for about 2 min., or until light and fluffy, scraping down bowl.
- With the mixer on low speed, add flour, oats, baking soda, salt, and cinnamon, blending for about 45 seconds. Don't overmix.
- Remove bowl from mixer and stir in chocolate chips and walnuts.
- Line the fryer basket with a grill mat or a sheet of parchment paper.
- Scoop about one Tbsp of dough onto a baking sheet lined with parchment paper about 2 inches apart.
- Air fry at 260F (130C) for 18-20 min..
- Remove from the air fryer and cool on a wired rack for about 1/2 hour.

773.Hotteok Korean Sweet Pancakes

Prep Time: 2 hrs 30 mins
Cook Time: 10 mins

Ingredients For The Dough:

- 1 1/4 cup all-purpose flour
- 1/2 tsp salt

- 1 tsp white sugar
- 1 tsp instant dry yeast
- 1/2 cup lukewarm milk
- Ingredients for the filling:
- 1/4 cup brown sugar
- 1/4 tsp cinnamon powder
- 1/4 cup chopped walnuts

Instructions

- In a mixing bowl, mix all the dough ingredients with a spatula.
- Lightly cover the bowl with saran wrap and let the dough rise for about 1-2 hours or until the dough doubles in size.
- Punch the dough down several times to release the air in the dough. Then, cover with saran wrap again and let it rest for about 20 minutes.
- In the meantime, mix all the filling ingredients in a bowl and set aside.
- Line the fryer basket with a grill mat or a sheet of lightly greased aluminum foil.
- Rub some cooking oil in your hands and take the dough out from the bowl. Roll the dough into a cylinder shape on the counter surface then cut it into six equal pieces. Roll each piece into a ball.
- Take one ball of dough and flatten it between the palms of your hand. Scoop about 1 Tbsp of filling and wrap it inside the dough. Place the dough inside the fryer basket, leaving about 2 inches between the balls. Repeat until done.
- Press the balls down with the palm of your hand. Spritz some oil on top and air fry at 300F (150C) for 8-10 minutes, flip once in the middle until the surface is golden brown.

774.Cinnamon Pear Slices

Prep Time: 5 mins Cook Time: 15 mins

Ingredients

- 1 medium-sized Asian pear peeled and cored
- 2 tbsp butter melted
- 1 tbsp brown sugar
- 1/2 tsp cinnamon
- Granola for garnish optional

Instructions

- Thinly cut the pear into 1/4 inch thick wedges.
- In a mixing bowl, combine and toss all the ingredients.
- Lightly grease a shallow baking pan.

Place the pear wedges in the pan, pour whatever is left in the bowl over the pear, and air fry at 340F (170C) for 14-16 mins until tender.

• Pair them with ice cream or sprinkle some granola over them to serve.

775. Rice Cake Spring Rolls

Prep Time: 10 mins Cook Time: 10 mins

Ingredients

• Spring roll wrapper
• Chinese sweet rice cake
• A small bowl of water
• Melted butter

Instructions

• Cut the rice cake into rectangles, about 1/4 inch thick.

• Cut the spring roll wrappers to the appropriate size, enough to wrap around the rice cake.

• Wrap the rice cake with spring roll paper. Smear a little water at the end of the wrapper so the wrapper will stick onto itself.

• Line the fryer basket with a grill mat or a sheet of lightly greased aluminum foil.

• Place the wrapped rice cake inside the fryer basket. Brush melted butter onto the wraps and air fry at 400F (2000C) for about 4-5 minutes.

• Flip the rolls over and brush them with butter again. Air fry again at 400F (200C) for another 4-5 mins until the surface looks crispy and golden brown.

• Let cool about 5 mins before serving.

776. Candied Kumquats

Prep Time: 5 mins Cook Time: 10 mins

Ingredients

• 2 cup kumquat
• 2 tbsp melted unsalted butter
• 1/4 cup brown sugar or to taste depending on the sweetness

Instructions

• Cut kumquats in half and pick out all the visible seeds. (Kumquat seeds are edible, therefore it is okay if the seeds cannot be removed completely.)

• In a large mixing bowl, gently stir and mix all the ingredients. Then, transfer the kumquats to a lightly greased bakeware.

Air fry at 300F (150C) for 10-12 minutes, stirring a couple of times in the middle until there is a slightly thickened sauce.

777. Pastry Wrapped Rice Cakes

Prep Time: 10 mins Cook Time: 10 mins

Ingredients

• Chinese rice cake (nian-ago)
• Pie crust or puff pastry
• Egg wash

Instructions

• Line the fryer basket with lightly greased aluminum foil.

• Cut rice cake into 1/2 inch thick pieces. Wrap the rice cake with pie crust or puff pastry. Lightly press down on the overlapping pie crust to prevent it from opening up. Then, place them in the fryer basket.

• Brush the top side with egg wash. Air fry at 350F (175C) for 4 minutes.

• Flip the rice cake over and brush with egg wash. Air fry again at 350F (175C) for another 4-5 mins until the surface is golden brown.

• The rice cake hardens when they are cold, so it is best to serve them warm.

778. Peanut Butter Cupcake Swirl

Prep Time: 10 mins Cook Time: 15 mins

Ingredients

• 1/4 cup butter softened
• 1/3 cup creamy peanut butter
• 2 tbsp sugar
• 1 egg
• 3/4 cup milk
• 1/2 tsp vanilla extract
• 3/4 cup cake flour
• 1 tsp baking soda
• 1/2 tsp baking powder
• 1/2 tsp salt
• 1/4 cup Nutella divided warmed

Instructions

• Line the muffin tins with cupcake liners and set them aside.

• Cream together the butter, sugar, and peanut butter using a whisk or an electric mixer. Then, add the egg, milk, and vanilla extract. Mix until homogenous. Finally, add the rest of the dry ingredients and mix until well combined.

• Scoop the batter into the liners about 2/3 full. Then, use a spoon to drop about 1/2 Tsp. of Nutella into the center of the cupcake. Insert a toothpick into the center of the Nutella and create a swirl by making circles in

the batter.

• Air fry at 300F (150C) for about 12-14 min.. Insert a toothpick to test. When the toothpick comes out clean, then the cupcake is cooked through.

779. Chocolate Sponge Cake

Prep Time: 10 mins Cook Time: 15 mins

Ingredients

• 3 large eggs
• 1 1/2 tbsp melted butter let cool until almost to room temperature
• 2 tbsp milk
• 2 tbsp sugar
• 1/4 tsp vanilla extract
• 1/3 cup cake flour
• 1/2 tsp baking powder
• 1 1/2 tbsp cocoa powder

Instructions

• Crack 3 eggs. Put the egg whites in a mixing bowl and egg yolks in a large bowl.

• To the egg yolks, add in the cooled butter, milk, sugar, and vanilla extract and mix until well combined. Sieve the cake flour, baking powder, and cocoa powder and whisk to combine the wet and dry ingredients to form a thick batter.

• In the meantime, use the electric mixer (or a whisk) to beat the egg whites until they can form a stiff peak. When done, pour this fluffy egg whites into the batter and gently combine them with a spatula until it is almost homogenous.

• Lightly grease the ramekins and put them inside the fryer basket. Preheat the air fryer at 400F (200C) for about 2 minutes.

• Scoop the batter into the preheated ramekins and air fry at 280F (140C) for about 10-12 minutes, until the toothpick comes out clean.

780. Red Bean Wheel Pie

Prep Time: 10 mins Cook Time: 10 mins

Ingredients

• 2 tbsp melted butter
• 2 eggs
• 2 tbsp sugar
• 1 tbsp honey
• 1/4 tsp vanilla extract
• 1/4 cup milk
• 1 cupcake flour

- 3/4 tsp baking powder
- 6 tbsp mashed sweetened red bean canned or homemade filling to taste

Instructions

- Lightly grease 4 ramekins with butter and place them in the fryer basket. Preheat at 400F (200C) for 2 min..
- In a large bowl, use a whisk to mix the egg, sugar, vanilla extract, and honey. Add in milk and whisk until the mixture is homogeneous. Finally, add in the sifted cake flour and baking powder. Continue to mix until everything is well blended.
- The total weight of the batter is about 280g. Spoon about 30g into the ramekin. Air fry at 300F (150C) for about 3 min..
- Take the desired amount of red bean (about 1 1/2 Tbsp for mine) and roll it into a ball using the palms of your hand. Flatten it into a circular disc that is smaller than the diameter of the ramekin. Place it in the center of the ramekin on top of the pancake. Scoop about 40g of the batter into the ramekins to cover the red beans.
- Air fry again at 300F (150C) for about 3 minutes. Brush some butter on top and air fry again at 300F (150C) for 1-2 mins until the top is slightly golden brown.

781.Sesame Crusted Sweet Potato Cakes

Prep Time: 15 mins Cook Time: 10 mins

Ingredients

- 400 g mashed sweet potato
- 70 g tapioca starch
- 20 g cake flour
- sugar to taste
- 1/4 cup toasted sesame seeds

Instructions

- In a large mixing bowl, combine the mashed sweet potato, tapioca starch, cake flour, and sugar until homogenous.
- Roll the dough into a long strip. Cut the dough into one-inch pieces and roll them into a round ball. Flatten the balls with the palm of your hand to form patties.
- Sprinkle sesame seeds onto the patties and press the sesame seeds into the patties. Repeat this step for the other side.

- Spray oil to both sides and air fry at 380F (190C) for about 10 min., flip once in between.

782.Strawberry Puff Pastry Twists

Prep Time: 10 mins Cook Time: 10 mins

Ingredients

- 1 Puff pastry sheet defrosted and cut into two equal pieces
- 4-5 Tbsp strawberry preserve

Instructions

- Spread the strawberry preserve on one piece of the puff pastry. Place the other piece on top. Using a sharp knife or a dough blade, cut the pastry dough "sandwich" into 1/2 inch wide strips.
- Twist each strip and place them in a parchment paper-lined fryer basket and air fry at 360F (180C) for 9-10 min., flip once in between.
- Let cool completely before serving.

783. Maple Sponge Cake

Prep Time: 10 mins Cook Time: 15 mins

Ingredients

- 50 g cake flour
- 1/2 Tsp. baking powder
- 35 g melted butter and let it cool to almost room temperature
- 2 Tbsp milk
- 2 1/2 Tbsp maple syrup
- 1/4 Tsp. vanilla extract
- 3 large eggs

Instructions

- Crack 3 eggs and put the egg whites in the mixing bowl and egg yolks in a medium-sized bowl.
- To the egg yolks, add in the cooled butter, maple syrup, and vanilla extract and mix until well combined.
- In a separate large bowl, sieve the cake flour and baking powder and mix them. Pour the egg yolk mixture into this large bowl and gently whisk to combine the wet and dry ingredients to form a thick batter.
- In the meantime, use the electric mixer (or a whisk) to beat the egg whites until they can form a stiff peak. When done, pour this fluffy egg whites into the batter and gently combine them with a spatula until it is almost homogenous.
- Put the muffin tins inside the fryer basket, hold them down with a steamer rack and preheat the air fryer at 400F

(200C) for about 2 min..
- Pour the batter into the preheated muffin tins and air fry at 260F (130C) for about 13 mins until the toothpick comes out clean. Air fry at 380F (190C) again for about 1-2 mins until the color turns golden brown.

784.Almond Flour Chocolate Banana Nut Brownie

Prep Time: 5 mins Cook Time: 8 mins

Ingredients For Brownie:

- 1 large ripe banana
- 3 Tbsps coconut oil melted
- 1 Tsp. vanilla extract
- 1 1/2 cups almond flour
- 1/3 cup chocolate whey protein powder
- 1/2 Tsp. baking soda
- 1/4 Tsp. salt

Other Ingredients:

- 1/4 cup chocolate chips or to taste
- 1/4 cup chopped walnuts or to taste

Instructions

- In a mixing bowl, mix all the ingredients, except chocolate chips and walnuts, until well combined. Fold in the chocolate chips and walnuts if desired.
- Line parchment paper in a 7-inch springform pan. Pour the batter into the pan and air fry at 300F (150C) for about 8 min..
- Let cool on a cooling rack. When cooled, cut it into 1-inch squares to serve.

785.Marshmallow Chocolate Chip Explosion Cookies

Prep Time: 10 mins Cook Time: 10 mins

Ingredients

- 2/3 cup all-purpose flour
- 1/4 Tsp. baking soda
- 1/8 Tsp. salt
- 1/4 cup unsalted butter softened at room temperature
- 1/3 cup brown sugar
- 1 egg yolk
- 1/2 Tsp. vanilla extract
- 1/2 cup chocolate chips or to taste
- 1/4 cup marshmallow or to taste chopped into about 1/4 inch cubes

Instructions

- Preheat the air fryer at 350F (175C) for about 3-4 min..

- Line a small cookie sheet or bakeware with parchment paper and set it aside. This step is crucial. Without some kind of bakeware under the parchment paper, the edges of the paper may be lifted off during the air frying process which may cause the cookies to bunch together.
- In a medium bowl, combine the flour, baking soda, and salt.
- In a large bowl, whisk together the butter and brown sugar until smooth. Add in the egg yolk and vanilla extract and whisk again.
- Combine the two bowls and mix well. Scoop one Tbspful of the dough and roll it into a ball. Flatten it with the palm of your hand and put the desired amount of marshmallow and chocolate chip in the middle. Wrap the dough around to form a ball again. Place the balls of dough on the parchment paper, making sure they are about 2 inches apart from each other.
- Air fry at 350F (175C) for 5-6 mins until the cookies look crispy. Remove the cookies and let them cool on a rack. Repeat the same process for the remaining dough if necessary.
- For your enjoyment, my little baker recommends the cookies to be warmed up a bit and topped with a scoop of ice cream.

786. Simple Cheesecake

Prep time: 10 mins Cook time: 15 mins
Ingredients
- Cream cheese – 1 pound
- Vanilla extract – ½ tsp.
- Eggs – 2
- Sugar – 4 tbsp.
- Graham crackers – 1 cup, crumbled
- Butter – 2 tbsp.

Directions:
- Mix crackers with the butter in a bowl.
- Press crackers mixture on the bottom of a lined cake pan.
- Place in the air fryer and cook at 350F for 4 minutes.
- Meanwhile, in a bowl, mix eggs, cream cheese, sugar and vanilla, and whisk
- well.
- Spread filling over crackers crust and cook in the air fryer at 310F for 15

minutes.
- Cool and keep in the refrigerator for 3 hours.
- Slice and serve.

787. Bread Pudding

Prep time: 10 mins Cook time: 1 hour
Ingredients
- Glazed doughnuts – 6, crumbled
- Cherries – 1 cup
- Egg – 4 yolks
- Whipping cream – 1 ½ cups
- Raisins – ½ cup
- Sugar – ¼ cup
- Chocolate chips – ½ cup

Directions:
- In a bowl, mix cherries with egg yolks and whipping cream, and stir well.
- In another bowl, mix doughnuts, chocolate chips, sugar and raisins.
- Combine 2 mixtures and transfer everything to a greased pan that fits in your air fryer and cook at 310F for 1 hour.
- Chill pudding before cutting then serve.

788. Cinnamon Rolls and Cream Cheese Dip

Prep time: 2 hours Cook time: 15 mins
Ingredients
- Bread dough – 1 pound
- Brown sugar – ¾ cup
- Cinnamon – 1 ½ tbsp., ground
- Butter – ¼ cup, melted
 For the cream cheese dip
- Butter – 2 tbsp.
- Cream cheese – 4 ounces
- Sugar – 1 ¼ cups
- Vanilla – ½ tsp.

Directions:
- Roll dough on a floured working surface, shape a rectangle and brush with ¼ cup butter.
- Mix sugar and cinnamon in a bowl. Sprinkle this over dough. Roll dough
- into a log. Seal well and cut into 8 pieces.
- Leave rolls to rise for 2 hours. Place them in the air fryer basket.
- Cook at 350F for 5 minutes. Then flip and cook for 4 mins more.
- Transfer to a platter.
- In a bowl, mix butter, cream cheese, sugar and vanilla. Whisk well.
- Serve cinnamon rolls with this cream

cheese dip.

789. Pumpkin Pie

Prep time: 10 mins Cook time: 15 mins
Ingredients
- Sugar – 1 tbsp.
- Flour – 2 tbsp.
- Butter – 1 tbsp.
- Water – 2 tbsp.
For the pumpkin pie filling
- Pumpkin flesh – 5 ounces, chopped
- Mixed spice – 1 tsp.
- Nutmeg – 1 tsp.
- Water – 3 ounces
- Egg – 1, whisked
- Sugar – 1 tbsp.

Directions:
- Put 3 ounces water in a pot. Bring to a boil and add pumpkin, 1 tbsp. sugar,
- egg, spice and nutmeg. Stir and boil for 20 minutes.
- Remove from the heat and blend with a hand mixer.
- In a bowl, mix butter, flour, 2 tbsp. water and 1 tbsp. sugar. Knead the dough well.
- Grease a pie pan with butter. Press dough into the pan. Fill with pumpkin
- pie filling.
- Place in the air fryer basket and cook at 360F for 15 minutes.
- Serve.

790. Cocoa Cake

Prep time: 10 mins Cook time: 17 mins
Ingredients
- Butter – 5 ounces, melted
- Eggs – 3
- Sugar – 3 ounces
- Cocoa powder – 1 tsp.
- Flour – 3 ounces
- Lemon juice – ½ tsp.

Directions:
- In a bowl, mix cocoa powder with 1 tbsp. butter and whisk.
- In another bowl, mix the rest of the butter with lemon juice, flour, eggs and sugar. Whisk well and pour half into a cake pan.
- Add half of the cocoa mix, spread, add the rest of the butter layer and top with the rest of the cocoa.
- Cook in the air fryer at 360F for 17 minutes.
- Cool, slice and serve.

791. Apple Bread

Prep time: 10 mins Cook time: 40 mins
Servings: 6
•Apples – 3, cored and cubed
•Sugar – 1 cup
•Vanilla – 1 tbsp.
•Eggs – 2
•Apple pie spice – 1 tbsp.
•White flour – 2 cups
•Baking powder – 1 tbsp.
•Butter – 1 stick
•Water – 1 cup
Directions:
• In a bowl, mix 1 stick butter, egg, apple pie spice and sugar. Stir with a mixer.
• Add apples and stir well.
• In another bowl, mix flour and baking powder.
• Combine the 2 mixtures. Stir and pour into a springform pan.
• Put springform pan in the air fryer and cook at 320F for 40 minutes.
• Slice and serve.

792.Mini Lava Cakes

Prep time: 10 mins Cook time: 20 mins
Ingredients
•Egg – 1
•Sugar – 4 tbsp.
•Olive oil – 2 tbsp.
•Milk – 4 tbsp.
•Flour – 4 tbsp.
•Cocoa powder – 1 tbsp.
•Baking powder – ½ tsp.
•Orange zest – ½ tsp.
Directions:
• In a bowl, combine oil, sugar, milk, egg, flour, salt, cocoa powder, baking powder and orange zest.
• Mix well and pour into greased ramekins.
• Add ramekins to the air fryer and cook at 320F for 20 minutes.
• Serve.

793.Ginger Cheesecake

Prep time: 2 hours and 10 mins
Cook time: 20 mins
Ingredients
•Butter – 2 tsp., melted
•Ginger cookies – ½ cup, crumbled
•Cream cheese – 16 ounces, soft
•Eggs – 2
•Sugar – ½ cup
•Rum – 1 tsp.
•Vanilla extract – ½ tsp.

•Nutmeg – ½ tsp., ground
Directions:
• Grease a pan with butter and spread cookie crumbs on the bottom.
• In a bowl, beat cream cheese, eggs, rum, vanilla and nutmeg. Whisk well and spread over the cookie crumbs.
• Place in the air fryer and cook at 340F for 20 minutes.
• Cool and keep in the refrigerator.
• Slice and serve.

794.Coffee Cheesecake

Prep time: 10 mins Cook time: 20 mins
Servings: 6
Ingredients
•Butter – 2 tbsp.
•Cream cheese – 8 ounces
•Coffee – 3 tbsp.
•Eggs – 3
•Sugar – 1/3 cup
•Caramel syrup – 1 tbsp.
For the frosting
•Caramel syrup – 3 tbsp.
•Butter – 3 tbsp.
•Mascarpone cheese – 8 ounces, soft
•Sugar – 2 tbsp.
Directions:
• In the blender, mix eggs, cream cheese, 1/3 cup sugar, 1 tbsp. caramel syrup, coffee and 2 tbsp. butter. Pulse very well and spoon into a cupcake pan.
• Cook in the air fryer at 320F for 20 minutes.
• Cool and keep in the freezer for 3 hours.
• Meanwhile, in a bowl, mix mascarpone, 2 tbsp. sugar, 3 tbsp. caramel syrup and 3 tbsp. butter.
• Blend well and spoon over cheesecakes then serve

795.Fiesta Pastries

Preparation time: 15 mins
Cooking time: 20 mins
Ingredients :
• ½ of apple, peeled, cored and chopped
• 1 teaspoon fresh orange zest, grated finely
• 05-ounce prepared frozen puff pastry, cut into 16 squares
• ½ tablespoon white sugar
• ½ teaspoon ground cinnamon
Directions:
• Preheat the Air fryer to 390 o F and

grease an Air fryer basket.
• Mix all ingredients in a bowl except puff pastry.
• Arrange about 1 teaspoon of this mixture in the center of each square.
• Fold each square into a triangle and slightly press the edges with a fork.
• Arrange the pastries in the Air fryer basket and cook for about 10 minutes.
• Dish out and serve immediately.

796.Classic Buttermilk Biscuits

Preparation time: 15 mins
Cooking time: 8 mins
Ingredients :
• ½ cup cake flour
• 1¼ cups all-purpose flour
• ¾ teaspoon baking powder
• ¼ cup + 2 tablespoons butter, cut into cubes
• ¾ cup buttermilk
• 1 teaspoon granulated sugar
• Salt, to taste
Directions:
• Preheat the Air fryer to 400 o F and grease a pie pan lightly.
• Sift together flours, baking soda, baking powder, sugar and salt in a large
• bowl.
• Add cold butter and mix until a coarse crumb is formed.
• Stir in the buttermilk slowly and mix until a dough is formed.
• Press the dough into ½ inch thickness onto a floured surface and cut out cir-
• cles with a 1¾-inch round cookie cutter.
• Arrange the biscuits in a pie pan in a single layer and brush butter on them.
• Transfer into the Air fryer and cook for about 8 mins until golden brown

797.Carrot brownies

Preparation time: 10 mins
Cooking time: 25 mins
Ingredients :
• 1 teaspoon almond extract
• 2 eggs, whisked
• ½ cup butter, melted
• 4 tablespoons sugar
• 2 cups almond flour
• ½ cup carrot, peeled and grated
Directions:
• In a bowl, combine the eggs with the butter and the other ingredients, whisk,

spread this into a pan that fits your air fryer, introduce in the fryer and cook at 340 degrees f for 25 minutes.

- Cool down, slice and serve.

798. Carrots bread

Preparation time: 10 mins
Cooking time: 40 mins

Ingredients :

- 2 cups carrots, peeled and grated
- 1 cup sugar
- 3 eggs, whisked
- 2 cups white flour
- 1 tablespoon baking soda
- 1 cup almond milk

Directions:

- In a bowl, combine the carrots with the sugar and the other ingredients, whisk well, pour this into a lined loaf pan, introduce the pan in the air fryer and cook at 340 degrees f for 40 minutes.
- Cool the bread down, slice and serve.

799. Yogurt cake

Preparation time: 10 mins
Cooking time: 30 mins

Ingredients :

- 6 eggs, whisked
- 1 teaspoon vanilla extract
- 1 teaspoon baking soda
- 9 ounces almond flour
- 4 tablespoons sugar
- 2 cups yogurt

Directions:

- In a blender, combine the eggs with the vanilla and the other ingredients, pulse, spread into a cake pan lined with parchment paper, put it in the air fryer and cook at 330 degrees f for 30 minutes.
- Cool the cake down, slice and serve.

800. Carrots bread

Preparation time: 10 mins
Cooking time: 40 mins

Ingredients :

- 2 cups carrots, peeled and grated
- 1 cup sugar
- 3 eggs, whisked
- 2 cups white flour
- 1 tablespoon baking soda
- 1 cup almond milk

Directions:

- In a bowl, combine the carrots with the sugar and the other ingredients ,

whisk well, pour this into a lined loaf pan, introduce the pan in the air fryer and cook at 340 degrees f for 40 minutes.

- Cool the bread down, slice and serve.

801. Lime cake

Preparation time: 10 mins
Cooking time: 30 mins

Ingredients :

- 1 egg, whisked
- 2 tablespoons sugar
- 2 tablespoons butter, melted
- ½ cup almond milk
- 2 tablespoons lime juice
- 1 tablespoon lime zest, grated
- 1 cup heavy cream
- ½ teaspoon baking powder

Directions:

- In a bowl, combine the egg with the sugar, butter and the other ingredients whisk well and transfer to a cake pan lined with parchment paper.
- Put the pan in your air fryer and cook at 320 degrees f for 30 minutes.
- Serve the cake cold.

802. Pear stew

Preparation time: 10 mins
Cooking time: 20 mins

Ingredients :

- 2 teaspoons cinnamon powder
- 4 pears, cored and cut into wedges
- 1 cup water
- 2 tablespoons sugar

Directions:

- In your air fryer's pan, combine the pears with the water and the other Ingredients , cook at 300 degrees f for 20 minutes, divide into cups and serve cold.

803. Avocado cream

Preparation time: 10 mins
Cooking time: 10 mins

Ingredients :

- 2 avocados, peeled, pitted and mashed
- 2 cups heavy cream
- 2 tablespoons sugar
- 1 tablespoon lemon juice

Directions:

- In a blender, combine the avocados with the cream and the other ingredients, pulse well, divide into 4 ramekins, introduce them in the fryer

and cook at 320 degrees f for 10 minutes.

- Serve the cream really cold.

804. Apples and wine sauce

Preparation time: 10 mins
Cooking time: 20 mins

Ingredients :

- 3 apples, cored and cut intro wedges
- 1 teaspoon nutmeg, ground
- 1 cup red wine
- ½ cup sugar

Directions:

- In your air fryer's pan, combine the apples with the nutmeg and the other Ingredients , toss and cook at 340 degrees f for 20 minutes.
- Divide into bowls and serve

805. Mandarin cream

Preparation time: 10 mins
Cooking time: 15 mins

Ingredients :

- 2 cups heavy cream
- 2 mandarins, peeled and chopped
- 1 teaspoon vanilla extract
- 2 tablespoons sugar

Directions:

- In a bowl, combine the cream with the mandarins and the other ingredients , whisk, transfer to 4 ramekins, put them in the air fryer's basket and cook at 300 degrees f for 15 minutes.
- Whisk the cream, divide it into cups and serve.

806. Avocado cake

Preparation time: 10 mins
Cooking time: 30 mins

Ingredients :

- 2 avocados, peeled, pitted and mashed
- 1 cup almond flour
- 2 teaspoons baking powder
- 1 cup sugar
- 1 cup butter, melted
- 3 tablespoons maple syrup
- 4 eggs, whisked

Directions:

- In a bowl, combine the avocados with the flour and the other ingredients, whisk, pour this into a lined cake pan, introduce the pan in the fryer and cook at 340 degrees f for 30 minutes.
- Leave the cake to cool down, slice and serve.

807. Quinoa pudding

Preparation time: 10 mins
Cooking time: 20 mins
Ingredients :
- 2 cups almond milk
- 1 teaspoon vanilla extract
- 1 teaspoon nutmeg, ground
- 1 cup quinoa
- ½ cup sugar

Directions:
- In your air fryer's pan, combine the almond milk with the quinoa and the other ingredients ,whisk, and cook at 320 degrees f for 20 minutes.
- Divide into bowls and serve.

808. Cake with cream and strawberries

Preparation time: 10 mins
Cooking time: 15 mins
Ingredients :
- 1 pure butter puff pastry to stretch
- 500g strawberries (clean and without skin)
- 1 bowl of custard
- 3 tbsp icing sugar baked at 210°C in the air fryer

Direction:
- Unroll the puff pastry and place it on the baking sheet. Prick the bottom with a fork and spread the custard. Arrange the strawberries in a circle and sprinkle with icing sugar.
- Cook in a fryer setting a 210°C for 15 minutes.
- Remove the cake from the fryer with the tongs and let cool.
- When serving sprinkle with icing sugar
- And why not, add some whipped cream.

809. Churros

Prep Time: 10 mins
Cooking time: 10 mins
Ingredients:
- 1 cup Water
- 1/3 cup Unsalted Butter
- 2 tbsp Granulated Sugar
- 1/4 tsp Salt
- 1 cup All-purpose Flour
- 2 large Eggs
- 1 tsp Vanilla Extract
- Oil spray

Directions:
- Fetch a small saucepan and add a cup of water into it. Then also add butter, salt, and sugar. Allow to boil for a little time.
- Bring down the heat and add some flour. Stir the mixture until both the
- dough and the other ingredients mix properly. Place the dough into a bowl and allow to get cool before continuing.
- In the bowl, add some eggs and vanilla extract. Then mix together: you can make use of an electric hand mixer to achieve the texture that you want. You can then make use of your hands to scoop them into a piping bag.
- Press the churros into a baking mat that has been lined. The length of the churros should be 4-inches.
- Place the baking mat into the refrigerator and leave in for at least 1 hour.
- After 1 hour, transfer the churros to the air fryer. Use some olive oil on the
- churros so they don't stick.
- Cooking time is 10 minutes. The air fryer should be set to about 372 degrees F.
- Fetch another bowl and put in the sugar and cinnamon.
- 9.When the churros are done, place each into the bowl containing the sugar and cinnamon and coat thoroughly.
- Serve.

810. Fried Banana S'mores

Prep time: 10 mins
Cooking time: 6 mins
Ingredients:
- 4 Bananas
- 3 tablespoons Mini Peanut Butter Chips
- 3 tablespoons Graham Cracker Cereal
- 3 tablespoons Mini Marshmallows
- 3 tablespoons Mini Sweet Chocolate Chips

Directions:
- Start by preheating the air fryer to about 400 degrees F. Set the timer for 6 minutes.
- Do not peel the bananas, simply slice the entire length. This should be done for the inside of the banana. Do not slice to the end. Leave some of the bottom intact so that the banana can be peeled back.
- For each banana, place chocolate chips, marshmallows and peanut butter chips into them.
- Force the graham cracker cereal into the filling.
- Put the bananas into the air fryer. Find a way to keep them together, and so
- that the slit side would be facing upwards.
- Cooking time is 6 minutes, and by that time the peel would have turned black and the banana would also have gotten soft. The marshmallows and chocolate would also have melted by this time.
- After they have gotten cool you can serve. They can be eaten with a spoon being used to scoop out the filling.

811. Chocolate Chip Cookie

Prep time: 15 mins
Cooking time: 10 mins
Ingredients:
- 1/2 cup Butter Softened
- 1/2 cup Sugar
- 1/2 cup Light Brown Sugar
- 1 Egg
- 1 tsp Vanilla
- 1/2 tsp Baking Soda
- 1/4 tsp Salt
- 1 1/2 cups All-purpose Flour
- 1 cup Chocolate Chips or Chocolate Chunks

Directions:
- Start by preheating the air fryer to about 350 degrees F. Set the timer for 25 minutes.
- Smear two metal pans with olive oil. They should be able to fit into your air fryer.
- Into the two metal pans, add some butter, sugar and brown sugar. Mix them properly. Also add some egg and vanilla, flour and salt. Stir and mix properly.
- Add in some chocolate chips.
- Put the pan into the air fryer and bake. The total time should be about 10 to 12 mins and by that time, the dough must have turned a light brown.

812. Grilled Pineapple.

Prep time: 10 mins
Cooking Time: 10 mins
Ingredients:
- 1 Pineapple
- ½ cup Brown Sugar
- 2 teaspoons Ground Cinnamon
- 3 tablespoons Melted Butter

Directions:

- Preheat the air fryer and set the temperature to 400 degrees F. Set the timer for 10 minutes.
- Mix together brown sugar and cinnamon in a bowl.
- Cut the pineapple into spears. Smear some butter on the pineapple spears.
- Also, sprinkle some cinnamon sugar on the pineapple spears. You can press slightly into the pineapple to make sure the pineapple absorbs the sugar.
- Place the pineapple spears into the air fryer basket. Midway into the cooking, remove the pineapple and smear with some more butter.
- Bring out the pineapples when you notice some bubbles forming on the surface.

813.Chocolate Mug Cake

Prep time: 2 mins
Cook time: 10 mins

Ingredients

- 3 teaspoon of Coconut Oil
- 3 tablespoon of Whole Milk
- 1 tablespoon of Cocoa Powder
- 5 tablespoon of Caster Sugar
- ¼ Cup of Self Raising Flour

Directions

- Combine together the ingredients in a mug that fits or ramekins.Mix very well.
- In the Air fryer, place the mug or ramekins and cook at 200c for 10 minutes.
- Repeat for the other mugs. Serve!

814.Fruit Crumble Mug Cakes

Prep time: 15 mins Cook time: 15 mins

Ingredients

- 1 tablespoon of Honey
- Handful Blueberries
- 1 Small Peach
- 1 Small Pear
- 1 Small Apple
- 4 Plums
- 25 grams of Brown Sugar
- 30 grams of Gluten Free Oats
- 30 grams of Caster Sugar
- 50 grams of Butter
- 110 grams of Plain Flour

Directions

- Heat up your Air fryer to 160c.
- Remove stones and cores from the

fruit using the corer and then chop into small square sizes.

- In the base of four mugs, evenly pour the fruit, spreading them out.
- Sprinkle with honey and brown sugar until nicely covered. Set aside.
- In a mixing bowl, add the butter, caster sugar and flour, rub the fat into the flour until it looks like a fine breadcrumbs. Add the oats and mix very well.
- Layer the mugs on top with the crumble, then Place in your Air fryer and cook for 10 mins. Once the 10 mins is completes, cook for additional 5 mins at 200c for a crunchy top.

815.Sweet Apple Tarte Tatin

Prep time: 15 mins Cook time: 25 mins

Ingredients

- Small, round 15 cm diameter fixed-base cake pan
- 30 grams of sugar
- 1 large, firm apple (Jonagold, Elstar), Peel, core and cut into 12 wedges
- 100 grams of flour
- 1 egg yolk
- 60 grams of cold butter, in thin slices

Directions

- Cut out 25 grams from the butter slices and cut into pieces, mix with the flour
- and egg yolk. Knead mixture into a smooth dough ball; add a little water, if needed.
- Roll the dough out on a floured work surface into a 15 cm round.
- Heat up your Air fryer to 400 F.
- Add the remainder 35 grams of butter slices into the cake pan and sprinkle with sugar. In a circular form, add the apple wedges over the top.
- Add the rolled-out dough over the apple wedges, press it down around the inner pan edge.
- Transfer the pan into the Air fryer basket and bake for 25 mins or until it's
- done. Once its set, invert onto a plate. Slice and serve immediately or lukewarm with vanilla sauce or ice cream.

816.Honey Pineapple With Coconut

Prep time: 10 mins
Cook time: 10 mins

Ingredients

- ¼ liter of ice cream or mango sorbet
- ½ tbsp of lime juice
- 1 tbsp of honey
- ½ small fresh pineapple

Directions

- Heat up your Air fryer to 400 F. Line the base of your Air fryer basket with parchment, leaving one cm of the edge open.
- Slice pineapple into 8 parts, lengthways. Peel off the skin and discard the tough core.
- In a bowl, Mix together the lime juice with honey. Brush honey all over the
- pineapple portion and place into the Air fryer basket. Sprinkle top with coconut.
- Cook pineapple for 12 mins in the Air fryer until golden brown. Serve each pineapple beside a large scoop of ice cream.

817.Cranberry Cinnamon Muffins

Prep time: 10 mins
Cook time: 15 mins

Ingredients

- 8 paper muffin cups
- 75 grams of dried cranberries
- 50 grams of butter, melted
- 75 ml of milk
- 1 small egg
- 3 tsp of sugar
- 1 tsp of cinnamon
- 1½ tsp of baking powder
- 75 grams of flour

Directions

- Heat up your Air fryer to 400 F. Place two muffin cups together, so you will have 4 cups in total.
- In a bowl, sift the flour, add cinnamon, baking powder, pinch of salt and sugar.
- Mix thoroughly.
- Beat the egg lightly in another bowl and add melted butter and milk. Mix well.
- Stir the wet **Ingredients** into the dry ingredients, add cranberries and stir well.
- Fill the muffin cups with the batter and transfer into the Air fryer basket. Bake for 15 mins until done and golden brown.
- Allow muffins to cool in cups

818. Lemon Ricotta Cheesecake

Prep time: 10 mins
Cook time: 25 mins
Ingredients
- 20 cm round oven dish
- 3 tablespoon of corn starch
- 3 eggs
- 2 teaspoon of vanilla essence
- 150 grams of sugar
- 500 grams of ricotta
- 1 (organic) lemon, Zest and juice

Directions
- Heat up your Air fryer to 160°C.
- In a bowl, combine together the vanilla essence, ricotta, sugar, 1 tablespoon of lemon zest and the lemon juice stirring until combined well. Stir the eggs one after another. Mix in corn starch until combined well.
- Transfer mixture to the oven dish and arrange the dish in the basket and bake
- for 25 mins 160°C until the center is set. Let dish cool on a wire rack. For an upside down cheesecake, top pudding with a crumbled digestive biscuit.

819. Chocolate Brownies.

Prep time: 20 mins
Cook time: 24 mins
Ingredients
- 1 cake tin 20 x 20 cm, greased
- 150 grams of chopped pecan nuts
- 100 grams of flour
- 2 tbsp of vanilla extract
- 200 grams of sugar
- 4 small eggs
- 100 grams of white chocolate
- 100 grams of dark chocolate
- 200 grams of butter

Directions
- Heat up the Air fryer to 160. In a thick-bottomed pan, melt dark chocolate with 1/2 of the butter. In another pan, melt the remaining butter with white chocolate.
- Let cool.
- Lightly beat the eggs, vanilla and sugar with the mixer. Half the flour into two and sprinkle each portion with a pinch of salt.
- Whisk 1/2 of the sugar/egg mix into the dark chocolate. Mix in 1/2 of the nuts and 1/2 of flour. Repeat step 3 with the white chocolate mixture.
- Grease the cake tin.
- Add the brown and white brownie mixture into separate sides inside the cake tin. Swirl both mix together partially with a spatula and bake 20 minutes or until set and the surface is dry when touched.

820. Cherry Sour Cream Clafoutis

Prep time: 15 mins
Cook time: 25 mins
Ingredients
- Small, low cake pan, 15 cm diameter
- Powdered sugar
- 10 grams of butter
- 125 ml of sour cream
- 1 egg
- 2 tbsp of sugar
- 50 grams of flour
- 2-3 tbsp of crème de cassis or vodka
- 200 grams of fresh cherries or 1 jar of cherries, well-drained, pitted

Directions
- Mix crème de cassis or kirsch with the cherries in a bowl.
- Heat up the Air fryer to 180°C.
- Mix together the flour, sour cream, egg, salt and sugar in another bowl until you have a thick and smooth dough. If needed, you can add little water.
- Pour batter in cake pan, top evenly with the cherries and add the rest butter in little chunks over the top.
- Transfer cake pan in the Air fryer basket and bake for 25 minutes until its done and golden brown.
- Dust the clafoutis generously with powdered sugar immediately after baking.
- Slice and serve lukewarm.

821. Coffee Cake

Prep Time: 15 mins Cook Time: 30 mins
Ingredients
- 1/2 cup oil
- 1 egg beaten
- 1/2 Tsp. vanilla extract
- 1/2 cup milk
- 1/2 cup sugar
- 1 1/2 cup cake flour
- 1 1/2 Tsp. baking powder
- 1/4 Tsp. salt
- 1/2 cup brown sugar
- 1 Tsp. cinnamon
- 1/4 cup melted butter

Instructions
- In a medium bowl, prepare streusel by combining brown sugar and cinnamon. Divide the streusel into two equal portions.
- In a large mixing bowl, combine oil, eggs, vanilla, and milk. In a medium bowl, blend sugar, flour, baking powder, and salt. Then, combine egg mixture with flour mixture, mix well, then divide the batter into two equal parts.
- Lightly grease the loaf pans. Pour 1/2 of the batter into each pan. Sprinkle 1/2 of streusel into the pan and top it off with the remaining batter
- Sprinkle the remaining streusel on top and drizzle with melted butter.
- Air fry at 320F (160C) for about 30 mins until the toothpick comes out clean.

822. Apple French Toast Cups

Prep Time: 10 mins Cook Time: 15 mins
Ingredients
- 1 apple peeled and cubed
- 1 Tbsp butter
- 6 oz bread or bread ends cut into one-inch cubes
- 1/3 cup brown sugar
- 1 teaspoons cornstarch
- 3 eggs
- 2/3 cups milk
- 1/2 Tsp. vanilla extract
- 1/2 Tsp. cinnamon
- 2 Tbsp maple syrup

Instructions
- In a microwave-safe bowl, microwave the apple cubes with butter for about 3 mins until the apples are tender. Let cool for a few minutes.
- Combine the bread, sugar, and cornstarch in a large mixing bowl.
- In a separate bowl, mix the eggs, milk, vanilla, cinnamon, apple (and its juices) and maple syrup then pour this mixture into the bread bowl and gently combine all ingredients.
- Scoop the mixture into a lightly greased muffin tin and air fry at 320F (160C) for about 12-14 mins until the surface is golden brown.

823. Air Fryer Apple Pies

Prep Time:30 mins Cook Time: 15 mins
Total Time: 45 mins

Ingredient
- 4 Tbsp butter
- 6 Tbsps brown sugar
- 1 Tsp. ground cinnamon
- 2 medium granny smith apples, diced
- 1 Tsp. cornstarch
- 2 teaspoons cold water
- ½ (14 ounces) package pastry for a 9-inch double-crust pie
- Cooking spray
- ½ Tbsp grapeseed oil
- ¼ cup powdered sugar
- 1 Tsp. milk, or more as needed

Instructions
- Combine apples, butter, brown sugar, and cinnamon in a non-stick skillet. Cook over medium heat until apples have softened, about 5 min..
- Dissolve cornstarch in cold water. Stir into apple mixture and cook until sauce thickens about 1 minute. Remove apple pie filling from heat and set aside to cool while you prepare the crust.
- Unroll pie crust on a lightly floured surface and roll out slightly to smooth the surface of the dough. Cut the dough into rectangles small enough so that 2 can fit in your air fryer at one time. Repeat with the remaining crust until you have 8 equal rectangles, re-rolling some of the scraps of dough if needed.
- Wet the outer edges of 4 rectangles with water and place some apple filling in the center about 1/2-inch from the edges. Roll out the remaining 4 rectangles so that they are slightly larger than the filled ones. Place these rectangles on top of the filling; crimp the edges with a fork to seal. Cut 4 small slits in the tops of the pies.
- Spray the basket of an air fryer with cooking spray. Brush the tops of 2 pies with grapeseed oil and transfer pies to the air fryer basket using a spatula.
- Insert basket and set the temperature to 385 degrees F (195 degrees C). Bake until golden brown, about 8 minutes. Remove pies from the basket and repeat with the remaining 2 pies.
- Mix powdered sugar and milk in a small bowl. Brush glaze on warm pies and allow to dry. Serve pies warm or at room temperature.

824.Air Fryer Oreos

Prep Time: 5 mins Cook Time: 5 mins Total Time: 10 mins

Ingredient
- ½ Cup complete pancake mix
- ⅓ cup water
- Cooking spray
- 9 chocolate sandwich cookies (such as oreo®)
- 1 Tbsp confectioners' sugar, or to taste

Instructions
- Mix pancake mix and water until well combined.
- Line an air fryer basket with parchment paper. Spray parchment paper with nonstick cooking spray. Dip each cookie into the pancake mixture and place it in the basket. Make sure they are not touching; cook in batches if necessary.
- Preheat the air fryer to 400 degrees F (200 degrees C). Add basket and cook for 4 to 5 minutes; flip and cook until golden brown, 2 to 3 mins more. Sprinkle with confectioners' sugar.

825.Air Fryer Churros

Prep Time: 5 mins Cook Time: 15 mins Additional Time: 5 mins Total Time: 25 mins

Ingredient
- ¼ cup butter
- ½ cup milk
- 1 pinch salt
- ½ cup all-purpose flour
- 2 eggs
- ¼ cup white sugar
- ½ Tsp. ground cinnamon

Instructions
- Melt butter in a saucepan over medium-high heat. Pour in milk and add salt. Lower heat to medium and bring to a boil, continuously stirring with a wooden spoon. Quickly add flour all at once. Keep stirring until the dough comes together.
- Remove from heat and let cool for 5 to 7 minutes. Mix in eggs with the wooden spoon until the pastry comes together. Spoon dough into a pastry bag fitted with a large star tip. Pipe dough into strips straight into the air fryer basket.
- Air fry churros at 340 degrees F (175 degrees C) for 5 min..

- Meanwhile, combine sugar and cinnamon in a small bowl and pour onto a shallow plate.
- Remove fried churros from the air fryer and roll in the cinnamon-sugar mixture.

826. Air Fryer Apple Fritters

Prep Time: 15 mins Cook Time: 10 mins Total Time: 25 mins

Ingredient
- Cooking spray
- 1 cup all-purpose flour
- ¼ cup white sugar
- ¼ cup milk
- 1 egg
- 1 ½ teaspoons baking powder
- 1 pinch salt
- 2 Tbsps white sugar
- ½ Tsp. ground cinnamon
- 1 apple - peeled, cored, and chopped

Glaze:
- ½ cup confectioners' sugar
- 1 Tbsp milk
- ½ Tsp. caramel extract
- ¼ Tsp. ground cinnamon

Instructions
- Preheat an air fryer to 350 degrees F (175 degrees C). Place a parchment paper round into the bottom of the air fryer. Spray with nonstick cooking spray.
- Mix flour, 1/4 cup sugar, milk, egg, baking powder, and salt together in a small bowl. Stir until combined.
- Mix 2 Tbsps sugar with cinnamon in another bowl and sprinkle over apples until coated. Mix apples into the flour mixture until combined.
- Drop fritters using a cookie scoop onto the bottom of the air fryer basket.
- Air-fry in the preheated fryer for 5 min.. Flip fritters and cook until golden, about 5 mins more.
- Meanwhile, mix confectioners' sugar, milk, caramel extract, and cinnamon in a bowl. Transfer fritters to a cooling rack and drizzle with glaze.

827.Air Fryer Roasted Bananas

Prep Time: 2 mins Cook Time: 7 mins Total Time: 9 mins

Ingredients
- 1 banana, sliced into 1/8-inch thick diagonals

- Avocado oil cooking spray

Instructions

- Line air fryer basket with parchment paper.
- Preheat an air fryer to 375 degrees F (190 degrees C).
- Place banana slices into the basket, making sure that they are not touching; cook in batches if necessary. Mist banana slices with avocado oil.
- Cook in the air fryer for 5 minutes. Remove the basket and flip banana slices carefully (they will be soft). Cook until banana slices are browning and caramelized, an additional 2 to 3 min.. Carefully remove from basket.

828. Triple-Chocolate Oatmeal Cookies

Prep Time: 15 mins Cook Time: 10 mins Total Time: 25 mins

Ingredient

- 3 cups quick-cooking oatmeal
- 1 ½ cups all-purpose flour
- ¼ cup cocoa powder
- 1 (3.4 ounces) package instant chocolate pudding mix
- 1 Tsp. baking soda
- 1 Tsp. salt
- 1 cup butter, softened
- ¾ cup brown sugar
- ¾ cup white sugar
- 2 eggs
- 1 Tsp. vanilla extract
- 2 cups chocolate chips
- 1 cup chopped walnuts (optional)
- Nonstick cooking spray

Instructions

- Preheat an air fryer to 350 degrees F (175 degrees C) according to the manufacturer's instructions. Spray the air fryer basket with nonstick cooking spray.
- Mix oatmeal, flour, cocoa powder, pudding mix, baking soda, and salt in a bowl until well combined. Set aside.
- Cream butter, brown sugar, and white sugar together in another bowl using an electric mixer. Add eggs and vanilla extract. Add oatmeal mixture and mix well. Stir in chocolate chips and walnuts.
- Drop dough into the air fryer using a large cookie scoop; flatten out and leave about 1 inch between each cookie.

- Cook until lightly browned, 6 to 10 min.. Cool on a wire rack before serving.

829. Air Fryer Beignets

Prep Time: 10 mins Cook Time: 15 mins Total Time: 25 mins

Ingredient

- Cooking spray
- ½ cup all-purpose flour
- ¼ cup white sugar
- ⅛ cup water
- 1 large egg, separated
- 1 ½ Tsp. melted butter
- ½ Tsp. baking powder
- ½ Tsp. vanilla extract
- 1 pinch salt
- 2 Tbsps confectioners' sugar, or to taste

Instructions

- Preheat air fryer to 370 degrees F (185 degrees C). Spray a silicone egg-bite mold with nonstick cooking spray.
- Whisk flour, sugar, water, egg yolk, butter, baking powder, vanilla extract, and salt together in a large bowl. Stir to combine.
- Beat egg white in a small bowl using an electric hand mixer on medium speed until soft peaks form. Fold into batter. Add batter to the prepared mold using a small hinged ice cream scoop.
- Place filled silicone mold into the basket of the air fryer.
- Fry in the preheated air fryer for 10 min.. Remove mold from the basket carefully; pop beignets out and flip over onto a parchment paper round.
- Place parchment round with beignets back into the air fryer basket. Cook for an additional 4 min.. Remove beignets from the air fryer basket and dust with confectioners' sugar.

830. Air-Fried Banana Cake

Prep Time: 10 mins Cook Time: 30 mins Total Time: 40 mins

Ingredient

- Cooking spray
- ⅓ cup brown sugar
- 3 ½ Tbsps butter, at room temperature
- 1 banana, mashed
- 1 egg
- 2 Tbsp honey
- 1 cup self-rising flour

- ½ Tsp. ground cinnamon
- 1 pinch salt

Instructions

- Preheat an air fryer to 320 degrees F (160 degrees C). Spray a small fluted tube pan with cooking spray.
- Beat sugar and butter together in a bowl using an electric mixer until creamy. Combine banana, egg, and honey in a separate bowl. Whisk banana mixture into butter mixture until smooth.
- Sift flour, cinnamon, and salt into the combined banana-butter mixture. Mix batter until smooth. Transfer to the prepared pan; level the surface using the back of a spoon.
- Place the cake pan in the air fryer basket. Slide the basket into the air fryer and set the timer for 30 min.. Bake until a toothpick inserted into the cake comes out clean.

831. Air-Fried Butter Cake

Prep Time: 10 mins Cook Time: 15 mins Additional Time: 5 mins Total Time: 30 mins

Ingredient

- Cooking spray
- 7 Tbsp butter, at room temperature
- ¼ cup white sugar
- 2 Tbsps white sugar
- 1 egg
- 1 ⅔ cups all-purpose flour
- 1 pinch salt, or to taste
- 6 Tbsp milk

Instructions

- Preheat an air fryer to 350 degrees F (180 degrees C). Spray a small fluted tube pan with cooking spray.
- Beat butter and 1/4 cup plus 2 Tbsps sugar together in a bowl using an electric mixer until light and creamy. Add egg and mix until smooth and fluffy. Stir in flour and salt. Add milk and mix batter thoroughly. Transfer batter to the prepared pan; use the back of a spoon to level the surface.
- Place the pan in the air fryer basket. Set the timer for 15 minutes. Bake until a toothpick inserted into the cake comes out clean.
- Turn the cake out of the pan and allow to cool for about 5 minutes.

832. Gluten-Free Fresh Cherry Crumble

Prep Time: 15 mins Cook Time: 25 mins Additional Time: 30 mins Total Time:1 hr 10 mins

Ingredient

- ⅓ cup butter
- 3 cups pitted cherries
- 10 Tbsps white sugar, divided
- 2 teaspoons lemon juice
- 1 cup gluten-free all-purpose baking flour
- 1 Tsp. vanilla powder
- 1 Tsp. ground nutmeg
- 1 Tsp. ground cinnamon

Instructions

- Cube butter and place in freezer until firm, about 15 minutes.
- Preheat air fryer to 325 degrees F (165 degrees C).
- Combine pitted cherries, 2 Tbsps sugar, and lemon juice in a bowl; mix well. Pour cherry mixture into baking dish.
- Mix flour and 6 Tbsps of sugar in a bowl. Cut in butter using fingers until particles are pea-size. Distribute over cherries and press down lightly.
- Stir 2 Tbsps sugar, vanilla powder, nutmeg, and cinnamon together in a bowl. Dust sugar topping over the cherries and flour.
- Bake in the preheated air fryer. Check at 25 min.; if not yet browned, continue cooking and checking at 5-minute intervals until slightly browned. Close drawer and turn off air fryer. Leave crumble inside for 10 min.. Remove and allow to cool slightly, about 5 min..

833. Easy Air Fryer Apple Pies

Prep Time: 15 mins Cook Time: 10 mins Total Time: 25 mins

Ingredient

- 1 (14.1 ounces) package refrigerated pie crusts (2 pie crusts)
- 1 (21 ounces) can apple pie filling
- 1 egg, beaten
- 2 Tbsps cinnamon sugar, or to taste
- 1 serving cooking spray

Instructions

- Place 1 pie crust onto a lightly floured surface and roll out the dough with a rolling pin. Using a 2-1/4-inch round biscuit or cookie cutter cut the pie crust into 10 circles. Repeat with the second pie crust for a total of 20 pie crust circles.
- Fill about 1/2 of each circle with apple pie filling. Place a second pie crust circle on top, making a mini pie. Do not overfill. Press down the edges of the mini pies, crimping with a fork to seal. Brush tops with beaten egg and sprinkles with cinnamon sugar.
- Preheat the air fryer to 360 degrees F (175 degrees C).
- Lightly spray the air fryer basket with cooking spray. Place a batch of the mini pies in the air fryer basket, leaving space around each for air circulation.
- Bake until golden brown, 5 to 7 min.. Remove from the basket and bake the remaining pies. Serve warm or at room temperature.

834. Chocolate Cake In An Air Fryer

Prep Time: 10 mins Cook Time: 15 mins Total Time: 25 mins

Ingredient

- Cooking spray
- ¼ cup white sugar
- 3 ½ Tbsp butter, softened
- 1 egg
- 1 Tbsp apricot jam
- 6 Tbsps all-purpose flour
- 1 Tbsp unsweetened cocoa powder
- Salt to taste

Instructions

- Preheat an air fryer to 320 degrees F (160 degrees C). Spray a small fluted tube pan with cooking spray.
- Beat sugar and butter together in a bowl using an electric mixer until light and creamy. Add egg and jam; mix until combined. Sift in flour, cocoa powder, and salt; mix thoroughly. Pour batter into the prepared pan. Level the surface of the batter with the back of a spoon.
- Place pan in the air fryer basket. Cook until a toothpick inserted into the center of the cake comes out cleanly, about 15 minutes.

835. Air Fryer Shortbread Cookie Fries

Prep Time: 20 mins Cook Time: 10 mins Total Time: 30 mins

Ingredient

- 1 ¼ cups all-purpose flour
- 3 Tbsps white sugar
- ½ cup butter
- ⅓ cup strawberry jam
- ⅛ Tsp. ground dried chipotle pepper

(Optional)

- ⅓ cup lemon curd

Instructions

- Combine flour and sugar in a medium bowl. Cut in butter with a pastry blender until the mixture resembles fine crumbs and starts to cling. Form the mixture into a ball and knead until smooth.
- Preheat an air fryer to 350 degrees F (190 degrees C).
- Roll dough to 1/4-inch thickness on a lightly floured surface. Cut into 1/2-inch-wide "fries" about 3- to 4-inch long. Sprinkle with additional sugar.
- Arrange fries in a single layer in the air fryer basket. Cook until lightly browned, 3 to 4 min.. Let cool in the basket until firm enough to transfer to a wire rack to cool completely. Repeat with the remaining dough.
- To make strawberry "ketchup," press jam through a fine-mesh sieve using the back of a spoon. Stir in ground chipotle. Whip the lemon curd to make it a dippable consistency for the "mustard."
- Serve sugar cookie fries with strawberry ketchup and lemon curd mustard.

836. Easy Air Fryer French Toast Sticks

Prep Time: 10 mins Cook Time: 10 mins Total Time: 20 mins

Ingredient

- 4 slices of slightly stale thick bread, such as Texas toast
- parchment paper
- 2 eggs, lightly beaten
- ¼ cup milk
- 1 Tsp. vanilla extract
- 1 Tsp. cinnamon
- 1 pinch ground nutmeg (optional)

Instructions

- Cut each slice of bread into thirds to make sticks. Cut a piece of parchment paper to fit the bottom of the air fryer basket.
- Preheat air fryer to 360 degrees F (180 degrees C).
- Stir together eggs, milk, vanilla extract, cinnamon, and nutmeg in a bowl until well combined. Dip each piece of bread into the egg mixture, making sure each piece is well submerged. Shake each breadstick to

remove excess liquid and place it in a single layer in the air fryer basket. Cook in batches, if necessary, to avoid overcrowding the fryer.
- Cook for 5 min., turn bread pieces and cook for an additional 5 min..

837. Air Fryer Peanut Butter & Jelly S'mores

Prep Time: 5 mins Cook Time: 5 mins Total Time: 10 mins

Ingredient
- 1 chocolate-covered peanut butter cup
- 2 chocolate graham cracker squares, divided
- 1 Tsp. seedless raspberry jam
- 1 large marshmallow

Instructions
- Preheat the air fryer to 400 degrees F (200 degrees C).
- Place peanut butter cup on 1 graham cracker square. Top with jelly and marshmallow. Carefully place in an air fryer basket.
- Cook in preheated air fryer until marshmallow is lightly browned and softened, about 1 minute. Immediately top with the remaining graham cracker square.

838. Air Fryer Apple Cider Donut Bites

Prep Time: 10 mins Cook Time: 10 mins
Additional Time: 30 mins
Total Time: 50 mins

Ingredient
- 2 ¼ cups all-purpose flour
- 3 Tbsps white sugar
- 4 teaspoons baking powder
- 1 ½ Tsp. apple pie spice
- ½ Tsp. salt
- 1 (4 ounces) container unsweetened applesauce
- ½ cup sparkling apple cider
- ¼ cup unsalted butter, melted and cooled
- 1 large egg
- 1 Tsp. apple cider vinegar

Glaze:
- 2 cups powdered sugar
- ½ Tsp. apple pie spice
- ¼ cup sparkling apple cider
- 1 Tsp. caramel extract (optional)

Instructions

- Preheat the air fryer to 400 degrees F (200 degrees C) for 5 minutes.
- Combine flour, sugar, baking powder, apple pie spice, and salt in a large bowl. Whisk together.
- Combine applesauce, sparkling apple cider, melted butter, egg, and vinegar in a small bowl; whisk until well combined. Add wet ingredients to the dry ingredients using a spatula and blend until just combined. Using a spring-hinged ice cream scoop, fill each cavity of the silicone donut mold with 2 Tbsps butter. Place the mold into the air fryer basket.
- Decrease temperature to 350 degrees F (175 degrees C) and cook for 8 min.. Carefully turn out the donut bites and cook for an additional 2 min..
- Remove donut bites from the basket when done and let cool completely on a wire rack before glazing, about 30 minutes.
- Combine powdered sugar and apple pie spice in a small bowl and whisk together. Add sparkling apple cider and caramel extract; whisk together until the glaze is smooth.
- Dip each donut bite into the glaze, rolling it so that all sides are covered with the glaze. Set on a wire rack to allow the glaze to dry and harden before eating.

839. Chocolate Chip Cookie Bites

Prep Time: 10 mins Cook Time: 30 mins
Total Time: 40 mins

Ingredient
- ½ cup butter softened
- ½ cup packed brown sugar
- ¼ cup white sugar
- ½ Tsp. baking soda
- ½ Tsp. salt
- 1 egg
- 1 ½ teaspoons vanilla extract
- 1 ⅓ cups all-purpose flour
- 1 cup miniature semisweet chocolate chips
- ⅓ cup finely chopped pecans, toasted

Instructions
- Cut a piece of parchment paper to fit an air fryer basket.
- Beat butter in a large bowl with an electric mixer on medium to high speed for 30 seconds. Add brown sugar, white

sugar, baking soda, and salt; beat on medium speed for 2 min., scraping bowl occasionally. Beat in egg and vanilla extract until combined. Add flour, beating in as much as you can. Stir in any remaining flour, chocolate chips, and pecans.
- Drop dough by teaspoonfuls 1 inch apart onto the parchment paper. Carefully transfer the parchment paper to the air fryer basket.
- Turn the air fryer to 300 degrees F (150 degrees C) and cook until golden brown and set about 8 minutes. Remove parchment paper to a wire rack to cool. Repeat with the remaining cookie dough.

840. Air Fryer Oreos recipe!

Prep Time: 5 Mins Cook Time: 5 Mins
Total Time: 10 mins

Ingredients
- 8 Oreo cookies or other brand sandwich cookies
- 1 package Pillsbury Crescent Roll (or crescent dough sheet)

Instructions
- Preheat your air fryer to 320 degrees.
- Spread out crescent dough onto a cutting board or counter.
- Using your finger, press down into each perforated line so it forms one big sheet.
- Cut the dough into eighths.
- Place an Oreo cookie in the center of each of the crescent roll squares and roll each corner up (see visual above in post).
- Bunch up the rest of the crescent roll to make sure it covers the entire Oreo
- Cookie. Do not stretch the crescent roll too thin or it will break.
- Gently place the Air Fried Oreos inside the air fryer in one even row so they
- Do not touch. If you have a smaller air fryer, cook in batches.
- Cook Oreos at 320 degrees for 5-6 mins until golden brown on the outside.
- Carefully remove the Air Fryer Oreos from the air fryer and immediately dust them with powdered sugar if desired.
- Let cool for two min., then enjoy!

Lean And Green Recipes

841. Air Fryer Green Beans

Prep Time: 5 mins Cook Time: 10 mins
Total Time: 15 mins
Ingredients
- 1 lb green beans
- 1 tbsp olive oil
- 1/2 tsp salt
- 1/4 tsp pepper

Instructions
- Trim the green beans, then toss with olive oil, salt, and pepper.
- Put prepared green beans in the air fryer basket and cook at 400F for 10 min., shaking the basket halfway through.

842. Chicken and Veggies (20 Minutes!)

Prep Time: 5 mins Cook Time: 15 mins
Total Time: 20 mins
Ingredients
- 1 pound chicken breast, chopped into bite-size pieces
- 1 cup broccoli florets (fresh or frozen)
- 1 zucchini chopped
- 1 cup bell pepper chopped (any colors you like)
- 1/2 onion chopped
- 2 cloves garlic minced or crushed
- 2 Tbsps olive oil
- 1/2 Tsp. EACH garlic powder, chili powder, salt, pepper
- 1 Tbsp Italian seasoning

Instructions
- Preheat air fryer to 400F.
- Chop the veggies and chicken into small bite-size pieces and transfer to a large mixing bowl.
- Add the oil and seasoning to the bowl and toss to combine.
- Add the chicken and veggies to the preheated air fryer and cook for 10 min., shaking halfway, or until the chicken and veggies are charred and chicken is cooked through. If your air fryer is small, you may have to cook them in 2-3 batches.

843. Fried Green Beans (Air Fryer)

Prep Time: 5 mins Cook Time: 5 mins
Total Time: 10 mins
Ingredients
- 1 lb. fresh green beans (cleaned and trimmed)
- 1 tsp. oil
- 1/4 tsp. garlic powder
- 1/8 tsp. sea salt

Instructions
- Toss all the ingredients together in a bowl to coat the green beans with oil and spices.
- Transfer about half of the green beans to the air fryer basket. (You'll have to do this in two batches or the beans won't cook properly) Spread them out as evenly as possible and return the basket to the air fryer.
- Adjust temp to 400 and set time to 5 min., or whichever time you chose from the chart above, and press start.
- When done, remove the basket from the fryer and turn the beans out onto a platter (repeat with the second half of the beans).
- If you try the beans and they aren't cooked enough to your liking, simply return them to the air fryer in the basket and cook in 2-minute increments until they are cooked to your liking.
- Cool slightly and serve.

844. Air Fryer Green Beans

Prep Time: 5 mins Cook Time: 15 mins
Total Time: 20 mins
Ingredients
- 1 pound (454 g) fresh green beans, ends trimmed and halved
- 1-2 Tbsps (15 ml) olive oil or spray
- 1/2 Tsp. (2.5 ml) garlic powder
- Salt and pepper, to taste
- Fresh lemon slices

Instructions
- In a bowl, combine green beans, oil, garlic powder, salt, and pepper. Place the seasoned green beans in an air fryer basket.
- Air Fry 360°F for about 10-14 mins depending on your preferred doneness. Toss and shake about 2 times during cooking.
- Season with salt and pepper, to taste. Serve with lemon slices or wedges

845. Air Fryer Green Beans With Bacon

Prep Time: 15 mins Cook Time: 10 mins
Total Time: 25 mins
Ingredients
- 3 cups (330 g) Frozen Cut Green Beans
- 3 slices (3 slices) bacon, diced
- 1/4 cup (62.5 ml) Water
- 1 Tsp. (1 teaspoon) Kosher Salt
- 1 Tsp. (1 teaspoon) Ground Black Pepper

Instructions
- Place the frozen green beans, onion, bacon, and water in a 6 x 3-inch heatproof pan.
- Place the pan in the air fryer basket. Set air fryer to 375°F for 15 min..
- Raise the air fryer temperature to 400°F for 5 min.. Add salt and pepper to taste and toss well.
- Remove from the air fryer and cover the pan. Let it rest for 5 mins and serve.
- I find that frozen vegetables often cook up better in an air fryer if you're looking for moist, tender beans.
- If you want crispy beans, you should start with fresh beans rather than frozen.
- You can also substitute cooked sausage for the bacon.
- If you use lean chicken sausage, then you may have to spray the beans with a little oil to get the best "air-fried" texture from them.

846. Air Fryer Stuffed Peppers

Prep Time: 15 Mins Cook Time: 15 Mins
Total Time: 30 Mins
Ingredients
- 6 Green Bell Peppers
- 1 Lb Lean Ground Beef
- 1 Tbsp Olive Oil
- 1/4 Cup Green Onion Diced
- 1/4 Cup Fresh Parsley
- 1/2 Tsp Ground Sage
- 1/2 Tsp Garlic Salt
- 1 Cup Cooked Rice
- 1 Cup Marinara Sauce More to Taste
- 1/4 Cup Shredded Mozzarella Cheese

Instructions
- Warm-up a medium-sized skillet with the ground beef and cook until well done.
- Drain the beef and return to the pan.
- Add in the olive oil, green onion, parsley, sage, and salt. Mix this well.
- Add in the cooked rice and marinara, mix well.
- Cut the top off of each pepper and clean the seeds out.
- Scoop the mixture into each of the peppers and place it in the basket of the air fryer. (I did 4 the first round, 2 the second to make them fit.)
- Cook for 10 mins at 355*, carefully open and add cheese.

- Cook for an additional 5 mins or until peppers are slightly soft and cheese is melted.
- Serve.

847. Weight Watchers Stuffed Peppers

Prep Time: 5 Mins Cook Time: 25 Mins Total Time: 30 Mins

Ingredients

- 6 bell peppers red, yellow, and orange
- 1/4 cup water
- 1/2 lb ground turkey breast LEAN
- 1 small zucchini small dice
- 2 cups crushed tomatoes no salt added
- 1 cup mushrooms small dice
- 1.5 cups cauliflower rice
- 1 tbsp Worcestershire sauce
- 1 tsp salt
- 3 Babybel Mini Light Cheese Rounds grated

Instructions

- Heat non-stick skillet on medium-high
- Add water, ground turkey, zucchini, and mushrooms
- Brown for five mins and add salt
- While turkey is browning, heat cauliflower rice in microwave according to package directions
- To the turkey, add Worcestershire, rice, and tomatoes and simmer for 2-3 mins
- While turkey mixture is cooking, prep peppers by slicing off tops and clean the insides (save the pepper tops to use in other recipes)
- Spoon turkey mixture into peppers
- Air Fryer **Instructions**: AF at 350 for 10 min.. Open AF and add shredded cheese. Air Fry 5 mins more until cheese melts and browns
- Oven **Instructions**: Cover with foil and bake at 350 for 30 min.. Uncover and add shredded cheese. Bake an additional 15 mins (uncovered)

848. Parmesan-Crusted Tilapia

Prep Time: 3 Mins Cook Time: 7 Mins Total Time: 10 Mins

Ingredients

- 2 thin tilapia fillets (about 4 ounces) fresh or frozen (times given for both below)
- Olive oil pump spray not aerosol or 1 Tbsp olive oil
- 1/4 Tsp. salt
- 1/4 Tsp. ground pepper (optional)
- 2 Tbsp grated Parmesan cheese
- 1/2 cup fine dry breadcrumbs

Instructions

- Place the frozen tilapia fillets on an aluminum or stainless steel baking pan while preheating the air fryer and measuring ingredients.
- Crazy Good Tip: These few mins on the baking pan will ever so slightly thaw the fillets just enough to allow the breadcrumbs to stick to the oil on them. Preheat the air fryer to 390-400 degrees for 3 min.. Most air fryers preset "air fryer" button is 390F to 400F degrees.
- Spray or coat fish fillets with olive oil sprayer or mister or brush with olive oil. (Not Pam aerosol vegetable cooking spray)
- Sprinkle both sides of fillets with salt and if desired, pepper.
- Sprinkle the top side of fillets with Parmesan cheese.
- Place the dry breadcrumbs on a plate and gently press the fish into the breadcrumbs to coat them. If you have trouble getting the breadcrumbs to stick to the fish, wait just a few mins or
- I like to spray the breaded fish again on top with a little bit of olive oil spray (again, not aerosol)
- Frozen fish: Air Fry at 390-400 degrees for 9 t0 11 minutes, without turning, depending on the thickness of fish until fish flakes easily in the center.
- Fresh fish: Air Fry at 390-400 degrees for 7 min., without turning, depending on the thickness of fish until fish flakes easily in the center.
- Carefully remove the fish with a silicone-coated spatula to prevent scraping the nonstick surface.

849. Air Fryer Plantain Chips

Prep Time: 5 Mins Cook Time: 12 Mins Total Time: 17 Mins

Ingredients

- 1 Green Plantain Evenly sliced
- 1 Tsp. Kosher Salt or to taste
- 1 Cup Water
- Lemon or Lime Juice Optional

Instructions

- Add the water and salt to a bowl. Stir. Set aside.
- Peel the plantains.
- Sliced the plantains in even slices. Best to use a mandolin.
- Add the plantain slices to the salted water, let soak for about 5-10 min..
- Transfer to the air fryer. Spray with olive oil, cook for 12 min., shaking and spraying with oil in between cooking. Increase the time for desired crispiness. Sprinkle with lemon or lime juice (optional). Enjoy!

850. Easy Green Bean Fries

Prep time: 15 MINS Total time: 15 MINS

Ingredients

- 1 pound of green beans, ends trimmed if needed
- 1 egg
- 1 Tbsp of low-carb ranch dressing, jalapeño ranch dressing, or mayonnaise
- 1 cup almond flour
- 1/2 Tsp. garlic salt
- 1/2 Tsp. pepper
- 1/2 Tsp. garlic powder
- 1/2 cup parmesan cheese

Air Fryer Instructions:

- Preheat your machine according to the directions at 390 degrees F.
- When hot, add in as many green beans as you comfortably can without overcrowding.
- Spray with cooking spray to help crisp.
- Cook 5 min., shaking the basket halfway through cooking to move them around.

851. Roasted Okra

Prep Time: 5 mins Cook Time: 15 mins Total Time: 20 mins

Ingredients

- 1/2 pound small whole okra, per person
- Salt to taste
- Pepper to taste (or seasonings of choice)
- Olive oil spray (optional, if needed to prevent sticking)

Instructions

- First, start with the smallest okra you can find. Larger okra tends to be woody, which wouldn't work in this recipe.
- Wash the okra. Trim off any excess stems, but do not cut into the okra pod itself.
- Preheat the oven to 450 F. Spray a

shallow baking dish with olive oil, if necessary, add okra, and season to taste. Give the okra one quick (1/2 second) spray with olive oil and put them into the oven. Bake, stirring every 5 mins until okra is browned on all sides, about 15 minutes. Serve hot out of the oven.

Air Fryer Instructions

• Preheat a standard air fryer to 390F or a Breville Air to 425F. Toss the freshly washed okra with seasoning and spread it in a single layer in the air fryer basket. Begin air frying, checking after about 7 minutes. Air fry until the okra is browning on all sides.

852. Easy Air Fryer Green Beans

Prep Time: 2 mins Cook Time: 6 mins
Total Time: 8 mins

Ingredients

• 1 lb (450g) green beans
• Cooking spray
• Salt

Instructions

• Preheat the air fryer to 400 F / 200C.
• Add the green beans to a bowl and spray with some low-calorie spray and the best salt ever and combine.
• Place the beans into the air fryer basket and cook for 6-8 min., turning a couple of times during cooking so that they brown evenly.
• Remove and serve topped with some extra salt and chopped herbs if you like.

853. Air Fryer Caramelized Stone Fruit

Prep Time: 3 mins Cook Time: 15 mins
Total Time: 15 mins

Ingredients

• 1 lbs / 2-3 stone fruits such as peaches, nectarines, plums, or apricots
• 1 tbsp maple syrup
• 1/2 tbsp coconut sugar
• 1/4 tsp cinnamon, optional
• Pinch of salt, optional

Instructions

• **Prepare Air Fryer:** Cut a sheet of parchment paper that will fit the floor of your air fryer basket and then place it inside the basket.
• **Prepare Fruit:** Slice the stone fruit down the middle and remove the seed. Then brush some maple syrup on the flesh and sprinkle with some coconut sugar. Add in a pinch of cinnamon and salt if desired.
• **Air Fry:** Place the stone fruit in the air fryer basket and air fry at 350 for 15 mins or until caramelized.

854. Air Fryer Green Beans With Lemon

Prep Time: 5 Mins Cook Time: 20 Mins
Total Time: 25 Mins

Ingredients

• 2 lbs green beans, washed & trimmed
• 2 Tbsp olive oil
• ¾ Tsp. salt
• 2 Tbsps lemon juice

Instructions

• Preheat the air fryer to 400 degrees for 5 minutes.
• In a large bowl, toss the beans in the olive oil until they are evenly covered with oil.
• Sprinkle the beans with ½ Tsp. salt and toss further until the salt evenly covers all the beans.
• Add the beans to the air fryer basket and air fry for 17-19 min., shaking the beans every 4 minutes, or until the beans are blistered and browning around the edges,
• Pour the beans into a large serving bowl and squeeze or pour the lemon juice over the beans. Toss the beans until they're covered with the lemon juice and season with up to an extra ¼ Tsp. salt to taste.

855. Asian-Inspired Green Beans

Prep Time: 5 mins Cook Time: 10 mins
Total Time: 15 mins

Ingredients

• 8 ounces fresh green beans
• 1 Tbsp tamari
• 1 Tsp. sesame oil

Instructions

• Break off the ends of the green beans, then snap them in half.
• Place the green beans in a resealable plastic bag or a container with a lid. Add the tamari and sesame oil and shake to coat.
• Put the green beans in the basket of your air fryer. Cook at 390 or 400 degrees (depending on your air fryer model) for 10 min., tossing halfway through.

856. Air Fryer Green Beans (II Version)

Prep Time: 10 mins Cook Time: 10 mins

Total Time: 20 mins

Ingredients

• 24 ounces fresh green beans - trimmed
• 2 cups sliced button mushrooms
• 1 fresh lemon - juiced
• 1 Tbsp garlic powder
• ¾ Tsp. ground sage
• 1 Tsp. onion powder
• ¾ Tsp. salt
• ¾ Tsp. black pepper
• Spray oil
• ⅓ cup french fried onions - for garnish, optional

Instructions

• In a large bowl, toss together the green beans, mushrooms, lemon juice, garlic powder, sage, onion powder, salt, and pepper. Transfer the mixture to your air fryer basket, then use spray oil to coat, shaking well.
• Air fry at 400° F for 10-12 min., shaking every 2-3 minutes.
• Serve topped with french fried onions, if you're using them.

857. Air Fryer Garlic Roasted Green Beans

Prep Time: 2 mins Cook Time: 8 mins
Total Time: 10 mins

Ingredients

• 3/4-1 pound fresh green beans (trimmed)
• 1 Tbsp olive oil
• 1 Tsp. garlic powder
• Salt and pepper to taste

Instructions

• Drizzle the olive oil over the green beans. Sprinkle the seasonings throughout. Toss to coat.
• Place the green beans in the air fryer basket.
• Cook the green beans for 7-8 mins at 370 degrees. Toss the basket halfway through the total cook time.
• Remove the green beans and serve.

Best Air Fryer Recipes

858. Easy Green Bean Fries

Prep Time: 15 Mins Total Time: 15 Mins
Ingredients

• 1 pound of green beans, ends

trimmed if needed
- One egg
- One tablespoon of low-carb ranch dressing, jalapeño ranch dressing, or mayonnaise
- 1 cup almond flour
- 1/2 teaspoon garlic salt
- 1/2 teaspoon pepper
- 1/2 teaspoon garlic powder
- 1/2 cup parmesan cheese

Directions:
- Preheat oven to 400 degrees F.
- Set up your breading station by setting up two shallow bowls and a baking sheet with a silicone baking sheet or sprayed well with cooking spray.
- In the first bowl, combine the egg and the ranch dressing, mix until completely combined
- In the second bowl, combine the almond flour, spices, and parmesan, mix well.
- Roll the green bean in the egg, then the almond flour crust, and place it on the pan.
- Lightly spray the breaded fries with cooking spray to help crisp them.
- Bake 10-12 Minsor until the green beans reach your desired tenderness.

859. Air Fryer Green Beans
Prep Time: 5 mins Cook Time: 10 mins Total Time: 15 mins
Ingredients
- 1 lb green beans
- 1 tbsp olive oil
- 1/2 tsp salt
- 1/4 tsp pepper

Directions:
- Trim the green beans, then toss with olive oil, salt, and pepper.
- Put prepared green beans in the air fryer basket and cook at 400F for 10 minutes, shaking the basket halfway through.

860. Healthy Air Fryer Baked Salmon
Prep Time: 3 Mins Cook Time: 10 Mins Total Time: 13 Mins
Ingredients
- 2 6 ounces (2 170 g) salmon fillets, skin, and bones removed
- One teaspoon (5 ml) olive oil or a light spray of organic cooking spray

- Kosher salt, to taste
- Black pepper, to taste

Directions:
- Coat salmon with light oil or cooking spray. Season both sides of salmon with salt and pepper.
- Place salmon in the basket. Air fry the salmon at 360°F for about 10 minutes or until cooked to your preferred texture.
- Check the salmon with a fork to make sure it's cooked the way you like it.
- Enjoy! It's that easy.

861. Air Fryer Roasted Cauliflower
Prep Time: 5 minutes Cook Time: 12 minutes Total Time: 17 minutes
Ingredients
- 4 cups chopped cauliflower
- 1 Tbs olive oil
- 1 tsp parsley
- 1 tsp thyme
- 1 tsp minced garlic
- 1 tsp salt
- ¼ cup parmesan cheese
- Salt and pepper to taste

Directions:
- In a large bowl, combine cauliflower with olive oil parsley, thyme, minced garlic, and salt.
- Toss to combine, and cauliflower is well coated.
- Place cauliflower in the air-fryer basket. Set air-fryer to 400 degrees for 20 minutes.
- Stir the cauliflower at 10 minutes, and add parmesan cheese.
- Serve immediately, season with salt and pepper to taste.

862. Air Fryer Mushrooms
Prep Time: 5 mins Cook Time: 10 mins Total Time: 15 mins
Ingredients
- 1 lb mushrooms sliced
- 2 tbsp olive oil
- 1/2 tsp salt
- 1/4 tsp pepper

Directions:
- Put sliced mushrooms in the air fryer basket.
- Add olive oil, salt, and pepper and toss to coat.
- Cook the mushrooms in the air fryer for 10 minutes at 400F, shaking the basket halfway through.

863. Air Fryer Eggplant
Prep Time: 5 mins Cook Time: 20 mins Total Time: 25 mins
Ingredients
- 2 tbsp olive oil
- 1 tsp garlic powder
- 1/2 tsp red pepper
- 1 tsp sweet paprika optional
- 1/2 tsp Italian seasoning
- One eggplant cut into 1-inch pieces

Directions:
- Combine all ingredients and toss until eggplant pieces are coated with olive oil and spices. Put the eggplant in the air fryer basket.
- Air fry the eggplant at 375F for 20 minutes, shaking the basket halfway through.

864. Zucchini Fries With Parmesan
Prep Time: 5 mins Cook Time: 10 mins Total Time: 15 mins
Ingredients
- Two zucchini
- 1/4 cup Parmesan cheese
- 1 tbsp olive oil
- 1/2 tsp salt
- 1/4 tsp pepper
- 1/2 tsp Italian seasoning

Directions:
- Cut off the ends of zucchini, cut zucchini lengthwise in half, then cut each half in half, then slice zucchini into the shape of fries.
- Put zucchini fries in a bowl and add olive oil, Parmesan cheese, Italian seasoning, salt, and pepper. Toss until combined.
- Put zucchini fries in the air fryer basket.
- Cook zucchini fries in the air fryer for 10 minutes at 400F.
- If desired, sprinkle with additional Parmesan cheese before serving.

865. Air Fryer Fries
Prep Time: 10 Mins Cook Time: 20 Mins Total Time: 30 minutes
- **Ingredients**
- One baker potato large, peeled
- 2 Tbsp vegetable oil
- 1/2 tsp kosher salt
- 1 tsp black pepper

Directions:
- Peel potato, and cut lengthwise into

1/4 inch thick slices. Then turn over and make additional cuts to make the fries, 1/4 inch square.

- Toss potatoes with vegetable oil and seasonings (salt and pepper) until well coated.
- Place fries in a single layer with space between them in an air-fryer basket. Work in batches if necessary or use a trivet to create two layers
- Set air fryer to 400 degrees.
- Cook at 400 degrees for 20 minutes, shaking the fries at the half way point
- When 20 Minsis up, check fries for desired crispiness and golden brownness; add time if desired.
- Remove from the air fryer, and serve with favorite dipping sauce.

866. Air Fryer Turkey Legs

Prep Time: 10 minutes Cook Time: 27 Mins Total Time: 37 minutes

Ingredients
- Four Turkey Legs
- 1 tsp salt
- 1 tsp pepper
- 1 Tbs butter
- 1/4 tsp rosemary
- 1/4 tsp oregano
- 1/4 tsp thyme

Directions:
- Pat turkey legs dry, then season with salt and pepper
- Combine butter with seasonings in a small bowl and mix well.
- Rub butter all over turkey legs and under the skin if possible
- Preheat the air fryer to 350 ° F
- Place the turkey leg into the air fryer basket and cook for 27 minutes until the internal temp is 165 degrees F.
- Check internal temp and add time if needed, then rest legs for 5 Minsand serve.

867. Air Fryer Turkey Breast

- Prep Time: 5 minutes
- Cook Time: 55 minutes
- Total Time: 1 hour
- Serving: 2-4 Serving
- Ingredients
- 4-pound turkey breast on the bone with skin (ribs removed)
- One tablespoon olive oil
- Two teaspoons kosher salt

- Butter Rub
- 2 Tbs butter
- 1/2 tsp paprika
- 1 tsp dried thyme
- 1/2 tsp dried oregano

Directions:
- Mix butter mixture in a small bowl, and gently spread it under the turkey breast skin
- Rub 1/2 tablespoon of oil all over the turkey breast. Season both sides with salt and then rub in the remaining half tablespoon of oil over the skin side.
- Preheat the air fryer 350F and cook skin side down 20 minutes, turn over and cook until the internal temperature is 160F using an instant-read thermometer about 30 to 40 Minsmore depending on the size of your breast.
- Let is rest 10 minutes before carving.

868. Air Fryer Chicken Tenders

Prep Time: 10 min Cook Time: 10 min Total Time: 20 min

Ingredients
- 1 pound of boneless skinless chicken tenders
- Two eggs, beaten
- 1 1/2 cups of bread crumbs (of choice)
- One teaspoon salt
- Cooking Spray

Directions:
- Preheat the air fryer if your brand requires preheating. Warm the air fryer by setting it to 400 degrees F for 5 minutes.
- Allow it to run without any food in the basket.
- Season both sides of your chicken tenders with salt and pepper. Prepare two shallows dishes.
- Add the egg to one dish and whisk it well until it looks like scrambled eggs. In another dish, add the breadcrumbs. Dip the chicken tenders into the egg wash and then press it into the bread crumbs.
- Turn to coat both sides. Add the breaded chicken tenders into the air fryer basket.
- Place the Fry Basket back into the air fryer and spray the bread chicken tenders with some
- Cooking Spray. Set the temperature to 400 degrees.
- Cook the chicken tenders for 5

minutes on one side, and then flip them.
- Continue cooking for another five minutes.

869. Easy Air Fryer Green Beans

Prep Time: 2 Minutes Cook Time: 8 Minutes Additional Time: 2 Minutes Total Time: 12 Mins

Ingredients
- 1 lb. fresh green beans
- 1/4 tsp garlic powder
- 1/2 tsp salt
- 1/8 tsp pepper

Directions:
- Trim the tops and tails of the beans.
- Add the green beans to a large mixing bowl.
- Spray green beans with canola or olive oil cooking spray. Season with salt, pepper, and garlic powder. Toss until well combined.
- Place green beans into the air fryer basket.
- Cook at 400 degrees for 8-10 minutes. Toss a few times during cooking, so they brown evenly.
- Remove from air fryer basket and serve immediately.

870. Mexican Air Fryer Corn On The Cob + Grill Version

Prep Time: 2 mins Cook Time: 10 mins Total Time: 12 mins

Ingredients
- Three corn on the cobb husks removed
- Low-Calorie spray
- Toppings
- Salt
- Lemon Zest
- Chopped cilantro fresh coriander

Directions:
- Preheat the air fryer to 400 F / 200C.
- Add the corn on the cob to a bowl and spray with some low-calorie spray and the best salt ever and combine.
- Place the corn into the air fryer basket and cook for 10 minutes, turning a couple of times during cooking to cook evenly.
- Remove and serve topped with some extra salt, lemon zest, and chopped cilantro.

871. Air Fryer Chickpeas

Prep Time: 2 mins Cook Time: 12 mins Total Time: 14 mins

Ingredients

- 14 oz (400g) tin of chickpeas rinsed, drained, and dried
- 2 tsp olive oil
- ½ tsp smoked paprika
- ½ tsp ground cumin
- Salt

Directions:

- Pre heat air fryer to 390F / 200C.
- Mix all the ingredients in a bowl.
- Add the chickpeas to the air fryer basket.
- Cook for 12-15 mins turning halfway through.

872.Maple Cinnamon Carrot Fries

Prep Time: 5 mins Cook Time: 12 mins

Ingredients

- 1 lb (450g carrots about four large carrots cut into sticks, or start with store-bought pre-cut carrots
- 1 tsp olive oil
- One tsp maple syrup
- 1/2 tsp ground cinnamon
- Salt to taste

Directions:

- In a bowl, combine all ingredients and then set aside.
- Preheat to 400F / Fan assisted 180C / 200C / gas 6.
- Place the carrots in a single layer on a baking tray.
- Bake in the preheated oven for 15-20 minutes, turning halfway through or till done.
- Serve and enjoy.

873.Air Fryer Feta Cheese Appetizer

Prep Time: 2 mins Cook Time: 15 mins Total Time: 18 mins

Ingredients

- 250 grams (1 block) feta cheese
- 2 tbsp olive oil
- 2 tbsp honey
- 1 tsp dried oregano
- 1/4 tsp chili flakes optional
- Oven-Baked Feta Cheese Appetizer

Directions:

- Preheat the oven to 400F /200C / fan-assisted 180C / gas 6.
- Put feta cheese in an oven-safe baking dish.
- Drizzle olive oil and honey over the

top of the feta cheese. Then sprinkle on the dried oregano and chili flakes.

- Bake for about 18 mins or until soft.
- Serve warm and enjoy!

874.Air Fryer Sweet Potato Fries

Prep Time: 10 mins Cook Time: 14 mins Total Time: 24 mins

Ingredients

- One tablespoon olive oil
- 1/4 teaspoon fine sea salt
- 2 (5 oz) sweet potatoes
- Cooking spray

Directions:

- Peel and cut each sweet potato into even 1/4 inch thick fries.
- Mix olive oil and salt and toss the sweet potato fries to coat thoroughly.
- Preheat the air fryer to 400F / 200C / Gas 6 and lightly spray the air fryer basket with cooking spray.
- Cook in batches (one layer), between 8 mins (thin fries) – to 14 mins (thick fries), flipping the fries halfway through the cooking time.

875.Air Fryer Butternut Squash Fries

- Prep Time: 5 mins
- Cook Time: 12 mins
- Servings: 4

Ingredients

- 3 cups (450g) butternut squash peeled and cut into 1-inch cubes
- 1 tbsp olive oil
- 1 tsp dried oregano
- 1/2 tsp smoked paprika
- Salt to taste
- Oven Roasted Butternut Squash

Directions:

- Preheat to 400F / Fan assisted 180C / 200C / gas 6.
- In a bowl, combine all ingredients, tossing to coat the squash well.
- Place the butternut squash in a single layer on a baking tray.
- Bake in the preheated oven for 20-25 minutes, turning halfway through or till done.
- Serve your oven-roasted butternut squash warm and enjoy.

876.Air Fryer Radishes

Prep Time: 5 mins Cook Time: 14 mins

Ingredients

- One bunch radishes stem and tips removed

- 1/2 tsp dried oregano
- Salt to taste

Directions:

- Preheat air fryer to 390 F / 200 C.
- Wash radishes, pat dry, and cut into quarters.
- Add all ingredients to a bowl and toss to combine.
- Place radishes in the air fryer basket.
- Cook for 9-14 mins, till done to your liking.

877.Air Fryer Roasted Almonds

Prep Time: 1 min Cook Time: 8 mins

Ingredients

- 1 cup (140g) whole raw almonds with skins on

Directions:

- Preheat the oven to 350 degrees F / 180 degree C.
- Spread nuts into a single layer on a large baking sheet.
- Roast for 10 minutes, making sure to turn halfway through. If they still need a little time, then roast for up to 6 more minutes, making sure to check after every 2 minutes.
- Watch them carefully, as they can burn quickly.
- Cool completely on the baking sheet before storing it in an airtight container.

878.Air Fryer Vegetable Kabobs

Prep Time: 5 mins Cook Time: 8 mins Total Time: 13 mins

Ingredients

- 1 cup (75g) button mushrooms
- 1 cup (200g) grape tomatoes or cherry tomatoes
- One small zucchini cut into chunks
- 1/2 tsp ground cumin
- 1/2 bell pepper sliced
- One small onion cut into chunks (or 3-4 small shallots, halved)
- Salt to taste

Directions:

- Soak skewers in water for at least 10 mins before using.
- Preheat air fryer to 390f / 198c.
- Thread vegetables onto the skewers.
- Place skewers in an air fryer and make sure they are not touching. If the air fryer basket is small, you may need to cut the ends of the skewers to fit.
- Cook for 10 mins, turning halfway

through the cooking time. Since air fryer temperatures can vary, start with less time and then add more as needed.

• Transfer veggie kabobs to a plate and serve.

879. Easy One-Pan Cauliflower Curry

Prep Time: 5 mins Cook Time: 15 mins Total Time: 20 mins

Ingredients

• ¾ cup (180ml) light coconut milk
• 1 ½ tsp garam masala
• 1 tsp mild curry powder
• 1 tsp garlic puree
• ½ tsp turmeric or to your taste
• Salt
• 12 oz (350 g) cauliflower florets
• 1 cup (200g) sweet corn kernels
• Three scallions (spring onions), sliced

Directions:

• Preheat air fryer to 375F / 190C.
• In a large bowl, mix all the ingredients from the coconut milk to pepper.
• Add in the vegetables and mix till coated.
• Transfer to a deep dish that is at least 4 inches deep.
• Cook for 12-15 mins till cauliflower is cooked, mixing a couple of times during cooking.

880. Fryer Brussels Sprouts

Prep Time: 2 mins Cook Time: 10 mins Total Time: 12 mins

Ingredients

• 1 lb (450g) Brussels sprouts stems cut up and halved and any loose leaves removed
• Calorie-controlled cooking spray
• Salt
• Black pepper

Directions:

• Preheat the air fryer to 350F / 180C.
• Place Brussels sprouts into a bowl, spray with cooking spray, add salt and black pepper, and mix until well coated.
• Add Brussels sprouts to the air fryer basket and fry between 8-12 mins, removing and shaking the basket a couple of times when cooking for even crisping.
• Serve warm or at room temperature.

881. Air Fryer Plantains

Prep Time: 2 mins Cook Time: 8 mins Total Time: 10 mins

Ingredients

• One plantain
• 3/4 tsp oil
• Salt to taste

Directions:

• Preheat air fryer to 350F /180C
• Peel the plantain and cut it into slices and add to a bowl.
• Gently mix in the oil and salt until plantains are coated on both sides.
• Put half the plantain slices in the air fryer basket in a single layer.
• Cook for 10 mins turning halfway through.
• Serve warm.

882. Fried Green Beans

Prep Time: 5 minutes Cook Time: 5 Mins Total Time: 10 minutes

Ingredients

• 1 lb. fresh green beans (cleaned and trimmed)
• 1 tsp. oil
• 1/4 tsp. garlic powder
• 1/8 tsp. sea salt

Directions:

• Toss all the ingredients together in a bowl to coat the green beans with oil and spices.
• Transfer about half of the green beans to the air fryer basket. (You'll have to do this in two batches, or the beans won't cook properly) Spread them out as evenly as possible and return the basket to the air fryer.
• Adjust temp to 400 and set time to 5 minutes, or whichever time you chose from the chart above, and press start.
• When done, remove the basket from the fryer and turn the beans out onto a platter (repeat with the second half of the beans).
• If you try the beans and aren't cooked enough to your liking, simply return them to the air fryer in the basket and cook in 2-minute increments until they are cooked to your liking.
• Cool slightly and serve.

883. Air Fryer Fried Green Tomatoes

Prep Time: 15 mins Cook Time: 20 mins Total Time: 35 mins

Ingredient

• Two green tomatoes, cut into 1/4-inch slices

• Salt and freshly ground black pepper to taste
• ⅓ cup all-purpose flour
• ½ cup buttermilk
• Two eggs, lightly beaten
• 1 cup plain panko bread crumbs
• 1 cup yellow cornmeal
• One teaspoon garlic powder
• ½ teaspoon paprika
• One tablespoon olive oil, or as needed

Directions:

• Season tomato slices with salt and pepper.
• Set up a breading station in 3 shallow dishes: pour flour into the first dish; stir together buttermilk and eggs in the second dish; and mix breadcrumbs, cornmeal, garlic powder, and paprika in the third dish.
• Dredge tomato slices in flour, shaking off the excess. Dip tomatoes into the egg mixture and then into the bread crumb mixture, making sure to coat both sides.
• Preheat the air fryer to 400 degrees F (200 degrees C). Brush the fryer basket with olive oil. Place breaded tomato slices in the fryer basket, making sure they do not touch each other; cook in batches if necessary. Brush the tops of tomatoes with olive oil.
• Cook for 12 minutes, then flip the tomatoes and brush again with olive oil. Cook until crisp and golden brown, 3 to 5 Minsmore. Remove tomatoes to a paper towel-lined rack to keep crisp. Repeat with the remaining tomatoes.

884. Air Fryer Chicken Fajitas

Prep Time: 5 minutes Cook Time: 15 Mins

Ingredients

• One large (about 10 ounces) chicken breast, sliced into 1/4-inch slices
• 1/2 medium onion, sliced
• 1/2 green bell pepper, sliced
• 1/2 red bell pepper, sliced
• 1 1/2 tablespoons olive or coconut oil
• Two teaspoons chili powder
• One teaspoon cumin
• 1/2 teaspoon salt
• 1/2 teaspoon paprika
• 1/2 teaspoon garlic powder
• 1/2 teaspoon onion powder

• 1/4 teaspoon dried oregano

Directions:

• Place chicken, onion, and bell peppers in a medium bowl.

• Drizzle with olive oil and sprinkle with seasonings. Stir to mix evenly.

• Place mixture in the Air Fryer basket. Set to cook for 15 Mins at 350 degrees. Open the Air Fryer halfway through and shake the basket.

885.Easy Air Fryer Chicken Breast

Prep Time: 5 Mins Cook Time: 15 Mins Total Time: 20 minutes

Ingredients

• 2 Boneless Skinless Chicken Breast

• Two tablespoon Salted Butter softened

• One teaspoon Dried Italian Seasoning

• 1/2 teaspoon Smoked paprika

• Kosher salt and pepper to taste

Directions:

• Place the chicken breast on a cutting board and, using a sharp knife, cut each breast in half lengthwise (see notes), resulting in 4 chicken cutlets.

• In a small bowl, mix the seasonings with the butter spread the mixture on top of each chicken breast cutlet.

• Place in the air fryer and cook at 370F for 10-15 minutes.

• Check after 10 minutes for doneness with an internal meat thermometer. It should be 165F.

• Continue cooking until the temperature is reached.

• Remove from air fryer and serve.

886.Air Fryer Chicken Thighs

Prep Time: 5 minutes Cook Time: 20 Mins Total Time: 25 minutes

Ingredients

• Four chicken thighs, skin on

• 1 tsp cumin

• 1 tsp garlic powder

• 1 tsp onion powder

• 1 tsp chili powder

• ½ tsp sea salt

• ¼ tsp pepper

• 1 tbsp olive oil

Directions:

• Toss all seasoning together in a small bowl.

• Pat chicken thighs dry with a paper towel and drizzle bother sides with olive

oil. Then sprinkle both sides with the seasoning. Be generous!

• Heat the air fryer to 350 degrees.

• Place chicken in the air fryer basket, so they are not touching. You don't want to overcrowd them, or they won't cook right.

• Set a timer for 20 minutes and flip the chicken at 10 minutes. The internal temperature should reach 165 degrees. Air Fryer Zucchini Fries

Prep Time: 7 mins Cook Time: 7 mins Servings: 4 servings

Ingredients

• Four large zucchini or eight mini zucchini, rinsed and ends removed

• One medium egg

• 1 TBS water

• 1/3 cup regular breadcrumbs

• 1/3 cup panko breadcrumbs

• 2 TBS everything but the bagel seasoning or garlic powder, onion powder, salt, pepper, poppy seeds- 1/8 tsp each

• 2 TBS parmesan cheese

• Oil spray

Directions:

• Prepare the zucchini by cutting off the stem and ends.

• Wash and dry. If using large zucchini, cut the zucchini in half length-wise, then cut it into 1/4ths.

• They are in 'fry' slices. If using mini zucchini, just cut into 1/4th slices.

• In a shallow bowl, add egg and 1 TBS of water, then whisk and beat until a little frothy. Add a handful of zucchini and toss around to coat.

• In a separate shallow dish or bowl, add panko breadcrumbs, regular breadcrumbs, cheese, and spices.

• Add the zucchini fries a few at a time, and toss until coated.

• Place them into the air fryer tray.

• Repeat until all zucchini are coated.

• Add fries to the air fryer basket, do not place them too close together.

• Lightly spray the tops with oil and close.

• Set air fryer for 400 degrees and 7 minutes.

• Check and if they are browned, then remove. If not, cook 1-2 more minutes.

• Serve with your favorite dipping

sauce!

887.Air Fryer Green Bean Fries

Prep Time: 5 mins Cook Time: 7 mins Total Time: 12 mins

Ingredients

• About 25 fresh green beans rinsed and dried

• One egg

• One egg white

• 1/4 cup panko breadcrumbs (Japanese style breadcrumbs)

• 1/4 cup regular whole-wheat breadcrumbs

• 2 TBS grated parmesan cheese

• 1/2 TBS garlic powder

• 1/8 tsp salt

• 1/8 tsp black pepper

Directions:

• Prep the green beans: rinse and dry them thoroughly. Cut off any funky-looking ends.

• Add egg and egg white to one shallow bowl; whisk for 30 seconds to completely combine. Set aside.

• In another shallow bowl, add panko, breadcrumbs, garlic powder, cheese, salt, and pepper; stir to mix well and set aside.

• Make an assembly line with the green beans, egg dip, breadcrumb mixture setup side by side.

• Taking a handful of green beans at a time, drop them into the egg, and toss around until coated.

• Using tongs, lift a few of the green beans out, let them drip a bit, then place them into the breadcrumb coating mixture. Shake the green beans around until they are fully coated with crumbs.

• Place them side-by-side with a little space in the air fryer, repeat coating for the rest of the green beans, and set them into the air fryer.

• Set the Air Fryer for 5 minutes and 400 degrees. When 5 Mins is up, carefully toss the green beans around, flipping if needed, then cook for two more minutes. Remove with tongs and serve immediately with your favorite dipping sauce!

888.Air Fryer Asparagus Fries

Prep Time: 5 mins Cook Time: 8 mins Total Time: 13 mins

Ingredients

- 16-20 spears of asparagus
- One medium egg
- 1 tsp water
- 1/3 cup regular breadcrumbs
- 1/4 cup panko breadcrumbs
- 1 tbs everything but the bagel seasoning
- Oil spray

Directions:

- Prepare the asparagus by cutting or snapping off the hard ends; about 1 inch up the stem and discard those pieces. Wash and dry the asparagus.
- In a shallow dish, add an egg and a bit of water, then whisk and beat until a little frothy. Add the asparagus and toss around to coat.
- In a separate shallow dish or bowl, add panko breadcrumbs, regular breadcrumbs, and spices.
- Add the asparagus spears a few at a time, and toss around until coated. Place them into the air fryer tray. Repeat until all asparagus are coated.
- Add fries to the air fryer basket, do not place them too close together. Lightly spray the tops with oil and close.
- Set air fryer for 400 degrees and 8 minutes. After 5 minutes, open and carefully flip fries over, then close and cook the remaining 3 minutes.
- Serve with your favorite dipping sauce!

889. Air Fryer Keto Fried Chicken | Paleo, Gluten-Free

Servings: 8 People Total Time: 35 Mins

Ingredients

- 16 Bone-In, Skin-On Chicken Pieces about 3lb
- ¾ cup Almond Flour
- 1-2 tsp Salt or to taste
- 2 tsp Tony Chachere's Creole Seasoning
- ½ tbsp Paprika
- 1 tsp Garlic Powder
- 1 tsp Black Pepper
- Avocado or Olive Oil Spray Optional

Directions:

- Combine everything except the chicken and oil spray in a large zip-top bag. Add four chicken pieces to the bag with the spices and seal the top.
- Shake the bag to coat the chicken,

then transfer to the air fryer. Arrange chicken in a single layer and spritz with avocado oil. (the oil helps the almond flour get brown, but isn't required)

- Repeat with the remaining chicken.
- Cook at 370 degrees for 30 Minsor until the internal temperature reaches 165 degrees F (75 degrees C), flipping the chicken halfway through the cooking time.
- Serve immediately

890. Air Fryer Stuffed Peppers

Prep Time: 25 MinsCook Time: 15 Mins Total Time: 40 Mins

Ingredients

- One tablespoon extra virgin olive oil
- 1/2 pound lean ground turkey
- 1/2 teaspoon chili powder
- 1/4 teaspoon garlic powder
- 1/4 teaspoon kosher salt
- 1 cup cooked brown rice
- 3/4 cup chunky medium salsa
- Three large bell peppers
- Three tablespoons grated tex mex cheese

Directions:

- Heat the oil over medium heat in a large skillet. Add the ground turkey, chili powder, garlic powder, and salt, and fry together until the turkey is fully cooked to a safe temperature of 165F.
- Stir in the cooked rice and salsa and let the mixture heat through for a few minutes.
- While the turkey mixture is cooking, prepare your peppers by cutting the tops off and scooping out the seeds and membranes.
- Grease the bottom and sides of the air fryer basket with non-stick cooking spray and arrange the unfilled peppers in the basket. Air fry on 400F for 5 minutes.
- Pull the air fryer basket out and carefully add the turkey filling to the peppers and continue air frying for 8-10 minutes.
- Add the grated cheese to the tops of the peppers for the last 2-3 minutes of air frying.
- Serve immediately with additional toppings such as salsa, guacamole, and chopped green onions.

891. Air Fryer Pork Chops & Broccoli

Yield: 2 Servings Prep Time: 5 Mins Cook Time: 10 MinsTotal Time: 15 Mins

Ingredients

- 2 5 ounce bone-in pork chops
- Two tablespoons avocado oil, divided
- 1/2 teaspoon paprika
- 1/2 teaspoon onion powder
- 1/2 teaspoon garlic powder
- One teaspoon salt, divided
- 2 cups broccoli florets
- Two cloves garlic, minced

Directions:

- Preheat air fryer according to manufacturer's instructions to 350 degrees. Spray basket with non-stick spray.
- Drizzle 1 tablespoon of oil on both sides of the pork chops.
- Season the pork chops on both sides with paprika, onion powder, garlic powder, and 1/2 teaspoon salt.
- Place pork chops in the air fryer basket and cook for 5 minutes.
- While pork chops are cooking, add the broccoli, garlic, remaining 1/2 teaspoon of salt, and remaining tablespoon of oil to a bowl and toss to coat.
- Open the air fryer and carefully flip the pork chops.
- Add the broccoli to the basket and return to the air fryer.
- Cook for five more minutes, stirring the broccoli halfway through.
- Carefully remove the food from the air fryer and serve.

892. Air Fryer Orange Chicken

Prep Time: 5 MinsCook Time: 15 Minutes Total Time: 20 Minutes

Ingredients

- 1 pound boneless skinless chicken breasts or chicken thighs
- Two tablespoons cornstarch or potato starch
- For The Orange Sauce
- 1/2 cup orange juice
- Two tablespoons brown sugar
- One tablespoon soy sauce
- One tablespoon rice wine vinegar
- 1/4 teaspoon ground ginger
- Dash of red pepper flakes
- Zest of one orange
- Two teaspoons cornstarch mixed with two teaspoons of water

Directions:

- Preheat the air fryer to 400 degrees.
- Combine chicken pieces and cornstarch into a bowl and mix until chicken is just fully coated (see notes above about not overcoating them).
- Cook chicken for 7-9 minutes, shaking the basket halfway through or until chicken is just at or above 165 degrees internally.
- Meanwhile, combine the orange juice, brown sugar, rice wine vinegar, soy sauce, ginger, red pepper flakes, and orange zest into a small saucepan on medium heat.
- Bring mixture to a simmer and simmer for 5 minutes.
- Mix cornstarch and water in a small bowl and add it to the orange sauce.
- Let simmer for one additional minute while stirring, then immediately remove from heat.
- Remove chicken from the air fryer and combine with sauce.
- Top with green onions and sesame seeds if desired and enjoyed immediately!

893. Air Fryer Healthy White Fish With Garlic & Lemon

Prep Time: 5 Mins Cook Time: 10 Mins
Total Time: 15 Mins

Ingredients

- 12 ounces (340 g) tilapia filets, or other white fish (2 filets-6 ounces each)
- 1/2 teaspoon (2.5 ml) garlic powder
- 1/2 teaspoon (2.5 ml) lemon pepper seasoning
- 1/2 teaspoon (2.5 ml) onion powder, optional
- Kosher salt or sea salt, to taste
- Fresh cracked black pepper, to taste
- Fresh chopped parsley
- Lemon wedges

Directions:

- Pre-heat Air Fryer to 360°F for 5 minutes. Rinse and pat dry the fish filets. Spray or coat with olive oil spray and season with garlic powder, lemon pepper, and onion power, salt, and pepper. Repeat for both sides.
- To help to stick, lay perforated air fryer baking paper inside the base of the air fryer. Lightly spray the paper.
- Lay the fish on top of the paper. Add a few lemon wedges next to the fish.
- Air Fry at 360°F for about 6-12 minutes, or until fish can be flaked with a fork.
- Timing will depend on how the thickness of the filets, how cold the filets are, & individual preference.

894. Air Fryer Chicken Fajita Dinner

Prep Time: 10 minutes Cook Time: 18 minutes

Ingredients

- 1 lb. Boneless, skinless chicken breast, sliced
- Two bell peppers, sliced
- One onion, sliced
- 2 tsp. Olive oil
- 2 tsp. Chili powder
- 1 tsp. Salt
- 1 tsp. Cumin
- 1/2 tsp. Black pepper
- One pinch cayenne
- For serving – tortillas, rice, lettuce, and any desired toppings

Directions:

- Combine the sliced chicken and vegetables in a bowl.
- Add the olive oil, chili powder, salt, cumin, pepper, and cayenne.
- Toss to combine and pour the contents out into the tray of an air fryer.
- Slide the tray into the air fryer and cook at 360°F for 16-20 minutes, checking and stirring halfway through.
- Once the fajitas have finished cooking, serve them in tortillas, over rice, or a salad with desired toppings.

895. Air-Fryer Jicama Fries

Prep Time: 5 Mins
Cook Time: 30 Minutes

Ingredients

- 1 1/2 cups peeled jicama spears (about 7 oz.)
- 1/8 tsp. salt, or more to taste
- Optional dip: ketchup

Directions

- Sprinkle jicama spears with salt, and place them in the air fryer in a single layer. Lightly spray with nonstick spray.
- Set air fryer to 365 degrees. Cook until golden brown and crispy, 25 - 30 minutes, shaking the basket halfway through.

896. Air Fryer Stuffed Peppers

Yield: 6
Prep Time: 15 Mins Cook Time: 15 Mins
Total Time: 30 Mins

Ingredients

- 6 Green Bell Peppers
- 1 Lb Lean Ground Beef
- 1 Tbsp Olive Oil
- 1/4 Cup Green Onion Diced
- 1/4 Cup Fresh Parsley
- 1/2 Tsp Ground Sage
- 1/2 Tsp Garlic Salt
- 1 Cup Cooked Rice
- 1 Cup Marinara Sauce More to Taste
- 1/4 Cup Shredded Mozzarella Cheese

Directions:

- Warm up a medium-sized skillet with the ground beef and cook until well done.
- Drain the beef and return to the pan.
- Add in the olive oil, green onion, parsley, sage, and salt. Mix this well.
- Add in the cooked rice and marinara, mix well.
- Cut the top off of each pepper and clean the seeds out.
- Scoop the mixture into each of the peppers and place it in the basket of the air fryer.
- Cook for 10 Mins at 355, carefully open and add cheese.
- Cook for an additional 5 minutes or until peppers are slightly soft and cheese is melted.
- Serve.

897. Air Fryer Butternut Squash With Cinnamon

Prep Time: 15 Mins Cook Time: 30 Mins
Total Time: 45 Mins

Ingredients

- 1 pound butternut squash cubes, no larger than 1-inch in size
- One tablespoon coconut oil, melted
- One teaspoon ground cinnamon

Instructions

- In a medium bowl, combine the cubed squash, melted coconut oil, and ground cinnamon. Toss to combine.
- Pour the squash into the basket of an air-fryer. Bake at 390 degrees F for 30 minutes. Toss the squash once during the cooking process.
- When the cooking time is up, transfer the squash to a serving bowl and enjoy the warmth.

898. Air Fryer Steak Tips

Prep Time: 5 Mins Cook Time: 9 minutes
Total Time: 14 Mins

Ingredients

- Beef chuck for a cheaper version cut to 3/4 inch cubes
- Air Fryer Steak Marinade
- 1 tsp oil
- 1/4 tsp salt
- 1/2 tsp black pepper, freshly ground
- 1/2 tsp dried garlic powder
- 1/2 tsp dried onion powder
- 1 tsp Montreal Steak Seasoning
- 1/8 tsp cayenne pepper
- Air Fryer Asparagus
- 1 lb Asparagus, tough ends trimmed (could replace with spears of zucchini)
- 1/4 tsp salt
- 1/2 tsp oil (optional)

Directions:

- Preheat the air fryer at 400F for about 5 minutes.
- Meanwhile, trim the steak of any fat and cut it into cubes. Then, toss with the ingredients for the marinade and massage the spices into the meat to coat evenly.
- Do this in a ziplock bag for easier cleanup.
- Spray the bottom of the air fryer basket with nonstick spray if you have any, and spread the prepared meat along its bottom. Cook the beef steak tips for about 4-6 minutes and check for doneness.
- Toss the asparagus with 1/2 tsp oil and 1/4 tsp salt until evenly coated.
- Once the steak bites are browned to your liking, toss them around and move to one side. Add the asparagus to the other side of the air fryer basket and cook for another 3 minutes.
- Remove the steak tips and the asparagus to a serving plate and serve while hot.

899. Easy Low Carb Stuffed Peppers

Prep Time: 10 Mins Cook Time: 20 minutes Total Time: 30 Mins

Ingredients

- Two bell peppers, sliced in half and cleaned
- 1/2 lb lean ground beef
- 1/4 cup cauliflower rice

- Two tablespoons Parmesan cheese
- 1/4 teaspoon pepper
- 1/4 teaspoon salt
- Three tablespoons tomato paste
- 1/2 teaspoon garlic powder
- 1/2 teaspoon onion powder

Directions:

- Mix the ground beef, cauliflower rice, Parmesan cheese, salt, and pepper, and then stuff the peppers.
- Mix the tomato paste, garlic powder, and onion powder, and a few tablespoons of water to thin. You still want the sauce to be thick because there is not much of it, and you want it to stay on the peppers.
- Place peppers in the basket of the air fryer and cook at 350°F for 20 minutes. Depending on how thick your peppers are, the cooking time may vary, so check them toward the end to make sure.
- To cook in the oven, preheat the oven to 350°F. Place peppers in a baking dish and cover with foil. Cook for 30 minutes and check for doneness. If the peppers are not soft, cook for another 10 minutes.

900. Soy And Onion Sugar Snap Peas

Prep Time: 3 mins Cook Time: 7 mins

Ingredients

- 1 tablespoon melted butter
- 2 tablespoon finely chopped onion
- 2 teaspoon minced garlic
- 1/2 tablespoon soy sauce
- 1/2 teaspoon onion powder
- 1/4 teaspoon black pepper or to taste
- 8 ounces sugar snap peas (about 250g)

Directions:

- Remove and discard the stem end and string from each pea pod.
- In a cake barrel, mix butter, onion, and garlic. Air fry at 380F (190C) for 2 minutes.
- Add in sugar snap peas and the rest of the ingredients. Stir to make sure the snap peas are coated with butter.
- Air fry at 360F (180C) for about 5-7 minutes, stirring once in the middle.

901. Easy Roasted Asparagus

Prep Time: 5 mins Cook Time: 8 mins

Ingredients

- 1 pound asparagus ends trimmed (about 500g)
- 1/4 tsp sea salt or to taste
- 1/8 teaspoon black pepper or to taste
- 1 tablespoon extra virgin olive oil

Directions:

- Rinse the asparagus and drain.
- Put the asparagus on a large plate and drizzle olive oil on it and season with salt, pepper. Mix gently.
- Line the fryer basket with a grill mat or a sheet of lightly greased aluminum foil.
- Put the asparagus in the fryer basket, without stacking if possible, and air fry at 360F (180C) for about 6-8 minutes until tender.

902. General Tso Tofu

Prep Time: 2 hrs Cook Time: 15 mins

Ingredients

- 10 oz firm tofu (about 285g)
- 2 tablespoon thinly sliced green onion
- 1 teaspoon sesame seeds
- **Ingredients** for the sauce:
- 1 Tablespoon chili oil
- 2 Tablespoon minced garlic
- 1 Tablespoon grated ginger
- 2 Tablespoon soy sauce
- 1 Tablespoon vinegar
- 1 1/2 Tablespoon sugar
- 2 teaspoon corn starch mix with 4 teaspoon water

Directions:

- Place a kitchen towel on the counter and place the tofu on top. Put a heavy item, such as a small pot, on top of the tofu for one hour to squeeze out excess water.
- Line the fryer basket with a grill mat or a sheet of lightly greased aluminum foil.
- Cut tofu into bite-size pieces and put them in a fryer basket without stacking. Spritz them with some oil and air fry at 400F (200C) for about 10-12 minutes, flip them once in the middle.
- In the meantime, prepare the sauce by mixing chili oil, minced garlic, grated ginger, soy sauce, vinegar, and sugar.
- Heat the sauce in a wok and bring it to a boil. Mix corn starch with water and add it to the sauce in the wok. Stir constantly until the sauce thickens.
- When the tofu is done, toss them in

the wok to coat.

- Sprinkle some sesame seeds and green onion to serve.

903.Roasted Cinnamon Sugar Orange

Prep Time: 5 mins Cook Time: 5 mins

Ingredients

- 4 Oranges
- 1/2 tsp cinnamon
- 2 tsp brown sugar

Directions:

- Mix cinnamon and sugar and set aside.
- Cut each half of the orange in half. Then, take a serrated knife to cut along the inner edges of the orange rind.
- Sprinkle the cinnamon sugar the orange.
- Air fry at 400F (200C) for about 4-5 minutes.
- Serve warm by itself or over ice cream.

904.Air Fryer Chicken Kiev Balls

Prep Time: 15 mins Cook Time: 10 mins Additional Time: 30 mins

Ingredient

- ½ Cup unsalted butter softened
- 2 tablespoons chopped fresh flat-leaf parsley
- 2 cloves garlic, crushed
- 1 (19.1 ounces) package ground chicken breast
- 2 eggs, beaten
- 1 cup panko bread crumbs
- 1 teaspoon paprika
- 1 teaspoon salt
- ½ teaspoon ground black pepper
- Cooking spray

Directions:

- Mix butter, parsley, and garlic in a bowl until evenly combined. Divide mixture into 12 equal parts on a baking sheet. Freeze until solid, about 20 minutes.
- Shape ground chicken into 12 balls.
- Make a deep thumbprint in the center of each ball.
- Place a piece of frozen herbed butter in the indention and wrap the meat around the butter until it is fully encased. Repeat with the remaining balls.
- Place beaten eggs in a bowl. Combine panko, paprika, salt, and pepper in a

separate bowl.

- Dip 1 ground chicken ball first in the beaten eggs, then in the seasoned bread crumbs. Dip the ball back into the egg and in the seasoned bread crumbs once more. Repeat with the remaining balls. Place on a baking sheet and freeze for 10 minutes.
- Preheat an air fryer to 400 degrees F (200 degrees C). Place 1/2 of the balls in the air fryer basket and spray with nonstick cooking spray.
- Cook for 5 minutes. Flip balls over with tongs and spray again with nonstick cooking spray. Cook for 5 minutes more. Repeat with remaining chicken balls.

905.Air Fryer Roasted Salsa

Prep Time: 15 mins Cook Time: 10 mins Additional Time:10 mins

Ingredient

- 4 Roma tomatoes, halved lengthwise
- 1 jalapeno pepper, halved and seeded
- ½ red onion, cut into 2 wedges
- Cooking spray
- 4 cloves garlic, peeled
- ½ cup chopped cilantro
- 1 lime, juiced
- Salt to taste

Directions:

- Preheat the air fryer to 390 degrees F (200 degrees C).
- Place tomatoes and jalapeno skin-side down into the air fryer basket, along with the red onion. Lightly spray vegetables with cooking spray to help the roasting process.
- Air fry vegetables for 5 minutes. Open the basket and add garlic cloves. Spray lightly with cooking spray and air fry for an additional 5 minutes.
- Transfer vegetables to a cutting board and allow to cool for 10 minutes.
- Remove skins from tomatoes and jalapeno, if desired; they should slip right off.
- Chop tomatoes, jalapeno, and onion into large chunks and add to the bowl of a food processor.
- Add garlic, cilantro, lime juice, and salt. Pulse several times until vegetables are finely chopped; do not over-process.
- Serve at room temperature or

refrigerate to let flavors meld.

906.Asparagus Fries

Prep Time: 20 mins Cook Time: 10 mins Resting Time: 30 mins

Ingredients

- 1 pound asparagus trimmed (thick if possible)
- Salt and pepper to taste
- 1 cup Parmesan cheese
- 3/4 cup almond flour
- 1/4 teaspoon cayenne pepper
- 1/4 teaspoon baking powder
- 4 eggs beaten
- Oil spray I used avocado oil

Directions:

- Preheat your air fryer to 400 degrees.
- Arrange the asparagus in a single layer, cooking in batches if necessary.
- Spray well with oil. Cook for 5 minutes. Flip, and respray. Cook for another 4 to 5 minutes, until the asparagus, is tender.
- Baked Asparagus Fries
- Preheat an oven to 420 degrees. Line a baking sheet with parchment paper.
- Arrange the asparagus in a single layer. Spray with oil. Bake for 15 to 20 minutes.

907.Air Fryer Shrimp & Sweet Chili Sauce

Prep Time: 10 Mins Cook Time: 10 minutes Total Time: 20 minutes

Ingredients

- Shrimp
- 1.5 lbs uncooked shrimp, peeled and deveined
- 1 1/3 cups almond flour
- 1/2 tsp garlic powder
- 1/2 tsp onion powder
- 1 tsp paprika
- 1/2 tsp sea salt
- 1/4 tsp pepper
- 2 tsp parsley
- 1 large egg, beaten
- Chili Sauce
- 1 1/2 tsp red pepper flakes
- 1/2 cup apple cider vinegar
- 1/2 cup water
- 1 1/2 tbsp coconut aminos
- 1/2 cup powdered sweetener
- 1 tsp ground ginger
- 1/4 tsp salt
- 2 tsp minced garlic

- 1/4 tsp xanthan gum

Directions:

- Air Fryer Shrimp
- Preheat the air fryer to 380 degrees.
- In a medium bowl, add the almond flour, garlic powder, onion powder, paprika, parsley, and salt/pepper and mix.
- In a small bowl, add the beaten egg.
- Dip each shrimp in the egg then the flour mixture. Place on a plate until all shrimp are completely coated.
- Spray the air fryer basket with cooking spray and add the shrimp to where they are not touching (You may have to cook in 2 batches).
- Spray the top of the shrimp with cooking spray and set the air fryer to 380F and cook for 9-10 minutes making sure to flip the shrimp halfway through. Once flipped, spray the shrimp with another round of cooking spray.
- Sweet Chili Sauce
- In a small saucepan, add all of the sauce ingredients except the xanthan gum.
- Heat over medium/high heat and bring to a boil.
- Reduce heat to low and add in the xanthan gum and stir until combined.
- Add to a jar and store in the fridge for up to 2 weeks.

908. Air Fryer Buffalo Wings

Prep Time: 5 minutes Cook Time: 45 minutes Total Time: 50 minutes

Ingredients

- 1 1/2 pounds chicken wings (about 16 wings)
- 1 tablespoon avocado oil
- 1 1/2 teaspoons garlic powder
- 1 1/2 teaspoons paprika
- 1/2-3/4 teaspoon cayenne pepper
- 1/3 cup homemade buffalo sauce (or more for your liking)
- Salt and pepper, to taste

Directions:

- Pat dry wings with a paper towel to remove excess moisture. Add to a large bowl and add avocado oil, 1 tablespoon buffalo sauce, garlic powder, paprika, cayenne, and salt and pepper. Mix well to combine.
- If desired, spray the bottom of your air fryer basket with oil

- Place wings in your air fryer basket, evenly spreading out and leaving a little room in between them so the air can easily flow through. Close drawer set air fryer on manual at 400°F for 22 minutes.
- Depending on the size of your air fryer, you will probably have to cook the wings in two batches to make sure they are not overcrowded.
- When the wings are almost done, either make or heat the buffalo sauce.
- Once wings are done, add to a large bowl and pour buffalo sauce over wings.
- Carefully mix to coat the wings. Serve with ranch or blue cheese, carrots, celery, and more hot sauce, and enjoy immediately

909. Air Fryer Potato Wedges

Prep Time: 5 Mins Cook Time: 15 Mins
Soaking Time: 30 Mins
Total Time: 50 Mins

Ingredients

- 2 medium Russet potatoes, cut into wedges
- 1 1/2 Tbsp olive oil
- 1/2 tsp paprika
- 1/4 tsp garlic powder
- 1/8 tsp cayenne pepper, (optional)
- 1 tsp sea salt
- 1/4 tsp ground black pepper

Directions:

- Place raw potato wedges in a bowl and add cold water and 2 cups of ice cubes. Let them soak for at least 30 min then drain them and pat them dry with paper towels.
- Preheat Air Fryer if it is recommended for your model.
- In a large bowl or ziplock bag combine olive oil, paprika, garlic powder, cayenne pepper, salt, and black pepper. Add the potato wedges and toss to coat the potatoes with the seasoning.
- Place wedges in the basket of the air fryer and cook for 15 minutes at 400F (200C). Shaking the basket every 5 minutes. Depending on your Air Fryer you might have to fry them in batches.
- In a bowl combine grated Parmesan cheese and parsley if using.
- Transfer cooked wedges to the bowl and toss until coated with the topping.

Serve with ketchup or sour cream on the side.

910. Crispy Air Fryer Cauliflower

Prep Time: 2 Minutes Cook Time: 13 Minutes Total Time: 15 Minutes

Ingredients

- 1 bag Trader Joe's Cauliflower Gnocchi
- Cooking oil spray

Directions:

- Spread the frozen Trader Joe's Cauliflower gnocchi on a microwave-safe plate. Microwave for 1 minute (if using the whole bag). Flip halfway to make sure they are thawed evenly.
- Toss the cauliflower gnocchi in the air fryer basket. Lightly spray with cooking oil.
- Cook 400 F for 13 - 15 minutes.
- Pair with your favorite sauce or sides.

911. Air Fryer Green Bean Fries

Prep Time: 5 minutes Cook Time: 9 minutes Total Time: 14 Mins

- 1 pound of green beans, ends trimmed
- 1 large egg
- 3/4 cup almond flour
- 2 tablespoons nutritional yeast
- 1 teaspoon garlic powder
- 1 teaspoon onion powder
- 3/4 tsp salt

Directions:

- Preheat air fryer to 390°F. Trim the ends of the green beans and rinse/dry.
- Prepare your two dipping bowls. One for the egg wash and the other with all the dry ingredients
- One at a time, dip green beans in the egg wash and then the dry mix.
- Place in an air fryer in an even layer and spray the beans with cooking spray. Cook for 8-9 Minsuntil golden brown. At the halfway mark, be sure to shake the basket and spray the tops with cooking spray to help get a crunch texture,
- Serve with my homemade ranch dressing.

912. Air Fryer Bang Bang Chicken

Prep Time: 10 Mins
Cook Time: 20 Mins

Ingredients

- Bang Bang Chicken
- 1 lb chicken breast (cut into 1-inch

pieces)
- 1 cup blanched almond flour
- 1/2 cup crushed plantain chips or tortilla chips
- 1/2 tsp sea salt
- 1 large egg
- 1 tbsp lime juice
- Bang Bang Sauce
- 1/2 cup mayonnaise
- 1 tbsp chili garlic sauce
- 1 tbsp rice vinegar
- 1 tbsp honey

Directions:
- Begin by prepping the chicken. In a shallow bowl, combine the almond flour, salt, and crushed up chips.
- In a separate bowl, whisk together lime juice and egg.
- Take each chicken piece and dip it into the egg mixture first, then dip it into the flour/chip mixture. Place all chicken pieces in one layer in the air fryer (you may have to do it in batches if you have a small air fryer).
- Set the air fryer to 380 and cook for 8-10 minutes, or until chicken is cooked through.
- Flip over each chicken piece, and cook for another 6-8 minutes, or until nice and crispy.
- While chicken is cooking, make the sauce. In a small bowl, whisk together the mayonnaise, chili garlic sauce, honey, and rice vinegar.
- Once the chicken is done place it on a large plate and drizzle with sauce. You can also use it as a dipping sauce.
- For The Oven:
- Preheat the oven to 450 degrees while you prepare the chicken. Lightly grease a large sheet pan. Place each chicken piece on the sheet pan and bake for 12 minutes, flip over the chicken, and bake another 10-12 minutes.

913. Air Fryer Zucchini
Prep Time: 5 MinsCook Time: 20 Minutes Total Time: 25 Minutes
Ingredients
- 2 medium zucchinis
- 1/2 cup shredded Parmesan
- 1 egg
- 2 heaping tbsp avocado oil
- 1/2 cup almond flour

- 2 tbsp coconut flour
- 1/2 tsp garlic powder
- 1/4 tsp smoked paprika
- Salt pepper to taste

Directions:
- Wash and dry zucchinis. Cut into strips about 3 inches long.A bowl of zucchinis cut into strips.
- In a shallow bowl, whisk together egg and avocado oil. In a separate bowl, whisk together almond flour, coconut flour, parmesan, and seasoning. Instruction on how to make air fryer zucchini fries, step by step.
- Dredge zucchini slices in the egg mixture. Then evenly coat zucchini slices with flour mixture. Make sure all surfaces are coated.
- Next, spray the air fryer basket then place zucchini slices in it with a little bit of space in between.
- Basket of zucchini fries before frying in the air fryer.
- Make sure to not overcrowd them. If they are too close or overlapping they won't cook properly.
- Fry in the air fryer at 400 F for 9-10 Mins

914. Easy, Crispy, And Perfect Bacon
Cook Time: 10 minutes Total Time: 10 Mins
Ingredients
- 6 slices Bacon

Directions:
- Line the air fryer basket with parchment paper. Parchment paper will soak up the grease and prevent the air fryer from smoking. Place the bacon on top of the paper. It's ok for the bacon to touch. I do not recommend stacking the bacon.
- Some air fryer brands may need a trivet placed on top of the bacon. If you have an air fryer that is older or is very loud, you may need a trivet to hold the bacon down. I did not need this while using a Power Air Fryer.
- Cook the bacon for 10 Minsat 380 degrees. I did not flip the bacon. Cook for additional time as necessary to reach your desired level of crunch.

915. Crispy Air Fryer Sweet Potato Hash Browns

Prep Time: 10 minutes Cook Time: 20 Mins Soak in water: 20 minutes
Total Time: 50 minutes
Ingredients
- 4 sweet potatoes peeled
- 2 garlic cloves minced
- 1 teaspoon cinnamon
- 1 teaspoon paprika
- salt and pepper to taste
- 2 teaspoons olive oil

Directions:
- largest holes of a cheese grater.
- Place the sweet potatoes in a bowl of cold water. Allow the sweet potatoes to soak for 20-25 minutes. Soaking the sweet potatoes in cold water will help remove the starch from the potatoes. This makes them crunchy.
- Drain the water from the potatoes and dry them completely using a paper towel.
- Place the potatoes in a dry bowl. Add the olive oil, garlic, paprika, and salt and pepper to taste. Stir to combine the ingredients.
- Add the potatoes to the air fryer.
- Cook for ten minutes at 400 degrees.
- Open the air fryer and shake the potatoes. Cook for an additional ten minutes.
- Cool before serving.
- Grate the sweet potatoes using the

916. Easy Air Fryer Cherry Turnovers
Prep Time: 15 Mins Cook Time: 10 minutes Total Time: 25 minutes
Ingredients
- 17 oz package puff pastry 4 sheets
- 10 oz can of cherry pie filling
- 1 egg beaten
- 2 tablespoons water
- cooking oil I use olive oil.

Directions:
- Lay the pastry sheets on a flat surface.
- Unfold both sheets of the puff pastry dough. Cut each sheet into 4 squares, making 8 squares total.
- Beat the egg in a small bowl along with the water to create an egg wash.
- Use a cooking brush or your fingers to brush along the edges of each square with the egg wash.
- Load 1 to 1 1/2 tablespoons of cherry pie filling into the middle of each square sheet. Do not overfill the pastry.

- Fold the dough over diagonally to create a triangle and seal the dough.
- Use the back of a fork to press lines into the open edges of each turnover to seal.
- Make 3 slits into the top of the crust to vent the turnovers.
- Brush the top of each turnover with the egg wash. (You can also do this step after you have placed them in the air fryer basket.)
- Spritz the air fryer basket with cooking oil and add the turnovers. Make sure they do not touch and do not stack the turnovers. Cook in batches if needed.
- Air fry at 370 degrees for 8 minutes. I did not flip.
- Allow the pastries to cool for 2-3 minutes before removing them from the air fryer. This will ensure they do not stick.

917. Green Smoothie Basics

Total Time: 15 mins
Ingredients
- 1 cup milk or juice
- 1 cup spinach or kale
- ½ cup banana or ½ cup plain yogurt
- 1 cup fruit today that's 1 kiwi and 1 pear
- 1 Tbsp optional superfood topping chia, flax, or hemp seeds
- 1 tsp optional flavor enhancer cinnamon, vanilla, honey

Directions:
- Combine liquid and greens in a blender until smooth.
- Add the rest of your ingredients and continue blending until smooth. Serve immediately.

918. Green Smoothie Recipe

Prep Time: 5 Mins
Total Time: 5 minutes
Ingredients
- 1 leaf kale - medium size
- 10 leaves dandelion greens
- 1 banana - frozen
- 1 green apple
- 1/2 cup orange juice - freshly squeezed (or 1 orange peel & seeds removed)
- 2 dates - pitted
- 1 tbsp hemp hearts

- 2 tsp apple cider vinegar
- 1/2 cup hemp milk or water + more to thin out to your liking
- 1 tsp spirulina powder

Directions:
- Add all of the above smoothie ingredients except the apple cider vinegar to a powerful blender.
- Process until smooth and creamy to your liking.
- Add more plant milk, juice, or water If you'd like a thinner consistency.
- Balance the flavors to your taste with the apple cider vinegar and enjoy!

919. Tropical Green Smoothies

Prep Time: 15 mins
Ingredients
- 1 large handful of ice
- 2 cup orange juice or coconut water
- 1 cup pineapple
- 1 cup mango cored and peeled
- 1 pear cored, peel left intact
- 1 Granny Smith apple cored, peel left intact
- 1 large handful of spinach
- 1 large handful of kale

Directions:
- Place items in a blender in the order listed.
- Blend until smooth. Keep covered with a lid in the refrigerator for up to 24 hours.

920. Keto Green Smoothie

Prep Time: 5 Mins Additional Time: 5 Mins Total Time: 10 Mins
Ingredients
- 2 cups baby spinach
- 1 1/2 cup unsweetened almond milk
- 1 cup frozen strawberry slices
- ½ cup frozen avocado chunks
- 2 tablespoons hemp seeds
- 3 drops Lakanto Monkfruit Extract, see note

Directions:
- Add all ingredients to a blender and blend until smooth.
- Divide between two glasses and drink immediately.

921. Glowing Green Smoothie Recipe

Prep Time: 5 mins
Ingredients
- 1/4 cup frozen pineapple chunks
- 1/4 cup frozen mango

- 1/2 banana
- 1/2 cup frozen or fresh baby spinach packed
- 1/2 cup water or milk of your choice
- 1 scoop truvani collagen (this is my favorite collagen)
- Flax seeds

Directions:
- Add pineapple chunks, mango, banana, spinach, water, and a scoop of Truvani Collagen into a blender. Blend for 1-2 minutes, or until the smoothie has a smooth texture.
- Pour into a tall glass. Garnish with flax seed and enjoy!

922. Spinach LOquat Smoothie

Prep Time: 10 minutes
Total Time: 10 minutes
Ingredients
- 1 banana
- 4 loquats pitted
- 1 cup spinach
- 1 cup water
- 1/2 tbsp chia seeds

Directions:
- Throw a banana, loquats, spinach leaves, and water in a blender.
- Blend it up, pour in a glass (or a jar!), and top with chia seeds.

923. Green Smoothie

Prep Time: 5 Mins
Total Time: 5 Mins
Ingredients
- 1 ½ cups packed kale
- ⅔ cup orange juice or as needed
- 1 cup vanilla yogurt
- 1 banana
- 2 cups frozen pineapple
- ½ cup ice

Directions:
- Blend kale and orange juice until smooth.
- Add remaining ingredients and blend until thickened and creamy.
- If your mixture is too thick, add orange juice as needed.

924. Easy Green Smoothie

Prep Time: 10 Mins Cook Time: 1 Minute Total Time: 11 Mins
Ingredients
- 1/2 Cup Water
- 1 cup Green Grapes
- 1/2 Cup Fresh Pineapple, Chunks

- 1/2 Banana
- 2 Cups Spinach, Lightly Packed
- 1/2 Cup Ice Cubes

Directions:
- Add all ingredients to the blender.
- Blend starting on low and increase speed to high.
- Blend 30 seconds to 1 minute or until your desired consistency.

925. Air Fryer Green Beans With Lemon (Healthy & Vegan!)

Prep Time: 5 Mins Cook Time: 20 Mins Total Time: 25 Mins

Ingredients
- 2 lbs green beans, washed & trimmed
- 2 tablespoon olive oil
- ¾ teaspoon salt
- 2 tablespoons lemon juice

Directions:
- Preheat the air fryer to 400 degrees for 5 minutes.
- In a large bowl, toss the beans in the olive oil until they are evenly covered with oil.
- Sprinkle the beans with ½ teaspoon salt and toss further until the salt evenly covers all the beans.
- Add the beans to the air fryer basket and air fry for 17-19 minutes, shaking the beans every 4 minutes, or until the beans are blistered and browning around the edges,
- Pour the beans into a large serving bowl and squeeze or pour the lemon juice over the beans.
- Toss the beans until they're covered with the lemon juice and season with up to an extra ¼ teaspoon salt to taste.

926. Garlic Shrimp With Lemon

Prep Time: 5 mins Cook Time: 10 mins Total Time: 15 mins

Ingredients
- 1 pound (454 g) raw shrimp, peeled deveined,
- Vegetable oil or spray, to coat shrimp
- 1/4 teaspoon (1.25 ml) garlic powder
- Salt, to taste
- Black pepper, to taste
- Lemon wedges
- Minced parsley and/or chili flakes (optional)

Directions:
- In a bowl, toss the shrimp with the oil

or spray to coat.
- Add garlic powder, salt, and pepper, and toss to evenly coat the shrimp.
- Add shrimp to the air fryer basket in a single layer.
- Air Fry at 400°F for about 8-14 minutes, gently shaking and flipping the shrimp over halfway through cooking.
- Cooking times will vary depending on the size of shrimp and on different air fryer brands and styles.
- Transfer shrimp to the bowl, squeeze lemon juice on top. Sprinkle parsley and/or chili flakes and serve hot.

927. Air Fried Shrimp With Garlic & Butter

Prep Time: 5 mins Cook Time: 6 mins Total Time: 12 mins

Ingredients
- 3 tbsp butter (or ghee) melted
- 3 cloves garlic minced or pressed
- 12 XL shrimp 16/20 or smaller
- 1 tsp sea salt
- 1 tsp freshly ground black pepper

Directions:
- Wash the shrimp in cold water. If needed, using kitchen shears, slit the top of the shrimps and devein. Keep the shells on and place the shrimp in a medium bowl.
- Turn on the air fryer to preheat to 360°F
- In a small bowl, mix the melted butter or ghee, and garlic.
- Pour the garlic and ghee mixture over the shrimp to marinate.
- Place the shrimp in the air fryer basket. Set the timer to 6 minutes.
- Reserve butter and garlic mixture for later.
- When the timer goes off, open the basket and check for doneness.
- If the color of the shrimps is red and the flesh is opaque white, they are cooked. These shrimps were XL and it only took 6 minutes. Depending on the size, the cooking time may vary.
- Place the shrimps back in the medium bowl and toss them with the reserved garlic butter mixture.
- Sprinkle sea salt and black pepper and toss well. Serve immediately.

928. Easy Shrimp & Vegetables

Prep Time: 15 minutes Cook Time: 15 minutes Total Time: 30 Mins

Ingredients
- 1 pound thawed shrimp, peeled, deveined and tails removed
- 1 red bell pepper, cut into 1-inch chunks
- 1/2 yellow onion, cut into 1-inch chunks
- 1 tablespoon avocado oil or olive oil
- 1 teaspoon chili powder
- 1/2 teaspoon garlic powder
- 1/8 teaspoon cayenne pepper
- 1/2 teaspoon salt
- 1/2 teaspoon fresh ground black pepper
- Optional To Serve: Rice, quinoa, pad thai noodles, more veggies, teriyaki sauce, etc

Directions:
- Prep: Thaw and remove the tails from the shrimp. You can cook them tails on but I like to get it over with so I can enjoy my meal tail-free. Place the shrimp in a strainer to remove the excess liquid. If you're serving with rice, start that now. Make sure the veggies are prepped and ready to go.
- Mix it: Add the shrimp, bell pepper, onion, oil, chili powder, garlic powder, cayenne pepper, salt & black pepper to a medium-sized mixing bowl and stir to combine.
- Cook: Place seasoned shrimp and vegetable mixture into your air fryer basket.
- Set the air fryer to about 330F degrees
- Air fry the shrimp and vegetables for 10-13 minutes total, shaking the basket halfway through.
- Serve: Serve with rice, quinoa, pad thai noodles, or any other carb you prefer. Store leftovers in an airtight container for up to 4 days.

929. Air Fryer Fish And Chips Healthy

Total Time: 20 Mins

Ingredients
- 4-6 oz Tilapia Filets
- 2 tablespoons of flour
- 1 egg
- 1/2 cup of panko bread crumbs
- Old Bay Seasoning
- Salt and pepper
- Frozen Crinkle Cut Fries such as Ore

Ida

Directions:

- Gather 3 small bowls. In one bowl add the flour, in the 2nd bowl add the egg and beat it with a wire whisk, in the 3rd bowl add the panko bread crumbs and Old Bay Seasoning.
- Take the fish and dredge it in the flour, then the egg, and next in the bread crumbs. Add to the air fryer along with 15 frozen french fries. Air Fry for 15 minutes at 390 degrees.
- Serving size: 1 tilapia filet. Use serving size on fry package for fries and measure out accordingly.

930. Kale Salad With Herb Chicken Breast

Prep Time: 20 mins Cook Time: 20 mins
Total Time: 40 mins

Ingredients

- 1 Tablespoon Panko (Bread Crumbs)
- 2 Tablespoons Mixed Dry Herbs Use your favorite blend
- 1 Teaspoon Smoked Paprika
- 1 Teaspoon Salt
- 1 Tablespoon Olive Oil
- 1.5 Pounds Chicken Breast Pounded Evenly
- 1 Cup Corn Kernels From about 2 years, if fresh
- 8 Strawberries, Sliced & Quartered
- 1/2 Ounce Goat Cheese
- 2 Avocados, halved and sliced
- 2 Hard Boiled Eggs, sliced
- 2 Tablespoons Extra Virgin Olive Oil
- 16 Ounce Bag Baby Kale Greens

Directions:

- Combine panko, herbs, smoked paprika, salt, and olive oil in a small bowl to make a paste. Apply this evenly to the chicken breast.
- Cook the chicken in a preheated air fryer for 20 minutes at 370 degrees. Let it rest outside of the air fryer for 5 minutes before slicing for the salad
- In a large salad bowl or serving plate, place your bed of salad greens and then add the corn, strawberries, goat cheese, avocado, hard-boiled eggs, and chicken
- Drizzle the extra virgin olive oil over the top and then season lightly with salt and pepper

931. Easy Air Fryer Broccoli

Prep Time: 5 Mins Cook Time: 6 Mins
Total Time: 11 Mins

Ingredients

- 2 heads of broccoli, cut into bite-sized pieces
- 2 tablespoons olive oil
- Sea salt, to taste
- Fresh cracked black pepper, to taste

Directions:

- 2 heads of broccoli, cut into bite-sized pieces
- 2 tablespoons olive oil
- Sea salt, to taste
- Fresh cracked black pepper, to taste

932. Air Fryer Vegetables

Prep Time: 3 mins Cook Time: 7 mins
Total Time: 10 mins

Ingredients

- 1/2 lb broccoli fresh
- 1/2 lb cauliflower fresh
- 1 TBSP olive oil
- 1/4 tsp seasoning can use pepper, salt, garlic salt - I prefer Flavor God Garlic Everything
- 1/3 c water

Directions:

- In a medium bowl, mix vegetables, olive oil, and seasonings.
- Pour 1/3 c. water in the Air Fryer base to prevent smoking.
- Place vegetables in the air fryer basket.
- Cook at 400 degrees for 7-10 minutes.
- Shake vegetables to make sure they get evenly cooked about halfway through the 7-10 minutes.

933. Airfried Vegetables

Prep time: 10 min Cook time: 20 min
Total time: 30 min

Ingredients

- 1 lb / 0.5kg of vegetables (broccoli, brussels sprouts, carrots, cauliflower, parsnips, potatoes, sweet potatoes, zucchini will all work), chopped evenly
- 1 Tbsp / 30 mL of cooking oil
- Some salt and pepper

Directions:

- Preheat air fryer for about 5 Minsat 360F / 182C degrees.
- Evenly chop veggies and toss with oil and some salt and pepper.
- If making potato or sweet potato fries, soak them in water for ~30

minutes to draw out excess starch for crispier results, and then pat dry thoroughly with paper towels before tossing with oil.

- Make
- Transfer veggies into frying compartment and fry for 15 to 20 minutes, stirring veggies every 5 to 8 minutes or so.
- Some veggies might need longer and some will need less – just use your judgment when you open the compartment to stir the veggies. You want the outside to be golden and crispy and the inside to be tender.
- Enjoy or toss with your favorite dipping sauce when done! If you need sauce ideas, check out 5 of our favorites.

934. Air Fryer Vegetables

Prep Time: 10 Mins Cook Time: 10 minutes

Ingredients

- 2 zucchini cut into dials
- 2 yellow squash cut into dials
- 1 container mushrooms cut in half
- 1/2 c olive oil
- 1/2 onion sliced
- 3/4 tsp Italian seasoning
- 1/2 tsp garlic salt
- 1/4 tsp Lawry's seasoned salt

Directions:

- Slice zucchini and yellow squash into dials.
- The thinner they are the softer they will get. I would recommend 3/4" thick so they all are the same consistency when done.
- Slice mushrooms in half. Put all vegetables in a bowl and toss together gently.
- Pour olive oil on top and toss gently, then sprinkle in all seasonings in a bowl and gently toss one more time.
- Add half of your vegetables into your air fryer, close, and set to 400 degrees for 10 minutes. I did not bother shaking or tossing halfway through and they came out amazing.
- Remove, enjoy, and add another half at 400 degrees for 10 minutes to finish the cooking batch.

935. Veg Cutlet Recipe

Prep Time: 15 Mins Cook Time: 40 Mins

Total Time: 55 Mins

Ingredients

- 2 cups Sweet Potatoes (Boiled, Peeled and Mashed) 1 cup is 250 ml
- 3/4 cup Carrot (finely grated)
- 1/2 cup Sweet Corn (steamed)
- 1/2 cup Capsicum (finely chopped)
- 1/3 cup Green Peas (Steamed)
- 1/2 cup Quick Cooking Oats Or Instant Oats
- 1 tbsp Ginger Paste
- 1 & 1/2 tbsp Oil For Cooking cutlets (1 tbsp oil is 15 ml)
- Salt to taste
- 2 to 3 tbsp Coriander Leaves (finely chopped)
- Spices
- 1 tsp Kashmiri Red chili powder 1 tsp is 5 ml
- 1 & 1/2 tsp Garam Masala Powder
- 1/2 tsp Turmeric Powder
- 1/4 tsp Chaat Masala Powder
- 1/2 tsp Amchur Powder or Dry Mango Powder

Directions:

- In a wide bowl, add boiled and mashed sweet potatoes, cooked peas, steamed sweet corn, grated carrots, and finely chopped capsicum.
- Add all the spices, ginger paste, quick-cooking oats, and salt to taste.
- Now add the finely chopped coriander leaves
- Mix everything together.
- Divide and take an equal portion of the cutlet mixture and shape them into an "oval" shape. Once the cutlets are shaped, preheat the Air Fryer at 200 Degrees C for 5 minutes
- Place around 12 cutlets, brush or spray oil and cook them for 15 minutes at 200 Degree C.
- Turn them after 8 to 10 minutes of cooking, repeat the process of spraying oil or brushing and air fry them until they are golden brown.
- Serve with the accompaniment of your choice.

936.Air Fryer Roasted Broccoli

Cook Time: 8 Mins Total Time: 8 Mins

Ingredients

- 5 cups broccoli florets
- 2 tablespoons butter
- 2 teaspoons minced garlic
- 1/3 cup shredded parmesan cheese
- Salt and pepper to taste
- Lemon slices (optional)

Directions:

- Melt the butter and combine with the minced garlic, set aside for later.
- Preheat your air fryer according to the manufactures directions at a temperature of 350 degrees.
- Add the chopped broccoli florets to the basket of the air fryer and spray very lightly with cooking oil.
- Roast the broccoli for 8 minutes total.
- I remove the basket after 4 minutes and shake or toss with tongs to make sure everything is cooking evenly, then cook for 4 more minutes.
- At this point, the broccoli should be fork tender at the thickest part of the stem and slightly crispy on the outside.
- Remove the broccoli from the basket and toss with the garlic butter, parmesan and add salt and pepper to taste.

937.Air Fryer Vegetables Recipe

Prep Time: 15 Mins Cook Time: 20 Mins
Total Time: 35 Mins

Ingredients

- 1 cup broccoli florets
- 1 cup cauliflower florets
- 1/2 cup baby carrots
- 1/2 cup yellow squash, sliced
- 1/2 cup baby zucchini, sliced
- 1/2 cup sliced mushrooms
- 1 onion, sliced
- 1/4 cup balsamic vinegar
- 1 tbsp olive oil
- 1 tbsp minced garlic
- 1 tsp sea salt
- 1 tsp black pepper
- 1 tsp red pepper flakes
- 1/4 cup parmesan cheese

Directions:

- Pre-heat Air Fryer at 400 for 3 Mins(you can skip this step if you'd like)
- In a large bowl, olive oil, balsamic vinegar, garlic, salt and pepper, and red pepper flakes.
- Whisk together.
- Add vegetables and toss to coat.
- Add vegetables to the Air Fryer basket.

- Cook for 8 minutes. Shake vegetables and cook for 6-8 additional minutes.
- Add cheese and bake for 1-2 minutes.

938.Air Fryer Broccoli

Prep Time: 5 min Cook Time: 6 min
Total Time: 11 Mins

Ingredients

- 12 oz fresh broccoli florets, cut/torn into toughly even, very-small pieces
- 2 tablespoons extra virgin olive oil
- 1/4 tsp garlic powder
- 1/4 tsp onion powder
- 1/8 tsp kosher salt
- 1/8 tsp freshly ground black pepper

Directions:

- Combine all ingredients in a bowl; toss well to fully incorporate seasonings into the broccoli florets
- Pour 1 TB water into the bottom of the air fryer pan (this helps prevent contents from smoking.)
- Add broccoli mixture evenly into the air fryer basket.
- Set to 400F for 6 minutes. Once the timer goes off, immediately remove the basket and serve.

939.Air Fryer Vegetables

Prep Time: 5 Mins Cook Time: 18 Mins
Total Time: 23 Mins

Ingredients

- Vegetables Of Choice. Used Here Are:
- 1 cup broccoli
- 1 cup cauliflower
- 1 cup carrots
- 1 Tablespoon Olive oil or oil of choice

Directions:

- Place the vegetables in a bowl and toss with the oil
- Add seasoning and toss
- Add the vegetable to the Vortex rotisserie basket (or your air fryer basket with other brands)
- Air fry on 380 or 18 Minsor until vegetables are roasted with golden brown parts
- Carefully remove the basket using the removal tool, serve, and enjoy!

940."Fried" Tempura Veggies

Total Time: 25 mins

Ingredients

- ½ Cup flour
- ½ teaspoon salt, plus more to taste
- ½ teaspoon black pepper

- 2 eggs
- 2 water
- 1 cup panko bread crumbs
- 2 teaspoons vegetable oil
- ¼ teaspoon seasoning, or more to taste
- 2 – 3 cups vegetable pieces cut 1/2 inch thick

Directions:

- Mix together flour, 1/4 tsp. salt, and the pepper in a shallow dish. Whisk together eggs and water in another shallow dish. Stir together panko and oil in a third shallow dish. Add the desired Seasoning to either panko and/or flour mixture.
- Sprinkle vegetables with remaining 1/4 tsp. salt. Dip in flour mixture, then in egg mixture, and finally in panko mixture to coat.
- Preheat air fryer to 400°F and oven to 200°F.
- Arrange half of the vegetables in a single layer in a fryer basket. Cook until golden brown, about 10 minutes.
- Sprinkle with additional salt, if desired. Transfer vegetables to the oven to keep warm.
- Repeat with remaining vegetables. Serve with dipping sauce.

941.Sweet And Sour Brussel Sprouts

Prep Time: 5 mins Cook Time: 20 mins

Ingredients

- 1 pound Brussels sprouts
- 1 tsp olive oil
- 1 tbsp minced garlic
- 1/4 tsp salt or to taste
- 2 tbsp Thai Sweet Chili Sauce
- 2-3 tsp lime juice

Directions:

- Rinse the Brussels sprouts with cold water and let dry in a colander.
- Trim off the ends and cut them in half.
- In a large mixing bowl, toss the Brussels sprouts and garlic with olive oil and wrap them in aluminum foil.
- Air fry at 380F (190C) for about about 18 minutes.
- In a mixing bowl, toss the Sprouts with Thai Sweet Chili Sauce and lime juice to serve.

942.Red Bean Wheel Pie

Prep Time: 10 mins Cook Time: 10 mins

Ingredients

- 2 tbsp melted butter
- 2 eggs
- 2 tbsp sugar
- 1 tbsp honey
- 1/4 tsp vanilla extract
- 1/4 cup milk
- 1 cupcake flour
- 3/4 tsp baking powder
- 6 tbsp mashed sweetened red bean canned or homemade filling to taste

Directions:

- Lightly grease 4 ramekins with butter and place them in the fryer basket. Preheat at 400F (200C) for 2 minutes.
- In a large bowl, use a whisk to mix the egg, sugar, vanilla extract, and honey. Add in milk and whisk until the mixture is homogeneous. Finally, add in the sifted cake flour and baking powder. Continue to mix until everything is well blended.
- The total weight of the batter is about 280g. Spoon about 30g into the ramekin. Air fry at 300F (150C) for about 3 minutes.
- Take the desired amount of red bean (about 1 1/2 Tablespoon for mine) and roll it into a ball using the palms of your hand. Flatten it into a circular disc that is smaller than the diameter of the ramekin. Place it in the center of the ramekin on top of the pancake. Scoop about 40g of the batter into the ramekins to cover the red beans.
- Air fry again at 300F (150C) for about 3 minutes. Brush some butter on top and air fry again at 300F (150C) for 1-2 minutes until the top is slightly golden brown.

943.Crispy Curry Chickpeas

Prep Time: 5 mins Cook Time: 25 mins

Ingredients

- 2 cups canned chickpeas drained
- 1 teaspoon olive oil
- 1/2 teaspoon curry powder
- 1/4 teaspoon onion powder
- 1/4 teaspoon paprika
- 1/4 teaspoon salt or to taste
- 1/8 teaspoon garlic powder
- 1/8 teaspoon cayenne pepper optional
- 1/8 teaspoon mushroom essence or Hondashi optional

Directions:

- Mix all the dry ingredients and set aside.
- In a large bowl, toss the chickpeas with olive oil. Then, add in the dry ingredients and toss, making sure all chickpeas are coated with seasoning.
- In a lightly greased cake pan or bakeware, air fry the chickpeas at 360F (180C) for about 23-25 minutes, shake the basket 3-4 times in the middle, until the surface is crisp and lightly golden brown.
- Pour the chickpeas onto a plate. Let cool completely before serving.

944.Cheesy Cauliflower Croquettes

Prep Time: 15 mins Cook Time: 10 mins

Ingredients

- 2 cups of cauliflower rice preparation see instruction
- 2 eggs beaten
- 1/2 cup Mexican blend cheese or your favorite cheese
- 1/4 cup grated Parmesan cheese
- 1/4 cup Mozzarella cheese
- 1/3 cup breadcrumbs
- 1 teaspoon garlic powder
- 1 teaspoon dried basil
- 1/2 teaspoon onion powder
- 1/4 teaspoon salt or to taste
- 1/4 teaspoon black pepper or to taste

Directions:

- Pulse the cauliflower in the food processor a few times until it is about the size of a grain of rice.
- Transfer the cauliflower rice to a microwave-safe bowl and microwave for about 5-6 minutes.
- In a large bowl, combine the cauliflower rice with all the other ingredients (except sriracha mayonnaise). Shape the mixture into the desired shape.
- Line the fryer basket with a grill mat or a sheet of lightly greased aluminum foil.
- Place the croquettes in the fryer basket and air fry at 400F (200C) for 8-9 minutes, flip once in the middle, until the surface is golden brown.
- Serve with sriracha mayo or your favorite dipping sauce.

945.Curry Roasted Cauliflower

Prep Time: 10 mins Cook Time: 10 mins

Ingredients

- 1/2 head cauliflower break them into small florets
- 2 teaspoon olive oil
- 1/2 teaspoon curry powder
- 1/4 teaspoon paprika
- 1/4 teaspoon cumin
- 1/4 teaspoon garlic powder
- 1/4 teaspoon sea salt or to taste

Directions:

- Put the cauliflower florets in a large microwave-safe bowl and microwave for about 4-5 minutes.
- When done, transfer the florets to a large mixing bowl.
- Add in olive oil and toss. Then, add the rest of the ingredients to the mixing bowl and toss again to coat.
- Air fry at 350F (175C) for about 5-6 minutes, shake the basket once in between. until you start seeing browning of the edges.

946. Broccoli And Mushroom Omelette

Prep Time: 10 mins Cook Time: 10 mins

Ingredients

- 2 eggs beaten
- 1/4 cup broccoli florets steamed
- 1/4 cup buttoned mushroom sliced
- 1/4 cup shredded cheese Mexican Blend
- 2-3 Tablespoon milk
- 1/8 teaspoon salt and pepper or to taste
- 4-5 slices of pickled jalapeno or to taste (optional)
- Extra cheese to sprinkle

Directions:

- Lightly grease a shallow baking pan and set it aside.
- In a large bowl, mix the eggs, broccoli, mushroom, 1/4 cup shredded cheese, milk, salt, and pepper, and pour it into the pan.
- Then, place the jalapeno slices on top (or can be chopped up and mix with the egg mixture).
- Air fry at 320F (160C) for about 6-8 minutes. Sprinkle some more cheese on top and air fry again at 320F (160C) for another 2 Minsor so until the eggs are set.

947. Low-Carb And Egg Cups

Prep Time: 10 Mins Cook Time: 10 Minutes Total Time: 20 Minutes

Ingredients

- 3 slices bacon, sliced in half
- 6 large eggs
- 1 bunch green onions, optional
- salt and pepper, optional

Directions:

- Arrange 6 baking cups (silicone or paper) in the air fryer basket. Spray with nonstick cooking spray.
- Line cups with bacon slice.
- Carefully crack an egg into each cup. Season with salt and pepper, if desired.
- Turn the air fryer on to 330° and cook for 10 minutes, until eggs are set.
- Carefully remove from air fryer and garnish with desired toppings.

948. Vegan Breakfast Potatoes

Cook Time: 40 minutes Total Time: 40 Mins

Ingredients

- 3 lb potatoes, diced
- 2 bell peppers, any color, diced
- 1 onion, diced
- 15 oz mushrooms, diced
- 1 1/2 cups or 1-14 oz can black beans, drained
- Lemon Miso Tahini Sauce, optional
- Spinach and avocado for serving, optional

Directions:

- If Air Frying: Add potatoes to the air fryer basket.
- Cook 20 minutes at 400 degrees F (or 205 degrees C), shaking basket frequently.
- Add beans and vegetables and cook 10 - 15 more minutes until potatoes are soft or crispy, according to preference.
- If Baking: Spread potatoes out on a lined baking tray and bake for 25-30 minutes in a 425 degree F (218 degrees C) oven.
- Remove the tray and flip the potatoes. Add your veggies and beans and stir. Put the tray back in the oven for 15-20 more minutes, until the potatoes have started to get crispy and lightly golden brown and until all the veggies have cooked.
- Make the lemon miso tahini sauce by mixing the ingredients in a bowl and thinning the sauce with water if needed.
- Add to a bowl with spinach and whatever else you like
- Top with sauce mixture and enjoy!
- Refrigerate leftovers in an airtight container for up to 5 days. Recommended reheating in the oven, skillet, or air fryer to retain crispiness.

949. Dry Rub Skirt Steak Sandwiches

Prep Time: 10 Mins Cook Time: 15 Minutes Inactive Time: 30 Minutes Total Time: 55 Mins

Ingredients

For The Dry Rub

- 3 tablespoons ground coriander
- 3 tablespoons smoked paprika
- 3 tablespoons ground smoked cumin
- 1 teaspoon allspice
- 1½ tablespoons ground cinnamon
- 2 tablespoons dried oregano
- 1½ tablespoons dry mustard
- 3 tablespoons salt
- 1½ tablespoons black pepper
- 2 tablespoons garlic powder
- 4 tablespoons brown sugar

For the sandwich

- 2 beef skirt steaks
- 1 tablespoon canola oil
- 3 green bell peppers, seeded and sliced
- 2 large sweet onions, peeled and sliced
- ½ teaspoon salt
- ¼ teaspoon pepper
- 8 crusty rolls
- 1½ cup beef broth for dipping, optional
- hot sauce, optional

Directions:

- In a large bowl with a lid, mix all the ingredients for the dry rub until well combined.
- Place the meat on the baking sheet and liberally sprinkle the dry rub on both sides of the meat and rub it in lightly.
- Allow the meat to sit for approximately 30 minutes.
- Meanwhile, heat a large skillet to medium, add the canola oil and the sliced peppers and onions.
- Sautee the green peppers and onions with ½ teaspoon salt and ¼ pepper until

they softened and cooked through. Remove from heat and keep warm.

- Place the steaks on a hot grill and cook for approximately 5 minutes per side.
- Remove the cooked steaks from the grill and allow them to sit, covered with aluminum foil, for at least 10 minutes.
- Slice the meat across the grain in thin slices.
- To serve pile the sliced beef onto crusty rolls and top with the sauteed peppers and onions.
- Spoon (or dip) the beef stock over the prepared sandwiches and a few shakes of hot sauce if desired.
- Serve hot!

950. Air Fryer Chicken Chimichangas

Prep Time: 35 min Total Time: 35 min

Ingredients

- Two teaspoons vegetable oil
- 2 cups shredded deli rotisserie chicken
- One packet (0.85 oz) Old El Paso chicken taco seasoning mix
- Three tablespoons water
- 3/4 cup (from 16-oz can) Old El Paso traditional refried beans
- One can (4.5 oz) Old El Paso chopped green chiles
- Eight flour tortillas (6 inches)
- 1 cup shredded Cheddar cheese (4 oz)
- Two tablespoons butter, melted

Directions:

- In 10-inch nonstick skillet, heat oil over medium heat.
- Add chicken, taco seasoning mix, and water; stir until well coated. Cook uncovered for 4 to 5 minutes, frequently stirring until chicken is heated through.
- In a small bowl, stir together beans and chiles. Place tortilla on a work surface, and spread about three tablespoons of the bean mixture in the middle of the tortilla.
- Top with about 1/4 cup of chicken and two tablespoons of cheese. Fold sides of the tortilla in. Fold bottom over filling and sides. Roll tightly to enclose filling. Repeat with remaining tortillas.
- Brush outside of each filled tortilla with melted butter; place 4 in the air fryer basket, seam side down. Set to 400°F; cook 4 minutes.

- Turn; cook 2 to 3 minutes or until lightly browned and heated through.
- Repeat with the remaining four filled tortillas.

951. Air Fryer Herbed Turkey Breast

Prep Time: 15 MIN Total Time: 1 HR 30 MIN

Ingredients

- One tablespoon butter softened
- One bone-in skin-on turkey breast half (2 to 2 1/2 lb), patted dry
- One teaspoon salt
- 1/2 teaspoon chopped fresh thyme leaves
- 1/2 teaspoon chopped fresh sage leaves
- 1/4 teaspoon ground pepper

Directions:

- Cut an 8-inch round of parchment paper; place in the bottom of the air fryer basket. Spray with cooking spray.
- Rub softened butter on all sides of turkey breast; season with salt, herbs, and pepper. Place skin side up in the basket of the air fryer.
- Set to 325°F; cook 30 minutes. Using tongs, carefully turn the breast over.
- Cook 27 to 32 minutes or until the internal temperature is at least 165°F.
- Remove from the basket; let stand 10 minutes before slicing.

952. Asian Shrimp With Yum Yum Sauce

Prep Time: 30 min Total Time: 30 min

Ingredients

- Yum Yum Sauce
- 1/3 cup mayonnaise
- One tablespoon butter, melted
- One tablespoon chili garlic sauce
- One tablespoon natural rice vinegar
- One tablespoon packed brown sugar
- One teaspoon smoked paprika
- One teaspoon toasted sesame oil
- Air Fryer Asian Shrimp
- Two tablespoons cornstarch
- 1/4 teaspoon salt
- One egg
- 1/2 cup Progresso plain panko crispy bread crumbs
- 1/2 lb uncooked deveined peeled large shrimp (with tails left on)
- One tablespoon finely chopped fresh cilantro leaves

Directions:

- In a small bowl, mix all Yum Yum Sauce ingredients. Cover and refrigerate until ready to serve.
- Cut an 8-inch round of cooking parchment paper. Place in bottom of air fryer basket.
- In a shallow dish, mix cornstarch and salt. In another shallow dish, beat egg. In the third shallow dish, place bread crumbs. Holding shrimp by tail, coat with cornstarch; dip into egg mixture, then coat with bread crumbs, pressing to adhere.
- Place shrimp on parchment in the air fryer basket, standing shrimp against sides of the basket if necessary.
- Set to 350°F; cook 4 minutes. Carefully turn shrimp; set to 400°F, and cook 3 to 5 minutes longer or until pink. Sprinkle with cilantro. Serve with sauce.

953. Air Fryer Fish Tacos

Prep Time: 30 min Total Time: 35 min

Ingredients

- Two tablespoons sour cream
- One tablespoon mayonnaise
- One clove garlic, finely chopped
- One teaspoon lime juice
- 1/4 teaspoon salt
- 1 1/2 cups shredded green cabbage
- 1/4 cup thinly sliced red onion
- Two tablespoons Old El Paso original taco seasoning mix (from 1-oz package)
- One egg
- One tablespoon water
- 1/2 cup Progresso plain panko crispy bread crumbs
- 1/2 lb skinless white fish fillets (such as halibut or mahi-mahi), cut into 1-inch strips
- One package (12 bowls) Old El Paso mini flour tortilla taco bowls, heated as directed on package
- Sliced avocado, thinly sliced radishes, chopped fresh cilantro leaves, and lime wedges

Directions:

- In a medium bowl, mix sour cream, mayonnaise, garlic, lime juice, and salt. Add cabbage and red onion; toss to coat.
- Cover and refrigerate cabbage mixture until ready to serve.
- Cut an 8-inch round of cooking

parchment paper.

- Place in bottom of air fryer basket.
- In a shallow dish, place taco seasoning mix. In another shallow dish, beat egg and water.
- In the third shallow dish, place bread crumbs. Coat fish with taco seasoning mix; dip into egg mixture, then coat with bread crumb mixture, pressing to adhere.
- Place fish on parchment in an air fryer basket. Set to 350°F; cook 8 minutes.
- Turn fish; cook 4 to 6 Minslonger or until fish flakes easily with a fork (at least 145°F). Cut fish into bite-size pieces.
- Divide cabbage mixture among taco bowls. Top with fish, then top with avocado, radishes, and cilantro. Serve with lime wedges.

954. Air Fryer Breakfast Biscuit Bombs

Prep Time: 30 min Total Time: 45 min

Ingredients

- Biscuit Bombs
- One tablespoon vegetable oil
- 1/4 lb bulk breakfast sausage
- Two eggs, beaten
- 1/8 teaspoon salt
- 1/8 teaspoon pepper
- One can (10.2 oz) Pillsbury Grands! Flaky Layers refrigerated biscuits (5 biscuits)
- 2 oz sharp Cheddar cheese, cut in ten 1/2-inch cubes
- Egg Wash
- One egg
- One tablespoon water

Directions:

- Cut two 8-inch rounds of cooking parchment paper.
- Place one round at the bottom of the air fryer basket. Spray with cooking spray.
- In 10-inch nonstick skillet, heat oil over medium-high heat.
- Cook sausage in oil for 2 to 5 minutes, occasionally stirring to crumble, until no longer pink; using a slotted spoon, transfer to a medium bowl. Reduce heat to medium.
- Add beaten eggs, salt, and pepper to drippings in skillet; cook until eggs are thickened but still moist, stirring frequently. Stir eggs into sausage in a

bowl. Cool 5 minutes.

- Meanwhile, separate dough into five biscuits; separate each biscuit into two layers. Press each into a 4-inch round.
- Spoon one heaping tablespoonful of egg mixture onto the center of each round. Top with one piece of cheese. Gently fold edges up and over filling; pinch to seal. In a small bowl, beat the remaining egg and water.
- Brush biscuits on all sides with egg wash.
- Place 5 of the biscuit bombs, seam sides down, on parchment in an air fryer basket.
- Spray both sides of the second parchment round with cooking spray.
- Top biscuit bombs in a basket with a second parchment round, then top with the remaining five biscuit bombs.
- Set to 325°F; cook 8 minutes. Remove top parchment round; using tongs, carefully turn biscuits, and place in basket in a single layer. Cook 4 to 6 minutes longer or until cooked through (at least 165°F).

955. Air Fryer Crispy Italian Chicken

Prep Time: 20 min Total Time: 50 min

Ingredients

- Crispy Italian Chicken Thighs
- Two tablespoons Gold Medal all-purpose flour
- One egg
- One tablespoon balsamic vinegar
- 1/4 teaspoon salt
- 3/4 cup Progresso Italian style panko crispy bread crumbs
- 1/4 cup grated Parmesan cheese
- One package (20 oz) boneless skinless chicken thighs
- Two tablespoons thinly sliced fresh basil leaves
- Arugula Tomato Salad
- Two tablespoons extra-virgin olive oil
- One teaspoon balsamic vinegar
- 1/4 teaspoon salt
- 1/8 teaspoon pepper
- 4 cups baby arugula
- 1 cup halved cherry tomatoes

Directions:

- Cut an 8-inch round of cooking parchment paper.
- Place in bottom of air fryer basket.

- In a shallow dish, place flour. In another shallow dish, beat egg, one tablespoon vinegar, and 1/4 teaspoon salt. In the third shallow dish, mix bread crumbs and Parmesan cheese.
- Coat chicken with flour; dip into egg mixture, then coat with bread crumb mixture, pressing to adhere.
- Place chicken on parchment in the air fryer basket, standing chicken against sides of the basket if necessary. Set to 325°F; cook 15 minutes.
- Turn chicken; cook 10 to 15 minutes longer or until the juice of the chicken is clear when the thickest part is cut (at least 165°F), turning once. Top with basil.
- Meanwhile, in a large bowl, beat olive oil, one teaspoon vinegar, 1/4 teaspoon salt, and pepper with whisk.
- Add arugula and tomatoes; toss to coat. Serve salad with chicken.

956. Bacon-Ranch Hasselback Potatoes

Prep Time: 15 min Total Time: 1 hr 10 min

Ingredients

- Four medium Yukon Gold potatoes (about 2 lb)
- One package (1 oz) gluten-free ranch dip mix
- 1/4 cup butter, melted
- 1/2 cup sour cream
- Four slices cooked gluten-free bacon, chopped (1/3 cup)
- One tablespoon thinly sliced green onion (1 medium)

Directions:

- Cut an 8-inch round of parchment paper; place in the bottom of the air fryer basket.
- Spray with cooking spray.
- Cut potatoes crosswise into 1/8-inch slices, leaving about 1/4 inch of bottom intact. In a small bowl, mix five teaspoons of the dip mix and the melted butter.
- Brush mixture all over potatoes and between slices. Place cut sides down in the basket of the air fryer.
- Set to 350°F; cook 35 minutes. Using tongs, carefully turn over. Cook 15 to 20 minutes or until potatoes are completely tender and tops are golden brown.

- Meanwhile, in a small bowl, mix sour cream and remaining (about three teaspoons) dip mix.
- Top potatoes with bacon and green onion; serve with seasoned sour cream.

957. Easy Air Fryer Parmesan-Crusted Tilapia

Prep Time: 3 mins Cook Time: 7 mins Total Time: 10 mins

Ingredients
- Two thin tilapia fillets (about 4 ounces) fresh or frozen (times given for both below)
- Olive oil pump spray, not aerosol or one tablespoon olive oil
- 1/4 teaspoon salt
- 1/4 teaspoon ground pepper (optional)
- Two tablespoons grated Parmesan cheese
- 1/2 cup fine dry breadcrumbs

Directions:
- Place the frozen tilapia fillets on an aluminum or stainless steel baking pan while preheating the air fryer and measuring ingredients.
- Crazy Good Tip: These few minutes on the baking pan will ever so slightly thaw the fillets just enough to allow the breadcrumbs to stick to the oil on them. Here's the article from The Kitchn spelling out the details of why placing frozen fish and meat on aluminum and stainless steel thaws significantly quicker than stone, wood, or plastic surfaces.
- Preheat the air fryer to 390-400 degrees for 3 minutes.
- Most air fryers preset "air fryer" button is 390F to 400F degrees.
- Spray or coat fish fillets with olive oil sprayer or mister or brush with olive oil.
- Sprinkle both sides of fillets with salt and, if desired, pepper.
- Sprinkle the top side of fillets with Parmesan cheese.
- Place the dry breadcrumbs on a plate and gently press the fish into the breadcrumbs to coat them.
- If you have trouble getting the breadcrumbs to stick to the fish, wait just a few Minsor
- I like to spray the breaded fish again on top with a little bit of olive oil spray

- Frozen fish: Air Fry at 390-400 degrees for nine t0 11 minutes, without turning, depending on the thickness of fish until fish flakes easily in the center.
- Fresh fish: Air Fry at 390-400 degrees for 7 minutes, without turning, depending on the thickness of fish until fish flakes easily in the center.
- Carefully remove the fish with a silicone-coated spatula to prevent scraping the nonstick surface.

958. Buffalo Chicken Tenders

Prep Time: 10 Mins Cook Time: 20 Mins Total Time: 30 Mins

Ingredients
- 1 lb. boneless skinless chicken breasts
- 1/4 c. buffalo wing sauce
- 2/3 c. Panko bread crumbs

Directions:
- Cut the chicken breasts into 1 inch thick strips. Pat the chicken dry with a paper towel.
- Pour the buffalo sauce into a small bowl. Add the Panko breadcrumbs to a separate small bowl.
- Dip the chicken strips into the buffalo sauce and, using your fingers, scrape off the excess sauce. Place the dipped chicken in the bowl of Panko bread crumbs and coat evenly.
- Carefully arrange the breaded chicken in your Airfryer basket. Cook at 300° for 15-20 minutes or the internal temperature reaches 165°. Serve immediately.

959. Air Fryer Tilapia

Prep Time: 5 Mins Cook Time: 5 Mins

Ingredients
- Four tilapia fish fillets
- Cajun seasoning
- Pinch of Cajun seasoning
- Pinch of salt
- Pinch of garlic powder
- Pinch of black pepper

Directions:
- Preheat your air fryer to 390 °F / 200 °C. If necessary, spray the inside of your air fryer with cooking spray to prevent the fish from sticking to it.
- You don't want to stack any fish fillets on top of each other. If you're cooking a large amount, you might have to air fry the fish in several batches.
- Using fresh fish

- Season the tilapia well on both sides with your choice of seasoning.
- Air fry the fish for about 4-7 minutes, depending on the size of your fillets and the efficiency of your air fryer.
- You can check if they have cooked through by touching the fillets with a fork. If the fish flakes at the touch, they are ready to serve.
- Using frozen tilapia
- Air fry the fish for about 5 minutes. This will allow the surface of the fish to thaw. Remove it from the air fryer basket, and season well on both sides.
- Add it back to the basket, and air fry for another 5-7 minutes, depending on the size of your fish. The tilapia is ready to serve when it flakes at the touch of a fork.

960. Crispy Breaded Pork Chops

Prep Time: 10 minutes Cook Time: 12 Mins

Ingredients
- Four pork chops, boneless, 5 ounces each
- One egg
- 1 cup Italian flavored bread crumbs
- Salt and pepper, to taste
- Olive oil spray

Directions:
- Preheat air fryer to 400°F. Spray air fryer basket with olive oil spray. Prepare the cutlets.
- In a bowl, whisk egg and season to taste with salt and pepper. Set aside.
- In another bowl, add Italian flavored bread crumbs.
- Dip the chops into the egg wash, then into flavored bread crumbs.
- Place the seasoned pork chop into the prepared air fryer basket. Spritz with olive oil spray. Repeat with remaining pieces.
- Cook the pork chops for about 6 minutes, flip the chops. Spritz again with olive oil spray and cook for another 6 minutes. The internal temperature of pork should be 145°.
- Serve with your favorite side dishes.

961. Easy Air Fryer Recipes

Prep Time: 5 Mins Cook Time: 15 minutes

Ingredients
- One bag of frozen french fries

- 1/4 tsp salt
- Olive oil spray

Directions:

- Preheat the air fryer to 400 degrees for 5 minutes.
- Pour in one layer of frozen fries, ensuring they are overlapping as little as possible.
- Set time to 15 minutes total. Open the basket and shake to flip fries over and rotate them every five minutes.
- Before cooking for the last 5 minutes, spray lightly with olive oil spray and sprinkle with salt.
- Enjoy once they're as crispy as you'd like them

962. Air Fryer Buffalo Cauliflower

Prep Time: 5 Mins Cook Time: 15 Mins
Total Time: 20 minutes

Ingredients

- ½ head cauliflower
- ½ cup buffalo sauce we used Frank's Red Hot Buffalo Wing Sauce, 120 mL
- 2 Tbsp olive oil 30 mL
- 1 tsp garlic powder
- ½ tsp salt
- To Serve: creamy dip (like ranch or bleu cheese) and celery stalks

Directions:

- Prep: Cut cauliflower into bite-sized florets. In a large bowl, gently stir together cauliflower and all remaining ingredients.
- Cook: Lightly grease your air fryer basket or rack. Arrange cauliflower in a single layer (working in batches if they don't fit in a single layer). Cook at 375°F (190°C) for 12 to 15 minutes, or until fork-tender and slightly browned.
- Serve: Serve warm with your favorite dipping sauce and celery sticks.

963. Turkey Italian Meatballs

Total Time: 45-1 hour Servings: 4 people

Ingredients

- 1 pound 93/7 ground turkey
- 1/2 cup Italian bread crumbs
- One large egg whisked
- One teaspoon garlic powder
- One teaspoon onion powder
- One teaspoon Italian seasoning
- 1/4 cup parmesan cheese
- Salt & pepper, to taste

- One package Green Giant Zucchini Veggie Spirals

Directions:

- Preheat air fryer to 400º.
- In a bowl, add all ingredients.
- Mix with a spoon until just combined. If the mixture is a bit too moist, add extra bread crumbs.
- Using a cookie scoop or tablespoon, make equal-sized meatballs. You should get around 20.
- Coat the basket of the air fryer with cooking spray. Add meatballs to the basket and cook for 12 minutes or until golden brown.
- While the meatballs are cooking, steam the green giant veggie spirals in the microwave. Drain after cooking. Heat marinara.
- To plate, toss zucchini noodles in warm sauce and top with meatballs. Sprinkle with Parmesan cheese, if desired.

964. Naked Chicken Tenders

Yield: 4 Servings Prep Time: 5 Mins
Cook Time: 10 Mins
Marination Time: 20 Mins
Total Time: 35 Mins

Ingredients

- 1 lb chicken tenderloins
- 2 tbsp canola oil
- 1 tbsp vinegar
- One tbsp butt rub (or your favorite BBQ seasoning)

Directions:

- Combine chicken tenders, oil, vinegar, and butt rub in a plastic bag or bowl.
- Toss until seasoning coats the tenders evenly.
- Refrigerate and marinate for at least 20 minutes.
- Place chicken tenders in a single layer in the air fryer basket.
- Air fry at 400 degrees for 10-12 Minsuntil chicken is cooked through. Verify that the inside of the chicken reaches at least 165 degrees.

965. Air Fryer Pork Chops

Yields: 4 Servings Prep Time: 5 Mins
Total Time: 20 Mins

Ingredients

- Four boneless pork chops
- 2 tbsp. extra-virgin olive oil
- 1/2 c. freshly grated Parmesan

- 1 tsp. kosher salt
- 1 tsp. paprika
- 1 tsp. garlic powder
- 1 tsp. onion powder
- 1/2 tsp. freshly ground black pepper

Directions

- Pat pork chops dry with paper towels, then coat both sides with oil.
- In a medium bowl, combine Parmesan and spices.
- Coat both sides of pork chops with Parmesan mixture.
- Place pork chops in the air fryer basket and cook at 375° for 9 minutes, flipping halfway through.

966. Juicy Pork Chops With Rub

Prep Time: 5 Mins Cook Time: 12 Mins
Total Time: 17 Mins

Ingredients

- 2-4 boneless pork chops (1 1/2 lb for four chops)
- 2 Tbsp+ pork rub (or homemade version)
- 1 Tbsp olive oil

Directions:

- Brush both sides of the pork chops with olive oil.
- You'll use about 1 Tbsp+ of olive oil for four boneless pork chops.
- Spread pork rub seasoning on both sides of the pork chops. It works well to gently press the rub into the pork chops to help get the seasoning stick.
- Spray the aluminum air fryer basket with cooking spray to help make clean-up easier.
- If it's already non-stick, do not use a spray like Pam.
- Put 2-4 boneless pork chops into the air fryer basket.
- Set the temperature setting to 400F with a total cooking time of 12 minutes.
- Cook the air fryer pork chops for 7 minutes on one side.
- Flip them over and continue cooking for five more minutes or until the internal temperature reaches 145F.
- If you're baking four pork chops in an air fryer, make sure to flip and ROTATE the pan to ensure an even cooking time.
- Meaning, the pork chops in the front for the first 7 minutes, don't just flip them and put them in the back of the pan when they finish cooking.

- Let rests 5+ minutes before serving. Very important!
- Enjoy

967. Best Boneless Pork Chops

Prep Time: 5 Minutes Cook Time: 12 Minutes Additional Time: 2 Mins Total Time: 19 Minutes

Ingredients

- 1 lb boneless pork chops (1.5 in thick)
- One teaspoon olive oil
- 1 Tablespoon dijon mustard
- 1 Tablespoon balsamic vinegar
- Salt and pepper to taste
- For the peaches
- Two medium peaches, sliced
- One teaspoon balsamic vinegar

Directions:

- In a small bowl mix, the Dijon mustard and balsamic vinegar are set aside.
- Pat dry the boneless pork chops with a paper towel;
- Lightly coat them with olive oil, season with salt and pepper to taste.
- Brush the Dijon mustard and balsamic vinegar mixture on the boneless pork chops.
- Place in the air fryer. Cook at 400° for 10 -12 minutes, turning the pork chops over at 6 minutes.
- The pork chops are done when they reach 145° F measured in the center; this is the lowest safe point for pork chops. Go to about 155-160 for well-done pork chops.
- Once the pork chops are done, let them rest cover for 2-3 minutes.
- For The Peaches
- In a medium bowl, add the peaches, coat with balsamic vinegar, place in the air fryer, cook at 400F for 2 minutes, or until desire doneness.
- Serve the pork chops with the peaches. Enjoy it!

968. Crispy Baked Sweet Potato Fries

Prep Time: 10 Mins Cook Time: 25 Mins Total Time: 35 Mins

Ingredients

- Three large sweet potatoes
- 1.5 tablespoons cornstarch
- 2.5 tablespoons olive oil, divided
- Salt and fresh cracked pepper, to taste

Directions:

- Preheat oven to 425°F. Line a large cookie sheet with parchment paper or non-stick aluminum foil.
- Peel sweet potatoes and slice into fries. You want fries to be as even in width as possible for even cooking.
- Place sweet potatoes in one of those giant-size zip locks and drizzle in 2 tablespoons olive oil. Shake like crazy to evenly coat.
- Then sprinkle in the cornstarch and shake, shake, shake.
- Drizzle in the last tablespoon of olive oil and shake until cornstarch disappears. Sprinkle in the salt and pepper and shake one last time!
- Layout the sweet potatoes in a single layer and bake 25-30 minutes, flipping halfway through. Serve immediately.

969. Taquitos With Beef

Prep Time: 5 Mins Cook Time: 25 minutes Total Time: 30 Mins

Ingredients

- Two teaspoons extra virgin olive oil
- 1/3 cup chopped onion
- One teaspoon minced garlic
- 8 oz lean Ground Beef
- 8 oz finely chopped mushrooms
- 1 cup chopped bell peppers
- One teaspoon dried oregano
- 1/2 teaspoon ground cumin
- 1/4 teaspoon cayenne pepper
- 1/4 teaspoon salt
- 8-10 each whole wheat tortillas
- 1/4 cup shredded cheese optional
- 1/3 cup plain Greek yogurt optional
- 1/3 cup guacamole optional
- 1/3 cup salsa optional

Directions:

- Begin by sautéing onions and garlic in oil for about 3 to 4minutes. Then, add ground beef, mushrooms, bell peppers, and spices and cook over medium heat on the stovetop. Sauté until beef is browned and fully cooked to an internal temperature of 160 degrees F (or for about 10minutes.) *Note, if using 80% lean/ 20% fat beef, sauté the beef first, then strain the fat out, and sauté the other ingredients in the oil then add back in the beef at the end.
- Using a slotted spoon, portion out the ground beef mixture onto your tortillas in the center. Leave about 1-inch space

on the sides to allow the tortilla to roll into the taquito form. Sprinkle cheese on top.

- Repeat adding the meat mixture into the tortillas until all are filled. Then, roll the tortilla up tightly, ensuring the opposite side is tightly tucked under the center.
- Lightly spray the air fryer basket with an olive oil mist, then place rolled taquitos in the air fryer basket and set the temperature to 370 degrees for 7 minutes. *Note, if your air fryer requires a preheat, be sure to turn it on during the sauté period above.
- Once taquitos are golden brown, remove and let cool 2 to 3minutes before serving. Repeat cooking with remaining taquitos depending on the size of your air fryer basket.
- Garnish with desired toppings like plain Greek yogurt (a nutrient-rich swap for sour cream), guacamole, and salsa.

970. Turkey Meatloaf

Prep Time: 13 mins Cook Time: 35 mins Resting: 10 mins Total Time: 47 mins

Ingredients

- 1 Egg, beaten
- 1/3 cup Bread Crumbs
- 1/3 cup Milk
- 2 tsp Garlic Powder
- 1 tsp Onion Powder
- 1 tsp Salt
- 1/2 tsp Pepper
- 2 tsp Italian Seasoning
- 1/2 cup Ketchup
- 3 tsp Dijon Mustard
- 1 1/2 lbs Ground Turkey, 85% Lean
- 1/4 lb Thick Cut Bacon (optional)
- Topping Sauce
- 1/2 cup Ketchup
- 3 Tbsp Real Maple Syrup
- 1/2 tsp Liquid Smoke

Directions:

- In a large mixing bowl, add the egg and beat it. Then add the bread crumbs, milk, garlic powder, onion powder, salt, pepper, and Italian seasoning. Mix well.
- Add the ketchup and Dijon. Mix well.
- Add the ground turkey and thoroughly combine the meat with the seasoning mixture.
- Shape into a loaf that is even in thickness and will fit in the air fryer

basket. This recipe works best in a minimum 7-inch wide basket. A smaller basket will yield a thicker meatloaf, which means a longer cook time.

- Put the meatloaf into the air fryer basket and then drape the strips of bacon evenly over the loaf. Tuck the bottoms of the bacon under the loaf.
- Cook at 350° F for 20 minutes.
- While the meatloaf is cooking, mix up the topping sauce. After the 20 minute cook time, open the air fryer and apply a generous amount of the sauce over the top of the meatloaf (try not to double-dip into the sauce so you can use the rest to serve with the meatloaf).
- Place a piece of sprayed foil loosely over the meatloaf. Cook at 350° F for another 10 minutes.
- Open the air fryer and check the temperature with an instant-read thermometer. If it says 160°, then let the meatloaf rest for 10 minutes before serving. It will come up to 165°.
- If the meatloaf is below 160°, cook for another 5 minutes. You can take off the foil for the last couple of minutes.
- Always rest meatloaf for 5-10 minutes after cooking.
- Transfer to a serving platter and slice. Serve with the remaining topping sauce.

971.Sour Cream And Onion Chicken

Prep Time: 10 Mins Cook Time: 10 Mins

Ingredients

- Marinade
- Four skinless, boneless chicken breasts halved to make four breasts
- ¼ cup fresh parsley chopped
- ½ cup sour cream plus an additional two tablespoons
- 2 tsp onion powder
- 1 ½ tbsp chives
- 1 ½ tbsp green onions
- ½ tbsp fresh lemon juice
- 2 ½ tsp salt and pepper
- 1 tsp sugar
- Cooking spray
- For the dredge
- One ¾ cups Panko breadcrumbs
- ¼ cup parmesan
- 1 tsp lemon zest
- One egg

Directions:

- Add all of the marinade ingredients to a plastic zip bag or bowl.
- Mix well. Add the chicken. Make sure to coat the chicken all over with the marinade. Zip the bag up. Place it into the fridge and marinate overnight.
- Let the chicken come to room temperature.
- Add the egg to a shallow bowl. Lightly beat it. In a separate shallow bowl, add the bread crumbs, Parmesan cheese, and lemon zest. Mix to combine.
- Dip both sides of the chicken into the eggs. Let excess drip back into the bowl.
- Next, dip the chicken into the panko crumbs. Cover both sides with panko, pressing very well to adhere. Shake off excess. *See notes below.
- Spray some oil into the air fryer. Place chicken in the air fryer. Spray the top of the chicken with a bit of oil.
- Set air fryer to 400 degree at 5 Minsper side or until internal temperature reaches 165 degrees Fahrenheit. Cooking times will vary depending on the thickness and size of the breast.

972.Pork Loin Roast

Prep Time: 15 Mins Cook Time: 30 Mins
Total Time: 45 Mins

Ingredients

- 2 lb. pork loin roast
- 1 T olive oil
- 1 T Rosemary and Garlic Rub

Directions:

- Trim the pork roast slightly, cutting off some of the fat if there is a lot of it.
- If your roast has a layer of fat over the top, cut that fat crosswise in slits.
- Rub the roast all over with olive oil.
- We rubbed our pork with the same Rosemary and Garlic Herb Rub that we used for the Instant Pot and Slow Cooker pork roasts, but you can use any kind of rub or spice and herb mixture that's good on pork.
- Be sure the roast has come to room temperature when you're ready to cook.
- Set Air Fryer to 360F/180C. If your Air Fryer has multiple functions, be sure it is on Air Fry.
- If your Air Fryer has different heights to put the tray, I will put it in the lower slot.
- Cook the pork roast for 30 minutes or until it reaches 145F/60C on an Instant Read Meat Thermometer (affiliate link).
- Our fat got a bit dark, but even those dark parts tasted great when we ate it.
- Let the roast rest a few minutes before slicing.
- Serve hot for a tasty low-carb main dish.
- The leftovers will also be good cold for sandwiches or to use in a salad or stir-fry.

973.Taco Zucchini Boats

Prep Time: 15 Minutes Cook Time: 12 Minutes

Ingredients

- 2 Medium zucchini Trimmed and scooped
- 16 Ounces 93% lean ground turkey
- 1/2 Medium onion Chopped finely
- 1 Package taco seasoning
- 1 cup water
- 2 Ounces Monteray Jack Cheese Shredded

Directions:

- Using a small scoop, hollow out medium-size zucchini. They should look like small boat shape zucchini that will fit your air fryer basket. Chop the scooped-out zucchini into small pieces to be cooked with ground turkey meat.
- Brown ground turkey chopped fine onions and chopped zucchini pieces that were scooped from the zucchini boat. Add the taco seasoning mix to browned ground turkey moisture.
- Add water to the turkey taco meat mixture and cook for 5 minutes. The mixture should be nice and thick.
- Place the hollowed-out zucchini boats into the air fryer basket. Fill each boat with as much filling as you can. Then top with shredded Monterey Jack Cheese. Note you will have some leftover Taco Turkey Meat, which can be used for other dishes.
- Place air fryer basket with Taco Zucchini Boats into Air Fryer set for 10 minutes at 370°f. Check after 10 Minsof cooking time and adjust the extra amount of cooking time if need. This all depends on the size of zucchini boats.
- Plate cooked zucchini boat and drizzle

with favorite hot sauce or salsa. My favorite is sriracha sauce garnished with cherry tomatoes and cilantro.

974.The Best Chicken Tikka Recipe

Prep Time: 30 Mins Cook Time: 15 Mins Marination Time: 6 Hrs Total Time: 6 Hrs 45 Mins

Ingredients

- 1 lb. Chicken breast boneless or 500 gm.
- For marinade
- 2 tbsp. ginger and garlic paste or minced ginger and garlic
- 3 tbsp. Greek yogurt
- 1 tsp. garam masala powder or curry powder
- 1 tsp. cayenne
- 1 tsp. black pepper coarsely ground skip if you prefer less spice
- 1 tbsp. Tandoori chicken masala optional
- 1 tsp. paprika or Kashmiri chili powder
- 1 tsp. coriander powder
- 1 tsp. lemon juice
- 1 tsp. Kasuri methi or dry fenugreek
- 1 tsp. oil/butter for marination and some more for basting
- 2 tsp. chickpea flour or besan
- Salt

Directions:

- The key to making good chicken tikka is in its marination.
- Take all the ingredients of the marinade and mix to form a thick paste.
- Evenly coat chicken pieces with this marinade and keep for 4-6 hours or overnight for the flavors to get absorbed.
- For Oven
- Preheat oven at 240 C or 460 F for 10 minutes. Line a baking tray with foil and arrange a grill tray on it. Line your tikka on skewers and bake for about 25-30 Minstill it is well cooked. You can do the same in a conventional grill.
- Serve hot with lemon slices, slices of onion, and chaat masala. Enjoy

975.Baked Chicken Egg Rolls

Prep Time: 20 minutes Cook Time: 15 minutes Total Time: 35 minutes
Servings: 12 Egg rolls

Ingredients

- ½ Lb minced chicken breast

- 12 egg roll wrappers
- 2 c red cabbage shredded
- 1 c carrots shredded
- 1 c red radish shredded
- ¼ c cilantro optional
- 2 tbsp scallions
- Four garlic cloves chopped
- 2 tsp ginger finely grated
- 2 tbsp canola oil and1 tbsp oyster sauce
- 2 tsp soy sauce low sodium
- 1 tsp fish sauce
- ¼ tsp kosher salt
- ¼ tsp white pepper
- Cooking spray

Directions:

- In a skillet over medium heat, add the canola oil.
- Allow the oil to heat, and add the minced chicken, scallion, garlic, ginger, salt, and white pepper. Mix well and allow to cook, controlling the heat.
- Cook about ¾ths of the way and add the cabbage, carrots, and radish. Stir, then add the oyster, soy, and fish sauce. Toss to blend and allow to cook another 2 minutes. Top with cilantro and turn off the heat to cool.
- Divide the filling evenly between the wrappers.
- About 1 ½ tbsp each. To fold the egg rolls, follow the instructions on the package or see the tutorial above and line on a baking sheet.
- Generously spray the egg rolls with cooking spray or brush with canola oil.
- Bake in a 425 degree preheated oven for 15-20 Minsor until they brown and the edges crisp.

Air Fryer Method

- To make chicken egg rolls in the air fryer, like the air fryer tray with the rolls without overcrowding. Set the temp to 390 degrees for 6-8 Minsbefore turning and cooking for 4-6 minutes more.

976.Air Fryer Kale Chips

Prep Time: 5 Mins Cook Time: 15 Mins Total Time: 20 Mins

Ingredients

- 10 oz lacinato or leafy kale, washed and cut into 1.5-2" pieces
- Two tablespoons olive oil or avocado oil
- Two tablespoons coconut liquid

amigos
- One teaspoon toasted sesame oil
- Two tablespoons sesame seeds
- ½ teaspoon garlic powder
- ¾ teaspoon onion powder
- ¼ teaspoon salt

Directions:

- In a large bowl, combine the kale, olive oil, coconut aminos, and toasted sesame oil.
- Toss the kale in the oil and liquid aminos until the kale is evenly covered with the oil and amino.
- Sprinkle the kale with sesame seeds, dried garlic, dried onion, and salt. Toss the kale further to distribute all the seasonings evenly throughout the kale.
- Add the kale to the basket of the air fryer. Air fry at 400 degrees for 13-14 minutes, shaking every 3-4 minutes, or until the kale gets crispy and the sesame seeds are starting to brown. Remove the kale from the air fryer and serve!

977.Crispy Air Fryer Brussels Sprouts

Prep Time: 5 Mins Cook Time: 15 Mins Total Time: 20 Mins

Ingredients

- 16 oz. brussels sprouts, trimmed and cut into halves or quarters
- One tablespoon olive oil or avocado oil
- ¼ teaspoon salt
- 1 ½ tablespoon lemon juice

Instructions

- Place the air fryer basket in the air fryer and preheat the air fryer for 3-5 minutes.
- In a large mixing bowl, toss the brussels sprouts, olive oil, and salt until combined.
- Add the brussels sprouts to the air fryer and air fry for 12-15 minutes, shaking the basket every 4-5 minutes, or until the brussels sprouts are cooked through and crispy.
- Squeeze or drizzle the lemon juice over the brussels sprouts and toss or gently stir until covered. Serve hot!

978.Potato Skins

Prep Time: 10 Mins Bake Time: 1 Hour Cook Time: 10 Mins Total Time: 1 Hour 20 Mins

Ingredients

- Air fryer potato skins
- Eight smaller russet potatoes scrubbed thoroughly
- Non-stick cooking spray
- 3-4 green onions (or ⅓ cup), green and white parts sliced
- ⅓ cup sliced black olives
- ⅓ cup bacon bits (optional)
- ½ cup shredded sharp cheddar cheese
- Potato skin garnishes
- ¼ cup sour cream or 2-4% greek yogurt
- 2-3 tablespoons sliced cilantro leaves

Directions:
- Preheat the oven to 375 degrees Fahrenheit. Pierce each potato 2-3 times with a sharp knife.
- Place the potatoes in the oven, directly on the baking rack. Bake the potatoes for 50-60 minutes, or until the potatoes are tender and cooked through.
- Remove the potatoes from the oven. Very carefully slice the potatoes in half and scoop out all but ¼-inch of the potato flesh next to the skin
- Spray the pulp and skin sides of the potato skin with non-stick cooking spray. With the pulp side up, sprinkle two teaspoons black olives, two teaspoons green onions, and two teaspoons bacon bits (if using) into each skin. Sprinkle one tablespoon shredded cheese over the toppings.
- Preheat the air fryer fitted with a rack or big basket to 350 degrees for 2-3 minutes.
- Add the potato skins, filling side up, to the air fryer rack or basket, leaving 1-1 ½ inches between the skins. Air fry for 5-7 minutes, or until the cheese is bubbling and turning golden.
- Remove the skins from the air fryer and serve hot with sour cream, Greek yogurt, cilantro, and any of your other favorite garnishes.

979. Crispy Keto Air Fryer Pork Chops
Prep Time: 15 Mins Cook Time: 10 minutes Total Time: 25 minutes
Ingredients
- Boneless pork chops
- 4-6 center-cut boneless pork chops (4-6 oz each, ~ ¾ inch thick)
- Keto pork chops coating

- ⅓ cup almond flour
- ⅓ cup grated parmesan (or sub additional almond flour)
- 1 tsp garlic powder
- 1 tsp paprika
- ½ tsp onion powder
- ½ tsp salt
- ½ tsp black pepper
- Two eggs

Directions:
- Preheat oven to 425°F (210°C).
- Spray both sides of coated pork chops with cooking spray and add to a baking rack on top of a lined baking sheet.
- Bake for 20 minutes, flipping halfway through. (May need to bake longer for thicker chops or bone-in chops.)
- Near the end of cook time, check oven fried pork chops temperature as explained above.

980. Chicken Nuggets
Prep Time: 15 Mins Cook Time: 7 Mins Total Time: 22 Mins
Ingredients
- 1/4 cup whole wheat flour
- 1/4 teaspoon salt, or to taste
- 1/4 teaspoon black pepper
- One large egg
- 2/3 cup whole-wheat panko bread crumbs
- 1/3 cup grated Parmesan cheese
- Two teaspoons dried parsley flakes
- 1 pound boneless, skinless chicken breasts, cut into 1-inch cubes
- Olive oil spray

Directions:
- Preheat air fryer at 400ºF for 8-10 minutes.
- Set out three small shallow bowls. In the first bowl, place flour, salt, and pepper; mix lightly. In the second bowl, add egg and beat lightly.
- In the third bowl, combine Panko, parmesan cheese, and parsley flakes.
- One at a time, coat chicken pieces in the flour mixture, then dip into the beaten egg, and finally coat with the Panko mixture, pressing lightly to help the coating adhere.
- Place chicken nuggets in the basket of the air fryer in a single layer. Spray the nuggets with olive oil spray (this helps them get golden brown and crispy). You

will not be able to cook them all at once. Cook each batch of chicken nuggets for 7 minutes or until the internal temperature reaches 165ºF. Do not overcook.

981. Chicken Legs
Prep Time: 5 Mins Cook Time: 30 minutes Total Time: 35 minutes
Ingredients
- Eight chicken drumsticks plus thigh
- 1/2 tsp kosher salt (plus more to taste)
- 2 Tbsp olive oil
- 1 Tbsp sesame oil
- 4 Tbsp low sodium soy sauce
- 1 Tbsp Worcestershire sauce
- 2 Tbsp lime juice (or lemon juice)
- 2 Tbsp honey
- 1 Tbsp garlic powder
- 1 Tbsp onion powder
- 1/4 tsp cayenne pepper

Directions:
- In a large bowl, mix all of the ingredients except chicken until well blended. Add the chicken legs.
- Mix and massage the drumsticks by hand for about 2-3 minutes, or until all the liquids are almost completely absorbed by the meat.
- Make sure that the seasoning sauce evenly covers the chicken. Massaging the chicken will allow the sauce to get quickly absorbed by the meat, flavoring it inside.
- Place the chicken legs on the air fryer rack, leaving some space in between.
- Depending on the size of your air fryer, you may need to do the frying in two batches.
- Fry at 400F for 15 min.
- Flip and fry for 10 min more, again at 400F. Flip again and fry for 5 Minsmore. If the legs look quite well-browned, you may not need to do the final 5 Minsof frying.
- Remove the drumsticks from the air fryer and transfer them to a serving platter. Serve hot with your favorite side dish or a salad.

982. Shrimp Tacos
Prep Time: 20 minutes Cook Time: 10 Mins Total Time: 30 minutes
Ingredients
- 1 tbsp vegetable oil

- 24 jumbo frozen (raw) shrimp peeled, deveined, and without tail
- 1 1/2 tsp light brown sugar
- 1 tsp chipotle chili powder
- 1/2 tsp smoked paprika
- 1/2 tsp garlic powder
- 1/4 tsp salt
- 1 cup fresh avocado sliced
- 1 cup purple cabbage chopped
- 1/2 cup green salsa
- 1/2 cup sour cream
- 1/2 cup red onion finely chopped
- Lime wedges
- 12 street sized flour tortillas

Directions:

- Thaw the shrimp according to package directions. I used the quick thaw method, which is just rinsing the frozen shrimp under cold water.
- Brush the air fryer basket lightly with the vegetable oil. Preheat the air fryer to 400 degrees F.
- Stir together the brown sugar, chipotle chili powder, smoked paprika. Garlic powder and salt.
- Dry the shrimp with paper towels. Place the shrimp in a zippered plastic bag. Pour in the seasoning mixture and shake to coat the shrimp fully.
- Place the shrimp in a single layer in the air fryer basket. You may need to fry them in two batches. Cook for 3 - 4 minutes. Turn the shrimp over and cook for an additional 3 - 4 minutes.
- The shrimp will shrink in size quite a bit, and they will be firm to the touch when cooked.
- Mix the green salsa and sour cream for your sauce. Serve the air-fried shrimp with the rest of the ingredients and assemble as tacos. Tortilla, sliced avocado, purple cabbage, shrimp, sauce, red onion, and a squeeze of lime.

983. Air Fryer Ravioli

Prep Time: 5 minutes Cook Time: 5 minutes Total Time: 10 minutes

Ingredients

- Vegetable oil
- One pkg premium refrigerated ravioli about 16 pieces
- Three large egg whites
- 2 tbsp water
- 1 cup italian seasoned panko breadcrumbs

- 1/2 cup parmesan cheese
- 1 cup pizza or marinara sauce

Directions:

- Lightly brush the basket of an air fryer with vegetable oil. Preheat the air fryer to 400 degrees.
- While the air fryer is preheating, whisk together the egg whites and water in a shallow bowl.
- Whisk the Panko breadcrumbs and Parmesan cheese together in a separate shallow bowl.
- Dip each ravioli on both sides first in the egg and water mixture and then in the breadcrumb and cheese mixture.
- Open the air fryer and place the coated ravioli in a single layer in the basket. You'll have to fry the ravioli in two or three batches, depending on the size of your air fryer.
- Fry the ravioli for about 4 minutes, or until puffed and starting to brown.
- Serve with pizza or marinara sauce for dipping.

984. Mashed Potato Pancakes

Prep Time: 5 Mins Cook Time: 15 Mins Total Time: 20 Minutes

Ingredients

- 2 Cups Mashed Potatoes
- 1 cup cheddar cheese
- 1 green onion chopped
- 2 strips cooked bacon
- 1 egg
- 2 tbsp flour
- 1 cup panko bread crumbs
- Salt and Pepper to taste

Instructions

- Mix Potatoes, egg, cheese, bacon, green onion, and flour
- Make into a patty form.
- Coat in panko bread crumbs
- Place in the freezer for 10 Mins to hold the form.
- Place foil over your rack on your ninja food or air fryer
- Cook on 390 for 10 minutes
- Flip over and cook for an additional 5 minutes.

985. Donut Bites

Prep Time: 5 minutes Cook Time: 5 minutes Total Time: 10 minutes

Ingredients

- One can (five) flaky buttermilk biscuits

I used Pillsbury Southern Homestyle
- 2 tbsp salted butter
- 1/4 cup powdered sugar
- 2 tbsp granulated sugar
- 1/2 tsp cinnamon

Directions:

- Melt the butter in a microwave-safe bowl.
- Use a silicone pastry brush to brush the air fryer basket lightly with melted butter.
- Put the basket into the air fryer and preheat it to 350 degrees.
- Separate the biscuits and cut each biscuit into four pieces, using a pizza cutter or sharp knife.
- Spread the biscuit pieces in a single layer into the air fryer basket. Close the air fryer and fry the biscuit pieces for 4 - 5 minutes, or until browned and cooked through.
- Pour the rest of the melted butter into a pie plate and pour the fried biscuit pieces into the plate. Stir them, so they are coated with the butter.
- Place the sugars and cinnamon in a half-gallon or gallon-sized zippered bag. Close the bag and shake, so the sugars and cinnamon are evenly combined.
- Place the donut bites covered in melted butter into the bag with the cinnamon and sugar. Close the bag and shake to coat the donut bites. Serve immediately.

986. Perfect Personal Pizza

Prep Time: 5 Mins Cook Time: 5 minutes Total Time: 10 minutes

Ingredients

- 1 Stonegate Mini Naan Round
- 2 tbsp jarred pizza sauce
- 2 tbsp shredded pizza cheese or shredded Mozzarella
- 6 or 7 mini Pepperoni

Directions:

- Top the mini naan round with the pizza sauce, shredded pizza cheese, and mini pepperoni.
- Place the topped personal pizza into the basket of an air fryer.
- Set the air fryer to about 375 degrees F. "Fry" the pizza for between 5 to 7 minutes or until cheese is completely melted and starting to brown. Serve immediately.

987. Lamb Chops With Dijon Garlic Marinade

Prep Time: 10 minutes (+time to marinate) Cook Time: 22 minutes Total Time: 32 minutes

Ingredients

- Two teaspoons Dijon mustard
- Two teaspoons olive oil
- One teaspoon soy sauce
- One teaspoon garlic, minced
- One teaspoon cumin powder
- One teaspoon cayenne pepper
- One teaspoon Italiano spice blend (optional)
- ¼ teaspoon salt
- Eight pieces of lamb chops

Directions:

- Make the marinade by combining Dijon mustard, olive oil, soy sauce, garlic, cumin powder, cayenne pepper, Italiano spice blend (optional), and salt in a medium bowl and mix well.
- Place lamb chops into a Ziploc bag and pour in the marinade. Press the air out of the bag and seal tightly. Press the marinade around the lamb chops to coat fully. Place into the fridge and marinate for at least 30 minutes, up to overnight.
- Place three pieces of marinated lamb chops onto a grill rack on top of the air frying basket, and space them out evenly. Cook at 350 F for 17 minutes, flipping the lamb chops once, halfway through, to ensure even cooking.
- Once done, leave the lamb chops inside the hot air fryer for another 5 minutes. This keeps the lamb chops warm and ensures that it is thoroughly cooked yet still tender.
- Season with additional salt and cumin to taste.

988. Plantain Chips

Prep Time: 5 Mins Cook Time: 12 Mins Total Time: 17 Mins

Ingredients

- 1 Green Plantain Evenly sliced
- 1 Tsp. Kosher Salt or to taste
- 1 Cup Water
- Lemon or Lime Juice Optional

Directions:

- Add the water and salt to a bowl. Stir. Set aside.
- Peel the plantains.
- Sliced the plantains in even slices. Best to use a mandolin.
- Add the plantain slices to the salted water, let soak for about 5-10 minutes.
- Transfer to the air fryer. Spray with olive oil, cook for 12 minutes, shaking and spraying with oil in between cooking. Increase the time for desired crispiness. Sprinkle with lemon or lime juice (optional). Enjoy!

989. Breaded Pork Chops

Prep Time: 5 minutes Cook Time: 12 minutes Resting time: 3 minutes Total Time: 20 minutes

Ingredients

- 4 (4) Bone-in center-cut pork chops, about 24 oz (1/2" thick)
- Non-fat cooking spray, like Pam cooking spray

Ingredients For Liquid Dredge Station:
- One egg, beaten
- 1/4 cup water

Ingredients For Dry Dredge Station:
- 1 cup Panko breadcrumbs
- 1/2 cup All-purpose flour, optional
- Four teaspoons paprika
- Two teaspoons dried parsley
- 1/2 teaspoon garlic powder
- 1/2 teaspoon black pepper
- 1/4 - 1/2 teaspoon cayenne pepper, more or less to taste
- 1/4 teaspoon dry mustard
- 1/2 teaspoon salt

Directions:

- Prepare The Chops: Trim all fat from chops. Rinse with water to remove any bone particles.
- Prepare The Dredge Stations: In one shallow dish or baking pan, beat the egg with water. In another shallow bowl or baking pan, mix Panko bread crumbs and spices.
- If adding the OPTIONAL flour dredge, set up the third pan with the flour.
- Coat The Chops: If using the optional flour step, first lightly coat the chop in flour. Shake off any excess flour.
- This step helps the egg wash adhere to the pork chop. If not using flour, skip to the next step.
- Place chops in egg wash mixture and turn to wet both sides.
- Next, dip chops into crumb mixture, turning to coat both sides.
- Into The Fryer: Place chops in the Air Fryer pan. Spray lightly with non-stick cooking spray. If necessary, add a wire rack to create a second tier of pork chops (See photos). Insert drawer into fryer and close.
- Cook The Chops: Set the temperature to 380 degrees F and the time for 12 minutes.
- Turn the chops halfway through the cooking time and lightly spray with cooking spray. Close the drawer and continue cooking. The chops are done when the internal temperature reaches 145 degrees F, and the center is no longer pink.
- Please Give It A Rest: Allow the chops to rest for 3-Minsbefore serving.
- Serving Suggestions: For an easy 20-minute meal, serve with steamed vegetables, quick-cooking rice, and a fresh cucumber-tomato salad.
- Storage: Leftovers may be stored in an air-tight container in the refrigerator for up to 3 days.

990. Garlic Parmesan Chicken

Prep Time: 15 minutes Cook Time: 12 minutes Total Time: 27 Mins

Ingredients

- Four medium bone-in, skin-on chicken thighs OR boneless, skinless chicken breasts
- ½ tsp sea salt
- ½ tsp pepper
- ½ tsp garlic powder
- ½ tsp smoked paprika
- ¼ cup Parmesan cheese, finely grated

Directions:

- Brine the chicken parts first. Add ¼ cup salt to a bowl (or zipper-closure bag) of slightly warm water. Add the chicken thighs or breasts and let them sit in this brine for 15 minutes.
- While the chicken is brining, combine the seasonings for the rub.
- Drain the saltwater mixture, rinse the chicken with cool water and thoroughly pat dry.
- Toss, the chicken parts with one tablespoon olive oil, then rub the spice mixture into both sides.
- For bone-in, skin-on chicken thighs, air fry at 375°F. For 8 minutes, then pause the air fryer and remove the

basket. Use tongs to flip the pieces over. For boneless, skinless breasts, air fry at 375°F. For 6 minutes.

• Place a tablespoon or so of grated parmesan cheese on top of each of the pieces of chicken. Return the basket to the fryer and fry at 350°F. for 4 minutes (both thighs and breasts.) With an instant-read meat thermometer, check that the internal temperature of the chicken has reached 165°F.

• Remove with tongs and serve.

991. Air Fryer Chicken Burger

Prep Time: 5 Mins Cook Time: 8 minutes Total Time: 13 Mins

Ingredients

• 1 lb. ground chicken
• 1 tsp. olive oil
• 1 tsp. Worcestershire sauce
• 3/4 tsp. salt
• 1/4 tsp. black pepper
• Cooking spray (or an oil sprayer like this)
• Four hamburger buns for serving
• Toppings
• Lettuce leaves and Tomato slices
• Onion slices
• Pickles and Ketchup
• Mayonnaise
• Mustard

Directions:

• Gently mix chicken, olive oil, Worcestershire sauce, salt, and pepper until just combined.

• Divide into four sections and lightly form into burger patties. Make an indent in the center of each burger.

• Grease the air fryer basket with oil and preheat the air fryer to 360°F.

• Cook at 360°F for 4 minutes. Flip burger over and cook for four more minutes at 400°F until it reaches an internal temperature of 165°F on an instant-read thermometer.

• Repeat with the remaining two burgers.

• Serve with buns and desired toppings.

992. Air Fryer Carrots

Prep Time: 5 mins Cook Time: 15 mins Total Time: 20 mins

Ingredients

• 1/2 pound carrots
• 1/2 tablespoon olive oil

• One teaspoon ground cumin
• 1/4 teaspoon chile powder
• 1/8 teaspoon garlic powder
• Pinch salt
• Toasted sesame seeds (optional garnish)
• Fresh cilantro coriander leaves, chopped (optional garnish)

Directions:

• Preheat the air fryer for 5 Minsat 390 F (200 C). Wash and chop the carrots while the air fryer preheats

• Place the carrots in the air fryer basket. Air fry for 10 Minsat 390 F (200 C).

• Transfer carrots to a medium-sized bowl. Combine olive oil, cumin, chile powder, garlic powder, and salt in the bowl with the carrots. Stir to coat the carrots well in seasoning and oil.

• Return carrots to air fryer basket and air fry at 390 F (200 C) for 5 minutes until the carrots are well browned on the edges.

• Remove carrots from the air fryer, garnish with sesame seeds and cilantro (if using) and serve immediately.

993. Weight Watchers Stuffed Peppers

Prep Time: 5 Mins Cook Time: 25 Mins Total Time: 30 Mins

Ingredients

• 6 bell peppers red, yellow, and orange
• 1/4 cup water
• 1/2 lb ground turkey breast LEAN
• 1 small zucchini small dice
• 2 cups crushed tomatoes no salt added
• 1 cup mushrooms small dice
• 1.5 cups cauliflower rice
• 1 tbsp Worcestershire sauce
• 1 tsp salt
• 3 Babybel Mini Light Cheese Rounds grated

Directions:

• Heat non-stick skillet on medium-high
• Add water, ground turkey, zucchini, and mushrooms
• Brown for five minutes and add salt
• While turkey is browning, heat cauliflower rice in microwave according to package directions
• To the turkey, add Worcestershire, rice, and tomatoes and simmer for 2-3

minutes
• While turkey mixture is cooking, prep peppers by slicing off tops and clean the insides (save the pepper tops to use in other recipes)
• Spoon turkey mixture into peppers
• Air Fryer Instructions: AF at 350 for 10 minutes. Open AF and add shredded cheese. Air Fry 5 minutes more until cheese melts and browns
• Oven Instructions: Cover with foil and bake at 350 for 30 minutes.
• Uncover and add shredded cheese. Bake an additional 15 minutes (uncovered)

994. Air Fryer Zucchini Fritters

Prep Time: 15 mins Cook Time: 12 mins Servings: 9 Serving

Ingredients

• Three medium zucchini (about 2.5 cups shredded zucchini)
• 1/2 tsp fine sea salt
• One large egg
• 1/2 cup superfine blanched almond flour
• 1/4 cup grated Parmesan cheese (sub with nutritional yeast for dairy-free / paleo / Whole30)
• 1/2 teaspoon baking powder
• 1/4 teaspoon lemon pepper
• 1/2 teaspoon garlic powder
• 1/2 teaspoon smoked paprika
• 1/2 teaspoon Italian seasoning
• Two green onions, finely sliced
• Avocado oil or olive oil
• For Serving:
• A dollop of sour cream, chopped green onions, or dill plus lemon wedges

Directions:

• Grate Zucchini: Use a box grater to grated zucchini. Place in a bowl and stir in 1/2 tsp salt. Allow resting for 10 minutes.

• Squeeze Out Excess Water: Use thick paper towels or a tea towel.

• Make The Zucchini Patties: Add egg, 1/4 cup grated Parmesan cheese, almond flour, green onions, and seasonings and mix until combined.

• If the batter seems too soggy, add a little bit more almond flour. If the batter seems too dry, add a little bit of water.

• Scoop 1.5 tablespoonfuls Portions into THE air fryer basket, an inch apart.

Press to flatten zucchini cakes and lightly spray with oil.

• Close air fryer and cook at 385F for 11-12 minutes (or until desired crispness), flipping and spraying halfway through.

• Serve warm with a dollop of sour cream and top with chopped green onions or dill along with lemon wedges.

995. Cajun Shrimp Dinner

Prep Time: 10 Mins Cook Time: 20 Mins
Total Time: 30 Mins

Ingredients

• One tablespoon Cajun or Creole seasoning
• 24 (1 pound) cleaned and peeled extra-jumbo shrimp
• 6 ounces fully cooked Turkey/Chicken Andouille sausage
• One medium zucchini, 8 ounces, sliced into 1/4-inch thick half-moons
• One medium yellow squash, 8 ounces, sliced into 1/4-inch thick half-moons
• One large red bell pepper, seeded and cut into thin 1-inch pieces
• 1/4 teaspoon kosher salt
• Two tablespoons olive oil

Directions:

• In a large bowl, combine the Cajun seasoning and shrimp, toss to coat.
• Add the sausage, zucchini, squash, bell peppers, and salt, and toss with the oil.
• Preheat the air fryer to 400F.
• In 2 batches (for smaller baskets), transfer the shrimp and vegetables to the air fryer basket and cook for 8 minutes, shaking the basket 2 to 3 times.
• Set aside, repeat with remaining shrimp and veggies.
• Once both batches are cooked, return the first batch to the air fryer and cook for 1 minute.

996. Stuffed Turkey Breast "Roll" With Bacon, Spinach/Kale, & Parmesan

Prep Time: 15 Mins Cook Time: 45 Mins
Total Time: 1 Hr

Ingredients

• 2 -1.5 Lb. (680g) Deboned Turkey Breasts
• Salt, To Taste
• Black Pepper, To Taste
• Filling:

• Four slices of bacon, cut into bite-sized pieces
• 4 oz. (113 g) mushrooms, sliced
• 1/2 small onion, diced
• Two cloves garlic, minced
• 2 cups (480 ml) chopped fresh kale or spinach (if frozen, use 1 cup, thawed, then squeeze out water)
• 1/2 teaspoon (2.5 ml) dried thyme, oregano, or rosemary (or 1/2 Tablespoon fresh)
• 1/4 teaspoon (1.25 ml) dried sage or 1/2 tablespoon fresh chopped
• 1/4 teaspoon (1.25 ml) kosher salt, or to taste
• 1/4 teaspoon (1.25 ml) black pepper, or to taste
• 1/4 cup (25 g) shredded parmesan cheese or crumbled feta

Directions:

• Make The Filling:
• Heat pan, adds bacon, and cook until bacon starts to become crispy. Add onion, garlic, and mushrooms. Cook until mushrooms shrink and release moisture.
• Add kale/spinach and cook until softened. Add dried herbs, salt, and pepper, and stir. Remove pan from heat.
• Stir in cheese and set filling aside.
• Prepare The Turkey:
• Place plastic wrap on top of each turkey breast and pound thinner into an even thickness, about 1/2-inch thick.
• Place the turkey breast skin side down. Lay the filling on top of the turkey breast. Fold one edge of turkey breast over. Tie turkey breasts.
• Season top of tied breasts with additional salt and pepper. Coat the air fryer basket with oil, and then place the turkey skin-side down in the basket.
• Air Fry at 360°F for 20 minutes. Flip the turkey breast to be skin-side up and Air Fry again for 10-20 minutes or until the turkey's internal temperature reaches 165°F, the thickest part. Allow to rest for 5 minutes and then slice and serve.

997. Air Fryer Tot Broccoli

Prep Time: 5 Mins Cook Time: 10 Mins
Total Time: 15 Mins

Ingredients

• 1 pound (454 g) broccoli, cut into bite-sized pieces
• Two tablespoons (30 ml) oil (approximately)
• 1/2 teaspoon (2.5 ml) garlic powder
• Salt, to taste
• Fresh cracked black pepper, to taste
• Fresh lemon wedges

Directions:

• Add broccoli to a large bowl and drizzle evenly with olive oil. Season broccoli with garlic powder, salt, and pepper.
• Add broccoli to the air fryer basket/tray in an even layer.
• Air Fry 380°F for 12-15 minutes, flipping and shaking three times through cooking.
• Or cook until crispy. Serve with lemon wedges.

998. Vietnamese Vegetarian Egg MeatloafAll Round Avocado Fries

Prep time: 10 mins Cook time: 10 mins

Ingredients

• Cooking spray
• 1/2 cup of panko bread crumbs
• 1 ripe avocado, peeled, halved, and cut into 8 slices
• 1 tsp of water
• 1 egg
• 1/4 tsp of salt
• 1/2 tsp of ground black pepper
• 1/4 cup of all-purpose flour

Directions

• Heat up the Air fryer to 400°F.
• In a shallow bowl, combine together the flour salt and pepper.
• In a separate shallow bowl, beat water and egg together. Add panko into a different shallow bowl.
• Dip oneslice of avocado in the flour, shake to remove any excess. Dip into the bowl of egg, allowing excess to drip off. Lastly coat both side of the avocado slice with panko. Place on a plate or bowl and repeat the process with other slices.
• Generously coat cooking spray on avocado slices and place sprayed-side down in the bowl of the Air fryer, then spray the avocado top side.
• Cook at 400 Degrees for 4 minutes.

Flip and cook more for 3 minutes until golden.

999.Air-Fried Calzones

Prep time: 15 mins Cook time: 27 mins

Ingredients

- Cooking spray
- 1 1/2 (about 6 tablespoons) oz of pre-shredded part-skim mozzarella cheese
- 6 oz of fresh prepared whole-wheat pizza dough
- 2 (about 1/3 cup) oz. shredded rotisserie chicken breast
- 1/3 cup of lower-sodium marinara sauce
- 3 (about 3 cups) oz of baby spinach leaves
- 1 small red onion, finely chopped
- 1 tsp of olive oil

Directions

- Heat oil over medium-high in a medium nonstick skillet. Sauté onion 2 minutes, stirring not too often until tender.
- Add spinach and sauté for 1 1/2 minutes until wilted.
- Withdraw skillet from heat and stir in chicken and marinara sauce.
- Divide dough evenly into four portion. Lightly flour a work surface and Roll each dough piece on the surface into a 6-inch circle.
- Fill the center of each dough circle with 1/4 of the spinach mixture and then add 1/4 of the cheese on top. Fold dough in half moon shape to cover the filling, crimp the edges to seal.
- Spritz calzones generously with cooking spray.
- Cook for 12 minutes at 325°F in Air fryer basket, turning over after 8 minutes until dough is golden brown.

1000. Sweet Potato Fries

Prep time: 10 mins Cook time: 1 hr

Ingredients

- Cooking spray
- 2 (6-ounces) sweet potatoes, peeled and cut into 1/4-inch
- 1/4 tsp of garlic powder
- 1/4 tsp of fine sea salt
- 1 tsp of chopped fresh thyme
- 1 tbsp of olive oil

Directions

- In a medium bowl, mix together garlic powder, thyme, olive oil and salt. Add in the potato, and toss until well coated well.
- Spritz the Air fryer basket lightly with cooking spray. Add potatoes in the basket in a single layer. Cook potato for 14 minutes at 400°F in batches, turning fries over halfway through cooking until lightly browned and tender on the inside.

1001. Cranberries Butternut Squash

Prep time: 20 mins

Cook time: 25-35 mins

Ingredients

- 4 cups of diced butternut squash - (about 1-inch pieces).
- 1 cup of sliced green onions
- 8 oz of button mushrooms, stemmed and quartered
- 1 tbsp of olive oil, optional
- 1 tbsp of balsamic vinegar
- 1 tbsp of soy sauce
- 1 tbsp of maple syrup
- Spray oil
- 4 cloves of fresh garlic
- 1/4 cup of dried cranberries
- (Optional) extra green onion - for garnish,

Directions

- Combine together the button mushrooms, green onions and squash in a large bowl, and set aside.
- Puree the garlic, vinegar, maple syrup, soy sauce, and olive oil in the food processor or blender until smooth. Toss the squash mixture with the sauce until well coated.
- Transfer the coated squash in the Air fryer basket, spritz with spray oil to coat.
- Air fry for 25-35 minutes at 400F, shaking after each 5 minutes interval, until the squash pieces outside are browned and inside are tender. Toss cooked squash
- with cranberries and top with the extra green onion if desired.
- Notes about cooking time:
- Cooking time may vary based on the size your Air fryer, size of your squash pieces and how fresh the squash you are using is.